SUPER A-Z SC/
GREAT BRITAIN
NORTHERN IRELAND

C000179460

Journey Route Planning maps

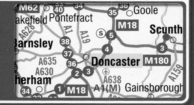

Southern Britain......II–III

Northern Britain and Northern Ireland......IV–V

Mileage Chart..........2

Britain & Northern Ireland Road maps

Key to map pages inside front cover

Reference..........3

Britain......4-173

Northern Ireland......174-179

Detailed Main Route maps

London..........180-187

Birmingham..........188-189

Manchester..........190

City and Town centre maps

Plans of 70 principal cities and towns in Britain

Reference..........191

Cities and Towns......192-203

Sea Port & Channel Tunnel plans

Access maps to principal sea ports..........204

Folkestone and Calais Terminals..........29

Airport plans

Access maps to principal Airports in Britain..........205

Over 32,000 Index References

Including cities, towns, villages, hamlets and locations..........206-232

	.2F 49	Gulden Down. *Shrp*	.2F 59	Hainw.
	3H 59	Gulden Morden. *Cambs*	.1C 52	Haisth.
	3C 88	Gulden Sutton. *Ches W*	.4G 83	Hakin.
	4G 75	**Guildford.** *Surr*	.1A 26 & 195	Halam.
	2A 92	Guildtown. *Per*	.5A 144	Halber.
	2D 90	Guisborough. *Nptn*	.3D 62	Halber.
	3B 170	Guilsfield. *Powy*	.4E 70	Halcro.
	D 170	Guineaford. *Devn*	.3F 19	Hale.
	3H 21	**Guisborough.** *Red C*	.3D 106	**Hale.**
	7F 173	Guiseley. *W Yor*	.5D 98	Hale.
	4B 108	Guist. *Norf*	.3B 78	Hale.

Index to Places of Interest

Full postcodes to easily locate popular places of interest on your SatNav 233-235

Penshurst Place & Gdns. (TN11 8DG)	.1G 27
Peover Hall (WA16 9HW)	.3B 84
Perth Mus. & Art Gallery (PH1 5LB)	.201
Peterborough Cathedral (PE1 1XZ)	.201
Petworth House & Pk. (GU28 0AE)	.3A 26
Pevensey Castle (BN24 5LE)	.5H 27
Peveril Castle (S33 8WQ)	.2F 85
Philipps House (SP3 5HH)	.3F 23
Pickering Castle (YO18 7AX)	.1C 100
Picton Castle (SA62 4AS)	.3E 43
Piel Castle (LA13 0QN)	.3B 96

Motorway Junctions

Details of motorway junctions with limited interchange..........236

Junction		M1
2	Northbound	No exit, access from A1 only
	Southbound	No access, exit to A1 only
4	Northbound	No exit, access from A41 only
	Southbound	No access, exit to A41 only
6a	Northbound	No exit, access from M25 only
	Southbound	No access, exit to M25 only

Safety Camera Information

Details of Safety Camera symbols used on the maps, and the responsible use of camera information ....Inside back cover

Edition 22 2013. Copyright © Geographers' A-Z Map Company Ltd. An AtoZ Publication.

Fairfield Road, Borough Green, Sevenoaks, Kent TN15 8PP   Retail Sales: 01732 783422   Trade Sales: 01732 781000   www.az.co.uk

Direct
Customer Service

If you experience difficulty obtaining any of our 300 titles, please contact us direct for help and advice.

www.az.co.uk

Tel: 01732 783422   Fax: 01732 780677

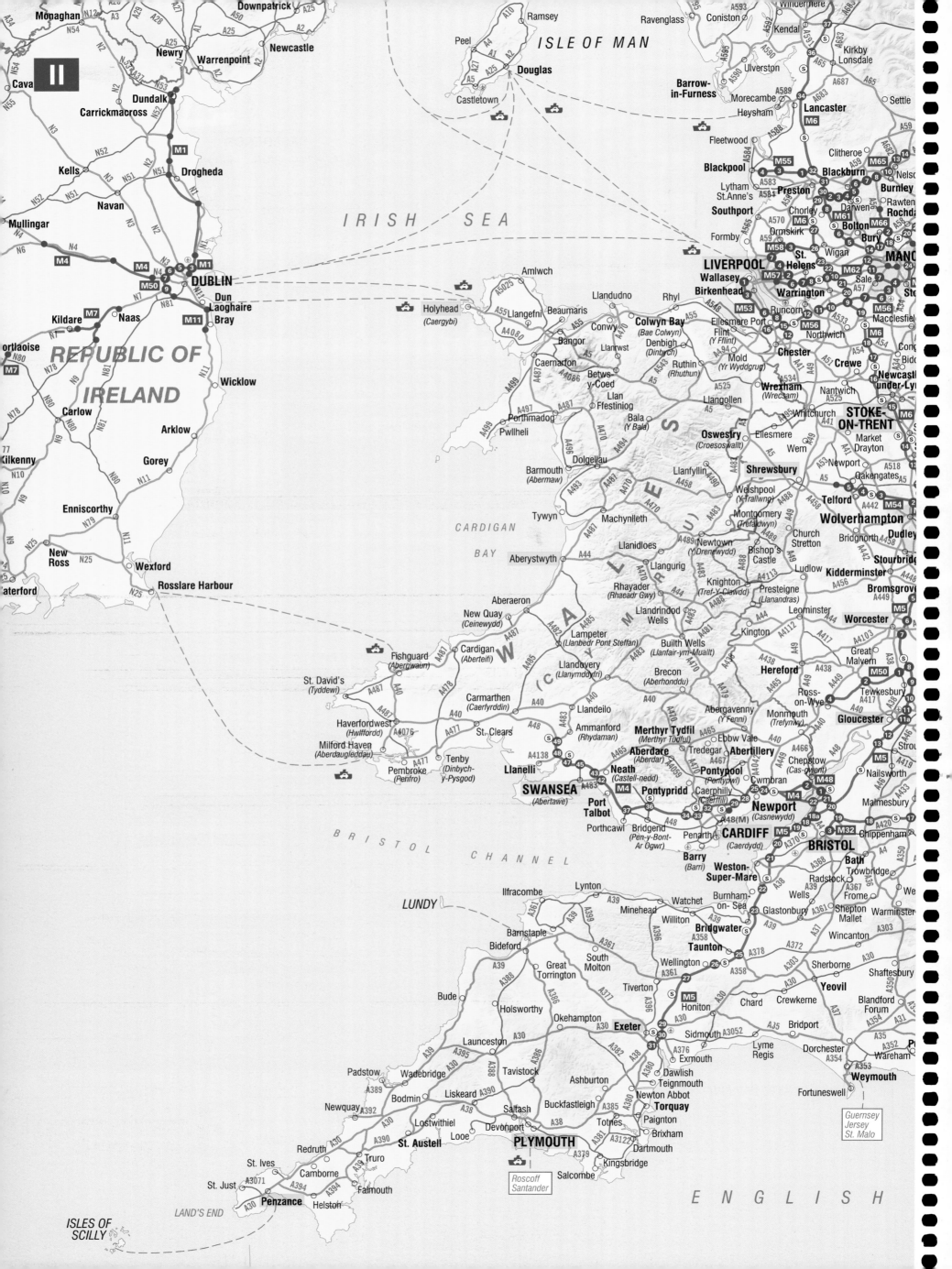

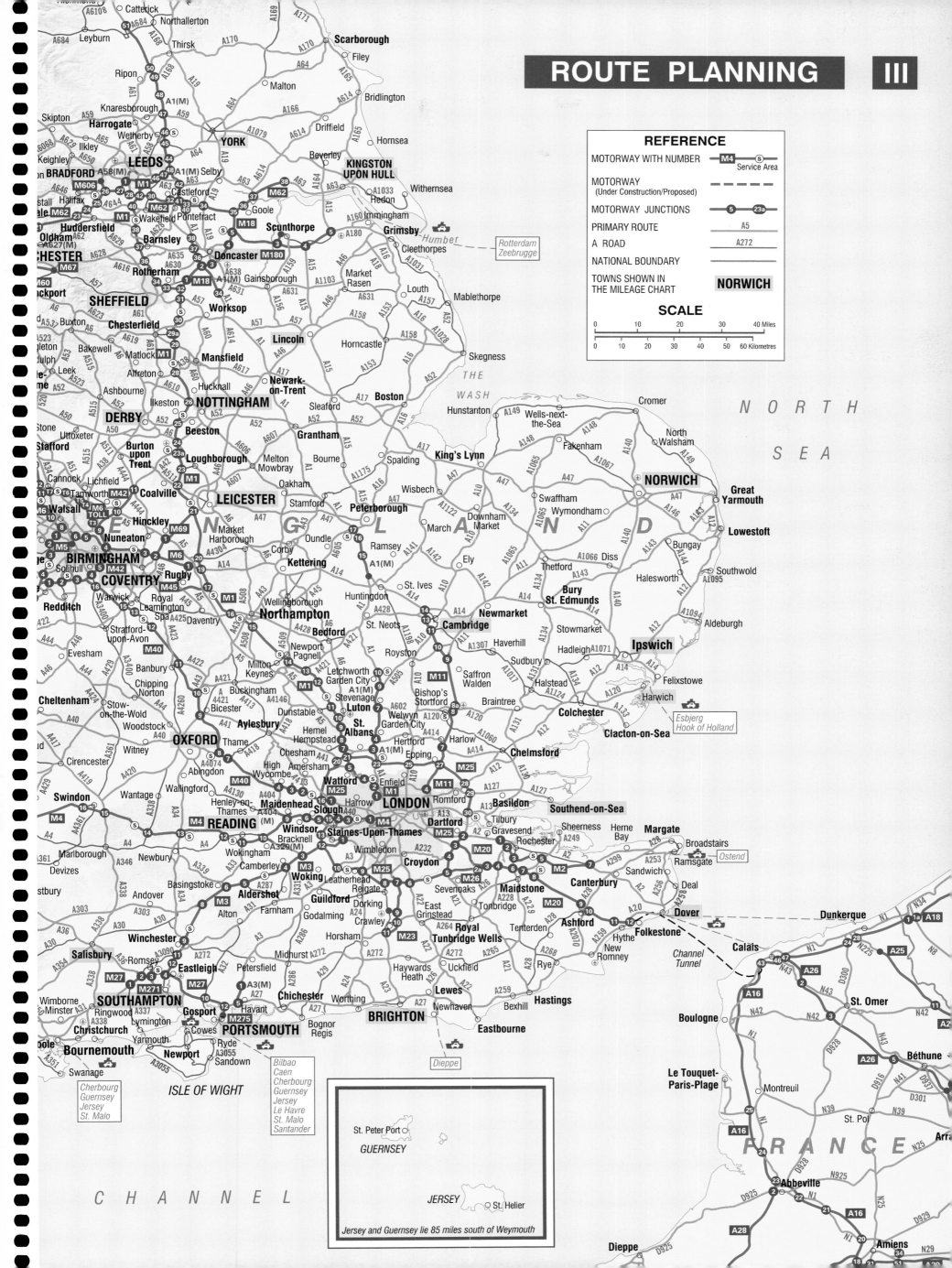

REFERENCE

MOTORWAY WITH NUMBER	M4 — S Service Area
MOTORWAY (Under Construction/Proposed)	- - - -
MOTORWAY JUNCTIONS	5 — 23a
PRIMARY ROUTE	A5
A ROAD	A272
NATIONAL BOUNDARY	
TOWNS SHOWN IN THE MILEAGE CHART	NORWICH

SCALE

0   10   20   30   40 Miles

0   10   20   30   40   50   60 Kilometres

NORTH SEA

THE WASH

ENGLAND

CHANNEL

FRANCE

Cherbourg
Guernsey
Jersey
St. Malo

Bilbao
Caen
Cherbourg
Guernsey
Jersey
Le Havre
St. Malo
Santander

Dieppe

Rotterdam Zeebrugge

Esbjerg Hook of Holland

Ostend

ISLE OF WIGHT

St. Peter Port
GUERNSEY

JERSEY   St. Helier

Jersey and Guernsey lie 85 miles south of Weymouth

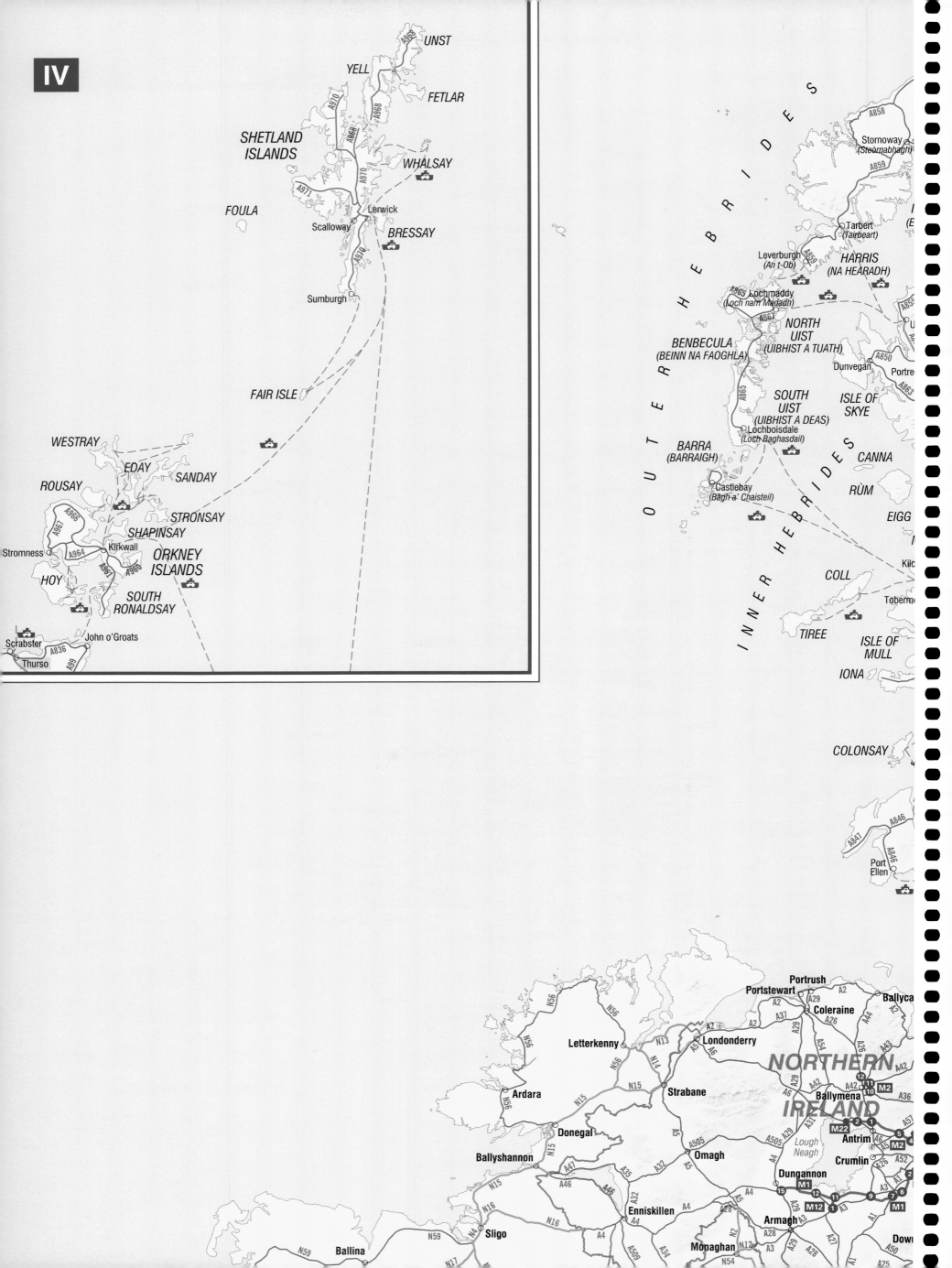

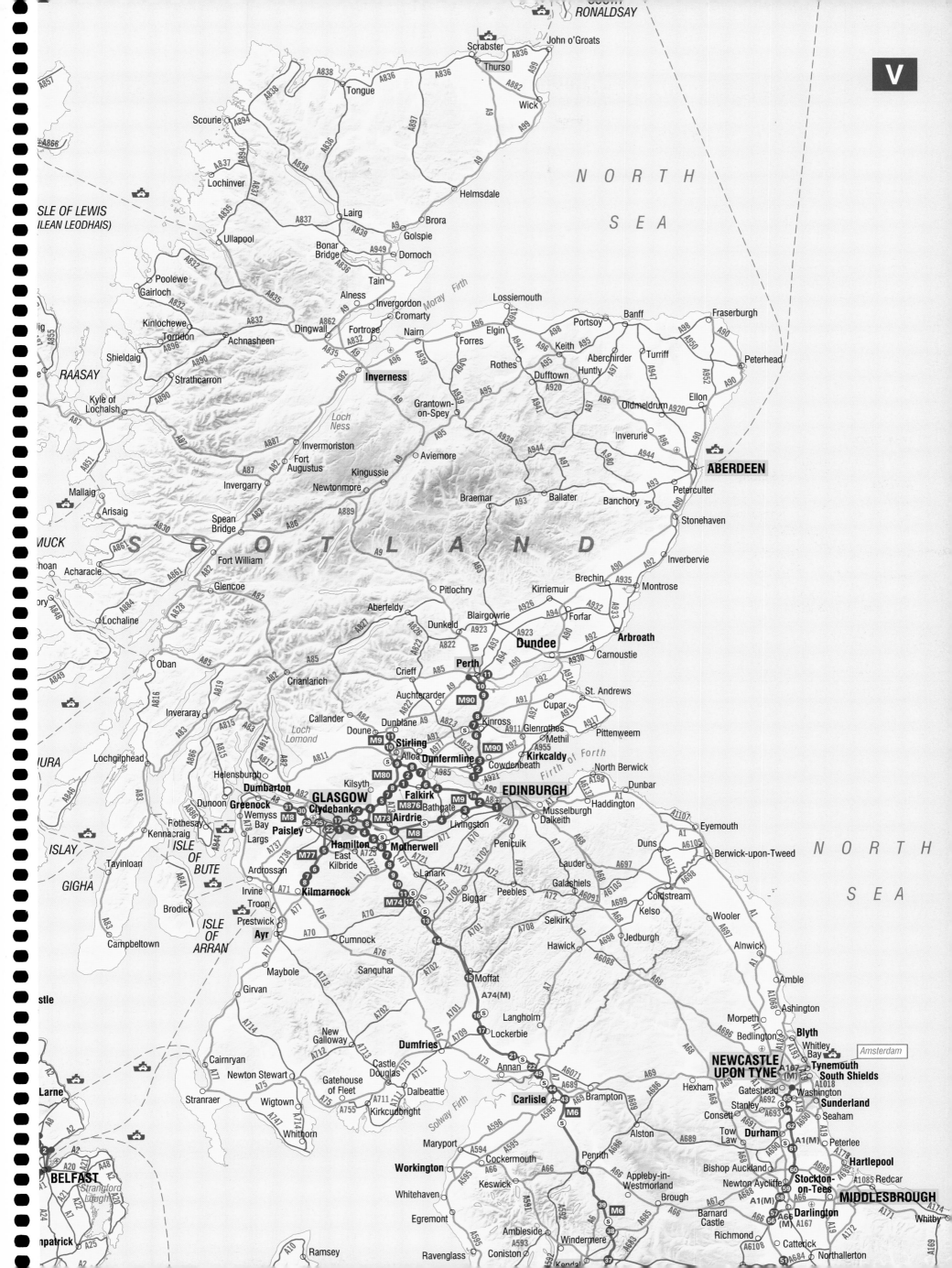

This chart shows the distance in miles and journey time between two cities or towns in Great Britain. Each route has been calculated using a combination of motorways, primary routes and other major roads. This is normally the quickest, though not always the shortest route.

Average journey times are calculated whilst driving at the maximum speed limit. These times are approximate and do not include traffic congestion or convenience breaks.

To find the distance and journey time between two cities or towns, follow a horizontal line and vertical column until they meet each other.

For example, the 285 mile journey from London to Penzance is approximately 4 hours and 59 minutes.

Northern Ireland

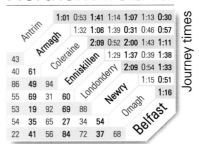

Journey times

				Antrim	1:01	0:53	1:41	1:14	1:07	1:13	0:30
					Armagh	1:32	1:06	1:39	0:31	0:46	0:57
				43		Coleraine	2:09	0:52	2:00	1:43	1:11
			40	61		Enniskillen	1:29	1:37	0:39	1:38
		86	49	94		Londonderry	2:09	0:54	1:33
	55	69	31	60		Newry	1:15	0:51
53	19	92	69	88		Omagh	1:16
54	35	65	27	34	54		**Belfast**
22	41	56	84	72	37	68	

Distance in miles

Belfast to London = 440m / 9:46h (excluding ferry)
Belfast to Glasgow = 104m / 4:46h (excluding ferry)

Britain

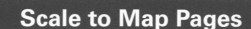

(Mileage chart and journey times between British towns and cities — a large triangular matrix of distances in miles and journey times, with labels: Aberdeen, Aberystwyth, Ayr, Birmingham, Bradford, Brighton, Bristol, Cambridge, Cardiff, Carlisle, Coventry, Derby, Doncaster, Dover, Edinburgh, Exeter, Fort William, Glasgow, Gloucester, Harwich, Holyhead, Inverness, Ipswich, Kendal, Kingston upon Hull, Leeds, Leicester, Lincoln, Liverpool, Manchester, Middlesbrough, Newcastle upon Tyne, Norwich, Nottingham, Oxford, Penzance, Perth, Plymouth, Portsmouth, Reading, Salisbury, Sheffield, Shrewsbury, Southampton, Southend-on-Sea, Stoke-on-Trent, Swansea, Thurso, Worcester, York, London.)

Distance in miles

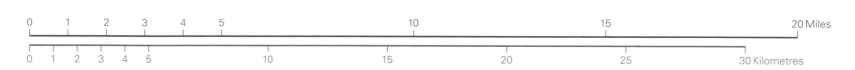

| 0 | 1 | 2 | 3 | 4 | 5 | | 10 | | 15 | | 20 Miles |

| 0 | 1 | 2 | 3 | 4 | 5 | | 10 | 15 | 20 | 25 | 30 Kilometres |

Reference Légende Zeichenerklärung

3

Motorway
Autoroute
Autobahn
M1

Motorway Under Construction
Autoroute en construction
Autobahn im Bau

Motorway Proposed
Autoroute prévue
Geplante Autobahn

Motorway Junctions with Numbers
Unlimited Interchange **4**
Limited Interchange **5**
Autoroute échangeur numéroté
Echangeur complet
Echangeur partiel
Autobahnanschlußstelle mit Nummer
Unbeschränkter Fahrtrichtungswechsel
Beschränkter Fahrtrichtungswechsel

Motorway Service Area (with fuel station)
with access from one carriageway only
Aire de services d'autoroute (avec station service)
accessible d'un seul côté
Rastplatz oder Raststätte (mit tankstelle)
Einbahn

Major Road Service Areas (with fuel station) with 24 hour facilities
Primary Route **S**   Class A Road **S**
Aire de services sur route prioritaire (avec station service) Ouverte 24h sur 24
Route à grande circulation   Route de type A
Raststätte (mit tankstelle) Durchgehend geöffnet
Hauptverkehrsstraße   A- Straße

Truckstop (selection of)
Sélection d'aire pour poids lourds
Auswahl von Fernfahrerrastplatz
T

Primary Route
Route à grande circulation
Hauptverkehrsstraße
A41

Primary Route Junction with Number
Echangeur numéroté
Hauptverkehrsstraßenkreuzung mit Nummer
5

Primary Route Destination
Route prioritaire, direction
Hauptverkehrsstraße Richtung
DOVER

Dual Carriageways (A & B roads)
Route à double chaussées séparées (route A & B)
Zweispurige Schnellstraße (A- und B- Straßen)

Class A Road
Route de type A
A-Straße
A129

Class B Road
Route de type B
B-Straße
B177

Narrow Major Road (passing places)
Route prioritaire étroite (possibilité de dépassement)
Schmale Hauptverkehrsstraße (mit Überholmöglichkeit)

Major Roads Under Construction
Route prioritaire en construction
Hauptverkehrsstaße im Bau

Major Roads Proposed
Route prioritaire prévue
Geplante Hauptverkehrsstraße

Safety Cameras with Speed Limits
Single Camera **30**
Multiple Cameras located along road **50**
Single & Multiple Variable Speed Cameras **V V**
Radars de contrôle de vitesse
Radar simple
Radars multiples situés le long de la route
Radars simples et multiples de contrôle de vitesse variable
Sicherheitskameras mit Tempolimit
Einzelne Kamera
Mehrere Kameras entlang der Straße
Einzelne und mehrere Kameras für variables Tempolimit

Fuel Station
Station service
Tankstelle

Gradient 1:5 (20%) **& steeper**
(ascent in direction of arrow)
Pente égale ou supérieure à 20% (dans le sens de la montée)
20% Steigung und steiler (in Pfeilrichtung)

Toll
Barrière de péage
Gebührenpflichtig
TOLL

Mileage between markers
Distence en miles entre les flèches
Strecke zwischen Markierungen in Meilen
8

Railway and Station
Voie ferrée et gare
Eisenbahnlinie und Bahnhof

Level Crossing and Tunnel
Passage à niveau et tunnel
Bahnübergang und Tunnel

River or Canal
Rivière ou canal
Fluß oder Kanal

County or Unitary Authority Boundary
Limite de comté ou de division administrative
Grafschafts- oder Verwaltungsbezirksgrenze

National Boundary
Frontière nationale
Landesgrenze

Built-up Area
Agglomération
Geschloßene Ortschaft

Village or Hamlet
Village ou hameau
Dorf oder Weiler

Wooded Area
Zone boisée
Waldgebiet

Spot Height in Feet
Altitude (en pieds)
Höhe in Fuß
• 813

Relief above 400' (122m)
Relief par estompage au-dessus de 400' (122m)
Reliefschattierung über 400' (122m)

National Grid Reference (kilometres)
Coordonnées géographiques nationales (Kilomètres)
Nationale geographische Koordinaten (Kilometer)
100

Page Continuation
Suite à la page indiquée
Seitenfortsetzung
48

Area covered by Main Route map
Répartition des cartes des principaux axes routiers
Von Karten mit Hauptverkehrsstrecken
MAIN ROUTE 180

Area covered by Town Plan
Ville ayant un plan à la page indiquée
Von Karten mit Stadtplänen erfaßter Bereich
SEE PAGE 194

Tourist Information Information Touristeninformationen

i

Airport
Aéroport
Flughafen

Airfield
Terrain d'aviation
Flugplatz

Heliport
Héliport
Hubschrauberlandeplatz

Battle Site and Date
Champ de bataille et date
Schlachtfeld und Datum
1066

Castle (open to public)
Château (ouvert au public)
Schloß / Burg (für die Öffentlichkeit zugänglich)

Castle with Garden (open to public)
Château avec parc (ouvert au public)
Schloß mit Garten (für die Öffentlichkeit zugänglich)

Cathedral, Abbey, Church, Friary, Priory
Cathédrale, abbaye, église, monastère, prieuré
Kathedrale, Abtei, Kirche, Mönchskloster, Kloster

Country Park
Parc régional
Landschaftspark

Ferry (vehicular, sea)
(vehicular, river)
(foot only)
Bac (véhicules, mer)
(véhicules, rivière)
(piétons)
Fähre (auto, meer)
(auto, fluß)
(nur für Personen)

Garden (open to public)
Jardin (ouvert au public)
Garten (für die Öffentlichkeit zugänglich)

Golf Course (9 hole) (18 hole)
Terrain de golf (9 trous) (18 trous)
Golfplatz (9 Löcher) (18 Löcher)

Historic Building (open to public)
Monument historique (ouvert au public)
Historisches Gebäude (für die Öffentlichkeit zugänglich)

Historic Building with Garden (open to public)
Monument historique avec jardin (ouvert au public)
Historisches Gebäude mit Garten (für die Öffentlichkeit zugänglich)

Horse Racecourse
Hippodrome
Pferderennbahn

Lighthouse
Phare
Leuchtturm

Motor Racing Circuit
Circuit Automobile
Automobilrennbahn

Museum, Art Gallery
Musée
Museum, Galerie

National Park
Parc national
Nationalpark

National Trust Property
(open) *NT*
(restricted opening) *NT*
(National Trust for Scotland) *NTS NTS*
National Trust Property
(ouvert)
(heures d'ouverture)
(National Trust for Scotland)
National Trust- Eigentum
(geöffnet)
(beschränkte Öffnungszeit)
(National Trust for Scotland)

Nature Reserve or Bird Sanctuary
Réserve naturelle botanique ou ornithologique
Natur- oder Vogelschutzgebiet

Nature Trail or Forest Walk
Chemin forestier, piste verte
Naturpfad oder Waldweg

Place of Interest *Monument* •
Site, curiosité
Sehenswürdigkeit

Picnic Site
Lieu pour pique-nique
Picknickplatz

Railway, Steam or Narrow Gauge
Chemin de fer, à vapeur ou à voie étroite
Eisenbahn, Dampf- oder Schmalspurbahn

Theme Park
Centre de loisirs
Vergnügungspark

Tourist Information Centre
Syndicat d'initiative
Information

Viewpoint (360 degrees) (180 degrees)
Vue panoramique (360 degrés) (180 degrés)
Aussichtspunkt (360 Grade) (180 Grade)

Visitor Information Centre
Centre d'information touristique
Besucherzentrum

Wildlife Park
Réserve de faune
Wildpark

Windmill
Moulin à vent
Windmühle

Zoo or Safari Park
Parc ou réserve zoologique
Zoo oder Safari-Park

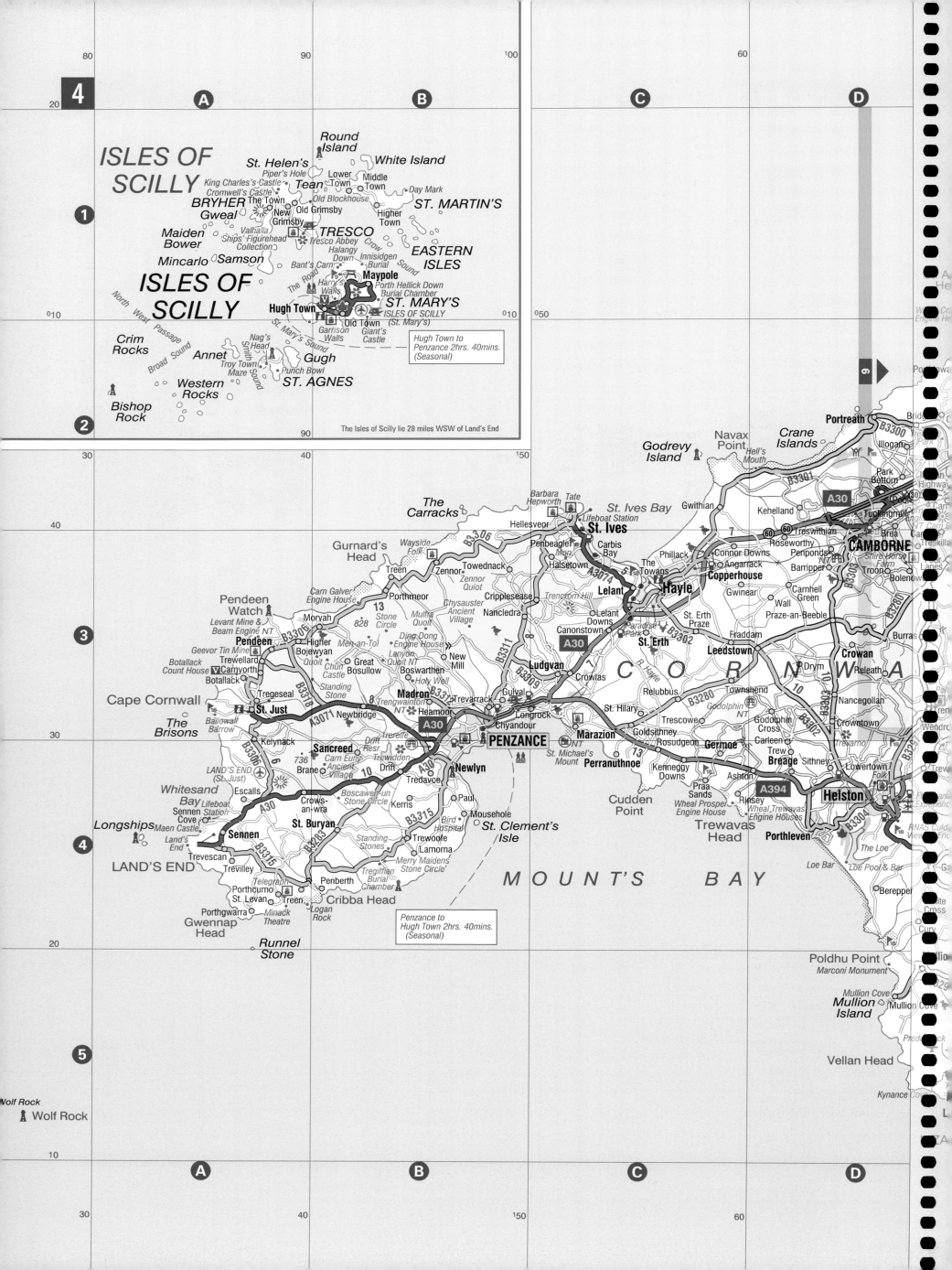

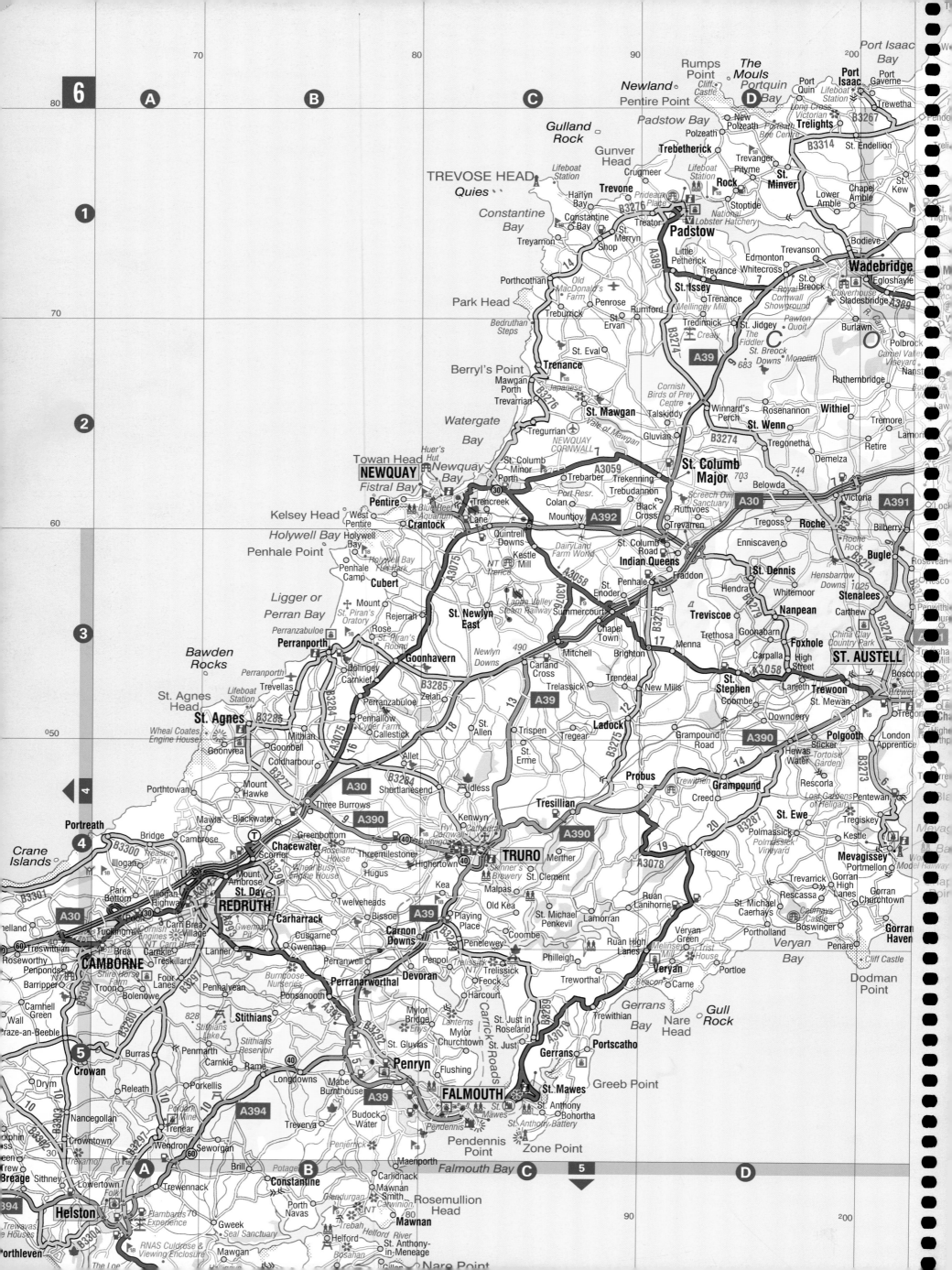

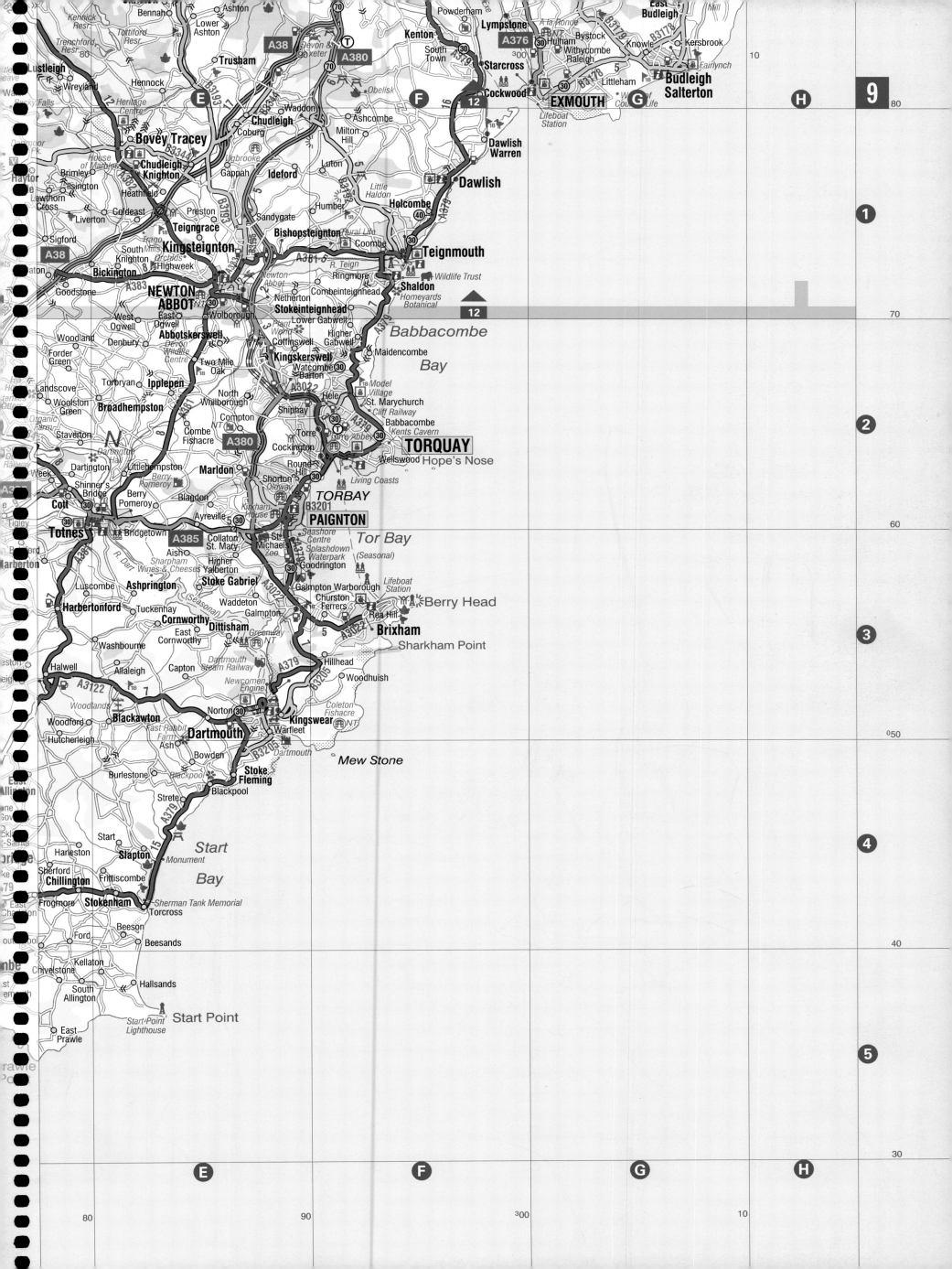

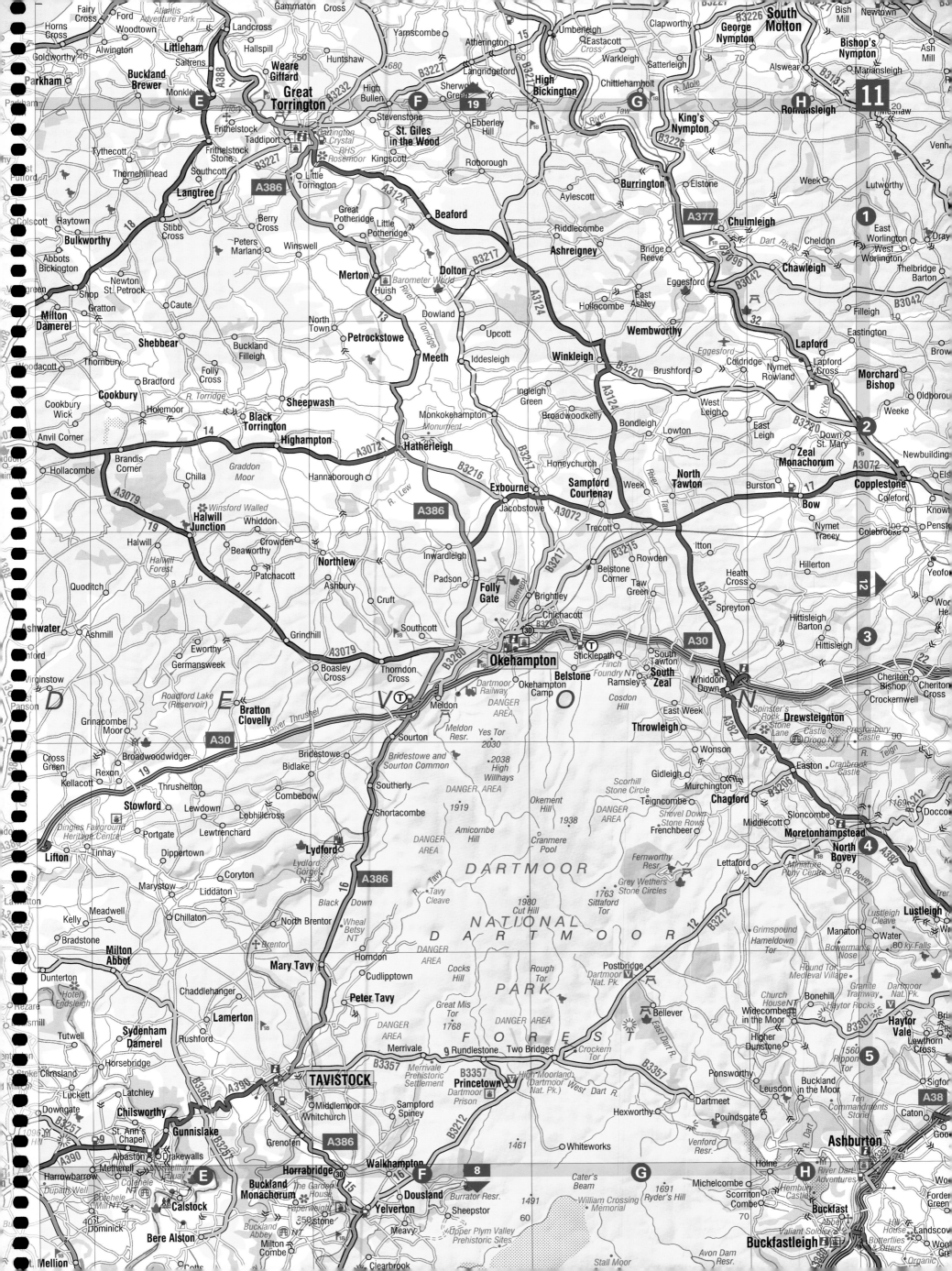

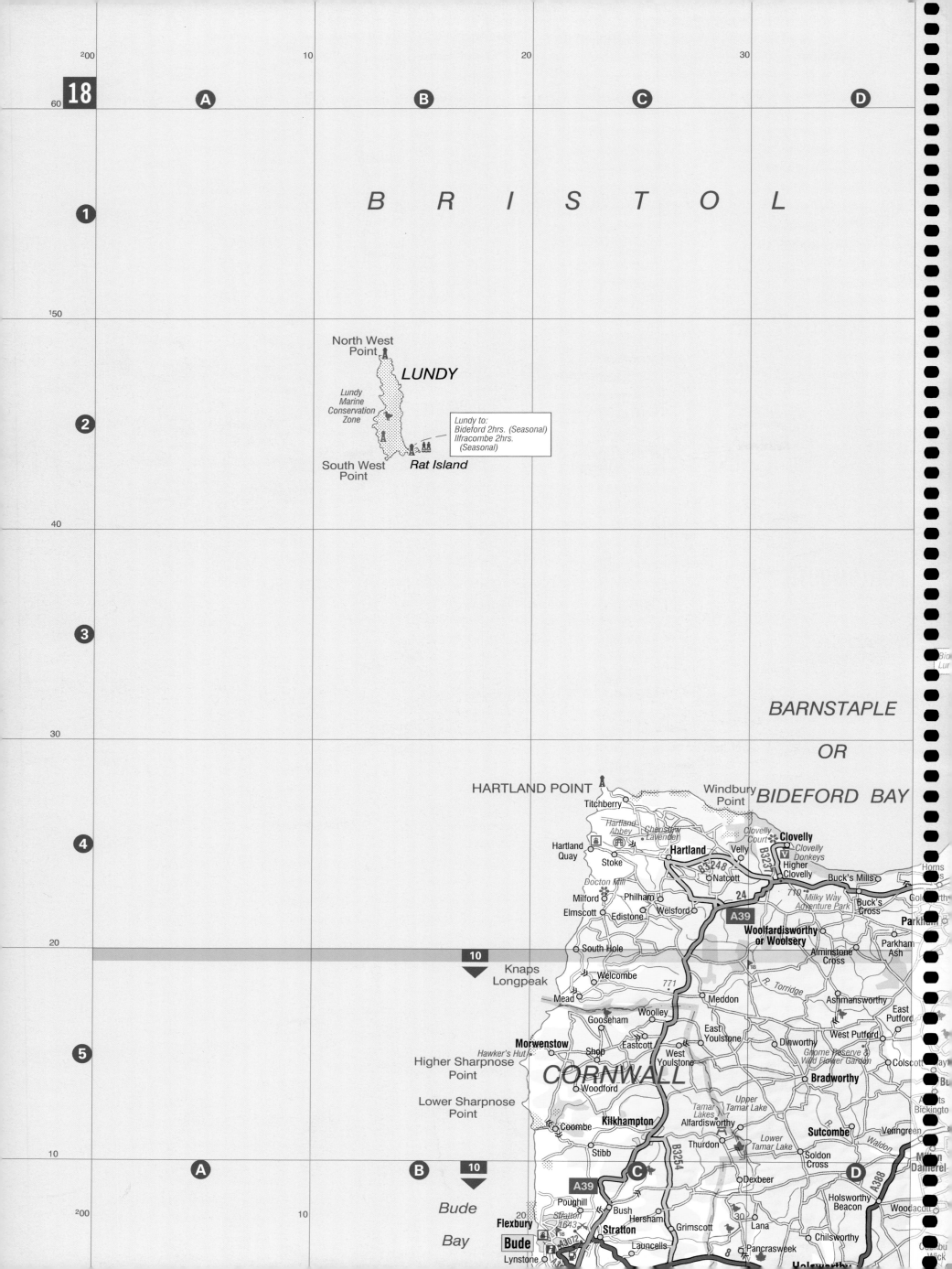

B R I S T O L

LUNDY

North West
Point

Lundy
Marine
Conservation
Zone

South West
Point

Rat Island

Lundy to:
Bideford 2hrs. (Seasonal)
Ilfracombe 2hrs.
(Seasonal)

BARNSTAPLE

OR

BIDEFORD BAY

HARTLAND POINT

Windbury
Point

Titchberry

Hartland
Abbey

Cheristow
Lavender

Clovelly
Court

Clovelly

Clovelly
Donkeys

Hartland
Quay

Hartland

Velly

Higher
Clovelly

Stoke

B3248

B3237

Buck's Mills

Docton Mill

Natcott

24

Milky Way
Adventure Park

Buck's
Cross

Milford

Philham

A39

Horns

Elmscott

Edistone

Welsford

Woolfardisworthy
or Woolsery

Parkham

Parkham
Ash

South Hole

Alminstone
Cross

10

Knaps
Longpeak

Welcombe

771

Meddon

R. Torridge

Ashmansworthy

East
Putford

Mead

Woolley

East
Youlstone

Dinworthy

West Putford

Gooseham

Morwenstow

Hawker's Hut

Shop

Eastcott

West
Youlstone

Gnome Reserve &
Wild Flower Garden

Colscott

Higher Sharpnose
Point

CORNWALL

Woodford

Bradworthy

Lower Sharpnose
Point

Tamar
Lakes

Upper
Tamar Lake

Sutcombe

Venngreen

Coombe

Kilkhampton

Alfardisworthy

Lower
Tamar Lake

Bickingto

Stibb

Thurdon

B3254

Soldon
Cross

Waldon

Milton
Damerel

A39

Dexbeer

Lana

A3072

Poughill

Bush

Hersham

Grimscott

Holsworthy
Beacon

Woodacott

Flexbury

Stratton
1643

Stratton

Lynstone

Launcells

Pancrasweek

8

Bude

Bude
Bay

Chilsworthy

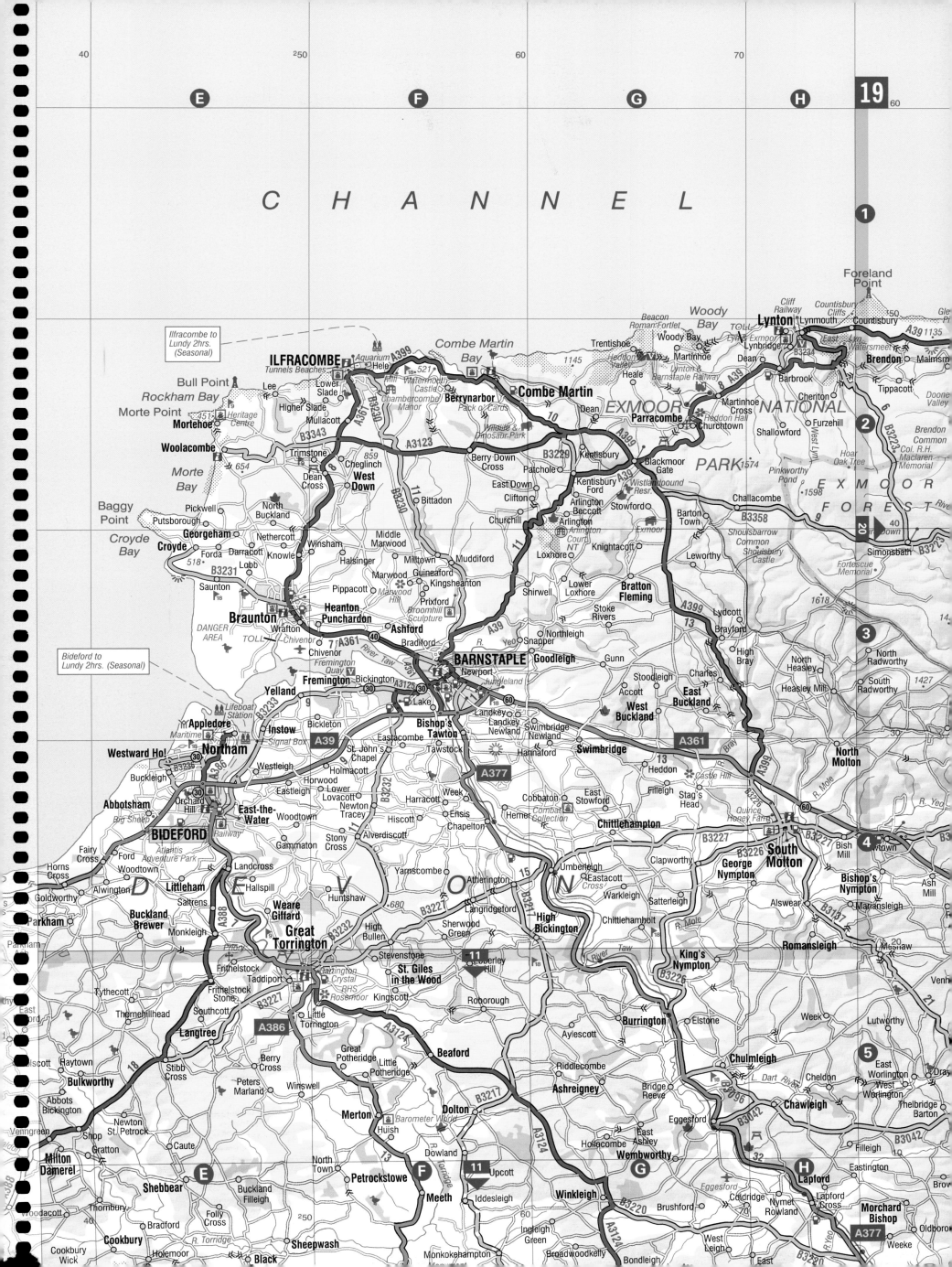

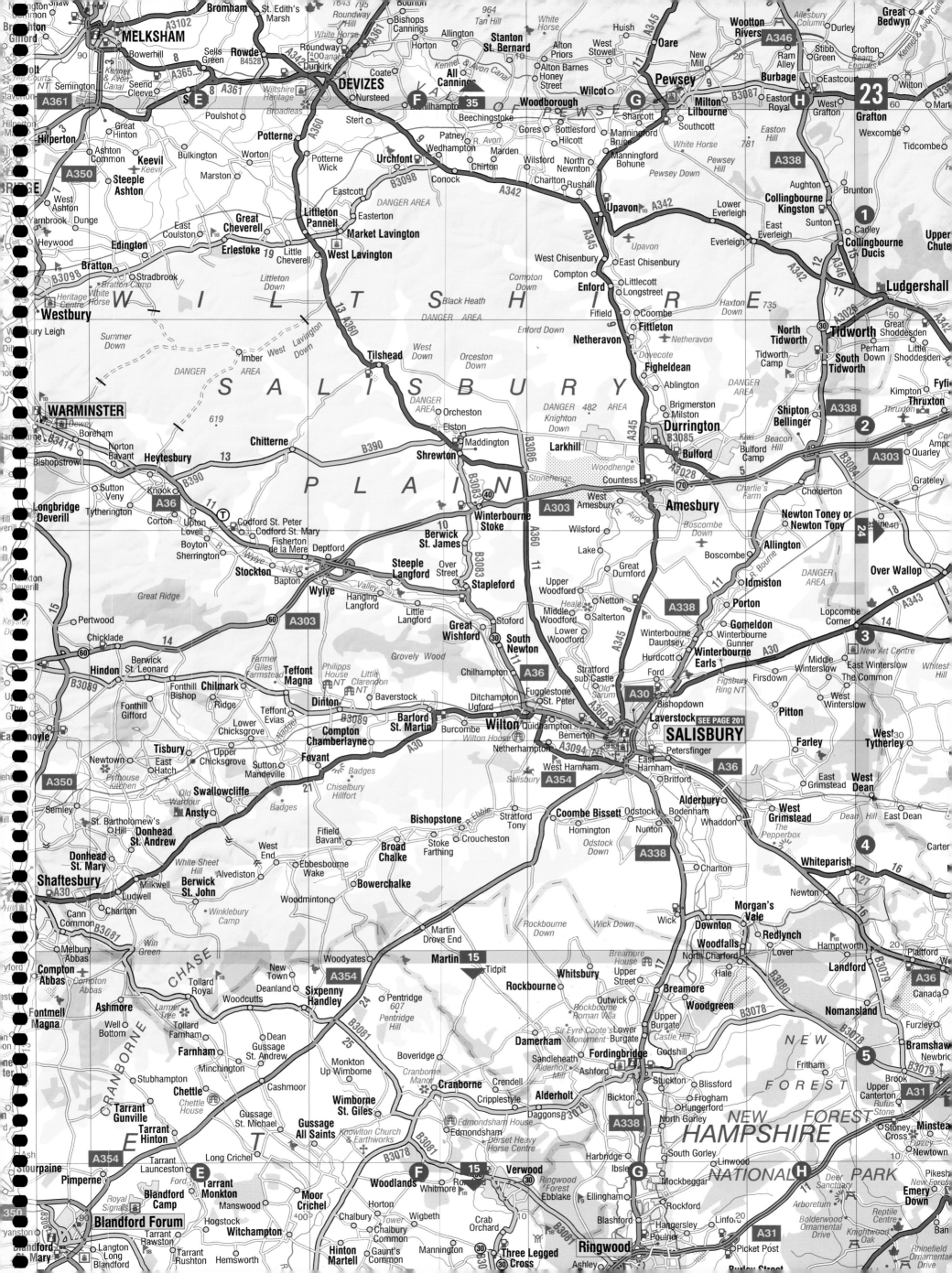

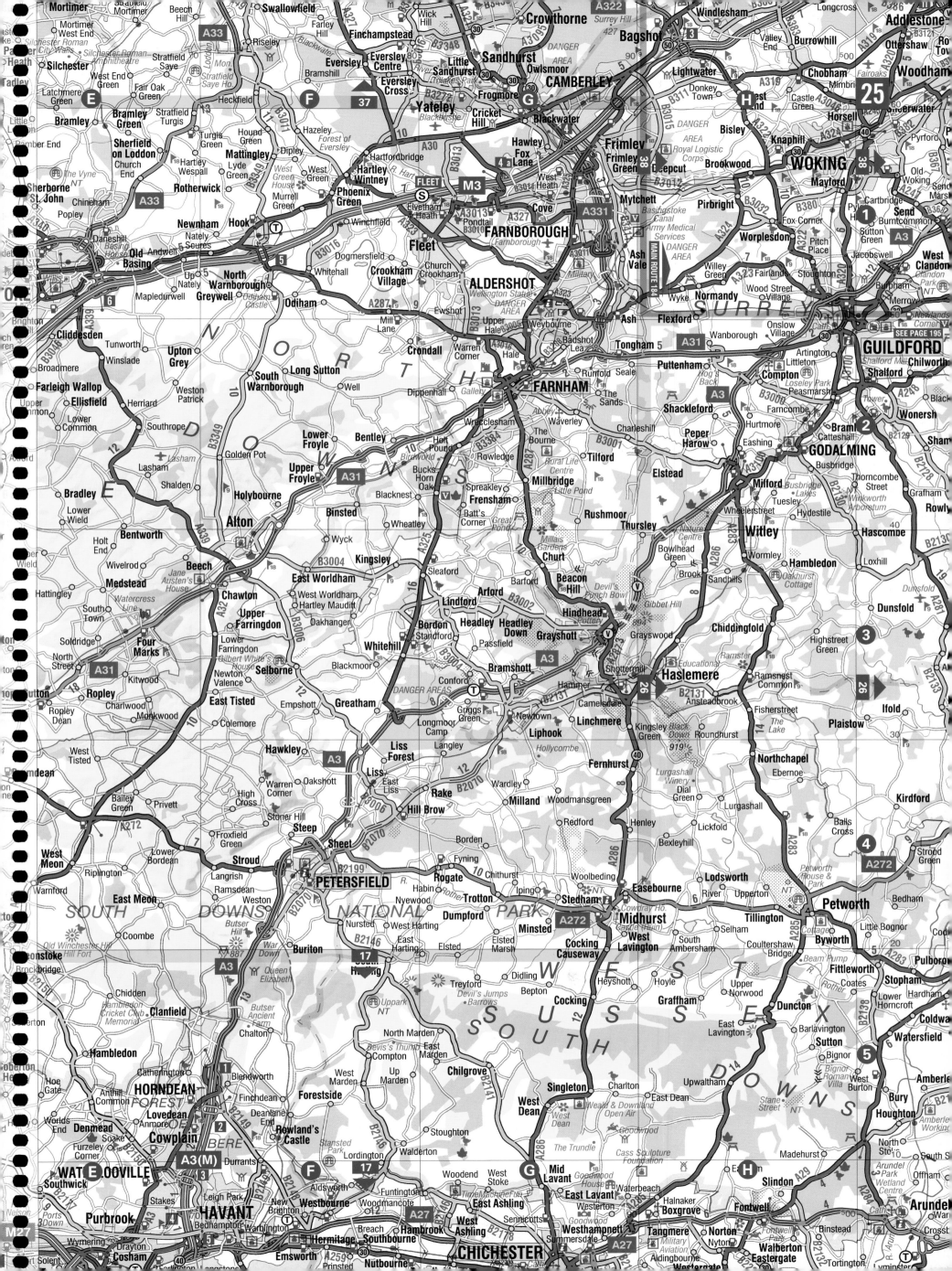

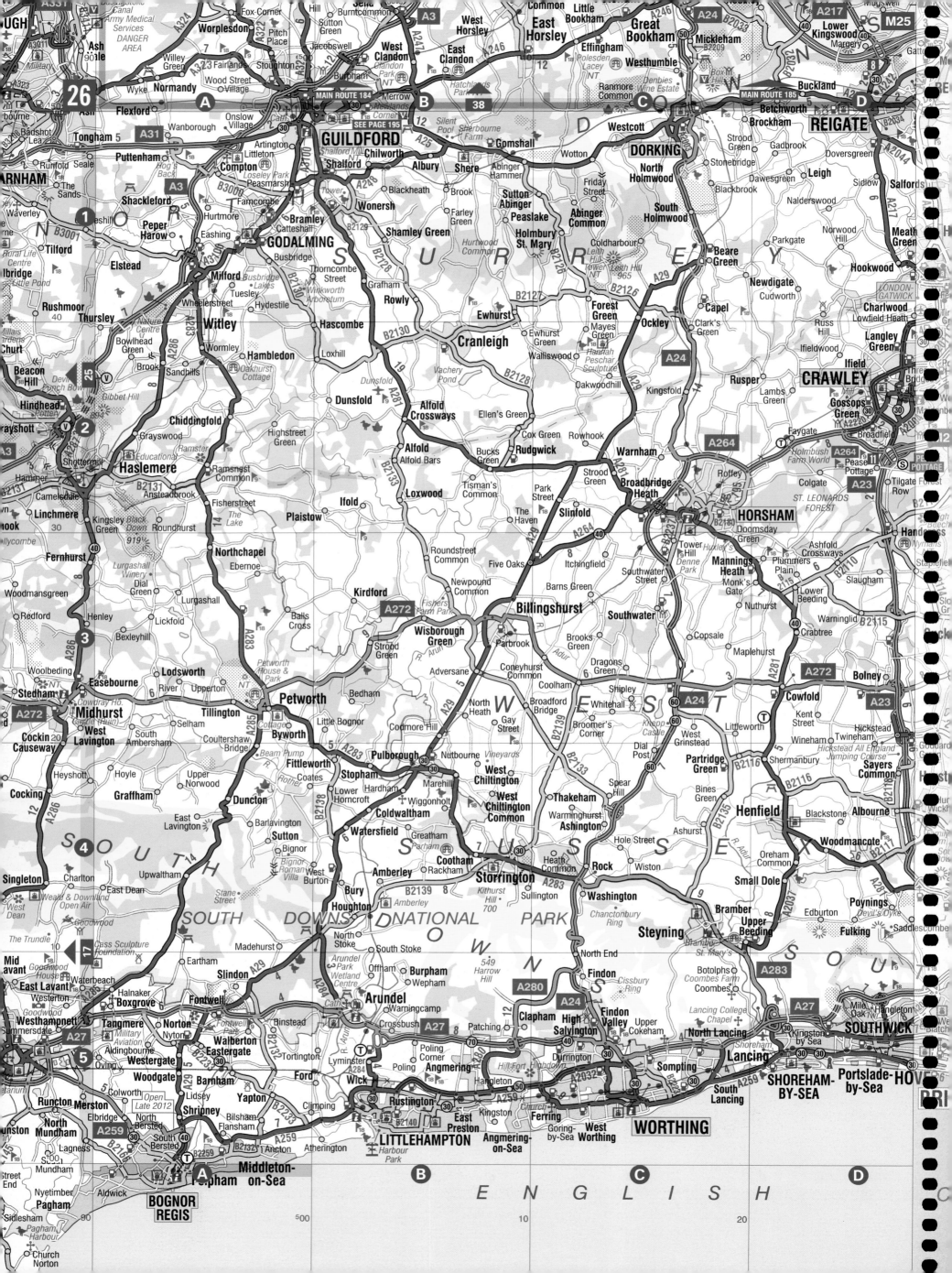

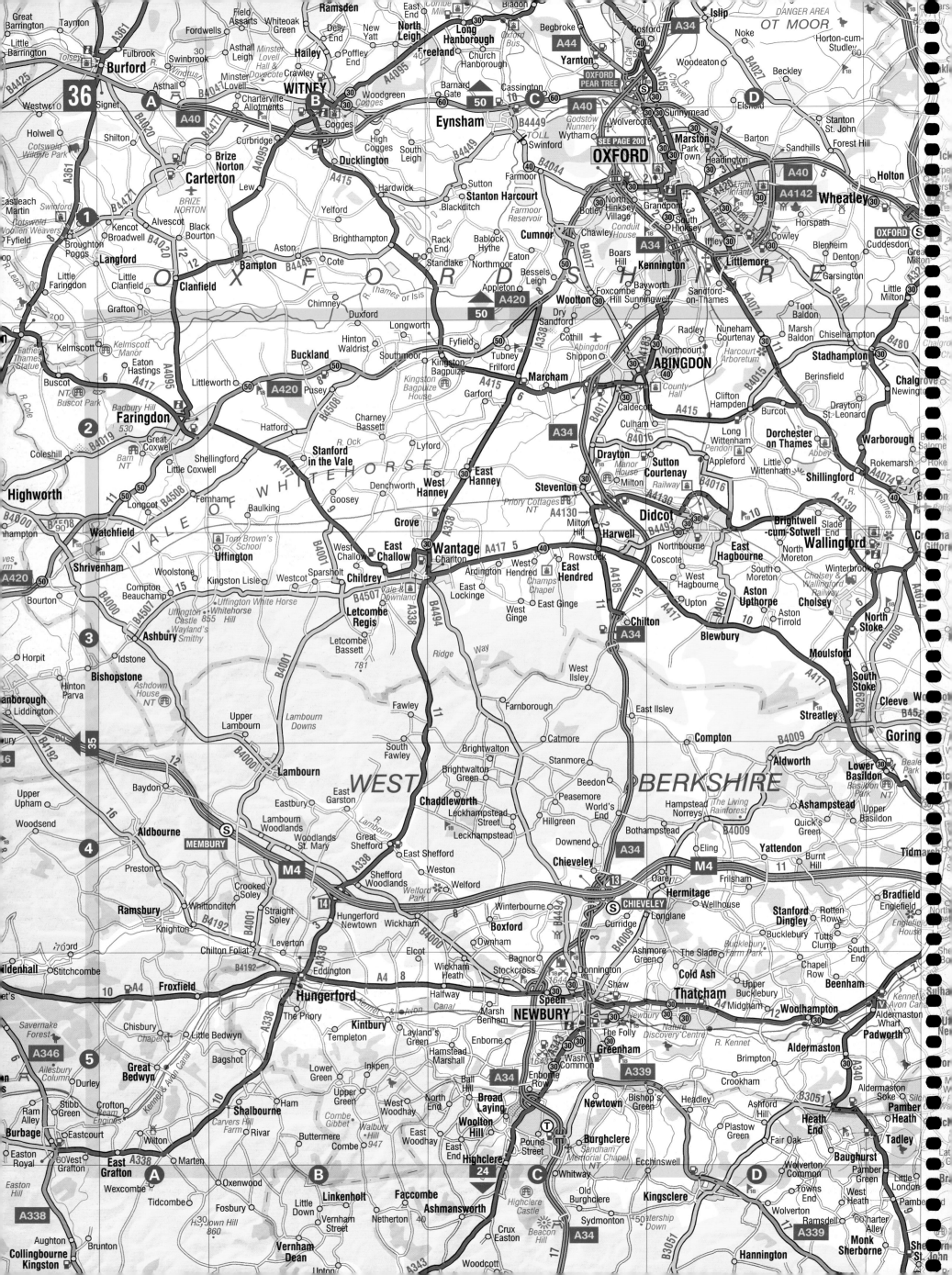

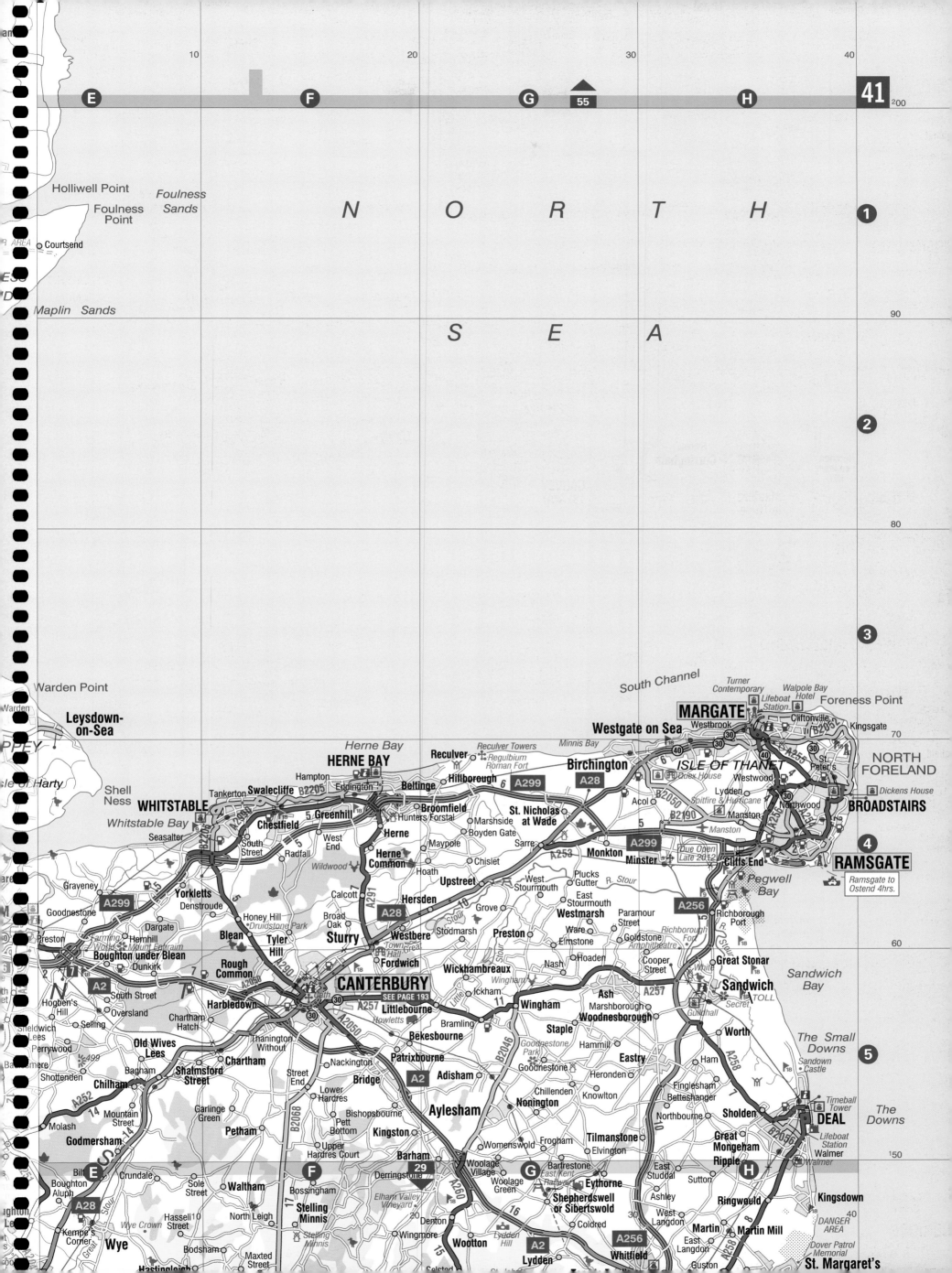

10 20 30 40

N O R T H

Holliwell Point
Foulness
Sands
Foulness
Point

Courtsend

S E A

Maplin Sands

1

90

2

80

3

South Channel
Turner
Contemporary
Walpole Bay
Hotel Foreness Point
Lifeboat
Station

Warden Point

MARGATE
Kingsgate

Westbrook
Cliftonville

**Leysdown-
on-Sea**

Westgate on Sea
Minnis Bay
**NORTH
FORELAND**

Herne Bay
Reculver Towers
Regulbium
Roman Fort

ISLE OF THANET

Isle of Harty

Shell
Ness

HERNE BAY
Reculver

Birchington

Acol
Westwood

Spitfire & Hurricane
Lydden

Hampton
Hillborough

Northwood

St.
Peter's

WHITSTABLE
Tankerton
Swalecliffe
B2205
Eddington
Beltinge

BROADSTAIRS

Manston
Whitstable Bay
Chestfield
Broomfield
**St. Nicholas
at Wade**
Manston

Dickens House

Seasalter
Greenhill
Hunters Forstal
Marshside
Sarre
A299

South
Street
West
End
Herne
Maypole
Boyden Gate
Monkton
Cliffs End
4
RAMSGATE

Radfall
**Herne
Common**
Hoath
Chislet
Minster

*Ramsgate to
Ostend 4hrs.*

Graveney
Wildwood
Upstreet
West
Stourmouth
Plucks
Gutter
Pegwell
Bay

Goodnestone
Yorkletts
Denstroude
Calcott
Hersden
Grove
East
Stourmouth
Richborough
Port

Preston
Dargate
Honey Hill
Druidstone Park
Broad
Oak
Westbere
Stodmarsh
Preston
Westmarsh
Paramour
Street
Richborough
Fort

Hernhill
Blean
Sturry
Ware
Goldstone
Amphitheatre

Boughton under Blean
Dunkirk
**Tyler
Hill**
Wickhambreaux
Nash
Elmstone
Great Stonar

Hogben's
Hill
South Street
**Rough
Common**
Fordwich
Ickham
Ash
Hoaden
Cooper
Street
Sandwich
*Sandwich
Bay*

Overland
CANTERBURY
Harbledown
SEE PAGE 193
Littlebourne
Wingham
Marshborough
*The Small
Downs*

Sheldwich
Lees
Selling
Chartham
Hatch
Howletts
Bramling
Woodnesborough
Worth
Sandown
Castle

Perrywood
**Old Wives
Lees**
Thanington
Without
Bekesbourne
Hammill
Eastry
Ham

Chartham
Street
End
Patrixbourne
Staple
Heronden
Finglesham
Betteshanger
Northbourne

Chilham
**Shalmsford
Street**
Nackington
Lower
Hardres
Adisham
Chillenden
Knowlton
Sholden
Timeball
Tower

Bagham
Bridge
Nonington
Womenswold
Frogham
Tilmanstone
Great
Mongeham
DEAL

Molash
Mountain
Street
Garlinge
Green
Kingston
Aylesham
Elvington
Ripple

Godmersham
Petham
Bishopsbourne
Pett
Bottom
Barham
Womenswold
Bartrestone
East
Studdal
Sutton
Walmer
*The
Downs*

Lifeboat
Station
Walmer

Boughton
Aluph
Waltham
Sole
Street
Derringstone
Woolage
Village
Woolage
Green
Eythorne
Ashley
West
Langdon
Ringwould
Kingsdown

Kempe's
Corner
Bossingham
North Leigh
**Stelling
Minnis**
*Elham Valley
Vineyard*
Shepherdswell
or Sibertswold
West
Langdon
Martin
Martin Mill
*DANGER
AREA*

Wye
Hassell
Stelling
Minnis
Denton
Coldred
*Dover Patrol
Memorial*

Bodsham
Maxted
Street
Wingmore
Wootton
A2
Whitfield
Guston

Hastingleigh
Selstad
Lydden
St. Margaret's

70

60

150

40

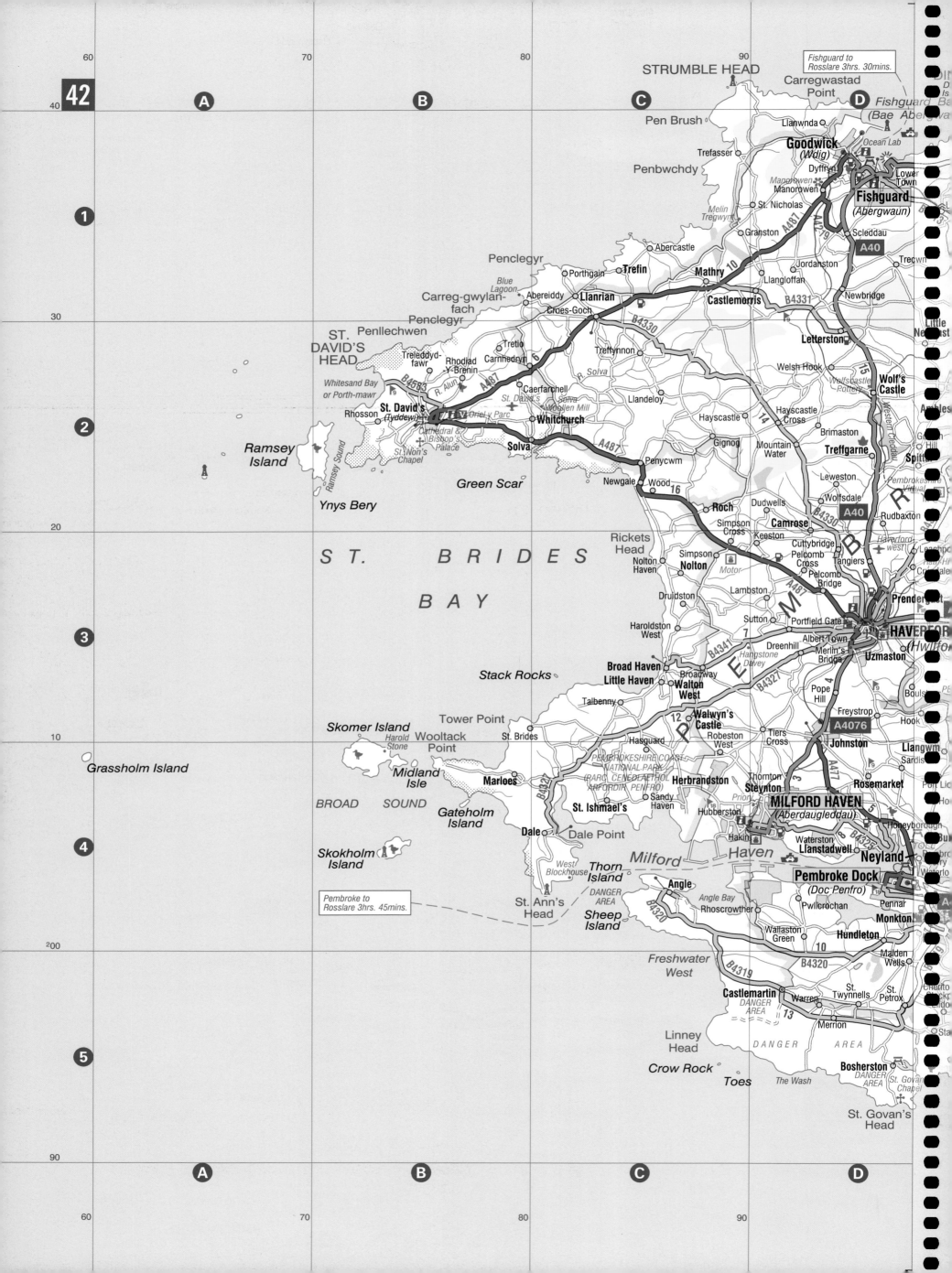

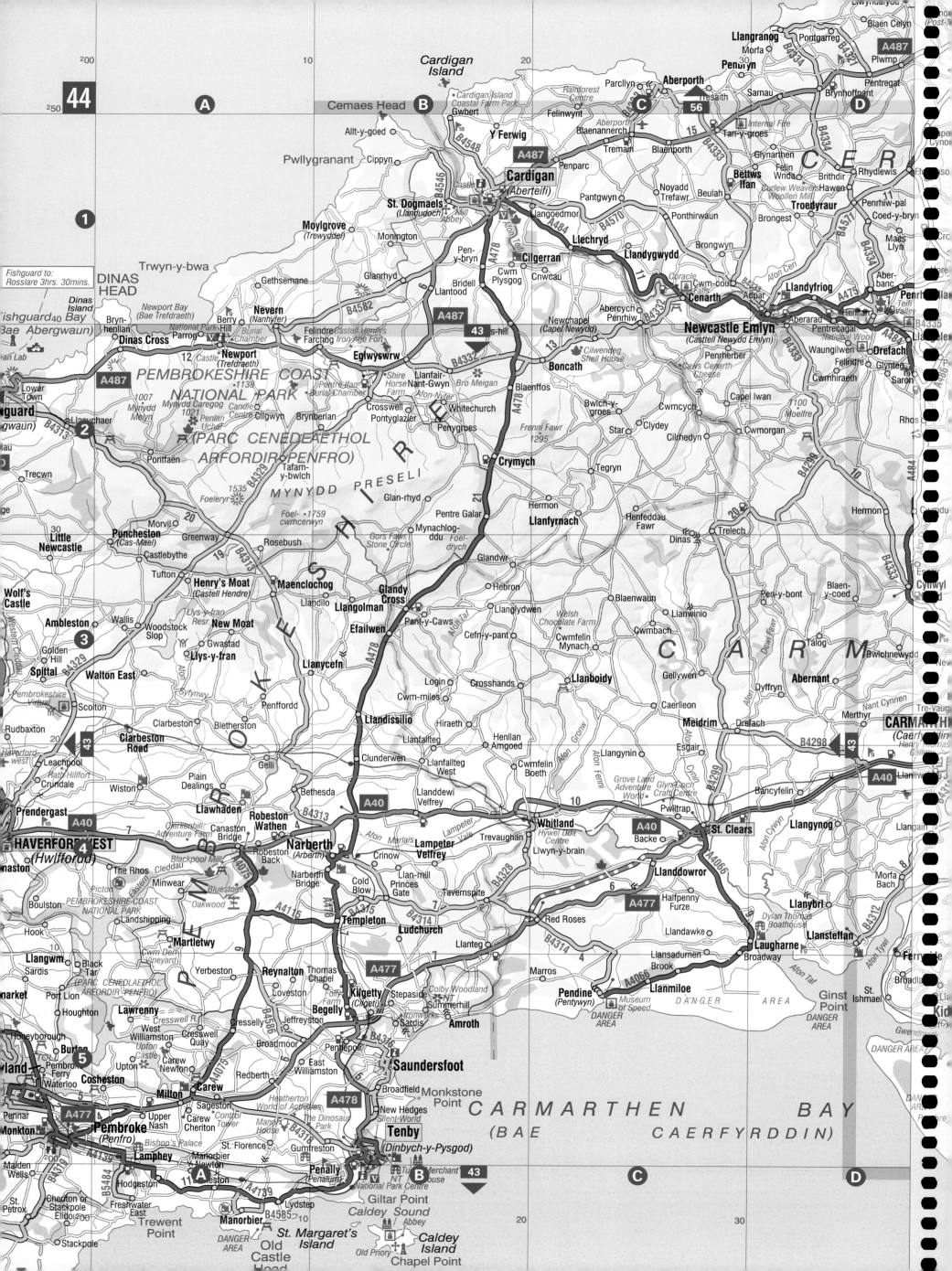

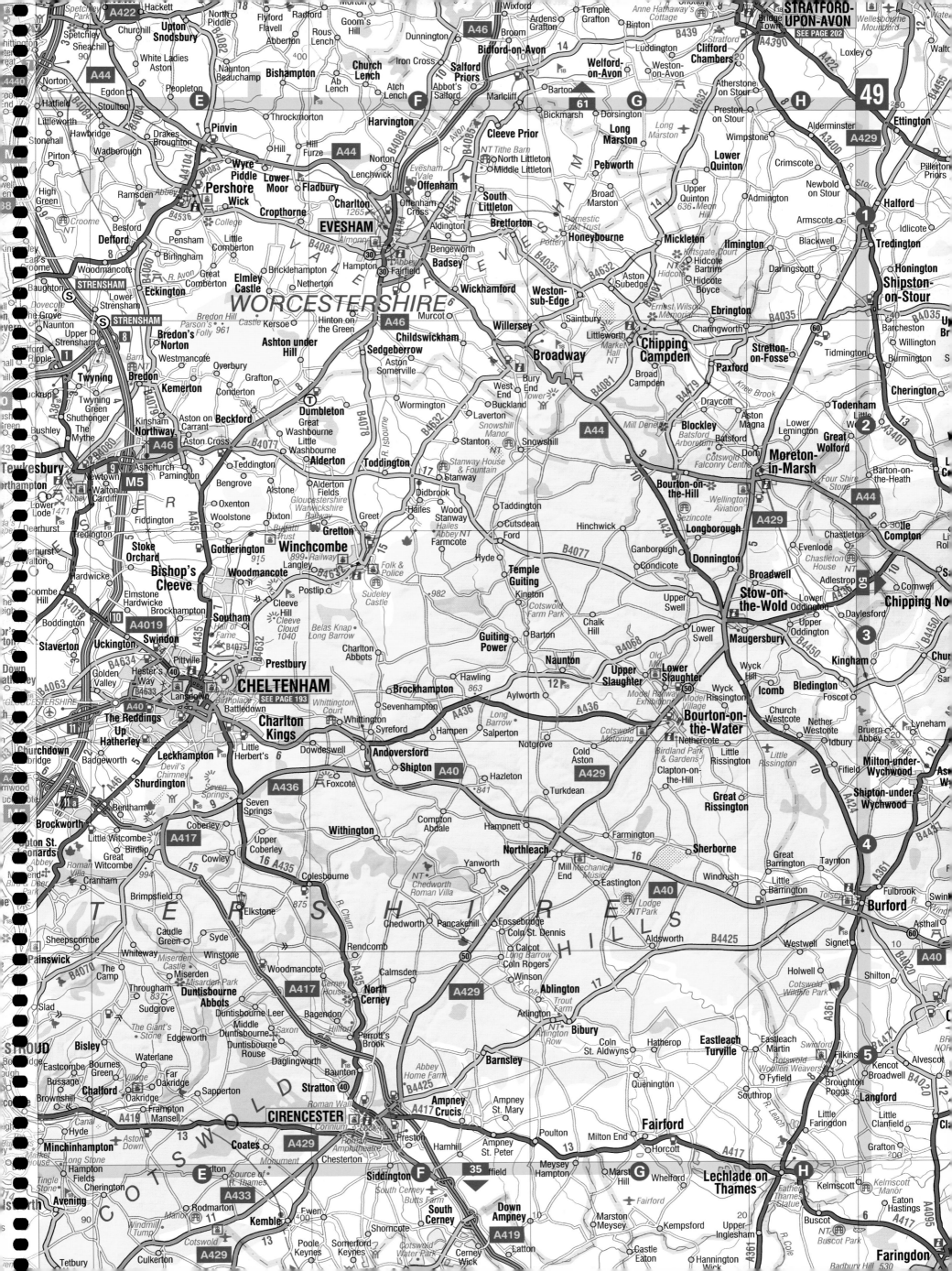

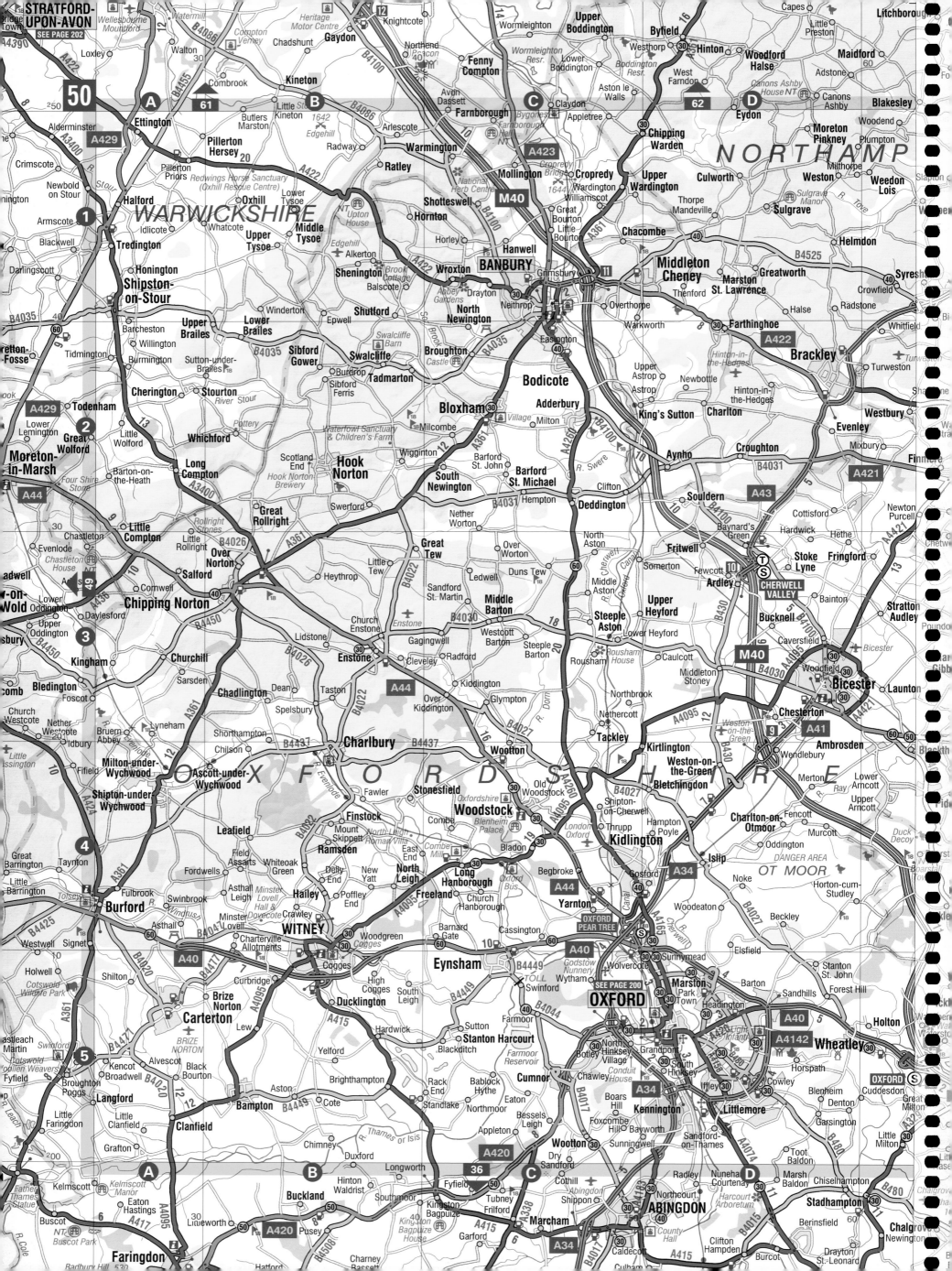

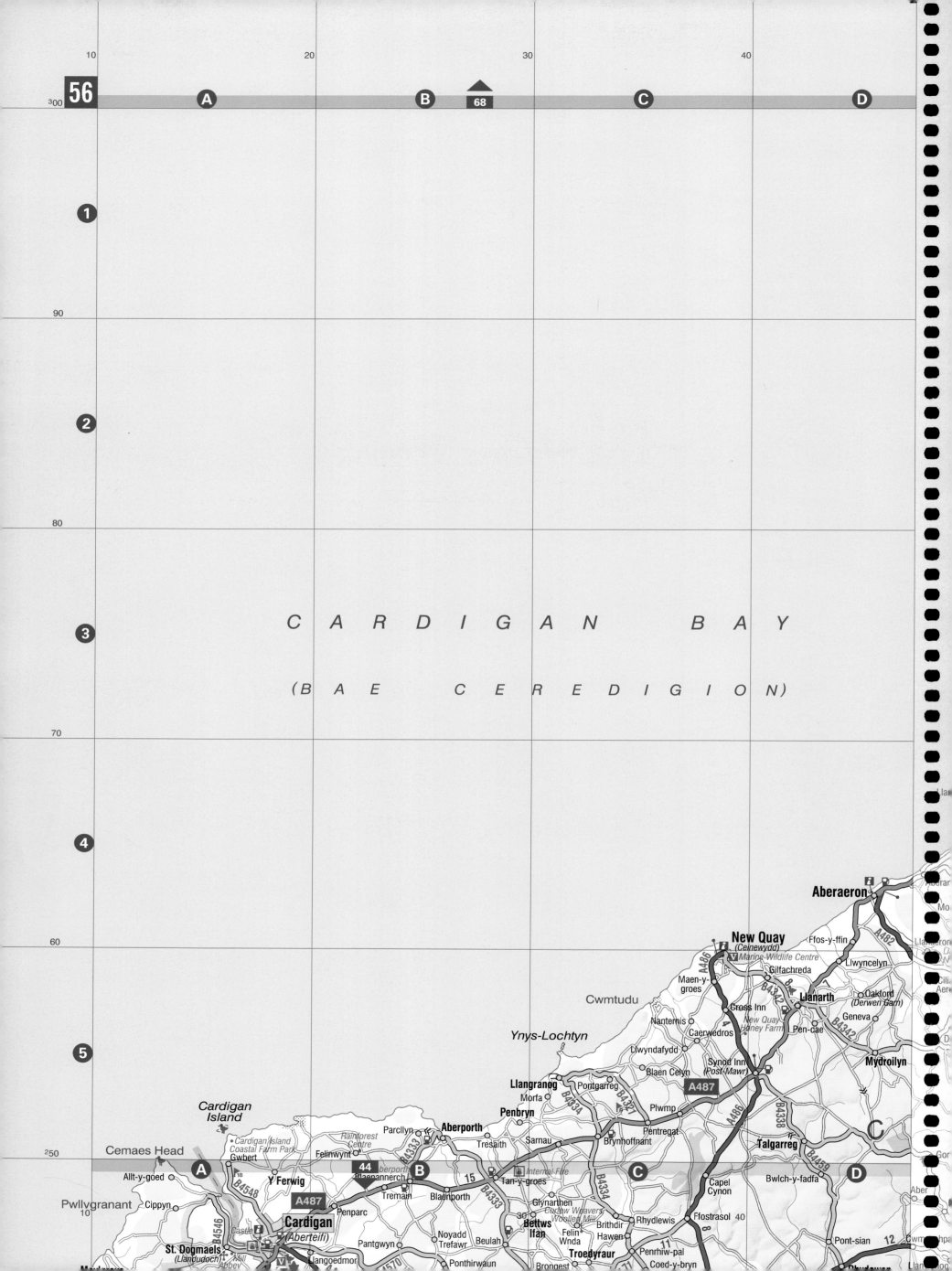

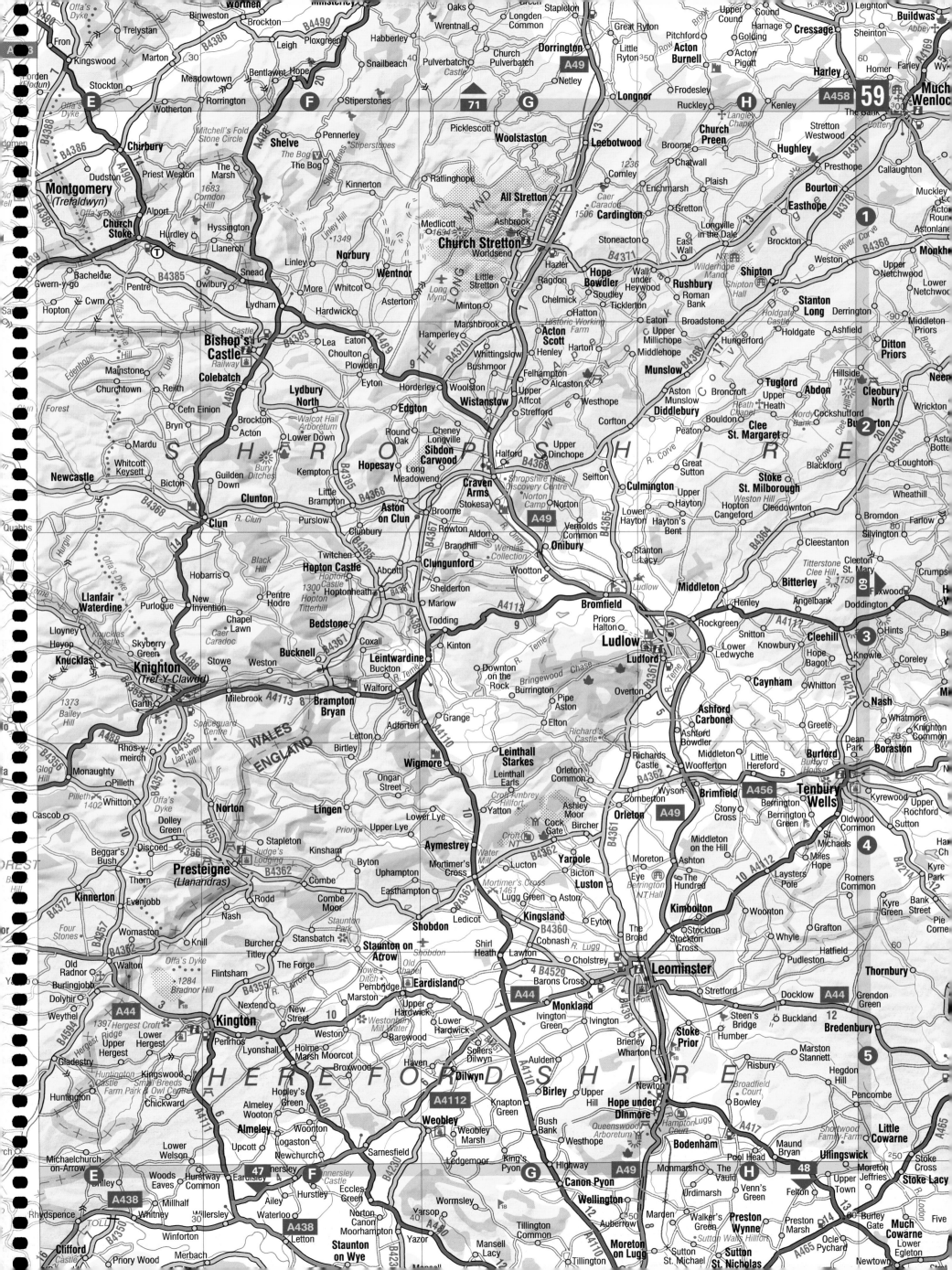

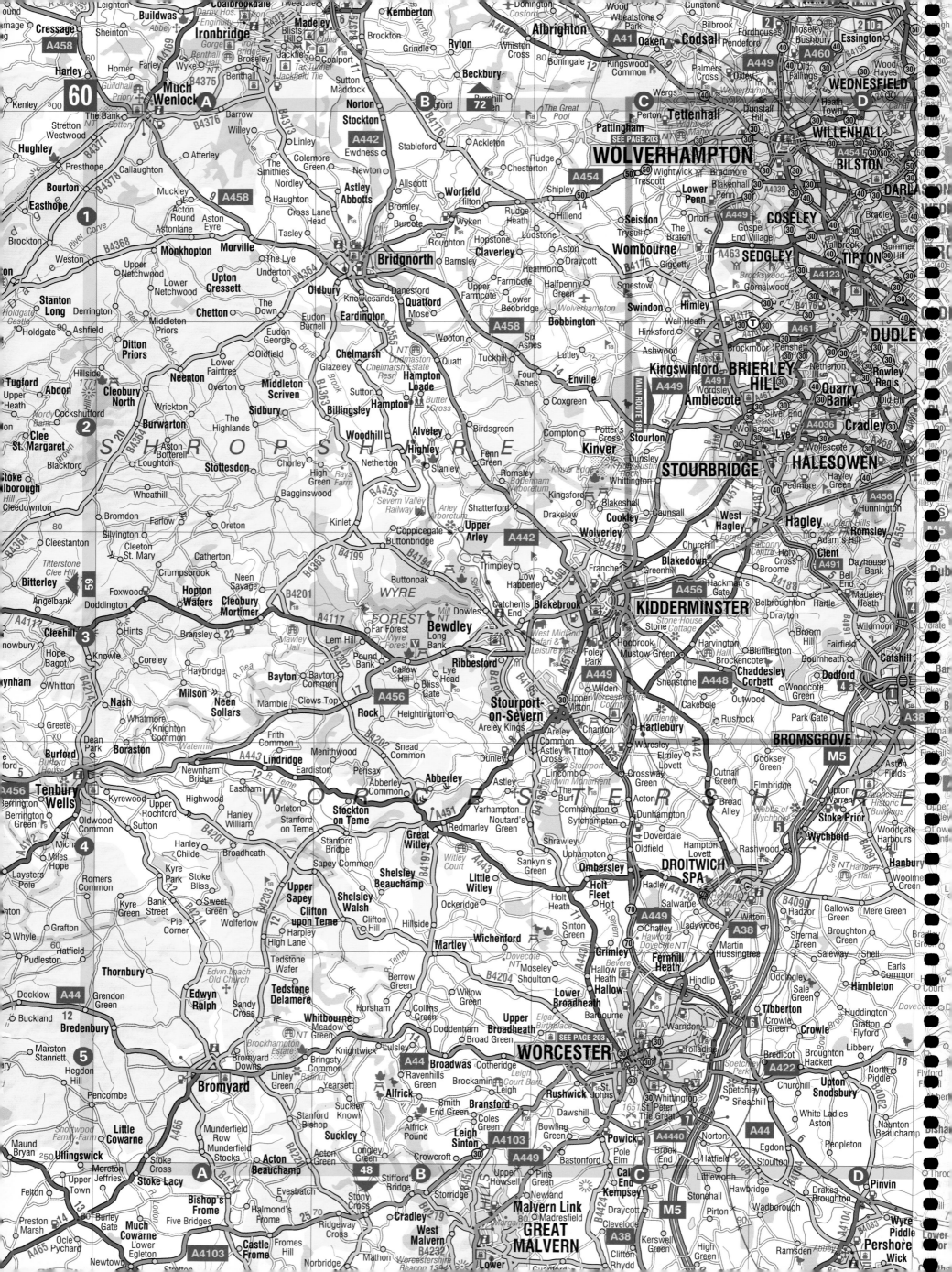

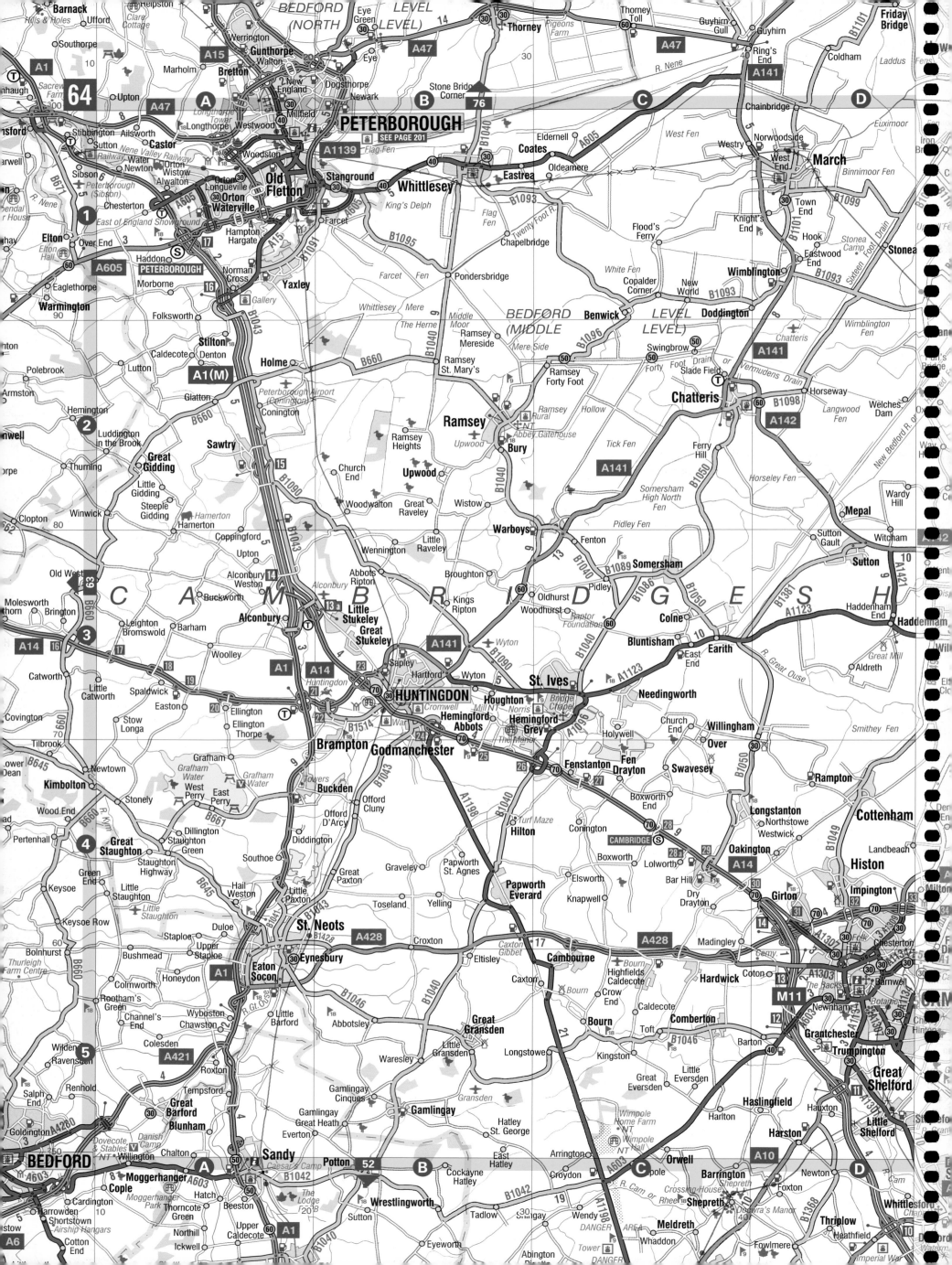

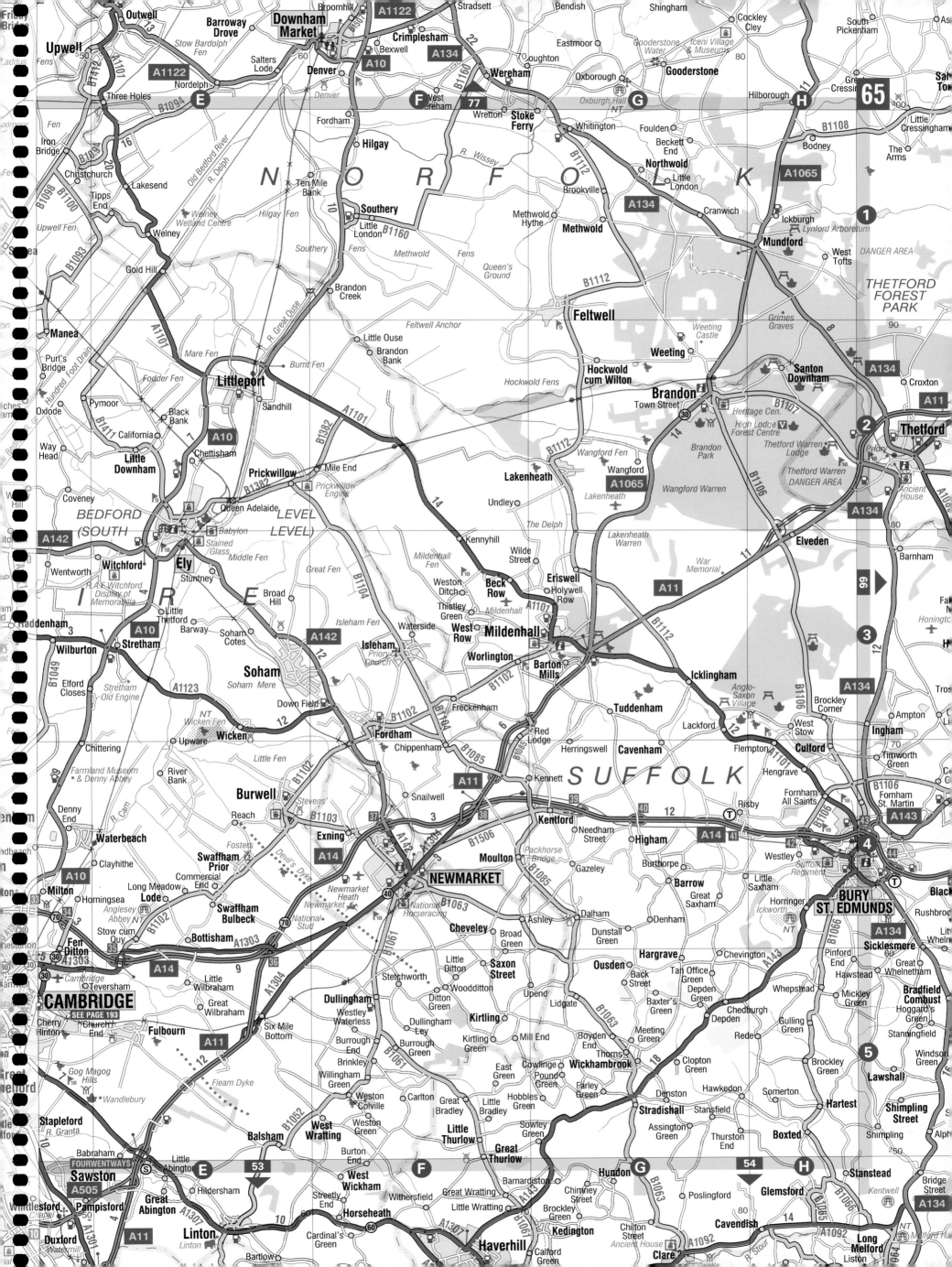

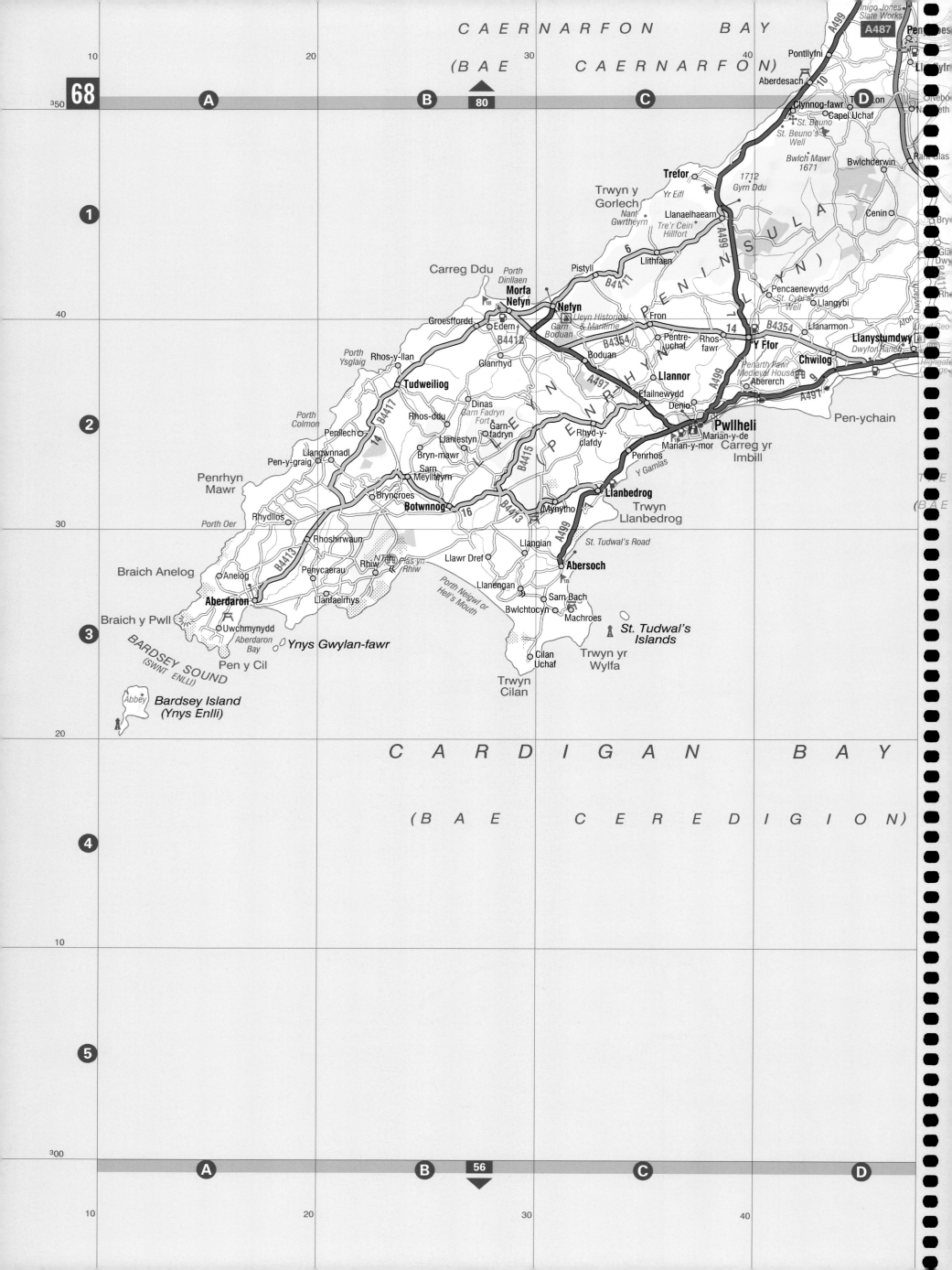

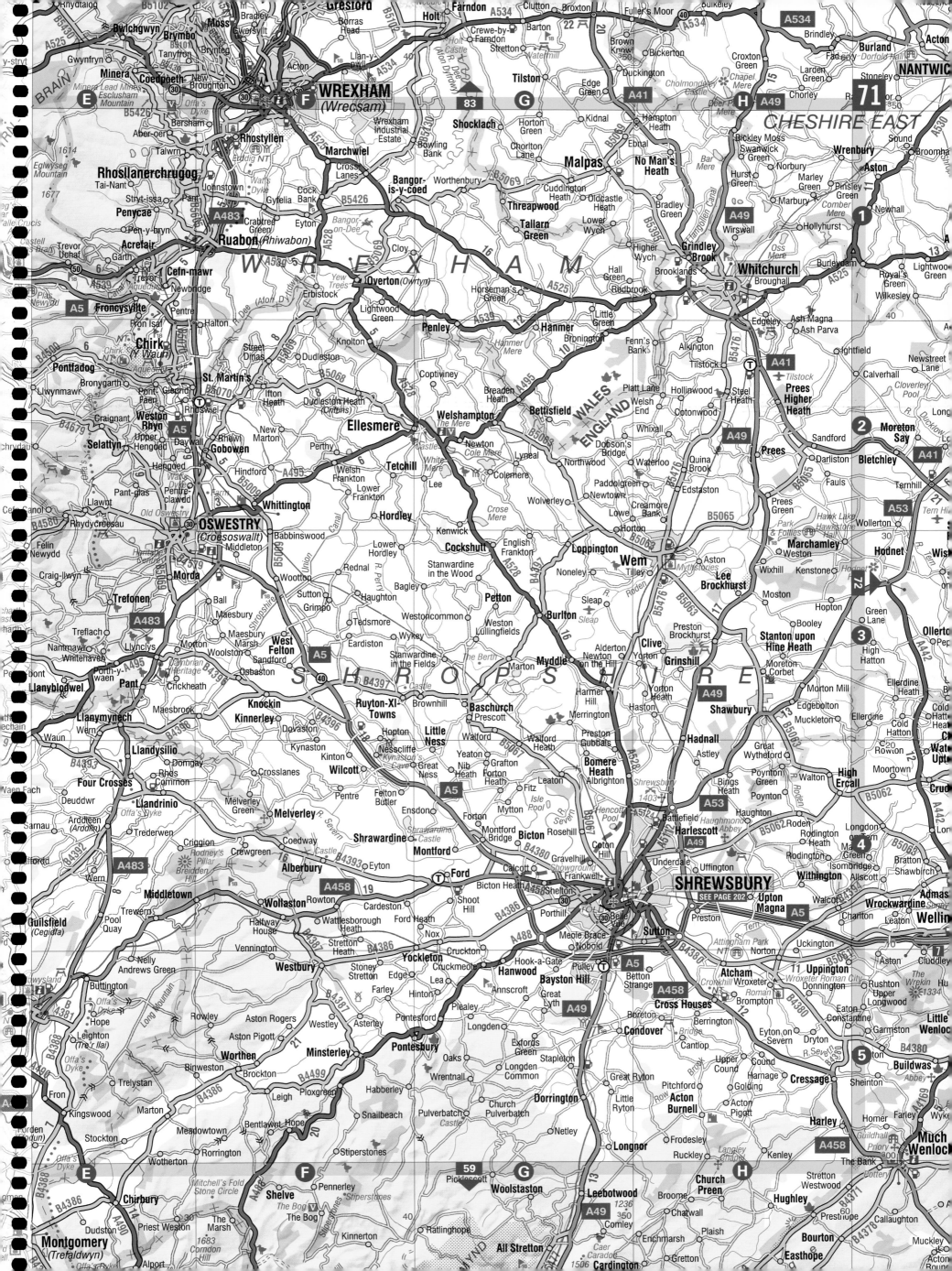

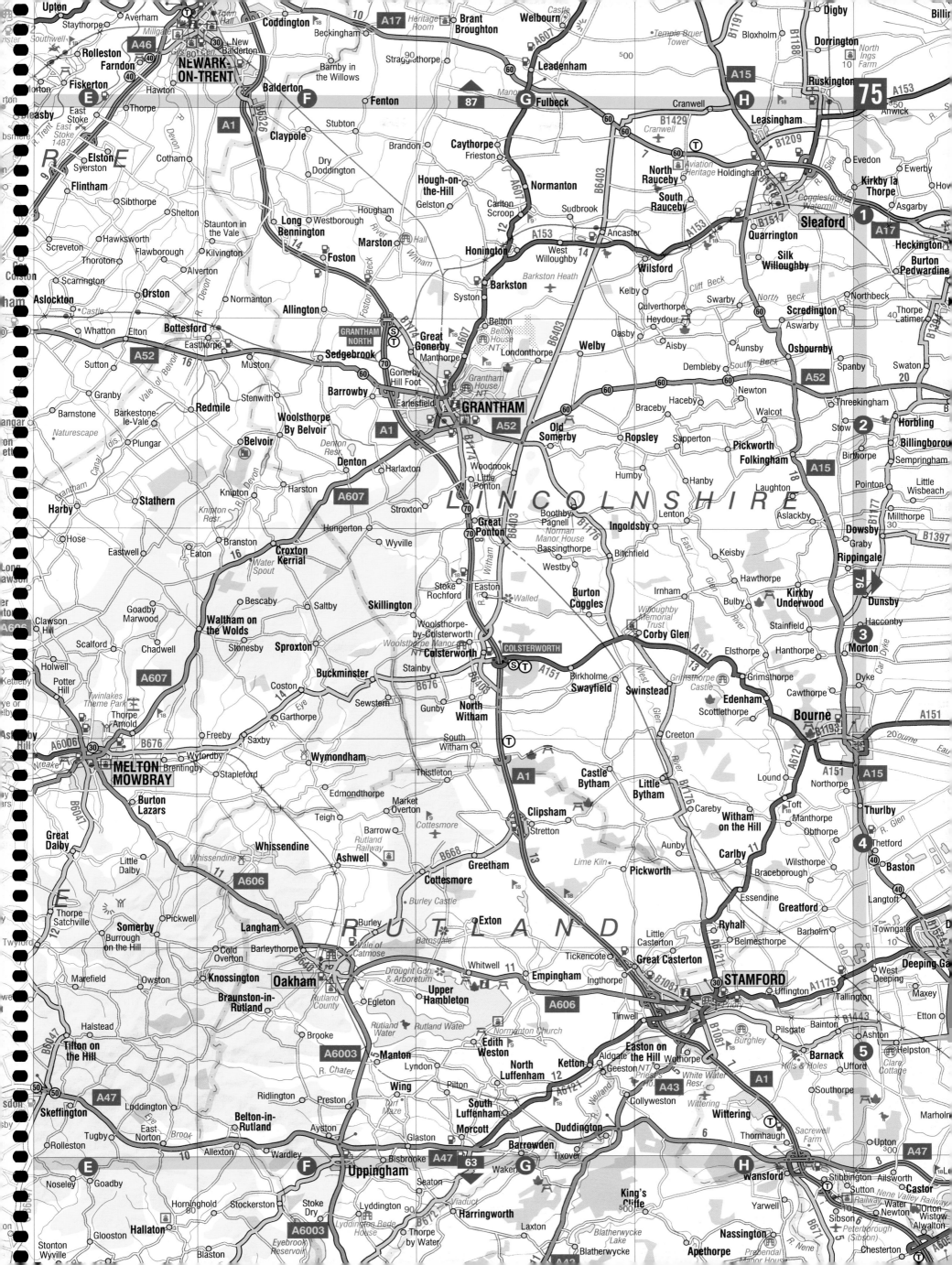

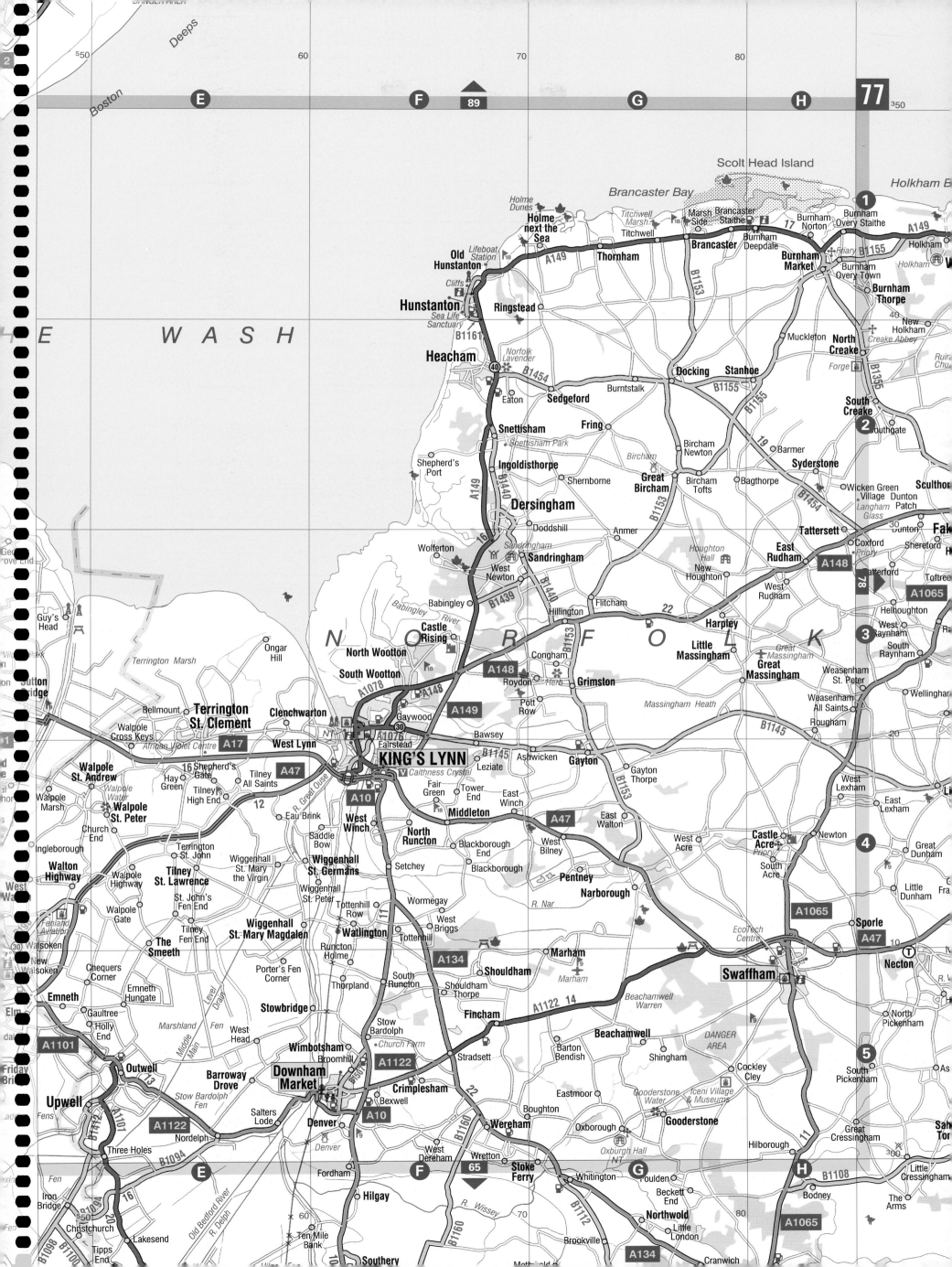

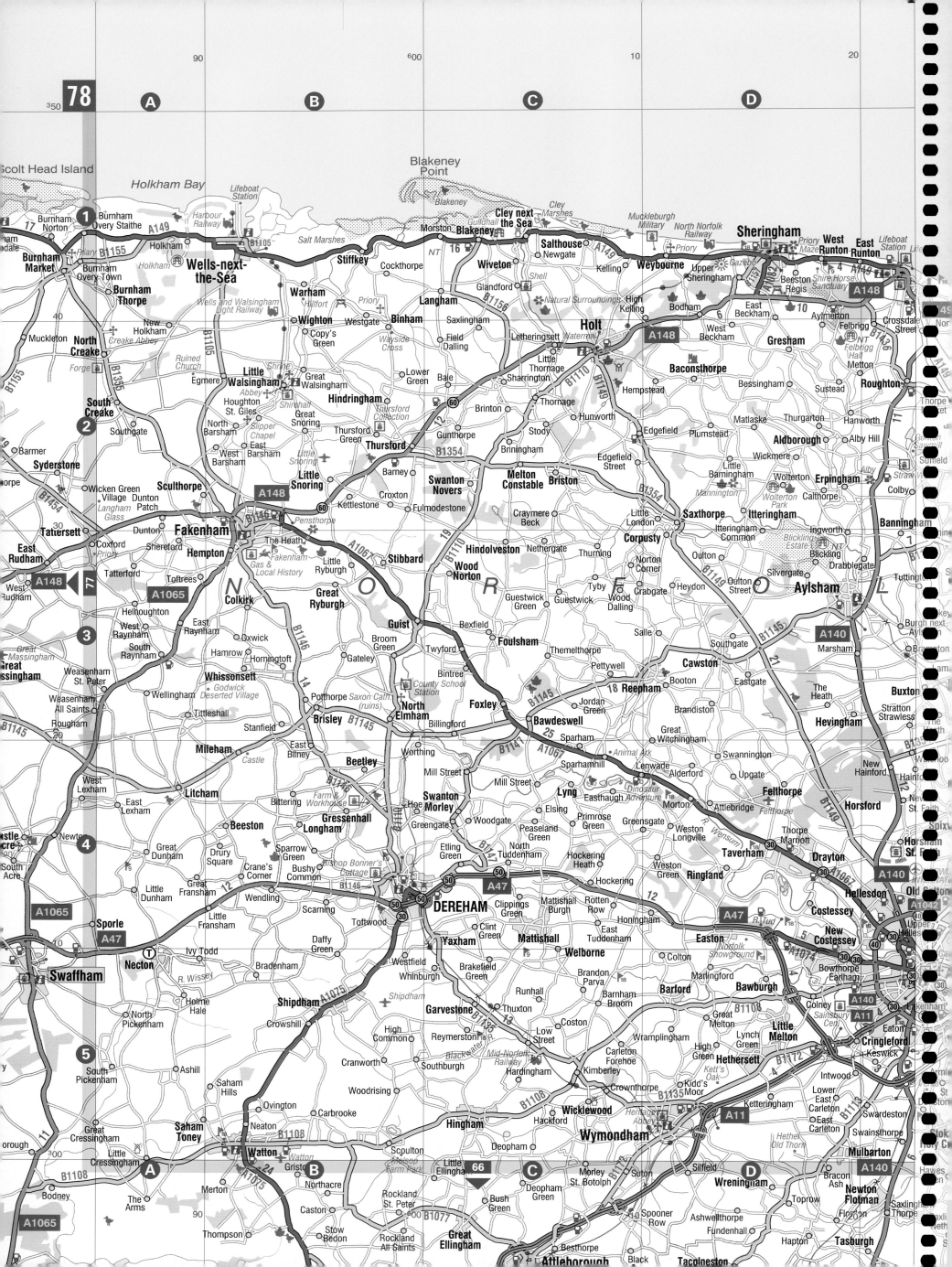

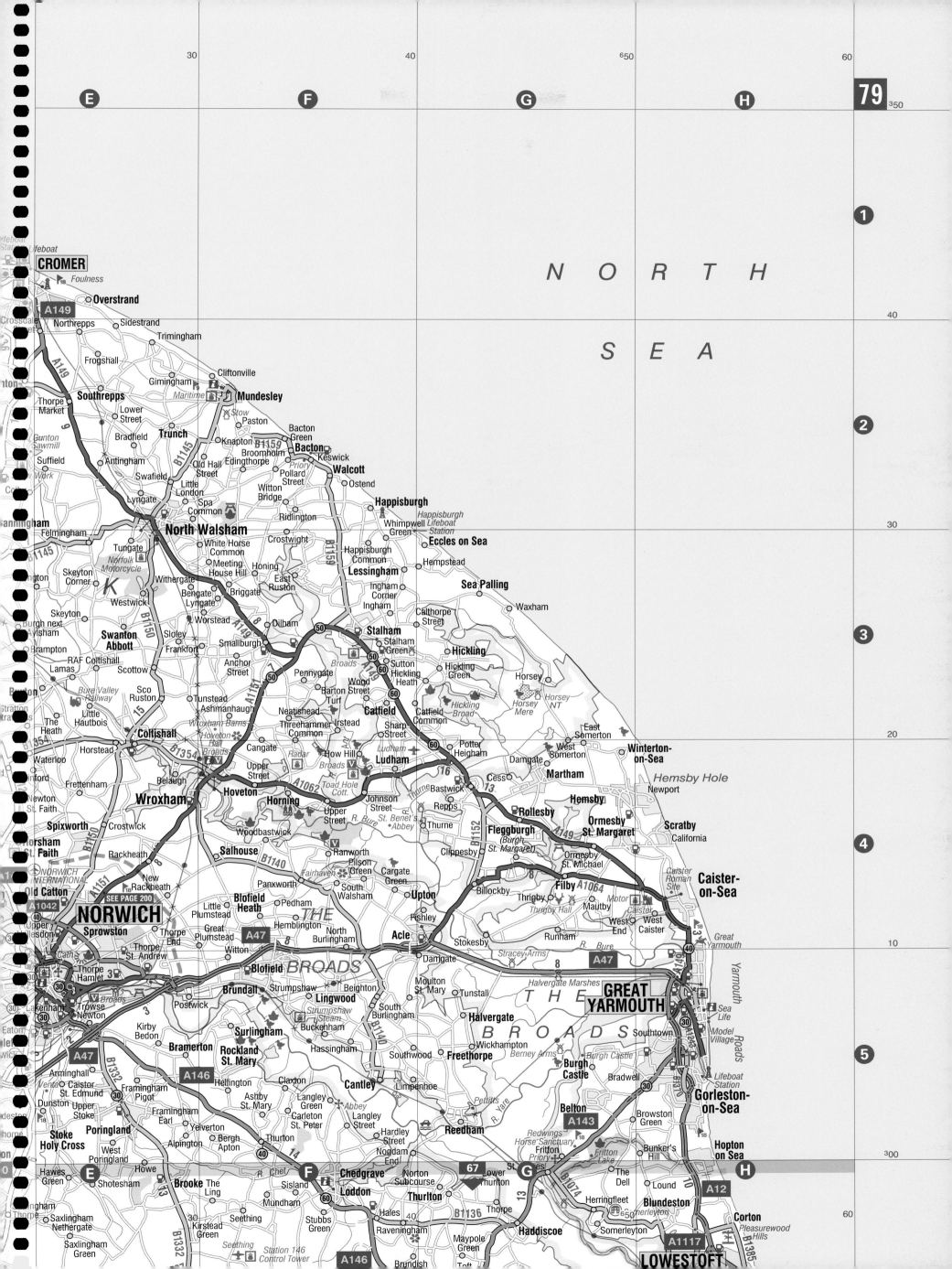

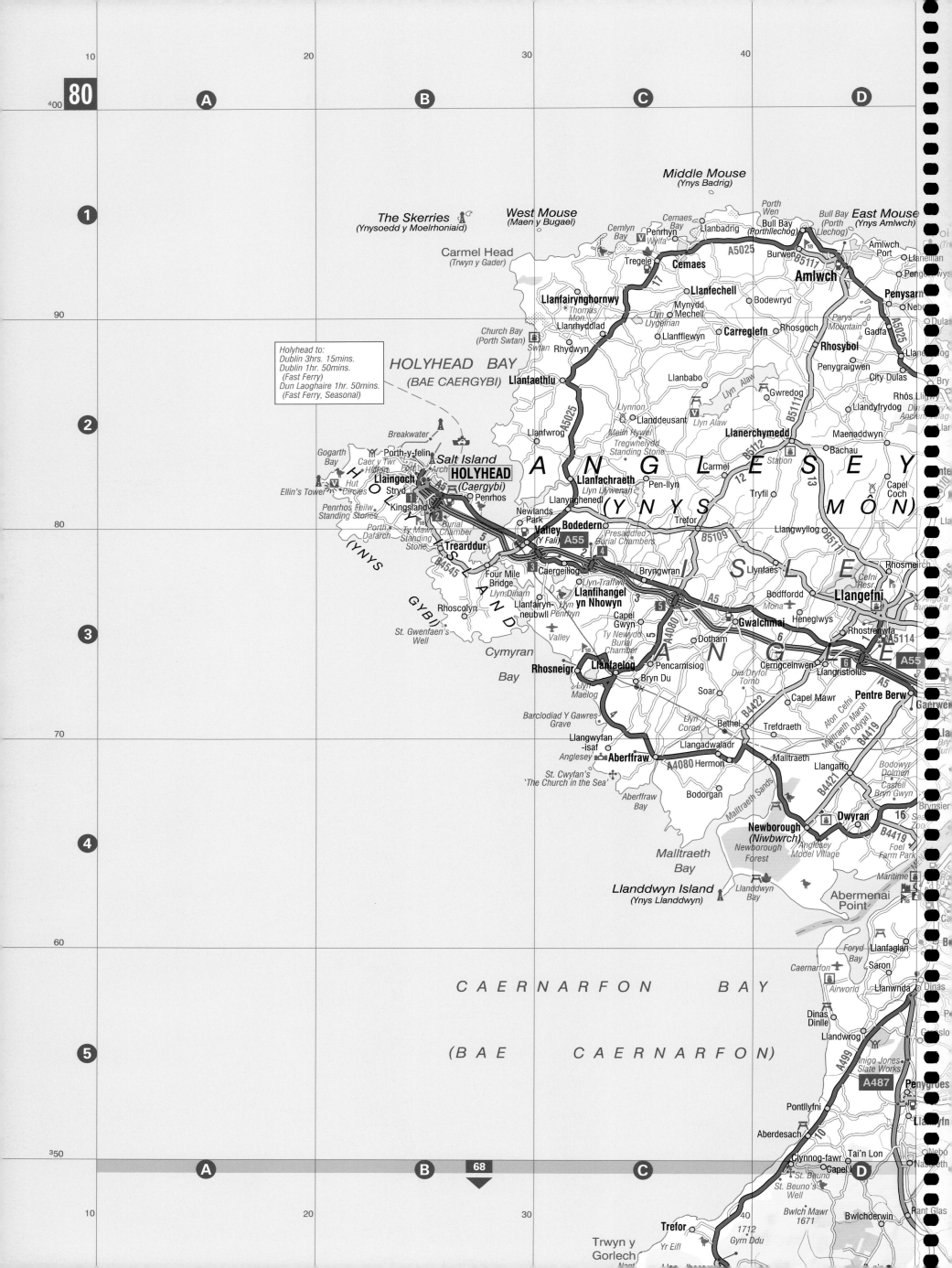

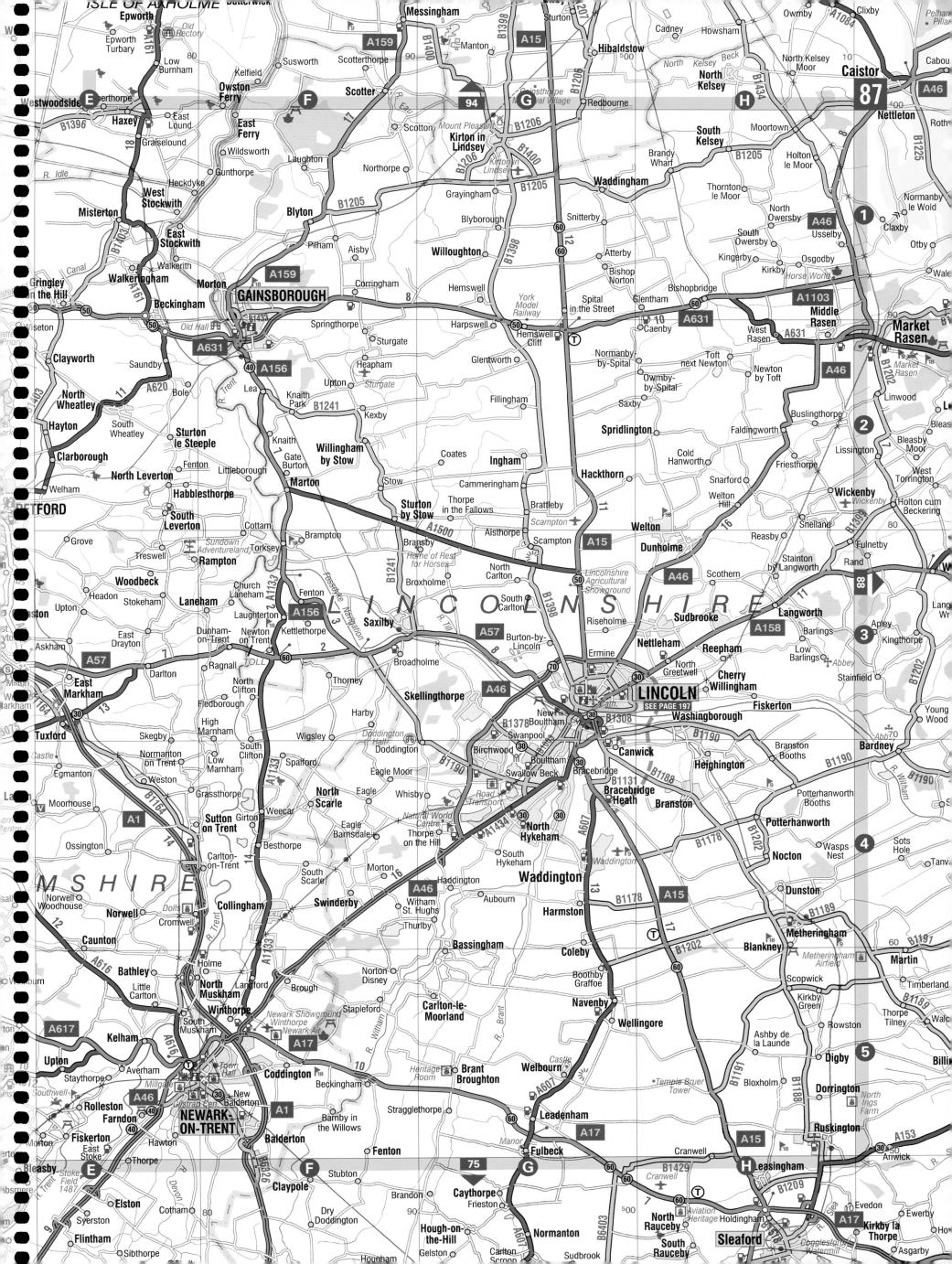

N O R T H

S E A

Theddlethorpe
St. Helen

Seal Sanctuary &
Wildlife Centre

Meers
Bridge

Mablethorpe
Lifeboat Station
Ye Olde
Curiosity

Thorpe

Trusthorpe

Maltby
le Marsh

Sutton on Sea

Sandilands

A1111   Hannah

Markby

Thurlby   **Huttoft**   Anderby
Creek

Drainage

B1449   13   Anderby
15

Farlesthorpe   **Mumby**

Cumberworth   Authorpe
Row

Helsey   **Chapel**
St. Leonards

Bonthorpe

Willoughby   **Hogsthorpe**

B1196   Sloothby   Slackholme
End

Hasthorpe   Hardys
Animal
Farm

Welton   Addlethorpe   **Ingoldmells**
le Marsh   Ingoldmells
Point

Orby   Skegness
(Ingoldmells)   Butlin's

Orby   Water
Marsh   Leisure Park

Winthorpe   **Seathorne**

7   **Burgh**
le Marsh   Natureland
Seal Sanctuary

A158   Church
Farm   Bottons
Pleasure Beach

Model Village   **SKEGNESS**

Thorpe
St. Peter   Croft

5   Seacroft

Croft Marsh

Batemans
Brewery   Magdalen   Gibraltar Point

Wainfleet
All Saints   Gibraltar

Wainfleet
St. Mary

Key's Toft

A52

DANGER AREA

Deeps

Boston   350

Scolt Head
Island

Brancaster Bay   Holkham B

Holme
Dunes   Titchwell   Marsh Brancaster   Burnham   Burnham

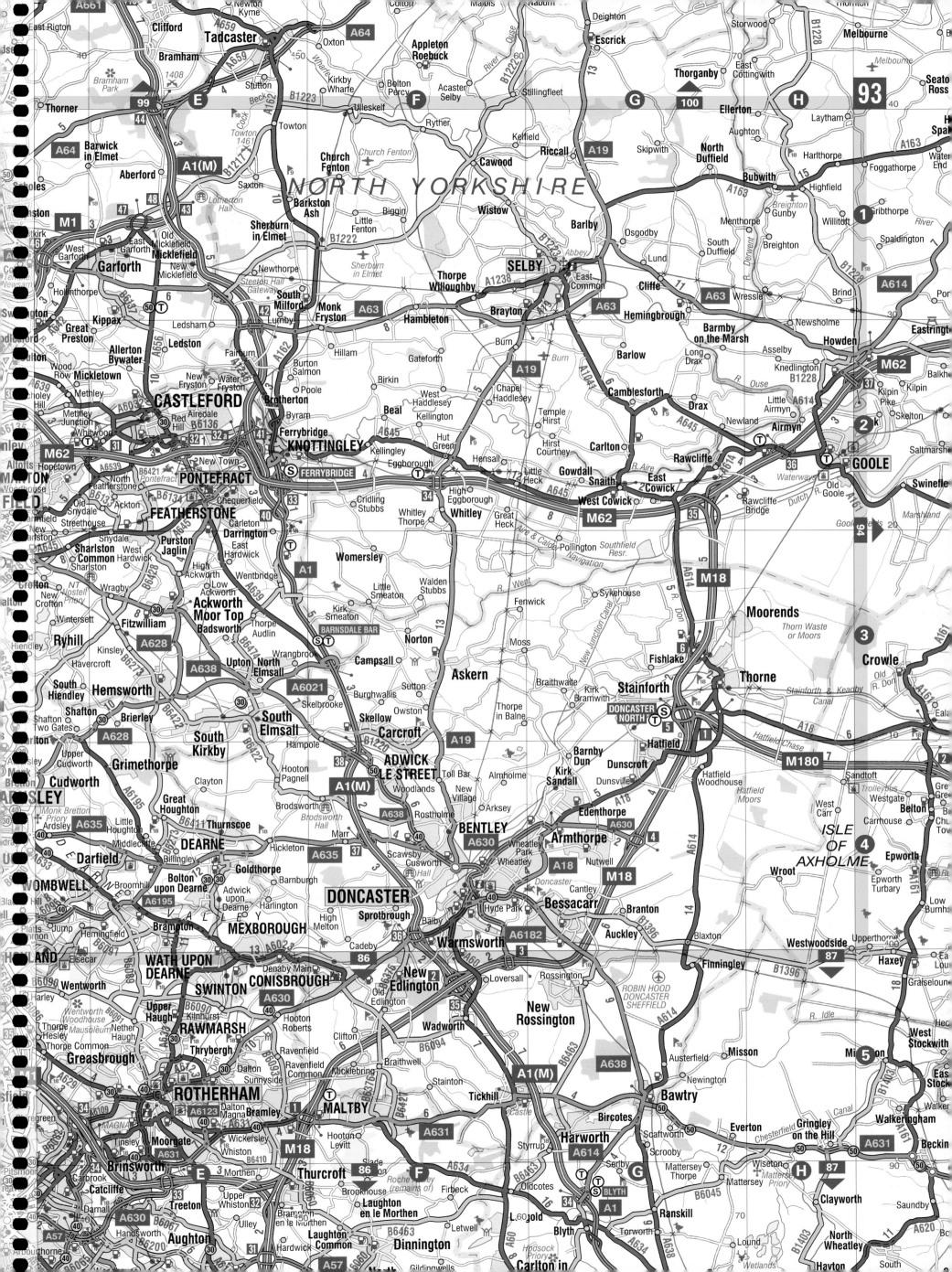

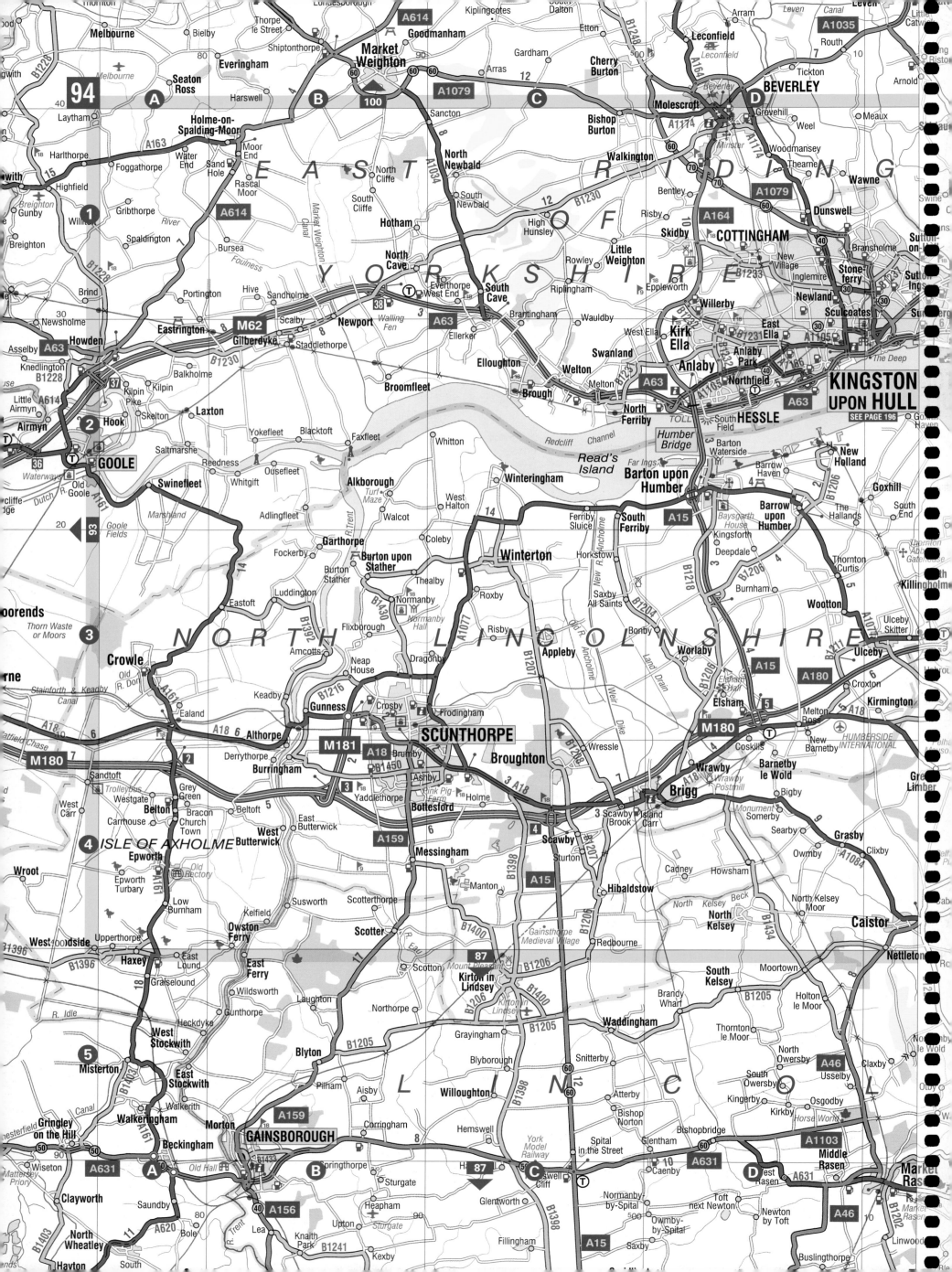

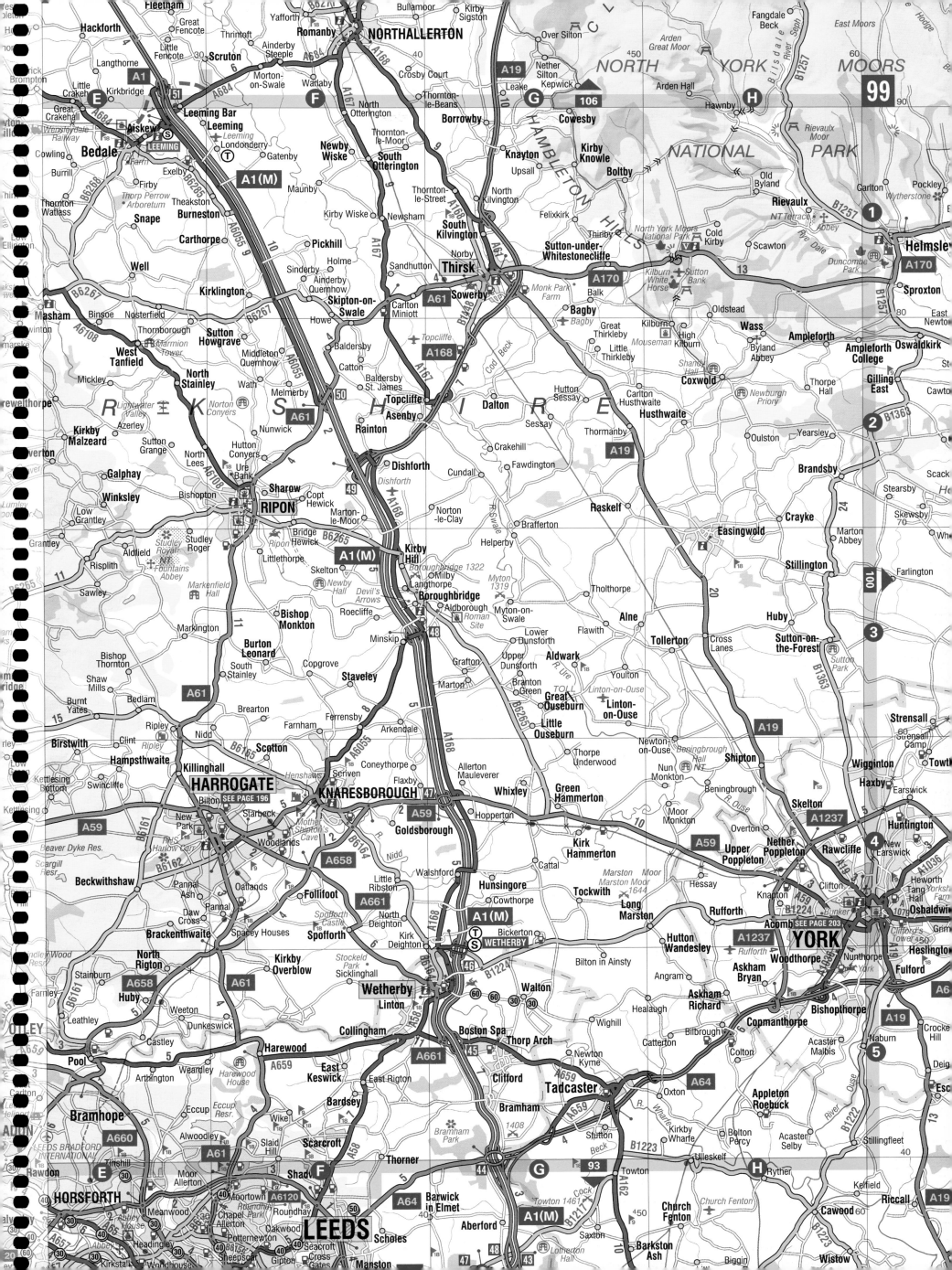

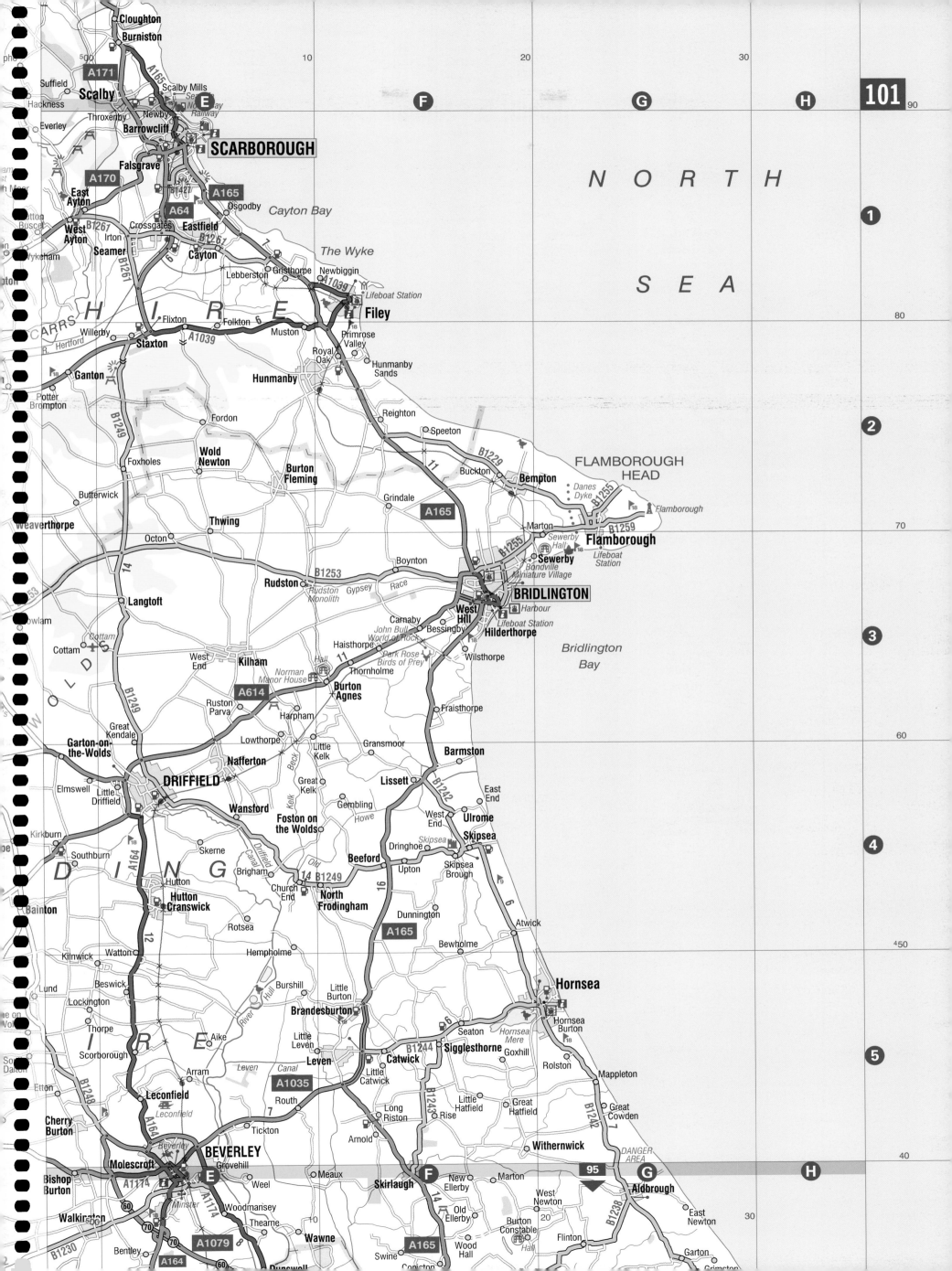

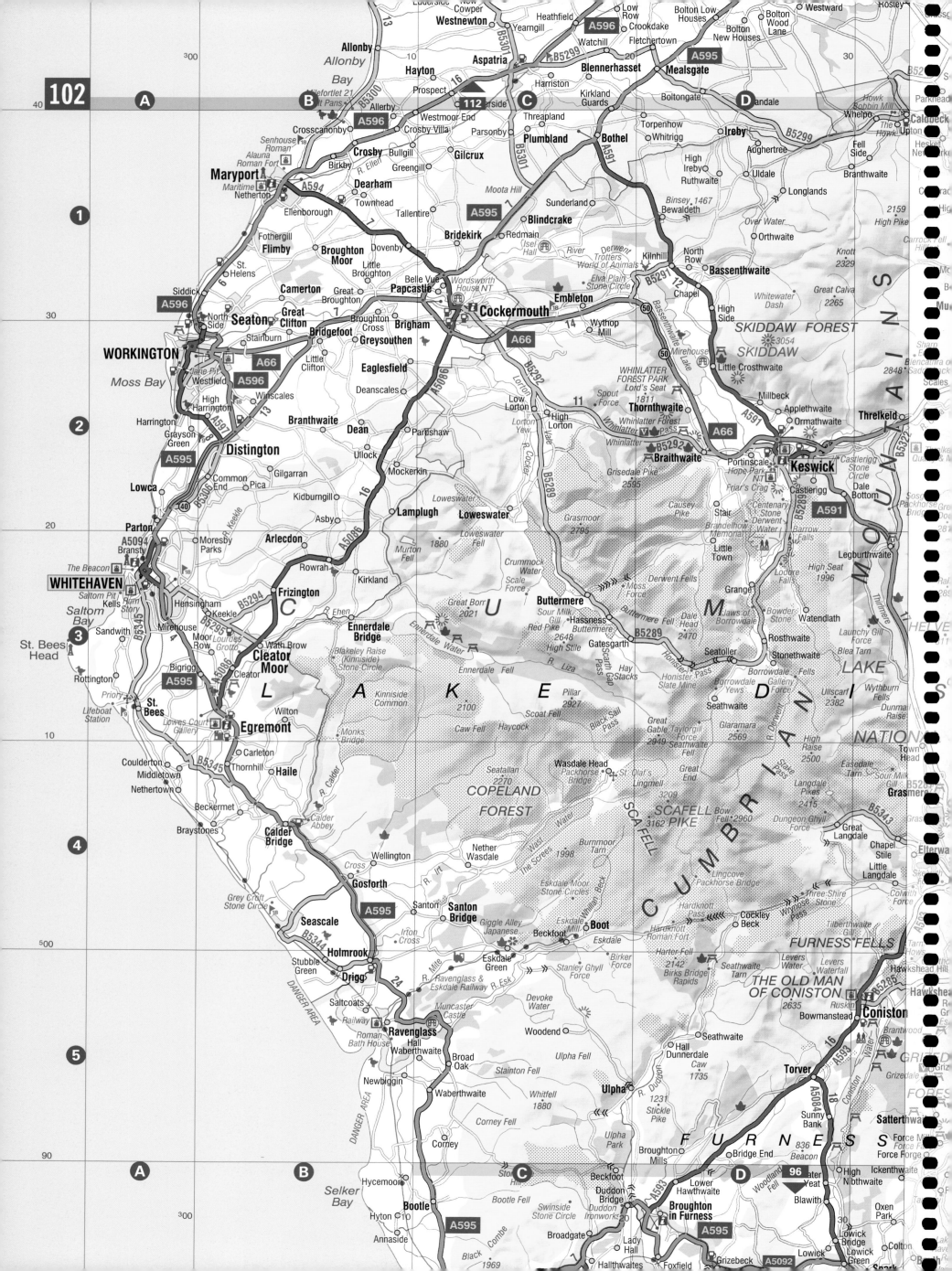

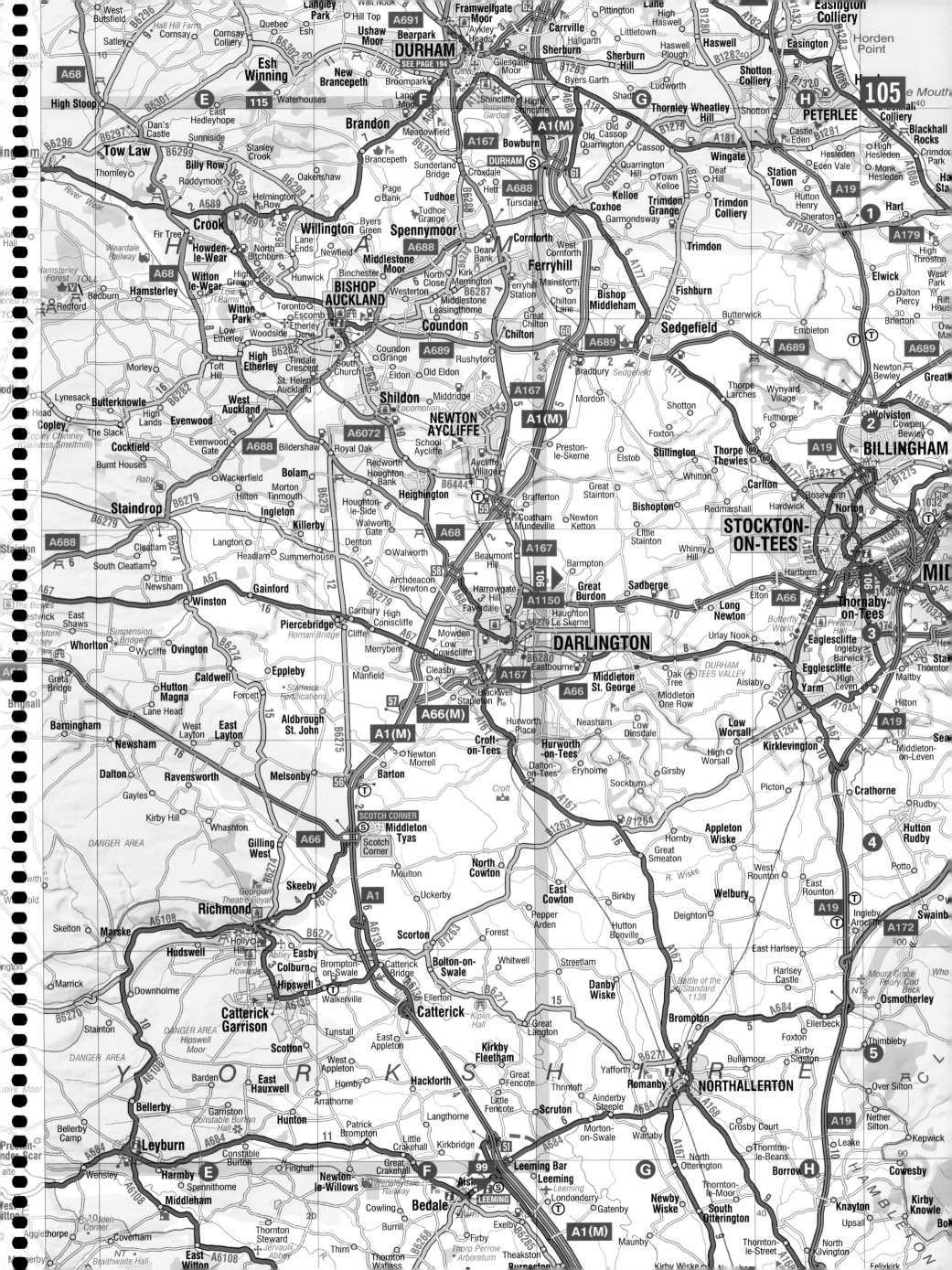

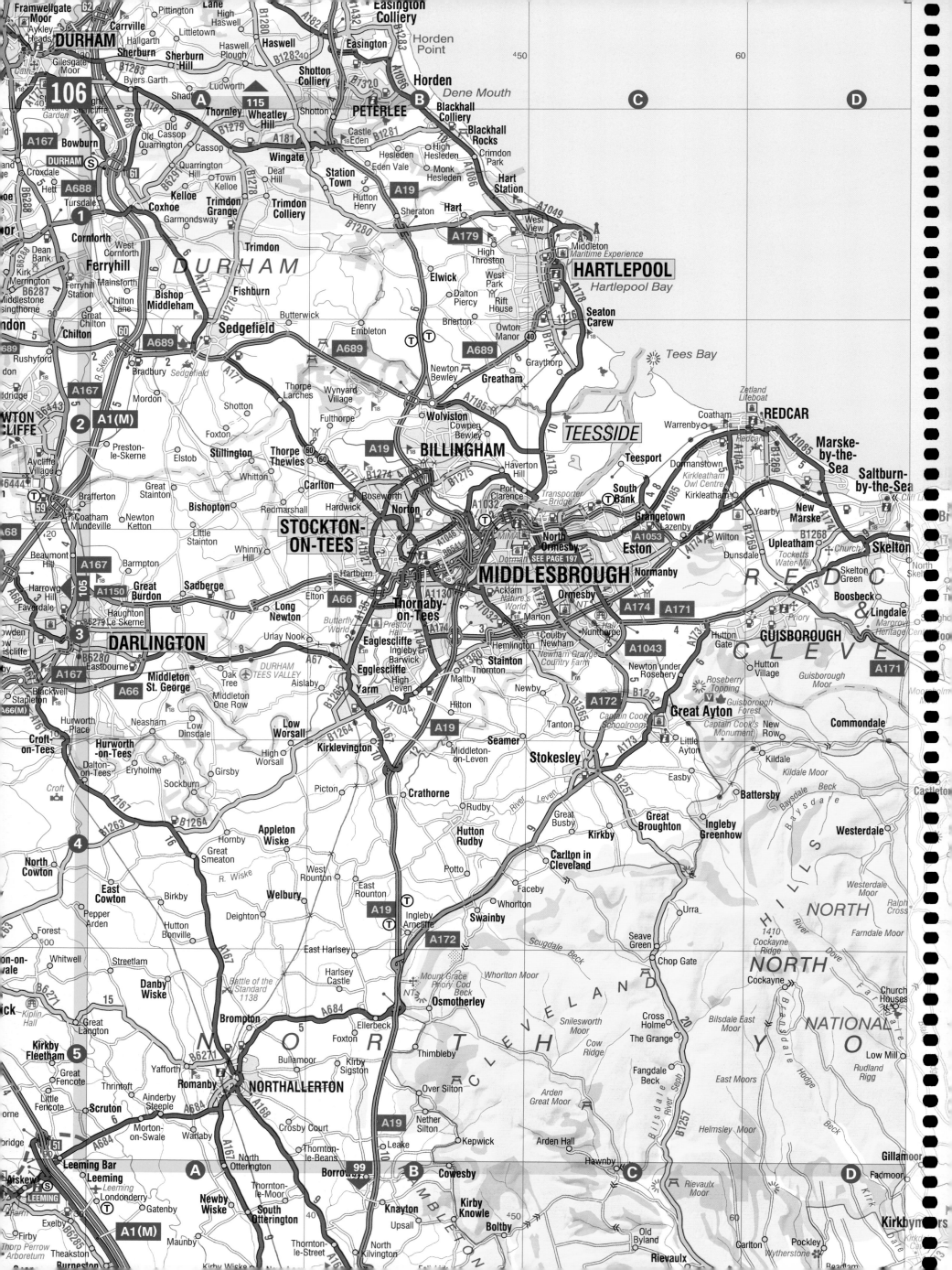

POINT OF AYRE

Rue Point

The Ayres

The L'hen

Cranstal

Dhowin

Bride

A10 A19 B6 B2

Jurby East

Shellag Point

Andreas

A9

B3

Jurby West

B14

B7

Regaby

500

Jurby Head

B5

Sandygate

Ballasalla

Civil War Fort

Dhoor Grove

Ramsey Bay

The Cronk

A13

A14

St. Judes

B14

A13

RAMSEY

B8

Sulby

A3

Lhergy Frissel

Orrisdale

Curraghs

Churchtown

6

Glen Auldyn

Elfin Glen

B16

A2

Port e Vullen

Maughold Head

Orrisdale Head

A10

Ballaugh

30

A3 T.T. Course

Gate

A18

Lewaigue

Maughold

90

Ravensdale

Glen Wyllin

Bishopscourt Glen

KIRK MICHAEL

Gate

1854 North Barrule

B19

Ballajora

Crosses

Port Mooar

90

Ballaleigh

SNAEFELL

Corrany

Cornaa

Manx Electric Railway

Ballacarnane Beg

Glen Mooar

Barregarrow

Slieau Dhoo 1601

Clagh Ouyr

Glen Mona

Cashtal yn Ard

Dhoon

Port Cornaa

Gob y Deigan

T.T. Course

B10

Sulby Resr.

A14 Gate

14

Snaefell Mountain Railway

Dhoon Glen

Knocksharry

A4

Cronk-y-Voddy

A18

B11

Bulgham Bay

St. Patrick's Isle

A3

Lambfell Moar

1599 Colden

Injebreck Resr.

B10

Great Laxey Mine Railway

Laxey Wheel

Laxey Glen

3

Ballagyr

Rhenass Waterfall

B22

LAXEY

Minorca

Contrary Head

PEEL

A20

Glen Helen

A18

Old Laxey

Laxey Head

Patrick

A1

Ballig

Slieau Ruy 1570

T.T. Course

Ballaheannagh

B12

B12

Ballacannell

80

A27

A30

ST. JOHN'S

Greeba Castle

A1

11

Baldwin

B21

B20

Laxey Bay

80

Glen Maye

Mill

Crosby

B22

Hillberry

A18

Baldrine

Clay Head

Dalby Point

Glen Maye

Lower Foxdale

Glen Vine

Strang

A22

ONCHAN

Groudle Glen Railway

A3

Garth

B35

Braaid

Cooil

Union Mills

A1

Willaston

A2

Port Groudle

Dalby

A27

Foxdale

Eairy

A26

B32

Spring Valley

Groudle Glen

Niarbyl

A36

A24

DOUGLAS

Onchan Head

4

Niarbyl Bay

A13

1586 Hill South Fort Barrule 12

B36

B35

B37

B18

Kewaigue

Manx

Douglas Bay

Stroin Vuigh

B39

A3

Close Clark

30

St. Mark's

Newtown

Quine's Hill

Horses Home

A25

B80

Douglas Head

Ronague

Ballamodha

B41

A5

A26

B29

A24

Keristal

Little Ness

Fleshwick Bay

Lingague

A27

Grenaby

B40

Port Soderick

Bradda Head

A36

B44

B42

Ballabeg

A26

B25

Isle of Man Steam railway

Bradda

Surby

A7

Colby

5

A3

A5

BALLASALLA

10

Santon Head

Port Erin

A5

Four Roads

A7

Derby Fort

St. Michael's Island

70

Bradda Glen

A31

Port St. Mary

CASTLETOWN

Ship Bunal

ISLE OF MAN

Derbyhaven

The Howe

Chambered Cairn

Cregneash

Nautical

The Sound

Kitterland

National Folk

Old House of Keys

V

SPANISH HEAD

5

Calf of Man

Dreswick Point

Douglas to:
Belfast 2hrs.45mins.
(Fast Ferry, Seasonal)
Birkenhead 4hrs. 15mins.
(Seasonal)
Heysham 3hrs. 30mins.
Dublin 2hrs. 45mins.
(Fast Ferry, Seasonal)
Liverpool 2hrs.30mins.
(Fast Ferry, Seasonal)

PAGE NOT CONTINUED

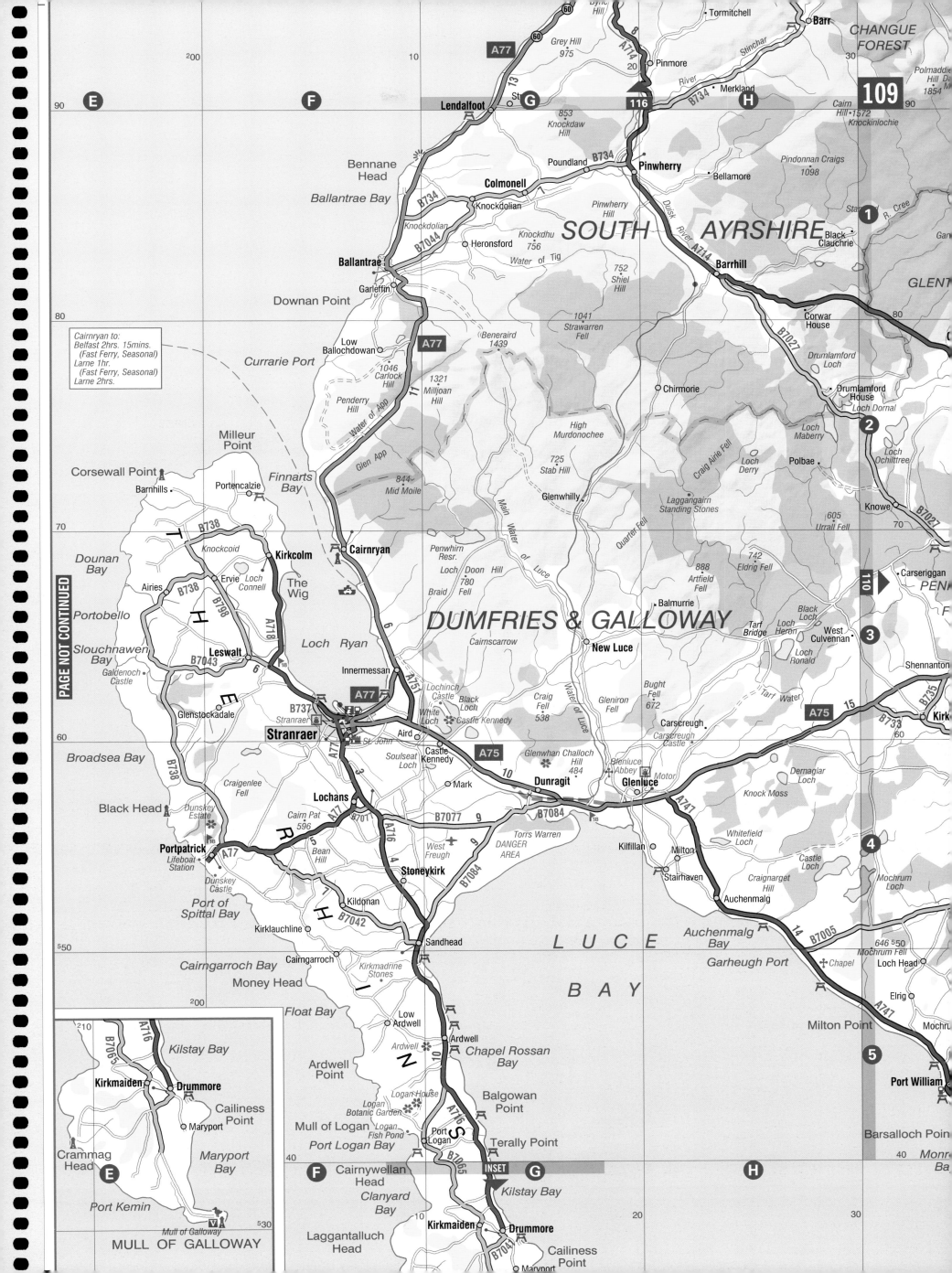

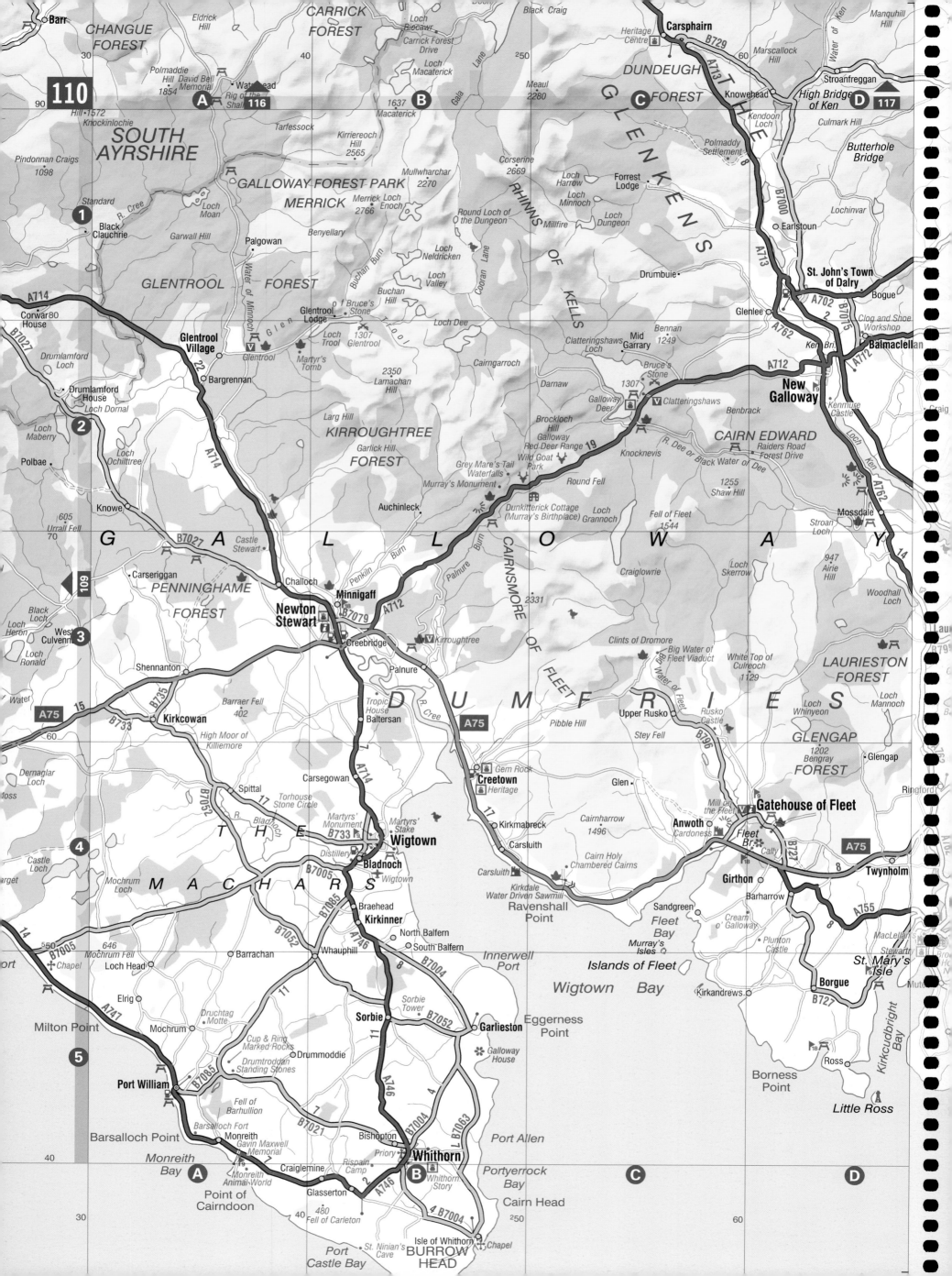

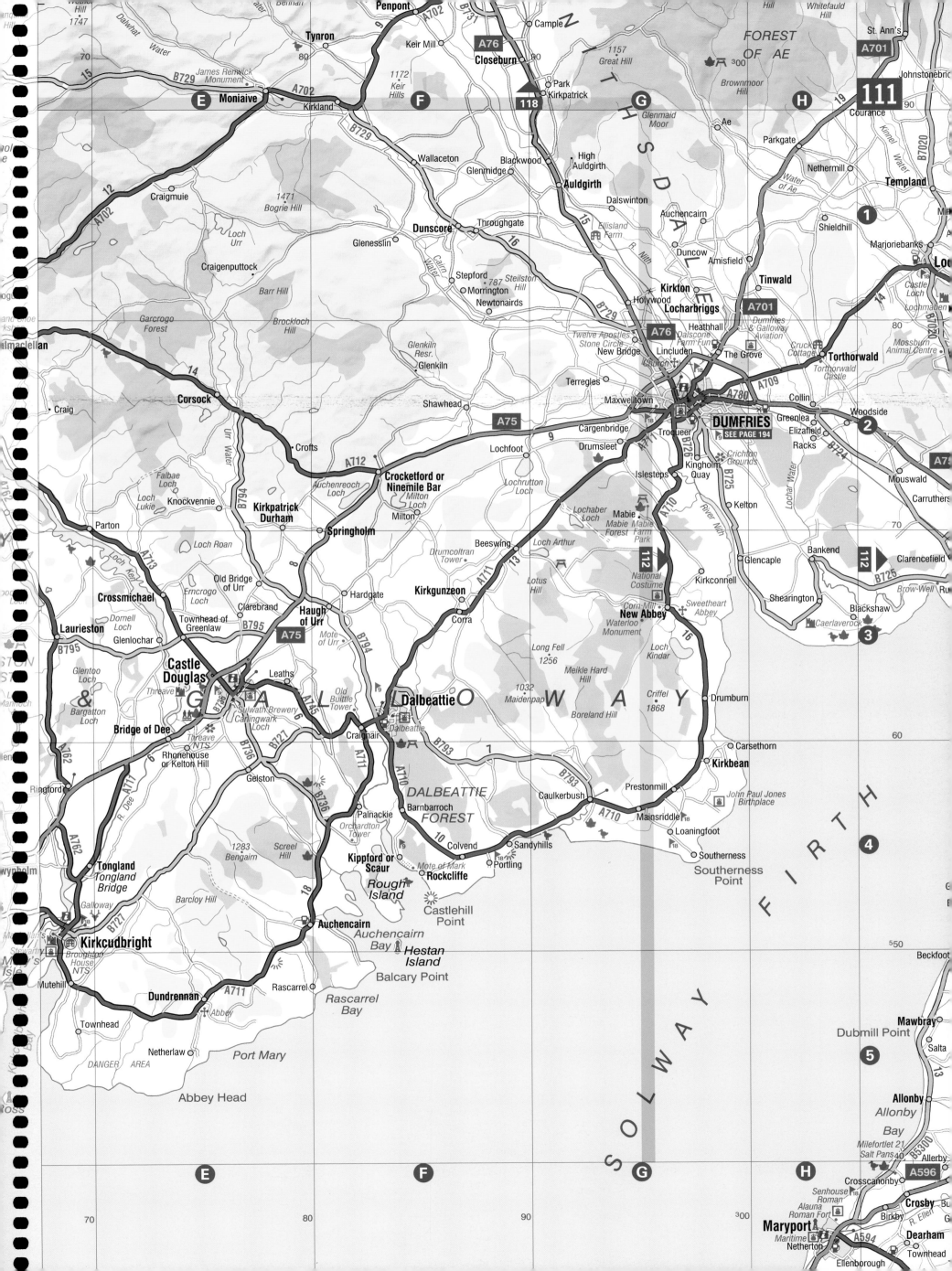

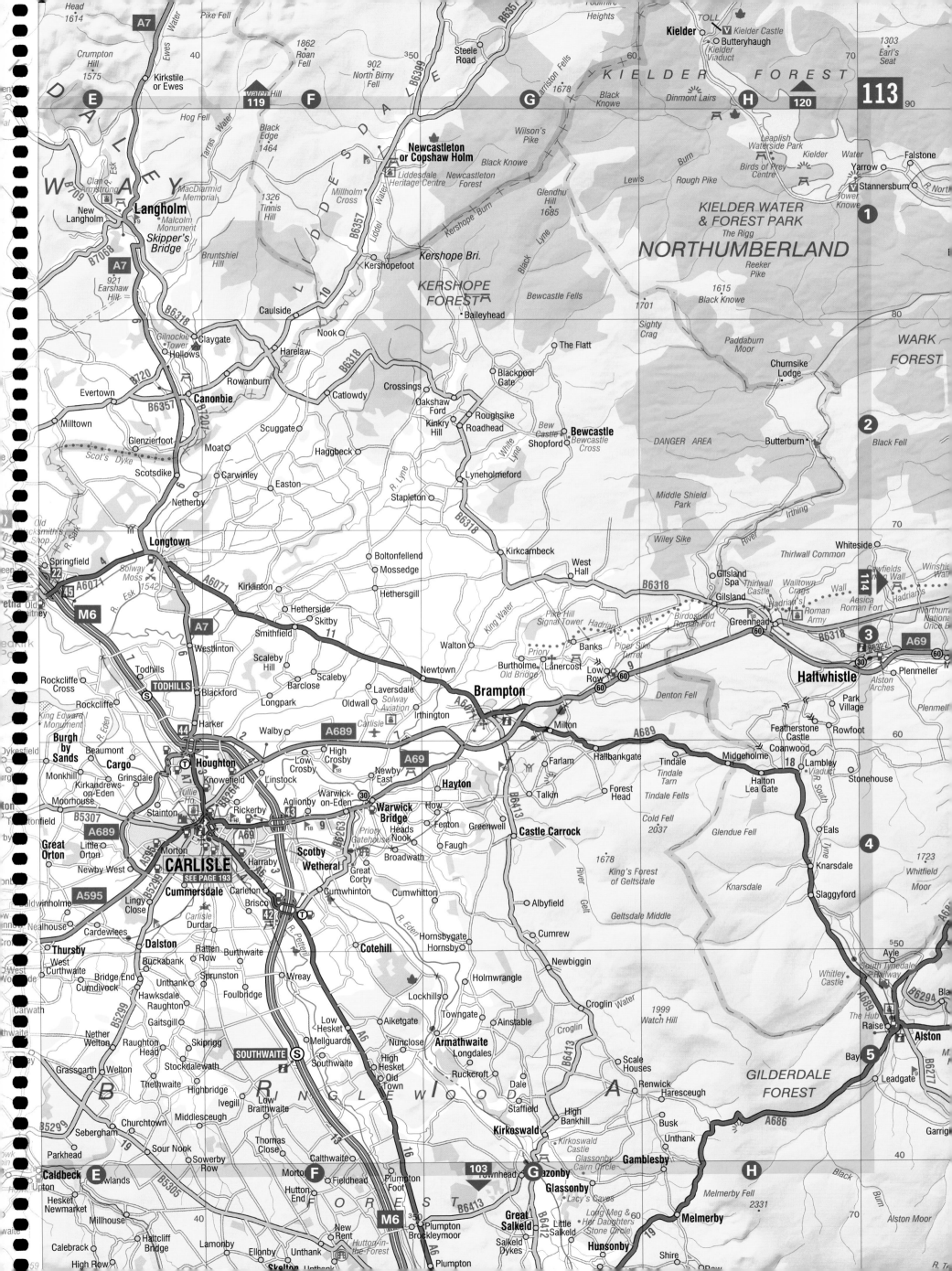

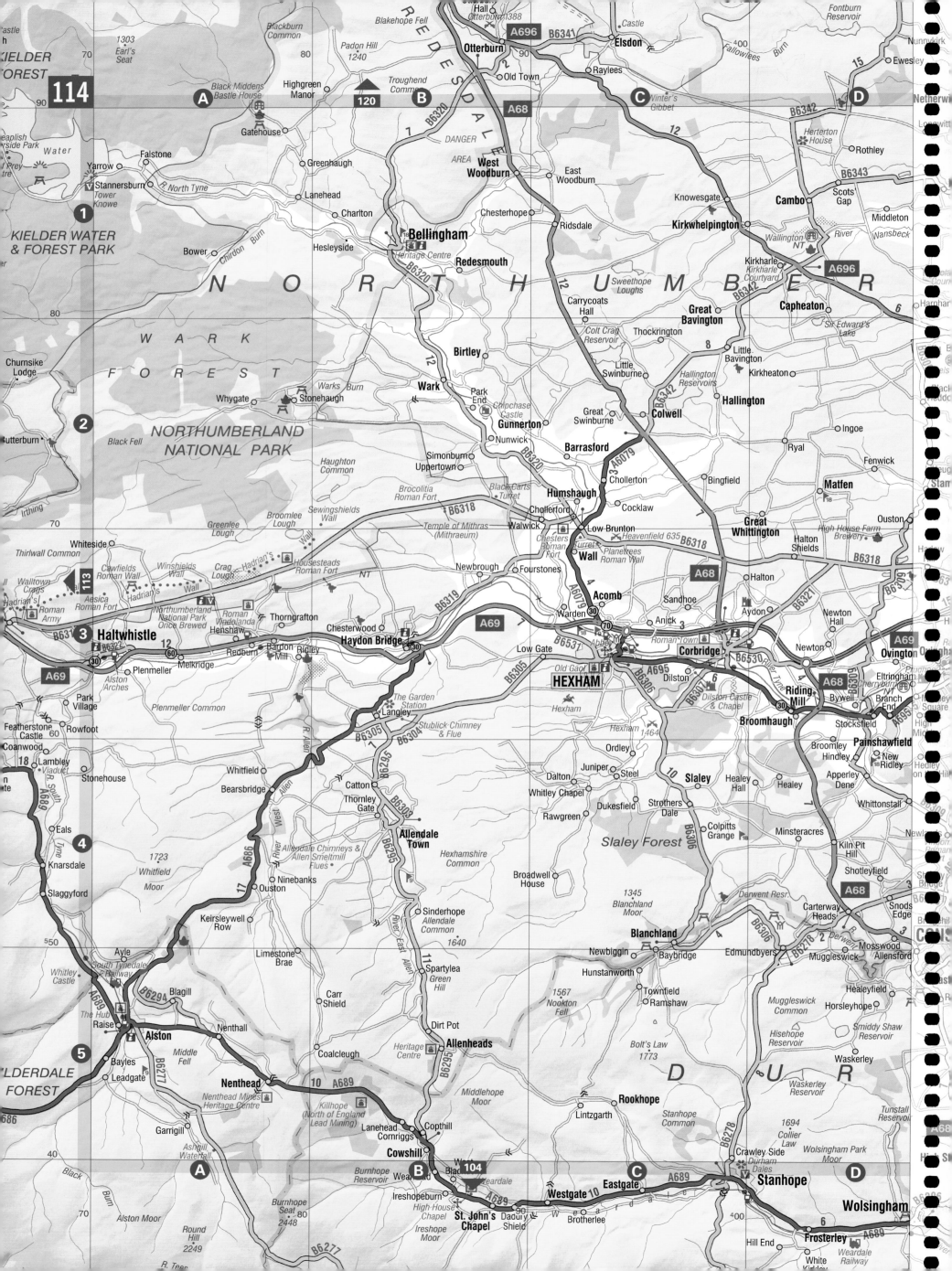

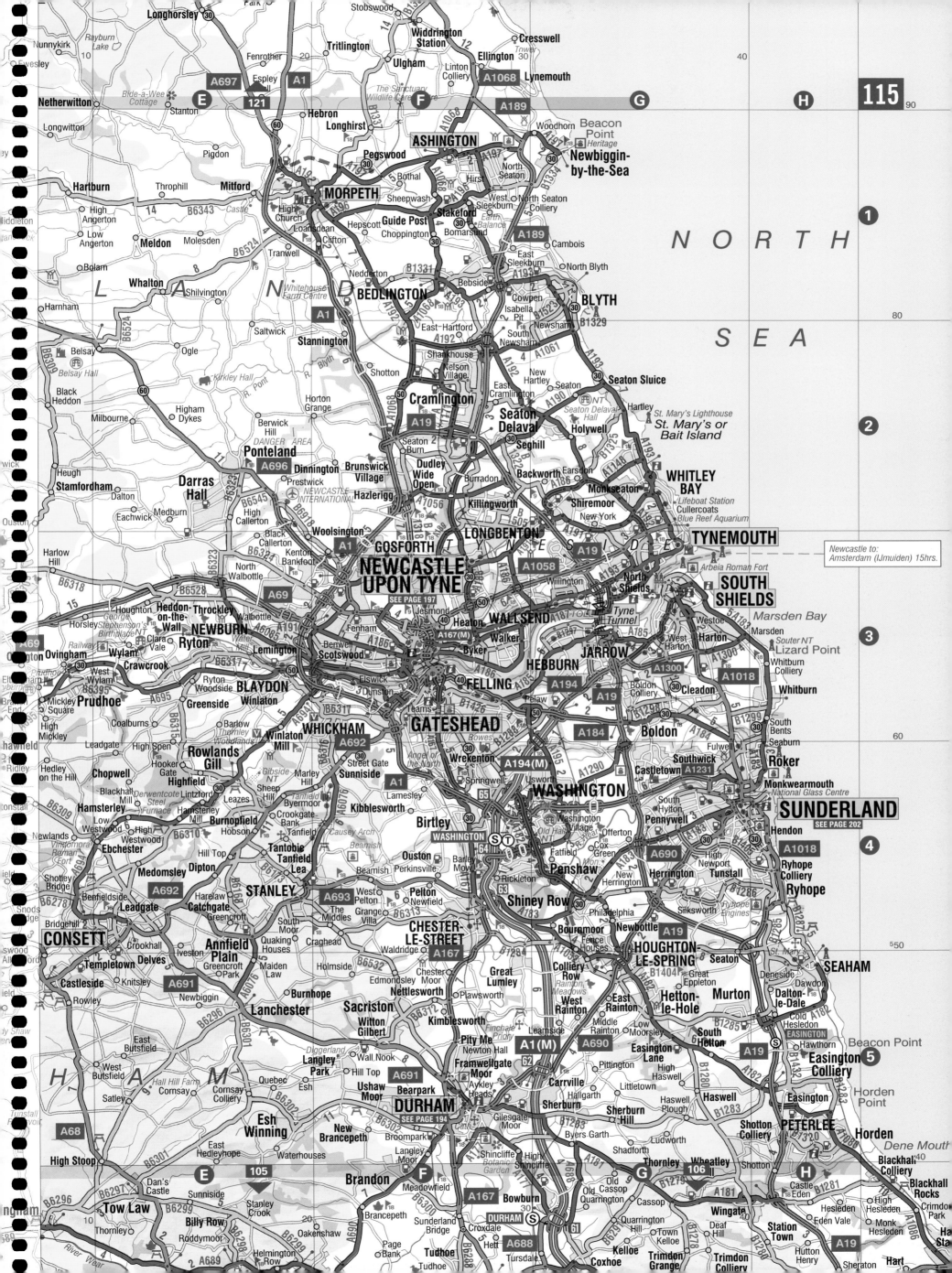

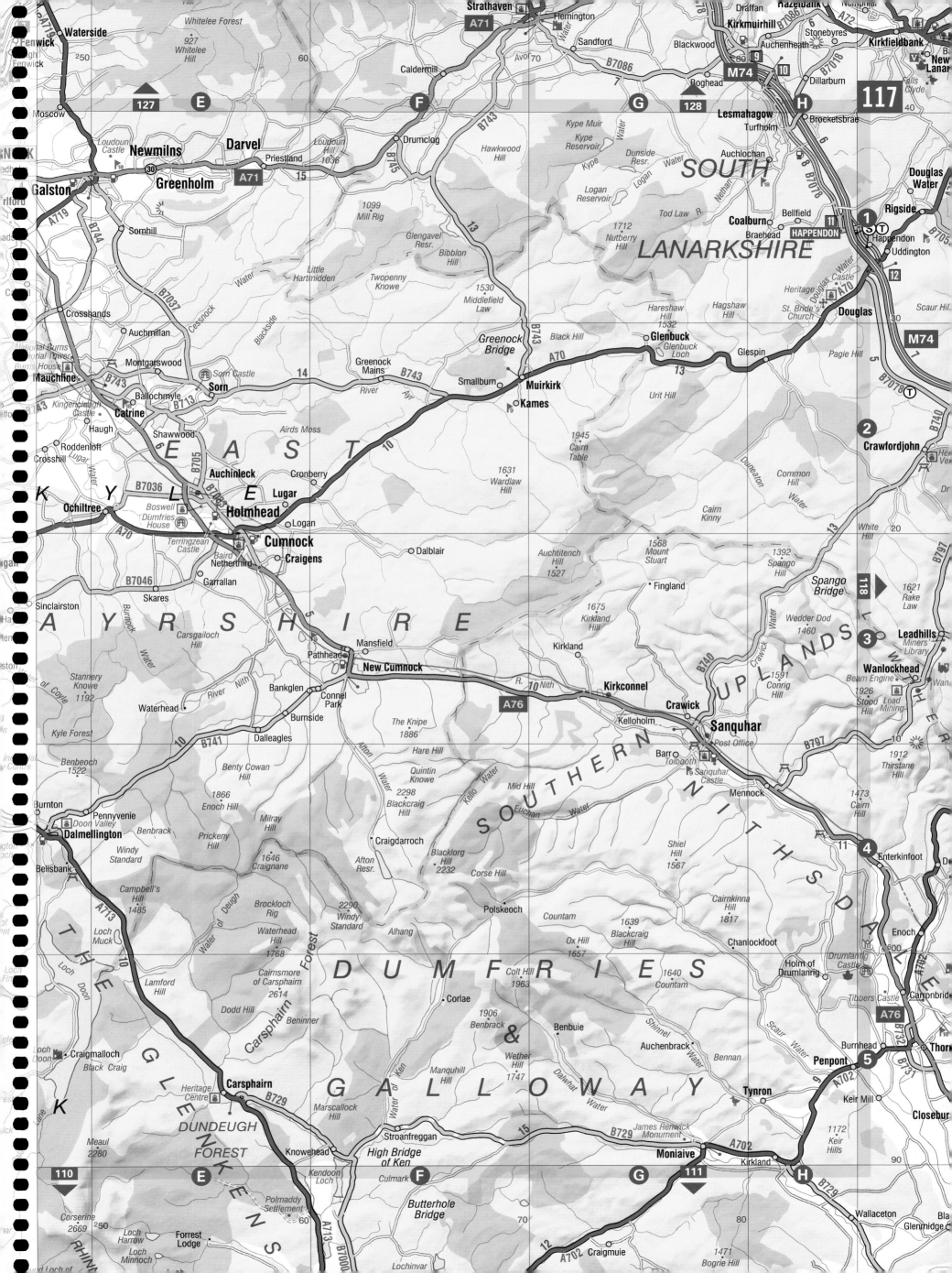

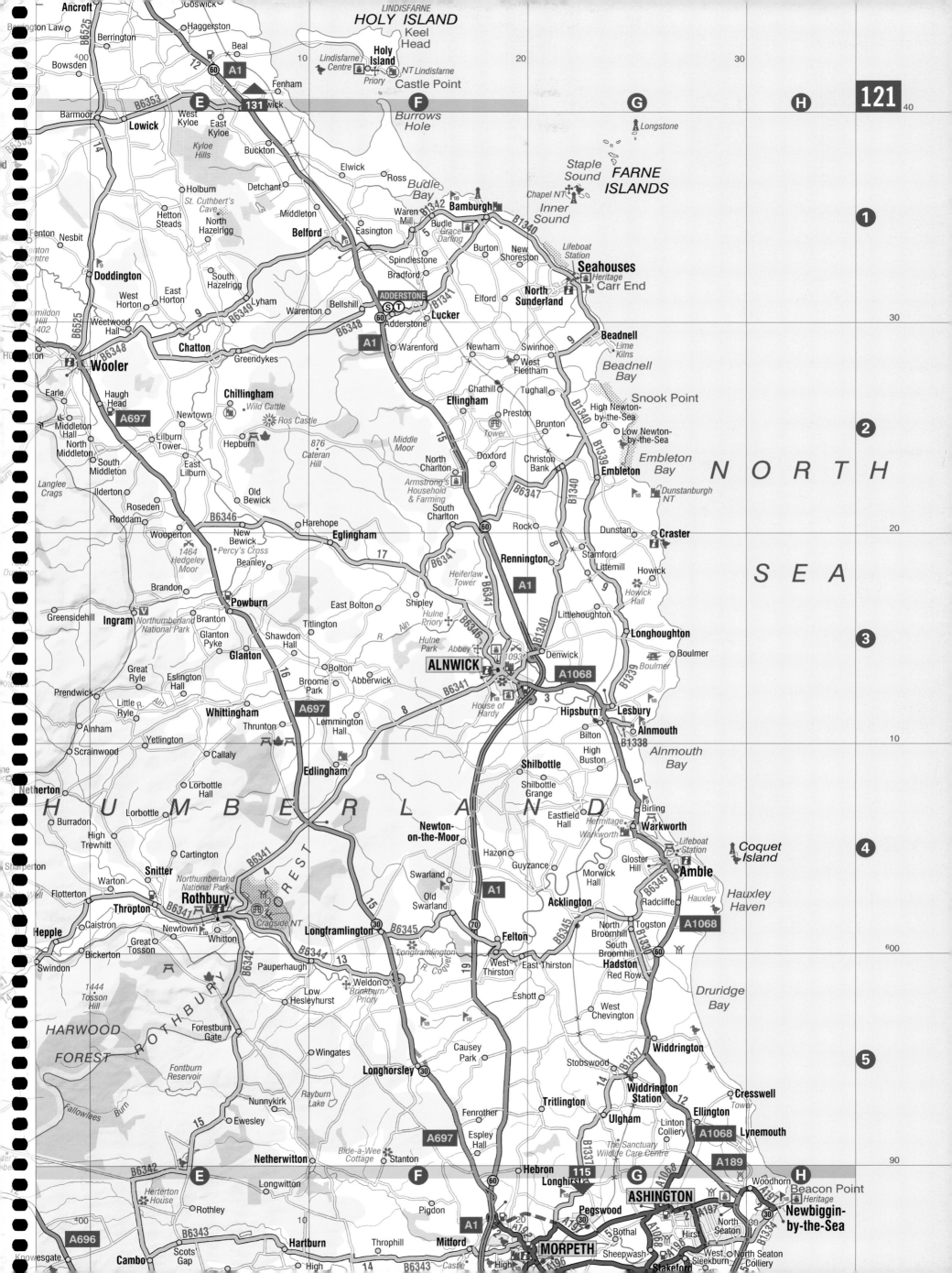

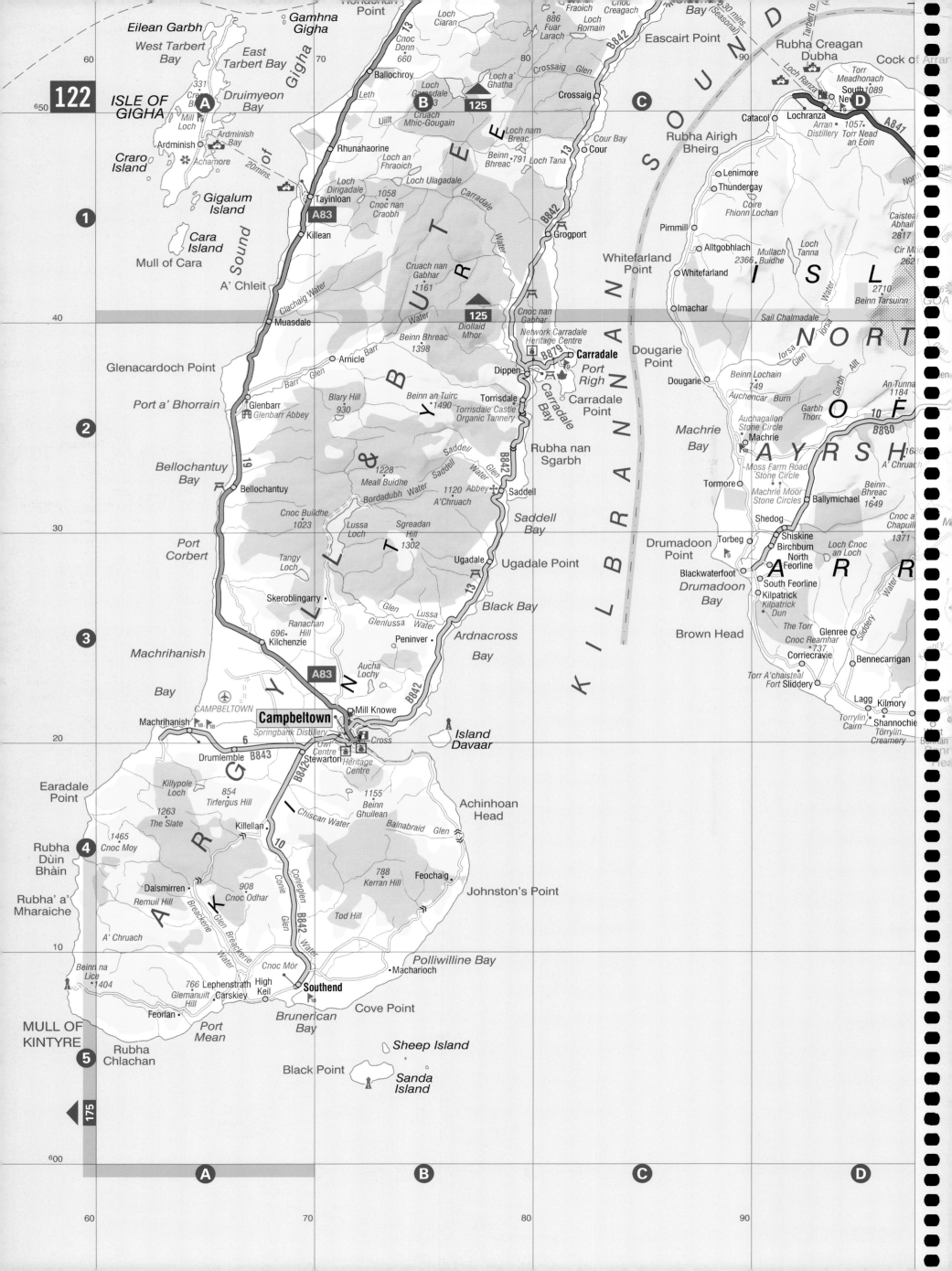

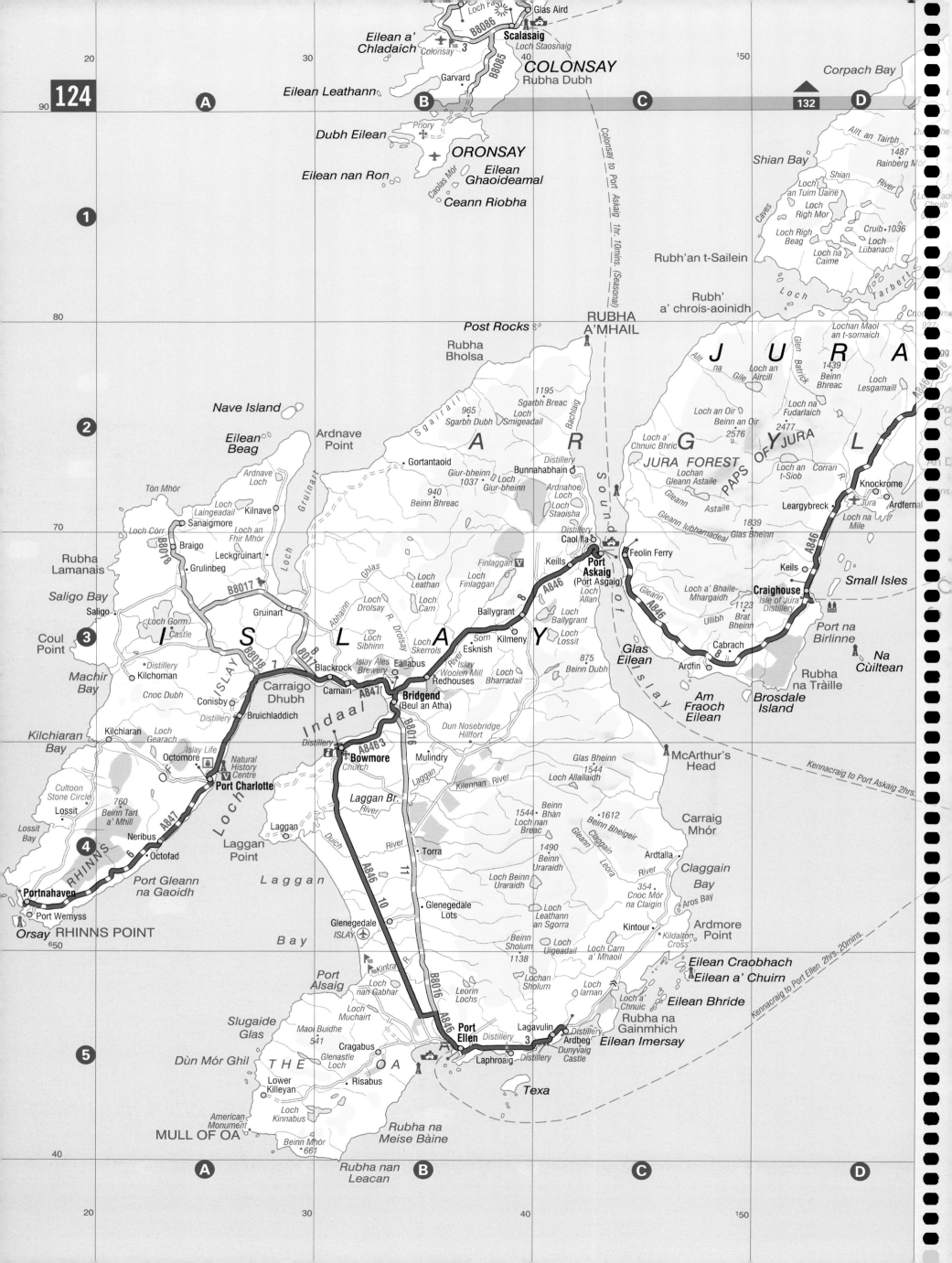

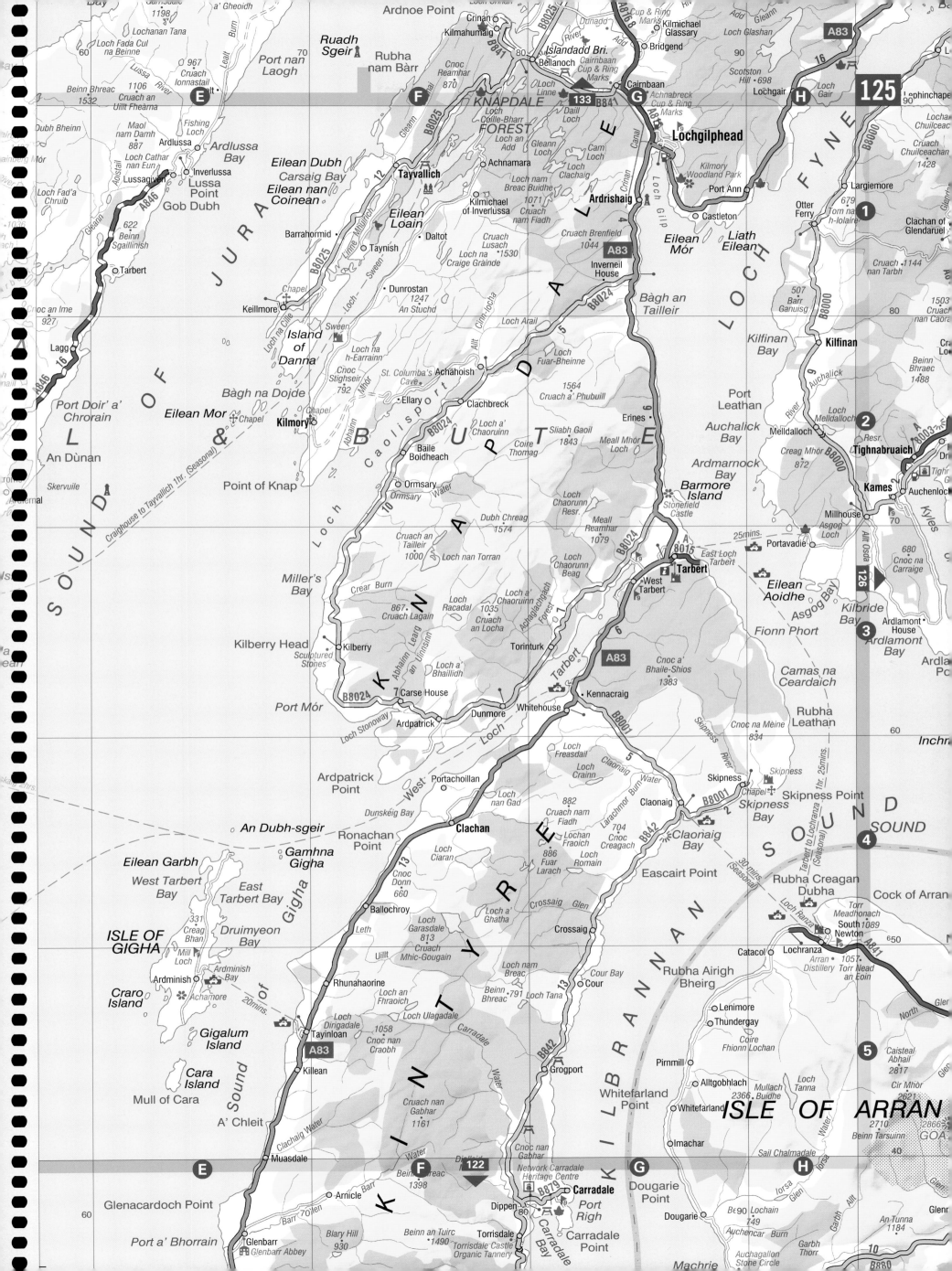

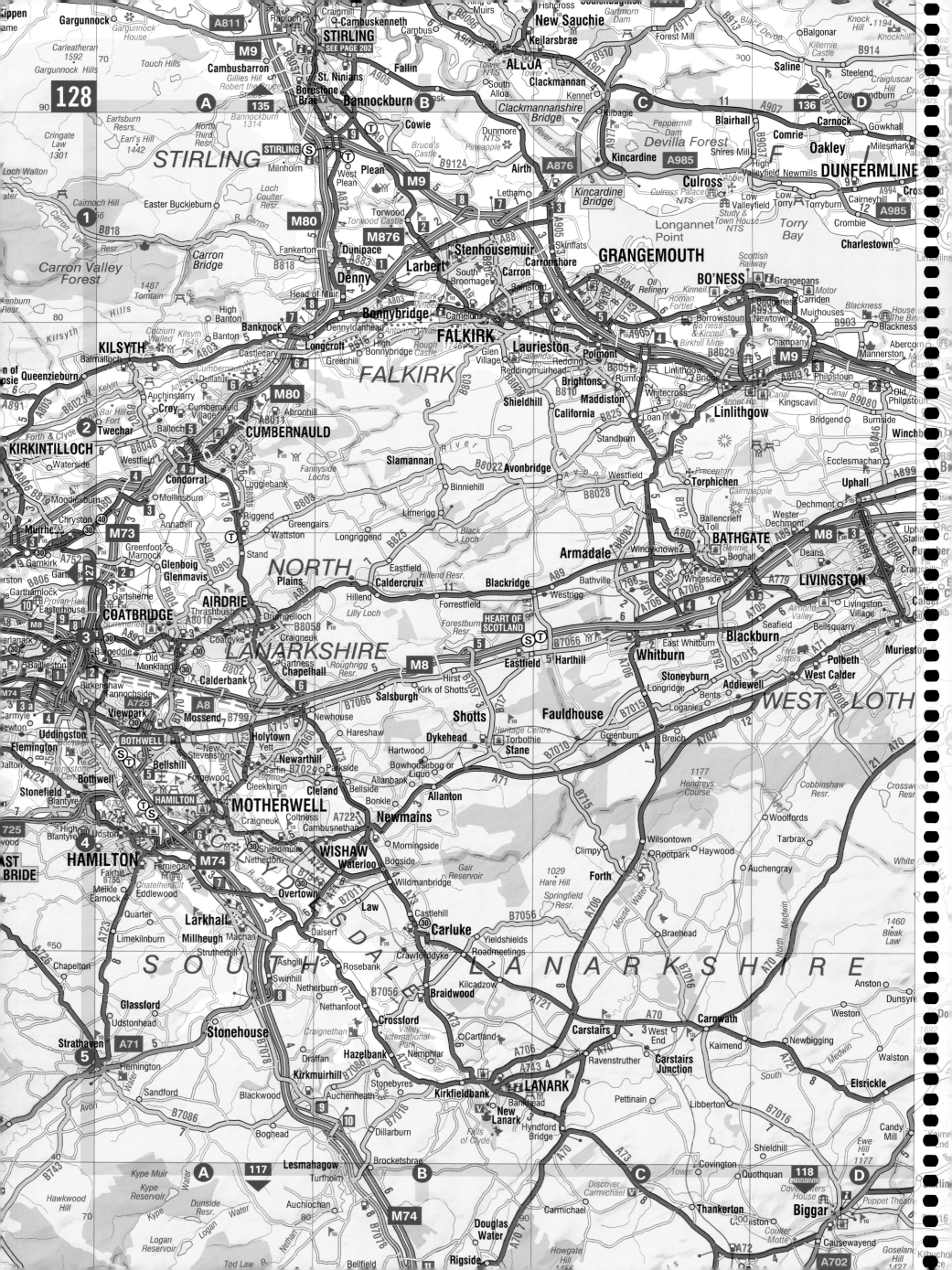

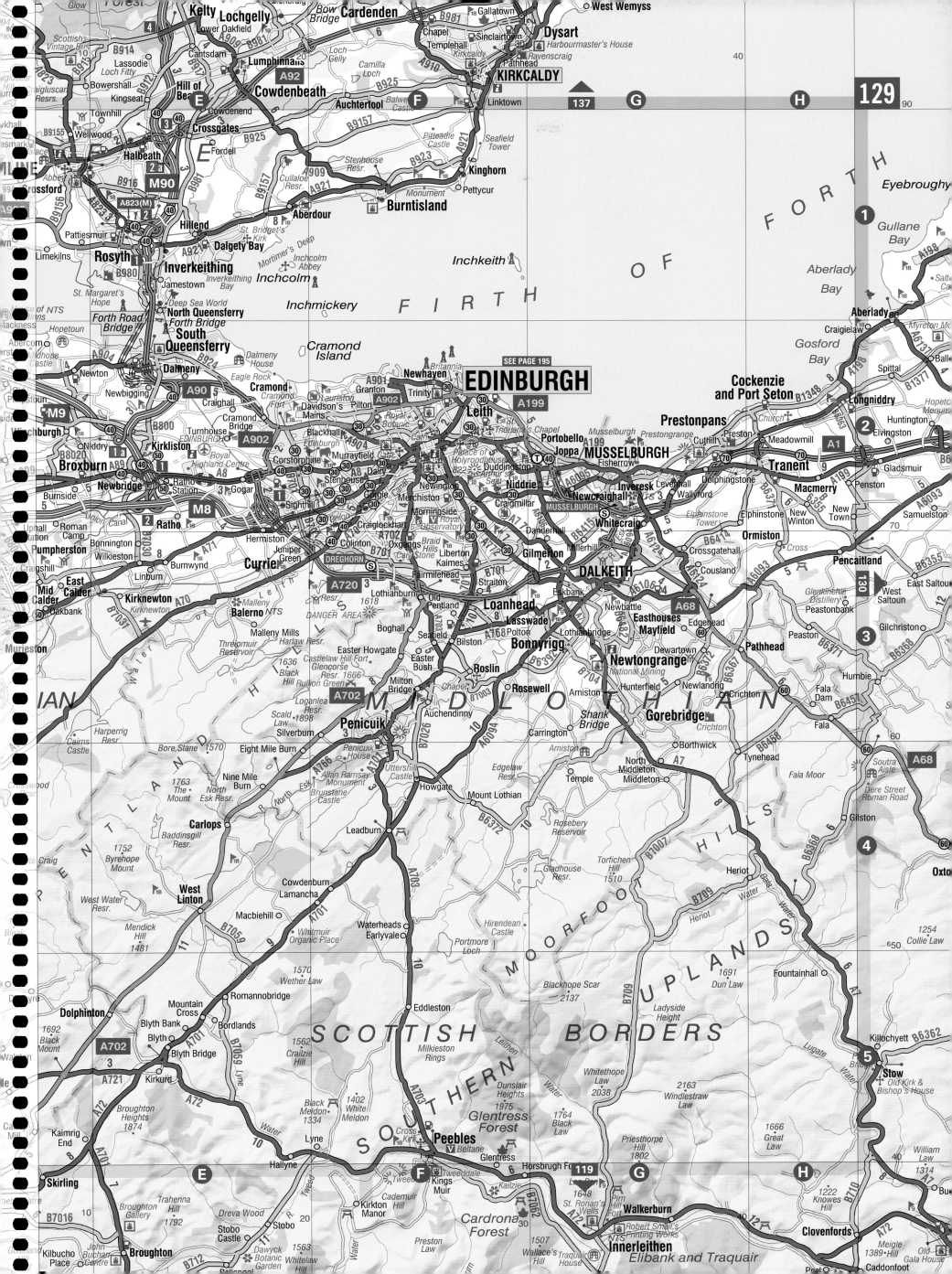

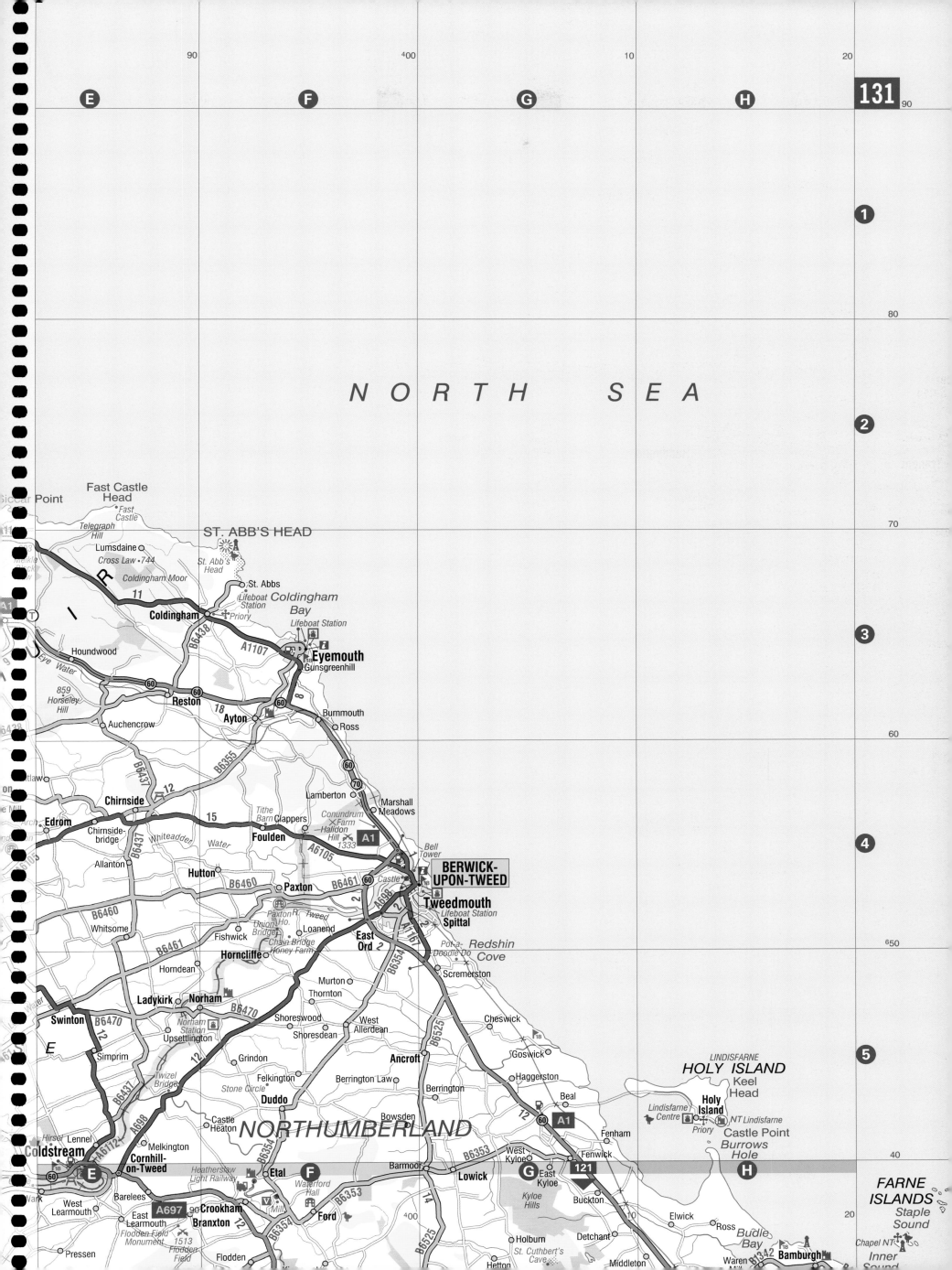

NORTH SEA

Siccar Point

Fast Castle Head
Fast Castle
Telegraph Hill
Lumsdaine
Cross Law •744
Coldingham Moor

ST. ABB'S HEAD
St. Abb's Head
St. Abbs
Lifeboat Station
Coldingham Bay
Priory
Lifeboat Station

Coldingham
B6438
A1107

Houndwood
Eye Water

Reston
859
Horseley Hill
60
60

Ayton
Burnmouth
Ross

Auchencrow

B6437
B6355

Chirnside
Lamberton
Marshall Meadows

Edrom
Chirnside-bridge
Whiteadder Water
Foulden
15
Tithe Barn Clappers
Conundrum Farm
Halidon Hill 1333
A1

Allanton

Hutton
B6460
Paxton
B6461
60
Bell Tower
BERWICK-UPON-TWEED
Castle
Tweedmouth
Spittal
Lifeboat Station

Whitsome
B6460
Paxton Ho.
R. Tweed
Union Bridge
Loanend
East Ord
Pot-a-Doodle-Do
Redshin Cove

Fishwick
Chain Bridge Honey Farm

Horncliffe
B6461
Horndean
Murton
Thornton
Scremerston

Ladykirk
Norham
Shoreswood
West Allerdean
Cheswick

Swinton
B6470
Norham Station
B6470
Shoresdean
B6525
Goswick

Upsettlington
12
Simprim
Grindon
Berrington Law
Ancroft
Haggerston
LINDISFARNE
HOLY ISLAND
Keel Head

Twizel Bridge
Stone Circle
Felkington
Berrington
Beal
Lindisfarne Centre
Holy Island
Lindisfarne Priory
NT Lindisfarne

Duddo
Bowsden
12
60
A1
Castle Point
Burrows Hole

Castle Heaton
NORTHUMBERLAND
Fenham

Coldstream
Hirsel Lennel
Melkington
B6354
West Kyloe
Fenwick

Cornhill-on-Tweed
Heatherslaw Light Railway
Etal
Barmoor
Lowick
East Kyloe
121

Waterford Hall
B6353
FARNE ISLANDS
Staple Sound

West Learmouth
Bareless
A697
Mill
Ford
Kyloe Hills
Buckton

East Learmouth
Crookham
Branxton
B6354
400
Elwick
Ross
Budle Bay

Flodden Field Monument 1513 Flodden Field
Holburn
Detchant
Bamburgh

Pressen
Flodden
St. Cuthbert's Cave
Waren
Middleton

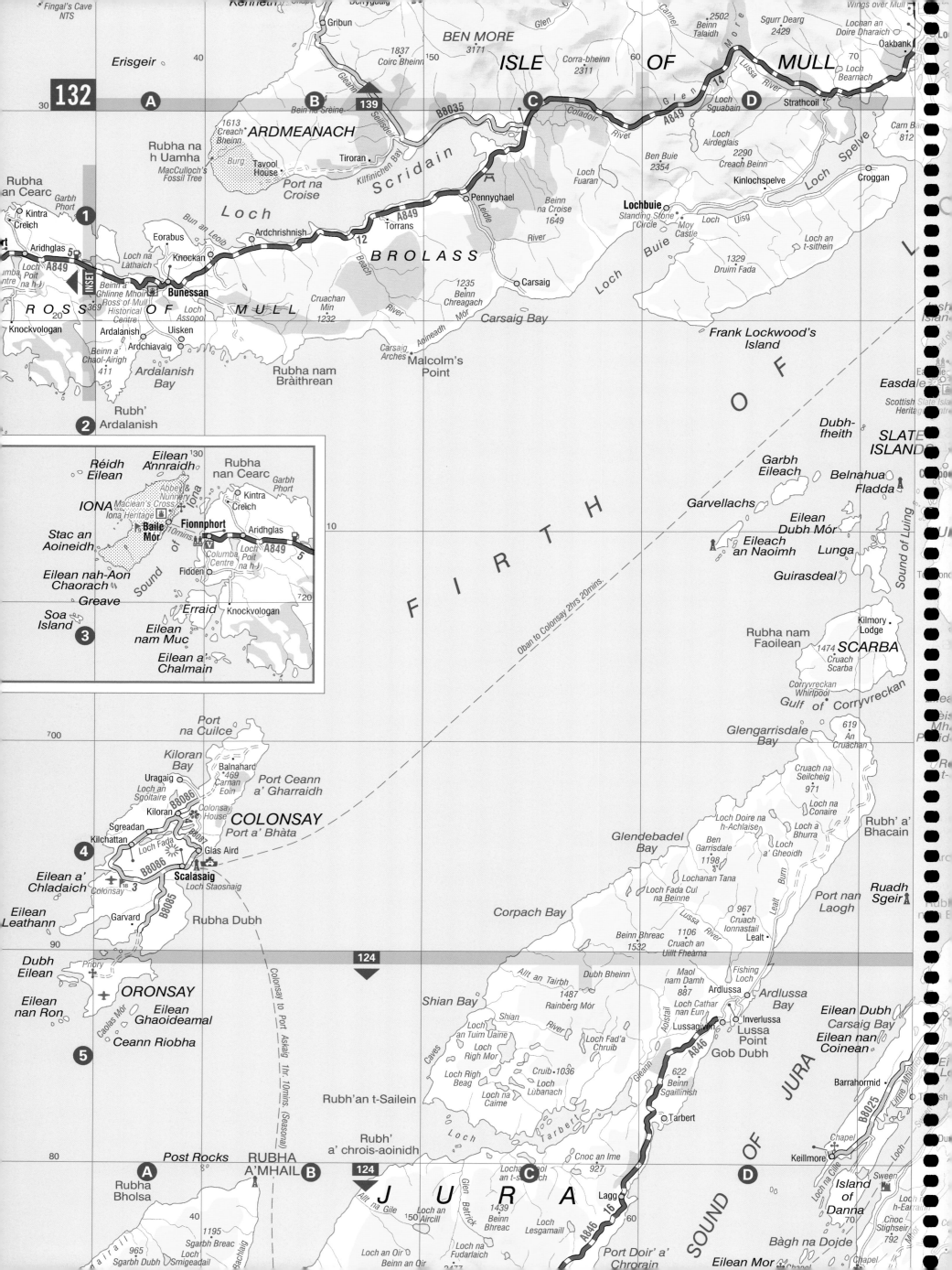

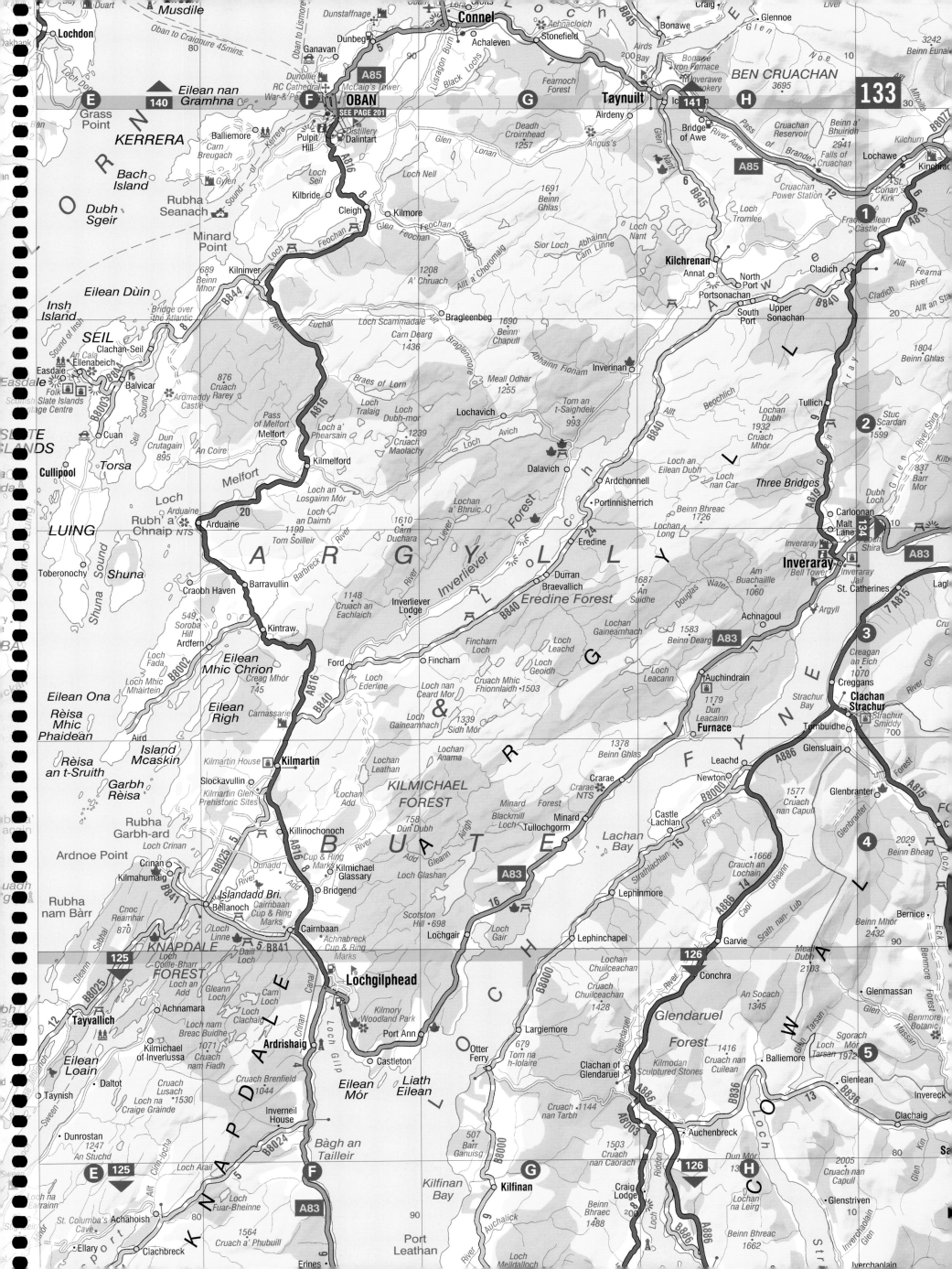

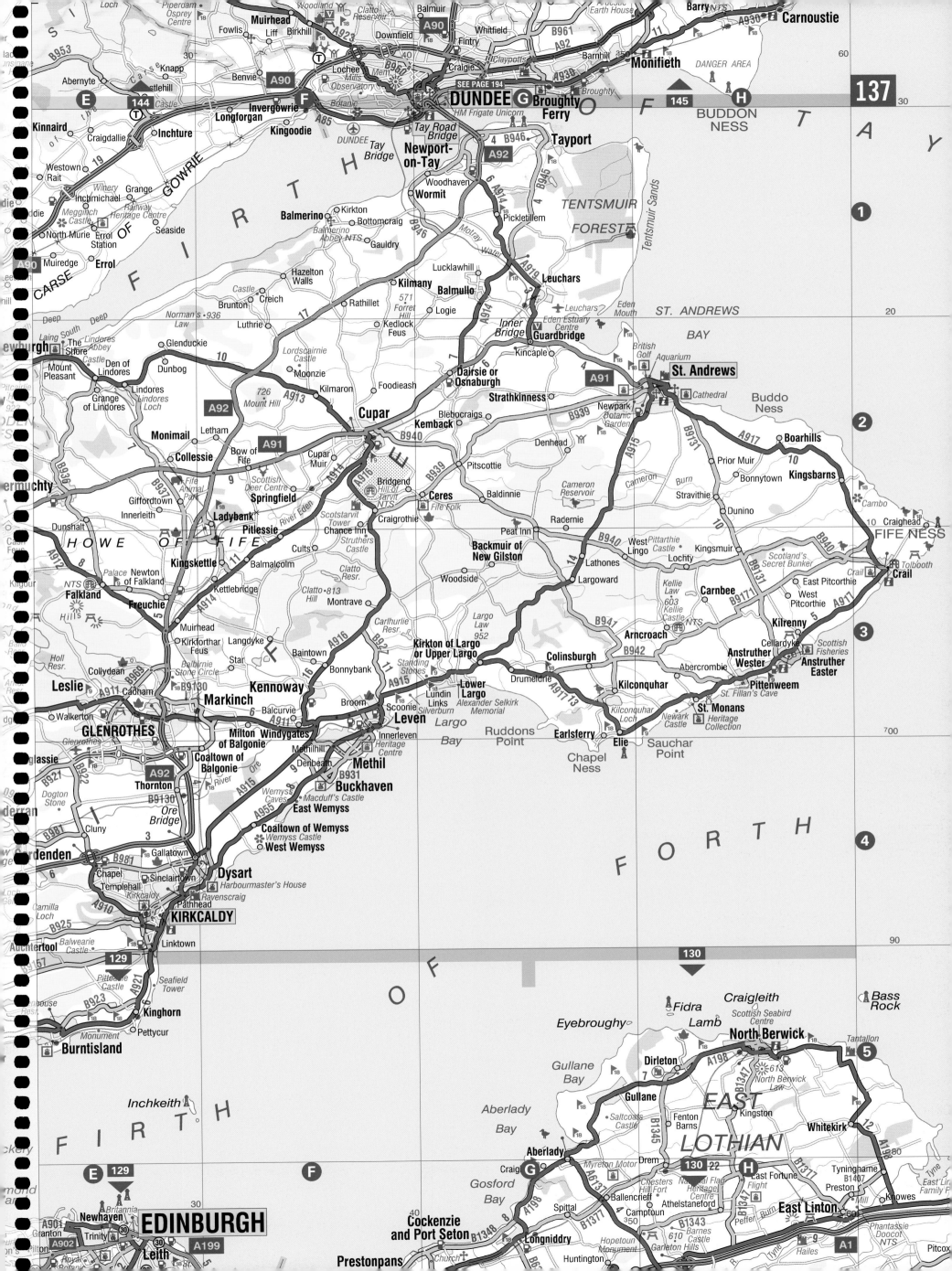

80

100   A   10   B   C   20   D   30

1

Oban to
Lochboisdale 5hrs. 20mins.
(Seasonal)

70

Oban to
Castlebay 5hrs.

Cairns of Coll

Eag na
Maoile

Eilean Mór

Rubha Mór

Bousd

2

Cornaigmore   Sorisdale

Rubh'a' Bhinnein   B8072

COLL

Loch
Fada

Cliad Bay

60

Grishipoll

Rubha Hogh

B8071

Clabhach   Loch Cliad   Bagh Feisdlum

B8071

Hogh Bay   340   **Arinagour**
Ben
Nogh   Loch nan
Cinneachan

Totronald   **V** Stables

Loch
Anlaimh   B8070

3   Tiree to
Barra 2hrs. 45mins.
(Seasonal)   + Coll
Feall   Uig   Acha   **Eilean
Bay   Ornsay**

       5   Loch
Etharna

Calgary Point   Port na
h-Eathar   Oban to Tiree 3hrs. 20mins. (Seasonal)

Gunna   Caolas Ban   Crossapol   Friesland
Port   Bay
a' Mhurain   **Bay**

   Soa

750

Miodar   Gunna Sound

Vaul
Bay   Carnan

**Hough
Skerries**   Balephetrish
Bay   Vaul   Salum   Rubhà Dubh

Treshnish

Cornaigmore   Balephetrish   Loch   B8069   Caolas   Coll to Tiree 55mins.

Sraid Ruadh   Riaghain   Ruaig

Balevullin   Kilmoluaig   Cornaigbeg   5   Kirkapol   **Gott Bay**

Hough   Kenovayo   B8068   Gott   Cairn na
Burgh Beg

4   TIREE
(Port Adhair Thiriodh)   5

Kilkenneth   B8068   B8065   **Scarinish**   Fladda

Sandaig   Moss   Loch an
Eilein   An Iodhlann

Middleton   Heylipol   4   Baugh   Lunga

Port Mor   Barrapol   Crossapol   Heanish

Island Life   B8065   2   Hynish   Rubha Tràigh
an Duin

Port   Loch a'
Bharrapool   Phuill   **Bay**   **TIREE**

B8067   **I N N E R**

Balephuil   **Balemartine**   Bac Mor or
Dutchman's Cap

40   Mannal

Balephuil   West   Bac Beag
Bay   Hynish
Hynish

Port Snoig   Skerryvore
Lighthouse

5

30

      A   B   C   D

100   10   20   30

Réidh   Eilean
Eilean   Annraidh   Rubha
nan Cearc

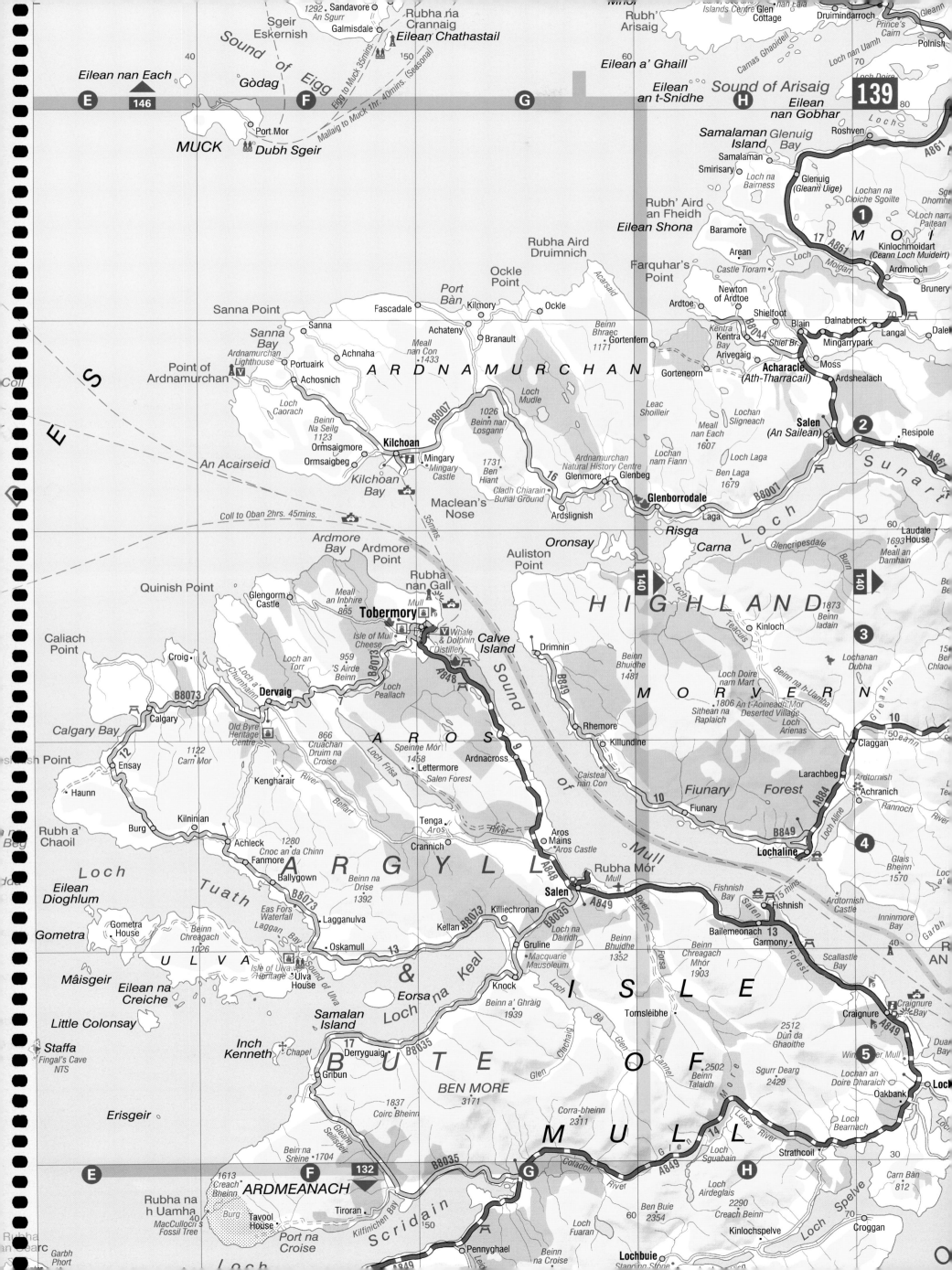

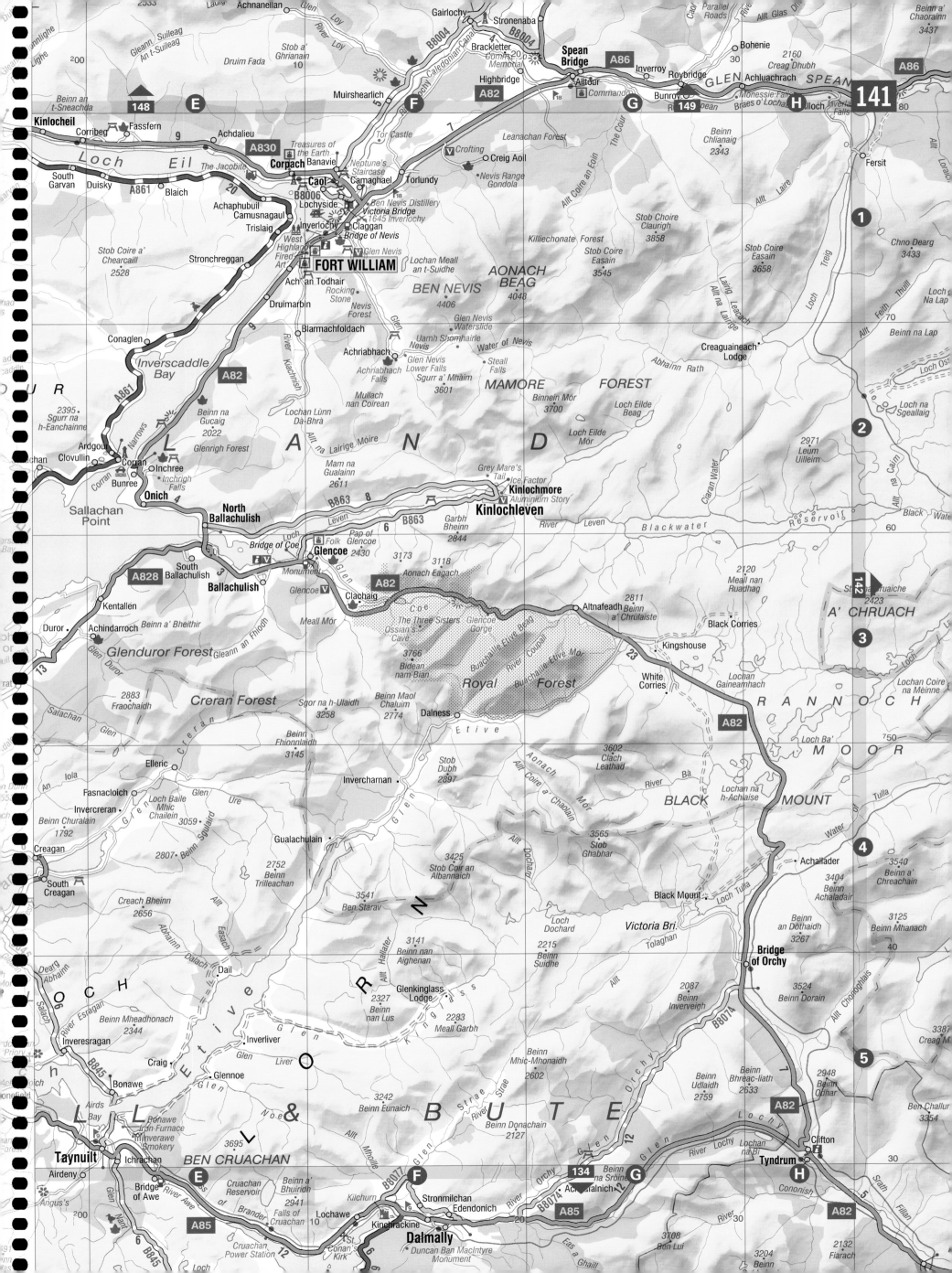

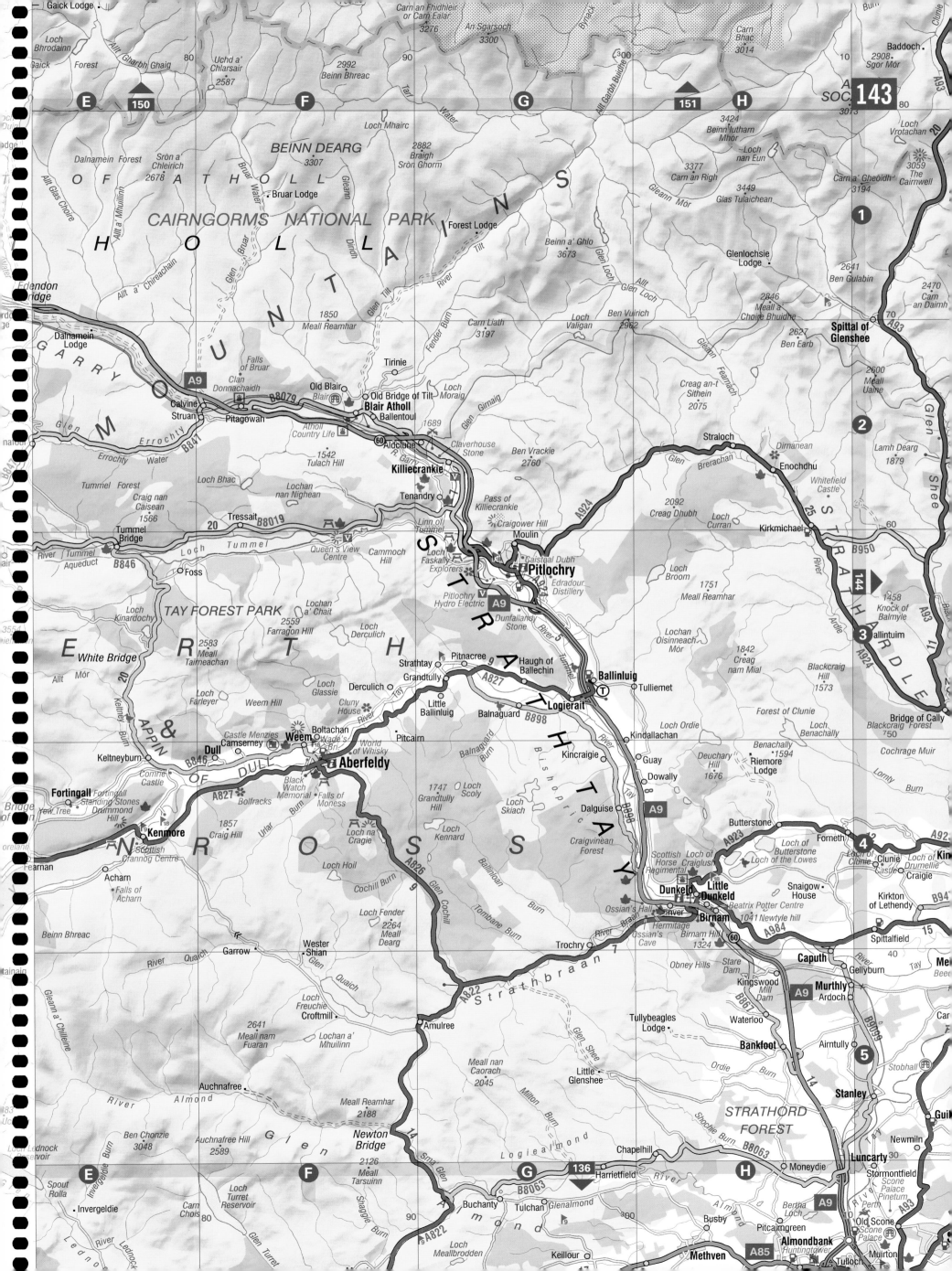

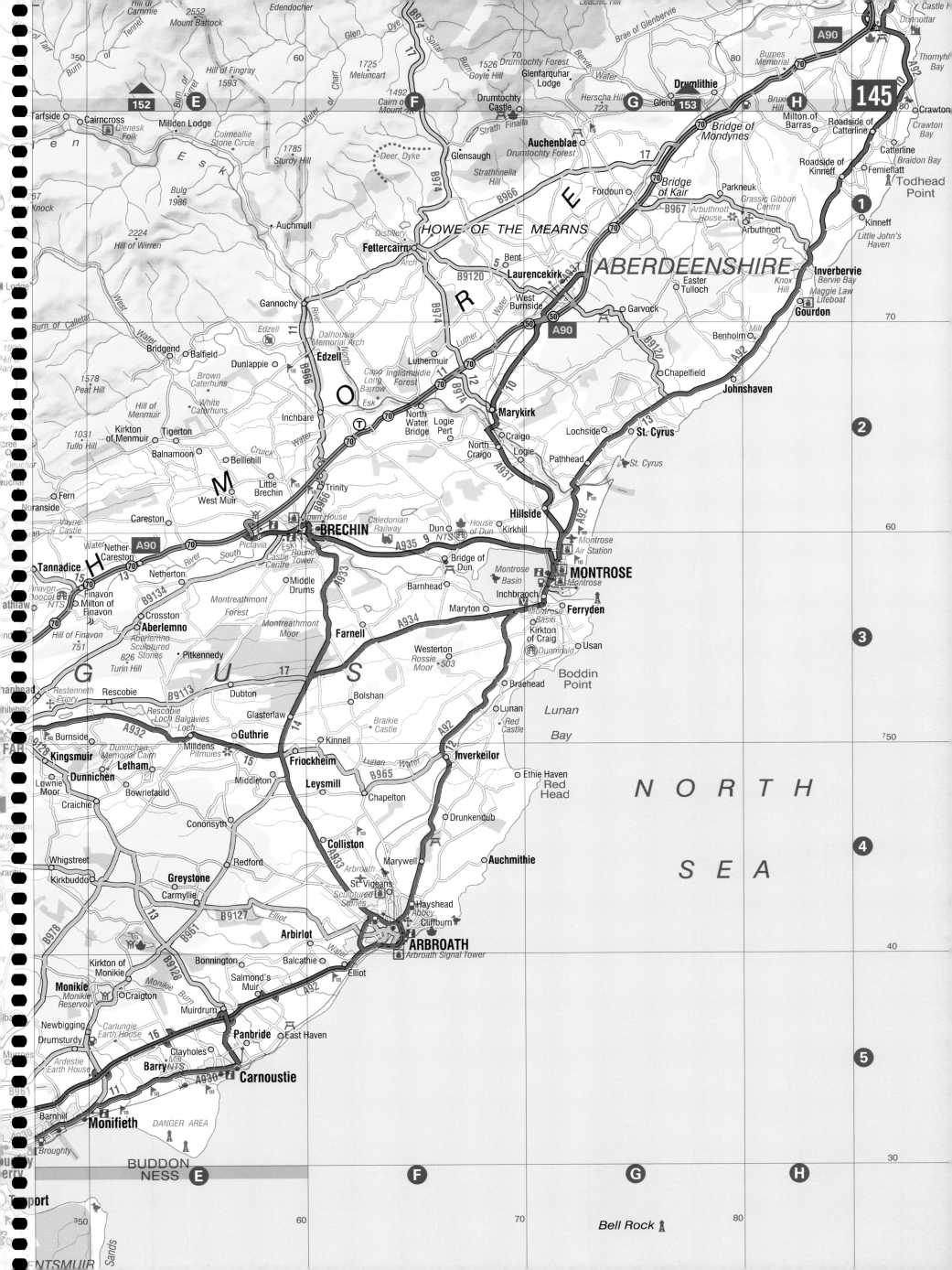

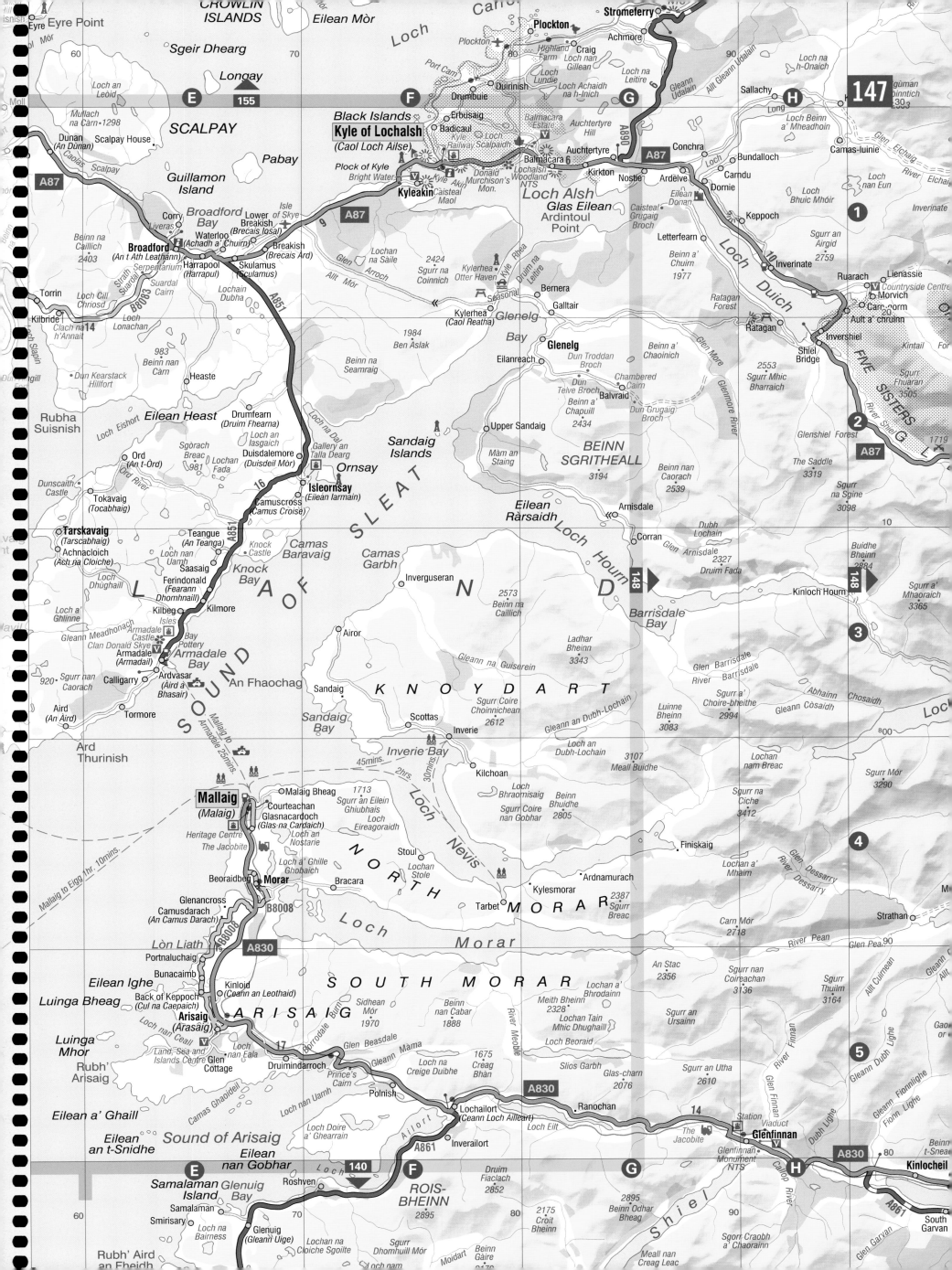

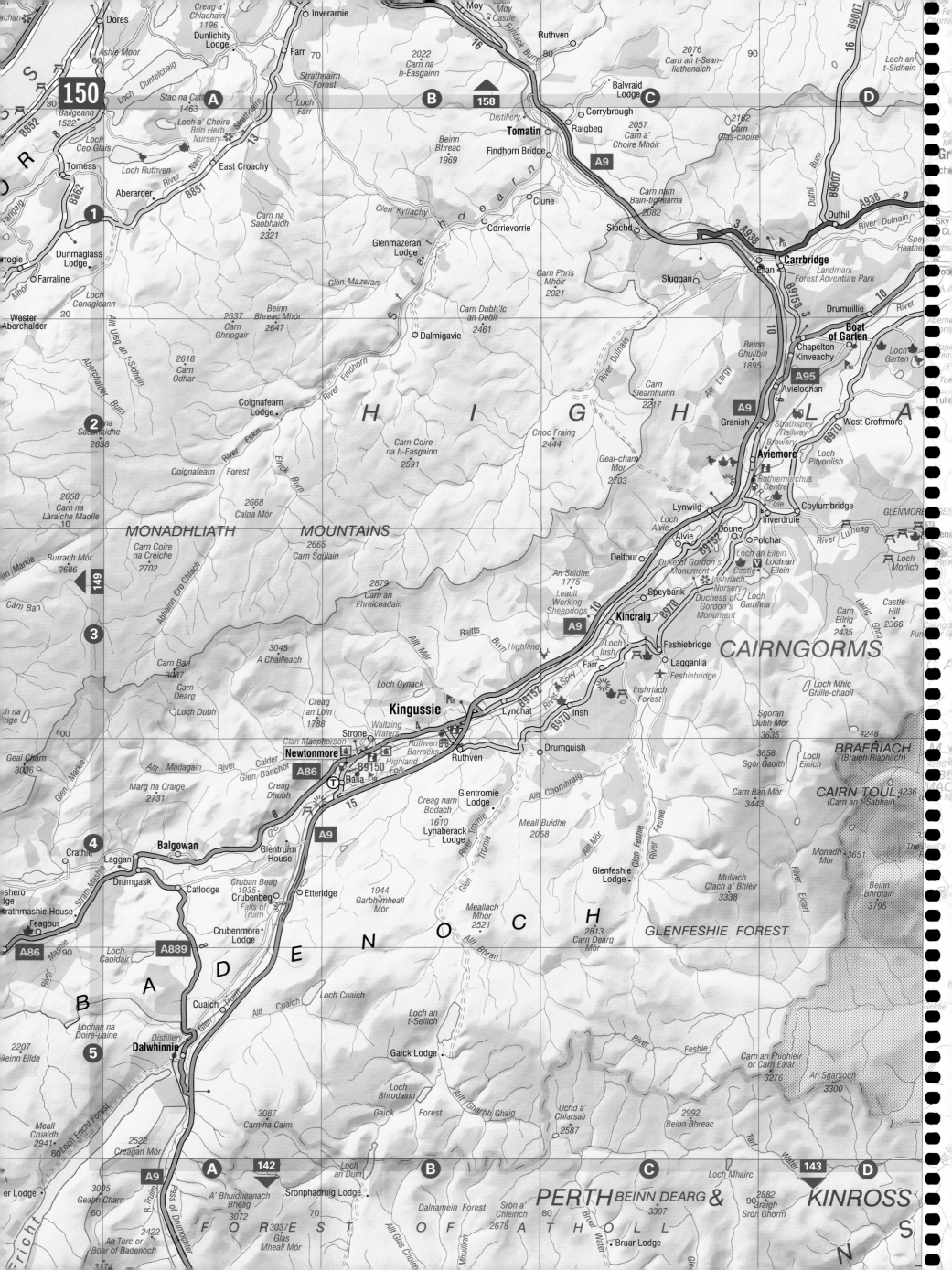

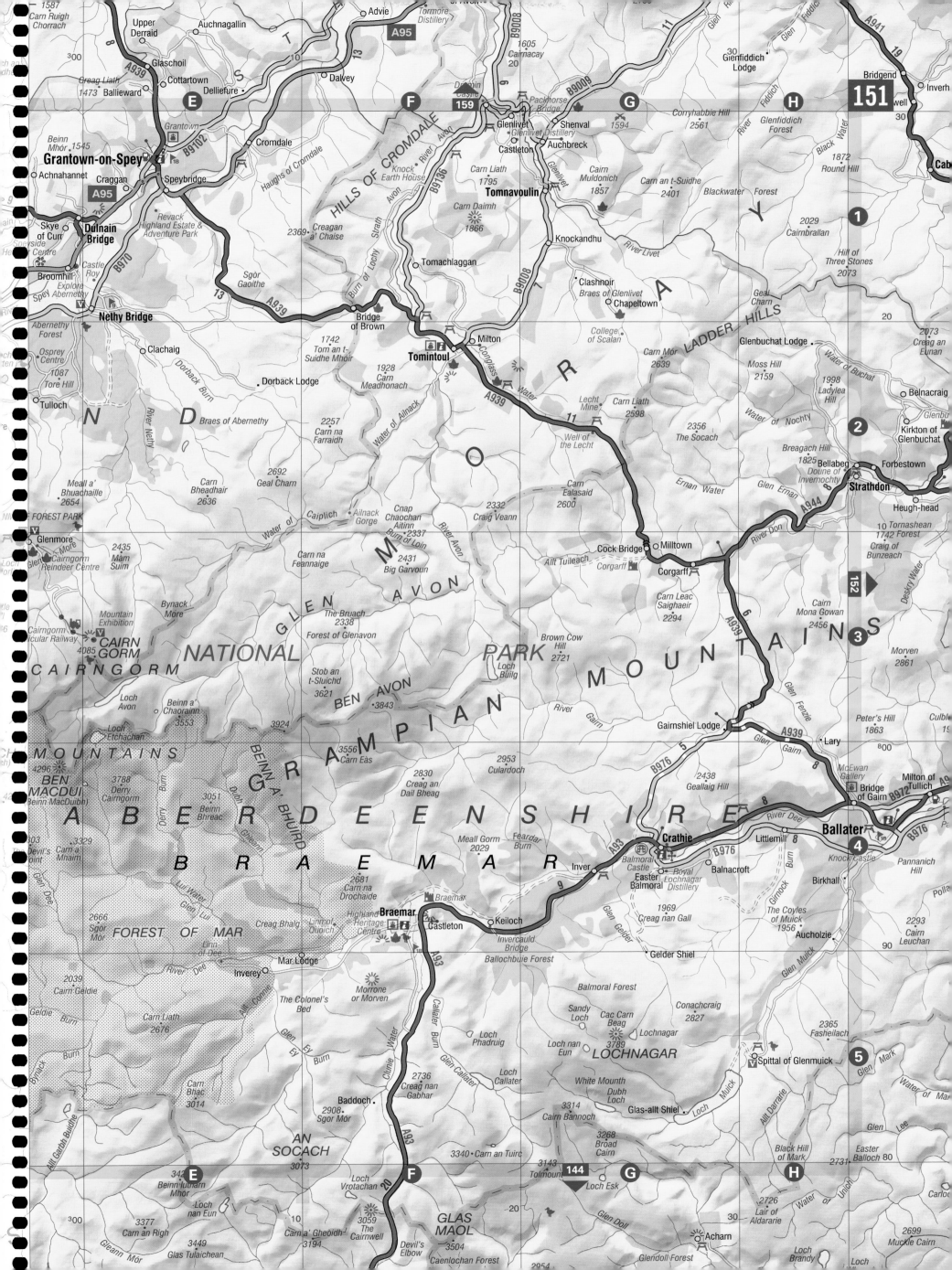

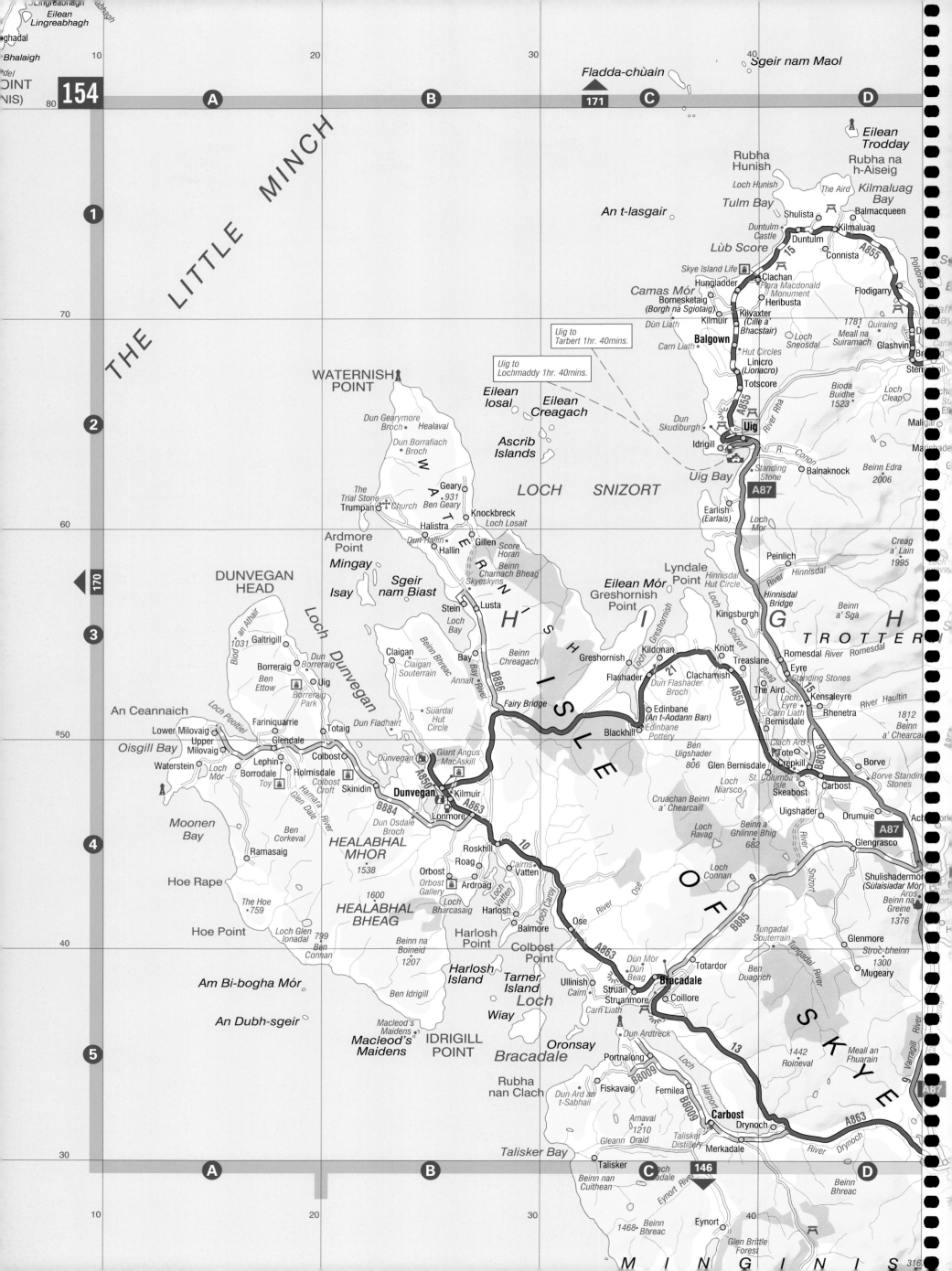

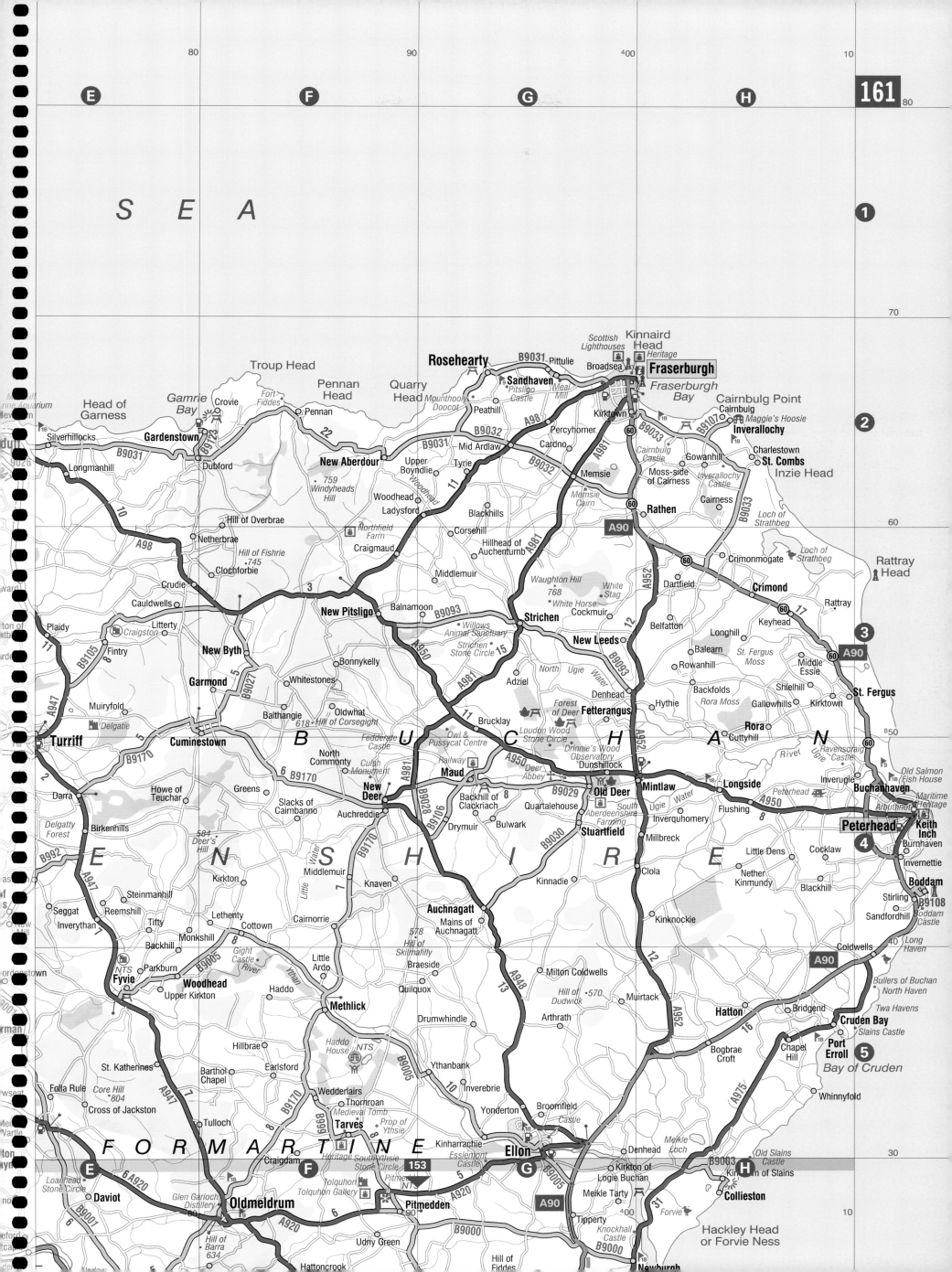

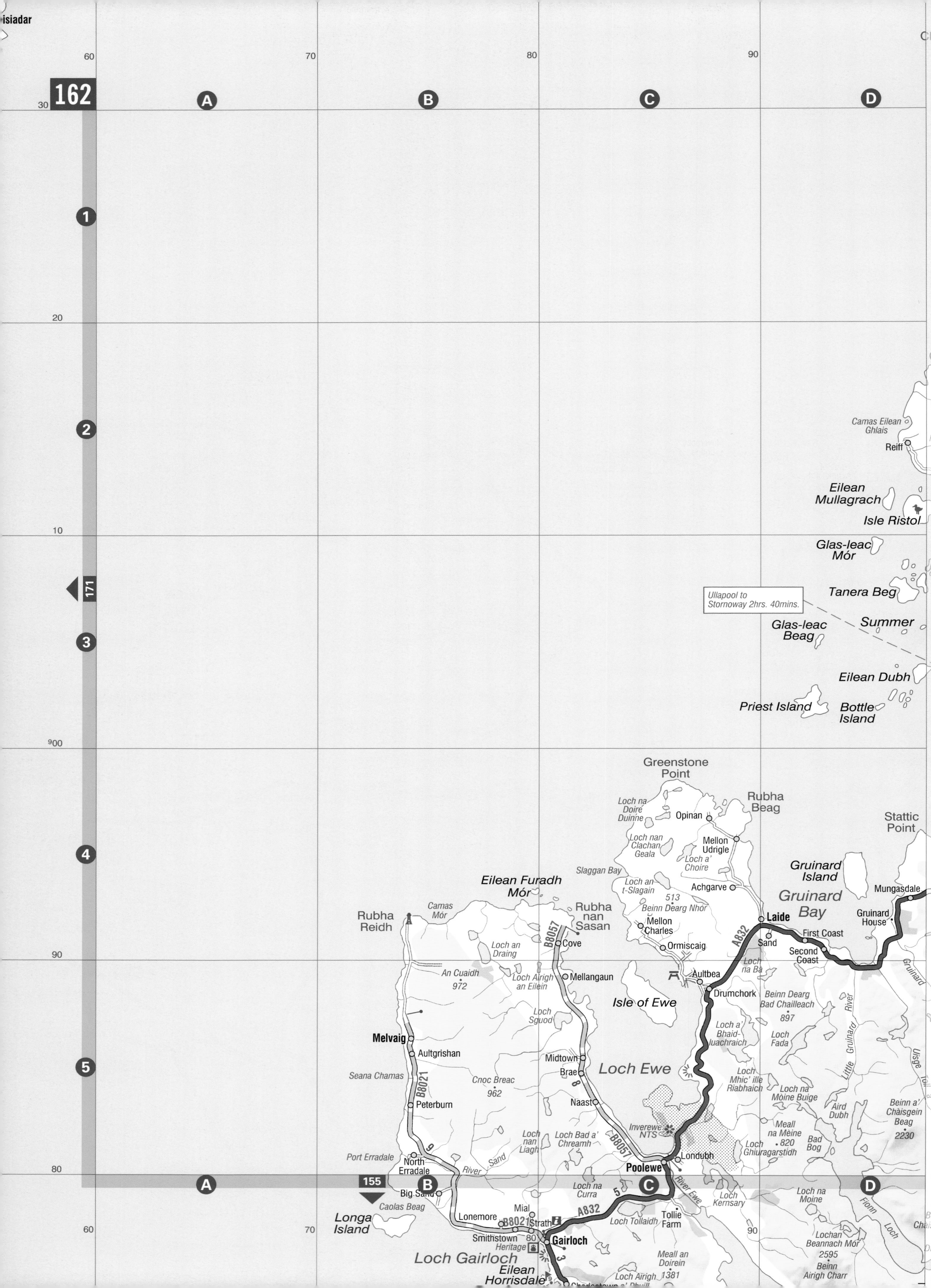

isiadar
A
B
C
D
1
2
3
4
5
171
155
Camas Eilean Ghlais
Reiff
Eilean Mullagrach
Isle Ristol
Glas-leac Mór
Tanera Beg
Ullapool to Stornoway 2hrs. 40mins.
Summer
Glas-leac Beag
Eilean Dubh
Priest Island
Bottle Island
Greenstone Point
Rubha Beag
Loch na Doire Duinne
Opinan
Loch nan Clachan Geala
Mellon Udrigle
Loch a' Choire
Stattic Point
Gruinard Island
Slaggan Bay
Eilean Furadh Mór
Loch an t-Slagain
Achgarve
513
Beinn Dearg Nhor
Gruinard Bay
Mungasdale
Rubha Reidh
Camas Mór
Rubha nan Sasan
Mellon Charles
Laide
Gruinard House
B8057
Cove
Sand
First Coast
Loch an Draing
Ormiscaig
A832
Second Coast
Loch na Bà
Aultbea
An Cuaidh 972
Loch Airigh an Eilein
Mellangaun
Drumchork
Beinn Dearg Bad Chailleach 897
Isle of Ewe
Loch Sguod
Loch a' Bhaid-luachraich
Melvaig
Loch Fada
Aultgrishan
Midtown
Brae
Loch Ewe
Loch Mhic' ille Riabhaich
Loch na Moine Buige
Seana Chamas
B8021
Cnoc Breac 962
Peterburn
Naast
Aird Dubh
Beinn a' Chaisgein Beag 2230
Inverewe NTS
Meall na Mèine 820
Loch nan Liagh
Loch Bad a' Chreamh
B8057
Bad Bog
Loch Ghiuragarstidh
Port Erradale
North Erradale
River Sand
Londubh
Poolewe
Big Sand
Loch na Curra
River Ewe
Loch Kernsary
Loch na Moine
Caolas Beag
Longa Island
Mial
Lonemore
B8021
Strath
A832
Tollie Farm
Loch Tollaidh
Smithstown
Gairloch Heritage
Gairloch
Lochan Beannach Mór 2595
Beinn Airigh Charr
Loch Gairloch
Eilean Horrisdale
Meall an Doirein 1381
Loch Airigh a' Phuill
Charlestown
Fionn Loch
Gruinard River
Little Gruinard River
60
70
80
90
30
20
10
900
90
80

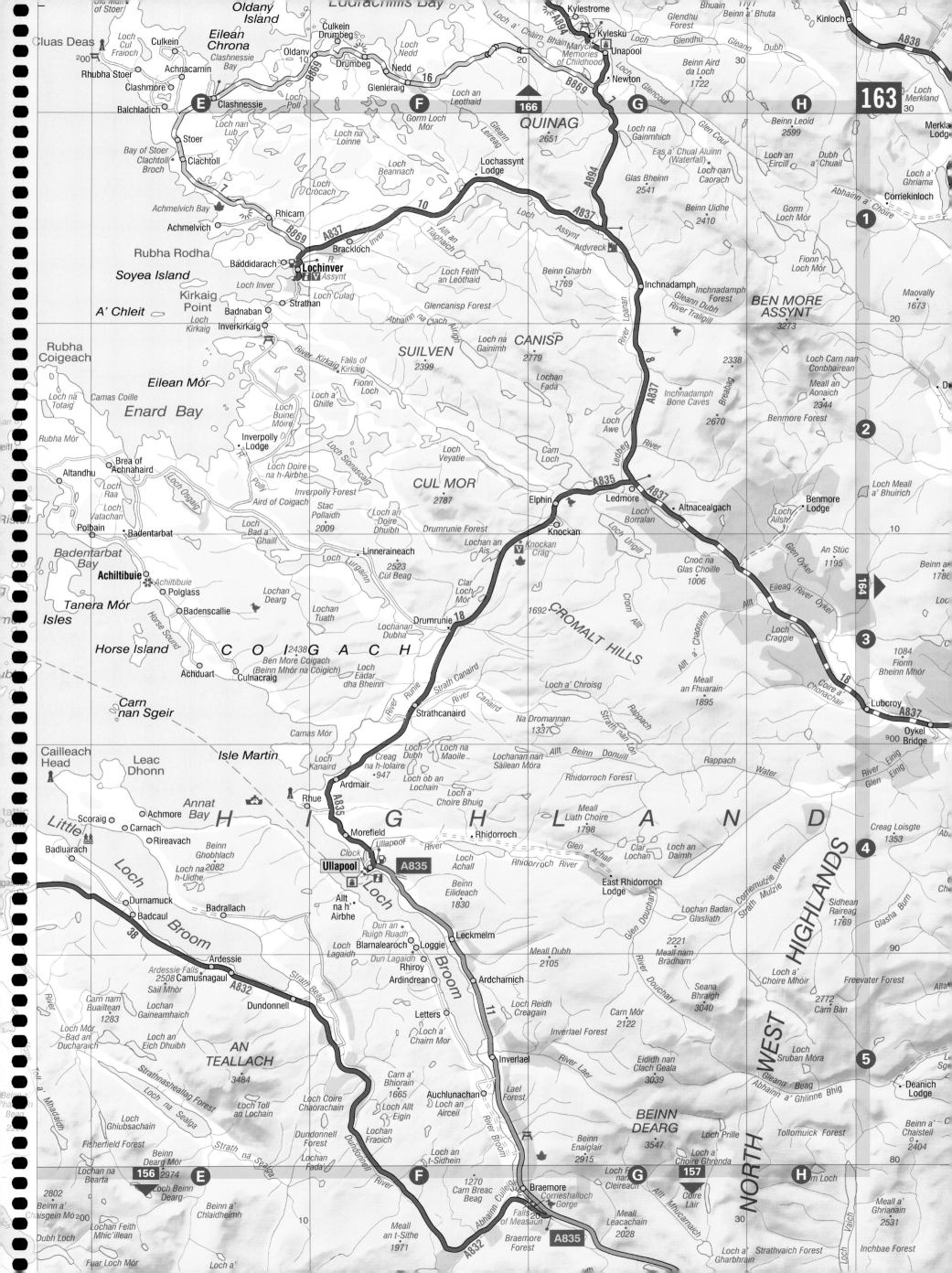

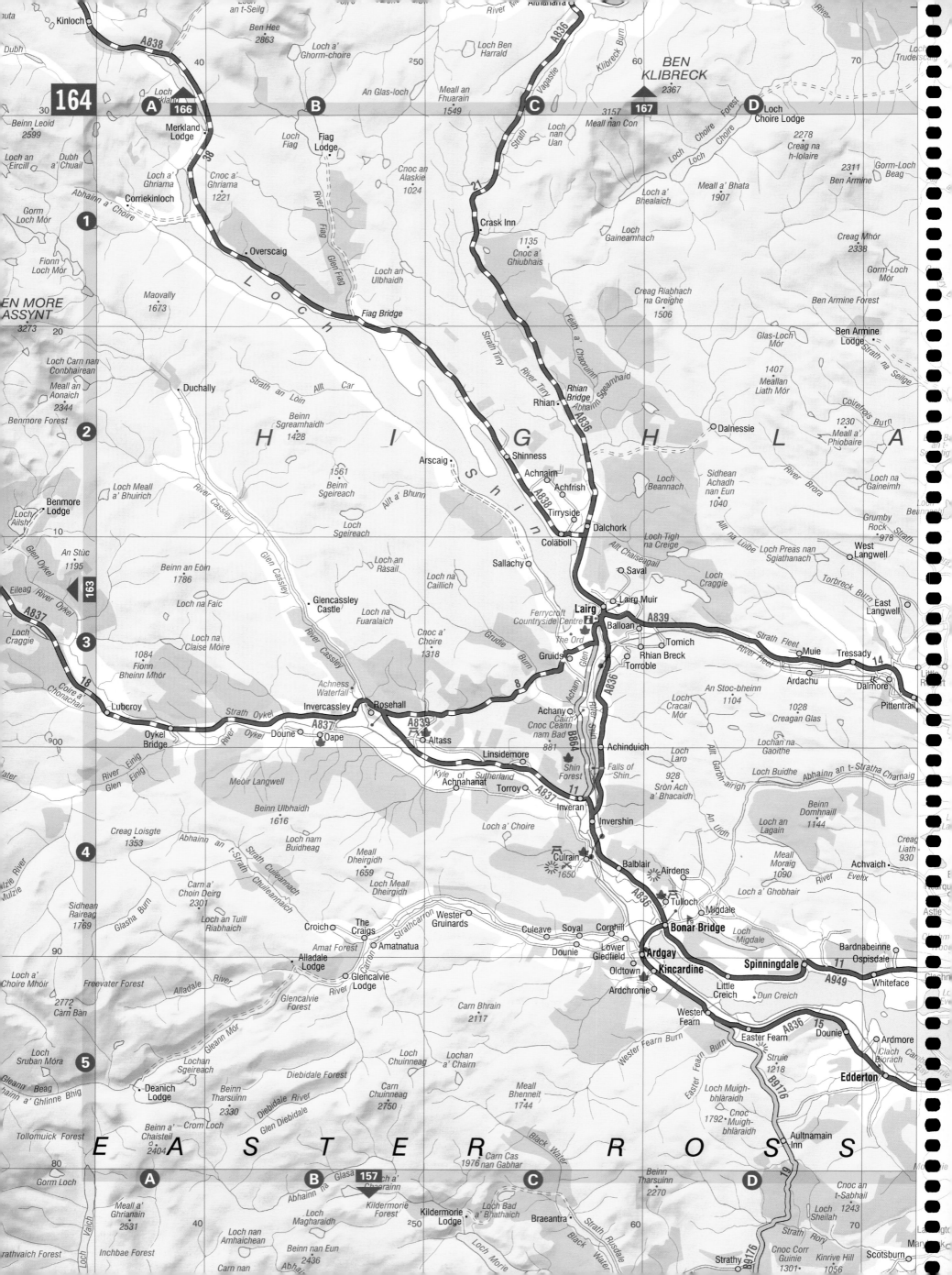

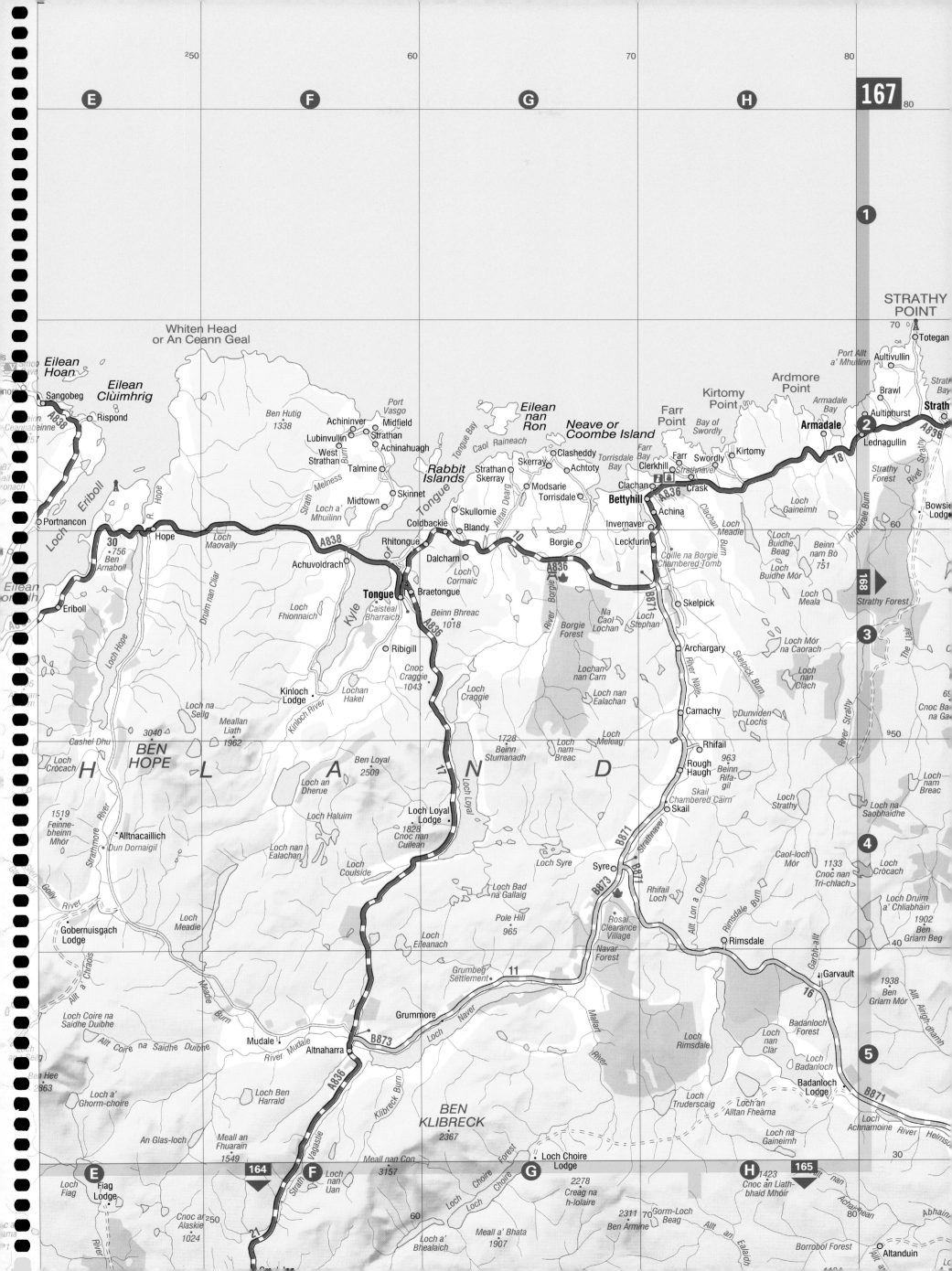

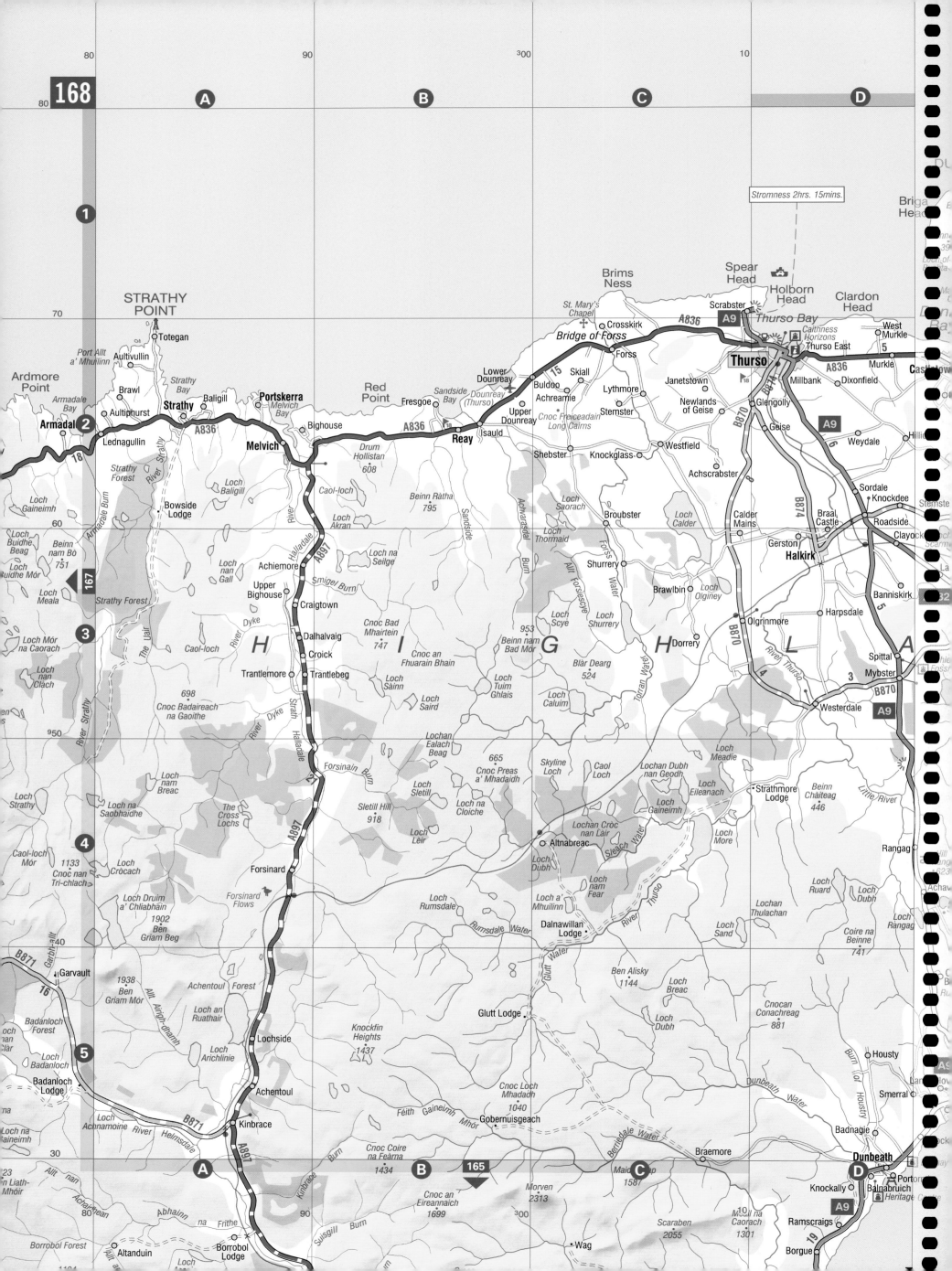

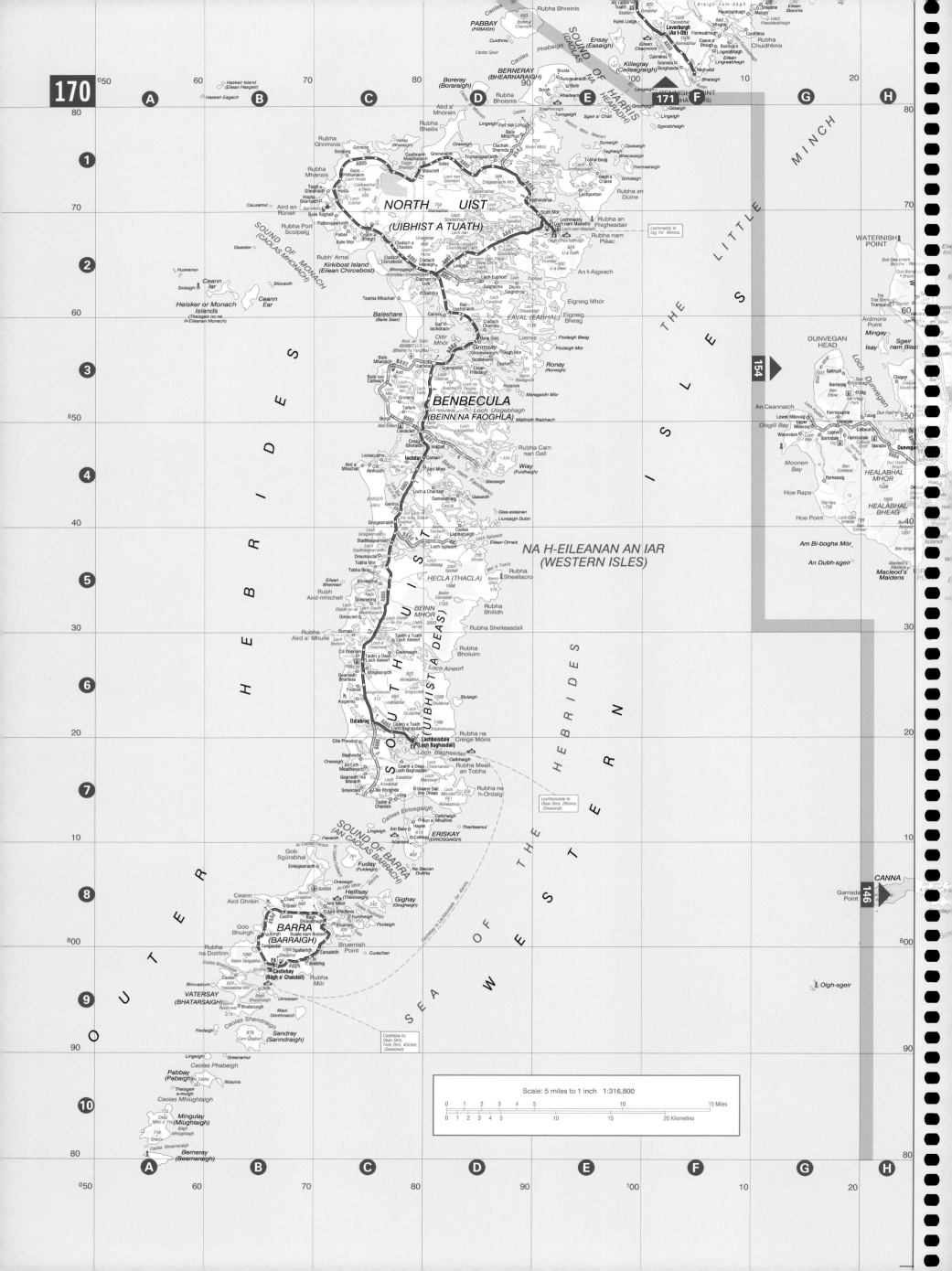

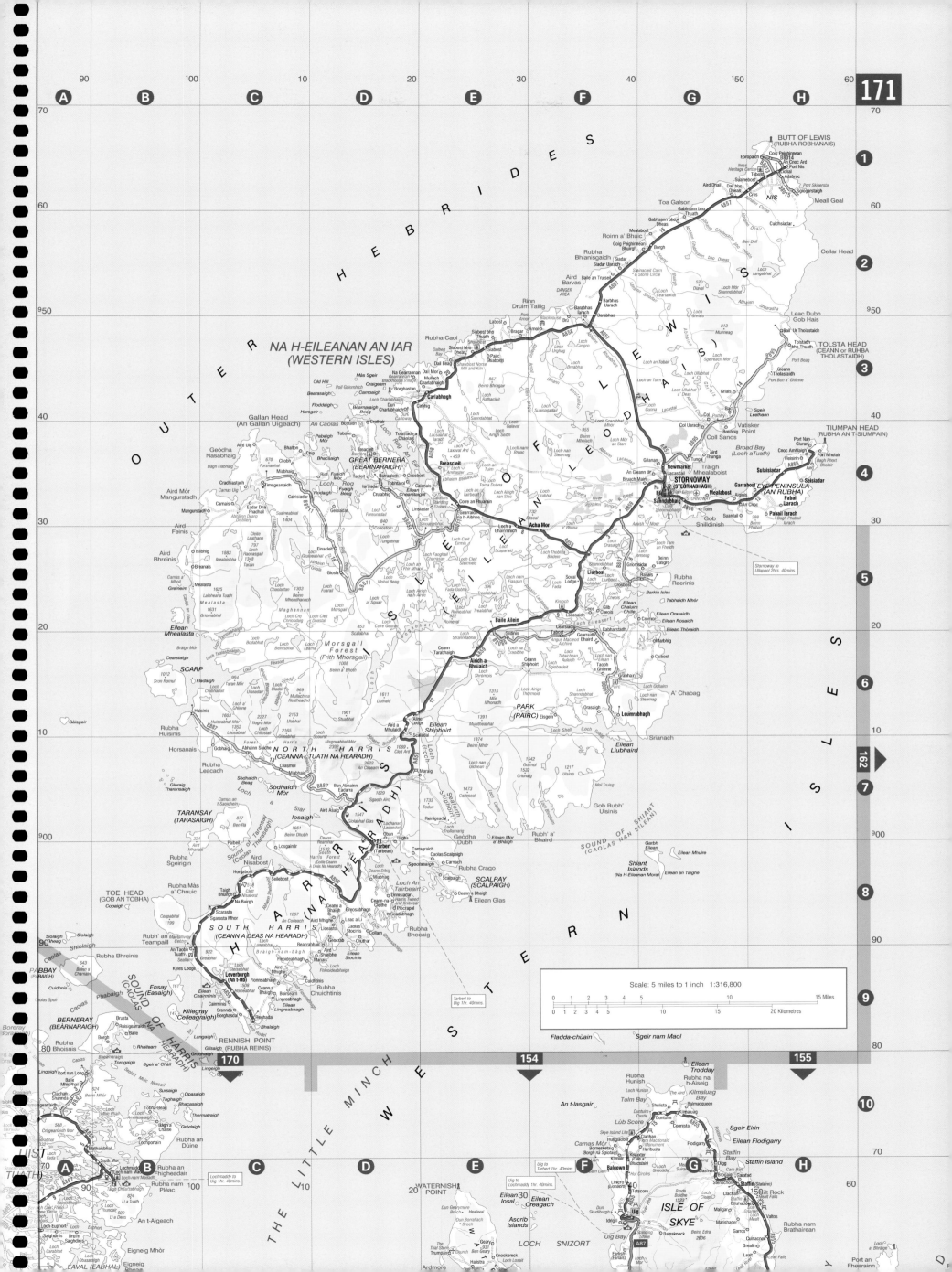

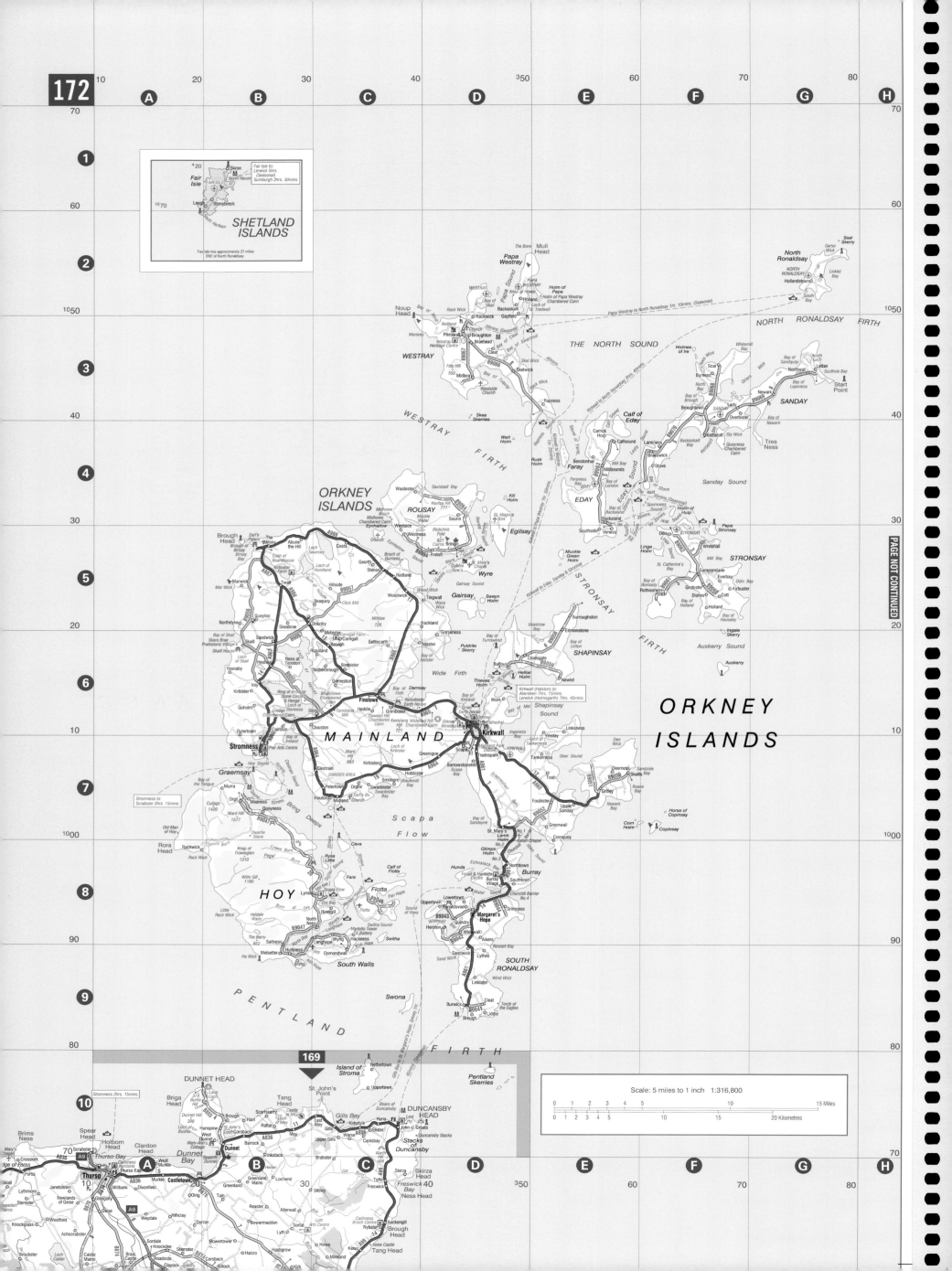

SHETLAND ISLANDS

Fair Isle

Fair Isle to:
Lerwick 5hrs. (Seasonal)
Sumburgh 2hrs. 30mins.

Fair Isle lies approximately 27 miles
ENE off North Ronaldsay

ORKNEY ISLANDS

Papa Westray

Mull Head

North Ronaldsay

Seal Skerry

Garso Wick

Linklet Bay

Noup Head

WESTRAY

THE NORTH SOUND

NORTH RONALDSAY FIRTH

Papa Westray to North Ronaldsay 1hr. 10mins. (Seasonal)

Start Point

SANDAY

WESTRAY FIRTH

Calf of Eday

Sanday Sound

FARAY

Tres Ness

ROUSAY

EDAY

STRONSAY FIRTH

Egilsay

Wyre

Gairsay

STRONSAY

Papa Stronsay

MAINLAND

Finstown

Kirkwall

SHAPINSAY

Auskerry Sound

ORKNEY

ISLANDS

Stromness

Kirkwall (Hatston) to:
Aberdeen 7hrs. 15mins.
Lerwick (Holmsgarth) 7hrs. 45mins.

DANGER AREA

Scapa
Flow

Deer Sound

Copinsay

Graemsay

Stromness to Scrabster 2hrs. 15mins.

HOY

Old Man
of Hoy

Rora
Head

Flotta

Burray

St. Margaret's
Hope

South Walls

SOUTH
RONALDSAY

PENTLAND

Swona

Tomb
of the Eagles

FIRTH

169

Stromness 2hrs. 15mins.

DUNNET HEAD

Island of
Stroma

Pentland
Skerries

DUNCANSBY
HEAD

Scale: 5 miles to 1 inch   1:316,800

0   1   2   3   4   5   10   15 Miles

0 1 2 3 4 5   10   15   20 Kilometres

St. John's
Point

Gills Bay

Thurso

Dunnet
Bay

Dunnet

Castletown

A9

A836

PAGE NOT CONTINUED

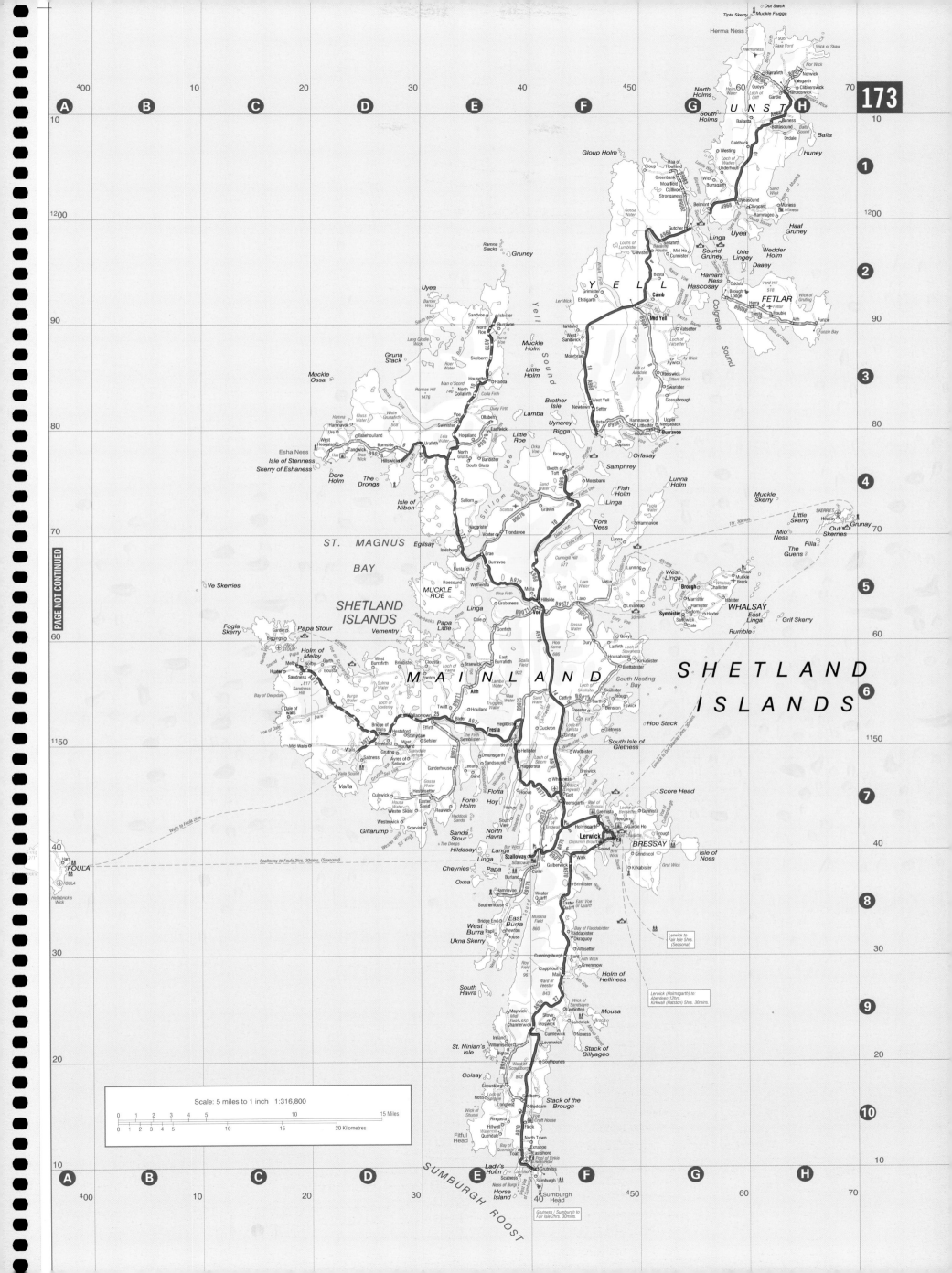

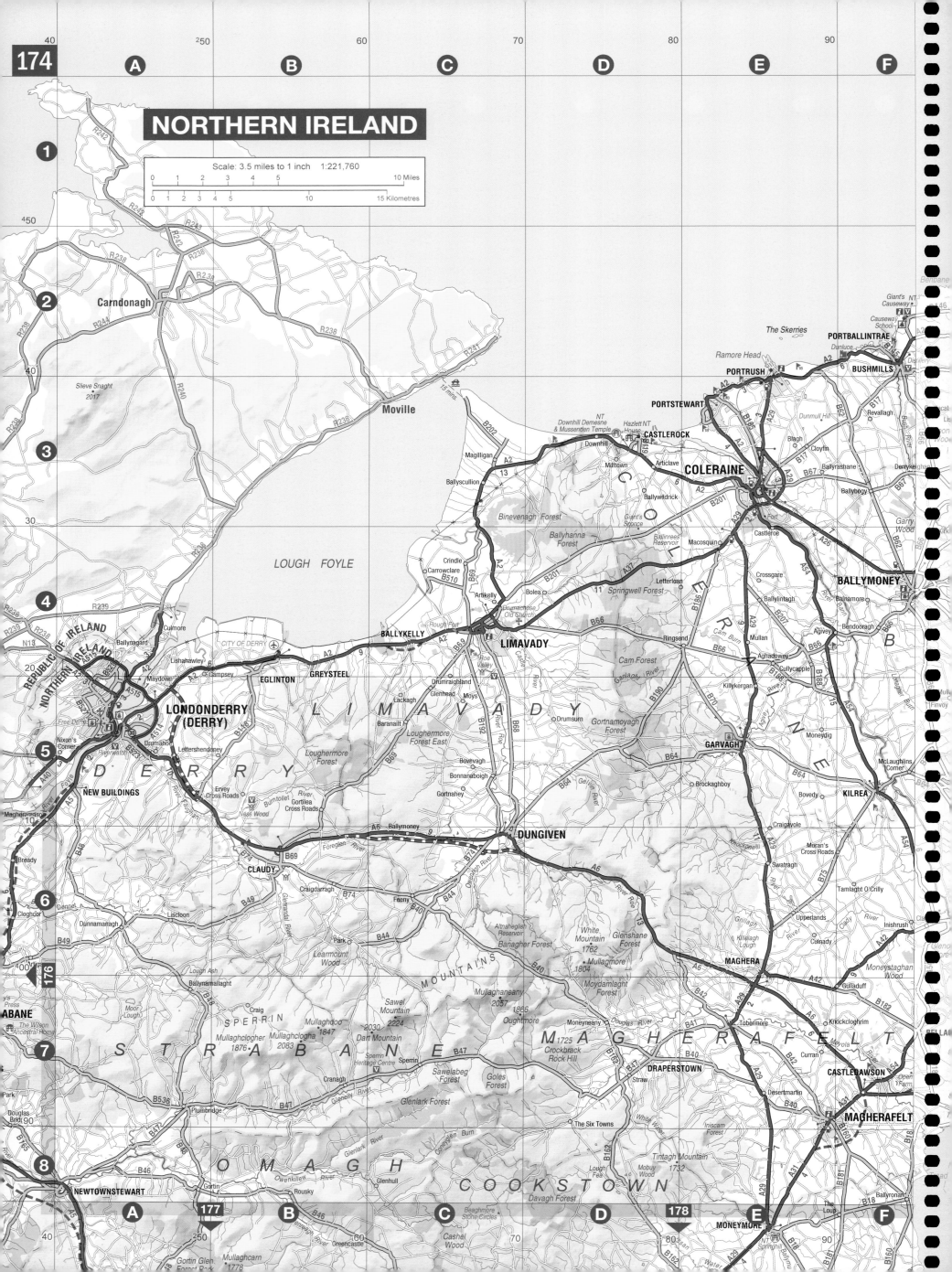

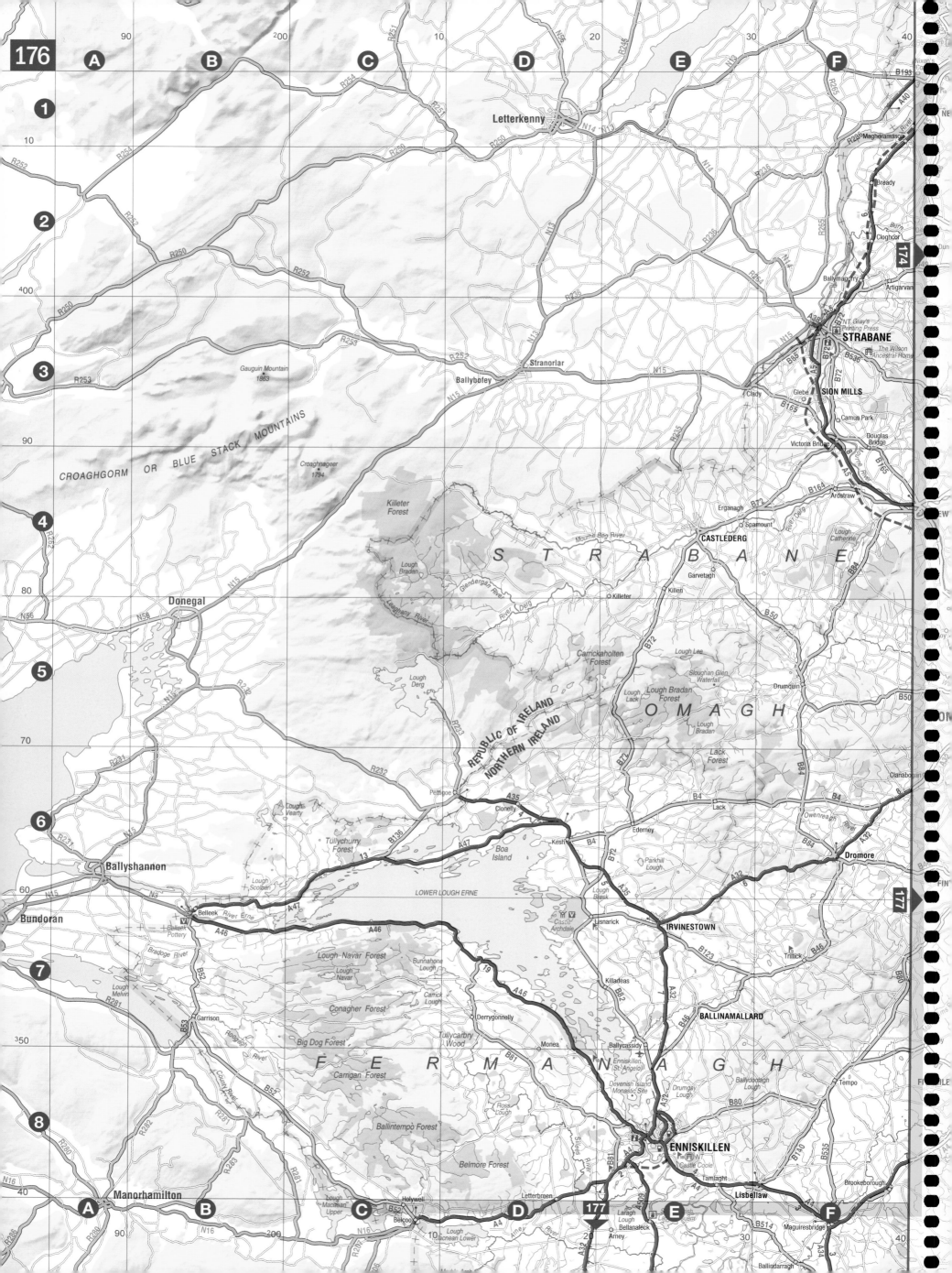

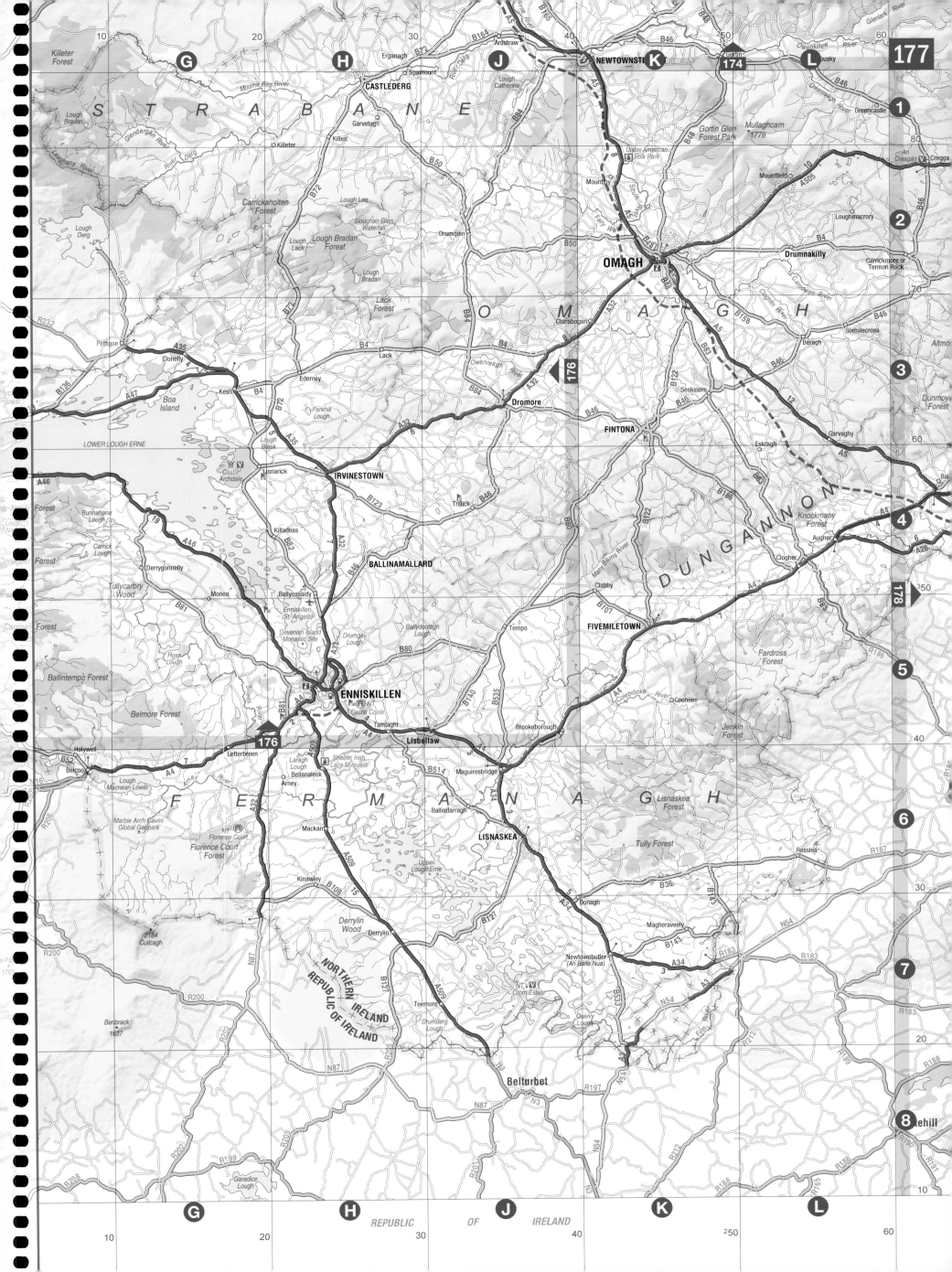

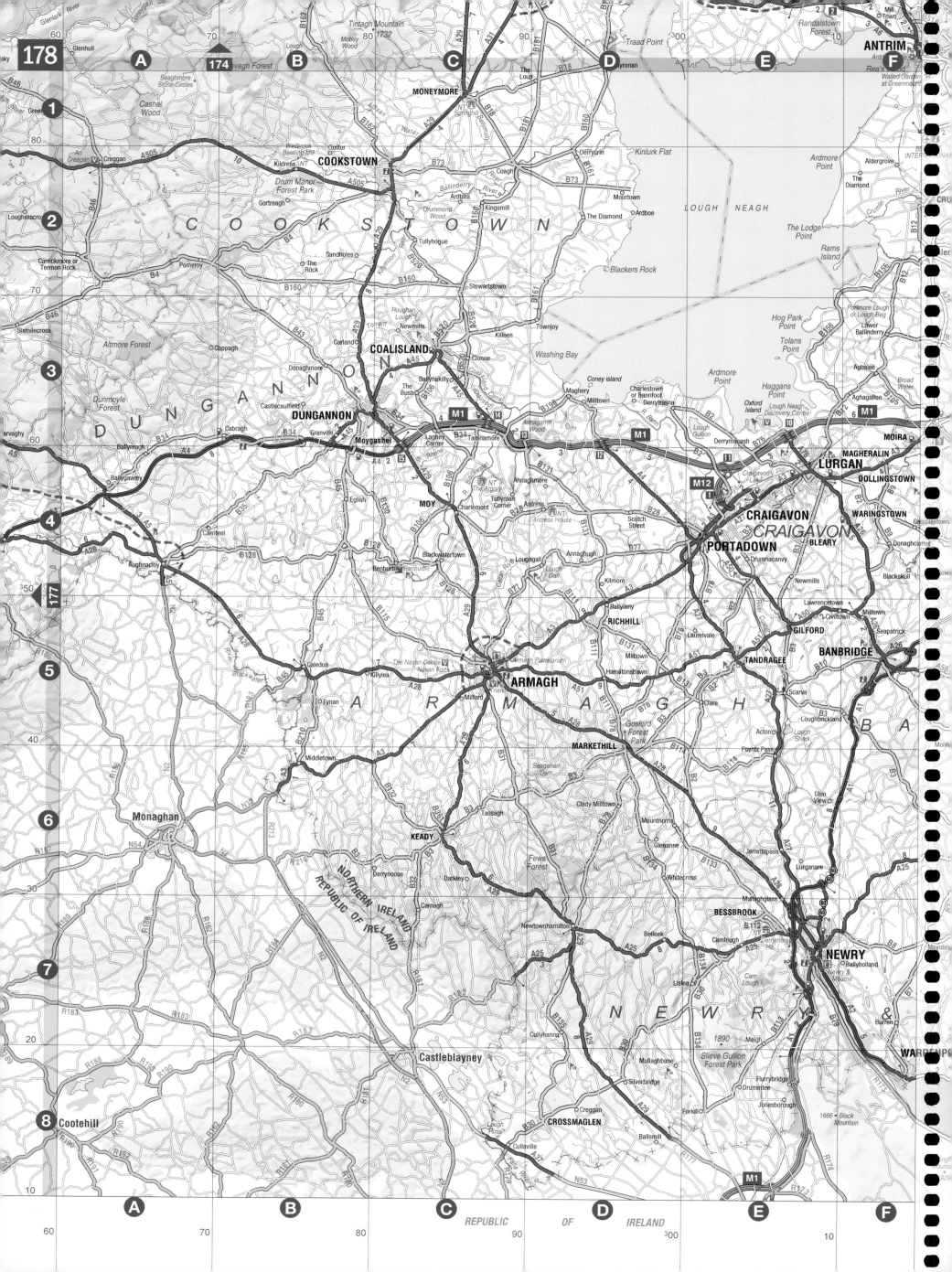

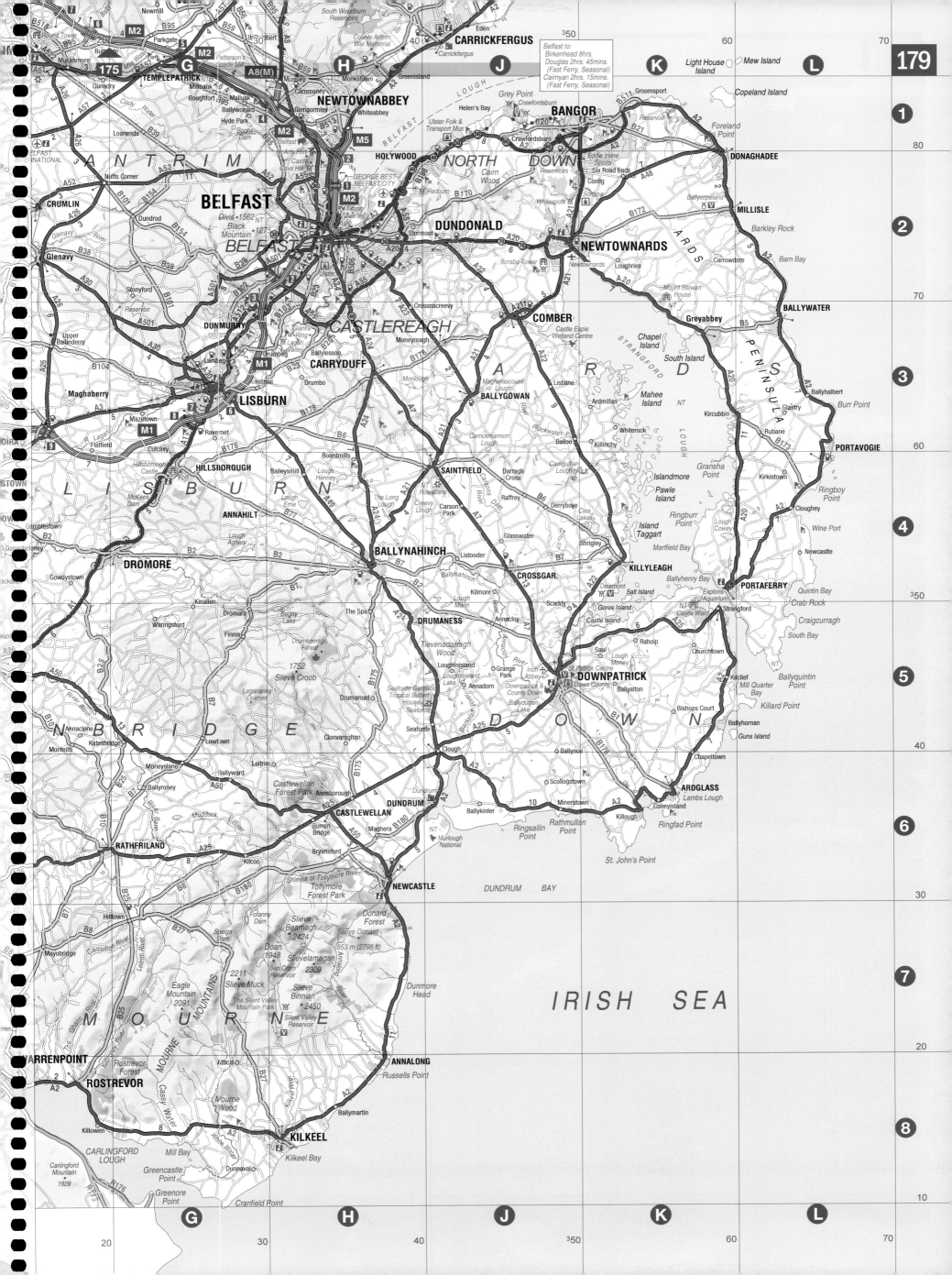

REFERENCE

MOTORWAY	M25
MOTORWAY JUNCTION NUMBERS	
Unlimited interchange 18 Limited interchange 19	
MILEAGES BETWEEN MOTORWAY JUNCTIONS	6
MOTORWAY SERVICE AREA	HESTON Ⓢ
PRIMARY ROUTE DESTINATION	WATFORD
JUNCTION NAMES	HYDE PARK CORNER
PRIMARY ROUTE	A1
PRIMARY ROUTE JUNCTION NUMBERS	12
A ROAD	A5
B ROAD	B450
NORTH & SOUTH CIRCULAR ROADS and INNER RING ROAD	
TRANSPORT FOR LONDON ROAD NETWORK and WEST MIDLANDS RED ROUTE	
SAFETY CAMERA WITH SPEED LIMIT	(30)
Ⓒ CONGESTION CHARGING ZONE (for full information - www.cclondon.com)	
LOW EMISSION ZONE (for full information - www.tfl.gov.uk/roadusers/lez)	

SCALE: approx. 1¼ Miles to 1 Inch

0 1 2 Miles

0 1 2 3 4 Kilometres

KEY TO LONDON MAIN ROUTES MAPS

180 NW	181	182	183
184 SW	185	186 SE	187

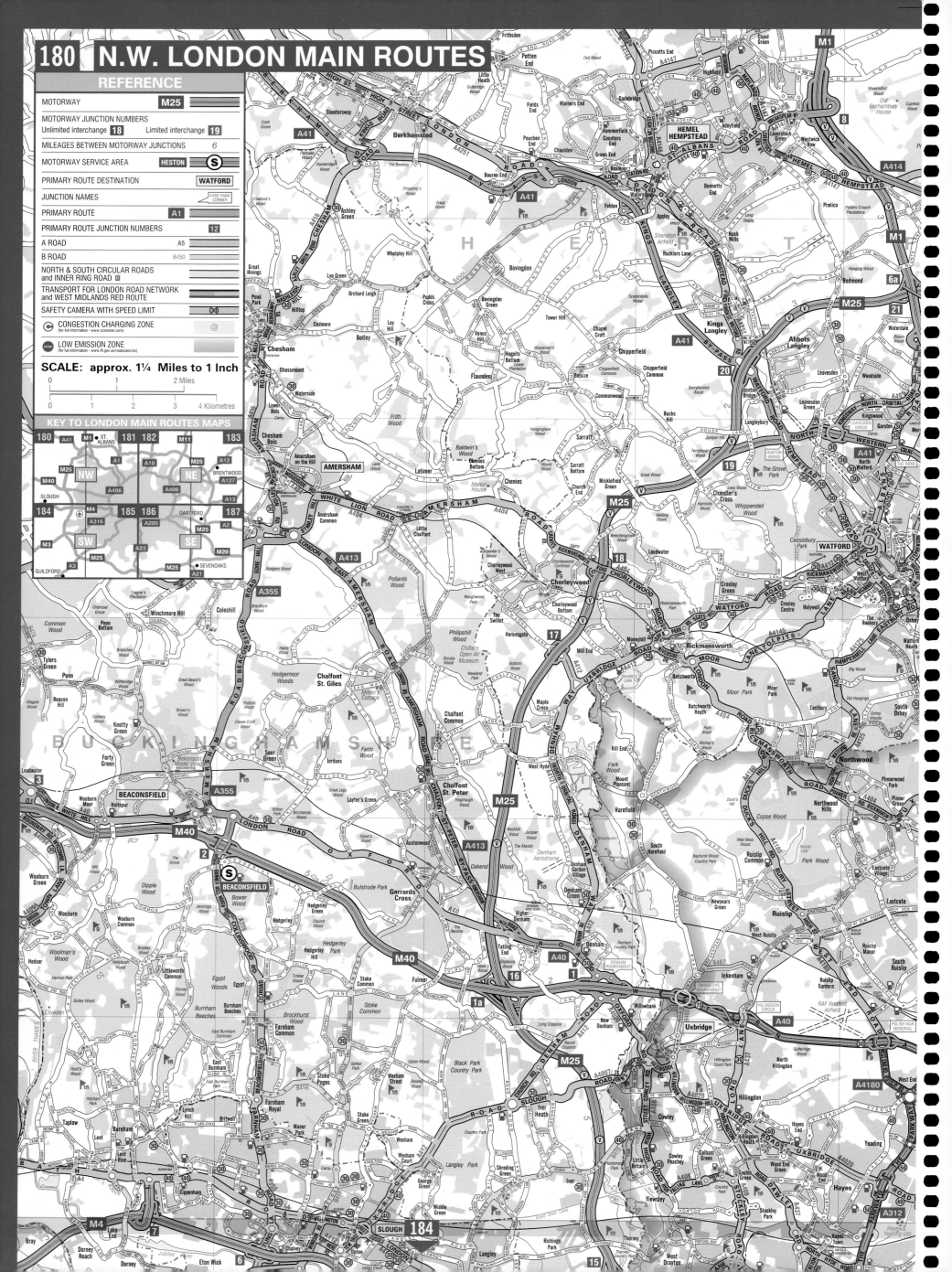

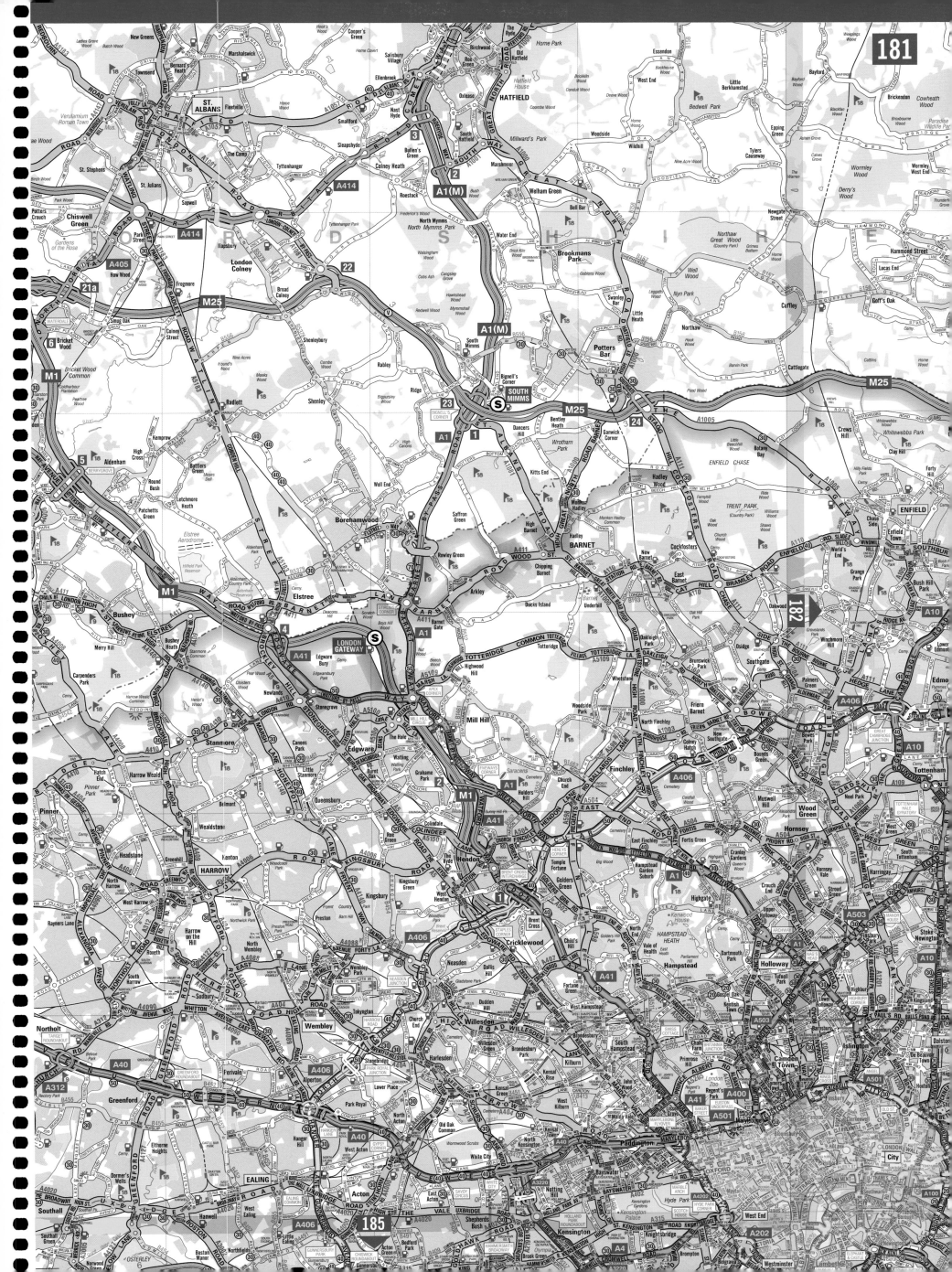

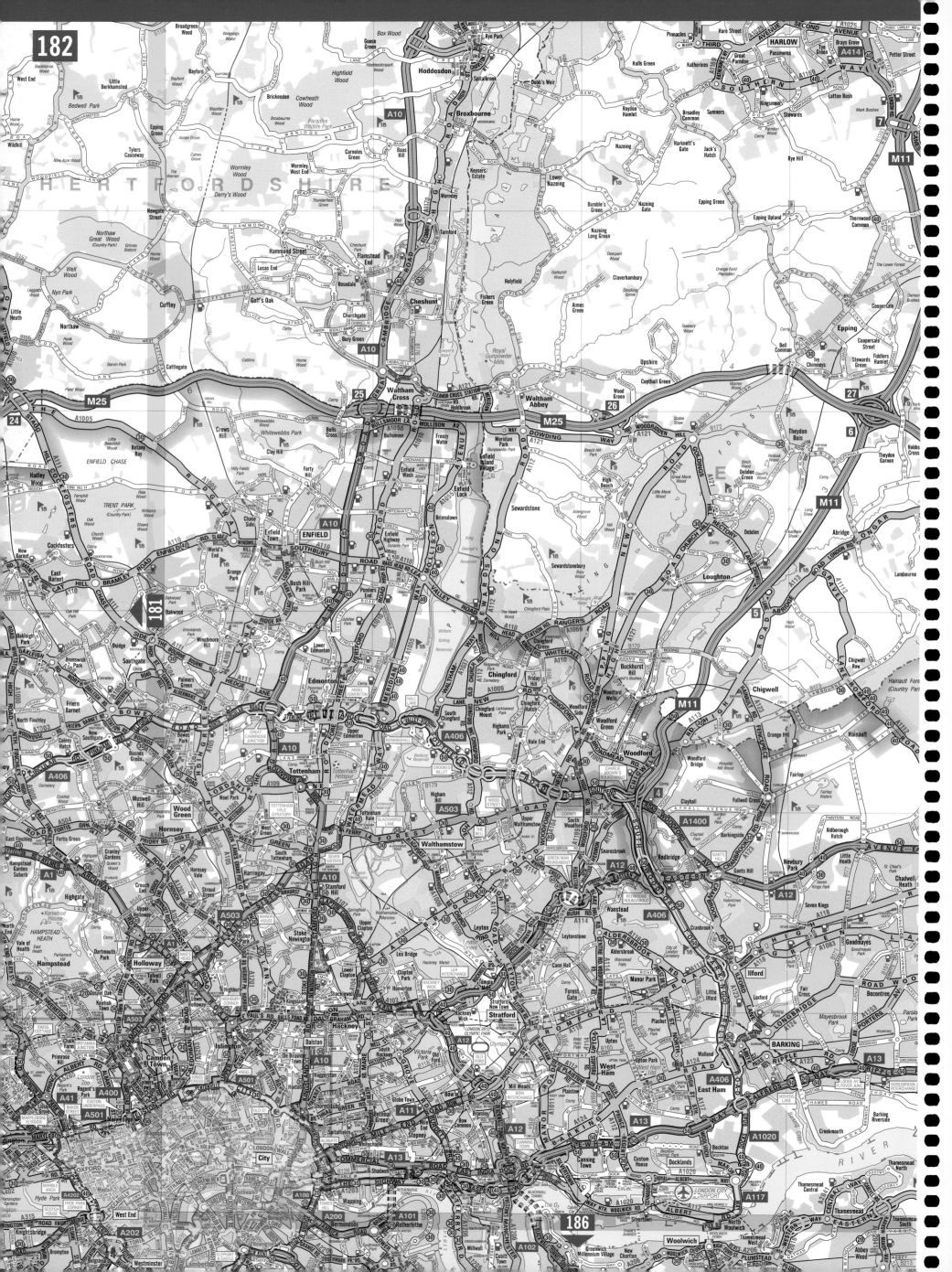

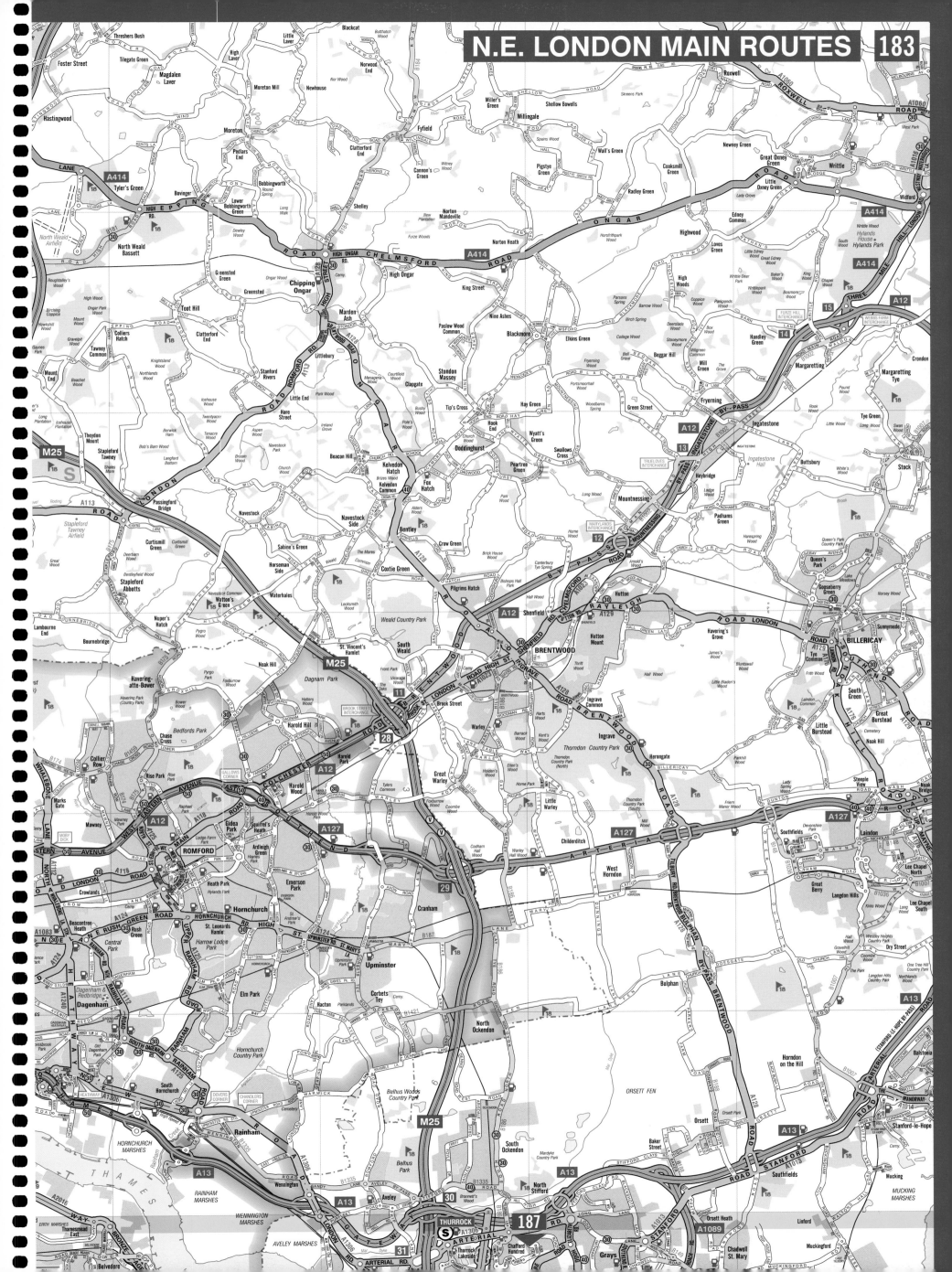

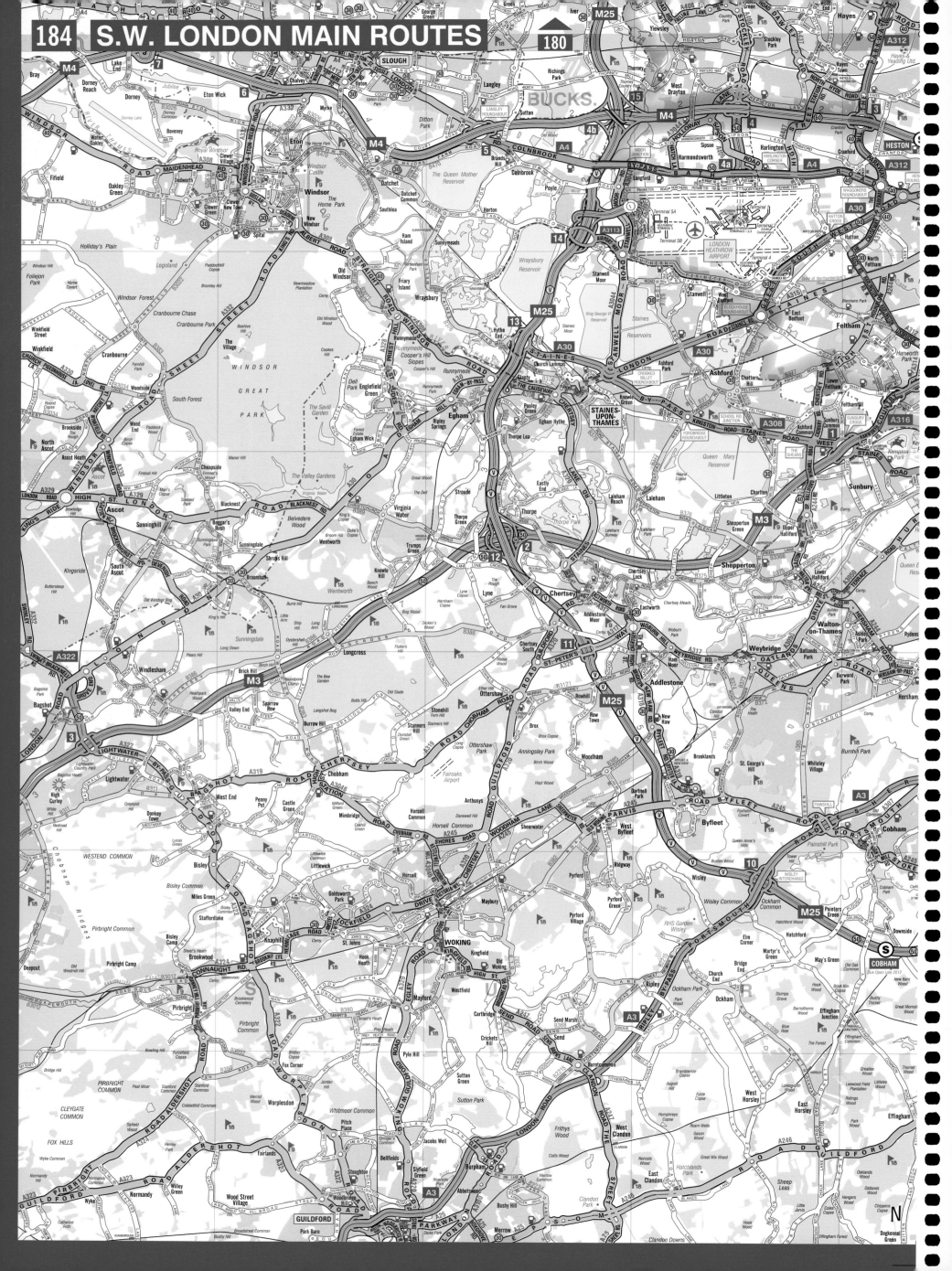

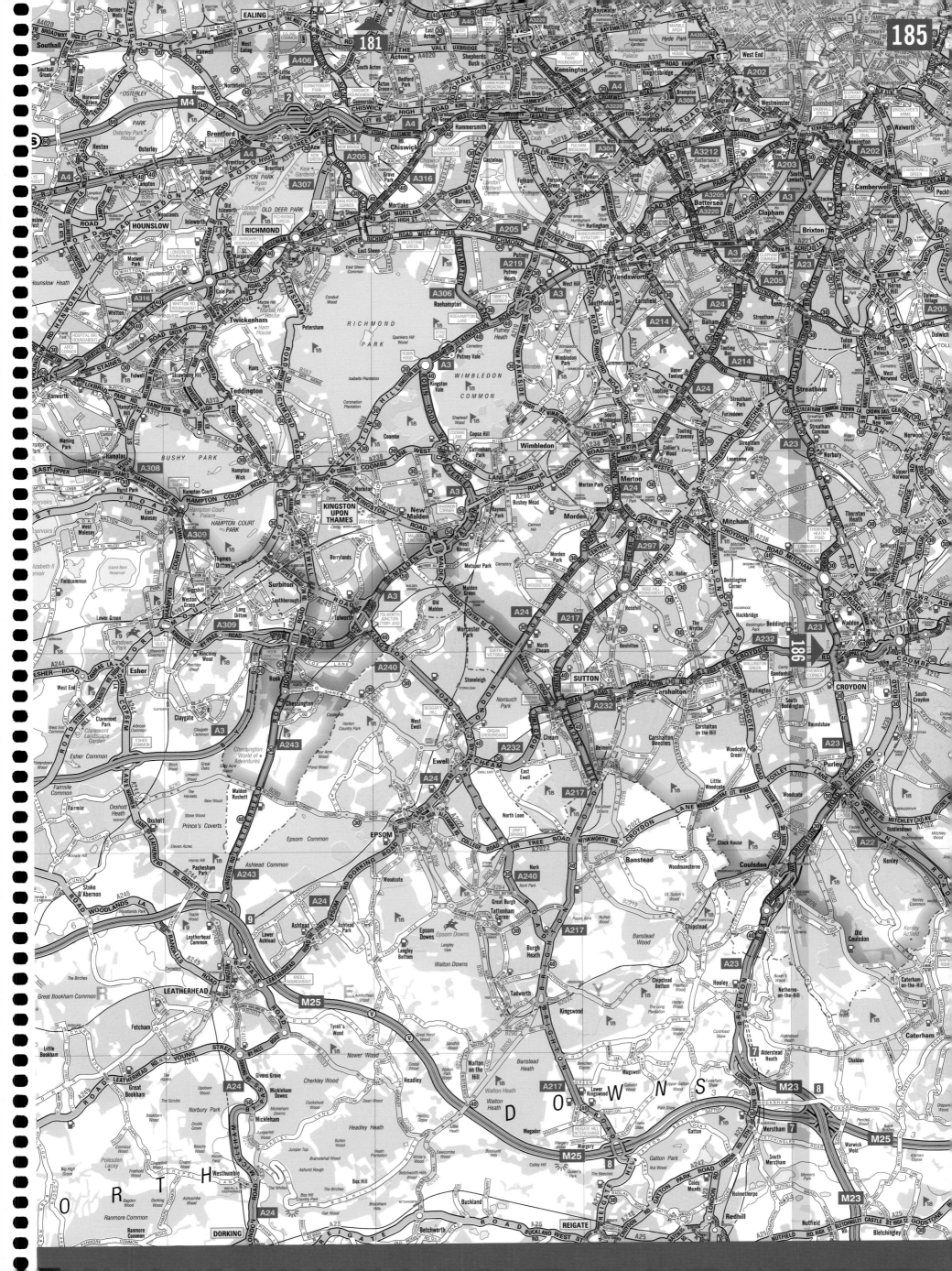

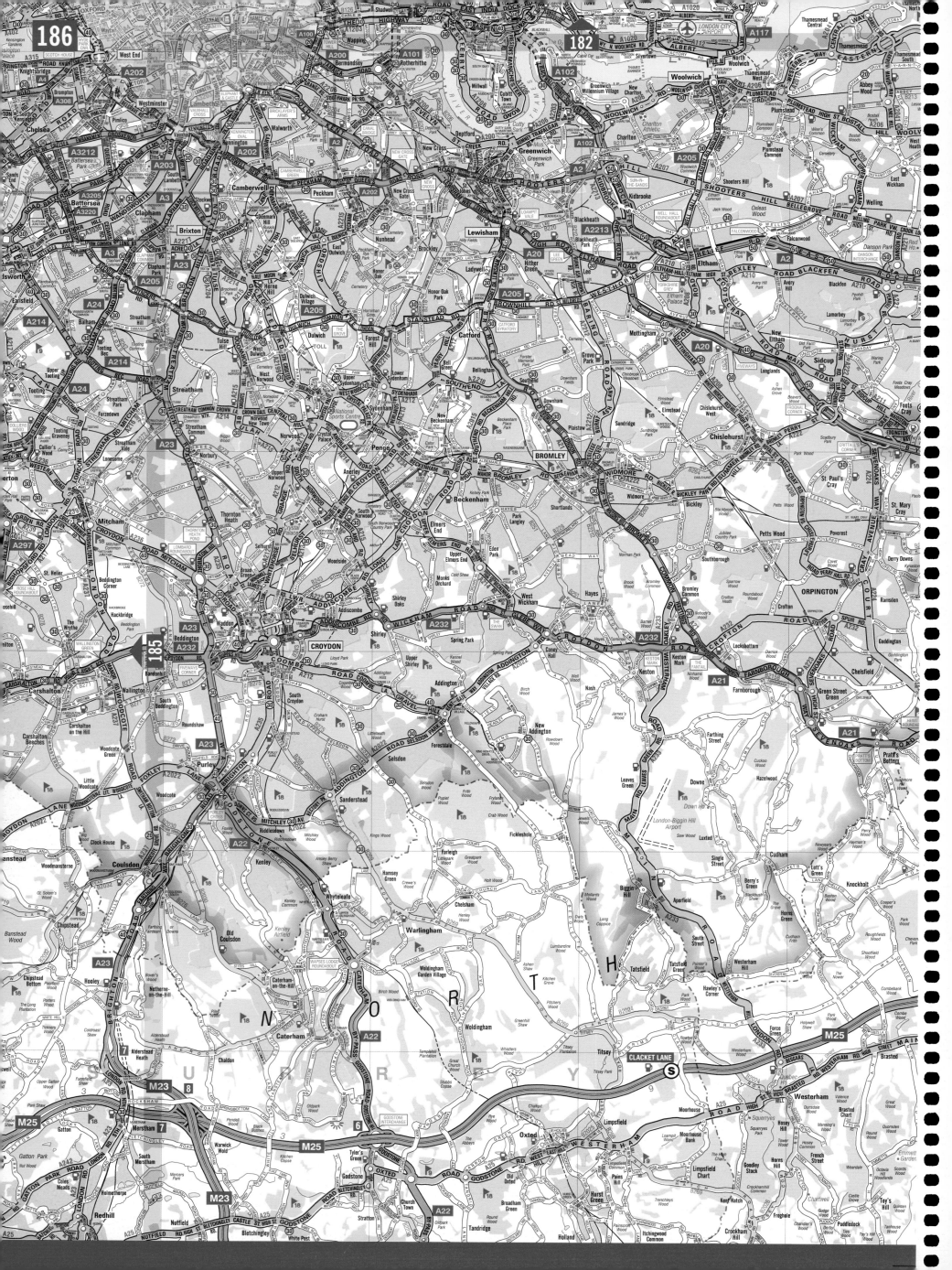

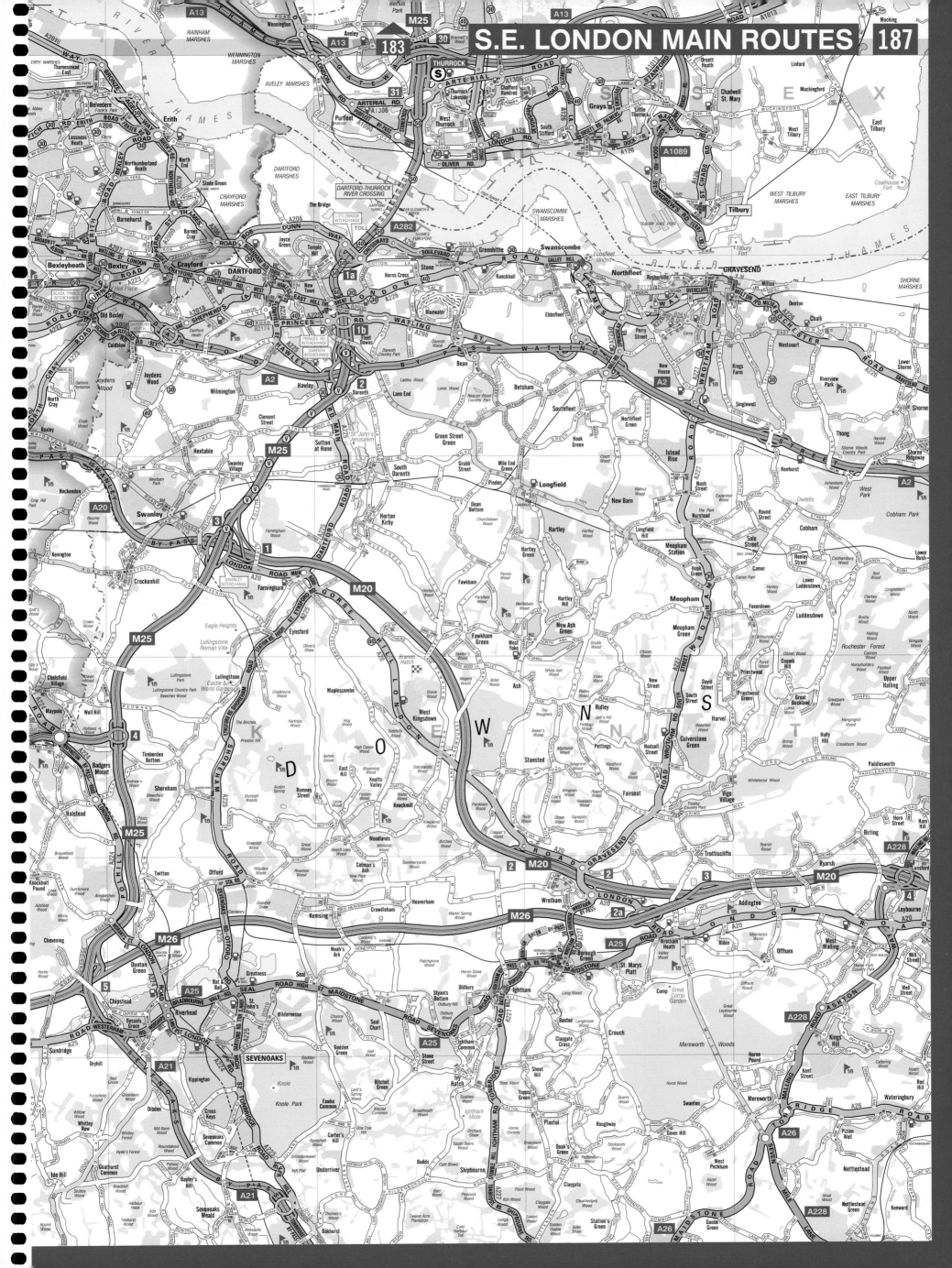

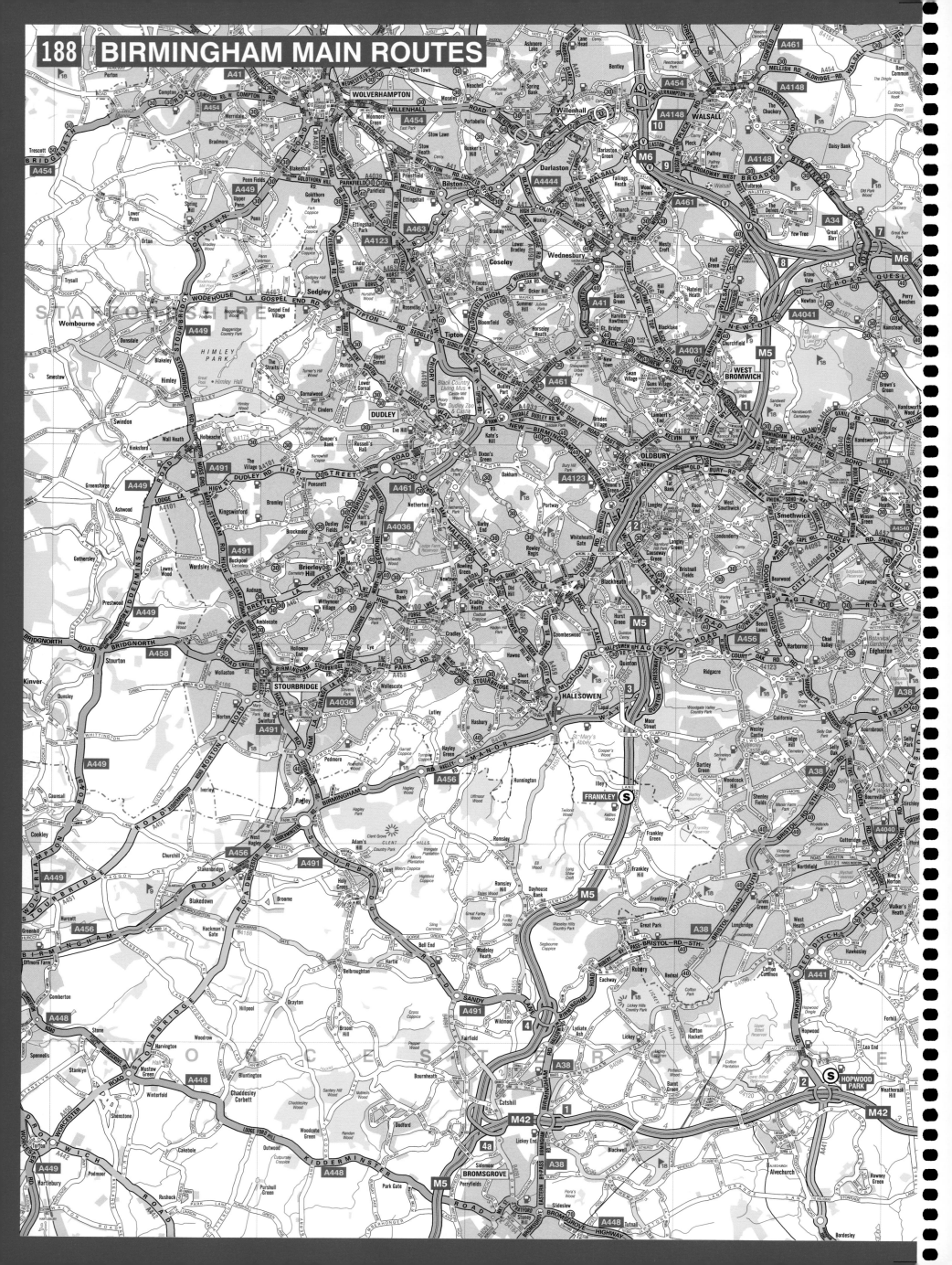

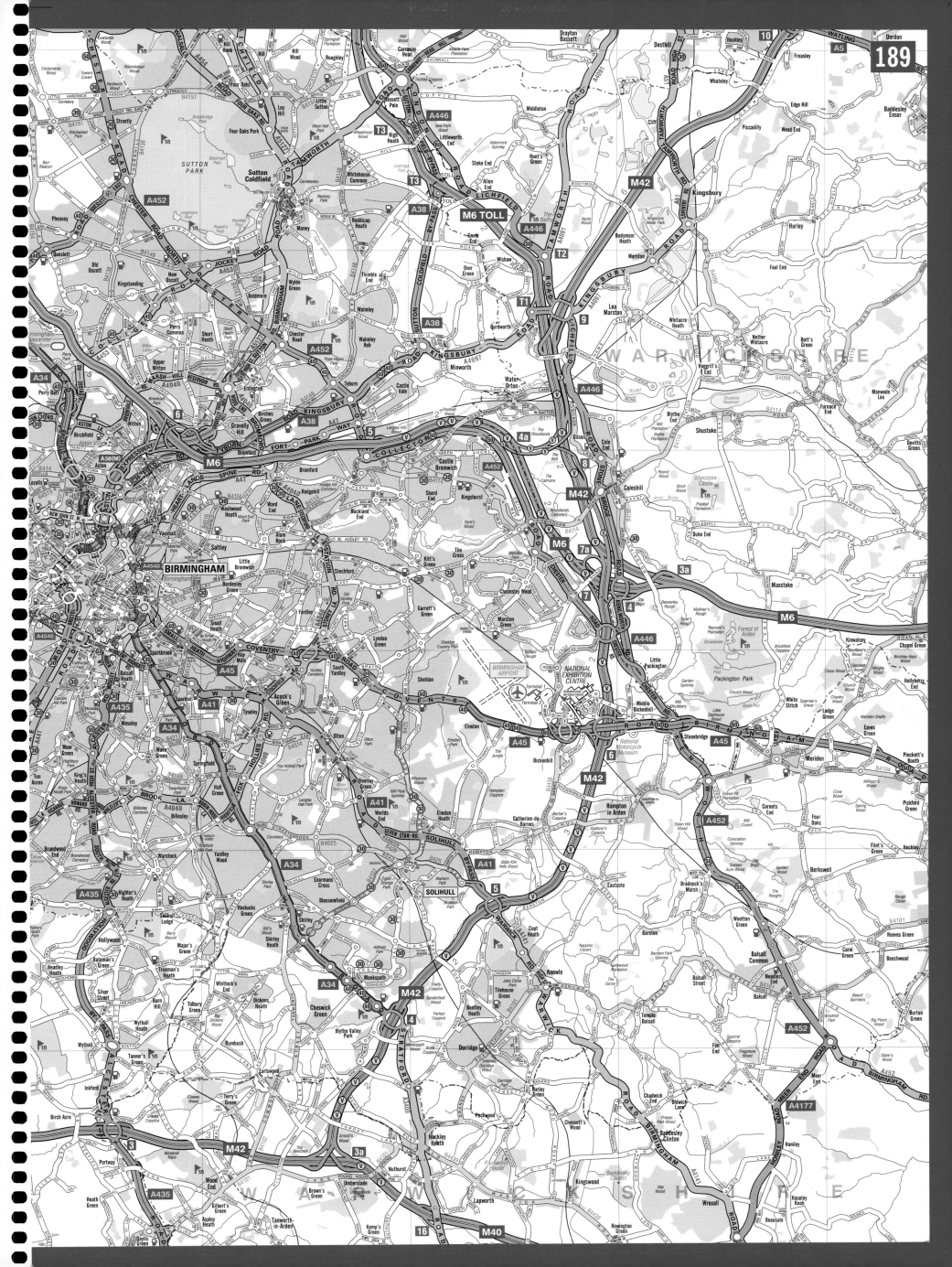

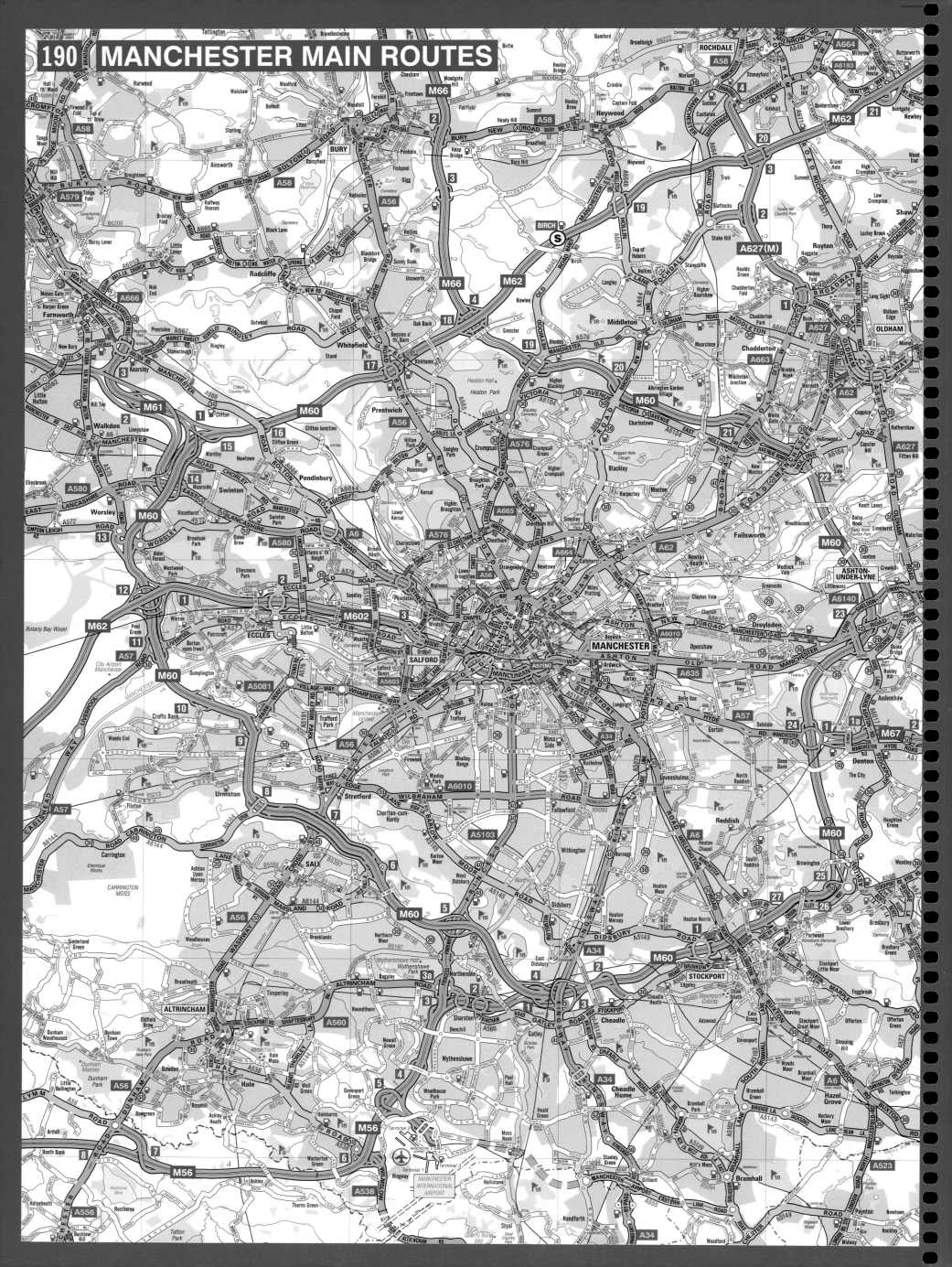

City & Town Centre Plans

Port Plans

Additional port plans included with city and town plans:

Airport Plans

Reference to City & Town Plans   Légende   Zeichenerklärung

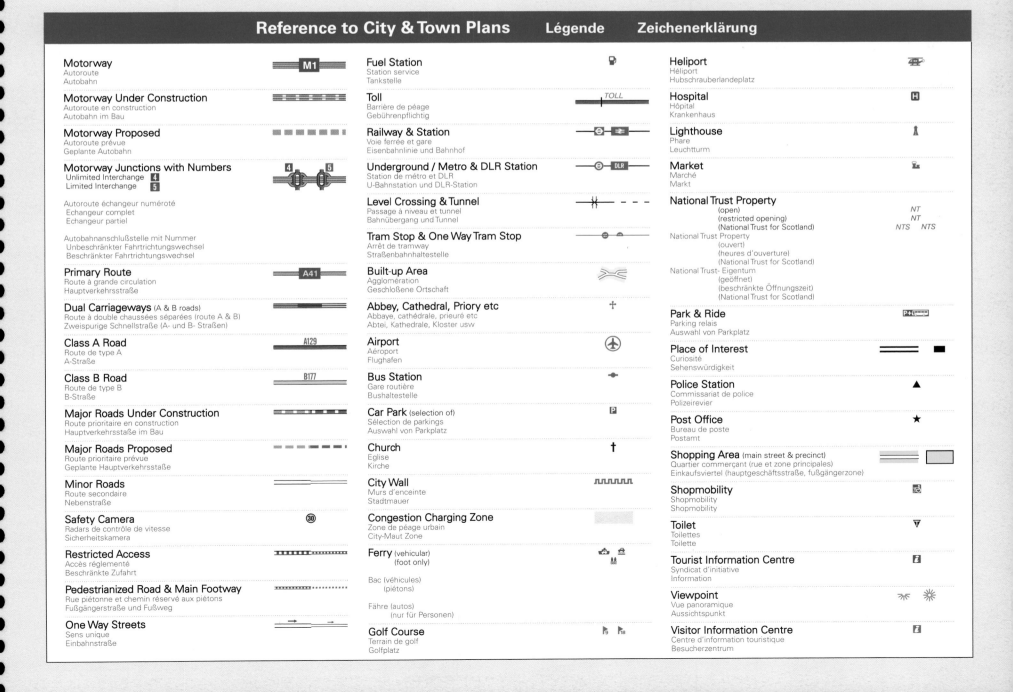

Motorway — Autoroute / Autobahn — M1

Motorway Under Construction — Autoroute en construction / Autobahn im Bau

Motorway Proposed — Autoroute prévue / Geplante Autobahn

Motorway Junctions with Numbers
Unlimited Interchange 4
Limited Interchange 5
Autoroute échangeur numéroté
Echangeur complet
Echangeur partiel
Autobahnanschlußstelle mit Nummer
Unbeschränkter Fahrtrichtungswechsel
Beschränkter Fahrtrichtungswechsel

Primary Route — Route à grande circulation / Hauptverkehrsstraße — A41

Dual Carriageways (A & B roads) — Route à double chaussées séparées (route A & B) / Zweispurige Schnellstraße (A- und B- Straßen)

Class A Road — Route de type A / A-Straße — A129

Class B Road — Route de type B / B-Straße — B177

Major Roads Under Construction — Route prioritaire en construction / Hauptverkehrsstraße im Bau

Major Roads Proposed — Route prioritaire prévue / Geplante Hauptverkehrsstraße

Minor Roads — Route secondaire / Nebenstraße

Safety Camera — Radars de contrôle de vitesse / Sicherheitskamera — 30

Restricted Access — Accès réglementé / Beschränkte Zufahrt

Pedestrianized Road & Main Footway — Rue piétonne et chemin réservé aux piétons / Fußgängerstraße und Fußweg

One Way Streets — Sens unique / Einbahnstraße

Fuel Station — Station service / Tankstelle

Toll — Barrière de péage / Gebührenpflichtig — TOLL

Railway & Station — Voie ferrée et gare / Eisenbahnlinie und Bahnhof

Underground / Metro & DLR Station — Station de métro et DLR / U-Bahnstation und DLR-Station — DLR

Level Crossing & Tunnel — Passage à niveau et tunnel / Bahnübergang und Tunnel

Tram Stop & One Way Tram Stop — Arrêt de tramway / Straßenbahnhaltestelle

Built-up Area — Agglomération / Geschlossene Ortschaft

Abbey, Cathedral, Priory etc — Abbaye, cathédrale, prieuré etc / Abtei, Kathedrale, Kloster usw — †

Airport — Aéroport / Flughafen

Bus Station — Gare routière / Bushaltestelle

Car Park (selection of) — Sélection de parkings / Auswahl von Parkplatz — P

Church — Eglise / Kirche — †

City Wall — Murs d'enceinte / Stadtmauer

Congestion Charging Zone — Zone de péage urbain / City-Maut Zone

Ferry (vehicular) (foot only) — Bac (véhicules) (piétons) / Fähre (autos) (nur für Personen)

Golf Course — Terrain de golf / Golfplatz

Heliport — Héliport / Hubschrauberlandeplatz

Hospital — Hôpital / Krankenhaus — H

Lighthouse — Phare / Leuchtturm

Market — Marché / Markt

National Trust Property
(open) — NT
(restricted opening) — NT
(National Trust for Scotland) — NTS NTS
National Trust Property
(ouvert)
(heures d'ouverture)
(National Trust for Scotland)
National Trust- Eigentum
(geöffnet)
(beschränkte Öffnungszeit)
(National Trust for Scotland)

Park & Ride — Parking relais / Auswahl von Parkplatz

Place of Interest — Curiosité / Sehenswürdigkeit

Police Station — Commissariat de police / Polizeirevier — ▲

Post Office — Bureau de poste / Postamt — ★

Shopping Area (main street & precinct) — Quartier commerçant (rue et zone principales) / Einkaufsviertel (hauptgeschäftsstraße, fußgängerzone)

Shopmobility — Shopmobility / Shopmobility

Toilet — Toilettes / Toilette — ▽

Tourist Information Centre — Syndicat d'initiative / Information

Viewpoint — Vue panoramique / Aussichtspunkt

Visitor Information Centre — Centre d'information touristique / Besucherzentrum

ABERDEEN

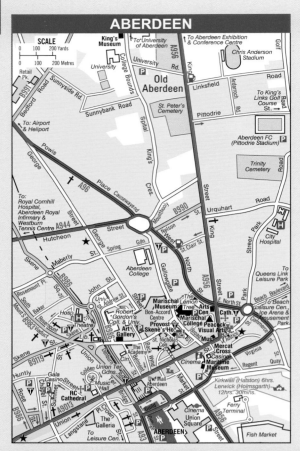

BATH

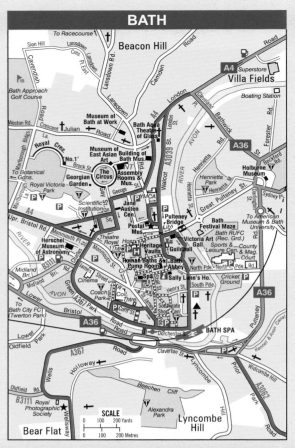

BLACKPOOL

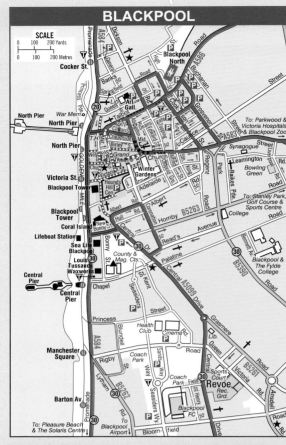

BIRMINGHAM (CITY CENTRE)

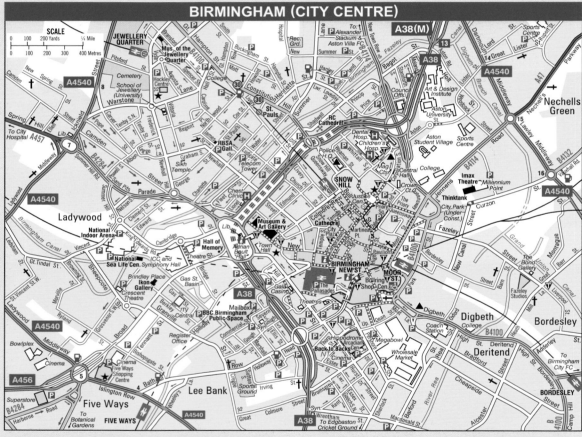

BOURNEMOUTH

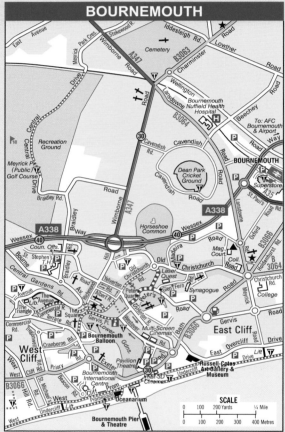

BRADFORD

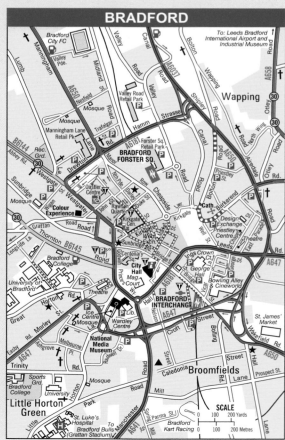

BRIGHTON and HOVE

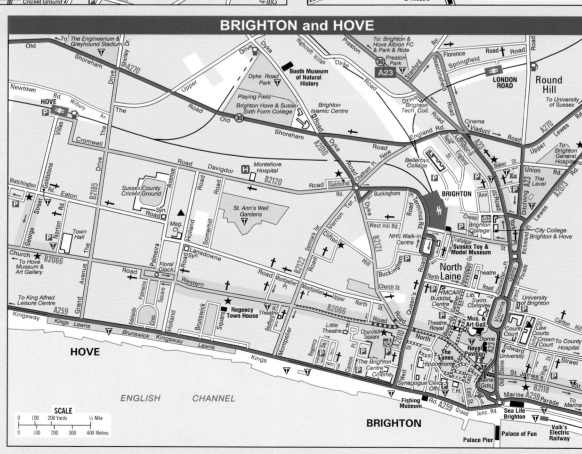

BRISTOL

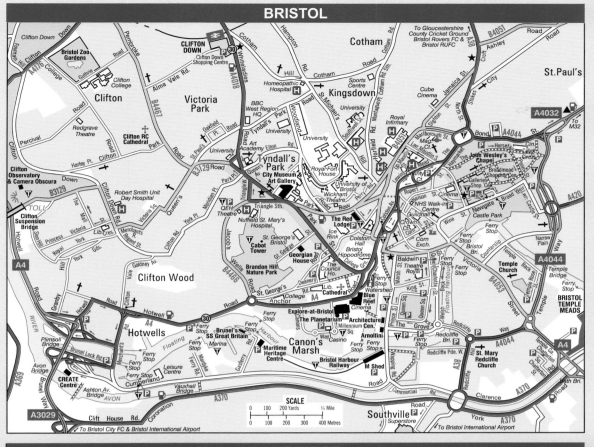

CANTERBURY

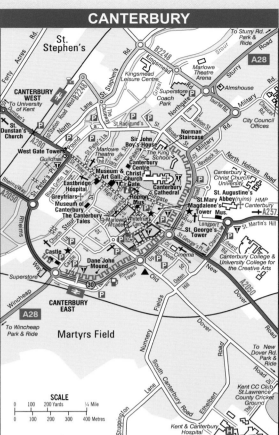

CAMBRIDGE

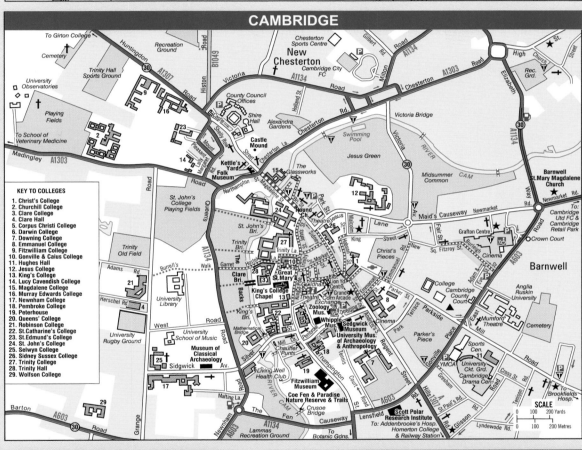

CARLISLE

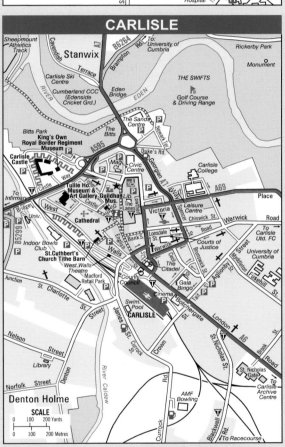

CARDIFF (CAERDYDD)

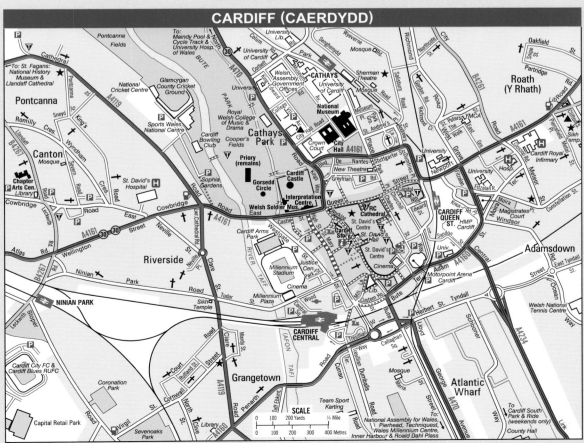

CHELTENHAM

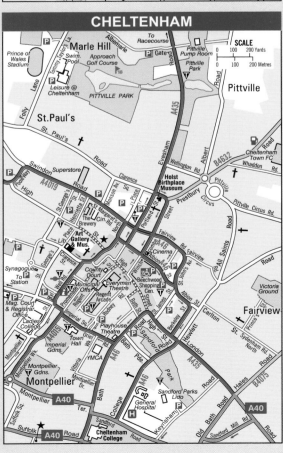

CHESTER

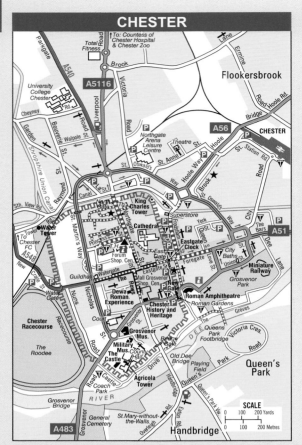

COVENTRY

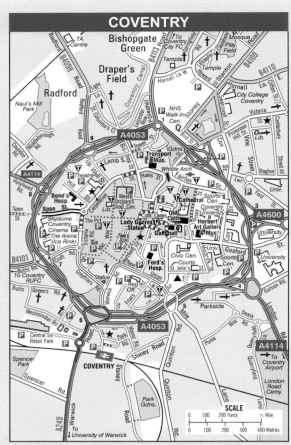

DERBY

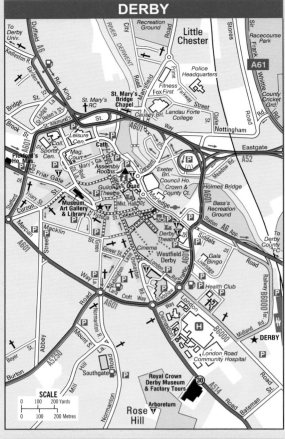

DOVER

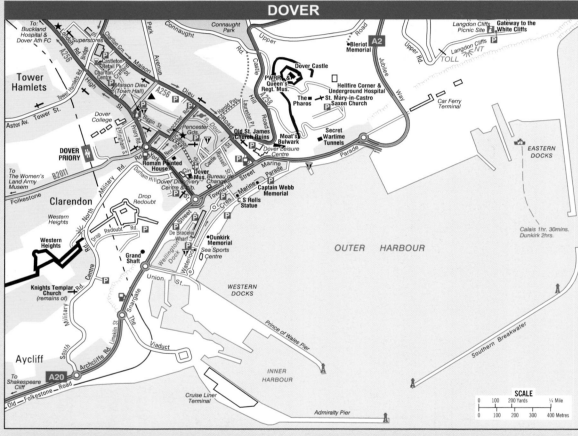

DUMFRIES

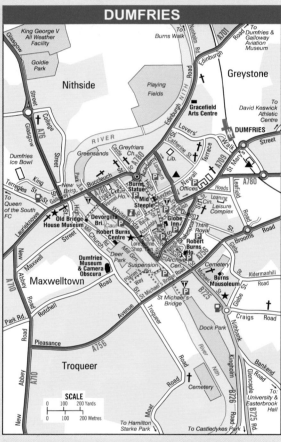

DUNDEE

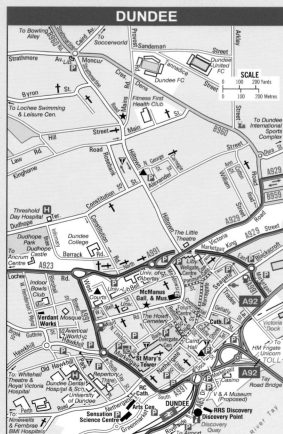

DURHAM

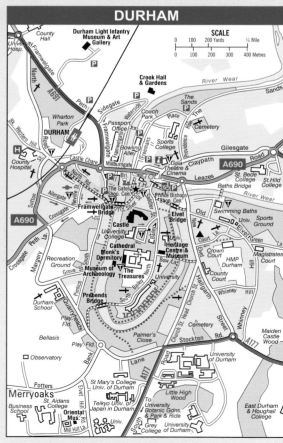

EASTBOURNE

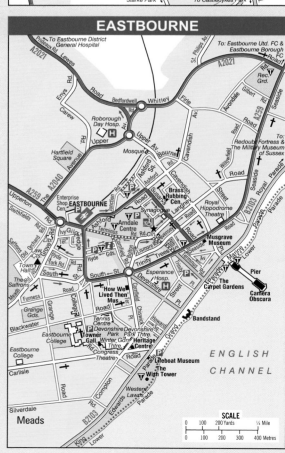

EDINBURGH

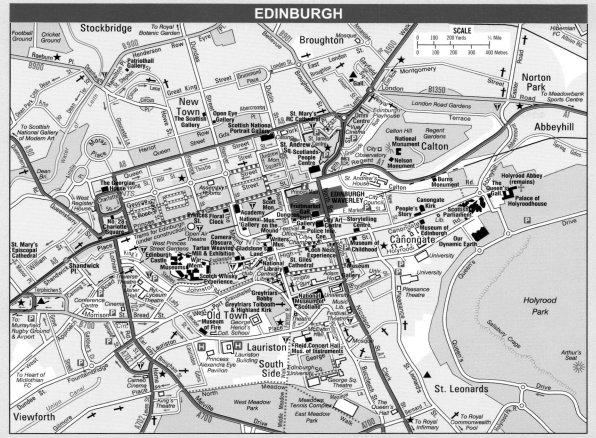

FOLKESTONE

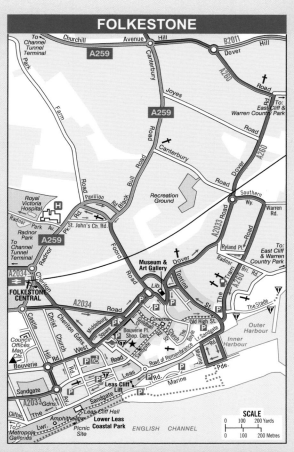

EXETER

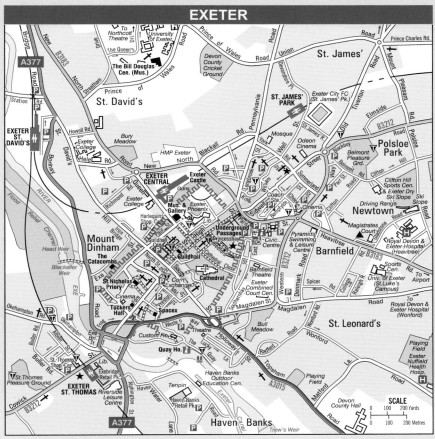

GUILDFORD

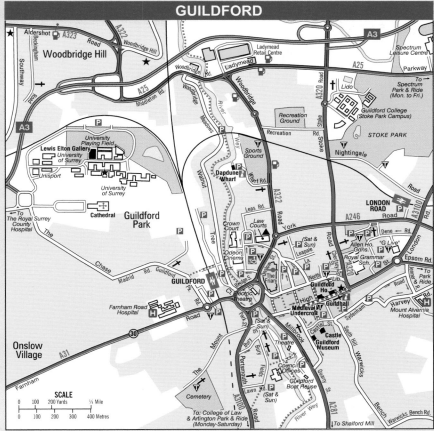

GLASGOW

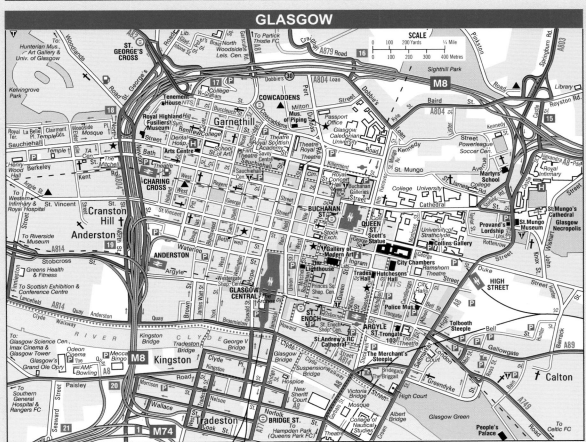

GLOUCESTER

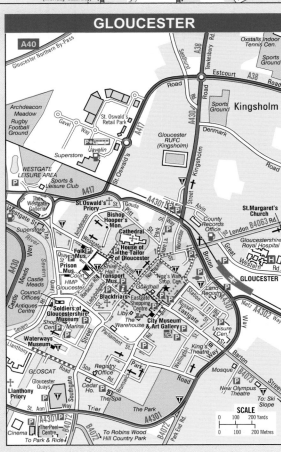

HARROGATE
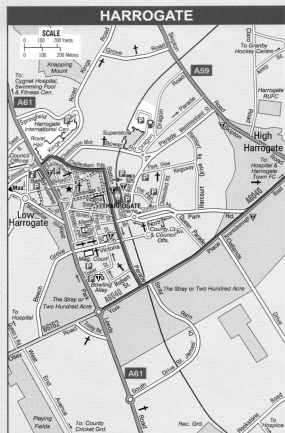

INVERNESS
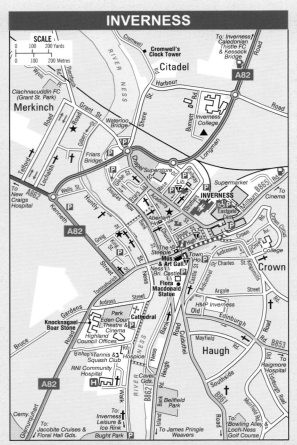

IPSWICH
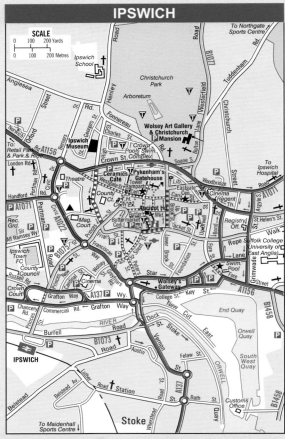

KILMARNOCK
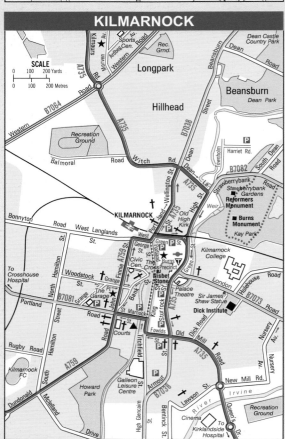

LEEDS
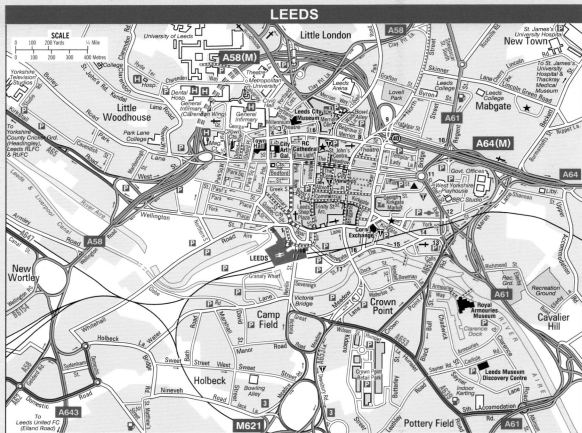

KINGSTON UPON HULL
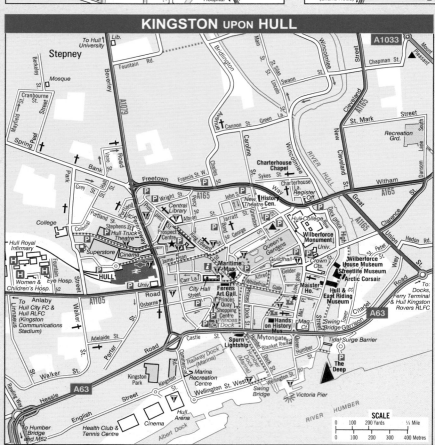

LEICESTER
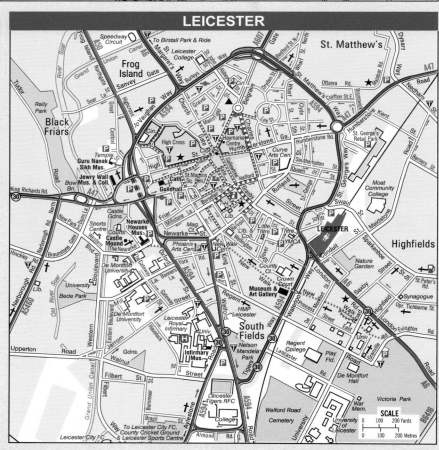

LINCOLN
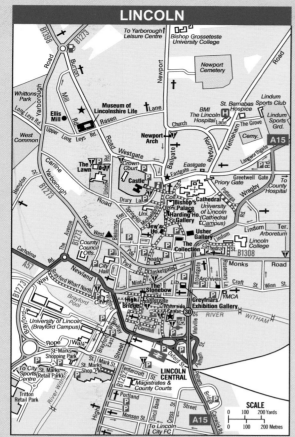

LIVERPOOL
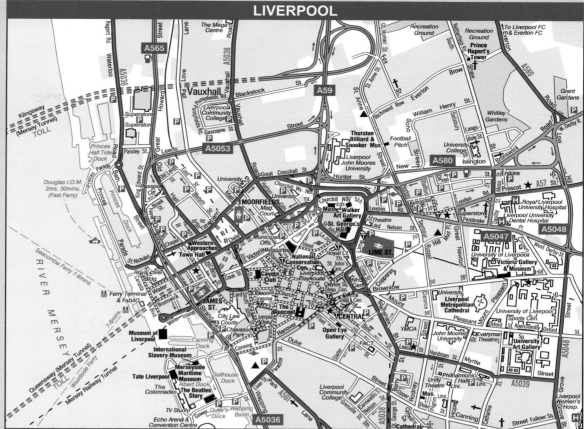

MANCHESTER (CITY CENTRE)
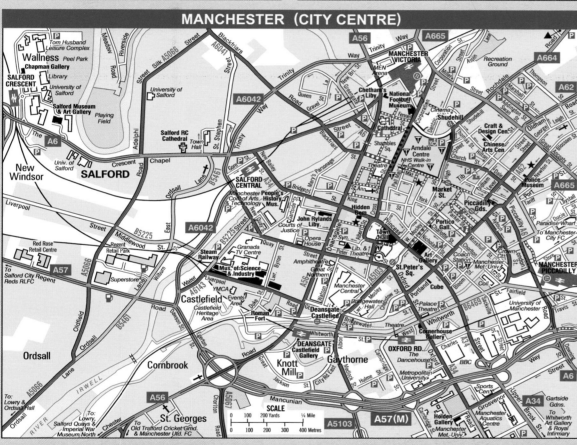

MIDDLESBROUGH
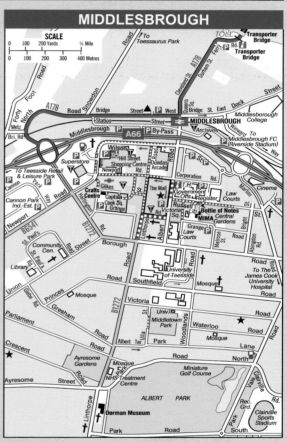

MEDWAY TOWNS
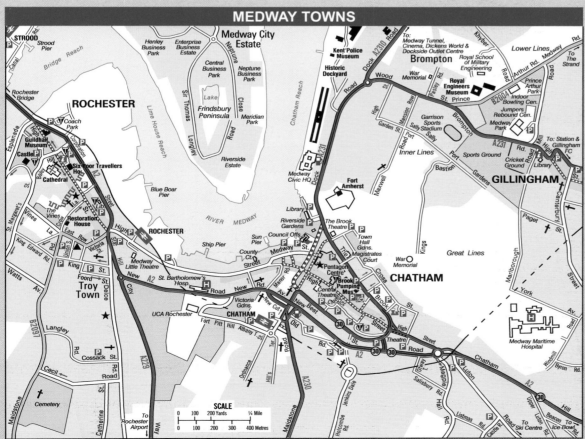

NEWCASTLE UPON TYNE
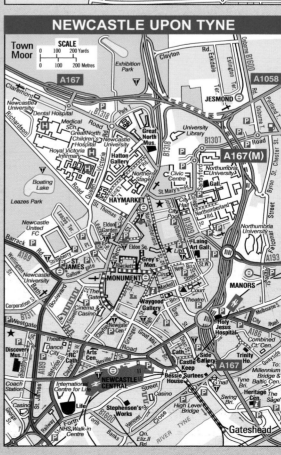

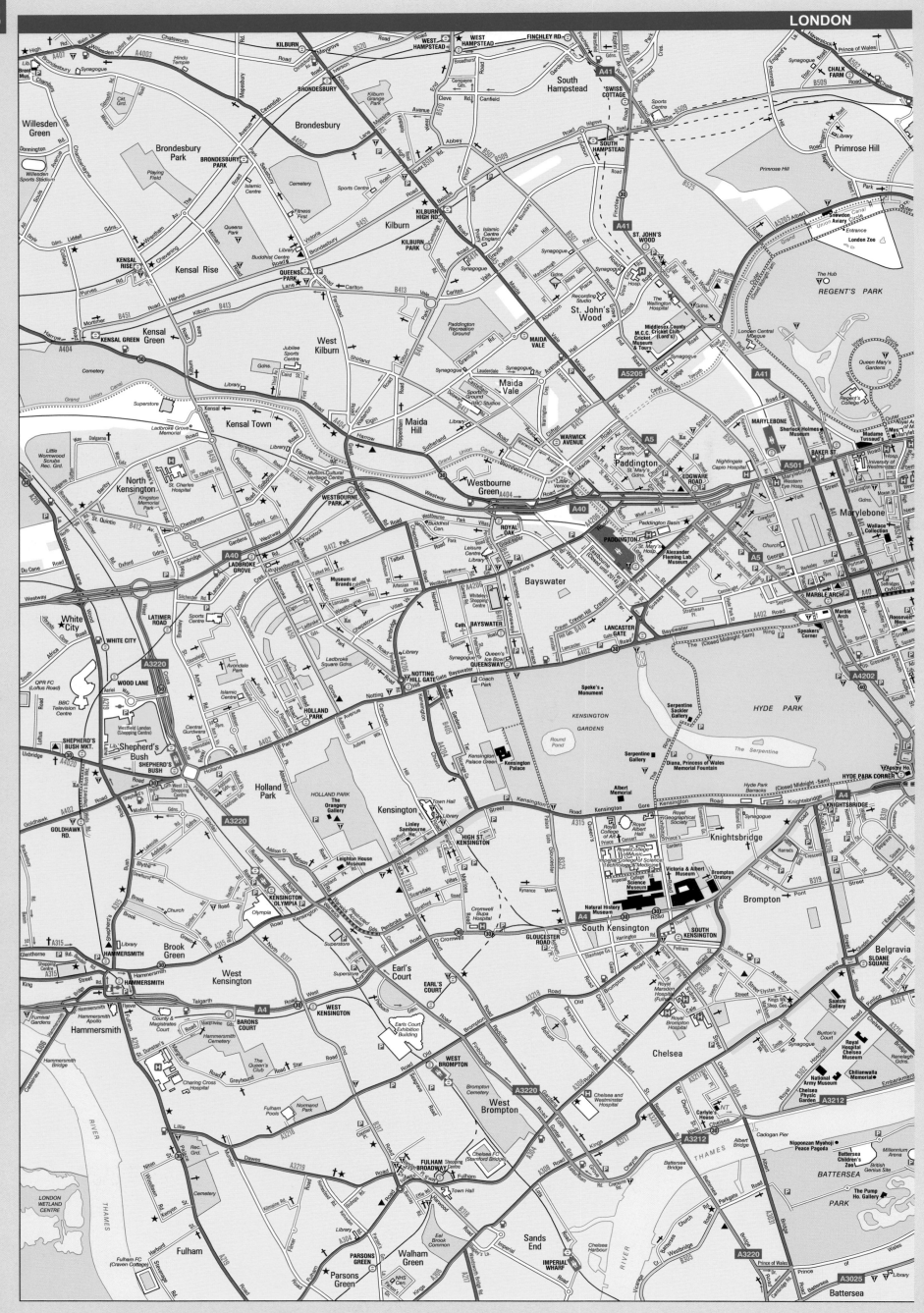

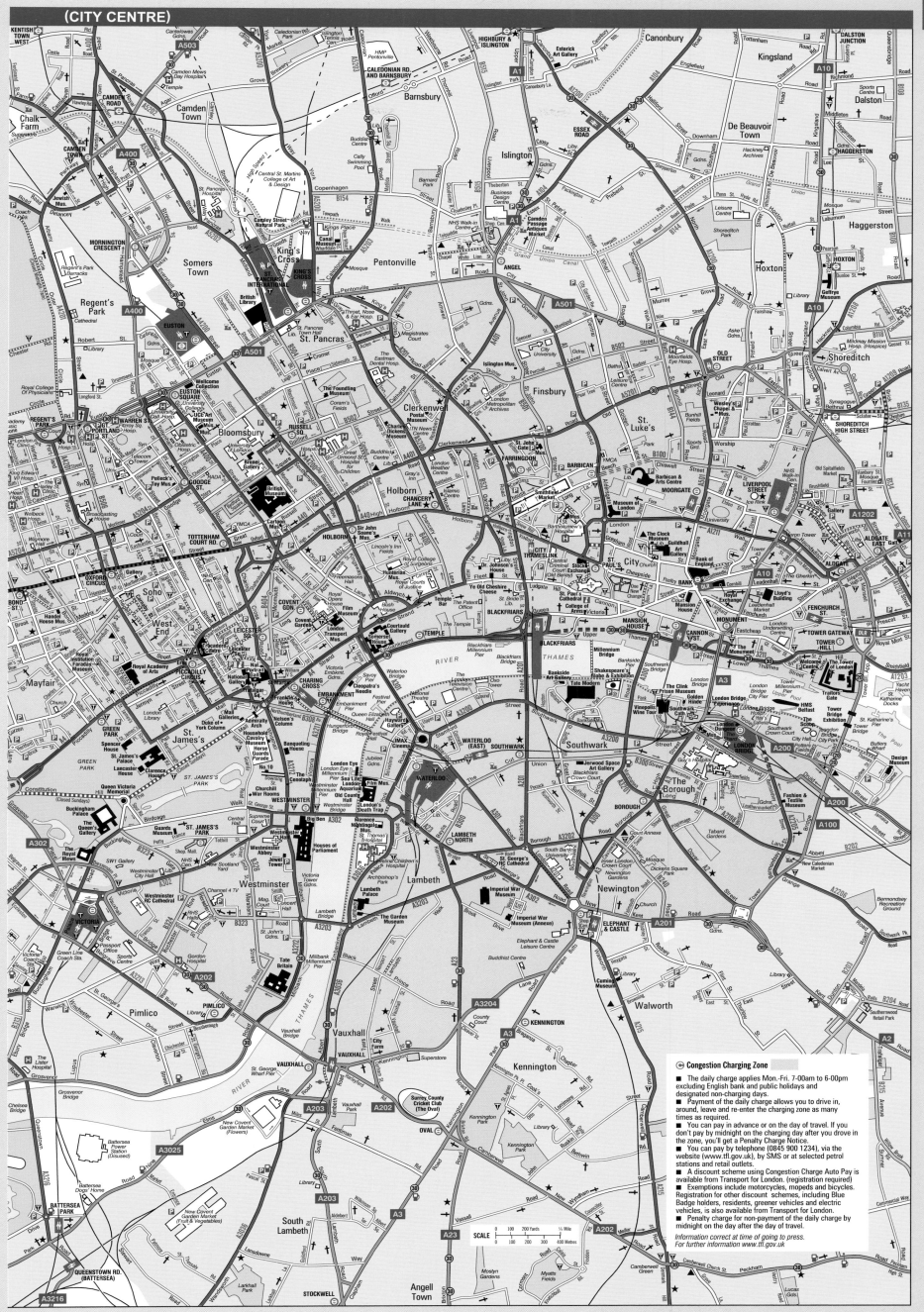

MILTON KEYNES

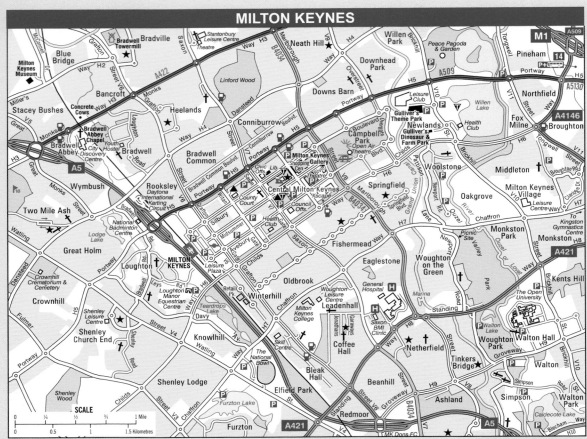

NEWPORT (CASNEWYDD)

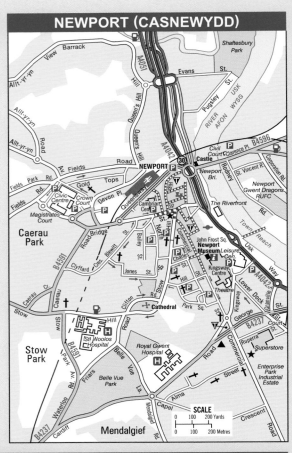

NORWICH

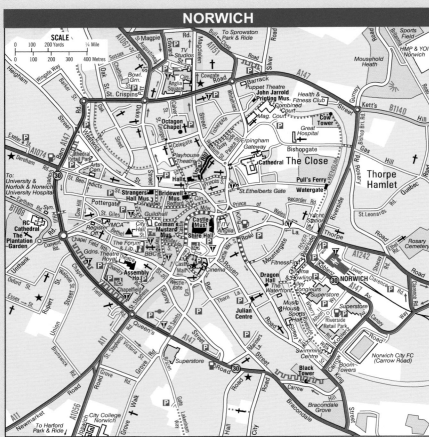

NOTTINGHAM

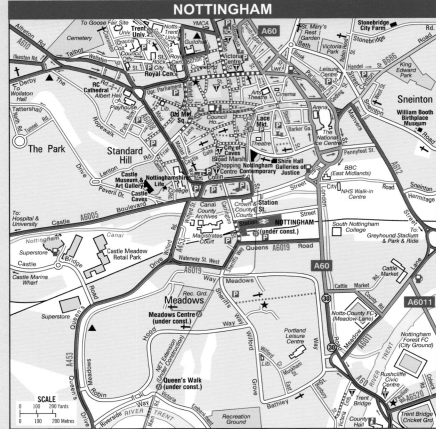

NORTHAMPTON

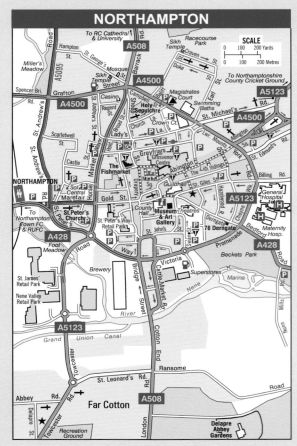

OXFORD

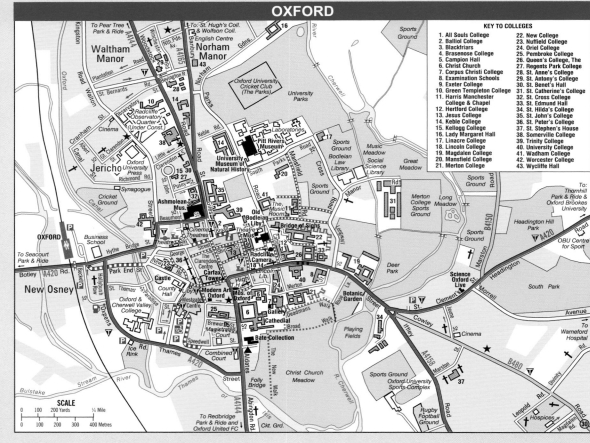

KEY TO COLLEGES

1. All Souls College
2. Balliol College
3. Blackfriars
4. Brasenose College
5. Campion Hall
6. Christ Church
7. Corpus Christi College
8. Examination Schools
9. Exeter College
10. Green Templeton College
11. Harris Manchester College & Chapel
12. Hertford College
13. Jesus College
14. Keble College
15. Kellogg College
16. Lady Margaret Hall
17. Linacre College
18. Lincoln College
19. Magdalen College
20. Mansfield College
21. Merton College
22. New College
23. Nuffield College
24. Oriel College
25. Pembroke College
26. Queen's College, The
27. Regents Park College
28. St. Anne's College
29. St. Antony's College
30. St. Benet's Hall
31. St. Catherine's College
32. St. Cross College
33. St. Edmund Hall
34. St. Hilda's College
35. St. John's College
36. St. Peter's College
37. St. Stephen's House
38. Somerville College
39. Trinity College
40. University College
41. Wadham College
42. Worcester College
43. Wycliffe Hall

OBAN
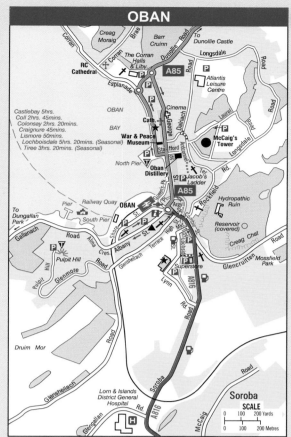

PERTH
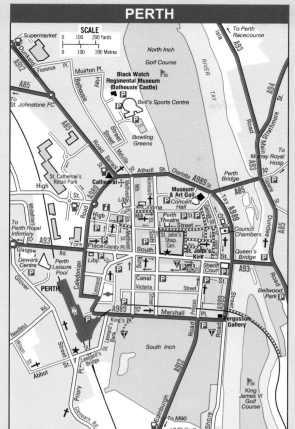

PETERBOROUGH
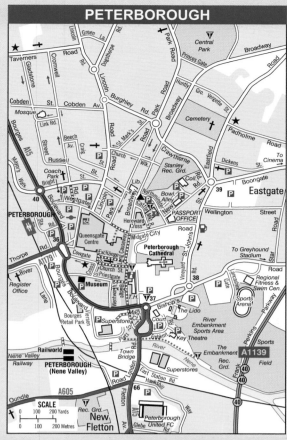

PLYMOUTH
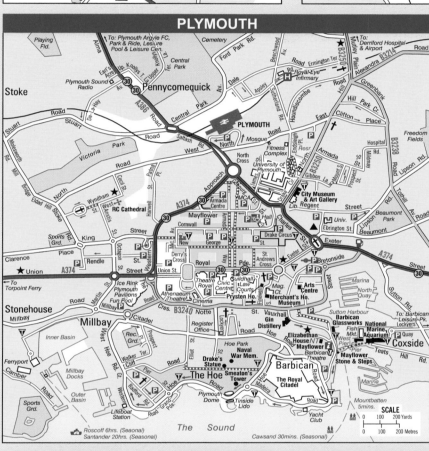

PORTSMOUTH
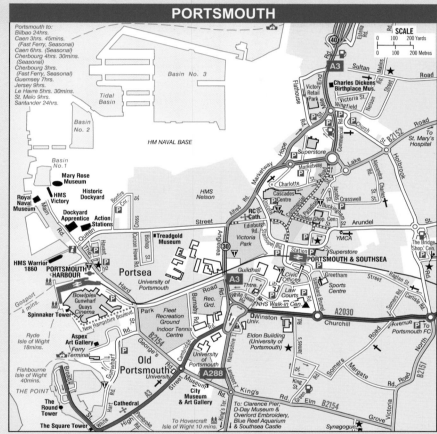

PRESTON
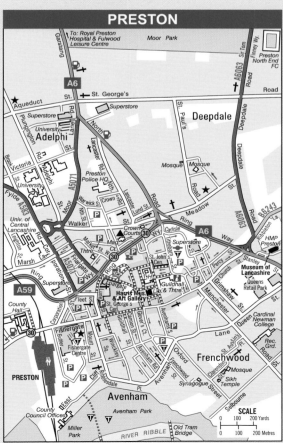

READING
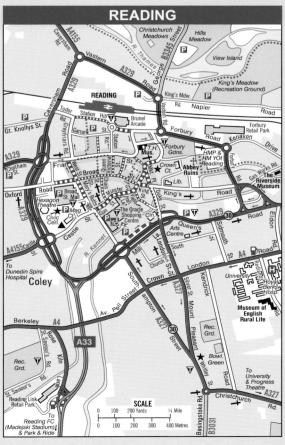

SALISBURY
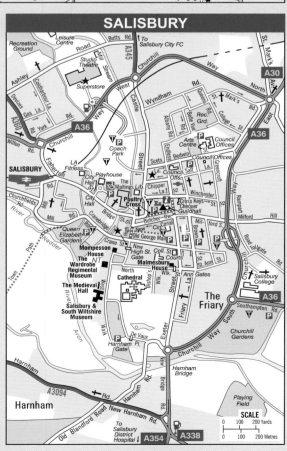

SHEFFIELD

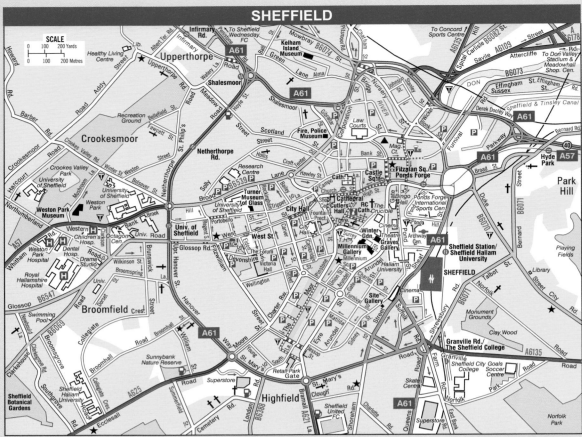

SHREWSBURY

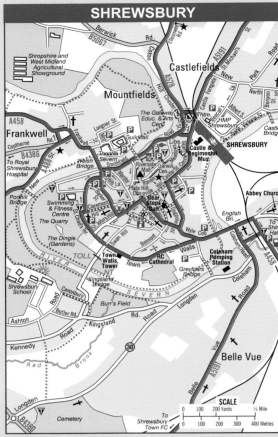

SOUTHAMPTON

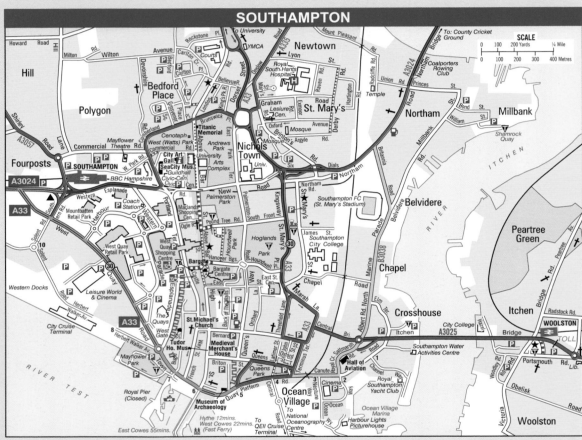

STIRLING

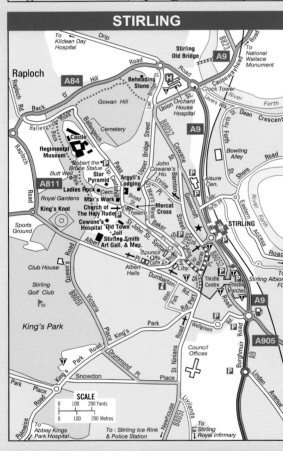

STOKE-ON-TRENT

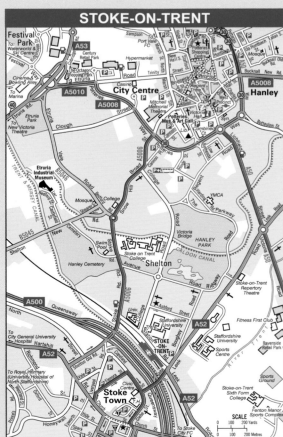

STRATFORD UPON AVON

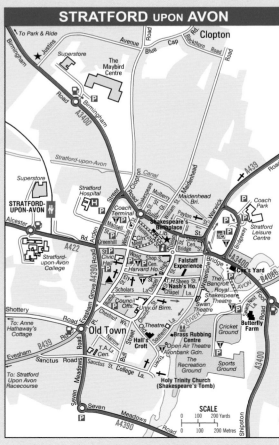

SUNDERLAND

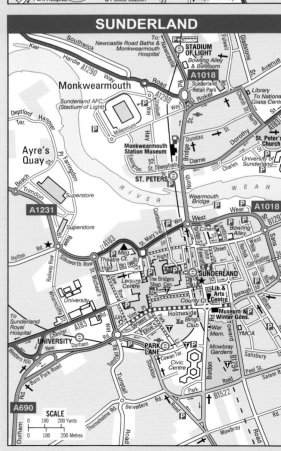

SWANSEA (ABERTAWE)
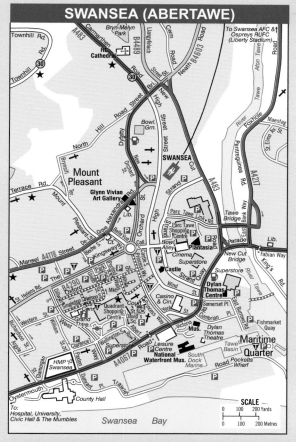

SWINDON
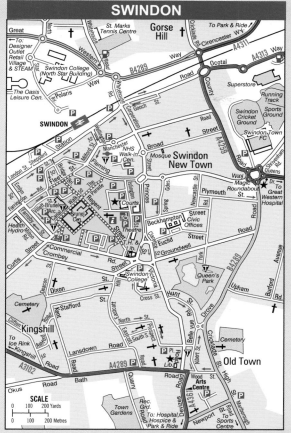

TAUNTON
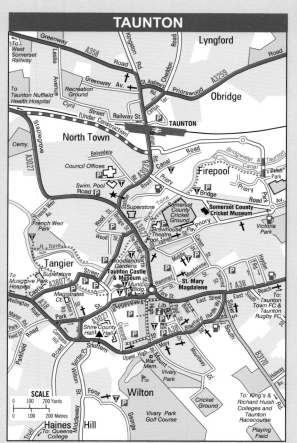

WINCHESTER
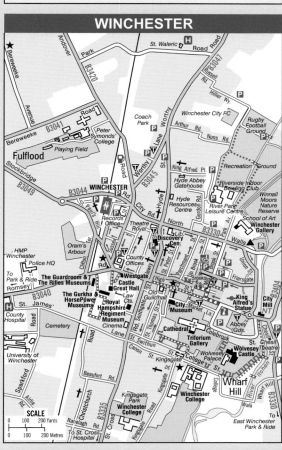

WINDSOR
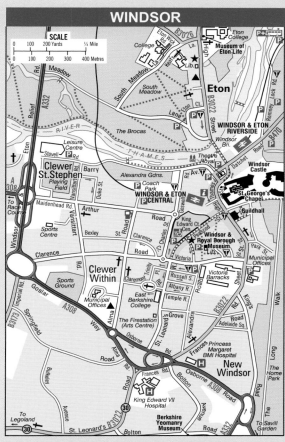

WOLVERHAMPTON
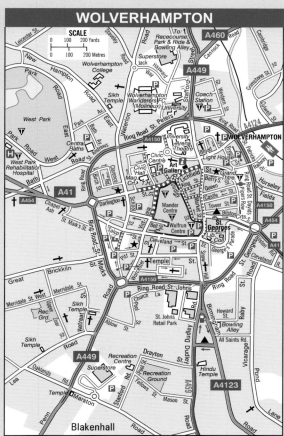

WORCESTER
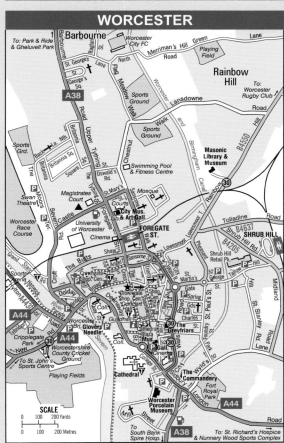

YORK
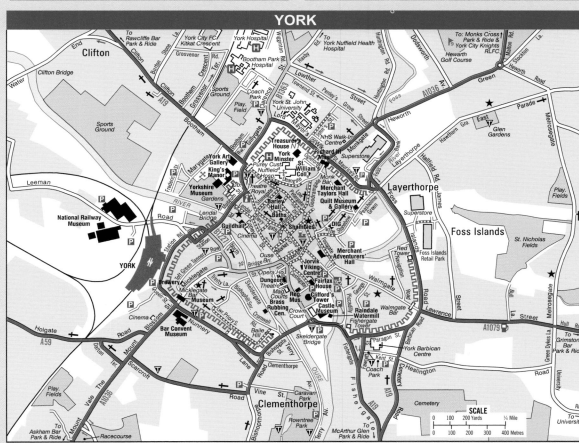

HARWICH

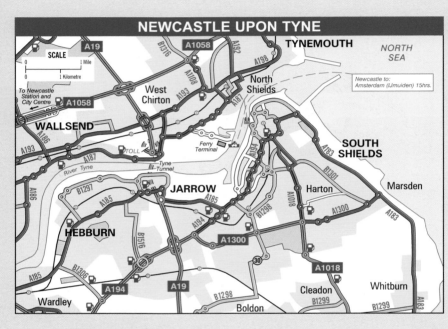

Harwich to:
Esbjerg 18hrs.
Hook of Holland 6hrs. 15mins.

KINGSTON UPON HULL

Hull to:
Rotterdam (Europoort) 10hrs.
Zeebrugge 12hrs. 30mins.

NEWCASTLE UPON TYNE

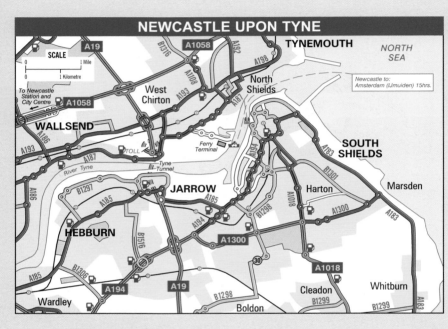

Newcastle to:
Amsterdam (IJmuiden) 15hrs.

NEWHAVEN

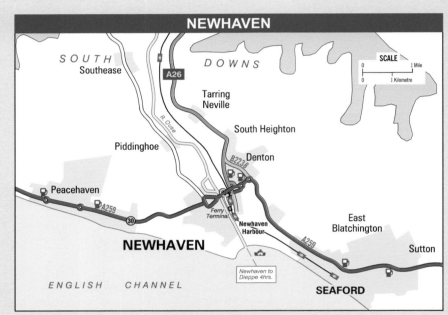

Newhaven to:
Dieppe 4hrs.

PEMBROKE DOCK (DOC PENFRO)

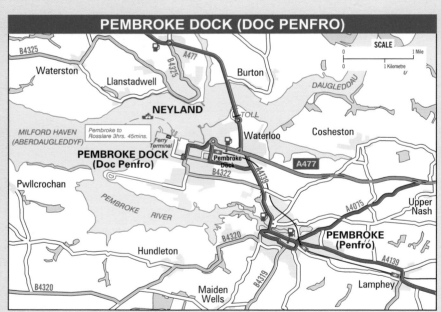

Pembroke to:
Rosslare 3hrs. 45mins.

POOLE

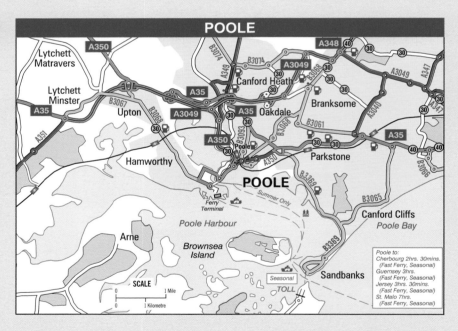

Poole to:
Cherbourg 2hrs. 30mins.
(Fast Ferry, Seasonal)
Guernsey 3hrs.
(Fast Ferry, Seasonal)
Jersey 3hrs. 30mins.
(Fast Ferry, Seasonal)
St. Malo 7hrs.
(Fast Ferry, Seasonal)

PORTSMOUTH

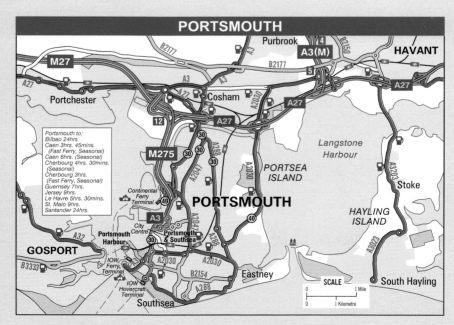

Portsmouth to:
Bilbao 24hrs.
Caen 3hrs. 45mins.
(Fast Ferry, Seasonal)
Caen 6hrs. (Seasonal)
Cherbourg 4hrs. 30mins.
(Seasonal)
Cherbourg 3hrs.
(Fast Ferry, Seasonal)
Guernsey 7hrs.
Jersey 9hrs.
Le Havre 5hrs. 30mins.
St. Malo 9hrs.
Santander 24hrs.

WEYMOUTH

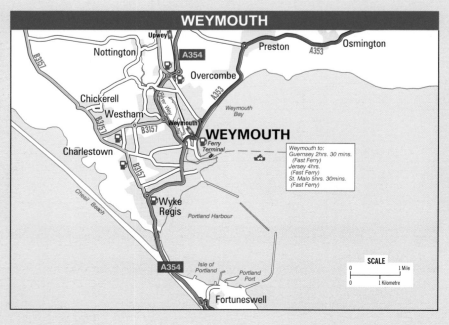

Weymouth to:
Guernsey 2hrs. 30 mins.
(Fast Ferry)
Jersey 4hrs.
(Fast Ferry)
St. Malo 5hrs. 30mins.
(Fast Ferry)

BIRMINGHAM

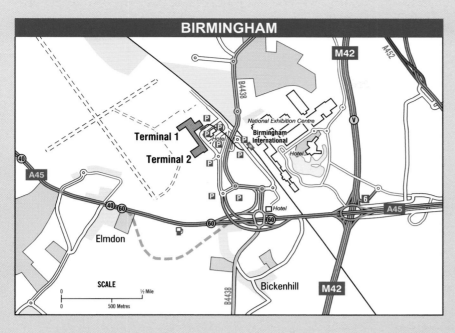

EAST MIDLANDS

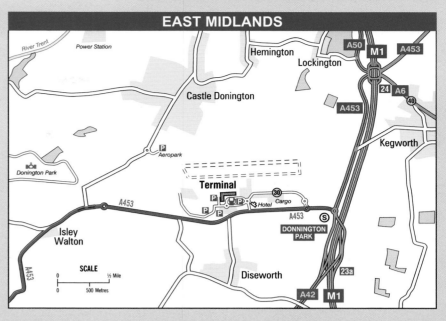

GLASGOW

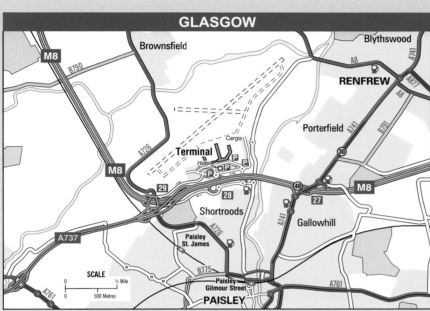

LONDON GATWICK

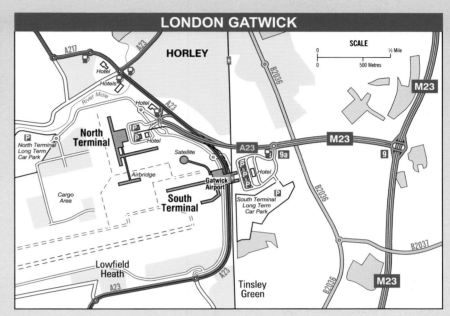

LONDON HEATHROW

LONDON LUTON

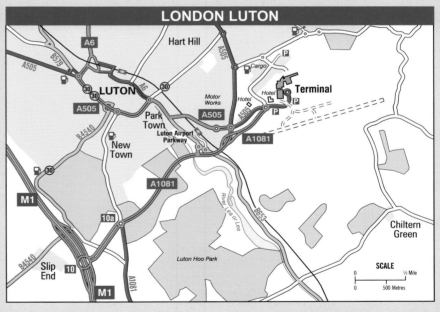

LONDON STANSTED

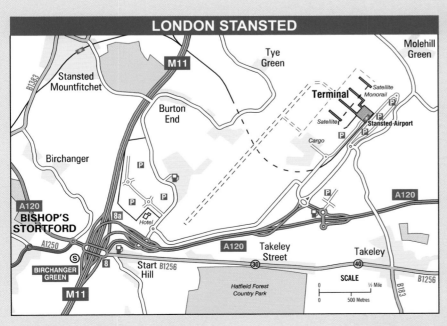

MANCHESTER INTERNATIONAL

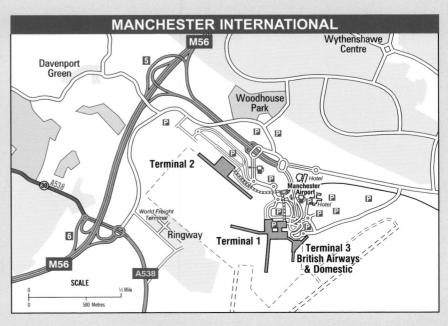

INDEX TO CITIES, TOWNS, VILLAGES, HAMLETS, LOCATIONS, AIRPORTS & PORTS

(1) A strict alphabetical order is used e.g. An Dùnan follows Andreas but precedes Andwell.

(2) The map reference given refers to the actual map square in which the town spot or built-up area is located and not to the place name.

(3) Major towns, selected airports and ports are shown in bold, i.e. **Aberdeen**. *Aber* . . . 3G **153** & **192**
Where they appear on a Town Plan a second page reference is given.

(4) Where two or more places of the same name occur in the same County or Unitary Authority, the nearest large town is also given; e.g. Achiemore. *High* . . . 2D **166** (nr. Durness) indicates that Achiemore is located in square 2D on page **166** and is situated near Durness in the Unitary Authority of Highland.

(5) Only one reference is given although due to page overlaps the place may appear on more than one page.

COUNTIES and UNITARY AUTHORITIES with the abbreviations used in this index

Aberdeen : *Aber*
Aberdeenshire : *Abers*
Angus : *Ang*
Antrim : *Ant*
Ards : *Ards*
Argyll & Bute : *Arg*
Armagh : *Arm*
Ballymena : *Bmna*
Ballymoney : *Bmny*
Banbridge : *Ban*
Bath & N E Somerset : *Bath*
Bedford : *Bed*
Belfast : *Bel*
Blackburn with Darwen : *Bkbn*
Blackpool : *Bkpl*
Blaenau Gwent : *Blae*
Bournemouth : *Bour*
Bracknell Forest : *Brac*
Bridgend : *B'end*
Brighton & Hove : *Brig*
Bristol : *Bris*
Buckinghamshire : *Buck*
Caerphilly : *Cphy*
Cambridgeshire : *Cambs*
Cardiff : *Card*
Carmarthenshire : *Carm*
Carrickfergus : *Carr*
Castlereagh : *Cast*
Central Bedfordshire : *C Beds*
Ceredigion : *Cdgn*
Cheshire East : *Ches E*
Cheshire West & Chester : *Ches W*
Clackmannanshire : *Clac*
Coleraine : *Cole*
Conwy : *Cnwy*
Cookstown : *Cook*
Cornwall : *Corn*
Craigavon : *Cgvn*
Cumbria : *Cumb*
Darlington : *Darl*
Denbighshire : *Den*
Derby : *Derb*
Derbyshire : *Derbs*
Derry : *Derr*
Devon : *Devn*
Dorset : *Dors*
Down : *Down*
Dumfries & Galloway : *Dum*
Dundee : *D'dee*
Dungannon : *Dngn*
Durham : *Dur*
East Ayrshire : *E Ayr*
East Dunbartonshire : *E Dun*
East Lothian : *E Lot*
East Renfrewshire : *E Ren*
East Riding of Yorkshire : *E Yor*
East Sussex : *E Sus*
Edinburgh : *Edin*
Essex : *Essx*
Falkirk : *Falk*
Fermanagh : *Ferm*
Fife : *Fife*
Flintshire : *Flin*
Glasgow : *Glas*
Gloucestershire : *Glos*
Greater London : *G Lon*
Greater Manchester : *G Man*
Gwynedd : *Gwyn*
Halton : *Hal*
Hampshire : *Hants*
Hartlepool : *Hart*
Herefordshire : *Here*
Hertfordshire : *Herts*
Highland : *High*
Inverclyde : *Inv*
Isle of Anglesey : *IOA*
Isle of Man : *IOM*
Isle of Wight : *IOW*
Isles of Scilly : *IOS*
Kent : *Kent*
Kingston upon Hull : *Hull*
Lancashire : *Lanc*
Larne : *Lar*
Leicester : *Leic*
Leicestershire : *Leics*
Limavady : *Lim*
Lincolnshire : *Linc*
Lisburn : *Lis*
Luton : *Lutn*
Magherafelt : *Mag*
Medway : *Medw*
Merseyside : *Mers*
Merthyr Tydfil : *Mer T*
Middlesbrough : *Midd*
Midlothian : *Midl*
Milton Keynes : *Mil*
Monmouthshire : *Mon*
Moray : *Mor*
Moyle : *Moy*
Neath Port Talbot : *Neat*
Newport : *Newp*
Newry & Mourne : *New M*
Newtownabbey : *Newt*
Norfolk : *Norf*
Northamptonshire : *Nptn*
North Ayrshire : *N Ayr*
North Down : *N Dwn*
North East Lincolnshire : *NE Lin*
North Lanarkshire : *N Lan*
North Lincolnshire : *N Lin*
North Somerset : *N Som*
Northumberland : *Nmbd*
North Yorkshire : *N Yor*
Nottingham : *Nott*
Nottinghamshire : *Notts*
Omagh : *Omag*
Orkney : *Orkn*
Oxfordshire : *Oxon*
Pembrokeshire : *Pemb*
Perth & Kinross : *Per*
Peterborough : *Pet*
Plymouth : *Plym*
Poole : *Pool*
Portsmouth : *Port*
Powys : *Powy*
Reading : *Read*
Redcar & Cleveland : *Red C*
Renfrewshire : *Ren*
Rhondda Cynon Taff : *Rhon*
Rutland : *Rut*
Scottish Borders : *Bord*
Shetland : *Shet*
Shropshire : *Shrp*
Slough : *Slo*
Somerset : *Som*
Southampton : *Sotn*
South Ayrshire : *S Ayr*
Southend-on-Sea : *S'end*
South Gloucestershire : *S Glo*
South Lanarkshire : *S Lan*
South Yorkshire : *S Yor*
Staffordshire : *Staf*
Stirling : *Stir*
Stockton-on-Tees : *Stoc T*
Stoke-on-Trent : *Stoke*
Strabane : *Strab*
Suffolk : *Suff*
Surrey : *Surr*
Swansea : *Swan*
Swindon : *Swin*
Telford & Wrekin : *Telf*
Thurrock : *Thur*
Torbay : *Torb*
Torfaen : *Torf*
Tyne & Wear : *Tyne*
Vale of Glamorgan, The : *V Glam*
Warrington : *Warr*
Warwickshire : *Warw*
West Berkshire : *W Ber*
West Dunbartonshire : *W Dun*
Western Isles : *W Isl*
West Lothian : *W Lot*
West Midlands : *W Mid*
West Sussex : *W Sus*
West Yorkshire : *W Yor*
Wiltshire : *Wilts*
Windsor & Maidenhead : *Wind*
Wokingham : *Wok*
Worcestershire : *Worc*
Wrexham : *Wrex*
York : *York*

INDEX

A

Abbas Combe. *Som* 4C 22
Abberley. *Worc* 4B 60
Abberley Common. *Worc* 4B 60
Abberton. *Essx* 4D 54
Abberton. *Worc* 5D 61
Abberwick. *Nmbd* 3F 121
Abbess Roding. *Essx* 4F 53
Abbey. *Devn* 1E 13
Abbey-cwm-hir. *Powy* 3C 58
Abbeydale. *S Yor* 2H 85
Abbeydale Park. *S Yor* 2H 85
Abbey Dore. *Here* 2G 47
Abbey Gate. *Devn* 3F 13
Abbey Hulton. *Stoke* 1D 72
Abbey St Bathans. *Bord* 3D 130
Abbeystead. *Lanc* 4E 97
Abbeytown. *Cumb* 4C 112
Abbey Village. *Lanc* 2E 91
Abbey Wood. *G Lon* 3F 39
Abbots Ann. *Hants* 2B 24
Abbots Bickington. *Devn* 1D 11
Abbots Bromley. *Staf* 3E 73
Abbotsbury. *Dors* 4A 14
Abbotsham. *Devn* 4E 19
Abbotskerswell. *Devn* 2E 9
Abbots Langley. *Herts* 5A 52
Abbots Leigh. *N Som* 4A 34
Abbotsley. *Cambs* 5B 64
Abbots Morton. *Worc* 5E 61
Abbots Ripton. *Cambs* 3B 64
Abbot's Salford. *Warw* 5E 61
Abbotstone. *Hants* 3D 24
Abbots Worthy. *Hants* 3C 24
Abcott. *Shrp* 3F 59
Abdon. *Shrp* 2H 59
Abenhall. *Glos* 4B 48
Aber. *Cdgn* 1E 45
Aberaeron. *Cdgn* 4D 56
Aberafan. *Neat* 3G 31
Aberaman. *Rhon* 5D 46
Aberangell. *Powy* 4H 69
Aberarad. *Carm* 1H 43
Aberarder. *High* 1A 150
Aberargie. *Per* 2D 136
Aberarth. *Cdgn* 4D 57
Aberavon. *Neat* 3G 31
Aber-banc. *Cdgn* 1D 44
Aberbargoed. *Cphy* 2E 33
Aberbechan. *Powy* 1D 58
Aberbeeg. *Blae* 5F 47
Aberbowlan. *Carm* 2G 45
Aberbran. *Powy* 3C 46
Abercanaid. *Mer T* 5D 46
Abercarn. *Cphy* 2F 33
Abercastle. *Pemb* 1C 42
Abercegir. *Powy* 5H 69
Aberchalder. *High* 3F 149
Aberchirder. *Abers* 3D 160
Abercorn. *W Lot* 2D 129
Abercraf. *Powy* 4B 46
Abercregan. *Neat* 2B 32
Abercrombie. *Fife* 3H 137
Abercwmboi. *Rhon* 2D 32
Abercych. *Pemb* 1C 44
Abercynon. *Rhon* 2D 32
Aber-Cywarch. *Gwyn* 4A 70
Aberdalgie. *Per* 1C 136
Aberdar. *Rhon* 5C 46
Aberdare. *Rhon* 5C 46
Aberdaron. *Gwyn* 3A 68
Aberdaugleddau. *Pemb* 4D 42
Aberdeen. *Aber* 3G 153 & 192
Aberdeen (Dyce) Airport. *Aber* 2F 153
Aberdesach. *Gwyn* 5D 80
Aberdour. *Fife* 1E 129
Aberdovey. *Gwyn* 1F 57
Aberdulais. *Neat* 5A 46
Aberdyfi. *Gwyn* 1F 57
Aberedw. *Powy* 1D 46
Abereiddy. *Pemb* 1B 42
Abererch. *Gwyn* 2C 68
Aberfan. *Mer T* 5D 46
Aberfeldy. *Per* 4F 143
Aberffraw. *IOA* 4C 80
Aberffrwd. *Cdgn* 3F 57
Aberford. *W Yor* 1E 93
Aberfoyle. *Stir* 3E 135
Abergarw. *B'end* 3C 32
Abergarwed. *Neat* 5B 46
Abergavenny. *Mon* 4G 47
Abergele. *Cnwy* 3B 82
Aber-Giar. *Carm* 1F 45
Abergorlech. *Carm* 2F 45
Abergwaun. *Pemb* 1D 42
Abergwesyn. *Powy* 5A 58
Abergwili. *Carm* 3E 45
Abergwynfi. *Neat* 2B 32
Abergwyngregyn. *Gwyn* 3F 81
Abergynolwyn. *Gwyn* 5F 69
Aberhafesp. *Powy* 1C 58
Aberhonddu. *Powy* 3D 46
Aberhosan. *Powy* 1H 57
Aberkenfig. *B'end* 3B 32
Aberlady. *E Lot* 2A 130
Aberlemno. *Ang* 3E 145
Aberllefenni. *Gwyn* 5G 69
Abermaw. *Gwyn* 4F 69
Abermeurig. *Cdgn* 5E 57
Aber-miwl. *Powy* 1D 58
Abermule. *Powy* 1D 58
Abernant. *Carm* 2H 43
Abernant. *Rhon* 5D 46
Abernethy. *Per* 2D 136
Abernyte. *Per* 5B 144
Aber-oer. *Wrex* 1E 71
Aberpennar. *Rhon* 2D 32
Aberporth. *Cdgn* 5B 56
Aberriw. *Powy* 5D 70
Abersoch. *Gwyn* 3C 68
Abersychan. *Torf* 5F 47
Abertawe. *Swan* 3F 31 & **Swansea** 203
Aberteifi. *Cdgn* 1B 44
Aberthin. *V Glam* 4D 32
Abertillery. *Blae* 5F 47
Abertridwr. *Cphy* 3E 32
Abertridwr. *Powy* 4C 70
Abertyleri. *Blae* 5F 47
Abertysswg. *Cphy* 5E 47
Aberuthven. *Per* 2B 136
Aber Village. *Powy* 3E 46
Aberyscir. *Powy* 3D 46
Aberystwyth. *Cdgn* 2E 57
Abhainn Suidhe. *W Isl* 7C 171
Abingdon. *Oxon* 2C 36
Abinger Common. *Surr* 1C 26
Abinger Hammer. *Surr* 1B 26
Abington. *S Lan* 2B 118
Abington Pigotts. *Cambs* 1D 52
Ab Kettleby. *Leics* 3E 74
Ab Lench. *Worc* 5E 61
Ablington. *Glos* 5G 49
Ablington. *Wilts* 2G 23
Abney. *Derbs* 3F 85
Aboyne. *Abers* 4C 152
Abram. *G Man* 4E 90
Abriachan. *High* 5H 157
Abridge. *Essx* 1F 39
Abronhill. *N Lan* 2A 128
Abson. *S Glo* 4C 34
Abthorpe. *Nptn* 1E 51
Abune-the-Hill. *Orkn* 5B 172
Aby. *Linc* 3D 88
Acairseid. *W Isl* 8C 170
Acaster Malbis. *York* 5H 99
Acaster Selby. *N Yor* 5H 99
Accott. *Devn* 3G 19
Accrington. *Lanc* 2F 91
Acha. *Arg* 3C 138
Achachork. *High* 4D 155
Achadh a' Chuirn. *High* 1E 147
Achahoish. *Arg* 2F 125
Achaleven. *Arg* 5D 140
Achallader. *Arg* 4H 141
Acha Mor. *W Isl* 5F 171
Achanalt. *High* 2E 157
Achandunie. *High* 1A 158
Ach'an Todhair. *High* 1E 141
Achany. *High* 3C 164
Achaphubuil. *High* 1E 141
Acharacle. *High* 2A 140
Acharn. *Ang* 1B 144
Acharn. *Per* 4E 143
Acharole. *High* 3E 169
Achateny. *High* 2G 139
Achavanich. *High* 4D 169
Achdalieu. *High* 1E 141
Achduart. *High* 3E 163
Achentoul. *High* 5A 168
Achfary. *High* 5C 166
Achfrish. *High* 2C 164
Achgarve. *High* 4C 162
Achiemore. *High* 2D 166 (nr. Durness)
Achiemore. *High* 3A 168 (nr. Thurso)
A'Chill. *High* 3A 146
Achiltibuie. *High* 3E 163
Achina. *High* 2H 167
Achinahuagh. *High* 2F 167
Achindarroch. *High* 3E 141
Achinduich. *High* 3C 164
Achinduin. *Arg* 5C 140
Achininver. *High* 2F 167
Achintee. *High* 4B 156
Achintraid. *High* 5H 155
Achleck. *Arg* 4F 139
Achlorachan. *High* 3F 157
Achluachrach. *High* 5E 149
Achlyness. *High* 3C 166
Achmelvich. *High* 1E 163
Achmony. *High* 5H 157
Achmore. *High* 5A 156 (nr. Stromeferry)
Achmore. *High* 4E 163 (nr. Ullapool)
Achnacarnin. *High* 1E 163
Achnacarry. *High* 5D 148
Achnaclerach. *High* 2G 157
Achnacloich. *High* 3D 147
Ach na Cloiche. *High* 3D 147
Achnaconeran. *High* 2G 149
Achnacroish. *Arg* 4C 140
Achnafalnich. *Arg* 1B 134
Achnagarron. *High* 1A 158
Achnaha. *High* 2F 139
Achnahanat. *High* 4C 164
Achnahannet. *High* 1D 151
Achnairn. *High* 2C 164
Achnamara. *Arg* 1F 125
Achnanellan. *High* 5C 148
Achnangoul. *Arg* 3H 133
Achnasheen. *High* 3D 156
Achnashellach. *High* 4C 156
Achosnich. *High* 2F 139
Achow. *High* 5E 169
Achranich. *High* 4B 140
Achreamie. *High* 2C 168
Achriabhach. *High* 2F 141
Achriesgill. *High* 3C 166
Achrimsdale. *High* 3G 165
Achscrabster. *High* 2C 168
Achtoty. *High* 2G 167
Achurch. *Nptn* 2H 63
Achuvoldrach. *High* 3F 167
Achvaich. *High* 4E 164
Achvoan. *High* 3E 165
Ackenthwaite. *Cumb* 1E 97
Ackergill. *High* 3F 169
Ackergillshore. *High* 3F 169
Acklam. *Midd* 3B 106
Acklam. *N Yor* 3B 100
Ackleton. *Shrp* 1B 60
Acklington. *Nmbd* 4G 121
Ackton. *W Yor* 2E 93
Ackworth Moor Top. *W Yor* 3E 93
Acle. *Norf* 4G 79
Acocks Green. *W Mid* 2F 61
Acol. *Kent* 4H 41
Acomb. *Nmbd* 3C 114
Acomb. *York* 4H 99
Aconbury. *Here* 2A 48
Acre. *G Man* 4H 91
Acre. *Lanc* 2F 91
Acrefair. *Wrex* 1E 71
Acrise. *Kent* 1F 29
Acton. *Arm* 5E 178
Acton. *Ches E* 5A 84
Acton. *Dors* 5E 15
Acton. *G Lon* 2C 38
Acton. *Shrp* 2F 59
Acton. *Staf* 1C 72
Acton. *Suff* 1B 54
Acton. *Worc* 4C 60
Acton. *Wrex* 5F 83
Acton Beauchamp. *Here* 5A 60
Acton Bridge. *Ches W* 3H 83
Acton Burnell. *Shrp* 5H 71
Acton Green. *Here* 5A 60
Acton Pigott. *Shrp* 5H 71
Acton Round. *Shrp* 1A 60
Acton Scott. *Shrp* 2G 59
Acton Trussell. *Staf* 4D 72
Acton Turville. *S Glo* 3D 34
Adabroc. *W Isl* 1H 171
Adam's Hill. *Worc* 3D 60
Adbaston. *Staf* 3B 72
Adber. *Dors* 4B 22
Adderbury. *Oxon* 2C 50
Adderley. *Shrp* 2A 72
Adderstone. *Nmbd* 1F 121
Addiewell. *W Lot* 3C 128
Addingham. *W Yor* 5C 98
Addington. *Buck* 3F 51
Addington. *G Lon* 4E 39
Addington. *Kent* 5A 40
Addinston. *Bord* 4B 130
Addiscombe. *G Lon* 4E 39
Addlestone. *Surr* 4B 38
Addlethorpe. *Linc* 4E 89
Adeney. *Telf* 4B 72
Adfa. *Powy* 5C 70
Adforton. *Here* 3G 59
Adgestone. *IOW* 4D 16
Adisham. *Kent* 5G 41
Adlestrop. *Glos* 3H 49
Adlingfleet. *E Yor* 2B 94
Adlington. *Ches E* 2D 84
Adlington. *Lanc* 3E 90
Admaston. *Staf* 3E 73
Admaston. *Telf* 4A 72
Admington. *Warw* 1G 49
Adpar. *Cdgn* 1D 44
Adsborough. *Som* 4F 21
Adstock. *Buck* 2F 51
Adstone. *Nptn* 5C 62
Adversane. *W Sus* 3B 26
Advie. *High* 5F 159
Adwalton. *W Yor* 2C 92
Adwell. *Oxon* 2E 37
Adwick le Street. *S Yor* 4F 93
Adwick upon Dearne. *S Yor* 4E 93
Adziel. *Abers* 3G 161
Ae. *Dum* 1A 112
Affleck. *Abers* 1F 153
Affpuddle. *Dors* 3D 14
Affric Lodge. *High* 1D 148
Afon-wen. *Flin* 3D 82
Agglethorpe. *N Yor* 1C 98
Aghagallon. *Cgvn* 3F 178
Aghalee. *Lis* 3F 178
Aglionby. *Cumb* 4F 113
Ahoghill. *Bmna* 6G 175
Aigburth. *Mers* 2F 83
Aiginis. *W Isl* 4G 171
Aike. *E Yor* 5E 101
Aikers. *Orkn* 8D 172
Aiketgate. *Cumb* 5F 113
Aikhead. *Cumb* 5D 112
Aikton. *Cumb* 4D 112
Ailey. *Here* 1G 47
Ailsworth. *Pet* 1A 64
Ainderby Quernhow. *N Yor* 1F 99
Ainderby Steeple. *N Yor* 5A 106
Aingers Green. *Essx* 3E 54
Ainsdale. *Mers* 3B 90
Ainsdale-on-Sea. *Mers* 3B 90
Ainstable. *Cumb* 5G 113
Ainsworth. *G Man* 3F 91
Ainthorpe. *N Yor* 4E 107
Aintree. *Mers* 1F 83
Aird. *Arg* 3E 133
Aird. *Dum* 3F 109
Aird. *High* 1G 155 (nr. Port Henderson)
Aird. *High* 3D 147 (nr. Tarskavaig)
Aird. *W Isl* 3C 170 (on Benbecula)
Aird. *W Isl* 4H 171 (on Isle of Lewis)
Àird a Bhasair. *High* 3E 147
Aird a Mhachair. *W Isl* 4C 170
Aird a Mhulaidh. *W Isl* 6D 171
Aird Asaig. *W Isl* 7D 171
Aird Dhail. *W Isl* 1G 171
Airdens. *High* 4D 164
Airdeny. *Arg* 1G 133
Aird Mhidhinis. *W Isl* 8C 170
Aird Mhighe. *W Isl* 8D 171 (nr. Ceann a Bhaigh)
Aird Mhighe. *W Isl* 9C 171 (nr. Fionnsabhagh)
Aird Mhor. *W Isl* 8C 170 (on Barra)
Aird Mhor. *W Isl* 4D 170 (on South Uist)
Airdrie. *N Lan* 3A 128
Aird Shleibhe. *W Isl* 9D 171
Aird, The. *High* 3D 154
Aird Thunga. *W Isl* 4G 171
Aird Uig. *W Isl* 4C 171
Airedale. *W Yor* 2E 93
Airidh a Bhruaich. *W Isl* 6E 171
Airies. *Dum* 3E 109
Airmyn. *E Yor* 2H 93
Airntully. *Per* 5H 143
Airor. *High* 3F 147
Airth. *Falk* 1C 128
Airton. *N Yor* 4B 98
Aisby. *Linc* 1F 87 (nr. Gainsborough)
Aisby. *Linc* 2H 75 (nr. Grantham)
Aisgernis. *W Isl* 6C 170
Aish. *Devn* 2C 8 (nr. Buckfastleigh)
Aish. *Devn* 3E 9 (nr. Totnes)
Aisholt. *Som* 3E 21
Aiskew. *N Yor* 1E 99
Aislaby. *N Yor* 1B 100 (nr. Pickering)
Aislaby. *N Yor* 4F 107 (nr. Whitby)
Aislaby. *Stoc T* 3B 106
Aisthorpe. *Linc* 2G 87
Aith. *Shet* 2H 173 (on Fetlar)
Aith. *Shet* 6E 173 (on Mainland)
Aithsetter. *Shet* 8F 173
Akeld. *Nmbd* 2D 120
Akeley. *Buck* 2F 51
Akenham. *Suff* 1E 55
Albaston. *Corn* 5E 11
Alberbury. *Shrp* 4F 71
Albert Town. *Pemb* 3D 42
Albert Village. *Leics* 4H 73
Albourne. *W Sus* 4D 26
Albrighton. *Shrp* 4G 71 (nr. Shrewsbury)
Albrighton. *Shrp* 5C 72 (nr. Telford)
Alburgh. *Norf* 2E 67
Albury. *Herts* 3E 53
Albury. *Surr* 1B 26
Albyfield. *Cumb* 4G 113
Alby Hill. *Norf* 2D 78
Alcaig. *High* 3H 157
Alcaston. *Shrp* 2G 59
Alcester. *Warw* 5E 61
Alciston. *E Sus* 5G 27
Alcombe. *Som* 2C 20
Alconbury. *Cambs* 3A 64
Alconbury Weston. *Cambs* 3A 64
Aldborough. *Norf* 2D 78
Aldborough. *N Yor* 3G 99
Aldbourne. *Wilts* 4A 36
Aldbrough. *E Yor* 1F 95
Aldbrough St John. *N Yor* 3F 105
Aldbury. *Herts* 4H 51
Aldcliffe. *Lanc* 3D 96
Aldclune. *Per* 2G 143
Aldeburgh. *Suff* 5G 67
Aldeby. *Norf* 1G 67
Aldenham. *Herts* 1C 38
Alderbury. *Wilts* 4G 23
Aldercar. *Derbs* 1B 74
Alderford. *Norf* 4D 78
Alderholt. *Dors* 1G 15
Alderley. *Glos* 2C 34
Alderley Edge. *Ches E* 3C 84
Aldermaston. *W Ber* 5D 36
Aldermaston Stoke. *W Ber* 5E 36
Aldermaston Wharf. *W Ber* 5E 36
Alderminster. *Warw* 1H 49
Alder Moor. *Staf* 3G 73
Aldersey Green. *Ches W* 5G 83
Aldershot. *Hants* 1G 25
Alderton. *Glos* 2E 49
Alderton. *Nptn* 1F 51
Alderton. *Shrp* 3G 71
Alderton. *Suff* 1G 55
Alderton. *Wilts* 3D 34
Alderton Fields. *Glos* 2F 49
Alderwasley. *Derbs* 5H 85
Aldfield. *N Yor* 3E 99
Aldford. *Ches W* 5G 83
Aldgate. *Rut* 5G 75
Aldham. *Essx* 3C 54
Aldham. *Suff* 1D 54
Aldingbourne. *W Sus* 5A 26
Aldingham. *Cumb* 2B 96
Aldington. *Kent* 2E 29
Aldington. *Worc* 1F 49
Aldington Frith. *Kent* 2E 29
Aldochlay. *Arg* 4C 134
Aldon. *Shrp* 3G 59
Aldoth. *Cumb* 5C 112
Aldreth. *Cambs* 3D 64
Aldridge. *W Mid* 5E 73
Aldringham. *Suff* 4G 67
Aldsworth. *Glos* 4G 49
Aldsworth. *W Sus* 2F 17
Aldwark. *Derbs* 5G 85
Aldwark. *N Yor* 3G 99
Aldwick. *W Sus* 3H 17
Aldwincle. *Nptn* 2H 63
Aldworth. *W Ber* 4D 36
Alexandria. *W Dun* 1E 127
Aley. *Som* 3E 21
Aley Green. *C Beds* 4A 52
Alfardisworthy. *Devn* 1C 10
Alfington. *Devn* 3E 12
Alfold. *Surr* 2B 26
Alfold Bars. *W Sus* 2B 26
Alfold Crossways. *Surr* 2B 26
Alford. *Abers* 2C 152
Alford. *Linc* 3D 88
Alford. *Som* 3B 22
Alfreton. *Derbs* 5B 86
Alfrick. *Worc* 5B 60
Alfrick Pound. *Worc* 5B 60
Alfriston. *E Sus* 5G 27
Algarkirk. *Linc* 2B 76
Alhampton. *Som* 3B 22
Aline Lodge. *W Isl* 6D 171
Alkborough. *N Lin* 2B 94
Alkerton. *Oxon* 1B 50
Alkham. *Kent* 1G 29
Alkington. *Shrp* 2H 71
Alkmonton. *Derbs* 2F 73
Alladale Lodge. *High* 5B 164
Allaleigh. *Devn* 3E 9
Allanbank. *N Lan* 4B 128
Allanton. *N Lan* 4B 128
Allanton. *Bord* 4E 131
Allaston. *Glos* 5B 48
Allbrook. *Hants* 4C 24
All Cannings. *Wilts* 5F 35
Allendale Town. *Nmbd* 4B 114
Allen End. *Warw* 1F 61
Allenheads. *Nmbd* 5B 114
Allensford. *Dur* 5D 115
Allen's Green. *Herts* 4E 53
Allensmore. *Here* 2H 47
Allenton. *Derb* 2A 74
Aller. *Som* 4H 21
Allerby. *Cumb* 1B 102
Allercombe. *Devn* 3D 12
Allerford. *Som* 2C 20
Allerston. *N Yor* 1C 100
Allerthorpe. *E Yor* 5B 100
Allerton. *Mers* 2G 83
Allerton. *W Yor* 1B 92
Allerton Bywater. *W Yor* 2E 93
Allerton Mauleverer. *N Yor* 4G 99
Allesley. *W Mid* 2G 61
Allestree. *Derb* 2H 73
Allet. *Corn* 4B 6
Allexton. *Leics* 5F 75
Allgreave. *Ches E* 4D 84
Allhallows. *Medw* 3C 40
Allhallows-on-Sea. *Medw* 3C 40
Alligin Shuas. *High* 3H 155
Allimore Green. *Staf* 4C 72
Allington. *Kent* 5B 40
Allington. *Linc* 1F 75
Allington. *Wilts* 3H 23 (nr. Amesbury)
Allington. *Wilts* 5F 35 (nr. Devizes)
Allithwaite. *Cumb* 2C 96
Alloa. *Clac* 4A 136
Allonby. *Cumb* 5B 112
Allostock. *Ches W* 3B 84
Alloway. *S Ayr* 3C 116
Allowenshay. *Som* 1G 13
All Saints South Elmham. *Suff* 2F 67
Allscott. *Shrp* 1B 60
Allscott. *Telf* 4A 72
All Stretton. *Shrp* 1G 59
Allt. *Carm* 5F 45
Alltami. *Flin* 4E 83
Alltgobhlach. *N Ayr* 5G 125
Alltmawr. *Powy* 1D 46
Alltnacaillich. *High* 4E 167
Allt na h-Airbhe. *High* 4F 163
Alltour. *High* 5E 148
Alltsigh. *High* 2G 149
Alltwalis. *Carm* 2E 45
Alltwen. *Neat* 5H 45
Alltyblacca. *Cdgn* 1F 45
Allt-y-goed. *Pemb* 1B 44
Almeley. *Here* 5F 59
Almeley Wooton. *Here* 5F 59
Almer. *Dors* 3E 15
Almholme. *S Yor* 4F 93
Almington. *Staf* 2B 72
Alminstone Cross. *Devn* 4D 18
Almodington. *W Sus* 3G 17
Almondbank. *Per* 1C 136
Almondbury. *W Yor* 3B 92
Almondsbury. *S Glo* 3B 34
Alne. *N Yor* 3G 99
Alness. *High* 2A 158
Alnessferry. *High* 2A 158
Alnham. *Nmbd* 3D 121
Alnmouth. *Nmbd* 3G 121
Alnwick. *Nmbd* 3F 121
Alphamstone. *Essx* 2B 54
Alpheton. *Suff* 5A 66
Alphington. *Devn* 3C 12
Alpington. *Norf* 5E 79
Alport. *Derbs* 4G 85
Alport. *Powy* 1E 59
Alpraham. *Ches E* 5H 83
Alresford. *Essx* 3D 54
Alrewas. *Staf* 4F 73
Alsager. *Ches E* 5B 84
Alsagers Bank. *Staf* 1C 72
Alsop en le Dale. *Derbs* 5F 85
Alston. *Cumb* 5A 114
Alston. *Devn* 2G 13
Alstone. *Glos* 2E 49
Alstone. *Som* 2G 21
Alstonefield. *Staf* 5F 85
Alston Sutton. *Som* 1H 21
Alswear. *Devn* 4H 19
Altandhu. *High* 2D 163
Altanduin. *High* 1F 165
Altarnun. *Corn* 4C 10
Altass. *High* 3B 164
Alterwall. *High* 2E 169
Altgaltraig. *Arg* 2B 126
Altham. *Lanc* 1F 91
Althorne. *Essx* 1D 40
Althorpe. *N Lin* 4B 94
Altnabreac. *High* 4C 168
Altnacealgach. *High* 2G 163
Altnafeadh. *High* 3G 141
Altnaharra. *High* 5F 167
Altofts. *W Yor* 2D 92
Alton. *Derbs* 4A 86
Alton. *Hants* 3F 25
Alton. *Staf* 1E 73
Alton Barnes. *Wilts* 5G 35
Altonhill. *E Ayr* 1D 116
Alton Pancras. *Dors* 2C 14
Alton Priors. *Wilts* 5G 35
Altrincham. *G Man* 2B 84
Altrua. *High* 4E 149
Alva. *Clac* 4A 136
Alvanley. *Ches W* 3G 83
Alvaston. *Derb* 2A 74
Alvechurch. *Worc* 3E 61
Alvecote. *Warw* 5G 73
Alvediston. *Wilts* 4E 23
Alveley. *Shrp* 2B 60
Alverdiscott. *Devn* 4F 19
Alverstoke. *Hants* 3D 16
Alverstone. *IOW* 4D 16
Alverthorpe. *W Yor* 2D 92
Alverton. *Notts* 1E 75
Alves. *Mor* 2F 159
Alvescot. *Oxon* 5A 50
Alveston. *S Glo* 3B 34
Alveston. *Warw* 5G 61
Alvie. *High* 3C 150
Alvingham. *Linc* 1C 88
Alvington. *Glos* 5B 48
Alwalton. *Cambs* 1A 64
Alweston. *Dors* 1B 14
Alwington. *Devn* 4E 19
Alwinton. *Nmbd* 4D 120
Alwoodley. *W Yor* 5E 99
Alyth. *Per* 4B 144
Amatnatua. *High* 4B 164
Am Baile. *W Isl* 7C 170
Ambaston. *Derbs* 2B 74
Ambergate. *Derbs* 5H 85
Amber Hill. *Linc* 1B 76
Amberley. *Glos* 5D 48
Amberley. *W Sus* 4B 26
Amble. *Nmbd* 4G 121
Amblecote. *W Mid* 2C 60
Ambler Thorn. *W Yor* 2A 92
Ambleside. *Cumb* 4E 103
Ambleston. *Pemb* 2E 43
Ambrosden. *Oxon* 4E 50
Amcotts. *N Lin* 3B 94
Amersham. *Buck* 1A 38
Amerton. *Staf* 3D 73
Amesbury. *Wilts* 2G 23
Amisfield. *Dum* 1B 112
Amlwch. *IOA* 1D 80
Amlwch Port. *IOA* 1D 80
Ammanford. *Carm* 4G 45
Amotherby. *N Yor* 2B 100
Ampfield. *Hants* 4B 24
Ampleforth. *N Yor* 2H 99
Ampleforth College. *N Yor* 2H 99
Ampney Crucis. *Glos* 5F 49
Ampney St Mary. *Glos* 5F 49
Ampney St Peter. *Glos* 5F 49
Amport. *Hants* 2A 24
Ampthill. *C Beds* 2A 52
Ampton. *Suff* 3A 66
Amroth. *Pemb* 4F 43
Amulree. *Per* 5G 143
Amwell. *Herts* 4B 52
Anaheilt. *High* 2C 140
An Àird. *High* 3D 147
An Baile Nua. *Ferm* 7K 177
An Camus Darach. *High* 4E 147
Ancaster. *Linc* 1G 75
Anchor. *Shrp* 2D 58
Anchorsholme. *Bkpl* 5C 96
Anchor Street. *Norf* 3F 79
An Cnoc. *W Isl* 4G 171
An Cnoc Ard. *W Isl* 1H 171
An Coroghon. *High* 3A 146
Ancroft. *Nmbd* 5G 131
Ancrum. *Bord* 2A 120
Ancton. *W Sus* 5A 26
Anderby. *Linc* 3E 89
Anderby Creek. *Linc* 3E 89
Anderson. *Dors* 3D 15
Anderton. *Ches W* 3A 84
Andertons Mill. *Lanc* 3D 90
Andover. *Hants* 2B 24
Andover Down. *Hants* 2B 24
Andoversford. *Glos* 4F 49
Andreas. *IOM* 2D 108
An Dùnan. *High* 1D 147
Andwell. *Hants* 1E 25
Anelog. *Gwyn* 3A 68
Anfield. *Mers* 1F 83
Angarrack. *Corn* 3C 4
Angelbank. *Shrp* 3H 59
Angersleigh. *Som* 1F 13
Angerton. *Cumb* 4D 112
Angle. *Pemb* 4C 42
An Gleann Ur. *W Isl* 4G 171
Angmering. *W Sus* 5B 26
Angmering-on-Sea. *W Sus* 5B 26
Angram. *N Yor* 5B 104 (nr. Keld)
Angram. *N Yor* 5H 99 (nr. York)
Anick. *Nmbd* 3C 114
Ankerbold. *Derbs* 4A 86
Ankerville. *High* 1C 158
Anlaby. *E Yor* 2D 94
Anlaby Park. *Hull* 2D 94
An Leth Meadhanach. *W Isl* 7C 170
Anmer. *Norf* 3G 77
Anmore. *Hants* 1E 17
Annacloy. *Down* 5J 179
Annadorn. *Down* 5J 179
Annaghmore. *Arm* 4D 178
Annaghugh. *Arm* 4D 178
Annahilt. *Lis* 4G 179
Annalong. *New M* 8H 179
Annan. *Dum* 3D 112
Annaside. *Cumb* 1A 96
Annat. *Arg* 1H 133
Annat. *High* 3A 156
Annathill. *N Lan* 2A 128
Anna Valley. *Hants* 2B 24
Annbank. *S Ayr* 2D 116
Annesley. *Notts* 5C 86
Annesley Woodhouse. *Notts* 5C 86
Annfield Plain. *Dur* 4E 115
Annsborough. *Down* 6H 179
Annscroft. *Shrp* 5G 71
An Sailean. *High* 2A 140
Ansdell. *Lanc* 2B 90
Ansford. *Som* 3B 22
Ansley. *Warw* 1G 61
Anslow. *Staf* 3G 73
Anslow Gate. *Staf* 3F 73
Ansteadbrook. *Surr* 2A 26
Anstey. *Herts* 2E 53
Anstey. *Leics* 5C 74
Anston. *S Lan* 5D 128
Anstruther Easter. *Fife* 3H 137
Anstruther Wester. *Fife* 3H 137
Ansty. *Warw* 2A 62
Ansty. *W Sus* 3D 27
Ansty. *Wilts* 4E 23
An Taobh Tuath. *W Isl* 9B 171
An t-Aodann Ban. *High* 3C 154
An t Ath Leathann. *High* 1E 147
An Teanga. *High* 3E 147
Anthill Common. *Hants* 1E 17
Anthorn. *Cumb* 4C 112
Antingham. *Norf* 2E 79
An t-Ob. *W Isl* 9C 171
Anton's Gowt. *Linc* 1B 76
Antony. *Corn* 3A 8
An t-Òrd. *High* 2E 147
Antrim. *Ant* 8H 175
Antrobus. *Ches W* 3A 84
Anvil Corner. *Devn* 2D 10
Anwick. *Linc* 5A 88
Anwoth. *Dum* 4C 110
Apethorpe. *Nptn* 1H 63
Apeton. *Staf* 4C 72
Apley. *Linc* 3A 88
Apperknowle. *Derbs* 3A 86
Apperley. *Glos* 3D 48
Apperley Dene. *Nmbd* 4D 114
Appersett. *N Yor* 5B 104
Appin. *Arg* 4D 140
Appleby. *N Lin* 3C 94
Appleby-in-Westmorland. *Cumb* 2H 103
Appleby Magna. *Leics* 5H 73
Appleby Parva. *Leics* 5H 73
Applecross. *High* 4G 155
Appledore. *Devn* 3E 19 (nr. Bideford)
Appledore. *Devn* 1D 12 (nr. Tiverton)
Appledore. *Kent* 3D 28
Appledore Heath. *Kent* 2D 28
Appleford. *Oxon* 2D 36
Applegarthtown. *Dum* 1C 112
Applemore. *Hants* 2B 16
Appleshaw. *Hants* 2B 24
Applethwaite. *Cumb* 2D 102
Appleton. *Hal* 2H 83
Appleton. *Oxon* 5C 50
Appleton-le-Moors. *N Yor* 1B 100
Appleton-le-Street. *N Yor* 2B 100
Appleton Roebuck. *N Yor* 5H 99
Appleton Thorn. *Warr* 2A 84
Appleton Wiske. *N Yor* 4A 106
Appletree. *Nptn* 1C 50
Appletreehall. *Bord* 3H 119
Appletreewick. *N Yor* 3C 98
Appley. *Som* 4D 20
Appley Bridge. *Lanc* 4D 90
Apse Heath. *IOW* 4D 16
Apsley End. *C Beds* 2B 52
Apuldram. *W Sus* 2G 17
Arabella. *High* 1C 158
Arasaig. *High* 5E 147
Arbeadie. *Abers* 4D 152
Arberth. *Pemb* 3F 43
Arbirlot. *Ang* 4F 145
Arborfield. *Wok* 5F 37
Arborfield Cross. *Wok* 5F 37
Arborfield Garrison. *Wok* 5F 37
Arbourthorne. *S Yor* 2A 86
Arbroath. *Ang* 4F 145
Arbuthnott. *Abers* 1H 145
Arcan. *High* 3H 157
Archargary. *High* 3H 167
Archdeacon Newton. *Darl* 3F 105
Archiestown. *Mor* 4G 159
Arclid. *Ches E* 4B 84
Arclid Green. *Ches E* 4B 84
Ardachu. *High* 3D 164
Ardalanish. *Arg* 2A 132
Ardaneaskan. *High* 5H 155
Ardarroch. *High* 5H 155
Ardbeg. *Arg* 1C 126 (nr. Dunoon)
Ardbeg. *Arg* 5C 124 (on Islay)
Ardbeg. *Arg* 3B 126 (on Isle of Bute)
Ardboe. *Cook* 2D 178
Ardcharnich. *High* 5F 163
Ardchiavaig. *Arg* 2A 132
Ardchonnell. *Arg* 2G 133
Ardchrishnish. *Arg* 1B 132
Ardchronie. *High* 5D 164
Ardchullarie. *Stir* 2E 135
Ardchyle. *Stir* 1E 135
Ard-dhubh. *High* 4G 155
Arddleen. *Powy* 4E 71
Arddlîn. *Powy* 4E 71
Ardechive. *High* 4D 148
Ardeley. *Herts* 3D 52
Ardelve. *High* 1A 148
Arden. *Arg* 1E 127
Ardendrain. *High* 5H 157
Arden Hall. *N Yor* 5C 106
Ardens Grafton. *Warw* 5F 61
Ardentinny. *Arg* 1C 126
Ardeonaig. *Stir* 5D 142
Ardersier. *High* 3B 158
Ardery. *High* 2B 140
Ardessie. *High* 5E 163
Ardfern. *Arg* 3F 133
Ardfernal. *Arg* 2D 124
Ardfin. *Arg* 3C 124
Ardgartan. *Arg* 3B 134
Ardgay. *High* 4C 164
Ardglass. *Down* 6K 179
Ardgour. *High* 2E 141
Ardheslaig. *High* 3G 155
Ardindrean. *High* 5F 163
Ardingly. *W Sus* 3E 27
Ardington. *Oxon* 3C 36
Ardlamont House. *Arg* 3A 126
Ardleigh. *Essx* 3D 54
Ardler. *Per* 4B 144
Ardley. *Oxon* 3D 50
Ardlui. *Arg* 2C 134
Ardlussa. *Arg* 1E 125
Ardmair. *High* 4F 163
Ardmay. *Arg* 3B 134
Ardmillan. *Ards* 3K 179
Ardminish. *Arg* 5E 125
Ardmolich. *High* 1B 140
Ardmore. *High* 3C 166 (nr. Kinlochbervie)
Ardmore. *High* 5E 164 (nr. Tain)
Ardnacross. *Arg* 4G 139
Ardnadam. *Arg* 1C 126
Ardnagrask. *High* 4H 157
Ardnamurach. *High* 4G 147
Ardnarff. *High* 5A 156
Ardnastang. *High* 2C 140
Ardoch. *Per* 5H 143
Ardochy House. *High* 3E 148
Ardpatrick. *Arg* 3F 125
Ardrishaig. *Arg* 1G 125
Ardroag. *High* 4B 154
Ardross. *High* 1A 158
Ardrossan. *N Ayr* 5D 126
Ardshealach. *High* 2A 140
Ardsley. *S Yor* 4D 93
Ardslignish. *High* 2G 139
Ardstraw. *Strab* 4F 176
Ardtalla. *Arg* 4C 124
Ardtalnaig. *Per* 5E 142
Ardtoe. *High* 1A 140
Arduaine. *Arg* 2E 133
Ardullie. *High* 2H 157
Ardvasar. *High* 3E 147
Ardvorlich. *Per* 1F 135
Ardwell. *Dum* 5G 109
Ardwell. *Mor* 5A 160
Arean. *High* 1A 140
Areley Common. *Worc* 3C 60
Areley Kings. *Worc* 3B 60
Arford. *Hants* 3G 25
Argoed. *Cphy* 2E 33
Argoed Mill. *Powy* 4B 58
Aridhglas. *Arg* 2B 132
Arinacrinachd. *High* 3G 155
Arinagour. *Arg* 3D 138
Arisaig. *High* 5E 147
Ariundle. *High* 2C 140
Arivegaig. *High* 2A 140
Arkendale. *N Yor* 3F 99
Arkesden. *Essx* 2E 53
Arkholme. *Lanc* 2E 97
Arkle Town. *N Yor* 4D 104
Arkley. *G Lon* 1D 38
Arksey. *S Yor* 4F 93
Arkwright Town. *Derbs* 3B 86
Arlecdon. *Cumb* 3B 102
Arlescote. *Warw* 1B 50
Arlesey. *C Beds* 2B 52
Arleston. *Telf* 4A 72
Arley. *Ches E* 2A 84
Arlingham. *Glos* 4C 48
Arlington. *Devn* 2G 19
Arlington. *E Sus* 5G 27
Arlington. *Glos* 5G 49
Arlington Beccott. *Devn* 2G 19
Armadail. *High* 3E 147
Armadale. *High* 3E 147 (nr. Isleornsay)
Armadale. *High* 2H 167 (nr. Strathy)
Armadale. *W Lot* 3C 128
Armagh. *Arm* 5C 178

Armathwaite—Beauvale

Armathwaite. Cumb 5G 113
Arminghall. Norf 5E 79
Armitage. Staf 4E 73
Armitage Bridge. W Yor 3B 92
Armley. W Yor 1C 92
Armoy. Moy 3G 175
Armscote. Warw 1H 49
Arms, The. Norf 1A 66
Armston. Nptn 2H 63
Armthorpe. S Yor 4G 93
Arncliffe. N Yor 2B 98
Arncliffe Cote. N Yor 2B 98
Arncroach. Fife 3H 137
Arne. Dors 4E 15
Arnesby. Leics 1D 62
Arnicle. Arg 2B 122
Arnisdale. High 2G 147
Arnish. High 4E 155
Arniston. Midl 3G 129
Arnol. W Isl 3F 171
Arnold. E Yor 5F 101
Arnold. Notts 1C 74
Arnprior. Stir 4F 135
Arnside. Cumb 2D 96
Aros Mains. Arg 4G 139
Arpafeelie. High 3A 158
Arrad Foot. Cumb 1C 96
Arram. E Yor 5E 101
Arras. E Yor 5D 100
Arrathorne. N Yor 5E 105
Arreton. IOW 4D 16
Arrington. Cambs 5C 64
Arrochar. Arg 3B 134
Arrow. Warw 5E 61
Arscaig. High 2C 164
Artafallie. High 4A 158
Arthington. W Yor 5E 99
Arthingworth. Nptn 2E 63
Arthog. Gwyn 4F 69
Arthrath. Abers 5G 161
Arthurstone. Per 4B 144
Articlave. Cole 3D 174
Artigarvan. Strab 2F 176
Artikelly. Lim 4C 174
Artington. Surr 1A 26
Arundel. W Sus 5B 26
Asby. Cumb 2B 102
Ascog. Arg 3C 126
Ascot. Wind 4A 38
Ascott-under-Wychwood. Oxon 4B 50
Asenby. N Yor 2F 99
Asfordby. Leics 4E 74
Asfordby Hill. Leics 4E 74
Asgarby. Linc 4C 88 (nr. Horncastle)
Asgarby. Linc 1A 76 (nr. Sleaford)
Ash. Devn 4E 9
Ash. Dors 1D 14
Ash. Kent 5G 41 (nr. Sandwich)
Ash. Kent 4H 39 (nr. Swanley)
Ash. Som 4H 21
Ash. Surr 1G 25
Ashampstead. W Ber 4D 36
Ashbocking. Suff 5D 66
Ashbourne. Derbs 1F 73
Ashbrittle. Som 4D 20
Ashbrook. Shrp 1G 59
Ashburton. Devn 2D 8
Ashbury. Devn 3F 11
Ashbury. Oxon 3A 36
Ashby. N Lin 4B 94
Ashby by Partney. Linc 4D 88
Ashby cum Fenby. NE Lin 4F 95
Ashby de la Launde. Linc 5H 87
Ashby-de-la-Zouch. Leics 4A 74
Ashby Folville. Leics 4E 74
Ashby Magna. Leics 1C 62
Ashby Parva. Leics 2C 62
Ashby Puerorum. Linc 3C 88
Ashby St Ledgars. Nptn 4C 62
Ashby St Mary. Norf 5F 79
Ashchurch. Glos 2E 49
Ashcombe. Devn 5C 12
Ashcott. Som 3H 21
Ashdon. Essx 1F 53
Ashe. Hants 1D 24
Asheldham. Essx 5C 54
Ashen. Essx 1H 53
Ashendon. Buck 4F 51
Ashey. IOW 4D 16
Ashfield. Hants 1B 16
Ashfield. Here 3A 48
Ashfield. Shrp 2H 59
Ashfield. Stir 3G 135
Ashfield. Suff 4E 66
Ashfield Green. Suff 3E 67
Ashfold Crossways. W Sus 3D 26
Ashford. Devn 3F 19 (nr. Barnstaple)
Ashford. Devn 4C 8 (nr. Kingsbridge)
Ashford. Hants 1G 15
Ashford. Kent 1E 28
Ashford. Surr 3B 38
Ashford Bowdler. Shrp 3H 59
Ashford Carbonel. Shrp 3H 59
Ashford Hill. Hants 5D 36
Ashford in the Water. Derbs 4F 85
Ashgill. S Lan 5A 128
Ash Green. Warw 2H 61
Ashgrove. Mor 2G 159
Ashill. Devn 1D 12
Ashill. Norf 5A 78
Ashill. Som 1G 13
Ashingdon. Essx 1C 40
Ashington. Nmbd 1F 115
Ashington. W Sus 4C 26
Ashkirk. Bord 2G 119
Ashlett. Hants 2C 16
Ashleworth. Glos 3D 48
Ashley. Cambs 4F 65
Ashley. Ches E 2B 84
Ashley. Dors 2G 15
Ashley. Glos 2E 35
Ashley. Hants 3A 16 (nr. New Milton)
Ashley. Hants 3B 24 (nr. Winchester)
Ashley. Kent 1H 29
Ashley. Nptn 1E 63
Ashley. Staf 2B 72
Ashley. Wilts 5D 34
Ashley Green. Buck 5H 51
Ashley Heath. Dors 2G 15
Ashley Heath. Staf 2B 72
Ashley Moor. Here 4G 59
Ash Magna. Shrp 2H 71
Ashmanhaugh. Norf 3F 79
Ashmansworth. Hants 1C 24
Ashmansworthy. Devn 1D 10
Ashmead Green. Glos 2C 34
Ashmill. Devn 3D 11 (nr. Holsworthy)
Ash Mill. Devn 4A 20 (nr. South Molton)
Ashmore. Dors 1E 15
Ashmore Green. W Ber 5D 36
Ashover. Derbs 4A 86
Ashow. Warw 3H 61
Ash Parva. Shrp 2H 71
Ashperton. Here 1B 48
Ashprington. Devn 3E 9
Ash Priors. Som 4E 21
Ashreigney. Devn 1G 11
Ash Street. Suff 1D 54
Ashtead. Surr 5C 38
Ash Thomas. Devn 1D 12
Ashton. Corn 4D 4
Ashton. Here 4H 59
Ashton. Inv 2D 126
Ashton. Nptn 2H 63 (nr. Oundle)
Ashton. Nptn 1F 51 (nr. Roade)
Ashton. Pet 5A 76
Ashton Common. Wilts 1E 23
Ashton Hayes. Ches W 4H 83
Ashton-in-Makerfield. G Man 4D 90
Ashton Keynes. Wilts 2F 35
Ashton under Hill. Worc 2E 49
Ashton-under-Lyne. G Man 1D 84
Ashton upon Mersey. G Man 1B 84
Ashurst. Hants 1B 16
Ashurst. Kent 2G 27
Ashurst. Lanc 4C 90
Ashurst. W Sus 4C 26
Ashurst Wood. W Sus 2F 27
Ash Vale. Surr 1G 25
Ashwater. Devn 3D 11
Ashwell. Herts 2C 52
Ashwell. Rut 4F 75
Ashwellthorpe. Norf 1D 66
Ashwick. Som 2B 22
Ashwicken. Norf 4G 77
Ashwood. Staf 2C 60
Askam in Furness. Cumb 2B 96
Askern. S Yor 3F 93
Askerswell. Dors 3A 14
Askett. Buck 5G 51
Askham. Cumb 2G 103
Askham. Notts 3E 87
Askham Bryan. York 5H 99
Askham Richard. York 5H 99
Askrigg. N Yor 5C 104
Askwith. N Yor 5D 98
Aslackby. Linc 2H 75
Aslacton. Norf 1D 66
Aslockton. Notts 1E 75
Aspatria. Cumb 5C 112
Aspenden. Herts 3D 52
Asperton. Linc 2B 76
Aspley Guise. C Beds 2H 51
Aspley Heath. C Beds 2H 51
Aspull. G Man 4E 90
Asselby. E Yor 2H 93
Assington. Suff 2C 54
Assington Green. Suff 5G 65
Astbury. Ches E 4C 84
Astcote. Nptn 5D 62
Asterby. Linc 3B 88
Asterley. Shrp 5F 71
Asterton. Shrp 1F 59
Asthall. Oxon 4A 50
Asthall Leigh. Oxon 4B 50
Astle. High 4E 165
Astley. G Man 4F 91
Astley. Shrp 4H 71
Astley. Warw 2H 61
Astley. Worc 4B 60
Astley Abbotts. Shrp 1B 60
Astley Bridge. G Man 3F 91
Astley Cross. Worc 4C 60
Aston. Ches E 1A 72
Aston. Ches W 3H 83
Aston. Derbs 2F 85 (nr. Hope)
Aston. Derbs 2F 73 (nr. Sudbury)
Aston. Flin 4F 83
Aston. Here 4G 59
Aston. Herts 3C 52
Aston. Oxon 5B 50
Aston. Shrp 1C 60 (nr. Bridgnorth)
Aston. Shrp 3H 71 (nr. Wem)
Aston. S Yor 2B 86
Aston. Staf 1B 72
Aston. Telf 5A 72
Aston. W Mid 1E 61
Aston. Wok 3F 37
Aston Abbotts. Buck 3G 51
Aston Botterell. Shrp 2A 60
Aston-by-Stone. Staf 2D 72
Aston Cantlow. Warw 5F 61
Aston Clinton. Buck 4G 51
Aston Crews. Here 3B 48
Aston Cross. Glos 2E 49
Aston End. Herts 3C 52
Aston Eyre. Shrp 1A 60
Aston Fields. Worc 4D 60
Aston Flamville. Leics 1B 62
Aston Ingham. Here 3B 48
Aston juxta Mondrum. Ches E 5A 84
Astonlane. Shrp 1A 60
Aston le Walls. Nptn 5B 62
Aston Magna. Glos 2G 49
Aston Munslow. Shrp 2H 59
Aston on Carrant. Glos 2E 49
Aston on Clun. Shrp 2F 59
Aston-on-Trent. Derbs 3B 74
Aston Pigott. Shrp 5F 71
Aston Rogers. Shrp 5F 71
Aston Rowant. Oxon 2F 37
Aston Sandford. Buck 5F 51
Aston Somerville. Worc 2F 49
Aston Subedge. Glos 1G 49
Aston Tirrold. Oxon 3D 36
Aston Upthorpe. Oxon 3D 36
Astrop. Nptn 2D 50
Astwick. C Beds 2C 52
Astwood. Mil 1H 51
Astwood Bank. Worc 4E 61
Aswarby. Linc 2H 75
Aswardby. Linc 3C 88
Atcham. Shrp 5H 71
Atch Lench. Worc 5E 61
Athelhampton. Dors 3C 14
Athelington. Suff 3E 66
Athelney. Som 4G 21
Athelstaneford. E Lot 2B 130
Atherfield Green. IOW 5C 16
Atherington. Devn 4F 19
Atherington. W Sus 5B 26
Athersley. S Yor 4D 92
Atherstone. Warw 1H 61
Atherstone on Stour. Warw 5G 61
Atherton. G Man 4E 91
Ath-Tharracail. High 2A 140
Atlow. Derbs 1G 73
Attadale. High 5B 156
Attenborough. Notts 2C 74
Atterby. Linc 1G 87
Atterley. Shrp 1A 60
Atterton. Leics 1A 62
Attical. New M 8G 179
Attleborough. Norf 1C 66
Attleborough. Warw 1A 62
Attlebridge. Norf 4D 78
Atwick. E Yor 4F 101
Atworth. Wilts 5D 34
Auberrow. Here 1H 47
Aubourn. Linc 4G 87
Aucharnie. Abers 4D 160
Auchattie. Abers 4D 152
Auchavan. Ang 2A 144
Auchbreck. Mor 1G 151
Auchenback. E Ren 4G 127
Auchenblae. Abers 1G 145
Auchenbrack. Dum 5G 117
Auchenbreck. Arg 1B 126
Auchencairn. Dum 4E 111 (nr. Dalbeattie)
Auchencairn. Dum 1A 112 (nr. Dumfries)
Auchencarroch. W Dun 1F 127
Auchencrow. Bord 3E 131
Auchendennan. W Dun 1E 127
Auchendinny. Midl 3F 129
Auchengray. S Lan 4C 128
Auchenhalrig. Mor 2A 160
Auchenheath. S Lan 5B 128
Auchenlochan. Arg 2A 126
Auchenmade. N Ayr 5E 127
Auchenmalg. Dum 4H 109
Auchentiber. N Ayr 5E 127
Auchenvennel. Arg 1D 126
Auchindrain. Arg 3H 133
Auchininna. Abers 4D 160
Auchinleck. Dum 2B 110
Auchinleck. E Ayr 2E 117
Auchinloch. N Lan 2H 127
Auchinstarry. N Lan 2A 128
Auchleven. Abers 1D 152
Auchlochan. S Lan 1H 117
Auchlunachan. High 5F 163
Auchmillan. E Ayr 2E 117
Auchmithie. Ang 4F 145
Auchmuirbridge. Per 3E 136
Auchmull. Ang 1E 145
Auchnacree. Ang 4G 161
Auchnafree. Per 5F 143
Auchnagallin. High 5E 159
Auchnagatt. Abers 4G 161
Aucholzie. Abers 4H 151
Auchreddie. Abers 4F 161
Auchterarder. Per 2B 136
Auchteraw. High 3F 149
Auchterderran. Fife 4E 136
Auchterhouse. Ang 5C 144
Auchtermuchty. Fife 2E 137
Auchterneed. High 3G 157
Auchtertool. Fife 4E 136
Auchtertyre. High 1G 147
Auchtubh. Stir 1E 135
Auckengill. High 2F 169
Auckley. S Yor 4G 93
Audenshaw. G Man 1D 84
Audlem. Ches E 1A 72
Audley. Staf 5B 84
Audley End. Essx 2F 53
Audmore. Staf 3C 72
Auds. Abers 2D 160
Augher. Dngn 4L 177
Aughertree. Cumb 1D 102
Aughnacloy. Dngn 4A 178
Aughton. E Yor 1H 93
Aughton. Lanc 3E 97 (nr. Lancaster)
Aughton. Lanc 4B 90 (nr. Ormskirk)
Aughton. S Yor 2B 86
Aughton. Wilts 1H 23
Aughton Park. Lanc 4C 90
Auldearn. High 3D 158
Aulden. Here 5G 59
Auldgirth. Dum 1G 111
Auldhouse. S Lan 4H 127
Ault a' chruinn. High 1B 148
Aultbea. High 5C 162
Aultdearg. High 2E 157
Aultgrishan. High 5B 162
Aultguish Inn. High 1F 157
Ault Hucknall. Derbs 4B 86
Aultibea. High 1H 165
Aultiphurst. High 2A 168
Aultivullin. High 2A 168
Aultmore. Mor 3B 160
Aultnamain Inn. High 5D 164
Aunby. Linc 4H 75
Aunsby. Linc 2H 75
Aust. S Glo 3A 34
Austerfield. S Yor 1D 86
Austin Fen. Linc 1C 88
Austrey. Warw 5G 73
Austwick. N Yor 3G 97
Authorpe. Linc 2D 88
Authorpe Row. Linc 3E 89
Avebury. Wilts 5G 35
Avebury Trusloe. Wilts 5F 35
Aveley. Thur 2G 39
Avening. Glos 2D 35
Averham. Notts 5E 87
Aveton Gifford. Devn 4C 8
Avielochan. High 2D 150
Aviemore. High 2C 150
Avington. Hants 3D 24
Avoch. High 3B 158
Avon. Hants 3G 15
Avonbridge. Falk 2C 128
Avon Dassett. Warw 5B 62
Avonmouth. Bris 4A 34
Avonwick. Devn 3D 8
Awbridge. Hants 4B 24
Awliscombe. Devn 2E 13
Awre. Glos 5C 48
Awsworth. Notts 1B 74
Axbridge. Som 1H 21
Axford. Hants 2E 24
Axford. Wilts 5H 35
Axminster. Devn 3F 13
Axmouth. Devn 3F 13
Aycliffe Village. Dur 2F 105
Aydon. Nmbd 3D 114
Aykley Heads. Dur 5F 115
Aylburton. Glos 5B 48
Aylburton Common. Glos 5B 48
Ayle. Nmbd 5A 114
Aylesbeare. Devn 3D 12
Aylesbury. Buck 4G 51
Aylesby. NE Lin 4F 95
Aylescott. Devn 1G 11
Aylesford. Kent 5B 40
Aylesham. Kent 5G 41
Aylestone. Leic 5C 74
Aylmerton. Norf 2D 78
Aylsham. Norf 3D 78
Aylton. Here 2B 48
Aylworth. Glos 3G 49
Aymestrey. Here 4G 59
Aynho. Nptn 2D 50
Ayot Green. Herts 4C 52
Ayot St Lawrence. Herts 4B 52
Ayot St Peter. Herts 4C 52
Ayr. S Ayr 2C 116
Ayres of Selivoe. Shet 7D 173
Ayreville. Torb 2E 9
Aysgarth. N Yor 1C 98
Ayshford. Devn 1D 12
Ayside. Cumb 1C 96
Ayston. Rut 5F 75
Ayton. Bord 3F 131
Aywick. Shet 3G 173
Azerley. N Yor 2E 99

B

Babbacombe. Torb 2F 9
Babbinswood. Shrp 3F 71
Babb's Green. Herts 4D 53
Babcary. Som 4A 22
Babel. Carm 2B 46
Babell. Flin 3D 82
Babingley. Norf 3F 77
Bablock Hythe. Oxon 5C 50
Babraham. Cambs 5E 65
Babworth. Notts 2D 86
Bac. W Isl 3G 171
Bachau. IOA 2D 80
Bacheldre. Powy 1E 59
Bachymbyd Fawr. Den 4C 82
Backaland. Orkn 4E 172
Backaskaill. Orkn 2D 172
Backbarrow. Cumb 1C 96
Backe. Carm 3G 43
Backfolds. Abers 3H 161
Backford. Ches W 3G 83
Backhill. Abers 5E 161
Backhill of Clackriach. Abers 4G 161
Backies. High 3F 165
Backmuir of New Gilston. Fife 3G 137
Back of Keppoch. High 5E 147
Back Street. Suff 5G 65
Backwell. N Som 5H 33
Backworth. Tyne 2G 115
Bacon End. Essx 4G 53
Baconsthorpe. Norf 2D 78
Bacton. Here 2G 47
Bacton. Norf 2F 79
Bacton. Suff 4C 66
Bacton Green. Norf 2F 79
Bacup. Lanc 2G 91
Badachonacher. High 1A 158
Badachro. High 1G 155
Badanloch Lodge. High 5H 167
Badavanich. High 3D 156
Badbury. Swin 3G 35
Badby. Nptn 5C 62
Badcall. High 3C 166
Badcaul. High 4E 163
Baddeley Green. Stoke 5D 84
Baddesley Clinton. W Mid 3G 61
Baddesley Ensor. Warw 1G 61
Baddidarach. High 1E 163
Baddoch. Abers 5F 151
Badenscallie. High 3E 163
Badenscoth. Abers 5E 160
Badentarbat. High 2E 163
Badgall. Corn 4C 10
Badgers Mount. Kent 4F 39
Badgeworth. Glos 4E 49
Badgworth. Som 1G 21
Badicaul. High 1F 147
Badingham. Suff 4F 67
Badlesmere. Kent 5E 40
Badlipster. High 4E 169
Badluarach. High 4D 163
Badminton. S Glo 3D 34
Badnaban. High 1E 163
Badnabay. High 4C 166
Badnagie. High 5D 168
Badnellan. High 3F 165
Badninish. High 4E 165
Badrallach. High 4E 163
Badsey. Worc 1F 49
Badshot Lea. Surr 2G 25
Badsworth. W Yor 3E 93
Badwell Ash. Suff 4B 66
Bae Cinmel. Cnwy 2B 82
Bae Colwyn. Cnwy 3A 82
Bae Penrhyn. Cnwy 2H 81
Bagby. N Yor 1G 99
Bag Enderby. Linc 3C 88
Bagendon. Glos 5F 49
Bagginswood. Shrp 2A 60
Bàgh a Chàise. W Isl 1E 170
Bàgh a' Chaisteil. W Isl 9B 170
Bagham. Kent 5E 41
Baghasdal. W Isl 7C 170
Bagh Mor. W Isl 3D 170
Bagh Shiarabhagh. W Isl 8C 170
Bagillt. Flin 3E 83
Baginton. Warw 3H 61
Baglan. Neat 2A 32
Bagley. Shrp 3G 71
Bagley. Som 2H 21
Bagnall. Staf 5D 84
Bagnor. W Ber 5C 36
Bagshot. Surr 4A 38
Bagshot. Wilts 5B 36
Bagstone. S Glo 3B 34
Bagthorpe. Norf 2G 77
Bagthorpe. Notts 5B 86
Bagworth. Leics 5B 74
Bagwy Llydiart. Here 3H 47
Baildon. W Yor 1B 92
Baildon Green. W Yor 1B 92
Baile. W Isl 1E 170
Baile Ailein. W Isl 5E 171
Baile an Truiseil. W Isl 2F 171
Baile Boidheach. Arg 2F 125
Baile Glas. W Isl 3D 170
Bailemeonach. Arg 4A 140
Baile Mhanaich. W Isl 3C 170
Baile Mhartainn. W Isl 1C 170
Baile MhicPhail. W Isl 1D 170
Baile Mor. Arg 2A 132
Baile Mor. W Isl 2C 170
Baile nan Cailleach. W Isl 3C 170
Baile Raghaill. W Isl 2C 170
Bailey Green. Hants 4E 25
Baileyhead. Cumb 1G 113
Baileysmill. Lis 4H 179
Bailiesward. Abers 5B 160
Bail' Iochdrach. W Isl 3D 170
Baillieston. Glas 3H 127
Bailrigg. Lanc 4D 97
Bail' Uachdraich. W Isl 2D 170
Bail Ur Tholastaidh. W Isl 3H 171
Bainbridge. N Yor 5C 104
Bainsford. Falk 1B 128
Bainshole. Abers 5D 160
Bainton. E Yor 4D 100
Bainton. Oxon 3D 50
Bainton. Pet 5H 75
Baintown. Fife 3F 137
Baker Street. Thur 2H 39
Bakewell. Derbs 4G 85
Bala. Gwyn 2B 70
Balachuirn. High 4E 155
Balbeg. High 5G 157 (nr. Cannich)
Balbeg. High 1G 149 (nr. Loch Ness)
Balbeggie. Per 1D 136
Balblair. High 4C 164 (nr. Bonar Bridge)
Balblair. High 2B 158 (nr. Invergordon)
Balblair. High 4H 157 (nr. Inverness)
Balby. S Yor 4F 93
Balcathie. Ang 5F 145
Balchladich. High 1E 163
Balchraggan. High 4H 157
Balchrick. High 3B 166
Balcombe. W Sus 2E 27
Balcombe Lane. W Sus 2E 27
Balcurvie. Fife 3F 137
Baldersby. N Yor 2F 99
Baldersby St James. N Yor 2F 99
Balderstone. Lanc 1E 91
Balderton. Ches W 4F 83
Balderton. Notts 5F 87
Baldinnie. Fife 2G 137
Baldock. Herts 2C 52
Baldrine. IOM 3D 108
Baldslow. E Sus 4C 28
Baldwin. IOM 3C 108
Baldwinholme. Cumb 4E 113
Baldwin's Gate. Staf 2B 72
Bale. Norf 2C 78
Balearn. Abers 3H 161
Balemartine. Arg 4A 138
Balephretrish. Arg 4B 138
Balephuil. Arg 4A 138
Balerno. Edin 3E 129
Balevullin. Arg 4A 138
Balfield. Ang 2E 145
Balfour. Orkn 6D 172
Balfron. Stir 1G 127
Balgaveny. Abers 4D 160
Balgonar. Fife 4C 136
Balgowan. High 4A 150
Balgown. High 2C 154
Balgrochan. E Dun 2H 127
Balgy. High 3H 155
Balhalgardy. Abers 1E 153
Baliasta. Shet 1H 173
Baligill. High 2A 168
Balintore. Ang 3B 144
Balintore. High 1C 158
Balintraid. High 1B 158
Balk. N Yor 1G 99
Balkeerie. Ang 4C 144
Balkholme. E Yor 2A 94
Ball. Shrp 3F 71
Ballabeg. IOM 4B 108
Ballacannell. IOM 3D 108
Ballacarnane Beg. IOM 3C 108
Ballachulish. High 3E 141
Ballagyr. IOM 3B 108
Ballajora. IOM 2D 108
Ballaleigh. IOM 3C 108
Ballamodha. IOM 4B 108
Ballantrae. S Ayr 1F 109
Ballards Gore. Essx 1D 40
Ballasalla. IOM 4B 108 (nr. Castletown)
Ballasalla. IOM 2C 108 (nr. Kirk Michael)
Ballater. Abers 4A 152
Ballaugh. IOM 2C 108
Ballencrieff. E Lot 2A 130
Ballencrieff Toll. W Lot 2C 128
Ballentoul. Per 2F 143
Ball Hill. Hants 5C 36
Ballidon. Derbs 5G 85
Balliemore. Arg 1B 126 (nr. Dunoon)
Balliemore. Arg 1F 133 (nr. Oban)
Ballieward. High 5E 159
Ballig. IOM 3B 108
Ballimore. Stir 2E 135
Ballinamallard. Ferm 7E 176
Ballindarragh. Ferm 6J 177
Ballingdon. Suff 1B 54
Ballinger Common. Buck 5H 51
Ballingham. Here 2A 48
Ballingry. Fife 4D 136
Ballinluig. Per 3G 143
Ballintoy. Moy 2G 175
Ballintuim. Per 3A 144
Balliveolan. Arg 4C 140
Balloan. High 3C 164
Balloch. High 4B 158
Balloch. N Lan 2A 128
Balloch. Per 2H 135
Balloch. W Dun 1E 127
Ballochan. Abers 4C 152
Ballochgoy. Arg 3B 126
Ballochmyle. E Ayr 2E 117
Ballochroy. Arg 4F 125
Balloo. Ards 3J 179
Balls Cross. W Sus 3A 26
Ball's Green. E Sus 2F 27
Ballsmill. New M 8D 178
Ballyalton. Down 5K 179
Ballybogy. Bmny 3F 174
Ballycarry. Lar 7L 175
Ballycassidy. Ferm 7E 176
Ballycastle. Moy 2H 175
Ballyclare. Newt 7J 175
Ballyeaston. Newt 7J 175
Ballygally. Lar 6K 175
Ballygawley. Dngn 4A 178
Ballygowan. Ards 3J 179
Ballygown. Arg 4F 139
Ballygrant. Arg 3B 124
Ballyhalbert. Ards 3L 179
Ballyholland. New M 7F 178
Ballyhornan. Down 5K 179
Ballykelly. Lim 4C 174
Ballykinler. Down 6J 179
Ballylesson. Lis 3H 179
Ballymagorry. Strab 2F 176
Ballymartin. New M 8H 179
Ballymena. Bmna 6H 175
Ballymichael. N Ayr 2D 122
Ballymoney. Bmny 4F 174
Ballymoney. Lim 6C 174
Ballynagard. Derr 4A 174
Ballynahinch. Down 4H 179
Ballynakilly. Dngn 3C 178
Ballynoe. Down 5J 179
Ballynure. Newt 7K 175
Ballyrashane. Cole 3E 174
Ballyrobert. Newt 8J 175
Ballyronan. Cook 8F 174
Ballyroney. Ban 6G 179
Ballyscullion. Lim 3C 174
Ballystrudder. Lar 7L 175
Ballyvoy. Moy 2H 175
Ballyward. Ban 6G 179
Ballywater. Ards 3L 179
Ballywonard. Newt 1G 179
Balmacara. High 1G 147
Balmaclellan. Dum 2D 110
Balmacqueen. High 1D 154
Balmaha. Stir 4D 134
Balmalcolm. Fife 3F 137
Balmalloch. N Lan 2A 128
Balmeanach. High 5E 155
Balmedie. Abers 2G 153
Balmerino. Fife 1F 137
Balmerlawn. Hants 2B 16
Balmore. E Dun 2H 127
Balmore. High 4B 154
Balmuir. Ang 5D 144
Balmullo. Fife 1G 137
Balmurrie. Dum 3H 109
Balnaboth. Ang 2C 144
Balnabruaich. High 1B 158
Balnabruich. High 5D 168
Balnacoil. High 2F 165
Balnacra. High 4B 156
Balnacroft. Abers 4G 151
Balnageith. Mor 3E 159
Balnaglaic. High 5G 157
Balnagrantach. High 5G 157
Balnaguard. Per 3G 143
Balnahard. Arg 4B 132
Balnain. High 5G 157
Balnakeil. High 2D 166
Balnaknock. High 2D 154
Balnamoon. Abers 3G 161
Balnamoon. Ang 2E 145
Balnamore. Bmny 4F 174
Balnapaling. High 2B 158
Balornock. Glas 3H 127
Balquhidder. Stir 1E 135
Balsall. W Mid 3G 61
Balsall Common. W Mid 3G 61
Balscote. Oxon 1B 50
Balsham. Cambs 5E 65
Balstonia. Thur 2A 40
Baltasound. Shet 1H 173
Balterley. Staf 5B 84
Baltersan. Dum 3B 110
Balthangie. Abers 3F 161
Baltonsborough. Som 3A 22
Balvaird. High 3H 157
Balvaird. Per 2D 136
Balvenie. Mor 4H 159
Balvicar. Arg 2E 133
Balvraid. High 2G 147
Balvraid Lodge. High 5C 158
Bamber Bridge. Lanc 2D 90
Bamber's Green. Essx 3F 53
Bamburgh. Nmbd 1F 121
Bamford. Derbs 2G 85
Bamfurlong. G Man 4D 90
Bampton. Cumb 3G 103
Bampton. Devn 4C 20
Bampton. Oxon 5B 50
Bampton Grange. Cumb 3G 103
Banavie. High 1F 141
Banbridge. Ban 5F 178
Banbury. Oxon 1C 50
Bancffosfelen. Carm 4E 45
Banchory. Abers 4D 152
Banchory-Devenick. Abers 3G 153
Bancycapel. Carm 4E 45
Bancyfelin. Carm 3H 43
Banc-y-ffordd. Carm 2E 45
Banff. Abers 2D 160
Bangor. Gwyn 3E 81
Bangor. N Dwn 1K 179
Bangor-is-y-coed. Wrex 1F 71
Bangors. Corn 3C 10
Bangor's Green. Lanc 4B 90
Banham. Norf 2C 66
Bank. Hants 2A 16
Bankend. Dum 3B 112
Bankfoot. Per 5H 143
Bankglen. E Ayr 3E 117
Bankhead. Aber 2F 153
Bankhead. Abers 3D 152
Bankhead. S Lan 5B 128
Bankland. Som 4G 21
Bank Newton. N Yor 4B 98
Banknock. Falk 2A 128
Banks. Cumb 3G 113
Banks. Lanc 2B 90
Bankshill. Dum 1C 112
Bank Street. Worc 4A 60
Bank, The. Ches E 5C 84
Bank, The. Shrp 1A 60
Bank Top. Lanc 4D 90
Banners Gate. W Mid 1E 61
Banningham. Norf 3E 78
Banniskirk. High 3D 168
Bannister Green. Essx 3G 53
Bannockburn. Stir 4H 135
Banstead. Surr 5D 38
Bantham. Devn 4C 8
Banton. N Lan 2A 128
Banwell. N Som 1G 21
Banyard's Green. Suff 3F 67
Bapchild. Kent 4D 40
Bapton. Wilts 3E 23
Barabhas. W Isl 2F 171
Barabhas Iarach. W Isl 3F 171
Baramore. High 1A 140
Barassie. S Ayr 1C 116
Baravullin. Arg 4D 140
Barbaraville. High 1B 158
Barber Booth. Derbs 2F 85
Barber Green. Cumb 1C 96
Barbhas Uarach. W Isl 2F 171
Barbieston. S Ayr 3D 116
Barbon. Cumb 1F 97
Barbourne. Worc 5C 60
Barbridge. Ches E 5A 84
Barbrook. Devn 2H 19
Barby. Nptn 3C 62
Barby Nortoft. Nptn 3C 62
Barcaldine. Arg 4D 140
Barcheston. Warw 1A 50
Barclose. Cumb 3F 113
Barcombe. E Sus 4F 27
Barcombe Cross. E Sus 4F 27
Barden. N Yor 5E 105
Barden Scale. N Yor 4C 98
Bardfield End Green. Essx 2G 53
Bardfield Saling. Essx 3G 53
Bardister. Shet 4E 173
Bardnabeinne. High 4E 164
Bardney. Linc 4A 88
Bardon. Leics 4B 74
Bardon Mill. Nmbd 3A 114
Bardowie. E Dun 2G 127
Bardrainney. Inv 2E 127
Bardsea. Cumb 2C 96
Bardsey. W Yor 5F 99
Bardsley. G Man 4H 91
Bardwell. Suff 3B 66
Bare. Lanc 3D 96
Barelees. Nmbd 1C 120
Barewood. Here 5F 59
Barford. Hants 3G 25
Barford. Norf 5D 78
Barford. Warw 4G 61
Barford St John. Oxon 2C 50
Barford St Martin. Wilts 3F 23
Barford St Michael. Oxon 2C 50
Barfrestone. Kent 5G 41
Bargeddie. N Lan 3A 128
Bargod. Cphy 2E 33
Bargoed. Cphy 2E 33
Bargrennan. Dum 2A 110
Barham. Cambs 3A 64
Barham. Kent 5G 41
Barham. Suff 5D 66
Barharrow. Dum 4D 110
Bar Hill. Cambs 4C 64
Barholm. Linc 4H 75
Barkby. Leics 4D 74
Barkestone-le-Vale. Leics 2E 75
Barkham. Wok 5F 37
Barking. G Lon 2F 39
Barking. Suff 5C 66
Barkingside. G Lon 2F 39
Barking Tye. Suff 5C 66
Barkisland. W Yor 3A 92
Barkston. Linc 1G 75
Barkston Ash. N Yor 1E 93
Barkway. Herts 2D 53
Barlanark. Glas 3H 127
Barlaston. Staf 2C 72
Barlavington. W Sus 4A 26
Barlborough. Derbs 3B 86
Barlby. N Yor 1G 93
Barlestone. Leics 5B 74
Barley. Herts 2D 53
Barley. Lanc 5H 97
Barley Mow. Tyne 4F 115
Barleythorpe. Rut 5F 75
Barling. Essx 2D 40
Barlings. Linc 3H 87
Barlow. Derbs 3H 85
Barlow. N Yor 2G 93
Barlow. Tyne 3E 115
Barmby Moor. E Yor 5B 100
Barmby on the Marsh. E Yor 2G 93
Barmer. Norf 2H 77
Barming. Kent 5B 40
Barming Heath. Kent 5B 40
Barmoor. Nmbd 1E 121
Barmouth. Gwyn 4F 69
Barmpton. Darl 3A 106
Barmston. E Yor 4F 101
Barmulloch. Glas 3H 127
Barnack. Pet 5H 75
Barnacle. Warw 2A 62
Barnard Castle. Dur 3D 104
Barnard Gate. Oxon 4C 50
Barnardiston. Suff 1H 53
Barnbarroch. Dum 4F 111
Barnburgh. S Yor 4E 93
Barnby. Suff 2G 67
Barnby Dun. S Yor 4G 93
Barnby in the Willows. Notts 5F 87
Barnby Moor. Notts 2D 86
Barnes. G Lon 3D 38
Barnes Street. Kent 1H 27
Barnet. G Lon 1D 38
Barnetby le Wold. N Lin 4D 94
Barney. Norf 2B 78
Barnham. Suff 3A 66
Barnham. W Sus 5A 26
Barnham Broom. Norf 5C 78
Barnhead. Ang 3F 145
Barnhill. D'dee 5D 145
Barnhill. Mor 3F 159
Barnhill. Per 1D 136
Barnhills. Dum 2E 109
Barningham. Dur 3D 105
Barningham. Suff 3B 66
Barnoldby le Beck. NE Lin 4F 95
Barnoldswick. Lanc 5A 98
Barns Green. W Sus 3C 26
Barnsley. Glos 5F 49
Barnsley. Shrp 1B 60
Barnsley. S Yor 4D 92
Barnstaple. Devn 3F 19
Barnston. Essx 4G 53
Barnston. Mers 2E 83
Barnstone. Notts 2E 75
Barnt Green. Worc 3E 61
Barnton. Ches W 3A 84
Barnwell. Cambs 5D 64
Barnwell. Nptn 2H 63
Barnwood. Glos 4D 48
Barons Cross. Here 5G 59
Barony, The. Orkn 5B 172
Barr. Dum 4G 117
Barr. S Ayr 5B 116
Barra Airport. W Isl 8C 170
Barrachan. Dum 5A 110
Barraglom. W Isl 4D 171
Barrahormid. Arg 1F 125
Barrapol. Arg 4A 138
Barrasford. Nmbd 2C 114
Barravullin. Arg 3F 133
Barregarrow. IOM 3C 108
Barrhead. E Ren 4G 127
Barrhill. S Ayr 1H 109
Barri. V Glam 5E 32
Barrington. Cambs 1D 53
Barrington. Som 1G 13
Barripper. Corn 3D 4
Barrmill. N Ayr 4E 127
Barrock. High 1E 169
Barrow. Lanc 1F 91
Barrow. Rut 4F 75
Barrow. Shrp 5A 72
Barrow. Som 3C 22
Barrow. Suff 4G 65
Barroway Drove. Norf 5E 77
Barrow Bridge. G Man 3E 91
Barrowburn. Nmbd 3C 120
Barrowby. Linc 2F 75
Barrowcliff. N Yor 1E 101
Barrow Common. N Som 5A 34
Barrowden. Rut 5G 75
Barrowford. Lanc 1G 91
Barrow Gurney. N Som 5A 34
Barrow Haven. N Lin 2D 94
Barrow Hill. Derbs 3B 86
Barrow-in-Furness. Cumb 3B 96
Barrow Nook. Lanc 4C 90
Barrows Green. Cumb 1E 97
Barrow's Green. Hal 2H 83
Barrow Street. Wilts 3D 22
Barrow upon Humber. N Lin 2D 94
Barrow upon Soar. Leics 4C 74
Barrow upon Trent. Derbs 3A 74
Barry. Ang 5E 145
Barry. V Glam 5E 32
Barry Island. V Glam 5E 32
Barsby. Leics 4D 74
Barsham. Suff 2F 67
Barston. W Mid 3G 61
Bartestree. Here 1A 48
Barthol Chapel. Abers 5F 161
Bartholomew Green. Essx 3H 53
Barthomley. Ches E 5B 84
Bartley. Hants 1B 16
Bartley Green. W Mid 2E 61
Bartlow. Cambs 1F 53
Barton. Cambs 5D 64
Barton. Ches W 5G 83
Barton. Cumb 2F 103
Barton. Glos 3F 49
Barton. IOW 4D 16
Barton. Lanc 4B 90 (nr. Ormskirk)
Barton. Lanc 1D 90 (nr. Preston)
Barton. N Som 1G 21
Barton. N Yor 4F 105
Barton. Oxon 5D 50
Barton. Torb 2F 9
Barton. Warw 5F 61
Barton Bendish. Norf 5G 77
Barton Gate. Staf 4F 73
Barton Green. Staf 4F 73
Barton Hartsthorn. Buck 2E 51
Barton Hill. N Yor 3B 100
Barton in Fabis. Notts 2C 74
Barton in the Beans. Leics 5A 74
Barton-le-Clay. C Beds 2A 52
Barton-le-Street. N Yor 2B 100
Barton-le-Willows. N Yor 3B 100
Barton Mills. Suff 3G 65
Barton on Sea. Hants 3H 15
Barton-on-the-Heath. Warw 2A 50
Barton St David. Som 3A 22
Barton Seagrave. Nptn 3F 63
Barton Stacey. Hants 2C 24
Barton Town. Devn 2G 19
Barton Turf. Norf 3F 79
Barton-under-Needwood. Staf 4F 73
Barton-upon-Humber. N Lin 2D 94
Barton Waterside. N Lin 2D 94
Barugh Green. S Yor 4D 92
Barway. Cambs 3E 65
Barwell. Leics 1B 62
Barwick. Herts 4D 53
Barwick. Som 1A 14
Barwick in Elmet. W Yor 1D 93
Baschurch. Shrp 3G 71
Bascote. Warw 4B 62
Basford Green. Staf 5D 85
Bashall Eaves. Lanc 5F 97
Bashall Town. Lanc 5G 97
Bashley. Hants 3H 15
Basildon. Essx 2B 40
Basingstoke. Hants 1E 25
Baslow. Derbs 3G 85
Bason Bridge. Som 2G 21
Bassaleg. Newp 3F 33
Bassendean. Bord 5C 130
Bassenthwaite. Cumb 1D 102
Bassett. Sotn 1C 16
Bassingbourn. Cambs 1D 52
Bassingfield. Notts 2D 74
Bassingham. Linc 5G 87
Bassingthorpe. Linc 3G 75
Bassus Green. Herts 3D 52
Basta. Shet 2G 173
Baston. Linc 4A 76
Bastonford. Worc 5C 60
Bastwick. Norf 4G 79
Batchley. Worc 4E 61
Batchworth. Herts 1B 38
Batcombe. Dors 2B 14
Batcombe. Som 3B 22
Bate Heath. Ches E 3A 84
Bath. Bath 5C 34 & 192
Bathampton. Bath 5C 34
Bathealton. Som 4D 20
Batheaston. Bath 5C 34
Bathford. Bath 5C 34
Bathgate. W Lot 3C 128
Bathley. Notts 5E 87
Bathpool. Corn 5C 10
Bathpool. Som 4F 21
Bathville. W Lot 3C 128
Bathway. Som 1A 22
Batley. W Yor 2C 92
Batsford. Glos 2G 49
Batson. Devn 5D 8
Battersby. N Yor 4C 106
Battersea. G Lon 3D 39
Battisborough Cross. Devn 4C 8
Battisford. Suff 5C 66
Battisford Tye. Suff 5C 66
Battle. E Sus 4B 28
Battle. Powy 2D 46
Battleborough. Som 1G 21
Battledown. Glos 3E 49
Battlefield. Shrp 4H 71
Battlesbridge. Essx 1B 40
Battlesden. C Beds 3H 51
Battlesea Green. Suff 3E 66
Battleton. Som 4C 20
Battram. Leic 5B 74
Battramsley. Hants 3B 16
Batt's Corner. Surr 2G 25
Bauds of Cullen. Mor 2B 160
Baugh. Arg 4B 138
Baughton. Worc 1D 49
Baughurst. Hants 5D 36
Baulking. Oxon 2B 36
Baumber. Linc 3B 88
Baunton. Glos 5F 49
Baverstock. Wilts 3F 23
Bawburgh. Norf 5D 78
Bawdeswell. Norf 3C 78
Bawdrip. Som 3G 21
Bawdsey. Suff 1G 55
Bawdsey Manor. Suff 2G 55
Bawsey. Norf 4F 77
Bawtry. S Yor 1D 86
Baxenden. Lanc 2F 91
Baxterley. Warw 1G 61
Baxter's Green. Suff 5G 65
Baybridge. Hants 4D 24
Baybridge. Nmbd 4C 114
Baycliff. Cumb 2B 96
Baydon. Wilts 4A 36
Bayford. Herts 5D 52
Bayford. Som 4C 22
Bayles. Cumb 5A 114
Baylham. Suff 5D 66
Baynard's Green. Oxon 3D 50
Bayston Hill. Shrp 5G 71
Baythorn End. Essx 1H 53
Baythorpe. Linc 1B 76
Bayton. Worc 3A 60
Bayton Common. Worc 3B 60
Bayworth. Oxon 5D 50
Beach. S Glo 4C 34
Beachampton. Buck 2F 51
Beachamwell. Norf 5G 77
Beachley. Glos 2A 34
Beacon. Devn 2E 13
Beacon End. Essx 3C 54
Beacon Hill. Surr 3G 25
Beacon's Bottom. Buck 2F 37
Beaconsfield. Buck 1A 38
Beacontree. G Lon 2F 39
Beacrabhaicg. W Isl 8D 171
Beadlam. N Yor 1A 100
Beadnell. Nmbd 2G 121
Beaford. Devn 1F 11
Beal. Nmbd 5G 131
Beal. N Yor 2F 93
Bealsmill. Corn 5D 10
Beam Hill. Staf 3G 73
Beamhurst. Staf 2E 73
Beaminster. Dors 2H 13
Beamish. Dur 4F 115
Beamond End. Buck 1A 38
Beamsley. N Yor 4C 98
Bean. Kent 3G 39
Beanacre. Wilts 5E 35
Beanley. Nmbd 3E 121
Beanshanger. Nptn 2F 51
Beaquoy. Orkn 5C 172
Beardwood. Bkbn 2E 91
Beare Green. Surr 1C 26
Bearley. Warw 4F 61
Bearpark. Dur 5F 115
Bearsbridge. Nmbd 4A 114
Bearsden. E Dun 2G 127
Bearsted. Kent 5B 40
Bearstone. Shrp 2B 72
Bearwood. Pool 3F 15
Bearwood. W Mid 2E 61
Beattock. Dum 4C 118
Beauchamp Roding. Essx 5F 53
Beauchief. S Yor 2H 85
Beaufort. Blae 4E 47
Beaulieu. Hants 2B 16
Beauly. High 4H 157
Beaumaris. IOA 3F 81
Beaumont. Cumb 4E 113
Beaumont. Essx 3E 55
Beaumont Hill. Darl 3F 105
Beaumont Leys. Leic 5C 74
Beausale. Warw 3G 61
Beauvale. Notts 1B 74

Beauworth—Bourton

Beauworth. Hants 4D 24
Beaworthy. Devn 3E 11
Beazley End. Essx 3H 53
Bebington. Mers 2F 83
Bebside. Nmbd 1F 115
Beccles. Suff 2G 67
Becconsall. Lanc 2C 90
Beckbury. Shrp 5B 72
Beckenham. G Lon 4E 39
Beckermet. Cumb 4B 102
Beckett End. Norf 1G 65
Beckfoot. Cumb 1A 96
(nr. Broughton in Furness)
Beck Foot. Cumb 5H 103
(nr. Kendal)
Beckfoot. Cumb 4C 102
(nr. Seascale)
Beckfoot. Cumb 5B 112
(nr. Silloth)
Beckford. Worc 2E 49
Beckhampton. Wilts 5F 35
Beck Hole. N Yor 4F 107
Beckingham. Linc 5F 87
Beckingham. Notts 1E 87
Beckington. Som 1D 22
Beckley. E Sus 3C 28
Beckley. Hants 3H 15
Beckley. Oxon 4D 50
Beck Row. Suff 3F 65
Beck Side. Cumb 1C 96
(nr. Cartmel)
Beckside. Cumb 1F 97
(nr. Sedbergh)
Beck Side. Cumb 1B 96
(nr. Ulverston)
Beckton. G Lon 2F 39
Beckwithshaw. N Yor 4E 99
Becontree. G Lon 2F 39
Bedale. N Yor 1E 99
Bedburn. Dur 1E 105
Bedchester. Dors 1D 14
Beddau. Rhon 3D 32
Beddgelert. Gwyn 1E 69
Beddingham. E Sus 5F 27
Beddington. G Lon 4D 39
Bedfield. Suff 4E 66
Bedford. Bed 1A 52
Bedford. G Man 4E 91
Bedham. W Sus 3B 26
Bedhampton. Hants 2F 17
Bedingfield. Suff 4D 66
Bedingham Green. Norf 1E 67
Bedlam. N Yor 3E 99
Bedlar's Green. Essx 4F 53
Bedlington. Nmbd 1F 115
Bedlinog. Mer T 5D 46
Bedminster. Bris 4A 34
Bedmond. Herts 5A 52
Bednall. Staf 4D 72
Bedrule. Bord 3A 120
Bedstone. Shrp 3F 59
Bedwas. Cphy 3E 33
Bedwellty. Cphy 5E 47
Bedworth. Warw 2A 62
Beeby. Leics 5D 74
Beech. Hants 3E 25
Beech. Staf 2C 72
Beechcliffe. W Yor 5C 98
Beech Hill. W Ber 5E 37
Beechingstoke. Wilts 1F 23
Beedon. W Ber 4C 36
Beeford. E Yor 4F 101
Beeley. Derbs 4G 85
Beelsby. NE Lin 4F 95
Beenham. W Ber 5D 36
Beeny. Corn 3B 10
Beer. Devn 4F 13
Beer. Som 3H 21
Beercrocombe. Som 4G 21
Beer Hackett. Dors 1A 14
Beesands. Devn 4E 9
Beesby. Linc 2D 88
Beeson. Devn 4E 9
Beeston. C Beds 1B 52
Beeston. Ches W 5H 83
Beeston. Norf 4B 78
Beeston. Notts 2C 74
Beeston. W Yor 1C 92
Beeston Regis. Norf 1D 78
Beeswing. Dum 3F 111
Beetham. Cumb 2D 97
Beetham. Som 1F 13
Beetley. Norf 4B 78
Beffcote. Staf 4C 72
Began. Card 3F 33
Begbroke. Oxon 4C 50
Begdale. Cambs 5D 76
Begelly. Pemb 4F 43
Beggar Hill. Essx 5G 53
Beggar's Bush. Powy 4E 59
Beggearn Huish. Som 3D 20
Beguildy. Powy 3D 58
Beighton. Norf 5F 79
Beighton. S Yor 2B 86
Beighton Hill. Derbs 5G 85
Beinn Casgro. W Isl 5G 171
Beith. N Ayr 4E 127
Bekesbourne. Kent 5F 41
Belaugh. Norf 4E 79
Belbroughton. Worc 3D 60
Belchalwell. Dors 2C 14
Belchalwell Street. Dors 2C 14
Belchamp Otten. Essx 1B 54
Belchamp St Paul. Essx 1A 54
Belchamp Walter. Essx 1B 54
Belchford. Linc 3B 88
Belcoo. Ferm 6F 177
Belfast. Bel 2H 179
Belfast International Airport.
Ant 1F 179
Belfatton. Abers 3H 161
Belford. Nmbd 1F 121
Belgrano. Cnwy 3B 82
Belhaven. E Lot 2C 130
Belhelvie. Abers 2G 153
Belhinnie. Abers 1B 152
Bellabeg. Abers 2A 152
Belladrum. High 4H 157
Bellaghy. Mag 7F 175
Bellamore. S Ayr 1H 109
Bellanaleck. Ferm 6H 177
Bellanoch. Arg 4F 133
Bell Busk. N Yor 4B 98
Belleau. Linc 3D 88
Belleek. Ferm 7B 176
Belleek. New M 7D 178
Belleheiglash. Mor 5F 159
Bell End. Worc 3D 60
Bellerby. N Yor 5E 105
Bellerby Camp. N Yor 5D 105
Bellever. Devn 5G 11
Belle Vue. Cumb 1C 102
Belle Vue. Shrp 4G 71
Bellfield. S Lan 1H 117
Belliehill. Ang 2E 145
Bellingdon. Buck 5H 51
Bellingham. Nmbd 1B 114
Bellmount. Norf 3E 77
Bellochantuy. Arg 2A 122
Bellsbank. E Ayr 4D 117
Bell's Cross. Suff 5D 66
Bellshill. N Lan 4A 128
Bellshill. Nmbd 1F 121
Bellside. N Lan 4B 128
Bellspool. Bord 1D 118
Bellsquarry. W Lot 3D 128
Bells Yew Green. E Sus 2H 27
Belmaduthy. High 3A 158
Belmesthorpe. Rut 4H 75
Belmont. Bkbn 3E 91
Belmont. Shet 1G 173
Belmont. S Ayr 3C 116
Belnacraig. Abers 2A 152
Belnie. Linc 2B 76
Belowda. Corn 2D 6
Belper. Derbs 1A 74
Belper Lane End. Derbs 1H 73
Belph. Derbs 3C 86
Belsay. Nmbd 2E 115
Belsford. Devn 3D 8
Belsize. Herts 5A 52
Belstead. Suff 1E 55
Belston. S Ayr 2C 116
Belstone. Devn 3G 11
Belstone Corner. Devn 3G 11
Belthorn. Lanc 2F 91
Beltinge. Kent 4F 41
Beltoft. N Lin 4B 94
Belton. Leics 3B 74
Belton. Linc 2G 75
Belton. Norf 5G 79
Belton. N Lin 4A 94
Belton-in-Rutland. Rut 5F 75
Beltring. Kent 1A 28
Belts of Collonach.
Abers 4D 152
Belvedere. G Lon 3F 39
Belvoir. Leics 2F 75
Bembridge. IOW 4E 17
Bemersyde. Bord 1H 119
Bemerton. Wilts 3G 23
Bempton. E Yor 2F 101
Benacre. Suff 2H 67
Ben Alder Lodge. High 1C 142
Ben Armine Lodge. High 2E 164
Benbecula Airport. W Isl 3C 170
Benbuie. Dum 5G 117
Benburb. Dngn 4C 178
Benchill. G Man 2C 84
Benderloch. Arg 5D 140
Bendish. Herts 3B 52
Bendooragh. Bmny 4F 174
Bendronaig Lodge. High 5C 156
Benenden. Kent 2C 28
Benera. High 1G 147
Benfieldside. Dur 4D 115
Bengate. Norf 3F 79
Bengeworth. Worc 1F 49
Bengrove. Glos 2E 49
Benhall Green. Suff 4F 67
Benholm. Abers 2H 145
Beningbrough. N Yor 4H 99
Benington. Herts 3C 52
Benington. Linc 1C 76
Benington Sea End. Linc 1D 76
Benllech. IOA 2E 81
Benmore Lodge. High 2H 163
Bennacott. Corn 3D 10
Bennah. Devn 4B 12
Bennecarrigan. N Ayr 3D 122
Bennethead. Cumb 2F 103
Benniworth. Linc 2B 88
Benover. Kent 1B 28
Benson. Oxon 2E 37
Benston. Shet 6F 173
Benstonhall. Orkn 4E 172
Bent. Abers 1F 145
Benthall. Shrp 5A 72
Bentham. Glos 4E 49
Benthoul. Aber 3F 153
Bentlawnt. Shrp 5F 71
Bentley. E Yor 1D 94
Bentley. Hants 2F 25
Bentley. S Yor 4F 93
Bentley. Suff 2E 54
Bentley. Warw 1G 61
Bentley. W Mid 1D 61
Bentley Heath. Herts 1D 38
Bentley Heath. W Mid 3F 61
Bentpath. Dum 5F 119
Bents. W Lot 3C 128
Bentworth. Hants 2E 25
Benvie. D'dee 5C 144
Benville. Dors 2A 14
Benwell. Tyne 3F 115
Benwick. Cambs 1C 64
Beoley. Worc 4E 61
Beoraidbeg. High 4E 147
Bepton. W Sus 1G 17
Beragh. Omag 3L 177
Berden. Essx 3E 53
Bere Alston. Devn 2A 8
Bere Ferrers. Devn 2A 8
Berepper. Corn 4D 4
Bere Regis. Dors 3D 14
Bergh Apton. Norf 5F 79
Berinsfield. Oxon 2D 36
Berkeley. Glos 2B 34
Berkhamsted. Herts 5H 51
Berkley. Som 2D 22
Berkswell. W Mid 3G 61
Bermondsey. G Lon 3E 39
Berner. Arg 4A 134
Bernisdale. High 3D 154
Berrick Salome. Oxon 2E 36
Berriedale. High 1H 165
Berrier. Cumb 2F 103
Berriew. Powy 5D 70
Berrington. Nmbd 5G 131
Berrington. Shrp 5H 71
Berrington. Worc 4H 59
Berrington Green. Worc 4H 59
Berrington Law. Nmbd 5F 131
Berrow. Som 1G 21
Berrow Green. Worc 5B 60
Berry Cross. Devn 1E 11
Berry Down Cross. Devn 2F 19
Berry Hill. Glos 4A 48
Berry Hill. Pemb 1A 44
Berryhillock. Mor 2C 160
Berrynarbor. Devn 2F 19
Berry Pomeroy. Devn 2E 9
Berryscaur. Dum 5D 118
Berry's Green. G Lon 5F 39
Bersham. Wrex 1F 71
Berthengam. Flin 3D 82
Berwick. E Sus 5G 27
Berwick Bassett. Wilts 4G 35
Berwick Hill. Nmbd 2E 115
Berwick St James. Wilts 3F 23
Berwick St John. Wilts 4E 23
Berwick St Leonard. Wilts 3E 23
Berwick-upon-Tweed.
Nmbd 4G 131
Berwyn. Den 1D 70
Bescaby. Leics 3F 75
Bescar. Lanc 3B 90
Besford. Worc 1E 49
Bessacarr. S Yor 4G 93
Bessbrook. New M 7E 178
Bessels Leigh. Oxon 5C 50
Bessingby. E Yor 3F 101
Bessingham. Norf 2D 78
Best Beech Hill. E Sus 2H 27
Besthorpe. Norf 1C 66
Besthorpe. Notts 4F 87
Bestwood Village. Notts 1C 74
Beswick. E Yor 5E 101
Betchworth. Surr 5D 38
Bethania. Cdgn 4E 57
Bethania. Gwyn 1G 69
(nr. Blaenau Ffestiniog)
Bethania. Gwyn 5F 81
(nr. Caernarfon)
Bethel. Gwyn 2B 70
(nr. Bala)
Bethel. Gwyn 4E 81
(nr. Caernarfon)
Bethel. IOA 3C 80
Bethersden. Kent 1D 28
Bethesda. Gwyn 4F 81
Bethesda. Pemb 3E 43
Bethlehem. Carm 3G 45
Bethnal Green. G Lon 2E 39
Betishill. N Lan 3A 128
Betley. Staf 1B 72
Betsham. Kent 3H 39
Betteshanger. Kent 5H 41
Bettiscombe. Dors 3H 13
Bettisfield. Wrex 2G 71
Betton. Shrp 2A 72
Betton Strange. Shrp 5H 71
Bettws. B'end 3C 32
Bettws. Newp 2F 33
Bettws Bledrws. Cdgn 5E 57
Bettws Cedewain. Powy 1D 58
Bettws Gwerfil Goch. Den 1C 70
Bettws Ifan. Cdgn 1D 44
Bettws Newydd. Mon 5G 47
Bettyhill. High 2H 167
Betws. Carm 4G 45
Betws Garmon. Gwyn 5E 81
Betws-y-Coed. Cnwy 5G 81
Betws-yn-Rhos. Cnwy 3B 82
Beulah. Cdgn 1C 44
Beulah. Powy 5B 58
Beul an Atha. Arg 3B 124
Bevendean. Brig 5E 27
Bevercotes. Notts 3E 86
Beverley. E Yor 1D 94
Beverston. Glos 2D 34
Bevington. Glos 2B 34
Bewaldeth. Cumb 1D 102
Bewcastle. Cumb 2G 113
Bewdley. Worc 3B 60
Bewerley. N Yor 3D 98
Bewholme. E Yor 4F 101
Bexfield. Norf 3C 78
Bexhill. E Sus 5B 28
Bexley. G Lon 3F 39
Bexleyheath. G Lon 3F 39
Bexleyhill. W Sus 3A 26
Bexwell. Norf 5F 77
Beyton. Suff 4B 66
Bhalton. W Isl 4C 171
Bhatarsaigh. W Isl 9B 170
Bibbington. Derbs 3E 85
Bibury. Glos 5G 49
Bicester. Oxon 3D 50
Bickenhall. Som 1F 13
Bickenhill. W Mid 2F 61
Bicker. Linc 2B 76
Bicker Bar. Linc 2B 76
Bicker Gauntlet. Linc 2B 76
Bickershaw. G Man 4E 91
Bickerstaffe. Lanc 4C 90
Bickerton. Ches E 5H 83
Bickerton. Nmbd 4D 121
Bickerton. N Yor 4G 99
Bickford. Staf 4C 72
Bickington. Devn 3F 19
(nr. Barnstaple)
Bickington. Devn 5B 12
(nr. Newton Abbot)
Bickleigh. Devn 2B 8
(nr. Plymouth)
Bickleigh. Devn 2C 12
(nr. Tiverton)
Bickleton. Devn 3F 19
Bickley. N Yor 5G 107
Bickley Moss. Ches W 1H 71
Bickmarsh. Warw 5F 61
Bicknacre. Essx 5A 54
Bicknoller. Som 3E 20
Bicknor. Kent 5C 40
Bickton. Hants 1G 15
Bicton. Here 4G 59
Bicton. Shrp 2E 59
(nr. Bishop's Castle)
Bicton. Shrp 4G 71
(nr. Shrewsbury)
Bicton Heath. Shrp 4G 71
Bidborough. Kent 1G 27
Biddenden. Kent 2C 28
Biddenden Green. Kent 1C 28
Biddenham. Bed 1A 52
Biddestone. Wilts 4D 34
Biddisham. Som 1G 21
Biddlesden. Buck 1E 51
Biddlestone. Nmbd 4D 120
Biddulph. Staf 5C 84
Biddulph Moor. Staf 5D 84
Bideford. Devn 4E 19
Bidford-on-Avon. Warw 5E 61
Bidlake. Devn 4F 11
Bidston. Mers 2E 83
Bielby. E Yor 5B 100
Bieldside. Aber 3F 153
Bierley. IOW 5D 16
Bierley. W Yor 1B 92
Bierton. Buck 4G 51
Bigbury. Devn 4C 8
Bigbury-on-Sea. Devn 4C 8
Bigby. Linc 4D 94
Biggar. Cumb 3A 96
Biggar. S Lan 1C 118
Biggin. Derbs 5F 85
(nr. Hartington)
Biggin. Derbs 1G 73
(nr. Hulland)
Biggin. N Yor 1F 93
Biggings. Shet 5C 173
Biggin Hill. G Lon 5F 39
Biggleswade. C Beds 1B 52
Bighouse. High 2A 168
Bighton. Hants 3E 24
Biglands. Cumb 4D 112
Bignall End. Staf 5C 84
Bignor. W Sus 4A 26
Bigrigg. Cumb 3B 102
Big Sand. High 1G 155
Bigton. Shet 9E 173
Bilberry. Corn 2E 6
Bilborough. Nott 1C 74
Bilbrook. Som 2D 20
Bilbrook. Staf 5C 72
Bilbrough. N Yor 5H 99
Bilbster. High 3E 169
Bilby. Notts 2D 86
Bildershaw. Dur 2F 105
Bildeston. Suff 1C 54
Billericay. Essx 1A 40
Billesdon. Leics 5E 74
Billesley. Warw 5F 61
Billingborough. Linc 2A 76
Billinge. Mers 4D 90
Billingford. Norf 3C 78
(nr. Dereham)
Billingford. Norf 3D 66
(nr. Diss)
Billingham. Stoc T 2B 106
Billinghay. Linc 5A 88
Billingley. S Yor 4E 93
Billingshurst. W Sus 3B 26
Billingsley. Shrp 2B 60
Billington. C Beds 3H 51
Billington. Lanc 1F 91
Billington. Staf 3C 72
Billockby. Norf 4G 79
Billy Row. Dur 1E 105
Bilsborrow. Lanc 5E 97
Bilsby. Linc 3D 88
Bilsham. W Sus 5A 26
Bilsington. Kent 2E 29
Bilson Green. Glos 4B 48
Bilsthorpe. Notts 4D 86
Bilston. Midl 3F 129
Bilston. W Mid 1D 60
Bilstone. Leics 5A 74
Bilting. Kent 1E 29
Bilton. E Yor 1E 95
Bilton. Nmbd 3G 121
Bilton. N Yor 4E 99
Bilton. Warw 3B 62
Bilton in Ainsty. N Yor 5G 99
Bimbister. Orkn 6C 172
Binbrook. Linc 1B 88
Binchester. Dur 1F 105
Bincombe. Dors 4B 14
Bindal. High 5G 165
Binegar. Som 2B 22
Bines Green. W Sus 4C 26
Binfield. Brac 4G 37
Binfield Heath. Oxon 4F 37
Bingfield. Nmbd 2C 114
Bingham. Notts 1E 74
Bingham's Melcombe.
Dors 2C 14
Bingley. W Yor 1B 92
Bings Heath. Shrp 4H 71
Binham. Norf 2B 78
Binley. Hants 1C 24
Binley. W Mid 3A 62
Binnegar. Dors 4D 15
Binniehill. Falk 2B 128
Binsoe. N Yor 2E 99
Binstead. IOW 3D 16
Binstead. W Sus 5A 26
Binsted. Hants 2F 25
Binton. Warw 5F 61
Bintree. Norf 3C 78
Binweston. Shrp 5F 71
Birch. Essx 4C 54
Birchall. Staf 5D 85
Bircham Newton. Norf 2G 77
Bircham Tofts. Norf 2G 77
Birchanger. Essx 3F 53
Birchburn. N Ayr 3D 122
Birch Cross. Staf 2F 73
Bircher. Here 4G 59
Birch Green. Essx 4C 54
Birchgrove. Card 4E 33
Birchgrove. Swan 3G 31
Birch Heath. Ches W 4H 83
Birch Hill. Ches W 3H 83
Birchill. Devn 2G 13
Birchington. Kent 4G 41
Birch Langley. G Man 4G 91
Birchley Heath. Warw 1G 61
Birchmoor. Warw 5G 73
Birchmoor Green. C Beds 2H 51
Birchover. Derbs 4G 85
Birch Vale. Derbs 2E 85
Birchview. Mor 5F 159
Birchwood. Linc 4G 87
Birchwood. Som 1F 13
Birchwood. Warr 1A 84
Bircotes. Notts 1D 86
Birdbrook. Essx 1H 53
Birdham. W Sus 2G 17
Birdholme. Derbs 4A 86
Birdingbury. Warw 4B 62
Birdlip. Glos 4E 49
Birdsall. N Yor 3C 100
Birds Edge. W Yor 4C 92
Birds Green. Essx 5F 53
Birdsgreen. Shrp 2B 60
Birdsmoorgate. Dors 2G 13
Birdston. E Dun 2H 127
Birdwell. S Yor 4D 92
Birdwood. Glos 4C 48
Birgham. Bord 1B 120
Birichen. High 4E 165
Birkby. Cumb 1B 102
Birkby. N Yor 1A 106
Birkdale. Mers 3B 90
Birkenhead. Mers 2F 83
Birkenhills. Abers 4E 161
Birkenshaw. N Lan 3H 127
Birkenshaw. W Yor 2C 92
Birkhall. Abers 4H 151
Birkhill. Ang 5C 144
Birkholme. Linc 3G 75
Birkin. N Yor 2F 93
Birley. Here 5G 59
Birling. Kent 4A 40
Birling. Nmbd 4G 121
Birling Gap. E Sus 5G 27
Birlingham. Worc 1E 49
Birmingham.
W Mid 2E 61 & 192
Birmingham Airport.
W Mid 2F 61 & 205
Birnam. Per 4H 143
Birsay. Orkn 5B 172
Birse. Abers 4C 152
Birsemore. Abers 4C 152
Birstall. Leics 5C 74
Birstall. W Yor 2C 92
Birstall Smithies. W Yor 2C 92
Birstwith. N Yor 4E 99
Birthorpe. Linc 2A 76
Birtle. Lanc 3G 91
Birtley. Here 4F 59
Birtley. Nmbd 2B 114
Birtley. Tyne 4F 115
Birtsmorton. Worc 2D 48
Birts Street. Worc 2C 48
Bisbrooke. Rut 1F 63
Bisham. Wind 3G 37
Bishampton. Worc 5D 61
Bish Mill. Devn 4H 19
Bishop Auckland. Dur 2F 105
Bishopbridge. Linc 1H 87
Bishopbriggs. E Dun 2H 127
Bishop Burton. E Yor 1C 94
Bishopdown. Wilts 3G 23
Bishop Middleham. Dur 1A 106
Bishopmill. Mor 2G 159
Bishop Monkton. N Yor 3F 99
Bishop Norton. Linc 1G 87
Bishops Cannings. Wilts 5F 35
Bishop's Castle. Shrp 2F 59
Bishop's Caundle. Dors 1B 14
Bishop's Cleeve. Glos 3E 49
Bishop's Down. Dors 1B 14
Bishop's Frome. Here 1B 48
Bishop's Green. Essx 4G 53
Bishop's Green. Hants 5D 36
Bishop's Hull. Som 4F 21
Bishop's Itchington.
Warw 5A 62
Bishops Lydeard. Som 4E 21
Bishop's Norton. Glos 3D 48
Bishop's Nympton. Devn 4A 20
Bishop's Offley. Staf 3B 72
Bishop's Stortford. Herts 3E 53
Bishops Sutton. Hants 3E 24
Bishop's Tachbrook.
Warw 4H 61
Bishop's Tawton. Devn 3F 19
Bishopsteignton. Devn 5C 12
Bishopstoke. Hants 1C 16
Bishopston. Swan 4E 31
Bishopstone. Buck 4G 51
Bishopstone. E Sus 5F 27
Bishopstone. Here 1H 47
Bishopstone. Swin 3H 35
Bishopstone. Wilts 4F 23
Bishopstrow. Wilts 2D 23
Bishop Sutton. Bath 1A 22
Bishop's Waltham. Hants 1D 16
Bishopswood. Som 1F 13
Bishops Wood. Staf 5C 72
Bishopsworth. Bris 5A 34
Bishop Thornton. N Yor 3E 99
Bishopthorpe. York 5H 99
Bishopton. Darl 2A 106
Bishopton. Dum 5B 110
Bishopton. N Yor 2E 99
Bishopton. Ren 2F 127
Bishopton. Warw 5F 61
Bishop Wilton. E Yor 4B 100
Bishton. Newp 3G 33
Bishton. Staf 3E 73
Bisley. Glos 5E 49
Bisley. Surr 5A 38
Bispham. Bkpl 5C 96
Bispham Green. Lanc 3C 90
Bissoe. Corn 4B 6
Bisterne. Hants 2G 15
Bisterne Close. Hants 2H 15
Bitchfield. Linc 3G 75
Bittadon. Devn 2F 19
Bittaford. Devn 3C 8
Bittering. Norf 4B 78
Bitterley. Shrp 3H 59
Bitterne. Sotn 1C 16
Bitteswell. Leics 2C 62
Bitton. S Glo 5B 34
Bix. Oxon 3F 37
Bixter. Shet 6E 173
Blaby. Leics 1C 62
Blackawton. Devn 3E 9
Black Bank. Cambs 2E 65
Black Barn. Linc 3D 76
Blackborough. Devn 2D 12
Blackborough. Norf 4F 77
Blackborough End. Norf 4F 77
Black Bourton. Oxon 5A 50
Blackboys. E Sus 3G 27
Blackbrook. Derbs 1H 73
Blackbrook. Mers 1H 83
Blackbrook. Staf 2B 72
Blackbrook. Surr 1C 26
Blackburn. Abers 2F 153
Blackburn. Bkbn 2E 91
Blackburn. W Lot 3C 128
Black Callerton. Tyne 3E 115
Black Carr. Norf 1C 66
Black Clauchrie. S Ayr 1H 109
Black Corries. High 3G 141
Black Crofts. Arg 5D 140
Black Cross. Corn 2D 6
Blackden Heath. Ches E 3B 84
Blackditch. Oxon 5C 50
Blackdog. Abers 2G 153
Black Dog. Devn 2B 12
Blackdown. Dors 2G 13
Blackdyke. Cumb 4C 112
Blacker Hill. S Yor 4D 92
Blackfen. G Lon 3F 39
Blackfield. Hants 2C 16
Blackford. Cumb 3E 113
Blackford. Per 3A 136
Blackford. Shrp 2H 59
Blackford. Som 2H 21
(nr. Burnham-on-Sea)
Blackford. Som 4B 22
(nr. Wincanton)
Blackfordby. Leics 4H 73
Blackgang. IOW 5C 16
Blackhall. Edin 2F 129
Blackhall. Ren 3F 127
Blackhall Colliery. Dur 1B 106
Blackhall Mill. Tyne 4E 115
Blackhall Rocks. Dur 1B 106
Blackham. E Sus 2F 27
Blackheath. Essx 3D 54
Blackheath. G Lon 3E 39
Blackheath. Suff 3G 67
Blackheath. Surr 1B 26
Blackheath. W Mid 2D 61
Black Heddon. Nmbd 2D 115
Blackhill. Abers 4H 161
Blackhill. High 3C 154
Black Hill. Warw 5G 61
Blackhills. Abers 2G 161
Blackhills. High 3D 158
Blackjack. Linc 2B 76
Blackland. Wilts 5F 35
Black Lane. G Man 4F 91
Blackleach. Lanc 1C 90
Blackley. G Man 4G 91
Blackley. W Yor 3B 92
Blacklunans. Per 2A 144
Blackmill. B'end 3C 32
Blackmoor. G Man 4E 91
Blackmoor. Hants 3F 25
Blackmoor Gate. Devn 2G 19
Blackmore. Essx 5G 53
Blackmore End. Essx 2H 53
Blackmore End. Herts 4B 52
Black Mount. Arg 4G 141
Blackness. Falk 2D 128
Blacknest. Hants 2F 25
Blackney. Dors 3H 13
Blacknoll. Dors 4D 14
Black Notley. Essx 3A 54
Blacko. Lanc 5A 98
Black Pill. Swan 3F 31
Blackpool. Bkpl 1B 90 & 192
Blackpool. Devn 4E 9
Blackpool Airport. Lanc 1B 90
Blackpool Corner. Devn 3G 13
Blackpool Gate. Cumb 2G 113
Blackridge. W Lot 3B 128
Blackrock. Arg 3B 124
Blackrock. Mon 4F 47
Blackrod. G Man 3E 90
Blackshaw. Dum 3B 112
Blackshaw Head. W Yor 2H 91
Blackshaw Moor. Staf 5E 85
Blackskull. Cgvn 4F 178
Blacksmith's Green. Suff 4D 66
Blacksnape. Bkbn 2F 91
Blackstone. W Sus 4D 26
Black Street. Suff 2H 67
Black Tar. Pemb 4D 43
Blackthorn. Oxon 4E 50
Blackthorpe. Suff 4B 66
Blacktoft. E Yor 2B 94
Blacktop. Aber 3F 153
Black Torrington. Devn 2E 11
Blacktown. Newp 3F 33
Blackwall Tunnel. G Lon 2E 39
Blackwater. Corn 4B 6
Blackwater. Hants 1G 25
Blackwater. IOW 4D 16
Blackwater. Som 1F 13
Blackwaterfoot. N Ayr 3C 122
Blackwatertown. Arm 4C 178
Blackwell. Darl 3F 105
Blackwell. Derbs 5B 86
(nr. Alfreton)
Blackwell. Derbs 3F 85
(nr. Buxton)
Blackwell. Som 4D 20
Blackwell. Warw 1H 49
Blackwell. Worc 3D 61
Blackwood. Cphy 2E 33
Blackwood. Dum 1G 111
Blackwood. S Lan 5A 128
Blackwood Hill. Staf 5D 84
Blacon. Ches W 4F 83
Bladnoch. Dum 4B 110
Bladon. Oxon 4C 50
Blaenannerch. Cdgn 1C 44
Blaenau Dolwyddelan.
Cnwy 5F 81
Blaenau Ffestiniog. Gwyn 1G 69
Blaenavon. Torf 5F 47
Blaenawey. Mon 4F 47
Blaen Celyn. Cdgn 5C 56
Blaen Clydach. Rhon 2C 32
Blaendulais. Neat 5B 46
Blaenffos. Pemb 1F 43
Blaengarw. B'end 2C 32
Blaen-geuffordd. Cdgn 2F 57
Blaengwrach. Neat 5B 46
Blaengwynfi. Neat 2B 32
Blaenllechau. Rhon 2D 32
Blaenpennal. Cdgn 4F 57
Blaenplwyf. Cdgn 3E 57
Blaenporth. Cdgn 1C 44
Blaenrhondda. Rhon 2C 32
Blaenwaun. Carm 2G 43
Blaen-y-coed. Carm 2H 43
Blaenycwm. Rhon 2C 32
Blagdon. N Som 1A 22
Blagdon. Torb 2E 9
Blagdon Hill. Som 1F 13
Blagill. Cumb 5A 114
Blaguegate. Lanc 4C 90
Blaich. High 1E 141
Blain. High 2A 140
Blaina. Blae 5F 47
Blair Atholl. Per 2F 143
Blair Drummond. Stir 4G 135
Blairgowrie. Per 4A 144
Blairhall. Fife 1D 128
Blairingone. Per 4B 136
Blairlogie. Stir 4H 135
Blairmore. Abers 5B 160
Blairmore. Arg 1C 126
Blairmore. High 3B 166
Blairquhanan. W Dun 1F 127
Blaisdon. Glos 4C 48
Blakebrook. Worc 3C 60
Blakedown. Worc 3C 60
Blake End. Essx 3H 53
Blakemere. Here 1G 47
Blakeney. Glos 5B 48
Blakeney. Norf 1C 78
Blakenhall. Ches E 1B 72
Blakenhall. W Mid 1C 60
Blakeshall. Worc 2C 60
Blakesley. Nptn 5D 62
Blanchland. Nmbd 4C 114
Blandford Camp. Dors 2E 15
Blandford Forum. Dors 2D 15
Blandford St Mary. Dors 2D 15
Bland Hill. N Yor 4E 98
Blandy. High 3G 167
Blanefield. Stir 2G 127
Blankney. Linc 4H 87
Blantyre. S Lan 4H 127
Blarnachfoldach. High 2E 141
Blarnalearoch. High 4F 163
Blashford. Hants 2G 15
Blaston. Leics 1F 63
Blatchbridge. Som 2C 22
Blathaisbhal. W Isl 1D 170
Blatherwycke. Nptn 1G 63
Blawith. Cumb 1B 96
Blaxhall. Suff 5F 67
Blaxton. S Yor 4G 93
Blaydon. Tyne 3E 115
Bleadney. Som 2H 21
Bleadon. N Som 1G 21
Blean. Kent 4F 41
Bleary. Cgvn 4E 178
Bleasby. Linc 2A 88
Bleasby. Notts 1E 74
Bleasby Moor. Linc 2A 88
Blebocraigs. Fife 2G 137
Bleddfa. Powy 4E 58
Bledington. Glos 3H 49
Bledlow. Buck 5F 51
Bledlow Ridge. Buck 2F 37
Blencarn. Cumb 1H 103
Blencogo. Cumb 5C 112
Blendworth. Hants 1F 17
Blenheim. Oxon 5D 50
Blennerhasset. Cumb 5C 112
Bletchingdon. Oxon 4D 50
Bletchingley. Surr 5E 39
Bletchley. Mil 2G 51
Bletchley. Shrp 2A 72
Bletherston. Pemb 2E 43
Bletsoe. Bed 5H 63
Blewbury. Oxon 3D 36
Blickling. Norf 3D 78
Blidworth. Notts 5C 86
Blindburn. Nmbd 3C 120
Blindcrake. Cumb 1C 102
Blindley Heath. Surr 1E 27
Blindmoor. Som 1F 13
Blisland. Corn 5A 10
Blissford. Hants 1G 15
Bliss Gate. Worc 3B 60
Blists Hill. Telf 5A 72
Blisworth. Nptn 5E 63
Blithbury. Staf 3E 73
Blitterlees. Cumb 4C 112
Blockley. Glos 2G 49
Blofield. Norf 5F 79
Blofield Heath. Norf 4F 79
Blo' Norton. Norf 3C 66
Bloomfield. Bord 2H 119
Blore. Staf 1F 73
Blount's Green. Staf 2E 73
Bloxham. Oxon 2C 50
Bloxholm. Linc 5H 87
Bloxwich. W Mid 5E 73
Bloxworth. Dors 3D 15
Blubberhouses. N Yor 4D 98
Blue Anchor. Som 2D 20
Blue Anchor. Swan 3E 31
Blue Bell Hill. Kent 4B 40
Blue Row. Essx 4D 54
Bluetown. Kent 5D 40
Blundeston. Suff 1H 67
Blunham. C Beds 5A 64
Blunsdon St Andrew.
Swin 3G 35
Bluntington. Worc 3C 60
Bluntisham. Cambs 3C 64
Blunts. Corn 2H 7
Blurton. Stoke 1C 72
Blyborough. Linc 1G 87
Blyford. Suff 3G 67
Blymhill. Staf 4C 72
Blymhill Lawns. Staf 4C 72
Blyth. Nmbd 1G 115
Blyth. Notts 2D 86
Blyth. Bord 5E 129
Blyth Bank. Bord 5E 129
Blyth Bridge. Bord 5E 129
Blythburgh. Suff 3G 67
Blythe Bridge. Staf 1D 72
Blythe Marsh. Staf 1D 72
Blythe, The. Staf 3E 73
Blyton. Linc 1F 87
Boardmills. Lis 4H 179
Boarhills. Fife 2H 137
Boarhunt. Hants 2E 16
Boarshead. E Sus 2G 27
Boar's Head. G Man 4D 90
Boars Hill. Oxon 5C 50
Boarstall. Buck 4E 51
Boasley Cross. Devn 3E 11
Boath. High 1H 157
Boat of Garten. High 2D 150
Bobbing. Kent 4C 40
Bobbington. Staf 1C 60
Bobbingworth. Essx 5F 53
Bocaddon. Corn 3F 7
Bocking. Essx 3A 54
Bocking Churchstreet.
Essx 3A 54
Boddam. Abers 4H 161
Boddam. Shet 10E 173
Boddington. Glos 3D 49
Bodedern. IOA 2C 80
Bodelwyddan. Den 3C 82
Bodenham. Here 5H 59
Bodenham. Wilts 4G 23
Bodewryd. IOA 1C 80
Bodfari. Den 3C 82
Bodffordd. IOA 3D 80
Bodham. Norf 1D 78
Bodiam. E Sus 3B 28
Bodicote. Oxon 2C 50
Bodieve. Corn 1D 6
Bodinnick. Corn 3F 7
Bodle Street Green.
E Sus 4A 28
Bodmin. Corn 2E 7
Bodnant. Cnwy 3H 81
Bodney. Norf 1H 65
Bodorgan. IOA 4C 80
Bodrane. Corn 2G 7
Bodsham. Kent 1F 29
Boduan. Gwyn 2C 68
Bodymoor Heath. Warw 1F 61
Bogallan. High 3A 158
Bogbrae Croft. Abers 5H 161
Bogend. S Ayr 1C 116
Boghall. Midl 3F 129
Boghall. W Lot 3C 128
Boghead. S Lan 5A 128
Bogindollo. Ang 3D 144
Bogmoor. Mor 2A 160
Bogniebrae. Abers 4C 160
Bognor Regis. W Sus 3H 17
Bograxie. Abers 2E 152
Bogside. N Lan 4B 128
Bog, The. Shrp 1F 59
Bogton. Abers 3D 160
Bogue. Dum 1D 110
Bohenie. High 5E 149
Bohortha. Corn 5C 6
Boirseam. W Isl 9C 171
Bokiddick. Corn 2E 7
Bolam. Dur 2E 105
Bolam. Nmbd 1D 115
Bolberry. Devn 5C 8
Bold Heath. Mers 2H 83
Boldon. Tyne 3G 115
Boldon Colliery. Tyne 3G 115
Boldre. Hants 3B 16
Boldron. Dur 3D 104
Bole. Notts 2E 87
Bolehall. Staf 5G 73
Bolehill. Derbs 5G 85
Bolenowe. Corn 5A 6
Boleside. Bord 1G 119
Bolham. Devn 1C 12
Bolham Water. Devn 1E 13
Bolingey. Corn 3B 6
Bollington. Ches E 3D 84
Bognor Regis
Bolney. W Sus 3D 26
Bolnhurst. Bed 5H 63
Bolshan. Ang 3F 145
Bolsover. Derbs 3B 86
Bolsterstone. S Yor 1G 85
Bolstone. Here 2A 48
Boltachan. Per 3F 143
Boltby. N Yor 1G 99
Bolton. Cumb 2H 103
Bolton. E Lot 2B 130
Bolton. E Yor 4B 100
Bolton. G Man 4F 91
Bolton. Nmbd 3F 121
Bolton Abbey. N Yor 4C 98
Bolton-by-Bowland. Lanc 5G 97
Boltonfellend. Cumb 3F 113
Boltongate. Cumb 5D 112
Bolton Green. Lanc 3D 90
Bolton-le-Sands. Lanc 3D 97
Bolton Low Houses.
Cumb 5D 112
Bolton New Houses.
Cumb 5D 112
Bolton-on-Swale. N Yor 5F 105
Bolton Percy. N Yor 5H 99
Bolton Town End. Lanc 3D 97
Bolton upon Dearne.
S Yor 4E 93
Bolton Wood Lane.
Cumb 5D 112
Bolventor. Corn 5B 10
Bomarsund. Nmbd 1F 115
Bomere Heath. Shrp 4G 71
Bonar Bridge. High 4D 164
Bonawe. Arg 5E 141
Bonby. N Lin 3D 94
Boncath. Pemb 1G 43
Bonchester Bridge.
Bord 3H 119
Bonchurch. IOW 5D 16
Bond End. Staf 4F 73
Bondleigh. Devn 2G 11
Bonds. Lanc 5D 97
Bonehill. Devn 5H 11
Bonehill. Staf 5F 73
Bo'ness. Falk 1C 128
Boney Hay. Staf 4E 73
Bonham. Wilts 3C 22
Bonhill. W Dun 2E 127
Boningale. Shrp 5C 72
Bonjedward. Bord 2A 120
Bonkle. N Lan 4B 128
Bonnanaboigh. Lim 5C 174
Bonnington. Ang 5E 145
Bonnington. Edin 3E 129
Bonnington. Kent 2E 29
Bonnybank. Fife 3F 137
Bonnybridge. Falk 1B 128
Bonnykelly. Abers 3F 161
Bonnyrigg. Midl 3G 129
Bonnyton. Ang 5C 144
Bonnytown. Fife 2H 137
Bonsall. Derbs 5G 85
Bont. Mon 4G 47
Bontddu. Gwyn 4F 69
Bont Dolgadfan. Powy 5A 70
Bontgoch. Cdgn 2F 57
Bonthorpe. Linc 3D 89
Bontnewydd. Cdgn 4F 57
Bont-newydd. Cnwy 3C 82
Bontnewydd. Gwyn 4D 81
(nr. Caernarfon)
Bont Newydd. Gwyn 1G 69
(nr. Llan Ffestiniog)
Bontuchel. Den 5C 82
Bonvilston. V Glam 4D 32
Bon-y-maen. Swan 3F 31
Booker. Buck 2G 37
Booley. Shrp 3H 71
Boorley Green. Hants 1D 16
Boosbeck. Red C 3D 106
Boot. Cumb 4C 102
Booth. W Yor 2A 92
Boothby Graffoe. Linc 5G 87
Boothby Pagnell. Linc 2G 75
Booth Green. Ches E 2D 84
Booth of Toft. Shet 4F 173
Boothstown. G Man 4F 91
Boothville. Nptn 4E 63
Booth Wood. W Yor 3A 92
Bootle. Cumb 1A 96
Bootle. Mers 1F 83
Booton. Norf 3D 78
Booze. N Yor 4D 104
Boquhan. Stir 1G 127
Boraston. Shrp 3A 60
Borden. Kent 4C 40
Borden. W Sus 4G 25
Bordlands. Bord 5E 129
Bordley. N Yor 3B 98
Bordon. Hants 3G 25
Boreham. Essx 5A 54
Boreham. Wilts 2D 23
Boreham Street.
E Sus 4A 28
Borehamwood. Herts 1C 38
Boreland. Dum 5D 118
Borestone Brae. Stir 4H 135
Boreston. Devn 3D 8
Boreton. Shrp 5H 71
Borgh. W Isl 8B 170
(on Barra)
Borgh. W Isl 3C 170
(on Benbecula)
Borgh. W Isl 1E 170
(on Berneray)
Borgh. W Isl 2G 171
(on Isle of Lewis)
Borghasdal. W Isl 9C 171
Borghastan. W Isl 3D 171
Borgh na Sgiotaig. High 1C 154
Borgie. High 3G 167
Borgue. Dum 5D 110
Borgue. High 1H 165
Borley. Essx 1B 54
Borley Green. Essx 1B 54
Borley Green. Suff 4B 66
Borlum. High 1H 149
Bornais. W Isl 6C 170
Borness. Dum 5D 110
Boroughbridge. N Yor 3F 99
Borough Green. Kent 5H 39
Borras Head. Wrex 5F 83
Borreraig. High 3A 154
Borrobol Lodge. High 1F 165
Borrodale. High 4A 154
Borrowash. Derb 2B 74
Borrowby. N Yor 1G 99
(nr. Northallerton)
Borrowby. N Yor 3E 107
(nr. Whitby)
Borrowston. High 4F 169
Borrowstonhill. Orkn 7D 172
Borrowstoun. Falk 1C 128
Borstal. Medw 4B 40
Borth. Cdgn 2F 57
Borthwick. Midl 4G 129
Borth-y-Gest. Gwyn 2E 69
Borve. High 4D 154
Borwick. Lanc 2E 97
Bosbury. Here 1B 48
Boscastle. Corn 3A 10
Boscombe. Bour 3G 15
Boscombe. Wilts 3H 23
Boscoppa. Corn 3E 7
Bosham. W Sus 2G 17
Bosherston. Pemb 5D 42
Bosley. Ches E 4D 84
Bossall. N Yor 3B 100
Bossiney. Corn 4A 10
Bossingham. Kent 1F 29
Bossington. Som 2B 20
Bostadh. W Isl 3D 171
Bostock Green. Ches W 4A 84
Boston. Linc 1C 76
Boston Spa. W Yor 5G 99
Boswarthen. Corn 3B 4
Boswinger. Corn 4D 6
Botallack. Corn 3A 4
Botany Bay. G Lon 1D 39
Botcheston. Leics 5B 74
Botesdale. Suff 3C 66
Bothal. Nmbd 1F 115
Bothampstead. W Ber 4D 36
Bothamsall. Notts 3D 86
Bothel. Cumb 1C 102
Bothenhampton. Dors 3H 13
Bothwell. S Lan 4H 127
Botley. Buck 5H 51
Botley. Hants 1D 16
Botley. Oxon 5C 50
Botloe's Green. Glos 3C 48
Botolph Claydon. Buck 3F 51
Botolphs. W Sus 5C 26
Bottacks. High 2G 157
Bottesford. Leics 2F 75
Bottesford. N Lin 4B 94
Bottisham. Cambs 4E 65
Bottlesford. Wilts 1G 23
Bottomcraig. Fife 1F 137
Bottom o' th' Moor.
G Man 3E 91
Botton. N Yor 4D 107
Botton Head. Lanc 3F 97
Bottreaux Mill. Devn 4B 20
Botus Fleming. Corn 2A 8
Botwnnog. Gwyn 2B 68
Bough Beech. Kent 1F 27
Boughrood. Powy 2E 47
Boughspring. Glos 2A 34
Boughton. Norf 5F 77
Boughton. Nptn 4E 63
Boughton. Notts 4D 86
Boughton Aluph. Kent 1E 29
Boughton Green. Kent 5B 40
Boughton Lees. Kent 1E 28
Boughton Malherbe. Kent 1C 28
Boughton Monchelsea.
Kent 5B 40
Boughton under Blean.
Kent 5E 41
Boulby. Red C 3E 107
Bouldnor. IOW 4B 16
Bouldon. Shrp 2H 59
Boulmer. Nmbd 3G 121
Boulston. Pemb 3D 42
Boultham. Linc 4G 87
Boulton. Derb 2A 74
Boundary. Staf 1D 73
Bounds. Here 2B 48
Bourn. Cambs 5C 64
Bournbrook. W Mid 2E 61
Bourne. Linc 3H 75
Bourne End. Bed 4H 63
Bourne End. Buck 3G 37
Bourne End. C Beds 1H 51
Bourne End. Herts 5A 52
Bournemouth.
Bour 3F 15 & 192
Bournemouth Airport.
Dors 3G 15
Bournes Green. Glos 5E 49
Bournes Green. S'end 2D 40
Bourne, The. Surr 2G 25
Bournheath. Worc 3D 60
Bournmoor. Dur 4G 115
Bournville. W Mid 2E 61
Bourton. Dors 3C 22
Bourton. N Som 5G 33
Bourton. Oxon 3H 35
Bourton. Shrp 1H 59
Bourton. Wilts 5F 35

Bourton on Dunsmore—Burley Woodhead

Bourton on Dunsmore. *Warw* 3B **62**
Bourton-on-the-Hill. *Glos* 2G **49**
Bourton-on-the-Water. *Glos* 3G **49**
Bousd. *Arg* 2D **138**
Bousta. *Shet* 6D **173**
Boustead Hill. *Cumb* 4D **112**
Bouth. *Cumb* 1C **96**
Bouthwaite. *N Yor* 2D **98**
Boveney. *Buck* 3A **38**
Boveridge. *Dors* 1F **15**
Boverton. *V Glam* 5C **32**
Bovey Tracey. *Devn* 5B **12**
Bovingdon. *Herts* 5A **52**
Bovingdon Green. *Buck* 3G **37**
Bovinger. *Essx* 5F **53**
Bovington Camp. *Dors* 4D **14**
Bow. *Devn* 2H **11**
Bowbank. *Dur* 2C **104**
Bow Brickhill. *Mil* 2H **51**
Bowbridge. *Glos* 5D **48**
Bowburn. *Dur* 1A **106**
Bowcombe. *IOW* 4C **16**
Bowd. *Devn* 4E **12**
Bowden. *Devn* 4E **9**
Bowden. *Bord* 1H **119**
Bowden Hill. *Wilts* 5E **35**
Bowdens. *Som* 4H **21**
Bowderdale. *Cumb* 4H **103**
Bowdon. *G Man* 2B **84**
Bower. *Nmbd* 1A **114**
Bowerchalke. *Wilts* 4F **23**
Bowerhill. *Wilts* 5E **35**
Bower Hinton. *Som* 1H **13**
Bowermadden. *High* 2E **169**
Bowers. *Staf* 2C **72**
Bowers Gifford. *Essx* 2B **40**
Bowershall. *Fife* 4C **136**
Bowertower. *High* 2E **169**
Bowes. *Dur* 3C **104**
Bowgreave. *Lanc* 5D **97**
Bowhousebog. *N Lan* 4B **128**
Bowithick. *Corn* 4B **10**
Bowland Bridge. *Cumb* 1D **96**
Bowlees. *Dur* 2C **104**
Bowley. *Here* 5H **59**
Bowlhead Green. *Surr* 2A **26**
Bowling. *W Dun* 2F **127**
Bowling. *W Yor* 1B **92**
Bowling Bank. *Wrex* 1F **71**
Bowling Green. *Worc* 5C **60**
Bowlish. *Som* 2B **22**
Bowmanstead. *Cumb* 5E **102**
Bowmore. *Arg* 4B **124**
Bowness-on-Solway. *Cumb* 3D **112**
Bowness-on-Windermere. *Cumb* 5F **103**
Bow of Fife. *Fife* 2F **137**
Bowriefauld. *Ang* 4E **145**
Bowscale. *Cumb* 1E **103**
Bowsden. *Nmbd* 5F **131**
Bowside Lodge. *High* 2A **168**
Bowston. *Cumb* 5F **103**
Bow Street. *Cdgn* 2F **57**
Bowthorpe. *Norf* 5D **78**
Box. *Glos* 5D **48**
Box. *Wilts* 5D **34**
Boxbush. *Glos* 3B **48**
Box End. *Bed* 1A **52**
Boxford. *Suff* 1C **54**
Boxford. *W Ber* 4C **36**
Boxgrove. *W Sus* 5A **26**
Boxley. *Kent* 5B **40**
Boxmoor. *Herts* 5A **52**
Box's Shop. *Corn* 2C **10**
Boxted. *Essx* 2C **54**
Boxted. *Suff* 5H **65**
Boxted Cross. *Essx* 2D **54**
Boxworth. *Cambs* 4C **64**
Boxworth End. *Cambs* 4C **64**
Boyden End. *Suff* 5G **65**
Boyden Gate. *Kent* 4G **41**
Boylestone. *Derbs* 2F **73**
Boylestonfield. *Derbs* 2F **73**
Boyndlie. *Abers* 2D **160**
Boynton. *E Yor* 3F **101**
Boys Hill. *Dors* 1B **14**
Boythorpe. *Derbs* 4A **86**
Boyton. *Corn* 3D **10**
Boyton. *Suff* 1G **55**
Boyton. *Wilts* 3E **23**
Boyton Cross. *Essx* 5G **53**
Boyton End. *Essx* 2G **53**
Boyton End. *Suff* 1H **53**
Bozeat. *Nptn* 5G **63**
Braaid. *IOM* 4C **108**
Braal Castle. *High* 2D **168**
Brabling Green. *Suff* 4E **67**
Brabourne. *Kent* 1F **29**
Brabourne Lees. *Kent* 1E **29**
Brabster. *High* 2F **169**
Bracadale. *High* 5C **154**
Bracara. *High* 4F **147**
Braceborough. *Linc* 4H **75**
Bracebridge. *Linc* 4G **87**
Bracebridge Heath. *Linc* 4G **87**
Braceby. *Linc* 2H **75**
Bracewell. *Lanc* 5A **98**
Brackenber. *Cumb* 3A **104**
Brackenfield. *Derbs* 5A **86**
Brackenlands. *Cumb* 5D **112**
Brackenthwaite. *Cumb* 5D **112**
Brackenthwaite. *N Yor* 4E **99**
Brackla. *B'end* 4C **32**
Brackla. *High* 3C **158**
Bracklesham. *W Sus* 3G **17**
Brackletter. *High* 5D **148**
Brackley. *Nptn* 2D **50**
Brackley Hatch. *Nptn* 1E **51**
Brackloch. *High* 1F **163**
Bracknell. *Brac* 5G **37**
Braco. *Per* 3H **135**
Bracobrae. *Mor* 3C **160**
Bracon. *N Lin* 4A **94**
Bracon Ash. *Norf* 1D **66**
Bradbourne. *Derbs* 5G **85**
Bradbury. *Dur* 2A **106**
Bradda. *IOM* 4A **108**
Bradden. *Nptn* 1E **51**
Bradenham. *Buck* 2G **37**
Bradenham. *Norf* 5B **78**
Bradenstoke. *Wilts* 4F **35**
Bradfield. *Essx* 2E **55**
Bradfield. *Norf* 2E **79**
Bradfield. *W Ber* 4E **36**
Bradfield Combust. *Suff* 5A **66**
Bradfield Green. *Ches E* 5A **84**
Bradfield Heath. *Essx* 3E **55**
Bradfield St Clare. *Suff* 5B **66**
Bradfield St George. *Suff* 4B **66**
Bradford. *Derbs* 4G **85**
Bradford. *Devn* 2E **11**
Bradford. *Nmbd* 1F **121**
Bradford. *W Yor* 1B **92** & **192**
Bradford Abbas. *Dors* 1A **14**
Bradford Barton. *Devn* 1B **12**
Bradford Leigh. *Wilts* 5D **34**
Bradford-on-Avon. *Wilts* 5D **34**
Bradford-on-Tone. *Som* 4E **21**
Bradford Peverell. *Dors* 3B **14**
Bradiford. *Devn* 3F **19**
Brading. *IOW* 4E **16**
Bradley. *Ches W* 3H **83**
Bradley. *Derbs* 1G **73**
Bradley. *Glos* 2C **34**
Bradley. *Hants* 2E **25**
Bradley. *NE Lin* 4F **95**
Bradley. *N Yor* 1C **98**
Bradley. *Staf* 4C **72**
Bradley. *W Mid* 1D **60**
Bradley. *W Yor* 2B **92**
Bradley. *Wrex* 5F **83**
Bradley Cross. *Som* 1H **21**
Bradley Green. *Ches W* 1H **71**
Bradley Green. *Som* 3F **21**
Bradley Green. *Warw* 5G **73**
Bradley Green. *Worc* 4D **61**
Bradley in the Moors. *Staf* 1E **73**
Bradley Mount. *Ches E* 3D **84**
Bradley Stoke. *S Glo* 3B **34**
Bradlow. *Here* 2C **48**
Bradmore. *Notts* 2C **74**
Bradmore. *W Mid* 1C **60**
Bradninch. *Devn* 2D **12**
Bradnop. *Staf* 5E **85**
Bradpole. *Dors* 3H **13**
Bradshaw. *G Man* 3F **91**
Bradstone. *Devn* 4D **11**
Bradwall Green. *Ches E* 4B **84**
Bradway. *S Yor* 2H **85**
Bradwell. *Derbs* 2F **85**
Bradwell. *Essx* 3B **54**
Bradwell. *Mil* 2G **51**
Bradwell. *Norf* 5H **79**
Bradwell-on-Sea. *Essx* 5D **54**
Bradwell Waterside. *Essx* 5C **54**
Bradworthy. *Devn* 1D **10**
Brae. *High* 5C **162**
Brae. *Shet* 5E **173**
Braeantra. *High* 1H **157**
Braefield. *High* 5G **157**
Braefindon. *High* 3A **158**
Braegrum. *Per* 1C **136**
Braehead. *Ang* 3F **145**
Braehead. *Dum* 4B **110**
Braehead. *Mor* 4G **159**
Braehead. *Orkn* 3D **172**
Braehead. *S Lan* 1H **117** (nr. Coalburn)
Braehead. *S Lan* 4C **128** (nr. Forth)
Braehoulland. *Shet* 4D **173**
Braemar. *Abers* 4F **151**
Braemore. *High* 5C **168** (nr. Dunbeath)
Braemore. *High* 1D **156** (nr. Ullapool)
Brae of Achnahaird. *High* 2E **163**
Brae Roy Lodge. *High* 4F **149**
Braeside. *Abers* 5G **161**
Braeside. *Inv* 2D **126**
Braes of Coul. *Ang* 3B **144**
Braeswick. *Orkn* 4F **172**
Braetongue. *High* 3F **167**
Braeval. *Stir* 3E **135**
Braevallich. *Arg* 3G **133**
Braewick. *Shet* 6E **173**
Brafferton. *Darl* 2F **105**
Brafferton. *N Yor* 2G **99**
Brafield-on-the-Green. *Nptn* 5F **63**
Bragar. *W Isl* 3E **171**
Bragbury End. *Herts* 3C **52**
Bragleenbeg. *Arg* 1G **133**
Braichmelyn. *Gwyn* 4F **81**
Braides. *Lanc* 4D **96**
Braidwood. *S Lan* 5B **128**
Braigo. *Arg* 3A **124**
Brailsford. *Derbs* 1G **73**
Braintree. *Essx* 3A **54**
Braiseworth. *Suff* 3D **66**
Braishfield. *Hants* 4B **24**
Braithwaite. *Cumb* 2D **102**
Braithwaite. *S Yor* 3G **93**
Braithwaite. *W Yor* 5C **98**
Braithwell. *S Yor* 1C **86**
Brakefield Green. *Norf* 5C **78**
Bramber. *W Sus* 4C **26**
Brambledown. *Kent* 3D **40**
Brambridge. *Hants* 4C **24**
Bramcote. *Notts* 2C **74**
Bramcote. *Warw* 2B **62**
Bramdean. *Hants* 4E **24**
Bramerton. *Norf* 5E **79**
Bramfield. *Herts* 4C **52**
Bramfield. *Suff* 3F **67**
Bramford. *Suff* 1E **54**
Bramhall. *G Man* 2C **84**
Bramham. *W Yor* 5G **99**
Bramhope. *W Yor* 5E **99**
Bramley. *Hants* 1E **25**
Bramley. *S Yor* 1B **86**
Bramley. *Surr* 1B **26**
Bramley. *W Yor* 1C **92**
Bramley Green. *Hants* 1E **25**
Bramley Head. *N Yor* 4D **98**
Bramley Vale. *Derbs* 4B **86**
Bramling. *Kent* 5G **41**
Brampford Speke. *Devn* 3C **12**
Brampton. *Cambs* 3B **64**
Brampton. *Cumb* 2H **103** (nr. Appleby-in-Westmorland)
Brampton. *Cumb* 3G **113** (nr. Carlisle)
Brampton. *Linc* 3F **87**
Brampton. *Norf* 3E **78**
Brampton. *S Yor* 4E **93**
Brampton. *Suff* 2G **67**
Brampton Abbotts. *Here* 3B **48**
Brampton Ash. *Nptn* 2E **63**
Brampton Bryan. *Here* 3F **59**
Brampton en le Morthen. *S Yor* 2B **86**
Bramshall. *Staf* 2E **73**
Bramshaw. *Hants* 1A **16**
Bramshill. *Hants* 5F **37**
Bramshott. *Hants* 3G **25**
Branault. *High* 2G **139**
Brancaster. *Norf* 1G **77**
Brancaster Staithe. *Norf* 1G **77**
Brancepeth. *Dur* 1F **105**
Branch End. *Nmbd* 3D **114**
Branchill. *Mor* 3E **159**
Brand End. *Linc* 1C **76**
Branderburgh. *Mor* 1G **159**
Brandesburton. *E Yor* 5F **101**
Brandeston. *Suff* 4E **67**
Brand Green. *Glos* 3C **48**
Brandhill. *Shrp* 3G **59**
Brandis Corner. *Devn* 2E **11**
Brandish Street. *Som* 2C **20**
Brandiston. *Norf* 3D **78**
Brandon. *Dur* 1F **105**
Brandon. *Linc* 1G **75**
Brandon. *Nmbd* 3E **121**
Brandon. *Suff* 2G **65**
Brandon. *Warw* 3B **62**
Brandon Bank. *Cambs* 2F **65**
Brandon Creek. *Norf* 1F **65**
Brandon Parva. *Norf* 5C **78**
Brandsby. *N Yor* 2H **99**
Brandy Wharf. *Linc* 1H **87**
Brane. *Corn* 4B **4**
Bran End. *Essx* 3G **53**
Branksome. *Pool* 3F **15**
Bransbury. *Hants* 2C **24**
Bransby. *Linc* 3G **87**
Branscombe. *Devn* 4E **13**
Bransford. *Worc* 5B **60**
Bransgore. *Hants* 3G **15**
Bransholme. *Hull* 1D **94**
Bransley. *Shrp* 3A **60**
Branston. *Leics* 3F **75**
Branston. *Linc* 4H **87**
Branston. *Staf* 3G **73**
Branston Booths. *Linc* 4H **87**
Branstone. *IOW* 4D **16**
Bransty. *Cumb* 3A **102**
Brant Broughton. *Linc* 5G **87**
Brantham. *Suff* 2E **54**
Branthwaite. *Cumb* 1D **102** (nr. Caldbeck)
Branthwaite. *Cumb* 2B **102** (nr. Workington)
Brantingham. *E Yor* 2C **94**
Branton. *Nmbd* 3E **121**
Branton. *S Yor* 4G **93**
Branton Green. *N Yor* 3G **99**
Branxholme. *Bord* 3G **119**
Branxton. *Nmbd* 1C **120**
Brassington. *Derbs* 5G **85**
Brasted. *Kent* 5F **39**
Brasted Chart. *Kent* 5F **39**
Bratch, The. *Staf* 1C **60**
Brathens. *Abers* 4D **152**
Bratoft. *Linc* 4D **88**
Brattleby. *Linc* 2G **87**
Bratton. *Som* 2C **20**
Bratton. *Telf* 4A **72**
Bratton. *Wilts* 1E **23**
Bratton Clovelly. *Devn* 3E **11**
Bratton Fleming. *Devn* 3G **19**
Bratton Seymour. *Som* 4B **22**
Braughing. *Herts* 3D **53**
Braulen Lodge. *High* 5E **157**
Braunston. *Nptn* 4C **62**
Braunstone Town. *Leic* 5C **74**
Braunston-in-Rutland. *Rut* 5F **75**
Braunton. *Devn* 3E **19**
Brawby. *N Yor* 2B **100**
Brawl. *High* 2A **168**
Brawlbin. *High* 3C **168**
Bray. *Wind* 3A **38**
Braybrooke. *Nptn* 2E **63**
Brayford. *Devn* 3G **19**
Bray Shop. *Corn* 5D **10**
Braystones. *Cumb* 4B **102**
Brayton. *N Yor* 1G **93**
Bray Wick. *Wind* 4G **37**
Brazacott. *Corn* 3C **10**
Brea. *Corn* 4A **6**
Breach. *W Sus* 2F **17**
Breachwood Green. *Herts* 3B **52**
Breacleit. *W Isl* 4D **171**
Breaden Heath. *Shrp* 2G **71**
Breadsall. *Derbs* 1A **74**
Breadstone. *Glos* 5C **48**
Breage. *Corn* 4D **4**
Breakachy. *High* 4G **157**
Breakish. *High* 1E **147**
Bream. *Glos* 5B **48**
Breamore. *Hants* 1G **15**
Bream's Meend. *Glos* 5B **48**
Brean. *Som* 1F **21**
Breanais. *W Isl* 5B **171**
Brearton. *N Yor* 3F **99**
Breascleit. *W Isl* 4E **171**
Breaston. *Derbs* 2B **74**
Brecais Àrd. *High* 1E **147**
Brecais Iosal. *High* 1E **147**
Brechfa. *Carm* 2F **45**
Brechin. *Ang* 3F **145**
Breckles. *Norf* 1B **66**
Brecon. *Powy* 3D **46**
Brecon Beacons. *Powy* 3C **46**
Bredbury. *G Man* 1D **84**
Brede. *E Sus* 4C **28**
Bredenbury. *Here* 5A **60**
Breden's Norton. *Worc* 2E **49**
Bredfield. *Suff* 5E **67**
Bredgar. *Kent* 4C **40**
Bredhurst. *Kent* 4B **40**
Bredicot. *Worc* 5D **60**
Bredon. *Worc* 2E **49**
Bredwardine. *Here* 1G **47**
Breedon on the Hill. *Leics* 3B **74**
Breibhig. *W Isl* 9B **170** (on Barra)
Breibhig. *W Isl* 4G **171** (on Isle of Lewis)
Breich. *W Lot* 3C **128**
Breightmet. *G Man* 3F **91**
Breighton. *E Yor* 1H **93**
Breinton. *Here* 2H **47**
Breinton Common. *Here* 2H **47**
Breiwick. *Shet* 7F **173**
Brelston Green. *Here* 3A **48**
Bremhill. *Wilts* 4E **35**
Brenachie. *High* 1B **158**
Brenchley. *Kent* 1A **28**
Brendon. *Devn* 2A **20**
Brent Cross. *G Lon* 2D **38**
Brent Eleigh. *Suff* 1C **54**
Brentford. *G Lon* 3C **38**
Brentingby. *Leics* 4E **75**
Brent Knoll. *Som* 1G **21**
Brent Pelham. *Herts* 2E **53**
Brentwood. *Essx* 1H **39**
Brenzett. *Kent* 3E **28**
Brereton. *Staf* 4E **73**
Brereton Cross. *Staf* 4E **73**
Brereton Green. *Ches E* 4B **84**
Brereton Heath. *Ches E* 4C **84**
Bressingham. *Norf* 2C **66**
Bretby. *Derbs* 3G **73**
Bretford. *Warw* 3B **62**
Bretforton. *Worc* 1F **49**
Bretherdale Head. *Cumb* 4G **103**
Bretherton. *Lanc* 2C **90**
Brettabister. *Shet* 6F **173**
Brettenham. *Norf* 2B **66**
Brettenham. *Suff* 5B **66**
Bretton. *Flin* 4F **83**
Bretton. *Pet* 5A **76**
Brewer Street. *Surr* 5E **39**
Brewlands Bridge. *Ang* 2A **144**
Brewood. *Staf* 5C **72**
Briantspuddle. *Dors* 3D **14**
Bricket Wood. *Herts* 5B **52**
Bricklehampton. *Worc* 1E **49**
Bride. *IOM* 1D **108**
Bridekirk. *Cumb* 1C **102**
Bridell. *Pemb* 1B **44**
Bridestowe. *Devn* 4F **11**
Brideswell. *Abers* 5C **160**
Bridford. *Devn* 4B **12**
Bridge. *Corn* 4A **6**
Bridge. *Kent* 5F **41**
Bridge. *Som* 2G **13**
Bridge End. *Bed* 5H **63**
Bridge End. *Cumb* 5D **102** (nr. Broughton in Furness)
Bridge End. *Cumb* 5E **113** (nr. Dalston)
Bridge End. *Linc* 2A **76**
Bridge End. *Shet* 8E **173**
Bridgefoot. *Ang* 5C **144**
Bridgefoot. *Cumb* 2B **102**
Bridge Green. *Essx* 2E **53**
Bridgehampton. *Som* 4A **22**
Bridge Hewick. *N Yor* 2F **99**
Bridgehill. *Dur* 4D **115**
Bridgemary. *Hants* 2D **16**
Bridgemere. *Ches E* 1B **72**
Bridgemont. *Derbs* 2E **85**
Bridgend. *Abers* 5C **160** (nr. Huntly)
Bridgend. *Abers* 5H **161** (nr. Peterhead)
Bridgend. *Ang* 2E **145** (nr. Brechin)
Bridgend. *Ang* 4C **144** (nr. Kirriemuir)
Bridgend. *Arg* 4F **133** (nr. Lochgilphead)
Bridgend. *Arg* 3B **124** (on Islay)
Bridgend. *B'end* 3C **32**
Bridgend. *Cumb* 3F **103**
Bridgend. *Devn* 4B **8**
Bridgend. *Fife* 2F **137**
Bridgend. *High* 3F **157**
Bridgend. *Mor* 5A **160**
Bridgend. *Per* 1D **136**
Bridgend. *W Lot* 2D **128**
Bridgend of Lintrathen. *Ang* 3B **144**
Bridgeness. *Falk* 1D **128**
Bridge of Alford. *Abers* 2C **152**
Bridge of Allan. *Stir* 4G **135**
Bridge of Avon. *Mor* 5F **159**
Bridge of Awe. *Arg* 1H **133**
Bridge of Balgie. *Per* 4C **142**
Bridge of Brown. *High* 1F **151**
Bridge of Cally. *Per* 3A **144**
Bridge of Canny. *Abers* 4D **152**
Bridge of Dee. *Dum* 3E **111**
Bridge of Don. *Aber* 2G **153**
Bridge of Dun. *Ang* 3F **145**
Bridge of Dye. *Abers* 5D **152**
Bridge of Earn. *Per* 2D **136**
Bridge of Ericht. *Per* 3C **142**
Bridge of Feugh. *Abers* 4E **152**
Bridge of Forss. *High* 2C **168**
Bridge of Gairn. *Abers* 4A **152**
Bridge of Gaur. *Per* 3C **142**
Bridge of Muchalls. *Abers* 4F **153**
Bridge of Oich. *High* 3F **149**
Bridge of Orchy. *Arg* 5H **141**
Bridge of Walls. *Shet* 6D **173**
Bridge of Weir. *Ren* 3E **127**
Bridge Reeve. *Devn* 1G **11**
Bridgerule. *Devn* 2C **10**
Bridge Sollers. *Here* 1H **47**
Bridge Street. *Suff* 1B **54**
Bridgetown. *Devn* 2E **9**
Bridgetown. *Som* 3C **20**
Bridge Town. *Warw* 5G **61**
Bridge Trafford. *Ches W* 3G **83**
Bridgeyate. *S Glo* 4B **34**
Bridgham. *Norf* 2B **66**
Bridgnorth. *Shrp* 1B **60**
Bridgtown. *Staf* 5D **73**
Bridgwater. *Som* 3G **21**
Bridister. *Shet* 6D **173**
Bridlington. *E Yor* 3F **101**
Bridport. *Dors* 3H **13**
Bridstow. *Here* 3A **48**
Brierfield. *Lanc* 1G **91**
Brierley. *Glos* 4B **48**
Brierley. *Here* 5G **59**
Brierley. *S Yor* 3E **93**
Brierley Hill. *W Mid* 2D **60**
Brierton. *Hart* 1B **106**
Briestfield. *W Yor* 3C **92**
Brigg. *N Lin* 4D **94**
Briggate. *Norf* 3F **79**
Briggswath. *N Yor* 4F **107**
Brigham. *Cumb* 1B **102**
Brigham. *E Yor* 4E **101**
Brighouse. *W Yor* 2B **92**
Brighstone. *IOW* 4C **16**
Brightgate. *Derbs* 5G **85**
Brighthampton. *Oxon* 5B **50**
Brightholmlee. *S Yor* 1G **85**
Brightley. *Devn* 3G **11**
Brightling. *E Sus* 3A **28**
Brightlingsea. *Essx* 4D **54**
Brighton. *Brig* 5E **27** & **192**
Brighton. *Corn* 3D **6**
Brighton Hill. *Hants* 2E **24**
Brightons. *Falk* 2C **128**
Brightwalton. *W Ber* 4C **36**
Brightwalton Green. *W Ber* 4C **36**
Brightwell. *Suff* 1F **55**
Brightwell Baldwin. *Oxon* 2E **37**
Brightwell-cum-Sotwell. *Oxon* 2D **36**
Brigmerston. *Wilts* 2G **23**
Brignall. *Dur* 3D **104**
Brig o'Turk. *Stir* 3E **135**
Brigsley. *NE Lin* 4F **95**
Brigsteer. *Cumb* 1D **97**
Brigstock. *Nptn* 2G **63**
Brill. *Buck* 4E **51**
Brill. *Corn* 4E **5**
Brilley. *Here* 1F **47**
Brimaston. *Pemb* 2D **42**
Brimfield. *Here* 4H **59**
Brimington. *Derbs* 3B **86**
Brimley. *Devn* 5B **12**
Brimpsfield. *Glos* 4E **49**
Brimpton. *W Ber* 5D **36**
Brims. *Orkn* 9B **172**
Brimscombe. *Glos* 5D **48**
Brimstage. *Mers* 2F **83**
Brincliffe. *S Yor* 2H **85**
Brind. *E Yor* 1H **93**
Brindister. *Shet* 8F **173**
Brindle. *Lanc* 2E **90**
Brindley. *Ches E* 5H **83**
Brindley Ford. *Stoke* 5C **84**
Brineton. *Staf* 4C **72**
Bringhurst. *Leics* 1F **63**
Brington. *Cambs* 3H **63**
Brinian. *Orkn* 5D **172**
Briningham. *Norf* 2C **78**
Brinkhill. *Linc* 3C **88**
Brinkley. *Cambs* 5F **65**
Brinklow. *Warw* 3B **62**
Brinkworth. *Wilts* 3F **35**
Brinscall. *Lanc* 2E **91**
Brinscombe. *Som* 1H **21**
Brinsley. *Notts* 1B **74**
Brinsty Common. *Here* 5A **60**
Brinsworth. *S Yor* 2B **86**
Brinton. *Norf* 2C **78**
Brisco. *Cumb* 4F **113**
Brisley. *Norf* 3B **78**
Brislington. *Bris* 4B **34**
Brissenden Green. *Kent* 2D **28**
Bristol. *Bris* 4A **34** & **193**
Bristol International Airport. *N Som* 5A **34**
Briston. *Norf* 2C **78**
Britannia. *Lanc* 2G **91**
Britford. *Wilts* 4G **23**
Brithdir. *Cphy* 5E **47**
Brithdir. *Cdgn* 1D **44**
Brithdir. *Gwyn* 4G **69**
Briton Ferry. *Neat* 3G **31**
Britwell Salome. *Oxon* 2E **37**
Brixham. *Torb* 3F **9**
Brixton. *Devn* 3B **8**
Brixton. *G Lon* 3E **39**
Brixton Deverill. *Wilts* 3D **22**
Brixworth. *Nptn* 3E **63**
Brize Norton. *Oxon* 5B **50**
Broad Alley. *Worc* 4C **60**
Broad Blunsdon. *Swin* 2G **35**
Broadbottom. *G Man* 1D **85**
Broadbridge. *W Sus* 2G **17**
Broadbridge Heath. *W Sus* 2C **26**
Broad Campden. *Glos* 2G **49**
Broad Chalke. *Wilts* 4F **23**
Broadclyst. *Devn* 3C **12**
Broadfield. *Inv* 2E **127**
Broadfield. *Pemb* 4F **43**
Broadfield. *W Sus* 2D **26**
Broadford. *High* 1E **147**
Broadford Bridge. *W Sus* 3B **26**
Broadgate. *Cumb* 1A **96**
Broad Green. *Cambs* 5F **65**
Broad Green. *C Beds* 1H **51**
Broad Green. *Worc* 3D **61** (nr. Bromsgrove)
Broad Green. *Worc* 5B **60** (nr. Worcester)
Broadhaven. *High* 3F **169**
Broad Haven. *Pemb* 3C **42**
Broadheath. *G Man* 2B **84**
Broad Heath. *Staf* 3C **72**
Broadheath. *Worc* 4A **60**
Broadhembury. *Devn* 2E **12**
Broadhempston. *Devn* 2E **9**
Broad Hill. *Cambs* 3E **65**
Broad Hinton. *Wilts* 4G **35**
Broadholm. *Derbs* 1A **74**
Broadholme. *Linc* 3F **87**
Broadlay. *Carm* 5D **44**
Broad Laying. *Hants* 5C **36**
Broadley. *Lanc* 3G **91**
Broadley. *Mor* 2A **160**
Broadley Common. *Essx* 5E **53**
Broad Marston. *Worc* 1G **49**
Broadmayne. *Dors* 4C **14**
Broadmere. *Hants* 2E **24**
Broadmoor. *Pemb* 4E **43**
Broad Oak. *Carm* 3F **45**
Broad Oak. *Cumb* 5C **102**
Broad Oak. *Devn* 3D **12**
Broadoak. *Dors* 3H **13** (nr. Bridport)
Broad Oak. *Dors* 1C **14** (nr. Sturminster Newton)
Broad Oak. *E Sus* 4C **28** (nr. Hastings)
Broad Oak. *E Sus* 3H **27** (nr. Heathfield)
Broadoak. *Glos* 4B **48**
Broadoak. *Hants* 1C **16**
Broad Oak. *Here* 3H **47**
Broad Oak. *Kent* 4F **41**
Broadrashes. *Mor* 3B **160**
Broads. *Norf* 5G **79**
Broadsea. *Abers* 2G **161**
Broad's Green. *Essx* 4G **53**
Broadshard. *Som* 1H **13**
Broadstairs. *Kent* 4H **41**
Broadstone. *Pool* 3F **15**
Broadstone. *Shrp* 2H **59**
Broad Street. *E Sus* 4C **28**
Broad Street. *Kent* 1F **29** (nr. Ashford)
Broad Street. *Kent* 5C **40** (nr. Maidstone)
Broad Street Green. *Essx* 5B **54**
Broad, The. *Here* 4G **59**
Broad Town. *Wilts* 4F **35**
Broadwas. *Worc* 5B **60**
Broadwath. *Cumb* 4F **113**
Broadway. *Carm* 5D **45** (nr. Kidwelly)
Broadway. *Carm* 3G **43** (nr. Laugharne)
Broadway. *Pemb* 3C **42**
Broadway. *Som* 1G **13**
Broadway. *Suff* 3F **67**
Broadway. *Worc* 2G **49**
Broadwell. *Glos* 4A **48** (nr. Cinderford)
Broadwell. *Glos* 3H **49** (nr. Stow-on-the-Wold)
Broadwell. *Oxon* 5A **50**
Broadwell. *Warw* 4B **62**
Broadwell House. *Nmbd* 4C **114**
Broadwey. *Dors* 4B **14**
Broadwindsor. *Dors* 2H **13**
Broadwoodkelly. *Devn* 2G **11**
Broadwoodwidger. *Devn* 4E **11**
Broallan. *High* 4G **157**
Brobury. *Here* 1G **47**
Brochel. *High* 4E **155**
Brockaghboy. *Cole* 5E **174**
Brockamin. *Worc* 5B **60**
Brockbridge. *Hants* 1E **16**
Brockdish. *Norf* 3E **66**
Brockencote. *Worc* 3C **60**
Brockenhurst. *Hants* 2A **16**
Brocketsbrae. *S Lan* 1H **117**
Brockford Street. *Suff* 4D **66**
Brockhall. *Nptn* 4D **62**
Brockham. *Surr* 1C **26**
Brockhampton. *Glos* 3E **49** (nr. Bishop's Cleeve)
Brockhampton. *Glos* 3F **49** (nr. Sevenhampton)
Brockhampton. *Here* 2A **48**
Brockhill. *Bord* 2F **119**
Brockholes. *W Yor* 3B **92**
Brockhouse. *S Yor* 2C **86**
Brockhurst. *Hants* 2D **16**
Brocklesby. *Linc* 3E **95**
Brockley. *N Som* 5H **33**
Brockley Corner. *Suff* 3H **65**
Brockley Green. *Suff* 1H **53** (nr. Bury St Edmunds)
Brockley Green. *Suff* 5H **65** (nr. Haverhill)
Brockleymoor. *Cumb* 1F **103**
Brockmoor. *W Mid* 2C **60**
Brockton. *Shrp* 2F **59** (nr. Bishop's Castle)
Brockton. *Shrp* 5B **72** (nr. Madeley)
Brockton. *Shrp* 1H **59** (nr. Much Wenlock)
Brockton. *Shrp* 5F **71** (nr. Pontesbury)
Brockton. *Staf* 2C **72**
Brockton. *Telf* 4B **72**
Brockweir. *Glos* 5A **48**
Brockworth. *Glos* 4D **49**
Brocton. *Staf* 4D **72**
Brodick. *N Ayr* 2E **123**
Brodie. *Mor* 3D **159**
Brodiesord. *Abers* 3C **160**
Brodsworth. *S Yor* 4F **93**
Brogaig. *High* 2D **154**
Brogborough. *C Beds* 2H **51**
Brokenborough. *Wilts* 3E **35**
Broken Cross. *Ches E* 3C **84**
Bromborough. *Mers* 2F **83**
Bromdon. *Shrp* 2A **60**
Brome. *Suff* 3D **66**
Brome Street. *Suff* 3D **66**
Bromeswell. *Suff* 5F **67**
Bromfield. *Cumb* 5C **112**
Bromfield. *Shrp* 3G **59**
Bromford. *W Mid* 1F **61**
Bromham. *Bed* 5H **63**
Bromham. *Wilts* 5E **35**
Bromley. *G Lon* 4F **39**
Bromley. *Herts* 3E **53**
Bromley. *Shrp* 1B **60**
Bromley Cross. *G Man* 3F **91**
Bromley Green. *Kent* 2D **28**
Bromley Wood. *Staf* 3F **73**
Brompton. *Medw* 4B **40**
Brompton. *N Yor* 5A **106** (nr. Northallerton)
Brompton. *N Yor* 1D **100** (nr. Scarborough)
Brompton. *Shrp* 5H **71**
Brompton-on-Swale. *N Yor* 5F **105**
Brompton Ralph. *Som* 3D **20**
Brompton Regis. *Som* 3C **20**
Bromsash. *Here* 3B **48**
Bromsberrow. *Glos* 2C **48**
Bromsberrow Heath. *Glos* 2C **48**
Bromsgrove. *Worc* 3D **60**
Bromstead Heath. *Staf* 4B **72**
Bromyard. *Here* 5A **60**
Bromyard Downs. *Here* 5A **60**
Bronaber. *Gwyn* 2G **69**
Broncroft. *Shrp* 2H **59**
Brongest. *Cdgn* 1D **44**
Brongwyn. *Cdgn* 1C **44**
Bronington. *Wrex* 2G **71**
Bronllys. *Powy* 2E **47**
Bronnant. *Cdgn* 4F **57**
Bronwydd Arms. *Carm* 3E **45**
Bronydd. *Powy* 1F **47**
Bronygarth. *Shrp* 2E **71**
Brook. *Carm* 4G **43**
Brook. *Hants* 1A **16** (nr. Cadnam)
Brook. *Hants* 4B **24** (nr. Romsey)
Brook. *IOW* 4B **16**
Brook. *Kent* 1E **29**
Brook. *Surr* 1B **26** (nr. Guildford)
Brook. *Surr* 2A **26** (nr. Haslemere)
Brooke. *Norf* 1E **67**
Brooke. *Rut* 5F **75**
Brookeborough. *Ferm* 8F **176**
Brookenby. *Linc* 1B **88**
Brookend. *Glos* 5B **48**
Brook End. *Worc* 1D **48**
Brookfield. *Lanc* 1D **90**
Brookfield. *Ren* 3F **127**
Brookhouse. *Lanc* 3E **97**
Brookhouse Green. *Ches E* 4C **84**
Brookhouses. *Staf* 1D **73**
Brookhurst. *Mers* 2F **83**
Brookland. *Kent* 3D **28**
Brooklands. *G Man* 1B **84**
Brooklands. *Shrp* 1H **71**
Brookmans Park. *Herts* 5C **52**
Brooks. *Powy* 1D **58**
Brooksby. *Leics* 4D **74**
Brooks Green. *W Sus* 3C **26**
Brook Street. *Essx* 1G **39**
Brook Street. *Kent* 2D **28**
Brook Street. *W Sus* 3E **27**
Brookthorpe. *Glos* 4D **48**
Brookville. *Norf* 1G **65**
Brookwood. *Surr* 5A **38**
Broom. *C Beds* 1B **52**
Broom. *Fife* 3F **137**
Broom. *Warw* 5E **61**
Broome. *Norf* 1F **67**
Broome. *Shrp* 1H **59** (nr. Cardington)
Broome. *Shrp* 2G **59** (nr. Craven Arms)
Broome. *Worc* 3D **60**
Broomedge. *Warr* 2B **84**
Broomend. *Abers* 2E **153**
Broome Park. *Nmbd* 3F **121**
Broomer's Corner. *W Sus* 3C **26**
Broomfield. *Abers* 5G **161**
Broomfield. *Essx* 4H **53**
Broomfield. *Kent* 4F **41** (nr. Herne Bay)
Broomfield. *Kent* 5C **40** (nr. Maidstone)
Broomfield. *Som* 3F **21**
Broomfleet. *E Yor* 2B **94**
Broom Green. *Norf* 3B **78**
Broomhall. *Ches E* 1A **72**
Broomhall. *Wind* 4A **38**
Broomhaugh. *Nmbd* 3D **114**
Broomhill. *Bris* 4B **34**
Broom Hill. *Dors* 2F **15**
Broomhill. *High* 1D **151** (nr. Grantown-on-Spey)
Broomhill. *High* 1B **158** (nr. Invergordon)
Broomhill. *Norf* 5F **77**
Broomhill. *S Yor* 4E **93**
Broom Hill. *Worc* 3D **60**
Broomhillbank. *Dum* 5D **118**
Broomholm. *Norf* 2F **79**
Broomlands. *Dum* 4C **118**
Broomley. *Nmbd* 3D **114**
Broom of Moy. *Mor* 3E **159**
Broompark. *Dur* 5F **115**
Broom's Green. *Glos* 2C **48**
Brora. *High* 3G **165**
Broseley. *Shrp* 5A **72**
Brotherhouse Bar. *Linc* 4B **76**
Brotheridge Green. *Worc* 1D **48**
Brotherlee. *Dur* 1C **104**
Brothertoft. *Linc* 1B **76**
Brotherton. *N Yor* 2E **93**
Brotton. *Red C* 2D **107**
Broubster. *High* 2C **168**
Brough. *Cumb* 3A **104**
Brough. *Derbs* 2F **85**
Brough. *E Yor* 2C **94**
Brough. *High* 1E **169**
Brough. *Notts* 5F **87**
Brough. *Orkn* 6C **172** (nr. Finstown)
Brough. *Orkn* 9D **172** (nr. St Margaret's Hope)
Brough. *Shet* 6F **173** (nr. Benston)
Brough. *Shet* 4F **173** (nr. Booth of Toft)
Brough. *Shet* 7G **173** (on Bressay)
Brough. *Shet* 5G **173** (on Whalsay)
Broughall. *Shrp* 1H **71**
Brougham. *Cumb* 2G **103**
Brough Lodge. *Shet* 2G **173**
Broughshane. *Bmna* 6H **175**
Brough Sowerby. *Cumb* 3A **104**
Broughton. *Cambs* 3B **64**
Broughton. *Flin* 4F **83**
Broughton. *Hants* 3B **24**
Broughton. *Lanc* 1D **90**
Broughton. *Mil* 2G **51**
Broughton. *Nptn* 3F **63**
Broughton. *N Lin* 4C **94**
Broughton. *N Yor* 2B **100** (nr. Malton)
Broughton. *N Yor* 4B **98** (nr. Skipton)
Broughton. *Orkn* 3D **172**
Broughton. *Oxon* 2C **50**
Broughton. *Bord* 1D **118**
Broughton. *Staf* 2B **72**
Broughton. *V Glam* 4C **32**
Broughton Astley. *Leics* 1C **62**
Broughton Beck. *Cumb* 1B **96**
Broughton Cross. *Cumb* 1B **102**
Broughton Gifford. *Wilts* 5D **35**
Broughton Green. *Worc* 4D **60**
Broughton Hackett. *Worc* 5D **60**
Broughton in Furness. *Cumb* 1B **96**
Broughton Mills. *Cumb* 5D **102**
Broughton Moor. *Cumb* 1B **102**
Broughton Park. *G Man* 4G **91**
Broughton Poggs. *Oxon* 5H **49**
Broughtown. *Orkn* 3F **172**
Broughty Ferry. *D'dee* 5D **144**
Browland. *Shet* 6D **173**
Brownbread Street. *E Sus* 4A **28**
Brown Candover. *Hants* 3D **24**
Brown Edge. *Lanc* 3B **90**
Brown Edge. *Staf* 5D **84**
Brownhill. *Bkbn* 1E **91**
Brownhill. *Shrp* 3G **71**
Brownhills. *Shrp* 2A **72**
Brownhills. *W Mid* 5E **73**
Brown Knowl. *Ches W* 5G **83**
Brownlow. *Ches E* 4C **84**
Brownlow Heath. *Ches E* 4C **84**
Brown's Green. *W Mid* 1E **61**
Brownshill. *Glos* 5D **49**
Brownston. *Devn* 3C **8**
Brownstone. *Devn* 2A **12**
Browston Green. *Norf* 5G **79**
Broxa. *N Yor* 5G **107**
Broxbourne. *Herts* 5D **52**
Broxburn. *E Lot* 2C **130**
Broxburn. *W Lot* 2D **129**
Broxholme. *Linc* 3G **87**
Broxted. *Essx* 3F **53**
Broxton. *Ches W* 5G **83**
Broxwood. *Here* 5F **59**
Broyle Side. *E Sus* 4F **27**
Brù. *W Isl* 3F **171**
Bruach Mairi. *W Isl* 4G **171**
Bruairnis. *W Isl* 8C **170**
Bruan. *High* 5F **169**
Bruar Lodge. *Per* 1F **143**
Brucehill. *W Dun* 2E **127**
Brucklay. *Abers* 3G **161**
Bruera. *Ches W* 4G **83**
Bruern Abbey. *Oxon* 3A **50**
Bruichladdich. *Arg* 3A **124**
Bruisyard. *Suff* 4F **67**
Bruisyard Street. *Suff* 4F **67**
Brumby. *N Lin* 4B **94**
Brund. *Staf* 4F **85**
Brundall. *Norf* 5F **79**
Brundish. *Norf* 1F **67**
Brundish. *Suff* 4E **67**
Brundish Street. *Suff* 3E **67**
Brunery. *High* 1B **140**
Brunswick Village. *Tyne* 2F **115**
Brunthwaite. *W Yor* 5C **98**
Bruntingthorpe. *Leics* 1D **62**
Brunton. *Fife* 1F **137**
Brunton. *Nmbd* 2G **121**
Brunton. *Wilts* 1H **23**
Brushford. *Devn* 2G **11**
Brushford. *Som* 4C **20**
Brusta. *W Isl* 1E **170**
Bruton. *Som* 3B **22**
Bryansford. *Down* 6H **179**
Bryanston. *Dors* 2D **15**
Bryant's Bottom. *Buck* 2G **37**
Brydekirk. *Dum* 2C **112**
Brymbo. *Cnwy* 3H **81**
Brymbo. *Wrex* 5E **83**
Brympton D'Evercy. *Som* 1A **14**
Bryn. *Carm* 5F **45**
Bryn. *G Man* 4D **90**
Bryn. *Neat* 2B **32**
Bryn. *Shrp* 2E **59**
Brynamman. *Carm* 4H **45**
Brynberian. *Pemb* 1F **43**
Brynbryddan. *Neat* 2A **32**
Bryncae. *Rhon* 3C **32**
Bryncethin. *B'end* 3C **32**
Bryncir. *Gwyn* 1D **69**
Bryn-coch. *Neat* 3G **31**
Bryncroes. *Gwyn* 2B **68**
Bryncrug. *Gwyn* 5F **69**
Bryn Du. *IOA* 3C **80**
Bryn Eden. *Gwyn* 3G **69**
Bryneglwys. *Den* 1D **70**
Bryn Eglwys. *Gwyn* 4F **81**
Brynford. *Flin* 3D **82**
Bryn Gates. *G Man* 4D **90**
Bryn Golau. *Rhon* 3D **32**
Bryngwran. *IOA* 3C **80**
Bryngwyn. *Mon* 5G **47**
Bryngwyn. *Powy* 1E **47**
Bryn-henllan. *Pemb* 1E **43**
Brynhoffnant. *Cdgn* 5C **56**
Bryn-llwyn. *Flin* 2C **82**
Brynllywarch. *Powy* 2D **58**
Brynmawr. *Blae* 4E **47**
Bryn-mawr. *Gwyn* 2B **68**
Brynmenyn. *B'end* 3C **32**
Brynmill. *Swan* 3F **31**
Brynna. *Rhon* 3C **32**
Brynrefail. *Gwyn* 4E **81**
Brynrefail. *IOA* 2D **81**
Brynsadler. *Rhon* 3D **32**
Bryn-Saith Marchog. *Den* 5C **82**
Brynsiencyn. *IOA* 4D **81**
Brynteg. *IOA* 2D **81**
Brynteg. *Wrex* 5F **83**
Brynygwenyn. *Mon* 4G **47**
Bryn-y-maen. *Cnwy* 3H **81**
Buaile nam Bodach. *W Isl* 8C **170**
Bualintur. *High* 1C **146**
Bubbenhall. *Warw* 3A **62**
Bubwith. *E Yor* 1H **93**
Buccleuch. *Bord* 3F **119**
Buchanan Smithy. *Stir* 1F **127**
Buchanhaven. *Abers* 4H **161**
Buchanty. *Per* 1B **136**
Buchany. *Stir* 3G **135**
Buchley. *E Dun* 2G **127**
Buchlyvie. *Stir* 4E **135**
Buckabank. *Cumb* 5E **113**
Buckden. *Cambs* 4A **64**
Buckden. *N Yor* 2B **98**
Buckenham. *Norf* 5F **79**
Buckerell. *Devn* 2E **13**
Buckfast. *Devn* 2D **8**
Buckfastleigh. *Devn* 2D **8**
Buckhaven. *Fife* 4F **137**
Buckholm. *Bord* 1G **119**
Buckholt. *Here* 4A **48**
Buckhorn Weston. *Dors* 4C **22**
Buckhurst Hill. *Essx* 1F **39**
Buckie. *Mor* 2B **160**
Buckingham. *Buck* 2E **51**
Buckland. *Buck* 4G **51**
Buckland. *Glos* 2F **49**
Buckland. *Here* 5H **59**
Buckland. *Herts* 2D **52**
Buckland. *Kent* 1H **29**
Buckland. *Oxon* 2B **36**
Buckland. *Surr* 5D **38**
Buckland Brewer. *Devn* 4E **19**
Buckland Common. *Buck* 5H **51**
Buckland Dinham. *Som* 1C **22**
Buckland Filleigh. *Devn* 2E **11**
Buckland in the Moor. *Devn* 5H **11**
Buckland Monachorum. *Devn* 2A **8**
Buckland Newton. *Dors* 2B **14**
Buckland Ripers. *Dors* 4B **14**
Buckland St Mary. *Som* 1F **13**
Buckland-tout-Saints. *Devn* 4D **8**
Bucklebury. *W Ber* 4D **36**
Bucklegate. *Linc* 2C **76**
Buckleigh. *Devn* 4E **19**
Buckler's Hard. *Hants* 3C **16**
Bucklesham. *Suff* 1F **55**
Buckley. *Flin* 4E **83**
Buckley Green. *Warw* 4F **61**
Buckley Hill. *Mers* 1F **83**
Bucklow Hill. *Ches E* 2B **84**
Buckminster. *Leics* 3F **75**
Bucknall. *Linc* 4A **88**
Bucknall. *Stoke* 1D **72**
Bucknell. *Oxon* 3D **50**
Bucknell. *Shrp* 3F **59**
Buckpool. *Mor* 2B **160**
Bucksburn. *Aber* 3F **153**
Buck's Cross. *Devn* 4D **18**
Bucks Green. *W Sus* 2B **26**
Buckshaw Village. *Lanc* 2D **90**
Bucks Hill. *Herts* 5A **52**
Bucks Horn Oak. *Hants* 2G **25**
Buck's Mills. *Devn* 4D **18**
Buckton. *E Yor* 2F **101**
Buckton. *Here* 3F **59**
Buckton. *Nmbd* 1E **121**
Buckton Vale. *G Man* 4H **91**
Buckworth. *Cambs* 3A **64**
Budby. *Notts* 4D **86**
Bude. *Corn* 2C **10**
Budge's Shop. *Corn* 3H **7**
Budlake. *Devn* 2C **12**
Budle. *Nmbd* 1F **121**
Budleigh Salterton. *Devn* 4D **12**
Budock Water. *Corn* 5B **6**
Buerton. *Ches E* 1A **72**
Buffler's Holt. *Buck* 2E **51**
Bugbrooke. *Nptn* 5D **62**
Buglawton. *Ches E* 4C **84**
Bugle. *Corn* 3E **6**
Bugthorpe. *E Yor* 4B **100**
Buildwas. *Shrp* 5A **72**
Builth Road. *Powy* 5C **58**
Builth Wells. *Powy* 5C **58**
Bulbourne. *Herts* 4H **51**
Bulby. *Linc* 3H **75**
Bulcote. *Notts* 1D **74**
Buldoo. *High* 2B **168**
Bulford. *Wilts* 2G **23**
Bulford Camp. *Wilts* 2G **23**
Bulkeley. *Ches E* 5H **83**
Bulkington. *Warw* 2A **62**
Bulkington. *Wilts* 1E **23**
Bulkworthy. *Devn* 1D **11**
Bullamoor. *N Yor* 5A **106**
Bull Bay. *IOA* 1D **80**
Bullbridge. *Derbs* 5A **86**
Bullgill. *Cumb* 1B **102**
Bull Hill. *Hants* 3B **16**
Bullinghope. *Here* 2A **48**
Bull's Green. *Herts* 4C **52**
Bullwood. *Arg* 2C **126**
Bulmer. *Essx* 1B **54**
Bulmer. *N Yor* 3A **100**
Bulmer Tye. *Essx* 2B **54**
Bulphan. *Thur* 2H **39**
Bulverhythe. *E Sus* 5B **28**
Bulwark. *Abers* 4G **161**
Bulwell. *Nott* 1C **74**
Bulwick. *Nptn* 1G **63**
Bumble's Green. *Essx* 5E **53**
Bun Abhainn Eadarra. *W Isl* 7D **171**
Bunacaimb. *High* 5E **147**
Bun a' Mhuillinn. *W Isl* 7C **170**
Bunarkaig. *High* 5D **148**
Bunbury. *Ches E* 5H **83**
Bunchrew. *High* 4A **158**
Bundalloch. *High* 1A **148**
Buness. *Shet* 1H **173**
Bunessan. *Arg* 1A **132**
Bungay. *Suff* 2F **67**
Bunkegivie. *High* 2H **149**
Bunker's Hill. *Cambs* 5D **76**
Bunkers Hill. *Linc* 5B **88**
Bunker's Hill. *Norf* 5H **79**
Bunloit. *High* 1H **149**
Bunnahabhain. *Arg* 2C **124**
Bunny. *Notts* 3C **74**
Bunoich. *High* 3F **149**
Bunree. *High* 2E **141**
Bunroy. *High* 5E **149**
Buntait. *High* 5F **157**
Buntingford. *Herts* 3D **52**
Buntings Green. *Essx* 2B **54**
Bunwell. *Norf* 1D **66**
Burbage. *Derbs* 3E **85**
Burbage. *Leics* 1B **62**
Burbage. *Wilts* 5H **35**
Burcher. *Here* 4F **59**
Burchett's Green. *Wind* 3G **37**
Burcombe. *Wilts* 3F **23**
Burcot. *Oxon* 2D **36**
Burcot. *Worc* 3D **61**
Burcote. *Shrp* 1B **60**
Burcott. *Buck* 3G **51**
Burcott. *Som* 2A **22**
Burdale. *N Yor* 3C **100**
Burdrop. *Oxon* 2B **50**
Bures. *Suff* 2C **54**
Burford. *Oxon* 4A **50**
Burford. *Shrp* 4H **59**
Burf, The. *Worc* 4C **60**
Burg. *Arg* 4E **139**
Burgate Great Green. *Suff* 3C **66**
Burgate Little Green. *Suff* 3C **66**
Burgess Hill. *W Sus* 4E **27**
Burgh. *Suff* 5E **67**
Burgh by Sands. *Cumb* 4E **113**
Burgh Castle. *Norf* 5G **79**
Burghclere. *Hants* 5C **36**
Burghead. *Mor* 2F **159**
Burghfield. *W Ber* 5E **37**
Burghfield Common. *W Ber* 5E **37**
Burghfield Hill. *W Ber* 5E **37**
Burgh Heath. *Surr* 5D **38**
Burghill. *Here* 1H **47**
Burgh le Marsh. *Linc* 4E **89**
Burgh Muir. *Abers* 2E **153**
Burgh next Aylsham. *Norf* 3E **78**
Burgh on Bain. *Linc* 2B **88**
Burgh St Margaret. *Norf* 4G **79**
Burgh St Peter. *Norf* 1G **67**
Burghwallis. *S Yor* 3F **93**
Burgie. *Mor* 3E **159**
Burham. *Kent* 4B **40**
Buriton. *Hants* 4F **25**
Burland. *Ches E* 5A **84**
Burland. *Shet* 8E **173**
Burlawn. *Corn* 2D **6**
Burleigh. *Brac* 3A **38**
Burleigh. *Glos* 5D **48**
Burlescombe. *Devn* 1D **12**
Burleston. *Dors* 3C **14**
Burlestone. *Devn* 4E **9**
Burley. *Hants* 2H **15**
Burley. *Rut* 4F **75**
Burley. *W Yor* 1C **92**
Burley Gate. *Here* 1A **48**
Burley in Wharfedale. *W Yor* 5D **98**
Burley Street. *Hants* 2H **15**
Burley Woodhead. *W Yor* 5D **98**

A-Z Great Britain Road Atlas 209

Burlingjobb—Charlton

Burlingjobb. *Powy* 5E **59**
Burlington. *Shrp* 4B **72**
Burlton. *Shrp* 3G **71**
Burmantofts. *W Yor* 1D **92**
Burmarsh. *Kent* 2F **29**
Burmington. *Warw* 2A **50**
Burn. *N Yor* 2F **93**
Burnage. *G Man* 1C **84**
Burnaston. *Derbs* 2G **73**
Burnbanks. *Cumb* 3G **103**
Burnby. *E Yor* 5C **100**
Burncross. *S Yor* 1H **85**
Burneside. *Cumb* 5G **103**
Burness. *Orkn* 3F **172**
Burneston. *N Yor* 1F **99**
Burnett. *Bath* 5B **34**
Burnfoot. *E Ayr* 4D **116**
Burnfoot. *Per* 3B **136**
Burnfoot. *Bord* 3H **119**
(nr. Hawick)
Burnfoot. *Bord* 3G **119**
(nr. Roberton)
Burngreave. *S Yor* 2A **86**
Burnham. *Buck* 2A **38**
Burnham. *N Lin* 3D **94**
Burnham Deepdale. *Norf* 1H **77**
Burnham Green. *Herts* 4C **52**
Burnham Market. *Norf* 1H **77**
Burnham Norton. *Norf* 1H **77**
Burnham-on-Crouch. *Essx* 1D **40**
Burnham-on-Sea. *Som* 2G **21**
Burnham Overy Staithe. *Norf* 1H **77**
Burnham Overy Town. *Norf* 1H **77**
Burnham Thorpe. *Norf* 1A **78**
Burnhaven. *Abers* 4H **161**
Burnhead. *Dum* 5A **118**
Burnhervie. *Abers* 2E **153**
Burnhill Green. *Staf* 5B **72**
Burnhope. *Dur* 5E **115**
Burnhouse. *N Ayr* 4E **127**
Burniston. *N Yor* 5H **107**
Burnlee. *W Yor* 4B **92**
Burnley. *Lanc* 1G **91**
Burnleydam. *Ches E* 1A **72**
Burnmouth. *Bord* 3F **131**
Burn Naze. *Lanc* 5C **96**
Burn of Cambus. *Stir* 3G **135**
Burnopfield. *Dur* 4E **115**
Burnsall. *N Yor* 3C **98**
Burnside. *Ang* 3E **145**
Burnside. *Ant* 8H **175**
Burnside. *E Ayr* 3E **117**
Burnside. *Newt* 7J **175**
Burnside. *Per* 3D **136**
Burnside. *Shet* 4D **173**
Burnside. *S Lan* 4H **127**
Burnside. *W Lot* 2D **129**
(nr. Broxburn)
Burnside. *W Lot* 2D **128**
(nr. Winchburgh)
Burntcommon. *Surr* 5B **38**
Burntheath. *Derbs* 2G **73**
Burnt Heath. *Essx* 3D **54**
Burnt Hill. *W Ber* 4D **36**
Burnt Houses. *Dur* 2E **105**
Burntisland. *Fife* 1F **129**
Burnt Oak. *G Lon* 1D **38**
Burnton. *E Ayr* 4D **117**
Burntstalk. *Norf* 2G **77**
Burntwood. *Staf* 5E **73**
Burntwood Green. *Staf* 5E **73**
Burnt Yates. *N Yor* 3E **99**
Burnwynd. *Edin* 3E **129**
Burpham. *Surr* 5B **38**
Burpham. *W Sus* 5B **26**
Burradon. *Nmbd* 4D **121**
Burradon. *Tyne* 2F **115**
Burrafirth. *Shet* 1H **173**
Burragarth. *Shet* 1G **173**
Burras. *Corn* 5A **6**
Burraton. *Corn* 3A **8**
Burravoe. *Shet* 3E **173**
(nr. North Roe)
Burravoe. *Shet* 5E **173**
(on Mainland)
Burravoe. *Shet* 4G **173**
(on Yell)
Burray Village. *Orkn* 8D **172**
Burrells. *Cumb* 3H **103**
Burrelton. *Per* 5A **144**
Burren. *New M* 7F **178**
Burren Bridge. *Down* 6H **179**
Burridge. *Devn* 2G **13**
Burridge. *Hants* 1D **16**
Burrigill. *High* 5E **169**
Burrill. *N Yor* 1E **99**
Burringham. *N Lin* 4B **94**
Burrington. *Devn* 1G **11**
Burrington. *Here* 3G **59**
Burrington. *N Som* 1H **21**
Burrough End. *Cambs* 5F **65**
Burrough Green. *Cambs* 5F **65**
Burrough on the Hill. *Leics* 4E **75**
Burroughston. *Orkn* 5E **172**
Burrow. *Devn* 4D **12**
Burrow. *Som* 2C **20**
Burrowbridge. *Som* 4G **21**
Burrowhill. *Surr* 4A **38**
Burry. *Swan* 3D **30**
Burry Green. *Swan* 3D **30**
Burry Port. *Carm* 5E **45**
Burscough. *Lanc* 3C **90**
Burscough Bridge. *Lanc* 3C **90**
Bursea. *E Yor* 1B **94**
Burshill. *E Yor* 5E **101**
Bursledon. *Hants* 2C **16**
Burslem. *Stoke* 1C **72**
Burstall. *Suff* 1D **54**
Burstock. *Dors* 2H **13**
Burston. *Devn* 2H **11**
Burston. *Norf* 2D **66**
Burston. *Staf* 2D **72**
Burstow. *Surr* 1E **27**
Burstwick. *E Yor* 2F **95**
Burtersett. *N Yor* 1A **98**
Burtholme. *Cumb* 3G **113**
Burthorpe. *Suff* 4G **65**
Burthwaite. *Cumb* 5F **113**
Burtle. *Som* 2H **21**
Burtoft. *Linc* 2B **76**
Burton. *Ches W* 4H **83**
(nr. Kelsall)
Burton. *Ches W* 3F **83**
(nr. Neston)
Burton. *Dors* 3G **15**
(nr. Christchurch)
Burton. *Dors* 3B **14**
(nr. Dorchester)
Burton. *Nmbd* 1F **121**
Burton. *Pemb* 4D **43**
Burton. *Som* 2E **21**
Burton. *Wilts* 4D **34**
(nr. Chippenham)
Burton. *Wilts* 3D **22**
(nr. Warminster)
Burton. *Wrex* 5F **83**
Burton Agnes. *E Yor* 3F **101**
Burton Bradstock. *Dors* 4H **13**
Burton-by-Lincoln. *Linc* 3G **87**
Burton Coggles. *Linc* 3G **75**
Burton Constable. *E Yor* 1E **95**
Burton Corner. *Linc* 1C **76**
Burton End. *Cambs* 1G **53**
Burton End. *Essx* 3F **53**
Burton Fleming. *E Yor* 2E **101**
Burton Green. *W Mid* 3G **61**
Burton Green. *Wrex* 5F **83**
Burton Hastings. *Warw* 2B **62**
Burton-in-Kendal. *Cumb* 2E **97**
Burton in Lonsdale. *N Yor* 2F **97**
Burton Joyce. *Notts* 1D **74**
Burton Latimer. *Nptn* 3G **63**
Burton Lazars. *Leics* 4E **75**
Burton Leonard. *N Yor* 3F **99**
Burton on the Wolds. *Leics* 3C **74**
Burton Overy. *Leics* 1D **62**
Burton Pedwardine. *Linc* 1A **76**
Burton Pidsea. *E Yor* 1F **95**
Burton Salmon. *N Yor* 2E **93**
Burton's Green. *Essx* 3B **54**
Burton Stather. *N Lin* 3B **94**
Burton upon Stather. *N Lin* 3B **94**
Burton upon Trent. *Staf* 3G **73**
Burton Wolds. *Leics* 3D **74**
Burtonwood. *Warr* 1H **83**
Burwardsley. *Ches W* 5H **83**
Burwarton. *Shrp* 2A **60**
Burwash. *E Sus* 3A **28**
Burwash Common. *E Sus* 3H **27**
Burwash Weald. *E Sus* 3A **28**
Burwell. *Cambs* 4E **65**
Burwell. *Linc* 3C **88**
Burwen. *IOA* 1D **80**
Burwick. *Orkn* 9D **172**
Bury. *Cambs* 2B **64**
Bury. *G Man* 3G **91**
Bury. *Som* 4C **20**
Bury. *W Sus* 4B **26**
Burybank. *Staf* 2C **72**
Bury End. *Worc* 2F **49**
Bury Green. *Herts* 3E **53**
Bury Hill. *S Glo* 3C **34**
Bury St Edmunds. *Suff* 4A **66**
Burythorpe. *N Yor* 3B **100**
Busbridge. *Surr* 1A **26**
Busby. *E Ren* 4G **127**
Busby. *Per* 1C **136**
Buscot. *Oxon* 2H **35**
Bush. *Corn* 2C **10**
Bush Bank. *Here* 5G **59**
Bushbury. *W Mid* 5D **72**
Bushby. *Leics* 5D **74**
Bushey. *Dors* 4E **15**
Bushey. *Herts* 1C **38**
Bushey Heath. *Herts* 1C **38**
Bush Green. *Norf* 1C **66**
(nr. Attleborough)
Bush Green. *Norf* 2E **66**
(nr. Harleston)
Bush Green. *Suff* 5B **66**
Bushley. *Worc* 2D **48**
Bushley Green. *Worc* 2D **48**
Bushmead. *Bed* 4A **64**
Bushmills. *Moy* 2F **174**
Bushmoor. *Shrp* 2G **59**
Bush, The. *Dngn* 3C **178**
Bushton. *Wilts* 4F **35**
Bushy Common. *Norf* 4B **78**
Busk. *Cumb* 5H **113**
Buslingthorpe. *Linc* 2H **87**
Bussage. *Glos* 5D **49**
Bussex. *Som* 3G **21**
Busta. *Shet* 5E **173**
Bustard Green. *Essx* 3G **53**
Butcher's Cross. *E Sus* 3G **27**
Butcombe. *N Som* 5A **34**
Bute Town. *Cphy* 5E **46**
Butleigh. *Som* 3A **22**
Butleigh Wootton. *Som* 3A **22**
Butlers Marston. *Warw* 5H **61**
Butley. *Suff* 5F **67**
Butley High Corner. *Suff* 1G **55**
Butlocks Heath. *Hants* 2C **16**
Butterburn. *Cumb* 2H **113**
Buttercrambe. *N Yor* 4B **100**
Butterknowle. *Dur* 2E **105**
Butterleigh. *Devn* 2C **12**
Buttermere. *Cumb* 3C **102**
Buttermere. *Wilts* 5B **36**
Buttershaw. *W Yor* 2B **92**
Butterstone. *Per* 4H **143**
Butterton. *Staf* 5E **85**
(nr. Leek)
Butterton. *Staf* 1C **72**
(nr. Stoke-on-Trent)
Butterwick. *Dur* 2A **106**
Butterwick. *Linc* 1C **76**
Butterwick. *N Yor* 2B **100**
(nr. Malton)
Butterwick. *N Yor* 2D **101**
(nr. Weaverthorpe)
Butteryhaugh. *Nmbd* 5A **120**
Butt Green. *Ches E* 5A **84**
Buttington. *Powy* 5E **71**
Buttonbridge. *Shrp* 3B **60**
Buttonoak. *Shrp* 3B **60**
Buttsash. *Hants* 2C **16**
Butt's Green. *Essx* 5A **54**
Butt Yeats. *Lanc* 3E **97**
Buxhall. *Suff* 5C **66**
Buxted. *E Sus* 3F **27**
Buxton. *Derbs* 3E **85**
Buxton. *Norf* 3E **79**
Buxworth. *Derbs* 2E **85**
Bwcle. *Flin* 4E **83**
Bwlch. *Powy* 3E **47**
Bwlchderwin. *Gwyn* 1D **68**
Bwlchgwyn. *Wrex* 5E **83**
Bwlch-Llan. *Cdgn* 5E **57**
Bwlchnewydd. *Carm* 3D **44**
Bwlchtocyn. *Gwyn* 3C **68**
Bwlch-y-cibau. *Powy* 4D **70**
Bwlchyddar. *Powy* 3D **70**
Bwlch-y-fadfa. *Cdgn* 1E **45**
Bwlch-y-ffridd. *Powy* 1C **58**
Bwlch y Garreg. *Powy* 1C **58**
Bwlch-y-groes. *Pemb* 1G **43**
Bwlch-y-sarnau. *Powy* 3C **58**
Bybrook. *Kent* 1E **28**
Byermoor. *Tyne* 4E **115**
Byers Garth. *Dur* 5G **115**
Byers Green. *Dur* 1F **105**
Byfield. *Nptn* 5C **62**
Byfleet. *Surr* 4B **38**
Byford. *Here* 1G **47**
Bygrave. *Herts* 2C **52**
Byker. *Tyne* 3F **115**
Byland Abbey. *N Yor* 2H **99**
Bylchau. *Cnwy* 4B **82**
Byley. *Ches W* 4B **84**
Bynea. *Carm* 3E **31**
Byram. *N Yor* 2E **93**
Byrness. *Nmbd* 4B **120**
Bystock. *Devn* 4D **12**
Bythorn. *Cambs* 3H **63**
Byton. *Here* 4F **59**
Bywell. *Nmbd* 3D **114**
Byworth. *W Sus* 3A **26**

C

Cabharstadh. *W Isl* 6F **171**
Cabourne. *Linc* 4E **95**
Cabrach. *Arg* 3C **124**
Cabrach. *Mor* 1A **152**
Cabragh. *Dngn* 3B **178**
Cabus. *Lanc* 5D **97**
Cadbury. *Devn* 2C **12**
Cadder. *E Dun* 2H **127**
Caddington. *C Beds* 4A **52**
Caddonfoot. *Bord* 1G **119**
Cadeby. *Leics* 5B **74**
Cadeby. *S Yor* 4F **93**
Cadeleigh. *Devn* 2C **12**
Cade Street. *E Sus* 3H **27**
Cadgwith. *Corn* 5E **5**
Cadham. *Fife* 3E **137**
Cadishead. *G Man* 1B **84**
Cadle. *Swan* 3F **31**
Cadley. *Lanc* 1D **90**
Cadley. *Wilts* 1H **23**
(nr. Ludgershall)
Cadley. *Wilts* 5H **35**
(nr. Marlborough)
Cadmore End. *Buck* 2F **37**
Cadnam. *Hants* 1A **16**
Cadney. *N Lin* 4D **94**
Cadole. *Flin* 4E **82**
Cadoxton-Juxta-Neath. *Neat* 2A **32**
Cadwell. *Herts* 2B **52**
Cadwst. *Den* 2C **70**
Caeathro. *Gwyn* 4E **81**
Caehopkin. *Powy* 4B **46**
Caenby. *Linc* 2H **87**
Caenn-na-Cleithe. *W Isl* 8D **171**
Caerau. *B'end* 2B **32**
Caerau. *Card* 4E **33**
Cae'r-bont. *Powy* 4B **46**
Cae'r-bryn. *Carm* 4F **45**
Caerdeon. *Gwyn* 4F **69**
Caerdydd. *Card* 4E **33** & **Cardiff 193**
Caerfarchell. *Pemb* 2B **42**
Caerffili. *Cphy* 3E **33**
Caerfyrddin. *Carm* 4E **45**
Caergeiliog. *IOA* 3C **80**
Caergwrle. *Flin* 5F **83**
Caergybi. *IOA* 2B **80**
Caerlaverock. *Per* 2A **136**
Caerleon. *Newp* 2G **33**
Caerlleon. *Carm* 2G **43**
Caerllion. *Newp* 2G **33**
Caernarfon. *Gwyn* 4D **81**
Caerphilly. *Cphy* 3E **33**
Caersws. *Powy* 1C **58**
Caerwedros. *Cdgn* 5C **56**
Caerwent. *Mon* 2H **33**
Caerwys. *Flin* 3D **82**
Caim. *IOA* 2F **81**
Caio. *Carm* 2G **45**
Cairinis. *W Isl* 2D **170**
Cairisiadar. *W Isl* 4D **171**
Cairminis. *W Isl* 9C **171**
Cairnbaan. *Arg* 4F **133**
Cairnbulg. *Abers* 2H **161**
Cairncross. *Ang* 1D **145**
Cairndow. *Arg* 2A **134**
Cairness. *Abers* 2H **161**
Cairneyhill. *Fife* 1D **128**
Cairngarroch. *Dum* 5F **109**
Cairngorms. *High* 3D **151**
Cairnhill. *Abers* 5D **160**
Cairnie. *Abers* 4B **160**
Cairnorrie. *Abers* 4F **161**
Cairnryan. *Dum* 3F **109**
Cairston. *Orkn* 6B **172**
Caister-on-Sea. *Norf* 4H **79**
Caistor. *Linc* 4E **95**
Caistor St Edmund. *Norf* 5E **79**
Caistron. *Nmbd* 4D **121**
Cakebole. *Worc* 3C **60**
Calais Street. *Suff* 1C **54**
Calanais. *W Isl* 4E **171**
Calbost. *W Isl* 6G **171**
Calbourne. *IOW* 4C **16**
Calceby. *Linc* 3C **88**
Calcot. *Glos* 4F **49**
Calcot Row. *W Ber* 4E **37**
Calcott. *Kent* 4F **41**
Calcott. *Shrp* 4G **71**
Caldback. *Shet* 1H **173**
Caldbeck. *Cumb* 1E **102**
Caldbergh. *N Yor* 1C **98**
Caldecote. *Cambs* 5C **64**
(nr. Cambridge)
Caldecote. *Cambs* 2A **64**
(nr. Peterborough)
Caldecote. *Herts* 2C **52**
Caldecote. *Warw* 1A **62**
Caldecott. *Nptn* 4G **63**
Caldecott. *Oxon* 2C **36**
Caldecott. *Rut* 1F **63**
Calderbank. *N Lan* 3A **128**
Calder Bridge. *Cumb* 4B **102**
Calderbrook. *G Man* 3H **91**
Caldercruix. *N Lan* 3B **128**
Calder Grove. *W Yor* 3D **92**
Calder Mains. *High* 3C **168**
Caldermill. *S Lan* 5H **127**
Calder Vale. *Lanc* 5E **97**
Calderwood. *S Lan* 4H **127**
Caldescote. *Nptn* 5D **62**
Caldicot. *Mon* 3H **33**
Caldwell. *Derbs* 4G **73**
Caldwell. *N Yor* 3E **105**
Caldy. *Mers* 2E **83**
Calebrack. *Cumb* 1E **103**
Caledfwlch. *Carm* 3G **45**
Caledon. *Dngn* 5B **178**
Calf Heath. *Staf* 5D **72**
Calford Green. *Suff* 1G **53**
Calfsound. *Orkn* 4E **172**
Calgary. *Arg* 3E **139**
Califer. *Mor* 3E **159**
California. *Cambs* 2E **65**
California. *Falk* 2C **128**
California. *Norf* 4H **79**
California. *Suff* 1E **55**
Calke. *Derbs* 3A **74**
Callakille. *High* 3F **155**
Callaly. *Nmbd* 4E **121**
Callander. *Stir* 3F **135**
Callaughton. *Shrp* 1A **60**
Callendoun. *Arg* 1E **127**
Callestick. *Corn* 3B **6**
Calligarry. *High* 3E **147**
Callington. *Corn* 2H **7**
Callingwood. *Staf* 3F **73**
Callow. *Here* 2H **47**
Callowell. *Glos* 5D **48**
Callow End. *Worc* 1D **48**
Callow Hill. *Wilts* 3F **35**
Callow Hill. *Worc* 3B **60**
(nr. Bewdley)
Callow Hill. *Worc* 4E **61**
(nr. Redditch)
Calmore. *Hants* 1B **16**
Calmsden. *Glos* 5F **49**
Calne. *Wilts* 4E **35**
Calow. *Derbs* 3B **86**
Calshot. *Hants* 2C **16**
Calstock. *Corn* 2A **8**
Calstone Wellington. *Wilts* 5F **35**
Calthorpe. *Norf* 2D **78**
Calthorpe Street. *Norf* 3G **79**
Calthwaite. *Cumb* 5F **113**
Calton. *N Yor* 4B **98**
Calton. *Staf* 5F **85**
Calveley. *Ches E* 5H **83**
Calver. *Derbs* 3G **85**
Calverhall. *Shrp* 2A **72**
Calverleigh. *Devn* 1C **12**
Calverley. *W Yor* 1C **92**
Calvert. *Buck* 3E **51**
Calverton. *Mil* 2F **51**
Calverton. *Notts* 1D **74**
Calvine. *Per* 2F **143**
Calvo. *Cumb* 4C **112**
Cam. *Glos* 2C **34**
Camaghael. *High* 1F **141**
Camas-luinie. *High* 1B **148**
Camasnacroise. *High* 3C **140**
Camastianavaig. *High* 5E **155**
Camasunary. *High* 2D **146**
Camault Muir. *High* 4H **157**
Camb. *Shet* 2G **173**
Camber. *E Sus* 4D **28**
Camberley. *Surr* 5G **37**
Camberwell. *G Lon* 3E **39**
Camblesforth. *N Yor* 2G **93**
Cambo. *Nmbd* 1D **114**
Cambois. *Nmbd* 1G **115**
Camborne. *Corn* 3D **4**
Cambourne. *Cambs* 5C **64**
Cambridge. *Cambs* 5D **64** & **193**
Cambridge. *Glos* 5C **48**
Cambrose. *Corn* 4A **6**
Cambus. *Clac* 4A **136**
Cambusbarron. *Stir* 4G **135**
Cambuskenneth. *Stir* 4H **135**
Cambuslang. *S Lan* 3H **127**
Cambusnethan. *N Lan* 4B **128**
Cambus o'May. *Abers* 4B **152**
Camden Town. *G Lon* 2D **39**
Cameley. *Bath* 1B **22**
Camelford. *Corn* 4B **10**
Camelon. *Falk* 1B **128**
Camelsdale. *Surr* 2A **26**
Camer's Green. *Worc* 2C **48**
Camerton. *Bath* 1B **22**
Camerton. *Cumb* 1B **102**
Camerton. *E Yor* 2F **95**
Camghouran. *Per* 3C **142**
Camlough. *New M* 7E **178**
Cammachmore. *Abers* 4G **153**
Cammeringham. *Linc* 2G **87**
Camore. *High* 4E **165**
Campbelton. *N Ayr* 4C **126**
Campbeltown. *Arg* 3B **122**
Campbeltown Airport. *Arg* 3A **122**
Cample. *Dum* 5B **118**
Campmuir. *Per* 5B **144**
Campsall. *S Yor* 3F **93**
Campsea Ashe. *Suff* 5F **67**
Camps End. *Cambs* 1G **53**
Campsey. *Derr* 4A **174**
Camp, The. *Glos* 5E **49**
Campton. *C Beds* 2B **52**
Camptoun. *E Lot* 2B **130**
Camptown. *Bord* 3A **120**
Camrose. *Pemb* 2D **42**
Camserney. *Per* 4F **143**
Camster. *High* 4E **169**
Camus Croise. *High* 2E **147**
Camuscross. *High* 2E **147**
Camusdarach. *High* 4E **147**
Camusnagaul. *High* 1E **141**
(nr. Fort William)
Camusnagaul. *High* 5E **163**
(nr. Little Loch Broom)
Camus Park. *Strab* 3F **176**
Camusteel. *High* 4G **155**
Camusterrach. *High* 4G **155**
Camusvrachan. *Per* 4D **142**
Canada. *Hants* 1A **16**
Canadia. *E Sus* 4B **28**
Canaston Bridge. *Pemb* 3E **43**
Candlesby. *Linc* 4D **88**
Candle Street. *Suff* 3C **66**
Candy Mill. *S Lan* 5D **128**
Cane End. *Oxon* 4E **37**
Canewdon. *Essx* 1C **40**
Canford Cliffs. *Pool* 4F **15**
Canford Heath. *Pool* 3F **15**
Canford Magna. *Pool* 3F **15**
Cangate. *Norf* 3F **79**
Canham's Green. *Suff* 4C **66**
Canholes. *Derbs* 3E **85**
Canisbay. *High* 1F **169**
Canley. *W Mid* 3H **61**
Cann. *Dors* 4D **22**
Cann Common. *Dors* 4D **23**
Cannich. *High* 5F **157**
Cannington. *Som* 3F **21**
Cannock. *Staf* 4D **73**
Cannock Wood. *Staf* 4E **73**
Canonbie. *Dum* 2E **113**
Canon Bridge. *Here* 1H **47**
Canon Frome. *Here* 1B **48**
Canon Pyon. *Here* 1H **47**
Canons Ashby. *Nptn* 5C **62**
Canonstown. *Corn* 3C **4**
Canterbury. *Kent* 5F **41** & **193**
Cantley. *Norf* 5F **79**
Cantley. *S Yor* 4G **93**
Cantlop. *Shrp* 5H **71**
Canton. *Card* 4E **33**
Cantray. *High* 4B **158**
Cantraybruich. *High* 4B **158**
Cantraywood. *High* 4B **158**
Cantsdam. *Fife* 4D **136**
Cantsfield. *Lanc* 2F **97**
Canvey Island. *Essx* 2B **40**
Canwick. *Linc* 4G **87**
Canworthy Water. *Corn* 3C **10**
Caol. *High* 1F **141**
Caolas. *W Isl* 9B **170**
Caolas Liubharsaigh. *W Isl* 4D **170**
Caolas Scalpaigh. *W Isl* 8E **171**
Caolas Stocinis. *W Isl* 8D **171**
Caoles. *Arg* 4B **138**
Caol Ila. *Arg* 3C **124**
Caol Loch Ailse. *High* 1F **147**
Caol Reatha. *High* 1F **147**
Capel. *Kent* 1H **27**
Capel. *Surr* 1C **26**
Capel Bangor. *Cdgn* 2F **57**
Capel Betws Lleucu. *Cdgn* 5F **57**
Capel Coch. *IOA* 2D **80**
Capel Curig. *Cnwy* 5G **81**
Capel Cynon. *Cdgn* 1D **45**
Capel Dewi. *Carm* 3E **45**
Capel Dewi. *Cdgn* 2F **57**
(nr. Aberystwyth)
Capel Dewi. *Cdgn* 1E **45**
(nr. Llandysul)
Capel Garmon. *Cnwy* 5H **81**
Capel Green. *Suff* 1G **55**
Capel Gwyn. *IOA* 3C **80**
Capel Gwynfe. *Carm* 3H **45**
Capel Hendre. *Carm* 4F **45**
Capel Isaac. *Carm* 3F **45**
Capel Iwan. *Carm* 1G **43**
Capel-le-Ferne. *Kent* 2G **29**
Capel Llanilterne. *Card* 4D **32**
Capel Mawr. *IOA* 3D **80**
Capel Newydd. *Pemb* 1G **43**
Capel St Andrew. *Suff* 1G **55**
Capel St Mary. *Suff* 2D **54**
Capel Seion. *Carm* 4F **45**
Capel Seion. *Cdgn* 3F **57**
Capel Uchaf. *Gwyn* 1D **68**
Capel-y-ffin. *Powy* 2F **47**
Capenhurst. *Ches W* 3F **83**
Capernwray. *Lanc* 2E **97**
Capheaton. *Nmbd* 1D **114**
Cappagh. *Dngn* 3A **178**
Cappercleuch. *Bord* 2E **119**
Capplegill. *Dum* 4D **118**
Capton. *Devn* 3E **9**
Capton. *Som* 3D **20**
Caputh. *Per* 5H **143**
Caradon Town. *Corn* 5C **10**
Carbis Bay. *Corn* 3C **4**
Carbost. *High* 5C **154**
(nr. Loch Harport)
Carbost. *High* 4D **154**
(nr. Portree)
Carbrook. *S Yor* 2A **86**
Carbrooke. *Norf* 5B **78**
Carburton. *Notts* 3D **86**
Carcluie. *S Ayr* 3C **116**
Car Colston. *Notts* 1E **74**
Carcroft. *S Yor* 3F **93**
Cardenden. *Fife* 4E **136**
Cardeston. *Shrp* 4F **71**
Cardewlees. *Cumb* 4E **113**
Cardiff. *Card* 4E **33** & **193**
Cardiff International Airport. *V Glam* 5D **32**
Cardigan. *Cdgn* 1B **44**
Cardinal's Green. *Cambs* 1G **53**
Cardington. *Bed* 1A **52**
Cardington. *Shrp* 1H **59**
Cardinham. *Corn* 2F **7**
Cardno. *Abers* 2G **161**
Cardow. *Mor* 4F **159**
Cardross. *Arg* 2E **127**
Cardurnock. *Cumb* 4C **112**
Careby. *Linc* 4H **75**
Careston. *Ang* 2E **145**
Carew. *Pemb* 4E **43**
Carew Cheriton. *Pemb* 4E **43**
Carew Newton. *Pemb* 4E **43**
Carey. *Here* 2A **48**
Carfin. *N Lan* 4A **128**
Carfrae. *Bord* 4B **130**
Cargan. *Bmna* 5H **175**
Cargate Green. *Norf* 4F **79**
Cargenbridge. *Dum* 2G **111**
Cargill. *Per* 5A **144**
Cargo. *Cumb* 4E **113**
Cargreen. *Corn* 2A **8**
Carham. *Nmbd* 1B **120**
Carhampton. *Som* 2D **20**
Carharrack. *Corn* 4B **6**
Carie. *Per* 3D **142**
(nr. Loch Rannah)
Carie. *Per* 5D **142**
(nr. Loch Tay)
Carisbrooke. *IOW* 4C **16**
Cark. *Cumb* 2C **96**
Carkeel. *Corn* 2A **8**
Carlabhagh. *W Isl* 3E **171**
Carland Cross. *Corn* 3C **6**
Carlbury. *Darl* 3F **105**
Carlby. *Linc* 4H **75**
Carlecotes. *S Yor* 4B **92**
Carleen. *Corn* 4D **4**
Carlesmoor. *N Yor* 2D **98**
Carleton. *Cumb* 4F **113**
(nr. Carlisle)
Carleton. *Cumb* 4B **102**
(nr. Egremont)
Carleton. *Cumb* 2G **103**
(nr. Penrith)
Carleton. *Lanc* 1B **90**
Carleton. *N Yor* 5B **98**
Carleton. *W Yor* 2E **93**
Carleton Forehoe. *Norf* 5C **78**
Carleton Rode. *Norf* 1D **66**
Carleton St Peter. *Norf* 5F **79**
Carlidnack. *Corn* 4E **5**
Carlingcott. *Bath* 1B **22**
Carlin How. *Red C* 3E **107**
Carlisle. *Cumb* 4F **113** & **193**
Carloonan. *Arg* 2H **133**
Carlops. *Bord* 4E **129**
Carlton. *Bed* 5G **63**
Carlton. *Cambs* 5F **65**
Carlton. *Leics* 5A **74**
Carlton. *N Yor* 1A **100**
(nr. Helmsley)
Carlton. *N Yor* 1C **98**
(nr. Middleham)
Carlton. *N Yor* 2G **93**
(nr. Selby)
Carlton. *Notts* 1D **74**
Carlton. *S Yor* 3D **92**
Carlton. *Stoc T* 2A **106**
Carlton. *Suff* 4F **67**
Carlton. *W Yor* 2D **92**
Carlton Colville. *Suff* 1H **67**
Carlton Curlieu. *Leics* 1D **62**
Carlton Husthwaite. *N Yor* 2G **99**
Carlton in Cleveland. *N Yor* 4C **106**
Carlton in Lindrick. *Notts* 2C **86**
Carlton-le-Moorland. *Linc* 5G **87**
Carlton Miniott. *N Yor* 1F **99**
Carlton-on-Trent. *Notts* 4F **87**
Carlton Scroop. *Linc* 1G **75**
Carluke. *S Lan* 4B **128**
Carlyon Bay. *Corn* 3E **7**
Carmarthen. *Carm* 4E **45**
Carmel. *Carm* 4F **45**
Carmel. *Flin* 3D **82**
Carmel. *Gwyn* 5D **81**
Carmel. *IOA* 2C **80**
Carmichael. *S Lan* 1B **118**
Carmunnock. *Glas* 4H **127**
Carmyle. *S Lan* 3H **127**
Carmyllie. *Ang* 4E **145**
Carnaby. *E Yor* 3F **101**
Carnach. *High* 1C **148**
(nr. Lochcarron)
Carnach. *High* 4E **163**
(nr. Ullapool)
Carnach. *Mor* 4E **159**
Carnach. *W Isl* 8E **171**
Carnachy. *High* 3H **167**
Carnain. *Arg* 3B **124**
Carnais. *W Isl* 4C **171**
Carnan. *Arg* 4B **138**
Carnan. *W Isl* 4C **170**
Carnbee. *Fife* 3H **137**
Carnbo. *Per* 3C **136**
Carn Brea Village. *Corn* 4A **6**
Carndu. *High* 1A **148**
Carnduff. *Moy* 2G **175**
Carne. *Corn* 5D **6**
Carnell. *S Ayr* 1D **116**
Carnforth. *Lanc* 2E **97**
Carn-gorm. *High* 1B **148**
Carnhedryn. *Pemb* 2B **42**
Carnhell Green. *Corn* 3D **4**
Carnie. *Abers* 3F **153**
Carnkie. *Corn* 5B **6**
(nr. Falmouth)
Carnkie. *Corn* 5A **6**
(nr. Redruth)
Carnkief. *Corn* 3B **6**
Carnlough. *Lar* 5J **175**
Carnmoney. *Newt* 1H **179**
Carno. *Powy* 1B **58**
Carnock. *Fife* 1D **128**
Carnon Downs. *Corn* 4B **6**
Carnoustie. *Ang* 5E **145**
Carnteel. *Dngn* 4A **178**
Carntyne. *Glas* 3H **127**
Carnwath. *S Lan* 5C **128**
Carnyorth. *Corn* 3A **4**
Carol Green. *W Mid* 3G **61**
Carpalla. *Corn* 3D **6**
Carperby. *N Yor* 1C **98**
Carradale. *Arg* 2C **122**
Carragraich. *W Isl* 8D **171**
Carrbridge. *High* 1D **150**
Carr Cross. *Lanc* 3B **90**
Carreglefn. *IOA* 2C **80**
Carrhouse. *N Lin* 4A **94**
Carrick Castle. *Arg* 4A **134**
Carrickfergus. *Carr* 8L **175**
Carrick Ho. *Orkn* 4E **172**
Carrickmore. *Omag* 2A **178**
Carriden. *Falk* 1D **128**
Carrington. *G Man* 1B **84**
Carrington. *Linc* 5C **88**
Carrington. *Midl* 3G **129**
Carrog. *Cnwy* 1G **69**
Carrog. *Den* 1D **70**
Carron. *Falk* 1B **128**
Carron. *Mor* 4G **159**
Carronbridge. *Dum* 5A **118**
Carronshore. *Falk* 1B **128**
Carrowclare. *Lim* 4C **174**
Carrowdore. *Ards* 2K **179**
Carrow Hill. *Mon* 2H **33**
Carr Shield. *Nmbd* 5B **114**
Carrutherstown. *Dum* 2C **112**
Carr Vale. *Derbs* 4B **86**
Carrville. *Dur* 5G **115**
Carrycoats Hall. *Nmbd* 2C **114**
Carryduff. *Cast* 3H **179**
Carsaig. *Arg* 1C **132**
Carscreugh. *Dum* 3H **109**
Carsegowan. *Dum* 4B **110**
Carse House. *Arg* 3F **125**
Carseriggan. *Dum* 3A **110**
Carsethorn. *Dum* 4A **112**
Carshalton. *G Lon* 4D **38**
Carsington. *Derbs* 5G **85**
Carskiey. *Arg* 5A **122**
Carsluith. *Dum* 4B **110**
Carson Park. *Down* 4J **179**
Carsphairn. *Dum* 5E **117**
Carstairs. *S Lan* 5C **128**
Carstairs Junction. *S Lan* 5C **128**
Cartbridge. *Surr* 5B **38**
Carterhaugh. *Ang* 4D **144**
Carter's Clay. *Hants* 4B **24**
Carterton. *Oxon* 5A **50**
Carterway Heads. *Nmbd* 4D **114**
Carthew. *Corn* 3E **6**
Carthorpe. *N Yor* 1F **99**
Cartington. *Nmbd* 4E **121**
Cartland. *S Lan* 5B **128**
Cartmel. *Cumb* 2C **96**
Cartmel Fell. *Cumb* 1D **96**
Cartworth. *W Yor* 4B **92**
Carwath. *Cumb* 5E **112**
Carway. *Carm* 5E **45**
Carwinley. *Cumb* 2F **113**
Cascob. *Powy* 4E **59**
Cas-gwent. *Mon* 2A **34**
Cash Feus. *Fife* 3E **136**
Cashlie. *Per* 4B **142**
Cashmoor. *Dors* 1E **15**
Cas-Mael. *Pemb* 2E **43**
Casnewydd. *Newp* 3G **33** & **Newport 200**
Cassington. *Oxon* 4C **50**
Cassop. *Dur* 1A **106**
Castell. *Cnwy* 4G **81**
Castell. *Den* 4D **82**
Castell Hendre. *Pemb* 2E **43**
Castell-nedd. *Neat* 2A **32**
Castell Newydd Emlyn. *Carm* 1D **44**
Castell-y-bwch. *Torf* 2F **33**
Casterton. *Cumb* 2F **97**
Castle. *Som* 2A **22**
Castle Acre. *Norf* 4H **77**
Castle Ashby. *Nptn* 5F **63**
Castlebay. *W Isl* 9B **170**
Castle Bolton. *N Yor* 5D **104**
Castle Bromwich. *W Mid* 2F **61**
Castle Bytham. *Linc* 4G **75**
Castlebythe. *Pemb* 2E **43**
Castle Caereinion. *Powy* 5D **70**
Castle Camps. *Cambs* 1G **53**
Castle Carrock. *Cumb* 4G **113**
Castlecary. *N Lan* 2A **128**
Castle Cary. *Som* 3B **22**
Castlecaulfield. *Dngn* 3B **178**
Castle Combe. *Wilts* 4D **34**
Castlecraig. *High* 2C **158**
Castledawson. *Mag* 7F **174**
Castlederg. *Strab* 4E **176**
Castle Donington. *Leics* 3B **74**
Castle Douglas. *Dum* 3E **111**
Castle Eaton. *Swin* 2G **35**
Castle Eden. *Dur* 1B **106**
Castleford. *W Yor* 2E **93**
Castle Frome. *Here* 1B **48**
Castle Green. *Surr* 4A **38**
Castle Green. *Warw* 3G **61**
Castle Gresley. *Derbs* 4G **73**
Castle Heaton. *Nmbd* 5F **131**
Castle Hedingham. *Essx* 2A **54**
Castle Hill. *Kent* 1A **28**
Castlehill. *Per* 5B **144**
Castlehill. *S Lan* 4B **128**
Castle Hill. *Suff* 1E **55**
Castlehill. *W Dun* 2E **127**
Castle Kennedy. *Dum* 4G **109**
Castle Lachlan. *Arg* 4H **133**
Castlemartin. *Pemb* 5D **42**
Castlemilk. *Glas* 4H **127**
Castlemorris. *Pemb* 1D **42**
Castlemorton. *Worc* 2C **48**
Castle O'er. *Dum* 5E **119**
Castle Park. *N Yor* 3F **107**
Castlerigg. *Cumb* 2D **102**
Castle Rising. *Norf* 3F **77**
Castlerock. *Cole* 3D **174**
Castleroe. *Cole* 4E **174**
Castleside. *Dur* 5D **115**
Castlethorpe. *Mil* 1F **51**
Castleton. *Abers* 4F **151**
Castleton. *Arg* 1G **125**
Castleton. *Derbs* 2F **85**
Castleton. *G Man* 3G **91**
Castleton. *Mor* 1F **151**
Castleton. *Newp* 3F **33**
Castleton. *N Yor* 4D **107**
Castleton. *Per* 2B **136**
Castletown. *Cumb* 1G **103**
Castletown. *Dors* 5B **14**
Castletown. *High* 2D **169**
Castletown. *IOM* 5B **108**
Castletown. *Tyne* 4G **115**
Castlewellan. *Down* 6H **179**
Castley. *N Yor* 5E **99**
Caston. *Norf* 1B **66**
Castor. *Pet* 1A **64**
Caswell. *Swan* 4E **31**
Catacol. *N Ayr* 5H **125**
Catbrook. *Mon* 5A **48**
Catchems End. *Worc* 3B **60**
Catchgate. *Dur* 4E **115**
Catcleugh. *Nmbd* 4B **120**
Catcliffe. *S Yor* 2B **86**
Catcott. *Som* 3G **21**
Caterham. *Surr* 5E **39**
Catfield. *Norf* 3F **79**
Catfield Common. *Norf* 3F **79**
Catfirth. *Shet* 6F **173**
Catford. *G Lon* 3E **39**
Catforth. *Lanc* 1C **90**
Cathcart. *Glas* 3G **127**
Cathedine. *Powy* 3E **47**
Catherine-de-Barnes. *W Mid* 2F **61**
Catherington. *Hants* 1E **17**
Catherston Leweston. *Dors* 3G **13**
Catherton. *Shrp* 3A **60**
Catisfield. *Hants* 2D **16**
Catlodge. *High* 4A **150**
Catlowdy. *Cumb* 2F **113**
Catmore. *W Ber* 3C **36**
Caton. *Devn* 5A **12**
Caton. *Lanc* 3E **97**
Catrine. *E Ayr* 2E **117**
Cat's Ash. *Newp* 2G **33**
Catsfield. *E Sus* 4B **28**
Catsgore. *Som* 4A **22**
Catshill. *Worc* 3D **60**
Cattal. *N Yor* 4G **99**
Cattawade. *Suff* 2E **54**
Catterall. *Lanc* 5D **97**
Catterick. *N Yor* 5F **105**
Catterick Bridge. *N Yor* 5F **105**
Catterick Garrison. *N Yor* 5E **105**
Catterlen. *Cumb* 1F **103**
Catterline. *Abers* 1H **145**
Catterton. *N Yor* 5H **99**
Catteshall. *Surr* 1A **26**
Catthorpe. *Leics* 3C **62**
Cattistock. *Dors* 3A **14**
Catton. *Nmbd* 4B **114**
Catton. *N Yor* 2F **99**
Catwick. *E Yor* 5F **101**
Catworth. *Cambs* 3H **63**
Caudle Green. *Glos* 4E **49**
Caulcott. *Oxon* 3D **50**
Cauldhame. *Stir* 4F **135**
Cauldmill. *Bord* 3H **119**
Cauldon. *Staf* 1E **73**
Cauldon Lowe. *Staf* 1E **73**
Cauldwells. *Abers* 3E **161**
Caulkerbush. *Dum* 4G **111**
Caulside. *Dum* 1F **113**
Caunsall. *Worc* 2C **60**
Caunton. *Notts* 4E **87**
Causewayend. *S Lan* 1C **118**
Causewayhead. *Stir* 4H **135**
Causey Park. *Nmbd* 5F **121**
Caute. *Devn* 1E **11**
Cautley. *Cumb* 5H **103**
Cavendish. *Suff* 1B **54**
Cavendish Bridge. *Derbs* 2B **74**
Cavenham. *Suff* 4G **65**
Caversfield. *Oxon* 3D **50**
Caversham. *Read* 4F **37**
Caversham Heights. *Read* 4E **37**
Caverswall. *Staf* 1D **72**
Cawdor. *High* 4C **158**
Cawkwell. *Linc* 2B **88**
Cawood. *N Yor* 1F **93**
Cawsand. *Corn* 3A **8**
Cawston. *Norf* 3D **78**
Cawston. *Warw* 3B **62**
Cawthorne. *N Yor* 1B **100**
Cawthorne. *S Yor* 4C **92**
Cawthorpe. *Linc* 3H **75**
Cawton. *N Yor* 2A **100**
Caxton. *Cambs* 5C **64**
Caynham. *Shrp* 3H **59**
Caythorpe. *Linc* 1G **75**
Caythorpe. *Notts* 1D **74**
Cayton. *N Yor* 1E **101**
Ceallan. *W Isl* 3D **170**
Ceann a Bhàigh. *W Isl* 9C **171**
(on Harris)
Ceann a Bhaigh. *W Isl* 2C **170**
(on North Uist)
Ceann a Bhaigh. *W Isl* 8E **171**
(on Scalpay)
Ceann a Bhaigh. *W Isl* 8D **171**
(on South Harris)
Ceannacroc Lodge. *High* 2E **149**
Ceann a Deas Loch Baghasdail. *W Isl* 7C **170**
Ceann an Leothaid. *High* 5E **147**
Ceann a Tuath Loch Baghasdail. *W Isl* 6C **170**
Ceann Loch Ailleart. *High* 5F **147**
Ceann Loch Muideirt. *High* 1B **140**
Ceann Shìphoirt. *W Isl* 6E **171**
Ceann Tarabhaigh. *W Isl* 6E **171**
Cearsiadar. *W Isl* 5F **171**
Ceathramh Meadhanach. *W Isl* 1C **170**
Cefn Berain. *Cnwy* 4B **82**
Cefn-brith. *Cnwy* 5B **82**
Cefn-bryn-brain. *Carm* 4H **45**
Cefn Bychan. *Cphy* 2F **33**
Cefn-bychan. *Flin* 4D **82**
Cefncaeau. *Carm* 3E **31**
Cefn Canol. *Powy* 2E **71**
Cefn Coch. *Powy* 5C **70**
(nr. Llanfair Caereinion)
Cefn-coch. *Powy* 3D **70**
(nr. Llanrhaeadr-ym-Mochnant)
Cefn-coed-y-cymmer. *Mer T* 5D **46**
Cefn Cribwr. *B'end* 3B **32**
Cefn-ddwysarn. *Gwyn* 2B **70**
Cefn Einion. *Shrp* 2E **59**
Cefneithin. *Carm* 4F **45**
Cefn Glas. *B'end* 3B **32**
Cefngorwydd. *Powy* 1C **46**
Cefn Llwyd. *Cdgn* 2F **57**
Cefn-mawr. *Wrex* 1E **71**
Cefn-y-bedd. *Flin* 5F **83**
Cefn-y-coed. *Powy* 1D **58**
Cefn-y-pant. *Carm* 2F **43**
Cegidfa. *Powy* 4E **70**
Ceinewydd. *Cdgn* 5C **56**
Cellan. *Cdgn* 1G **45**
Cellardyke. *Fife* 3H **137**
Cellarhead. *Staf* 1D **72**
Cemaes. *IOA* 1C **80**
Cemmaes. *Powy* 5H **69**
Cemmaes Road. *Powy* 5H **69**
Cenarth. *Carm* 1C **44**
Cenin. *Gwyn* 1D **68**
Ceos. *W Isl* 5F **171**
Ceres. *Fife* 2G **137**
Ceri. *Powy* 2D **58**
Cerist. *Powy* 2B **58**
Cerne Abbas. *Dors* 2B **14**
Cerney Wick. *Glos* 2F **35**
Cerrigceinwen. *IOA* 3D **80**
Cerrigydrudion. *Cnwy* 1B **70**
Cess. *Norf* 4G **79**
Cessford. *Bord* 2B **120**
Ceunant. *Gwyn* 4E **81**
Chaceley. *Glos* 2D **48**
Chacewater. *Corn* 4B **6**
Chackmore. *Buck* 2E **51**
Chacombe. *Nptn* 1C **50**
Chadderton. *G Man* 4H **91**
Chaddesden. *Derb* 2A **74**
Chaddesden Common. *Derb* 2A **74**
Chaddesley Corbett. *Worc* 3C **60**
Chaddlehanger. *Devn* 5E **11**
Chaddleworth. *W Ber* 4C **36**
Chadlington. *Oxon* 3B **50**
Chadshunt. *Warw* 5H **61**
Chadstone. *Nptn* 5F **63**
Chad Valley. *W Mid* 2E **61**
Chadwell. *Leics* 3E **75**
Chadwell. *Shrp* 4B **72**
Chadwell Heath. *G Lon* 2F **39**
Chadwell St Mary. *Thur* 3H **39**
Chadwick End. *W Mid* 3G **61**
Chadwick Green. *Mers* 1H **83**
Chaffcombe. *Som* 1G **13**
Chafford Hundred. *Thur* 3H **39**
Chagford. *Devn* 4H **11**
Chailey. *E Sus* 4E **27**
Chainbridge. *Cambs* 5D **76**
Chain Bridge. *Linc* 1C **76**
Chainhurst. *Kent* 1B **28**
Chalbury. *Dors* 2F **15**
Chalbury Common. *Dors* 2F **15**
Chaldon. *Surr* 5E **39**
Chaldon Herring. *Dors* 4C **14**
Chale. *IOW* 5C **16**
Chale Green. *IOW* 5C **16**
Chalfont Common. *Buck* 1B **38**
Chalfont St Giles. *Buck* 1A **38**
Chalfont St Peter. *Buck* 2B **38**
Chalford. *Glos* 5D **49**
Chalgrove. *Oxon* 2E **37**
Chalk. *Kent* 3A **40**
Chalk End. *Essx* 4G **53**
Chalk Hill. *Glos* 3G **49**
Challaborough. *Devn* 4C **8**
Challacombe. *Devn* 2G **19**
Challister. *Shet* 5G **173**
Challoch. *Dum* 3A **110**
Challock. *Kent* 5E **40**
Chalton. *C Beds* 5A **64**
(nr. Bedford)
Chalton. *C Beds* 3A **52**
(nr. Luton)
Chalton. *Hants* 1F **17**
Chalvington. *E Sus* 5G **27**
Champany. *Falk* 2D **128**
Chance Inn. *Fife* 2F **137**
Chancery. *Cdgn* 3E **57**
Chandler's Cross. *Herts* 1B **38**
Chandler's Cross. *Worc* 2C **48**
Chandler's Ford. *Hants* 4C **24**
Chanlockfoot. *Dum* 4G **117**
Channel's End. *Bed* 5A **64**
Channel Tunnel. *Kent* 2F **29**
Channerwick. *Shet* 9F **173**
Chantry. *Som* 2C **22**
Chantry. *Suff* 1E **55**
Chapel. *Cumb* 1D **102**
Chapel. *Fife* 4E **137**
Chapel Allerton. *Som* 1H **21**
Chapel Allerton. *W Yor* 1D **92**
Chapel Amble. *Corn* 1D **6**
Chapel Brampton. *Nptn* 4E **63**
Chapelbridge. *Cambs* 1B **64**
Chapel Chorlton. *Staf* 2C **72**
Chapel Cleeve. *Som* 2D **20**
Chapel End. *C Beds* 1A **52**
Chapel-en-le-Frith. *Derbs* 2E **85**
Chapelfield. *Abers* 2G **145**
Chapelgate. *Linc* 3D **76**
Chapel Green. *Warw* 2G **61**
(nr. Coventry)
Chapel Green. *Warw* 4B **62**
(nr. Southam)
Chapel Haddlesey. *N Yor* 2F **93**
Chapelhall. *N Lan* 3A **128**
Chapel Hill. *Abers* 5H **161**
Chapel Hill. *Linc* 5B **88**
Chapel Hill. *Mon* 5A **48**
Chapelhill. *Per* 1E **136**
(nr. Glencarse)
Chapelhill. *Per* 5H **143**
(nr. Harrietfield)
Chapelknowe. *Dum* 2E **112**
Chapel Lawn. *Shrp* 3F **59**
Chapel le Dale. *N Yor* 2G **97**
Chapel Milton. *Derbs* 2E **85**
Chapel of Garioch. *Abers* 1E **152**
Chapel Row. *W Ber* 5D **36**
Chapels. *Cumb* 1B **96**
Chapel St Leonards. *Linc* 3E **89**
Chapel Stile. *Cumb* 4E **102**
Chapelthorne. *W Yor* 3D **92**
Chapelton. *Ang* 4F **145**
Chapelton. *Devn* 4F **19**
Chapelton. *High* 2D **150**
(nr. Grantown-on-Spey)
Chapelton. *High* 3H **157**
(nr. Inverness)
Chapelton. *S Lan* 5H **127**
Chapeltown. *Bkbn* 3F **91**
Chapel Town. *Corn* 3C **6**
Chapeltown. *Down* 6K **179**
Chapeltown. *Mor* 1G **151**
Chapeltown. *S Yor* 1H **85**
Chapmanslade. *Wilts* 2D **22**
Chapmans Well. *Devn* 3D **10**
Chapmore End. *Herts* 4D **52**
Chappel. *Essx* 3B **54**
Chard. *Som* 2G **13**
Chard Junction. *Dors* 2G **13**
Chardstock. *Devn* 2G **13**
Charfield. *S Glo* 2C **34**
Charing. *Kent* 1D **28**
Charing Heath. *Kent* 1D **28**
Charing Hill. *Kent* 5D **40**
Charingworth. *Glos* 2G **49**
Charlbury. *Oxon* 4B **50**
Charlcombe. *Bath* 5C **34**
Charlcutt. *Wilts* 4E **35**
Charlecote. *Warw* 5G **61**
Charlemont. *Arm* 4C **178**
Charles. *Devn* 3G **19**
Charlesfield. *Dum* 3C **112**
Charleshill. *Surr* 2G **25**
Charleston. *Ang* 4C **144**
Charleston. *Ren* 3F **127**
Charlestown. *Aber* 3G **153**
Charlestown. *Abers* 2H **161**
Charlestown. *Corn* 3E **7**
Charlestown. *Dors* 5B **14**
Charlestown. *Fife* 1D **128**
Charlestown. *G Man* 4G **91**
Charlestown. *High* 1H **155**
(nr. Gairloch)
Charlestown. *High* 4A **158**
(nr. Inverness)
Charlestown. *W Yor* 2H **91**
Charlestown of Aberlour. *Mor* 4G **159**
Charles Tye. *Suff* 5C **66**
Charlesworth. *Derbs* 1E **85**
Charlton. *G Lon* 3F **39**
Charlton. *Hants* 2B **24**
Charlton. *Herts* 3B **52**
Charlton. *Nptn* 2D **50**
Charlton. *Nmbd* 1B **114**
Charlton. *Oxon* 3C **36**
Charlton. *Som* 1B **22**
(nr. Radstock)
Charlton. *Som* 2B **22**
(nr. Shepton Mallet)
Charlton. *Som* 4F **21**
(nr. Taunton)
Charlton. *Telf* 4H **71**
Charlton. *W Sus* 1G **17**

Dam Green—Easter Tulloch

Dam Green. Norf 2C 66
Damhead. Mor 3E 159
Danaway. Kent 4C 40
Danbury. Essx 5A 54
Danby. N Yor 4E 107
Danby Botton. N Yor 4D 107
Danby Wiske. N Yor 5A 106
Danderhall. Midl 3G 129
Danebank. Ches E 2D 85
Danebridge. Ches E 4D 84
Dane End. Herts 3D 52
Danehill. E Sus 3F 27
Danesford. Shrp 1B 60
Daneshill. Hants 1E 25
Danesmoor. Derbs 4B 86
Danestone. Aber 2G 153
Dangerous Corner. Lanc 3D 90
Daniel's Water. Kent 1D 28
Dan's Castle. Dur 1E 105
Danzey Green. Warw 4F 61
Dapple Heath. Staf 3E 73
Daren. Powy 4F 47
Darenth. Kent 3G 39
Daresbury. Hal 2H 83
Darfield. S Yor 4E 93
Dargate. Kent 4E 41
Dargill. Per 2A 136
Darite. Corn 2G 7
Darkley. Arm 6C 178
Darlaston. W Mid 1D 60
Darley. N Yor 4E 98
Darley Abbey. Derb 2A 74
Darley Bridge. Derbs 4G 85
Darley Dale. Derbs 4G 85
Darley Head. N Yor 4D 98
Darlingscott. Warw 1H 49
Darlington. Darl 3F 105
Darliston. Shrp 2H 71
Darlton. Notts 3E 87
Darmsden. Suff 5C 66
Darnall. S Yor 2A 86
Darnford. Abers 4E 153
Darnford. Staf 5F 73
Darnhall. Ches W 4A 84
Darnick. Bord 1H 119
Darowen. Powy 5H 69
Darra. Abers 4E 161
Darracott. Devn 3E 19
Darragh Cross. Down 4J 179
Darras Hall. Nmbd 2E 115
Darrington. W Yor 3E 93
Darrow Green. Norf 2E 67
Darsham. Suff 4G 67
Dartfield. Abers 3H 161
Dartford. Kent 3G 39
Dartford-Thurrock River Crossing. Kent 3G 39
Dartington. Devn 2D 9
Dartmeet. Devn 5G 11
Dartmoor. Devn 4F 11
Dartmouth. Devn 3E 9
Darton. S Yor 3D 92
Darvel. E Ayr 1E 117
Darwen. Bkbn 2E 91
Dassels. Herts 3D 53
Datchet. Wind 3A 38
Datchworth. Herts 4C 52
Datchworth Green. Herts 4C 52
Daubhill. G Man 4F 91
Dauntsey. Wilts 3E 35
Dauntsey Green. Wilts 3E 35
Dauntsey Lock. Wilts 3E 35
Dava. Mor 5E 159
Davenham. Ches W 3A 84
Daventry. Nptn 4C 62
Davidson's Mains. Edin 2F 129
Davidston. High 2B 158
Davidstow. Corn 4B 10
David's Well. Powy 3C 58
Davington. Dum 4E 119
Daviot. Abers 1E 153
Daviot. High 5B 158
Davyhulme. G Man 1B 84
Daw Cross. N Yor 4E 99
Dawdon. Dur 5H 115
Dawesgreen. Surr 1D 26
Dawley. Telf 5A 72
Dawlish. Devn 5C 12
Dawlish Warren. Devn 5C 12
Dawn. Cnwy 3A 82
Daws Heath. Essx 2C 40
Dawshill. Worc 5C 60
Daw's House. Corn 4D 10
Dawsmere. Linc 2D 76
Dayhills. Staf 2D 72
Dayhouse Bank. Worc 3D 60
Daylesford. Glos 3H 49
Daywall. Shrp 2E 71
Ddol. Flin 3D 82
Ddol Cownwy. Powy 4C 70
Deadman's Cross. C Beds 1B 52
Deadwater. Nmbd 5A 120
Deaf Hill. Dur 1A 106
Deal. Kent 5H 41
Dean. Cumb 2B 102
Dean. Devn 2G 19 (nr. Combe Martin)
Dean. Devn 2H 19 (nr. Lynton)
Dean. Dors 1E 15
Dean. Hants 1D 16 (nr. Bishop's Waltham)
Dean. Hants 3C 24 (nr. Winchester)
Dean. Oxon 3B 50
Dean. Som 2B 22
Dean Bank. Dur 1F 105
Deanburnhaugh. Bord 3F 119
Dean Cross. Devn 2F 19
Deane. Hants 1D 24
Deanich Lodge. High 5A 164
Deanland. Dors 1E 15
Deanlane End. W Sus 1F 17
Dean Park. Shrp 4H 59
Dean Prior. Devn 2D 8
Dean Row. Ches E 2C 84
Deans. W Lot 3D 128
Deanscales. Cumb 2B 102
Deanshanger. Nptn 2F 51
Deanston. Stir 3G 135
Dearham. Cumb 1B 102
Dearne. S Yor 4E 93
Dearne Valley. S Yor 4D 93
Debach. Suff 5E 67
Debden. Essx 2F 53
Debden Green. Essx 1F 39 (nr. Loughton)
Debden Green. Essx 2F 53 (nr. Saffron Walden)
Debenham. Suff 4D 66
Dechmont. W Lot 2D 128
Deddington. Oxon 2C 50
Dedham. Essx 2D 54
Dedham Heath. Essx 2D 54
Deebank. Abers 4D 152
Deene. Nptn 1G 63
Deenethorpe. Nptn 1G 63
Deepcar. S Yor 1G 85
Deepcut. Surr 5A 38
Deepdale. Cumb 1G 97
Deepdale. N Lin 3D 94
Deepdale. N Yor 2A 98
Deeping Gate. Pet 5A 76
Deeping St James. Linc 5A 76
Deeping St Nicholas. Linc 4B 76
Deerhill. Mor 3B 160
Deerhurst. Glos 3D 48
Deerhurst Walton. Glos 3D 49
Deerness. Orkn 7E 172
Defford. Worc 1E 49
Defynnog. Powy 3C 46
Deganwy. Cnwy 3G 81
Deighton. N Yor 4A 106
Deighton. W Yor 3B 92
Deighton. York 5A 100
Deiniolen. Gwyn 4E 81
Delabole. Corn 4A 10
Delamere. Ches W 4H 83
Delfour. High 3C 150
Delliefure. High 5E 159
Dell, The. Suff 1G 67
Delly End. Oxon 4B 50
Delny. High 1B 158
Delph. G Man 4H 91
Delves. Dur 5E 115
Delves, The. W Mid 1E 61
Delvin End. Essx 2A 54
Dembleby. Linc 2H 75
Demelza. Corn 2D 6
Denaby Main. S Yor 1B 86
Denbeath. Fife 4F 137
Denbigh. Den 4C 82
Denbury. Devn 2E 9
Denby. Derbs 1A 74
Denby Common. Derbs 1B 74
Denby Dale. W Yor 4C 92
Denchworth. Oxon 2B 36
Dendron. Cumb 2B 96
Deneside. Dur 5H 115
Denford. Nptn 3G 63
Dengie. Essx 5C 54
Denham. Buck 2B 38
Denham. Suff 4G 65 (nr. Bury St Edmunds)
Denham. Suff 3D 66 (nr. Eye)
Denham Green. Buck 2B 38
Denham Street. Suff 3D 66
Denhead. Abers 3G 161 (nr. Ellon)
Denhead. Abers 3G 161 (nr. Strichen)
Denhead. Fife 2G 137
Denholm. Bord 3H 119
Denholme. W Yor 1A 92
Denholme Clough. W Yor 1A 92
Denholme Gate. W Yor 1A 92
Denio. Gwyn 2C 68
Denmead. Hants 1E 17
Dennington. Suff 4E 67
Denny. Falk 1B 128
Denny End. Cambs 4D 65
Dennyloanhead. Falk 1B 128
Den of Lindores. Fife 2E 137
Denshaw. G Man 3H 91
Denside. Abers 4F 153
Densole. Kent 1G 29
Denston. Suff 5G 65
Denstone. Staf 1F 73
Denstroude. Kent 4E 41
Dent. Cumb 1G 97
Den, The. N Ayr 4E 127
Denton. Cambs 2A 64
Denton. Darl 3F 105
Denton. E Sus 5F 27
Denton. G Man 1D 84
Denton. Kent 1G 29
Denton. Linc 2F 75
Denton. Norf 2E 67
Denton. Nptn 5F 63
Denton. N Yor 5D 98
Denton. Oxon 5D 50
Denver. Norf 5F 77
Denwick. Nmbd 3G 121
Deopham. Norf 5C 78
Deopham Green. Norf 1C 66
Depden. Suff 5G 65
Depden Green. Suff 5G 65
Deptford. G Lon 3E 39
Deptford. Wilts 3F 23
Derby. Derb 2A 74 & 194
Derbyhaven. IOM 5B 108
Derculich. Per 3F 143
Dereham. Norf 4B 78
Deri. Cphy 5E 47
Derril. Devn 2D 10
Derringstone. Kent 1G 29
Derrington. Shrp 1A 60
Derrington. Staf 3C 72
Derriton. Devn 2D 10
Derry. Derr 5A 174
Derryboye. Down 4J 179
Derrycrin. Cook 2D 178
Derrygonnelly. Ferm 7D 176
Derryguaig. Arg 5F 139
Derry Hill. Wilts 4E 35
Derrykeighan. Bmny 3F 175
Derrylin. Ferm 7H 177
Derrymacash. Cgvn 3E 178
Derrythorpe. N Lin 4B 94
Derrytrasna. Cgvn 3D 178
Dersingham. Norf 2F 77
Dervaig. Arg 3F 139
Dervock. Bmny 3F 175
Derwen. Den 5C 82
Derwen Gam. Cdgn 5D 56
Derwenlas. Powy 1G 57
Desborough. Nptn 2F 63
Desertmartin. Mag 7E 174
Desford. Leics 5B 74
Detchant. Nmbd 1E 121
Dethick. Derbs 5H 85
Detling. Kent 5B 40
Deuchar. Ang 2D 144
Deuddwr. Powy 4E 71
Devauden. Mon 2H 33
Devil's Bridge. Cdgn 3G 57
Devitts Green. Warw 1G 61
Devizes. Wilts 5F 35
Devonport. Plym 3A 8
Devonside. Clac 4B 136
Devoran. Corn 5B 6
Dewartown. Midl 3G 129
Dewlish. Dors 3C 14
Dewsbury. W Yor 2C 92
Dewshall Court. Here 2H 47
Dexbeer. Devn 2C 10
Dhoon. IOM 3D 108
Dhoor. IOM 2D 108
Dhowin. IOM 1D 108
Dial Green. W Sus 3A 26
Dial Post. W Sus 4C 26
Dibberford. Dors 2H 13
Dibden. Hants 2C 16
Dibden Purlieu. Hants 2C 16
Dickleburgh. Norf 2D 66
Didbrook. Glos 2F 49
Didcot. Oxon 2D 36
Diddington. Cambs 4A 64
Diddlebury. Shrp 2H 59
Didley. Here 2H 47
Didling. W Sus 1G 17
Didmarton. Glos 3D 34
Didsbury. G Man 1C 84
Didworthy. Devn 2C 8
Digby. Linc 5H 87
Digg. High 2D 154
Diggle. G Man 4A 92
Digmoor. Lanc 4C 90
Digswell. Herts 4C 52
Dihewyd. Cdgn 5D 57
Dilham. Norf 3F 79
Dilhorne. Staf 1D 72
Dillarburn. S Lan 5B 128
Dillington. Cambs 4A 64
Dilston. Nmbd 3C 114
Dilton Marsh. Wilts 2D 22
Dilwyn. Here 5G 59
Dimmer. Som 3B 22
Dimple. G Man 3F 91
Dinas. Carm 1G 43
Dinas. Gwyn 5D 81 (nr. Caernarfon)
Dinas. Gwyn 2B 68 (nr. Tudweiliog)
Dinas Cross. Pemb 1E 43
Dinas Dinlle. Gwyn 5D 80
Dinas Mawddwy. Gwyn 4A 70
Dinas Powys. V Glam 4E 33
Dinbych. Den 4C 82
Dinbych-y-Pysgod. Pemb 4F 43
Dinckley. Lanc 1E 91
Dinder. Som 2A 22
Dinedor. Here 2A 48
Dinedor Cross. Here 2A 48
Dingestow. Mon 4H 47
Dingle. Mers 2F 83
Dingleden. Kent 2C 28
Dingleton. Bord 1H 119
Dingley. Nptn 2E 63
Dingwall. High 3H 157
Dinmael. Cnwy 1C 70
Dinnet. Abers 4B 152
Dinnington. Som 1H 13
Dinnington. S Yor 2C 86
Dinnington. Tyne 2F 115
Dinorwig. Gwyn 4E 81
Dinton. Buck 4F 51
Dinton. Wilts 3F 23
Dinworthy. Devn 1D 10
Dipley. Hants 1F 25
Dippen. Arg 2B 122
Dippenhall. Surr 2G 25
Dippertown. Devn 4E 11
Dippin. N Ayr 3E 123
Dipple. S Ayr 4B 116
Diptford. Devn 3D 8
Dipton. Dur 4E 115
Dirleton. E Lot 1B 130
Dirt Pot. Nmbd 5B 114
Discoed. Powy 4E 59
Diseworth. Leics 3B 74
Dishes. Orkn 5F 172
Dishforth. N Yor 2F 99
Disley. Ches E 2D 85
Diss. Norf 3D 66
Disserth. Powy 5C 58
Distington. Cumb 2B 102
Ditchampton. Wilts 3F 23
Ditcheat. Som 3B 22
Ditchingham. Norf 1F 67
Ditchling. E Sus 4E 27
Ditteridge. Wilts 5D 34
Dittisham. Devn 3E 9
Ditton. Hal 2G 83
Ditton. Kent 5B 40
Ditton Green. Cambs 5F 65
Ditton Priors. Shrp 2A 60
Divach. High 1G 149
Dixonfield. High 2D 168
Dixton. Glos 2E 49
Dixton. Mon 4A 48
Dizzard. Corn 3B 10
Doagh. Newt 8J 175
Dobcross. G Man 4H 91
Dobs Hill. Flin 4F 83
Dobson's Bridge. Shrp 2G 71
Dobwalls. Corn 2G 7
Doccombe. Devn 4A 12
Dochgarroch. High 4A 158
Docking. Norf 2G 77
Docklow. Here 5H 59
Dockray. Cumb 2E 103
Doc Penfro. Pemb 4D 42 & 204
Dodbrooke. Devn 4D 8
Doddenham. Worc 5B 60
Doddinghurst. Essx 1G 39
Doddington. Cambs 1C 64
Doddington. Kent 5D 40
Doddington. Linc 4G 87
Doddington. Nmbd 1D 121
Doddington. Shrp 3A 60
Doddiscombsleigh. Devn 4B 12
Doddshill. Norf 2G 77
Dodford. Nptn 4D 62
Dodford. Worc 3D 60
Dodington. Som 2E 21
Dodington. S Glo 4C 34
Dodleston. Ches W 4F 83
Dods Leigh. Staf 2E 73
Dodworth. S Yor 4D 92
Doe Lea. Derbs 4B 86
Dogdyke. Linc 5B 88
Dogmersfield. Hants 1F 25
Dogsthorpe. Pet 5B 76
Dog Village. Devn 3C 12
Dolanog. Powy 4C 70
Dolau. Powy 4D 58
Dolau. Rhon 3D 32
Dolbenmaen. Gwyn 1E 69
Doley. Staf 3B 72
Dol-fach. Powy 5B 70 (nr. Llanbrynmair)
Dolfach. Powy 3B 58 (nr. Llanidloes)
Dolfor. Powy 2D 58
Dolgarrog. Cnwy 4G 81
Dolgellau. Gwyn 4G 69
Dolgoch. Gwyn 5F 69
Dol-gran. Carm 2E 45
Dolhelfa. Powy 3B 58
Doll. High 3F 165
Dollar. Clac 4B 136
Dolley Green. Powy 4E 59
Dollingstown. Cgvn 4F 178
Dollwen. Cdgn 2F 57
Dolphin. Flin 3D 82
Dolphinholme. Lanc 4E 97
Dolphinton. S Lan 5E 129
Dolton. Devn 1F 11
Dolwen. Cnwy 3A 82
Dolwyddelan. Cnwy 5G 81
Dol-y-Bont. Cdgn 2F 57
Dolyhir. Powy 5E 59
Domgay. Powy 4E 71
Donagh. Ferm 7J 177
Donaghadee. Ards 2K 179
Donaghcloney. Cgvn 5G 178
Donaghmore. Dngn 3B 178
Doncaster. S Yor 4F 93
Donhead St Andrew. Wilts 4E 23
Donhead St Mary. Wilts 4E 23
Doniford. Som 2D 20
Donington. Linc 2B 76
Donington. Shrp 5C 72
Donington Eaudike. Linc 2B 76
Donington le Heath. Leics 4B 74
Donington on Bain. Linc 2B 88
Donington South Ing. Linc 2B 76
Donisthorpe. Leics 4H 73
Donkey Street. Kent 2F 29
Donkey Town. Surr 4A 38
Donna Nook. Linc 1D 88
Donnington. Glos 3G 49
Donnington. Here 2C 48
Donnington. Shrp 5H 71
Donnington. Telf 4B 72
Donnington. W Ber 5C 36
Donnington. W Sus 2G 17
Donyatt. Som 1G 13
Doomsday Green. W Sus 2C 26
Doonfoot. S Ayr 3C 116
Doonholm. S Ayr 3C 116
Dorback Lodge. High 2E 151
Dorchester. Dors 3B 14
Dorchester on Thames. Oxon 2D 36
Dordon. Warw 5G 73
Dore. S Yor 2H 85
Dores. High 5H 157
Dorking. Surr 1C 26
Dorking Tye. Suff 2C 54
Dormansland. Surr 1F 27
Dormans Park. Surr 1E 27
Dormanstown. Red C 2C 106
Dormington. Here 1A 48
Dormston. Worc 5D 61
Dorn. Glos 2H 49
Dorney. Buck 3A 38
Dornie. High 1A 148
Dornoch. High 5E 165
Dornock. Dum 3D 112
Dorrery. High 3C 168
Dorridge. W Mid 3F 61
Dorrington. Linc 5H 87
Dorrington. Shrp 5G 71
Dorsington. Warw 1G 49
Dorstone. Here 1G 47
Dorton. Buck 4E 51
Dotham. IOA 3C 80
Dottery. Dors 3H 13
Doublebois. Corn 2F 7
Dougarie. N Ayr 2C 122
Doughton. Glos 2D 35
Douglas. IOM 4C 108
Douglas. S Lan 1H 117
Douglas Bridge. Strab 3F 176
Douglastown. Ang 4D 144
Douglas Water. S Lan 1A 118
Doulting. Som 2B 22
Dounby. Orkn 5B 172
Doune. High 3C 150 (nr. Kingussie)
Doune. High 3B 164 (nr. Lairg)
Doune. Stir 3G 135
Dounie. High 4C 164 (nr. Bonar Bridge)
Dounie. High 5D 164 (nr. Tain)
Dounreay. High 2B 168
Doura. N Ayr 5E 127
Dousland. Devn 2B 8
Dovaston. Shrp 3F 71
Dove Holes. Derbs 3E 85
Dovenby. Cumb 1B 102
Dover. Kent 1H 29 & 194
Dovercourt. Essx 2F 55
Doverdale. Worc 4C 60
Doveridge. Derbs 2F 73
Doversgreen. Surr 1D 26
Dowally. Per 4H 143
Dowbridge. Lanc 1C 90
Dowdeswell. Glos 4F 49
Dowlais. Mer T 5D 46
Dowland. Devn 1F 11
Dowlands. Devn 3F 13
Dowles. Worc 3B 60
Dowlesgreen. Wok 5G 37
Dowlish Wake. Som 1G 13
Downall Green. Mers 4D 90
Down Ampney. Glos 2F 35
Downderry. Corn 3H 7 (nr. Looe)
Downderry. Corn 3D 6 (nr. St Austell)
Downe. G Lon 4F 39
Downend. IOW 4D 16
Downend. S Glo 4B 34
Downend. W Ber 4C 36
Down Field. Cambs 3F 65
Downfield. D'dee 5C 144
Downgate. Corn 5D 10 (nr. Kelly Bray)
Downgate. Corn 5C 10 (nr. Upton Cross)
Downham. Essx 1B 40
Downham. Lanc 5G 97
Downham. Nmbd 1C 120
Downham Market. Norf 5F 77
Down Hatherley. Glos 3D 48
Downhead. Som 2B 22 (nr. Frome)
Downhead. Som 4A 22 (nr. Yeovil)
Downhill. Cole 3D 174
Downholland Cross. Lanc 4B 90
Downholme. N Yor 5E 105
Downies. Abers 4G 153
Downley. Buck 2G 37
Downpatrick. Down 5J 179
Down St Mary. Devn 2H 11
Downside. Som 1B 22 (nr. Chilcompton)
Downside. Som 2B 22 (nr. Shepton Mallet)
Downside. Surr 5C 38
Down, The. Shrp 1A 60
Down Thomas. Devn 3B 8
Downton. Hants 3A 16
Downton. Wilts 4G 23
Downton on the Rock. Here 3G 59
Dowsby. Linc 3A 76
Dowsdale. Linc 4B 76
Dowthwaitehead. Cumb 2E 103
Doxey. Staf 3D 72
Doxford. Nmbd 2F 121
Doynton. S Glo 4C 34
Drabblegate. Norf 3E 78
Draethen. Cphy 3F 33
Draffan. S Lan 5A 128
Dragonby. N Lin 3C 94
Dragons Green. W Sus 3C 26
Drakelow. Worc 2C 60
Drakemyre. N Ayr 4D 126
Drakes Broughton. Worc 1E 49
Drakes Cross. Worc 3E 61
Drakewalls. Corn 5E 11
Draperstown. Mag 7D 174
Draughton. Nptn 3E 63
Draughton. N Yor 4C 98
Drax. N Yor 2G 93
Draycot. Oxon 5E 51
Draycote. Warw 3B 62
Draycot Foliat. Swin 4G 35
Draycott. Derbs 2B 74
Draycott. Glos 2G 49
Draycott. Shrp 1C 60
Draycott. Som 1H 21 (nr. Cheddar)
Draycott. Som 4A 22 (nr. Yeovil)
Draycott. Worc 1D 48
Draycott in the Clay. Staf 3F 73
Draycott in the Moors. Staf 1D 73
Drayford. Devn 1A 12
Drayton. Leics 1F 63
Drayton. Linc 2B 76
Drayton. Norf 4D 78
Drayton. Nptn 4C 62
Drayton. Oxon 2C 36 (nr. Abingdon)
Drayton. Oxon 1C 50 (nr. Banbury)
Drayton. Port 2E 17
Drayton. Som 4H 21
Drayton. Warw 5F 61
Drayton. Worc 3D 60
Drayton Bassett. Staf 5F 73
Drayton Beauchamp. Buck 4H 51
Drayton Parslow. Buck 3G 51
Drayton St Leonard. Oxon 2D 36
Drebley. N Yor 4C 98
Dreenhill. Pemb 3D 42
Drefach. Carm 4F 45 (nr. Meidrim)
Drefach. Carm 2D 44 (nr. Newcastle Emlyn)
Drefach. Carm 2G 43 (nr. Tumble)
Drefach. Cdgn 1E 45
Dreghorn. N Ayr 1C 116
Drellingore. Kent 1G 29
Drem. E Lot 2B 130
Dreumasdal. W Isl 5C 170
Drewsteignton. Devn 3H 11
Driby. Linc 3C 88
Driffield. E Yor 4E 101
Driffield. Glos 2F 35
Drift. Corn 4B 4
Drigg. Cumb 5B 102
Drighlington. W Yor 2C 92
Drimnin. High 3G 139
Drimpton. Dors 2H 13
Dringhoe. E Yor 4F 101
Drinisiadar. W Isl 8D 171
Drinkstone. Suff 4B 66
Drinkstone Green. Suff 4B 66
Drointon. Staf 3E 73
Droitwich Spa. Worc 4C 60
Droman. High 3B 166
Dromara. Lis 5G 179
Dromore. Ban 4G 179
Dromore. Omag 6F 176
Dron. Per 2D 136
Dronfield. Derbs 3A 86
Dronfield Woodhouse. Derbs 3H 85
Drongan. E Ayr 3D 116
Dronley. Ang 5C 144
Droop. Dors 2C 14
Drope. V Glam 4E 32
Droxford. Hants 1E 16
Droylsden. G Man 1C 84
Druggers End. Worc 2C 48
Druid. Den 1C 70
Druid's Heath. W Mid 5E 73
Druidston. Pemb 3C 42
Druim. High 3D 158
Druimarbin. High 1E 141
Druim Fhearna. High 2E 147
Druimindarroch. High 5E 147
Druim Saighdinis. W Isl 2D 170
Drum. Per 3C 136
Drumaness. Down 5H 179
Drumaroad. Down 5H 179
Drumbeg. High 5B 166
Drumblade. Abers 4C 160
Drumbo. Lis 3H 179
Drumbuie. Dum 1C 110
Drumbuie. High 5G 155
Drumburgh. Cumb 4D 112
Drumburn. Dum 3A 112
Drumchapel. Glas 2G 127
Drumchardine. High 4H 157
Drumchork. High 5C 162
Drumclog. S Lan 1F 117
Drumeldrie. Fife 3G 137
Drumelzier. Bord 1D 118
Drumfearn. High 2E 147
Drumgask. High 4A 150
Drumgelloch. N Lan 3A 128
Drumgley. Ang 3D 144
Drumguish. High 4B 150
Drumin. Mor 5F 159
Drumindorsair. High 4G 157
Drumintee. New M 8E 178
Drumlamford House. S Ayr 2H 109
Drumlasie. Abers 3D 152
Drumlemble. Arg 4A 122
Drumlithie. Abers 5E 153
Drummoddie. Dum 5A 110
Drummond. High 2A 158
Drummore. Dum 5E 109
Drummuir. Mor 4A 160
Drumnacanvy. Cgvn 4E 178
Drumnadrochit. High 5H 157
Drumnagorrach. Mor 3C 160
Drumnakilly. Omag 2L 177
Drumoak. Abers 4E 153
Drumquin. Omag 5F 176
Drumraighland. Lim 4C 174
Drumrunie. High 3F 163
Drumry. W Dun 2G 127
Drums. Abers 1G 153
Drumsleet. Dum 2G 111
Drumsmittal. High 4A 158
Drums of Park. Abers 3C 160
Drumsturdy. Ang 5D 145
Drumsurn. Lim 5D 174
Drumtochty Castle. Abers 5D 152
Drumuie. High 4D 154
Drumuillie. High 1D 150
Drumvaich. Stir 3F 135
Drumwhindle. Abers 5G 161
Drunkendub. Ang 4F 145
Drury. Flin 4E 83
Drury Square. Norf 4B 78
Drybeck. Cumb 3H 103
Drybridge. Mor 2B 160
Drybridge. N Ayr 1C 116
Drybrook. Glos 4B 48
Drybrook. Here 4A 48
Dryburgh. Bord 1H 119
Dry Doddington. Linc 1F 75
Dry Drayton. Cambs 4C 64
Drym. Corn 3D 4
Drymen. Stir 1F 127
Drymuir. Abers 4G 161
Drynachan Lodge. High 5C 158
Drynie Park. High 3H 157
Drynoch. High 5D 154
Dry Sandford. Oxon 5C 50
Dryslwyn. Carm 3F 45
Dry Street. Essx 2A 40
Dryton. Shrp 5H 71
Dubford. Abers 2E 161
Dubiton. Abers 3D 160
Dubton. Ang 3E 145
Duchally. High 2A 164
Duck End. Essx 3G 53
Duckington. Ches W 5G 83
Ducklington. Oxon 5B 50
Duckmanton. Derbs 3B 86
Duck Street. Hants 2B 24
Dudbridge. Glos 5D 48
Duddenhoe End. Essx 2E 53
Duddingston. Edin 2F 129
Duddington. Nptn 5G 75
Duddleswell. E Sus 3F 27
Duddo. Nmbd 5F 131
Duddon. Ches W 4H 83
Duddon Bridge. Cumb 1A 96
Dudleston. Shrp 2F 71
Dudleston Heath. Shrp 2F 71
Dudley. Tyne 2F 115
Dudley. W Mid 2D 60
Dudston. Shrp 1E 59
Dudwells. Pemb 2D 42
Duffield. Derbs 1H 73
Duffryn. Neat 2B 32
Dufftown. Mor 4H 159
Duffus. Mor 2F 159
Dufton. Cumb 2H 103
Duggleby. N Yor 3C 100
Duirinish. High 5G 155
Duisdalemore. High 2E 147
Duisdeil Mòr. High 2E 147
Duisky. High 1E 141
Dukesfield. Nmbd 4C 114
Dukestown. Blae 5E 47
Dukinfield. G Man 1D 84
Dulas. IOA 2D 81
Dulcote. Som 2A 22
Dulford. Devn 2D 12
Dull. Per 4F 143
Dullatur. N Lan 2A 128
Dullingham. Cambs 5F 65
Dullingham Ley. Cambs 5F 65
Dulnain Bridge. High 1D 151
Duloe. Bed 4A 64
Duloe. Corn 3G 7
Dulverton. Som 4C 20
Dulwich. G Lon 3E 39
Dumbarton. W Dun 2F 127
Dumbleton. Glos 2F 49
Dumfin. Arg 1E 127
Dumfries. Dum 2A 112 & 194
Dumgoyne. Stir 1G 127
Dummer. Hants 2D 24
Dumpford. W Sus 4G 25
Dun. Ang 2F 145
Dunadry. Ant 1F 179
Dunaghy. Bmny 4F 175
Dunagoil. Arg 4B 126
Dunalastair. Per 3E 142
Dunan. High 1D 147
Dunball. Som 2G 21
Dunbar. E Lot 2C 130
Dunbeath. High 5D 168
Dunbeg. Arg 5C 140
Dunblane. Stir 3G 135
Dunbog. Fife 2E 137
Dunbridge. Hants 4B 24
Duncanston. Abers 1C 152
Duncanston. High 3H 157
Dun Charlabhaigh. W Isl 3D 171
Dunchideock. Devn 4B 12
Dunchurch. Warw 3B 62
Duncote. Nptn 5D 62
Duncow. Dum 1A 112
Duncrievie. Per 3D 136
Duncton. W Sus 4A 26
Dundee. D'dee 5D 144 & 194
Dundee Airport. D'dee 1F 137
Dundon. Som 3H 21
Dundonald. Cast 2J 179
Dundonald. S Ayr 1C 116
Dundonnell. High 5E 163
Dundraw. Cumb 5D 112
Dundreggan. High 2F 149
Dundrennan. Dum 5E 111
Dundridge. Hants 1D 16
Dundrod. Lis 2G 179
Dundrum. Down 6J 179
Dundry. N Som 5A 34
Dunecht. Abers 3E 153
Dunfermline. Fife 1D 129
Dunford Bridge. S Yor 4B 92
Dungannon. Dngn 3B 178
Dungate. Kent 5D 40
Dunge. Wilts 1D 23
Dungeness. Kent 4E 29
Dungiven. Lim 6C 174
Dungworth. S Yor 2G 85
Dunham-on-the-Hill. Ches W 3G 83
Dunham-on-Trent. Notts 3F 87
Dunhampton. Worc 4C 60
Dunham Town. G Man 2B 84
Dunham Woodhouses. G Man 2B 84
Dunholme. Linc 3H 87
Dunino. Fife 2H 137
Dunipace. Falk 1B 128
Dunira. Per 1G 135
Dunkeld. Per 4H 143
Dunkerton. Bath 1C 22
Dunkeswell. Devn 2E 13
Dunkeswick. N Yor 5F 99
Dunkirk. Kent 5E 41
Dunkirk. S Glo 3C 34
Dunkirk. Staf 5C 84
Dunkirk. Wilts 5E 35
Dunk's Green. Kent 5H 39
Dunlappie. Ang 2E 145
Dunley. Hants 1C 24
Dunley. Worc 4B 60
Dunlichity Lodge. High 5A 158
Dunlop. E Ayr 5F 127
Dunloy. Bmny 5G 175
Dunmaglass Lodge. High 1H 149
Dunmore. Arg 3F 125
Dunmore. Falk 1B 128
Dunmore. High 4H 157
Dunmurry. Lis 3G 179
Dunnamanagh. Strab 6A 174
Dunnaval. New M 8G 179
Dunnet. High 1E 169
Dunnichen. Ang 4E 145
Dunning. Per 2C 136
Dunnington. E Yor 4F 101
Dunnington. Warw 5E 61
Dunnington. York 4A 100
Dunningwell. Cumb 1A 96
Dunnockshaw. Lanc 2G 91
Dunoon. Arg 2C 126
Dunphail. Mor 4E 159
Dunragit. Dum 4G 109
Dunrostan. Arg 1F 125
Duns. Bord 4D 130
Dunsby. Linc 3A 76
Dunscar. G Man 3F 91
Dunscore. Dum 1F 111
Dunscroft. S Yor 4G 93
Dunsdale. Red C 3D 106
Dunsden Green. Oxon 4F 37
Dunsfold. Surr 2B 26
Dunsford. Devn 4B 12
Dunshalt. Fife 2E 137
Dunshillock. Abers 4G 161
Dunsley. N Yor 3F 107
Dunsley. Staf 2C 60
Dunsmore. Buck 5G 51
Dunsop Bridge. Lanc 4F 97
Dunstable. C Beds 3A 52
Dunstal. Staf 3E 73
Dunstall. Staf 3F 73
Dunstall Green. Suff 4G 65
Dunstall Hill. W Mid 5D 72
Dunstan. Nmbd 3G 121
Dunster. Som 2C 20
Duns Tew. Oxon 3C 50
Dunston. Linc 4H 87
Dunston. Norf 5E 79
Dunston. Staf 4D 72
Dunston. Tyne 3F 115
Dunstone. Devn 3B 8
Dunston Heath. Staf 4D 72
Dunsville. S Yor 4G 93
Dunswell. E Yor 1D 94
Dunsyre. S Lan 5D 128
Dunterton. Devn 5D 11
Duntisbourne Abbots. Glos 5E 49
Duntisbourne Leer. Glos 5E 49
Duntisbourne Rouse. Glos 5E 49
Duntish. Dors 2B 14
Duntocher. W Dun 2F 127
Dunton. Buck 3G 51
Dunton. C Beds 1C 52
Dunton. Norf 2A 78
Dunton Bassett. Leics 1C 62
Dunton Green. Kent 5G 39
Dunton Patch. Norf 2A 78
Duntulm. High 1D 154
Dunure. S Ayr 3B 116
Dunvant. Swan 3E 31
Dunvegan. High 4B 154
Dunwich. Suff 3G 67
Dunwood. Staf 5D 84
Durdar. Cumb 4F 113
Durgates. E Sus 2H 27
Durham. Dur 5F 115 & 194
Durham Tees Valley Airport. Darl 3A 106
Durisdeer. Dum 4A 118
Durisdeermill. Dum 4A 118
Durkar. W Yor 3D 92
Durleigh. Som 3F 21
Durley. Hants 1D 16
Durley. Wilts 5H 35
Durley Street. Hants 1D 16
Durlow Common. Here 2B 48
Durnamuck. High 4E 163
Durness. High 2E 166
Durno. Abers 1E 152
Durns Town. Hants 3A 16
Duror. High 3D 141
Durran. Arg 3G 133
Durran. High 2D 169
Durrant Green. Kent 2C 28
Durrants. Hants 1F 17
Durrington. W Sus 5C 26
Durrington. Wilts 2G 23
Dursley. Glos 2C 34
Dursley Cross. Glos 4B 48
Durston. Som 4F 21
Durweston. Dors 2D 14
Dury. Shet 6F 173
Duston. Nptn 4E 62
Duthil. High 1D 150
Dutlas. Powy 3E 58
Duton Hill. Essx 3G 53
Dutson. Corn 4D 10
Dutton. Ches W 3H 83
Duxford. Cambs 1E 53
Duxford. Oxon 2B 36
Dwygyfylchi. Cnwy 3G 81
Dwyran. IOA 4D 80
Dyce. Aber 2F 153
Dyffryn. B'end 2B 32
Dyffryn. Carm 2H 43
Dyffryn. Pemb 1D 42
Dyffryn. V Glam 4D 32
Dyffryn Ardudwy. Gwyn 3E 69
Dyffryn Castell. Cdgn 2G 57
Dyffryn Ceidrych. Carm 3H 45
Dyffryn Cellwen. Neat 5B 46
Dyke. Linc 3A 76
Dyke. Mor 3D 159
Dykehead. Ang 2C 144
Dykehead. N Lan 3B 128
Dykehead. Stir 4E 135
Dykend. Ang 3B 144
Dykesfield. Cumb 4E 112
Dylife. Powy 1A 58
Dymchurch. Kent 3F 29
Dymock. Glos 2C 48
Dyrham. S Glo 4C 34
Dysart. Fife 4F 137
Dyserth. Den 3C 82

E

Eachwick. Nmbd 2E 115
Eadar Dha Fhadhail. W Isl 4C 171
Eagland Hill. Lanc 5D 96
Eagle. Linc 4F 87
Eagle Barnsdale. Linc 4F 87
Eagle Moor. Linc 4F 87
Eaglescliffe. Stoc T 3B 106
Eaglesfield. Cumb 2B 102
Eaglesfield. Dum 2D 112
Eaglesham. E Ren 4G 127
Eaglethorpe. Nptn 1H 63
Eagley. G Man 3F 91
Eairy. IOM 4B 108
Eakley Lanes. Mil 5F 63
Eakring. Notts 4D 86
Ealand. N Lin 3A 94
Ealing. G Lon 2C 38
Eallabus. Arg 3B 124
Eals. Nmbd 4H 113
Eamont Bridge. Cumb 2G 103
Earby. Lanc 5B 98
Earcroft. Bkbn 2E 91
Eardington. Shrp 1B 60
Eardisland. Here 5G 59
Eardisley. Here 1G 47
Eardiston. Shrp 3F 71
Eardiston. Worc 4A 60
Earith. Cambs 3C 64
Earlais. High 2C 154
Earle. Nmbd 2D 121
Earlesfield. Linc 2G 75
Earlestown. Mers 1H 83
Earley. Wok 4F 37
Earlham. Norf 5D 78
Earlish. High 2C 154
Earls Barton. Nptn 4F 63
Earls Colne. Essx 3B 54
Earls Common. Worc 5D 60
Earl's Croome. Worc 1D 48
Earlsdon. W Mid 3H 61
Earlsferry. Fife 3G 137
Earlsford. Abers 5F 161
Earl's Green. Suff 4C 66
Earlsheaton. W Yor 2C 92
Earl Shilton. Leics 1B 62
Earl Soham. Suff 4E 67
Earl Sterndale. Derbs 4E 85
Earlston. E Ayr 1D 116
Earlston. Bord 1H 119
Earl Stonham. Suff 5D 66
Earlstoun. Dum 1D 110
Earlswood. Mon 2H 33
Earlswood. Warw 3F 61
Earlyvale. Bord 4F 129
Earnley. W Sus 3G 17
Earsairidh. W Isl 9C 170
Earsdon. Tyne 2G 115
Earsham. Norf 2F 67
Earsham Street. Suff 3E 67
Earswick. York 4A 100
Eartham. W Sus 5A 26
Earthcott Green. S Glo 3B 34
Easby. N Yor 4C 106 (nr. Great Ayton)
Easby. N Yor 4E 105 (nr. Richmond)
Easdale. Arg 2E 133
Easebourne. W Sus 4G 25
Easenhall. Warw 3B 62
Eashing. Surr 1A 26
Easington. Buck 4E 51
Easington. Dur 5H 115
Easington. E Yor 3G 95
Easington. Nmbd 1F 121
Easington. Oxon 2C 50 (nr. Banbury)
Easington. Oxon 2E 37 (nr. Watlington)
Easington. Red C 3E 107
Easington Colliery. Dur 5H 115
Easington Lane. Tyne 5G 115
Easingwold. N Yor 3H 99
Eassie. Ang 4C 144
Eassie and Nevay. Ang 4C 144
East Aberthaw. V Glam 5D 32
Eastacombe. Devn 4F 19
Eastacott. Devn 4G 19
East Allington. Devn 4D 8
East Anstey. Devn 4B 20
East Anton. Hants 2B 24
East Appleton. N Yor 5F 105
East Ardsley. W Yor 2D 92
East Ashley. Devn 1G 11
East Ashling. W Sus 2G 17
East Aston. Hants 2C 24
East Ayton. N Yor 1D 101
East Barkwith. Linc 2A 88
East Barnby. N Yor 3F 107
East Barnet. G Lon 1D 39
East Barns. E Lot 2D 130
East Barsham. Norf 2B 78
East Beach. W Sus 3G 17
East Beckham. Norf 1D 78
East Bedfont. G Lon 3B 38
East Bennan. N Ayr 3D 123
East Bergholt. Suff 2D 54
East Bierley. W Yor 2B 92
East Blatchington. E Sus 5F 27
East Bliney. Norf 4B 78
East Bloxworth. Dors 3D 15
East Boldre. Hants 2B 16
East Bolton. Nmbd 3F 121
Eastbourne. Darl 3F 105
Eastbourne. E Sus 5H 27 & 194
East Brent. Som 1G 21
East Bridge. Suff 4G 67
East Bridgford. Notts 1D 74
East Briscoe. Dur 3C 104
East Buckland. Devn 3G 19 (nr. Barnstaple)
East Buckland. Devn 4C 8 (nr. Thurlestone)
East Budleigh. Devn 4D 12
Eastburn. W Yor 5C 98
East Burnham. Buck 2A 38
East Burrafirth. Shet 6E 173
East Burton. Dors 4D 14
Eastbury. Herts 1B 38
Eastbury. W Ber 4B 36
East Butsfield. Dur 5E 115
East Butterleigh. Devn 2C 12
East Butterwick. N Lin 4B 94
Eastby. N Yor 4C 98
East Calder. W Lot 3D 129
East Carleton. Norf 5D 78
East Carlton. Nptn 2F 63
East Carlton. W Yor 5E 98
East Chaldon. Dors 4C 14
East Challow. Oxon 3B 36
East Charleton. Devn 4D 8
East Chelborough. Dors 2A 14
East Chiltington. E Sus 4E 27
East Chinnock. Som 1H 13
East Chisenbury. Wilts 1G 23
Eastchurch. Kent 3D 40
East Clandon. Surr 5B 38
East Claydon. Buck 3F 51
East Clevedon. N Som 4H 33
East Clyne. High 3F 165
East Clyth. High 5E 169
East Coker. Som 1A 14
Eastcombe. Glos 5D 49
East Combe. Som 3E 21
East Common. N Yor 1G 93
East Compton. Som 2B 22
East Cornworthy. Devn 3E 9
Eastcote. G Lon 2C 38
Eastcote. Nptn 5D 62
Eastcote. W Mid 3F 61
Eastcott. Corn 1C 10
Eastcott. Wilts 1F 23
East Cottingwith. E Yor 5B 100
Eastcourt. Wilts 1E 23 (nr. Pewsey)
Eastcourt. Wilts 2E 35 (nr. Tetbury)
East Cowes. IOW 3D 16
East Cowick. E Yor 2G 93
East Cowton. N Yor 4A 106
East Cramlington. Nmbd 2F 115
East Cranmore. Som 2B 22
East Creech. Dors 4E 15
East Croachy. High 1A 150
East Dean. E Sus 5G 27
East Dean. Glos 3B 48
East Dean. Hants 4A 24
East Dean. W Sus 4A 26
East Down. Devn 2G 19
East Drayton. Notts 3E 87
East Dundry. N Som 5A 34
East Ella. Hull 2D 94
East End. Cambs 3C 64
East End. Dors 3E 15
East End. E Yor 4F 101 (nr. Ulrome)
East End. E Yor 2F 95 (nr. Withernsea)
East End. Hants 3B 16 (nr. Lymington)
East End. Hants 5C 36 (nr. Newbury)
East End. Herts 3E 53
East End. Kent 3D 40 (nr. Minster)
East End. Kent 2C 28 (nr. Tenterden)
East End. N Som 4H 33
East End. Oxon 4B 50
East End. Som 1A 22
East End. Suff 2E 54
Easter Ardross. High 1A 158
Easter Balgedie. Per 3D 136
Easter Balmoral. Abers 4G 151
Easter Brae. High 2A 158
Easter Buckieburn. Stir 1A 128
Easter Bush. Midl 3F 129
Easter Compton. S Glo 3A 34
Easter Fearn. High 5D 164
Easter Galcantray. High 4C 158
Easterhouse. Glas 3H 127
Easter Howgate. Midl 3F 129
Easter Kinkell. High 3H 157
Easter Lednathie. Ang 2C 144
Easter Ogil. Ang 2D 144
Easter Ord. Abers 3F 153
Easter Quarff. Shet 8F 173
Easter Rhynd. Per 2D 136
Easter Skeld. Shet 7E 173
Easter Suddie. High 3A 158
Eastertown. Som 1G 21
Easter Tulloch. Abers 1G 145

East Everleigh—Firle

East Everleigh. Wilts 1H 23
East Farleigh. Kent 5B 40
East Farndon. Nptn 2E 62
East Ferry. Linc 1F 87
Eastfield. N Lan 3B 128
(nr. Caldercruix)
Eastfield. N Lan 3B 128
(nr. Harthill)
Eastfield. N Yor 1E 101
Eastfield. S Lan 3H 127
Eastfield Hall. Nmbd 4G 121
East Fortune. E Lot 2B 130
East Garforth. W Yor 1E 93
East Garston. W Ber 4B 36
Eastgate. Dur 1C 104
Eastgate. Norf 3D 78
East Ginge. Oxon 3C 36
East Gores. Essx 3B 54
East Goscote. Leics 4D 74
East Grafton. Wilts 5A 36
East Green. Suff 5F 65
East Grimstead. Wilts 4H 23
East Grinstead. W Sus 2E 27
East Guldeford. E Sus 3D 28
East Haddon. Nptn 4D 62
East Hagbourne. Oxon 3D 36
East Halton. N Lin 2E 95
East Ham. G Lon 2F 39
Eastham. Mers 2F 83
Eastham. Worc 4A 60
Eastham Ferry. Mers 2F 83
Easthampstead. Brac 5G 37
Easthampton. Here 4G 59
East Hanney. Oxon 2C 36
East Hanningfield. Essx 5A 54
East Hardwick. W Yor 3E 93
East Harling. Norf 2B 66
East Harlsey. N Yor 5B 106
East Harnham. Wilts 4G 23
East Harptree. Bath 1A 22
East Hartford. Nmbd 2F 115
East Harting. W Sus 1G 17
East Hatch. Wilts 4E 23
East Hatley. Cambs 5B 64
Easthaugh. Norf 4C 78
East Hauxwell. N Yor 5E 105
East Haven. Ang 5E 145
Eastheath. Wok 5G 37
East Heckington. Linc 1A 76
East Hedleyhope. Dur 5E 115
East Helmsdale. High 2H 165
East Hendred. Oxon 3C 36
East Heslerton. N Yor 2D 100
East Hoathly. E Sus 4G 27
East Holme. Dors 4D 15
Easthope. Shrp 1H 59
Easthorpe. Essx 3C 54
Easthorpe. Leics 2F 75
East Horrington. Som 2A 22
East Horsley. Surr 5B 38
East Horton. Nmbd 1E 121
Easthouses. Midl 3G 129
East Howe. Bour 3F 15
East Huntspill. Som 2G 21
East Hyde. C Beds 4B 52
East Ilsley. W Ber 3C 36
Eastington. Devn 2H 11
Eastington. Glos 4G 49
(nr. Northleach)
Eastington. Glos 5C 48
(nr. Stonehouse)
East Keal. Linc 4C 88
East Kennett. Wilts 5G 35
East Keswick. W Yor 5F 99
East Kilbride. S Lan 4H 127
East Kirkby. Linc 4C 88
East Knapton. N Yor 2C 100
East Knighton. Dors 4D 14
East Knowstone. Devn 4B 20
East Knoyle. Wilts 3D 23
East Kyloe. Nmbd 1E 121
East Lambrook. Som 1H 13
East Langdon. Kent 1H 29
East Langton. Leics 1E 63
East Langwell. High 3E 164
East Lavant. W Sus 2G 17
East Lavington. W Sus 4A 26
East Layton. N Yor 4E 105
Eastleach Martin. Glos 5H 49
Eastleach Turville. Glos 5G 49
East Leake. Notts 3C 74
East Learmouth. Nmbd 1C 120
Eastleigh. Devn 4E 19
(nr. Bideford)
East Leigh. Devn 2H 11
(nr. Crediton)
East Leigh. Devn 3C 8
(nr. Modbury)
Eastleigh. Hants 1C 16
East Lexham. Norf 4A 78
East Lilburn. Nmbd 2E 121
Eastling. Kent 5D 40
East Linton. E Lot 2B 130
East Liss. Hants 4F 25
East Lockinge. Oxon 3C 36
East Looe. Corn 3G 7
East Lound. N Lin 1E 87
East Lulworth. Dors 4D 14
East Lutton. N Yor 3D 100
East Lydford. Som 3A 22
East Lyng. Som 4G 21
East Mains. Abers 4D 152
East Malling. Kent 5B 40
East Marden. W Sus 1G 17
East Markham. Notts 3E 87
East Marton. N Yor 4B 98
East Meon. Hants 4E 25
East Mersea. Essx 4D 54
East Mey. High 1F 169
East Midlands Airport.
Leics 3B 74 & 205
East Molesey. Surr 4C 38
Eastmoor. Norf 5G 77
East Morden. Dors 3E 15
East Morton. W Yor 5D 98
East Ness. N Yor 2A 100
East Newton. E Yor 1F 95
East Newton. N Yor 2A 100
Eastney. Port 3E 17
Eastnor. Here 2C 48
East Norton. Leics 5E 75
East Nynehead. Som 4E 21
East Oakley. Hants 1D 24
Eastoft. N Lin 3B 94
East Ogwell. Devn 5B 12
Easton. Cambs 3A 64
Easton. Cumb 4D 112
(nr. Burgh by Sands)
Easton. Cumb 2F 113
(nr. Longtown)
Easton. Devn 4H 11
Easton. Dors 5B 14
Easton. Hants 3D 24
Easton. Linc 3G 75
Easton. Norf 4D 78
Easton. Som 2A 22
Easton. Suff 5E 67
Easton. Wilts 4D 35
Easton Grey. Wilts 3D 35
Easton-in-Gordano.
N Som 4A 34
Easton Maudit. Nptn 5F 63
Easton on the Hill. Nptn 5H 75
Easton Royal. Wilts 5H 35
East Orchard. Dors 1D 14
East Ord. Nmbd 4F 131
East Panson. Devn 3D 10
East Peckham. Kent 1A 28
East Pennard. Som 3A 22
East Perry. Cambs 4A 64
East Pitcorthie. Fife 3H 137
East Portlemouth. Devn 5D 8
East Prawle. Devn 5D 9
East Preston. W Sus 5B 26
East Putford. Devn 1D 10
East Quantoxhead. Som 2E 21
East Rainton. Tyne 5G 115
East Ravendale. NE Lin 1B 88
East Raynham. Norf 3A 78
Eastrea. Cambs 1B 64
East Rhidorroch Lodge.
High 4G 163
Eastriggs. Dum 3D 112
East Rigton. W Yor 5F 99
Eastrington. E Yor 1A 94
East Rounton. N Yor 4B 106
East Row. N Yor 3F 107
East Rudham. Norf 3H 77
East Runton. Norf 1D 78
East Ruston. Norf 3F 79
Eastry. Kent 5H 41
East Saltoun. E Lot 3A 130
East Shaws. Dur 3D 105
East Shefford. W Ber 4B 36
Eastshore. Shet 10E 173
East Sleekburn. Nmbd 1F 115
East Somerton. Norf 4G 79
East Stockwith. Linc 1E 87
East Stoke. Dors 4D 14
East Stoke. Notts 1E 75
East Stoke. Som 1H 13
East Stour. Dors 4D 22
East Stourmouth. Kent 4G 41
East Stowford. Devn 4G 19
East Stratton. Hants 2D 24
East Studdal. Kent 1H 29
East Taphouse. Corn 2F 7
East-the-Water. Devn 4E 19
East Thirston. Nmbd 5F 121
East Tilbury. Thur 3A 40
East Tisted. Hants 3F 25
East Torrington. Linc 2A 88
East Tuddenham. Norf 4C 78
East Tytherley. Hants 4A 24
East Tytherton. Wilts 4E 35
East Village. Devn 2B 12
Eastville. Linc 5D 88
East Wall. Shrp 1H 59
East Walton. Norf 4G 77
East Week. Devn 3G 11
Eastwell. Leics 3E 75
East Wellow. Hants 4B 24
East Wemyss. Fife 4F 137
East Whitburn. W Lot 3C 128
Eastwick. Herts 4E 53
Eastwick. Shet 4E 173
East Williamston. Pemb 4E 43
East Winch. Norf 4F 77
East Winterslow. Wilts 3H 23
East Wittering. W Sus 3F 17
East Witton. N Yor 1D 98
Eastwood. Notts 1B 74
Eastwood. S'end 2C 40
East Woodburn. Nmbd 1C 114
Eastwood End. Cambs 1D 64
East Woodhay. Hants 5C 36
East Woodlands. Som 2C 22
East Worldham. Hants 3F 25
East Worlington. Devn 1A 12
East Wretham. Norf 1B 66
East Youlstone. Devn 1C 10
Eathorpe. Warw 4A 62
Eaton. Ches E 4C 84
Eaton. Ches W 4H 83
Eaton. Leics 3E 75
Eaton. Norf 2F 77
(nr. Heacham)
Eaton. Norf 5E 78
(nr. Norwich)
Eaton. Notts 3E 86
Eaton. Oxon 5C 50
Eaton. Shrp 2F 59
(nr. Bishop's Castle)
Eaton. Shrp 1H 59
(nr. Church Stretton)
Eaton Bishop. Here 2H 47
Eaton Bray. C Beds 3H 51
Eaton Constantine. Shrp 5H 71
Eaton Hastings. Oxon 2A 36
Eaton Socon. Cambs 5A 64
Eaton upon Tern. Shrp 3A 72
Eau Brink. Norf 4E 77
Eaves Green. W Mid 2G 61
Ebberley Hill. Devn 1F 11
Ebberston. N Yor 1C 100
Ebbesbourne Wake. Wilts 4E 23
Ebblake. Dors 2G 15
Ebbsfleet. Kent 3H 39
Ebbw Vale. Blae 5E 47
Ebchester. Dur 4E 115
Ebernoe. W Sus 3A 26
Ebford. Devn 4C 12
Ebley. Glos 5D 48
Ebnal. Ches W 1G 71
Ebrington. Glos 1G 49
Ecchinswell. Hants 1D 24
Ecclefechan. Dum 2C 112
Eccles. G Man 1B 84
Eccles. Kent 4B 40
Eccles. Bord 5D 130
Ecclesall. S Yor 2H 85
Ecclesfield. S Yor 1A 86
Eccles Green. Here 1G 47
Eccleshall. Staf 3C 72
Eccleshill. W Yor 1B 92
Ecclesmachan. W Lot 2D 128
Eccles on Sea. Norf 3G 79
Eccles Road. Norf 1C 66
Eccleston. Ches W 4G 83
Eccleston. Lanc 3D 90
Eccleston. Mers 1G 83
Eccup. W Yor 5E 99
Echt. Abers 3E 153
Eckford. Bord 2B 120
Eckington. Derbs 3B 86
Eckington. Worc 1E 49
Ecton. Nptn 4F 63
Edale. Derbs 2F 85
Eday Airport. Orkn 4E 172
Edburton. W Sus 4D 26
Edderside. Cumb 5C 112
Edderton. High 5E 164
Eddington. Kent 4F 41
Eddington. W Ber 5B 36
Eddleston. Bord 5F 129
Eddlewood. S Lan 4A 128
Eden. Carr 8L 175
Edenbridge. Kent 1F 27
Edendonich. Arg 1A 134
Edenfield. Lanc 3G 91
Edenhall. Cumb 1G 103
Edenham. Linc 3H 75
Edensor. Derbs 4G 85
Edentaggart. Arg 4C 134
Edenthorpe. S Yor 4G 93
Eden Vale. Dur 1B 106
Edern. Gwyn 2B 68
Ederney. Ferm 6E 176
Edgarley. Som 3A 22
Edgbaston. W Mid 2E 61
Edgcott. Buck 3E 51
Edgcott. Som 3B 20
Edge. Glos 5D 48
Edge. Shrp 5F 71
Edgebolton. Shrp 3H 71
Edge End. Glos 4A 48
Edgefield. Norf 2C 78
Edgefield Street. Norf 2C 78
Edge Green. Ches W 5G 83
Edgehead. Midl 3G 129
Edgeley. Shrp 1H 71
Edgeside. Lanc 2G 91
Edgeworth. Glos 5E 49
Edgiock. Worc 4E 61
Edgmond. Telf 4B 72
Edgmond Marsh. Telf 3B 72
Edgton. Shrp 2F 59
Edgware. G Lon 1C 38
Edgworth. Bkbn 3F 91
Edinbane. High 3C 154
Edinburgh. Edin 2F 129 & 195
Edinburgh Airport. Edin 2E 129
Edingale. Staf 4G 73
Edingley. Notts 5D 86
Edingthorpe. Norf 2F 79
Edington. Som 3G 21
Edington. Wilts 1E 23
Edingworth. Som 1G 21
Edistone. Devn 4C 18
Edithmead. Som 2G 21
Edith Weston. Rut 5G 75
Edlaston. Derbs 1F 73
Edlesborough. Buck 4H 51
Edlingham. Nmbd 4F 121
Edlington. Linc 3B 88
Edmondsham. Dors 1F 15
Edmondsley. Dur 5F 115
Edmondthorpe. Leics 4F 75
Edmonstone. Orkn 5E 172
Edmonton. Corn 1D 6
Edmonton. G Lon 1E 39
Edmundbyers. Dur 4D 114
Ednam. Bord 1B 120
Ednaston. Derbs 1G 73
Edney Common. Essx 5G 53
Edrom. Bord 4E 131
Edstaston. Shrp 2H 71
Edstone. Warw 4F 61
Edwalton. Notts 2D 74
Edwardstone. Suff 1C 54
Edwardsville. Mer T 2D 32
Edwinsford. Carm 2G 45
Edwinstowe. Notts 4D 86
Edworth. C Beds 1C 52
Edwyn Ralph. Here 5A 60
Edzell. Ang 2F 145
Efail-fach. Neat 2A 32
Efail Isaf. Rhon 3D 32
Efailnewydd. Gwyn 2C 68
Efail-rhyd. Powy 3D 70
Efailwen. Carm 2F 43
Efenechtyd. Den 5D 82
Effingham. Surr 5C 38
Effingham Common. Surr 5C 38
Effirth. Shet 6E 173
Efflinch. Staf 4F 73
Efford. Devn 2B 12
Efstigarth. Shet 2F 173
Egbury. Hants 1C 24
Egdon. Worc 5D 60
Egerton. G Man 3F 91
Egerton. Kent 1D 28
Egerton Forstal. Kent 1C 28
Eggborough. N Yor 2F 93
Eggbuckland. Plym 3A 8
Eggesford. Devn 1G 11
Eggington. C Beds 3H 51
Egginton. Derbs 3G 73
Egglescliffe. Stoc T 3B 106
Eggleston. Dur 2C 104
Egham. Surr 3B 38
Egham Hythe. Surr 3B 38
Egleton. Rut 5F 75
Eglingham. Nmbd 3F 121
Eglinton. Derr 4B 174
Eglish. Dngn 4B 178
Egloshayle. Corn 5A 10
Egloskerry. Corn 4C 10
Eglwysbach. Cnwy 3H 81
Eglwys Brewis. V Glam 5D 32
Eglwys Fach. Cdgn 1F 57
Eglwyswrw. Pemb 1F 43
Egmanton. Notts 4E 87
Egmere. Norf 2B 78
Egremont. Cumb 3B 102
Egremont. Mers 1F 83
Egton. N Yor 4F 107
Egton Bridge. N Yor 4F 107
Egypt. Buck 2A 38
Egypt. Hants 2C 24
Eight Ash Green. Essx 3C 54
Eight Mile Burn. Midl 4E 129
Eignaig. High 4B 140
Eilanreach. High 2G 147
Eildon. Bord 1H 119
Eileanach Lodge. High 2H 157
Eilean Fhlodaigh. W Isl 3D 170
Eilean Iarmain. High 2F 147
Einacleit. W Isl 5D 171
Eisgein. W Isl 6F 171
Eisingrug. Gwyn 2F 69
Elan Village. Powy 4B 58
Elberton. S Glo 3B 34
Elbridge. W Sus 5A 26
Elburton. Plym 3B 8
Elcho. Per 1D 136
Elcombe. Swin 3G 35
Elcot. W Ber 5B 36
Eldernell. Cambs 1C 64
Eldersfield. Worc 2D 48
Elderslie. Ren 3F 127
Elder Street. Essx 2F 53
Eldon. Dur 2F 105
Eldroth. N Yor 3G 97
Eldwick. W Yor 5D 98
Elfhowe. Cumb 5F 103
Elford. Nmbd 1F 121
Elford. Staf 4F 73
Elford Closes. Cambs 3D 65
Elgin. Mor 2G 159
Elgol. High 2D 146
Elham. Kent 1F 29
Elie. Fife 3G 137
Eling. Hants 1B 16
Eling. W Ber 4D 36
Elishaw. Nmbd 5C 120
Elizafield. Dum 2B 112
Elkesley. Notts 3D 86
Elkington. Nptn 3D 62
Elkins Green. Essx 5G 53
Elkstone. Glos 4E 49
Ellan. High 1C 150
Elland. W Yor 2B 92
Ellary. Arg 2F 125
Ellastone. Staf 1F 73
Ellbridge. Corn 2A 8
Ellel. Lanc 4D 97
Ellemford. Bord 3D 130
Ellenabeich. Arg 2E 133
Ellenborough. Cumb 1B 102
Ellenbrook. Herts 5C 52
Ellenhall. Staf 3C 72
Ellen's Green. Surr 2B 26
Ellerbec. N Yor 5B 106
Ellerburn. N Yor 1C 100
Ellerby. N Yor 3E 107
Ellerdine. Telf 3A 72
Ellerdine Heath. Telf 3A 72
Ellerhayes. Devn 2C 12
Elleric. Arg 4E 141
Ellerker. E Yor 2C 94
Ellerton. E Yor 1H 93
Ellerton. N Yor 5F 105
Ellerton. Shrp 3B 72
Ellesborough. Buck 5G 51
Ellesmere. Shrp 2F 71
Ellesmere Port. Ches W 3G 83
Ellingham. Hants 2G 15
Ellingham. Norf 1F 67
Ellingham. Nmbd 2F 121
Ellingstring. N Yor 1D 98
Ellington. Cambs 3A 64
Ellington. Nmbd 5G 121
Ellington Thorpe. Cambs 3A 64
Elliot. Ang 5F 145
Ellisfield. Hants 2E 25
Ellishadder. High 2E 155
Ellistown. Leics 4B 74
Ellon. Abers 5G 161
Ellonby. Cumb 1F 103
Ellough. Suff 2G 67
Elloughton. E Yor 2C 94
Ellwood. Glos 5A 48
Elm. Cambs 5D 76
Elmbridge. Glos 4D 48
Elmbridge. Worc 4D 60
Elmdon. Essx 2E 53
Elmdon. W Mid 2F 61
Elmdon Heath. W Mid 2F 61
Elmesthorpe. Leics 1B 62
Elmfield. IOW 3D 16
Elm Hill. Dors 4D 22
Elmhurst. Staf 4F 73
Elmley Castle. Worc 1E 49
Elmley Lovett. Worc 4C 60
Elmore. Glos 4C 48
Elmore Back. Glos 4C 48
Elm Park. G Lon 2G 39
Elmscott. Devn 4C 18
Elmsett. Suff 1D 54
Elmstead. Essx 3D 54
Elmstead Heath. Essx 3D 54
Elmstead Market. Essx 3D 54
Elmsted. Kent 1F 29
Elmstone. Kent 4G 41
Elmstone Hardwicke.
Glos 3E 49
Elmswell. E Yor 4D 101
Elmswell. Suff 4B 66
Elmton. Derbs 3C 86
Elphin. High 2G 163
Elphinstone. E Lot 2G 129
Elrick. Abers 3F 153
Elrick. Mor 1B 152
Elrig. Dum 5A 110
Elsdon. Nmbd 5D 120
Elsecar. S Yor 1A 86
Elsenham. Essx 3F 53
Elsfield. Oxon 4D 50
Elsham. N Lin 3D 94
Elsing. Norf 4C 78
Elslack. N Yor 5B 98
Elsrickle. S Lan 5D 128
Elstead. Surr 1A 26
Elsted. W Sus 1G 17
Elsted Marsh. W Sus 4G 25
Elsthorpe. Linc 3H 75
Elstob. Dur 2A 106
Elston. Devn 2A 12
Elston. Lanc 1E 90
Elston. Notts 1E 75
Elston. Wilts 2F 23
Elstone. Devn 1G 11
Elstow. Bed 1A 52
Elstree. Herts 1C 38
Elstronwick. E Yor 1F 95
Elswick. Lanc 1C 90
Elswick. Tyne 3F 115
Elsworth. Cambs 4C 64
Elterwater. Cumb 4E 103
Eltham. G Lon 3F 39
Eltisley. Cambs 5B 64
Elton. Cambs 1H 63
Elton. Ches W 3G 83
Elton. Derbs 4G 85
Elton. Glos 4C 48
Elton. G Man 3F 91
Elton. Here 3G 59
Elton. Notts 2E 75
Elton. Stoc T 3B 106
Elton Green. Ches W 3G 83
Eltringham. Nmbd 3D 115
Elvanfoot. S Lan 3B 118
Elvaston. Derbs 2B 74
Elveden. Suff 3H 65
Elvetham Heath. Hants 1F 25
Elvingston. E Lot 2A 130
Elvington. Kent 5G 41
Elvington. York 5B 100
Elwick. Hart 1B 106
Elwick. Nmbd 1F 121
Elworth. Ches E 4B 84
Elworth. Dors 4A 14
Elworthy. Som 3D 20
Ely. Cambs 2E 65
Ely. Card 4E 33
Emberton. Mil 1G 51
Embleton. Cumb 1C 102
Embleton. Dur 2B 106
Embleton. Nmbd 2G 121
Embo. High 4F 165
Emborough. Som 1B 22
Embo Street. High 4F 165
Embsay. N Yor 4C 98
Emery Down. Hants 2A 16
Emley. W Yor 3C 92
Emmbrook. Wok 5F 37
Emmer Green. Read 4F 37
Emmington. Oxon 5F 51
Emneth. Norf 5D 77
Emneth Hungate. Norf 5E 77
Empingham. Rut 5G 75
Empshott. Hants 3F 25
Emsworth. Hants 2F 17
Enborne. W Ber 5C 36
Enborne Row. W Ber 5C 36
Enchmarsh. Shrp 1H 59
Enderby. Leics 1C 62
Endmoor. Cumb 1E 97
Endon. Staf 5D 84
Endon Bank. Staf 5D 84
Enfield. G Lon 1E 39
Enfield Wash. G Lon 1E 39
Enford. Wilts 1G 23
Engine Common. S Glo 3B 34
Englefield. W Ber 4E 36
Englefield Green. Surr 3A 38
Engleseabrook. Ches E 5B 84
English Bicknor. Glos 4A 48
Englishcombe. Bath 5C 34
English Frankton. Shrp 3G 71
Enham Alamein. Hants 2B 24
Enmore. Som 3F 21
Ennerdale Bridge. Cumb 3B 102
Enniscaven. Corn 3D 6
Enniskillen. Ferm 8E 176
Enoch. Dum 4A 118
Enochdhu. Per 2H 143
Ensay. Arg 4E 139
Ensbury. Bour 3F 15
Ensdon. Shrp 4G 71
Ensis. Devn 4F 19
Enson. Staf 3D 72
Enstone. Oxon 3B 50
Enterkinfoot. Dum 4A 118
Enville. Staf 2C 60
Eolaigearraidh. W Isl 8C 170
Eorabus. Arg 1A 132
Eoropaidh. W Isl 1H 171
Epney. Glos 4C 48
Epperstone. Notts 1D 74
Epping. Essx 5E 53
Epping Green. Essx 5E 53
Epping Green. Herts 5C 52
Epping Upland. Essx 5E 53
Eppleby. N Yor 3E 105
Eppleworth. E Yor 1D 94
Epsom. Surr 4D 38
Epwell. Oxon 1B 50
Epworth. N Lin 4A 94
Epworth Turbary. N Lin 4A 94
Erbistock. Wrex 1F 71
Erbusaig. High 1F 147
Erchless Castle. High 4G 157
Erdington. W Mid 1F 61
Eredine. Arg 3G 133
Erganagh. Strab 4E 176
Eriboll. High 3E 167
Ericstane. Dum 3C 118
Eridge Green. E Sus 2G 27
Erines. Arg 2G 125
Eriswell. Suff 3G 65
Erith. G Lon 3G 39
Erlestoke. Wilts 1E 23
Ermine. Linc 3G 87
Ermington. Devn 3C 8
Ernesettle. Plym 3A 8
Erpingham. Norf 2D 78
Erriottwood. Kent 5D 40
Errogie. High 1H 149
Errol. Per 1E 137
Errol Station. Per 1E 137
Erskine. Ren 2F 127
Erskine Bridge. Ren 2F 127
Ervie. Dum 3F 109
Erwarton. Suff 2F 55
Erwood. Powy 1D 46
Eryholme. N Yor 4A 106
Eryrys. Den 5E 82
Escalls. Corn 4A 4
Escomb. Dur 1E 105
Escrick. N Yor 5A 100
Esgair. Carm 3D 45
(nr. Carmarthen)
Esgair. Carm 3G 43
(nr. St Clears)
Esgairgeiliog. Powy 5G 69
Esh. Dur 5E 115
Esher. Surr 4C 38
Esholt. W Yor 5D 98
Eshott. Nmbd 5G 121
Eshton. N Yor 4B 98
Esh Winning. Dur 5E 115
Eskadale. High 5G 157
Eskbank. Midl 3G 129
Eskdale Green. Cumb 4C 102
Eskdalemuir. Dum 5E 119
Eskham. Linc 1C 88
Esknish. Arg 3B 124
Esk Valley. N Yor 4F 107
Eslington Hall. Nmbd 3E 121
Espley Hall. Nmbd 5F 121
Esprick. Lanc 1C 90
Essendine. Rut 4H 75
Essendon. Herts 5C 52
Essich. High 5A 158
Essington. Staf 5D 72
Eston. Red C 3C 106
Estover. Plym 3B 8
Eswick. Shet 6F 173
Etal. Nmbd 1D 120
Etchilhampton. Wilts 5F 35
Etchingham. E Sus 3B 28
Etchinghill. Kent 2F 29
Etchinghill. Staf 4E 73
Etherley Dene. Dur 2E 105
Ethie Haven. Ang 4F 145
Etling Green. Norf 4C 78
Etloe. Glos 5B 48
Eton. Wind 3A 38
Eton Wick. Wind 3A 38
Etteridge. High 4A 150
Ettersgill. Dur 2B 104
Ettiley Heath. Ches E 4B 84
Ettington. Warw 1A 50
Etton. E Yor 5D 101
Etton. Pet 5A 76
Ettrick. Bord 3E 119
Ettrickbridge. Bord 2F 119
Etwall. Derbs 2G 73
Eudon Burnell. Shrp 2B 60
Eudon George. Shrp 2A 60
Euston. Suff 3A 66
Euxton. Lanc 3D 90
Evanstown. B'end 3C 32
Evanton. High 2A 158
Evedon. Linc 1H 75
Evelix. High 4E 165
Evendine. Here 1C 48
Evenjobb. Powy 4E 59
Evenley. Nptn 2D 50
Evenlode. Glos 3H 49
Even Swindon. Swin 3G 35
Evenwood. Dur 2E 105
Evenwood Gate. Dur 2E 105
Everbay. Orkn 5F 172
Evercreech. Som 3B 22
Everdon. Nptn 5C 62
Everingham. E Yor 5C 100
Everleigh. Wilts 1H 23
Everley. N Yor 1D 100
Eversholt. C Beds 2H 51
Evershot. Dors 2A 14
Eversley. Hants 5F 37
Eversley Centre. Hants 5F 37
Eversley Cross. Hants 5F 37
Everthorpe. E Yor 1C 94
Everton. C Beds 5B 64
Everton. Hants 3A 16
Everton. Mers 1F 83
Everton. Notts 1D 86
Evertown. Dum 2E 113
Evesbatch. Here 1B 48
Evesham. Worc 1F 49
Evington. Leic 5D 74
Ewden Village. S Yor 1G 85
Ewdness. Shrp 1B 60
Ewell. Surr 4D 38
Ewell Minnis. Kent 1G 29
Ewelme. Oxon 2E 37
Ewen. Glos 2F 35
Ewenny. V Glam 4C 32
Ewerby. Linc 1A 76
Ewes. Dum 5F 119
Ewesley. Nmbd 5E 121
Ewhurst. Surr 1B 26
Ewhurst Green. E Sus 3B 28
Ewhurst Green. Surr 2B 26
Ewlo. Flin 4F 83
Ewloe. Flin 4F 83
Ewood Bridge. Lanc 2F 91
Eworthy. Devn 3E 11
Ewshot. Hants 1G 25
Ewyas Harold. Here 3G 47
Exbourne. Devn 2G 11
Exbury. Hants 2C 16
Exceat. E Sus 5G 27
Exebridge. Som 4C 20
Exelby. N Yor 1E 99
Exeter. Devn 3C 12 & 195
Exeter International Airport.
Devn 3D 12
Exford. Som 3B 20
Exfords Green. Shrp 5G 71
Exhall. Warw 5F 61
Exlade Street. Oxon 3E 37
Exminster. Devn 4C 12
Exmoor. Som 3B 20
Exmouth. Devn 4D 12
Exnaboe. Shet 10E 173
Exning. Suff 4F 65
Exton. Devn 4C 12
Exton. Hants 4E 24
Exton. Rut 4G 75
Exton. Som 3C 20
Exwick. Devn 3C 12
Eyam. Derbs 3G 85
Eydon. Nptn 5C 62
Eye. Here 4G 59
Eye. Pet 5B 76
Eye. Suff 3D 66
Eye Green. Pet 5B 76
Eyemouth. Bord 3F 131
Eyeworth. C Beds 1C 52
Eyhorne Street. Kent 5C 40
Eyke. Suff 5F 67
Eynesbury. Cambs 5A 64
Eynort. High 1B 146
Eynsford. Kent 4G 39
Eynsham. Oxon 5C 50
Eyre. High 3D 154
(on Isle of Skye)
Eyre. High 5E 155
(on Raasay)
Eythorne. Kent 1G 29
Eyton. Here 4G 59
Eyton. Shrp 2F 59
(nr. Bishop's Castle)
Eyton. Shrp 4F 71
(nr. Shrewsbury)
Eyton. Wrex 1F 71
Eyton on Severn. Shrp 5H 71
Eyton upon the Weald Moors.
Telf 4A 72

F

Faccombe. Hants 1B 24
Faceby. N Yor 4B 106
Faddiley. Ches E 5H 83
Fadmoor. N Yor 1A 100
Fagwyr. Swan 5G 45
Faichem. High 3E 149
Faifley. W Dun 2G 127
Fail. S Ayr 2D 116
Failand. N Som 4A 34
Failford. S Ayr 2D 116
Failsworth. G Man 4H 91
Fairbourne. Gwyn 4F 69
Fairbourne Heath. Kent 5C 40
Fairburn. N Yor 2E 93
Fairfield. Derbs 3E 85
Fairfield. Kent 3D 28
Fairfield. Worc 3D 60
(nr. Bromsgrove)
Fairfield. Worc 1F 49
(nr. Evesham)
Fairford. Glos 5G 49
Fair Green. Norf 4F 77
Fair Hill. Cumb 1G 103
Fairhill. S Lan 4A 128
Fair Isle Airport. Shet 1B 172
Fairlands. Surr 5A 38
Fairlie. N Ayr 4D 126
Fairlight. E Sus 4C 28
Fairlight Cove. E Sus 4C 28
Fairmile. Devn 3D 12
Fairmile. Surr 4C 38
Fairmilehead. Edin 3F 129
Fair Oak. Devn 1D 12
Fair Oak. Hants 1C 16
(nr. Eastleigh)
Fair Oak. Hants 5D 36
(nr. Kingsclere)
Fairoak. Staf 2B 72
Fair Oak Green. Hants 5E 37
Fairseat. Kent 4H 39
Fairstead. Essx 4A 54
Fairstead. Norf 4F 77
Fairwarp. E Sus 3F 27
Fairwater. Card 4E 33
Fairy Cross. Devn 4E 19
Fakenham. Norf 3B 78
Fakenham Magna. Suff 3B 66
Fala. Midl 3H 129
Fala Dam. Midl 3H 129
Falcon. Here 2B 48
Faldingworth. Linc 2H 87
Falfield. S Glo 2B 34
Falkenham. Suff 2F 55
Falkirk. Falk 2B 128
Falkland. Fife 3E 137
Fallin. Stir 4H 135
Fallowfield. G Man 1C 84
Falmer. E Sus 5E 27
Falmouth. Corn 5C 6
Falsgrave. N Yor 1E 101
Falstone. Nmbd 1A 114
Fanagmore. High 4B 166
Fancott. C Beds 3A 52
Fanellan. High 4G 157
Fangdale Beck. N Yor 5C 106
Fangfoss. E Yor 4B 100
Fankerton. Falk 1A 128
Fanmore. Arg 4F 139
Fanner's Green. Essx 4G 53
Fannich Lodge. High 2E 156
Fans. Bord 5C 130
Farcet. Cambs 1B 64
Far Cotton. Nptn 5E 63
Fareham. Hants 2D 16
Farewell. Staf 4E 73
Far Forest. Worc 3B 60
Farforth. Linc 3C 88
Far Green. Glos 5C 48
Far Hoarcross. Staf 3F 73
Faringdon. Oxon 2A 36
Farington. Lanc 2D 90
Farlam. Cumb 4G 113
Farleigh. N Som 5H 33
Farleigh. Surr 4E 39
Farleigh Hungerford.
Som 1D 22
Farleigh Wallop. Hants 2E 24
Farleigh Wick. Wilts 5D 34
Farlesthorpe. Linc 3D 88
Farleton. Cumb 1E 97
Farleton. Lanc 3E 97
Farley. High 4G 157
Farley. N Som 4H 33
Farley. Shrp 5F 71
(nr. Shrewsbury)
Farley. Shrp 5A 72
(nr. Telford)
Farley. Staf 1E 73
Farley. Wilts 4H 23
Farley Green. Suff 5G 65
Farley Green. Surr 1B 26
Farley Hill. Wok 5F 37
Farley's End. Glos 4C 48
Farlington. N Yor 3A 100
Farlington. Port 2E 17
Farlow. Shrp 2A 60
Farmborough. Bath 5B 34
Farmcote. Glos 3F 49
Farmcote. Shrp 1B 60
Farmington. Glos 4G 49
Far Moor. G Man 4D 90
Farmoor. Oxon 5C 50
Farmtown. Mor 3C 160
Farnah Green. Derbs 1H 73
Farnborough. G Lon 4F 39
Farnborough. Hants 1G 25
Farnborough. Warw 1C 50
Farnborough. W Ber 3C 36
Farncombe. Surr 1A 26
Farndish. Bed 4G 63
Farndon. Ches W 5G 83
Farndon. Notts 5E 87
Farnell. Ang 3F 145
Farnham. Dors 1E 15
Farnham. Essx 3E 53
Farnham. N Yor 3F 99
Farnham. Suff 4F 67
Farnham. Surr 2G 25
Farnham Common. Buck 2A 38
Farnham Green. Essx 3E 53
Farnham Royal. Buck 2A 38
Farnhill. N Yor 5C 98
Farningham. Kent 4G 39
Farnley. N Yor 5E 98
Farnley Tyas. W Yor 3B 92
Farnsfield. Notts 5D 86
Farnworth. G Man 4F 91
Farnworth. Hal 2H 83
Far Oakridge. Glos 5E 49
Farr. High 2H 167
(nr. Bettyhill)
Farr. High 5A 158
(nr. Inverness)
Farr. High 3C 150
(nr. Kingussie)
Farraline. High 1H 149
Farringdon. Devn 3D 12
Farrington. Dors 1D 14
Farrington Gurney. Bath 1B 22
Far Sawrey. Cumb 5E 103
Farsley. W Yor 1C 92
Farthinghoe. Nptn 2D 50
Farthingstone. Nptn 5D 62
Farthorpe. Linc 3B 88
Fartown. W Yor 3B 92
Farway. Devn 3E 13
Fasag. High 3A 156
Fascadale. High 1G 139
Fasnacloich. Arg 4E 141
Fassfern. High 1E 141
Fatfield. Tyne 4G 115
Faugh. Cumb 4G 113
Fauld. Staf 3F 73
Fauldhouse. W Lot 3C 128
Faulkbourne. Essx 4A 54
Faulkland. Som 1C 22
Fauls. Shrp 2H 71
Faverdale. Darl 3F 105
Faversham. Kent 4E 40
Fawdington. N Yor 2G 99
Fawfieldhead. Staf 4E 85
Fawkham Green. Kent 4G 39
Fawler. Oxon 4B 50
Fawley. Buck 3F 37
Fawley. Hants 2C 16
Fawley. W Ber 3B 36
Fawley Chapel. Here 3A 48
Fawton. Corn 2F 7
Faxfleet. E Yor 2B 94
Faygate. W Sus 2D 26
Fazakerley. Mers 1F 83
Fazeley. Staf 5F 73
Feabuie. High 4B 158
Feagour. High 4H 149
Fearann Dhomhnaill.
High 3E 147
Fearby. N Yor 1D 98
Fearn. High 1C 158
Fearnan. Per 4E 142
Fearnbeg. High 3G 155
Fearnhead. Warr 1A 84
Fearnmore. High 2G 155
Featherstone. Staf 5D 72
Featherstone. W Yor 2E 93
Featherstone Castle.
Nmbd 3H 113
Feckenham. Worc 4E 61
Feeny. Lim 6C 174
Feering. Essx 3B 54
Feetham. N Yor 5C 104
Feizor. N Yor 3G 97
Felbridge. Surr 2E 27
Felbrigg. Norf 2E 78
Felcourt. Surr 1E 27
Felden. Herts 5A 52
Felhampton. Shrp 2G 59
Felindre. Carm 3F 45
(nr. Llandeilo)
Felindre. Carm 2G 45
(nr. Llandovery)
Felindre. Carm 2D 44
(nr. Newcastle Emlyn)
Felindre. Powy 2D 58
Felindre. Swan 5G 45
Felindre Farchog. Pemb 1F 43
Felinfach. Cdgn 5E 57
Felinfach. Powy 2D 46
Felinfoel. Carm 5F 45
Felingwmisaf. Carm 3F 45
Felingwmuchaf. Carm 3F 45
Felin Newydd. Powy 5C 70
(nr. Newtown)
Felin Newydd. Powy 3E 70
(nr. Oswestry)
Felin Wnda. Cdgn 1D 44
Felinwynt. Cdgn 5B 56
Felixkirk. N Yor 1G 99
Felixstowe. Suff 2F 55
Felixstowe Ferry. Suff 2G 55
Felkington. Nmbd 5F 131
Fell End. Cumb 5A 104
Felling. Tyne 3F 115
Fell Side. Cumb 1E 102
Felmersham. Bed 5G 63
Felmingham. Norf 3E 79
Felpham. W Sus 3H 17
Felsham. Suff 5B 66
Felsted. Essx 3G 53
Feltham. G Lon 3C 38
Felthamhill. Surr 3B 38
Felthorpe. Norf 4D 78
Felton. Here 1A 48
Felton. N Som 5A 34
Felton. Nmbd 4F 121
Felton Butler. Shrp 4F 71
Feltwell. Norf 1G 65
Fenay Bridge. W Yor 3B 92
Fence. Lanc 1G 91
Fence Houses. Tyne 4G 115
Fencott. Oxon 4D 50
Fen Ditton. Cambs 4D 65
Fen Drayton. Cambs 4C 64
Fen End. Linc 3B 76
Fen End. W Mid 3G 61
Fenham. Nmbd 5G 131
Fenham. Tyne 3F 115
Fenhouses. Linc 1B 76
Feniscowles. Bkbn 2E 91
Feniton. Devn 3D 12
Fenn Green. Shrp 2B 60
Fenn's Bank. Wrex 2H 71
Fenn Street. Medw 3B 40
Fenny Bentley. Derbs 5F 85
Fenny Bridges. Devn 3E 12
Fenny Compton. Warw 5B 62
Fenny Drayton. Leics 1A 62
Fenny Stratford. Mil 2G 51
Fenrother. Nmbd 5F 121
Fenstanton. Cambs 4C 64
Fen Street. Norf 1C 66
Fenton. Cambs 3C 64
Fenton. Cumb 4G 113
Fenton. Linc 5F 87
(nr. Caythorpe)
Fenton. Linc 3F 87
(nr. Saxilby)
Fenton. Nmbd 1D 120
Fenton. Notts 2E 87
Fenton. Stoke 1C 72
Fentonadle. Corn 5A 10
Fenton Barns. E Lot 1B 130
Fenwick. E Ayr 5F 127
Fenwick. Nmbd 5G 131
(nr. Berwick-upon-Tweed)
Fenwick. Nmbd 2D 114
(nr. Hexham)
Fenwick. S Yor 3F 93
Feochaig. Arg 4B 122
Feock. Corn 5C 6
Feolin Ferry. Arg 3C 124
Feorlan. Arg 5A 122
Ferindonald. High 3E 147
Feriniquarrie. High 3A 154
Fern. Ang 2D 145
Ferndale. Rhon 2C 32
Ferndown. Dors 2F 15
Ferness. High 4D 158
Fernham. Oxon 2A 36
Fernhill. W Sus 1D 27
Fernhill Heath. Worc 5C 60
Fernhurst. W Sus 4G 25
Fernieflatt. Abers 1H 145
Ferniegair. S Lan 4A 128
Fernilea. High 5C 154
Fernilee. Derbs 3E 85
Ferrensby. N Yor 3F 99
Ferriby Sluice. N Lin 2C 94
Ferring. W Sus 5C 26
Ferrybridge. W Yor 2E 93
Ferryden. Ang 3G 145
Ferryhill. Aber 3G 153
Ferry Hill. Cambs 2C 64
Ferryhill. Dur 1F 105
Ferryhill Station. Dur 1F 105
Ferryside. Carm 4D 44
Ferryton. High 2A 158
Fersfield. Norf 2C 66
Fersit. High 1A 142
Feshiebridge. High 3C 150
Fetcham. Surr 5C 38
Fetterangus. Abers 3G 161
Fettercairn. Abers 1F 145
Fewcott. Oxon 3D 50
Fewston. N Yor 4D 98
Ffairfach. Carm 3G 45
Ffair Rhos. Cdgn 4G 57
Ffaldybrenin. Carm 1G 45
Ffarmers. Carm 1G 45
Ffawyddog. Powy 4F 47
Ffodun. Powy 5E 71
Ffont-y-gari. V Glam 5D 32
Fforest. Carm 5F 45
Fforest-fach. Swan 3F 31
Fforest Goch. Neat 5H 45
Ffostrasol. Cdgn 1D 44
Ffos-y-ffin. Cdgn 4D 56
Ffrith. Flin 5E 83
Ffrwdgrech. Powy 3D 46
Ffwl-y-mwn. V Glam 5D 32
Ffynnon-ddrain. Carm 3E 45
Ffynnongroyw. Flin 2D 82
Ffynnon Gynydd. Powy 1E 47
Ffynnonoer. Cdgn 5E 57
Fiag Lodge. High 1B 164
Fidden. Arg 2B 132
Fiddington. Glos 2E 49
Fiddington. Som 2F 21
Fiddleford. Dors 1D 14
Fiddlers Hamlet. Essx 5E 53
Field. Staf 2E 73
Field Assarts. Oxon 4B 50
Field Broughton. Cumb 1C 96
Field Dalling. Norf 2C 78
Fieldhead. Cumb 1F 103
Field Head. Leics 5B 74
Fifehead Magdalen. Dors 4C 22
Fifehead Neville. Dors 1C 14
Fifehead St Quintin. Dors 1C 14
Fife Keith. Mor 3B 160
Fifield. Oxon 4H 49
Fifield. Wilts 1G 23
Fifield. Wind 3A 38
Fifield Bavant. Wilts 4F 23
Figheldean. Wilts 2G 23
Filby. Norf 4G 79
Filey. N Yor 1F 101
Filford. Dors 3H 13
Filgrave. Mil 1G 51
Filkins. Oxon 5H 49
Filleigh. Devn 1H 11
(nr. Crediton)
Filleigh. Devn 4G 19
(nr. South Molton)
Fillingham. Linc 2G 87
Fillongley. Warw 2G 61
Filton. S Glo 4B 34
Fimber. E Yor 3C 100
Finavon. Ang 3D 145
Fincham. Norf 5F 77
Finchampstead. Wok 5F 37
Fincharn. Arg 3G 133
Finchdean. Hants 1F 17
Finchingfield. Essx 2G 53
Finchley. G Lon 1D 38
Findern. Derbs 2H 73
Findhorn. Mor 2E 159
Findhorn Bridge. High 1C 150
Findochty. Mor 2B 160
Findo Gask. Per 1C 136
Findon. Abers 4G 153
Findon. W Sus 5C 26
Findon Mains. High 2A 158
Findon Valley. W Sus 5C 26
Finedon. Nptn 3G 63
Fingal Street. Suff 3E 66
Fingest. Buck 2F 37
Finghall. N Yor 1D 98
Fingland. Cumb 4D 112
Fingland. Dum 3G 117
Finglesham. Kent 5H 41
Fingringhoe. Essx 3D 54
Finiskaig. High 4A 148
Finmere. Oxon 2E 51
Finnart. Per 3C 142
Finningham. Suff 4C 66
Finningley. S Yor 1D 86
Finnyguad. Abers 3D 160
Finsbury. G Lon 2E 39
Finstall. Worc 3D 61
Finsthwaite. Cumb 1C 96
Finstock. Oxon 4B 50
Finstown. Orkn 6C 172
Fintona. Omag 3K 177
Fintry. Abers 3E 161
Fintry. D'dee 5D 144
Fintry. Stir 1H 127
Finvoy. Bmny 5F 175
Finwood. Warw 4F 61
Finzean. Abers 4D 152
Fionnphort. Arg 2B 132
Fionnsabhagh. W Isl 9C 171
Firbeck. S Yor 2C 86
Firby. N Yor 1E 99
(nr. Bedale)
Firby. N Yor 3B 100
(nr. Malton)
Firgrove. G Man 3H 91
Firle. E Sus 5F 27

Firsdown—Golcar

Firsdown. Wilts 3H 23
First Coast. High 4D 162
Firth. Shet 4F 173
Fir Tree. Dur 1E 105
Fishbourne. IOW 3D 16
Fishbourne. W Sus 2G 17
Fishburn. Dur 1A 106
Fishcross. Clac 4B 136
Fisherford. Abers 5D 160
Fisherrow. E Lot 2G 129
Fisher's Pond. Hants 4C 24
Fisher's Row. Lanc 5D 96
Fisherstreet. W Sus 2A 26
Fisherton. High 3B 158
Fisherton. S Ayr 3B 116
Fisherton de la Mere. Wilts 3E 23
Fishguard. Pemb 1D 42
Fishlake. S Yor 3G 93
Fishley. Norf 4G 79
Fishnish. Arg 4A 140
Fishpond Bottom. Dors 3G 13
Fishponds. Bris 4B 34
Fishpool. Glos 3B 48
Fishpool. G Man 4G 91
Fishpools. Powy 4D 58
Fishtoft. Linc 1C 76
Fishtoft Drove. Linc 1C 76
Fishwick. Bord 4F 131
Fiskavaig. High 5C 154
Fiskerton. Linc 3H 87
Fiskerton. Notts 5E 87
Fitch. Shet 7E 173
Fitling. E Yor 1F 95
Fittleton. Wilts 2G 23
Fittleworth. W Sus 4B 26
Fitton End. Cambs 4D 76
Fitz. Shrp 4G 71
Fitzhead. Som 4E 20
Fitzwilliam. W Yor 3E 93
Fiunary. High 4A 140
Five Ash Down. E Sus 3F 27
Five Ashes. E Sus 3G 27
Five Bells. Som 2D 20
Five Bridges. Here 1B 48
Fivehead. Som 4G 21
Five Lane Ends. Lanc 4E 97
Fivelanes. Corn 4C 10
Fivemiletown. Dngn 5K 177
Five Oak Green. Kent 1H 27
Five Oaks. W Sus 3B 26
Five Roads. Carm 5E 45
Five Ways. Warw 3G 61
Flack's Green. Essx 4A 54
Flackwell Heath. Buck 3G 37
Fladbury. Worc 1E 49
Fladda. Shet 3E 173
Fladdabister. Shet 8F 173
Flagg. Derbs 4F 85
Flamborough. E Yor 2G 101
Flamstead. Herts 4A 52
Flansham. W Sus 5A 26
Flasby. N Yor 4B 98
Flash. Staf 4E 85
Flashader. High 3C 154
Flatt, The. Cumb 2G 113
Flaunden. Herts 5A 52
Flawborough. Notts 1E 75
Flawith. N Yor 3G 99
Flax Bourton. N Som 5A 34
Flaxby. N Yor 4F 99
Flaxholme. Derbs 1H 73
Flaxley. Glos 4B 48
Flaxley Green. Staf 4E 73
Flaxpool. Som 3E 21
Flaxton. N Yor 3A 100
Fleck. Shet 10E 173
Fleckney. Leics 1D 62
Flecknoe. Warw 4C 62
Fledborough. Notts 3F 87
Fleet. Dors 4B 14
Fleet. Hants 1G 25 (nr. Farnborough)
Fleet. Hants 2F 17 (nr. South Hayling)
Fleet. Linc 3C 76
Fleet Hargate. Linc 3C 76
Fleetville. Herts 5B 52
Fleetwood. Lanc 5C 96
Fleggburgh. Norf 4G 79
Fleisirin. W Isl 4H 171
Flemingston. V Glam 4D 32
Flemington. S Lan 3H 127 (nr. Glasgow)
Flemington. S Lan 5A 128 (nr. Strathaven)
Flempton. Suff 4H 65
Fleoideabhagh. W Isl 9C 171
Fletcher's Green. Kent 1G 27
Fletchertown. Cumb 5D 112
Fletching. E Sus 3F 27
Fleuchary. High 4E 165
Flexbury. Corn 2C 10
Flexford. Surr 5A 38
Flimby. Cumb 1B 102
Flimwell. E Sus 2B 28
Flint. Flin 3E 83
Flintham. Notts 1E 75
Flint Mountain. Flin 3E 83
Flinton. E Yor 1F 95
Flintsham. Here 5F 59
Flishinghurst. Kent 2B 28
Flitcham. Norf 3G 77
Flitton. C Beds 2A 52
Flitwick. C Beds 2A 52
Flixborough. N Lin 3B 94
Flixton. G Man 1B 84
Flixton. N Yor 2E 101
Flixton. Suff 2F 67
Flockton. W Yor 3C 92
Flodden. Nmbd 1D 120
Flodigarry. High 1D 154
Flood's Ferry. Cambs 1C 64
Flookburgh. Cumb 2C 96
Flordon. Norf 1D 66
Flore. Nptn 4D 62
Flotterton. Nmbd 4E 121
Flowton. Suff 1D 54
Flushing. Abers 4H 161
Flushing. Corn 5C 6
Fluxton. Devn 3D 12
Flyford Flavell. Worc 5D 61
Fobbing. Thur 2B 40
Fochabers. Mor 3H 159
Fochriw. Cphy 5E 46
Fockerby. N Lin 3B 94
Fodderty. High 3H 157
Foddington. Som 4A 22
Foel. Powy 4B 70
Foffarty. Ang 4D 144
Foggathorpe. E Yor 1A 94
Fogo. Bord 5D 130
Fogorig. Bord 5D 130
Foindle. High 4B 166
Folda. Ang 2A 144
Fole. Staf 2E 73
Foleshill. W Mid 2A 62
Foley Park. Worc 3C 60
Folke. Dors 1B 14
Folkestone. Kent 2G 29 & 195
Folkingham. Linc 2H 75
Folkington. E Sus 5G 27
Folksworth. Cambs 1A 64
Folkton. N Yor 2E 101
Folla Rule. Abers 5E 161
Follifoot. N Yor 4F 99
Folly Cross. Devn 2E 11
Folly Gate. Devn 3F 11
Folly, The. Herts 4B 52
Folly, The. W Ber 5C 36
Fonmon. V Glam 5D 32
Fonthill Bishop. Wilts 3E 23
Fonthill Gifford. Wilts 3E 23
Fontmell Magna. Dors 1D 14
Fontwell. W Sus 5A 26
Font-y-gary. V Glam 5D 32
Foodieash. Fife 2F 137
Foolow. Derbs 3F 85
Footdee. Aber 3G 153
Footherley. Staf 5F 73
Foots Cray. G Lon 3F 39
Forbestown. Abers 2A 152
Force Forge. Cumb 5E 103
Force Mills. Cumb 5E 103
Forcett. N Yor 3E 105
Ford. Arg 3F 133
Ford. Buck 5F 51
Ford. Derbs 2B 86
Ford. Devn 4E 19 (nr. Bideford)
Ford. Devn 3C 8 (nr. Holbeton)
Ford. Devn 4D 9 (nr. Salcombe)
Ford. Glos 3F 49
Ford. Nmbd 1D 120
Ford. Plym 3A 8
Ford. Shrp 4G 71
Ford. Som 1A 22 (nr. Wells)
Ford. Som 4D 20 (nr. Wiveliscombe)
Ford. Staf 5E 85
Ford. W Sus 5B 26
Ford. Wilts 4D 34 (nr. Chippenham)
Ford. Wilts 3G 23 (nr. Salisbury)
Forda. Devn 3E 19
Ford Barton. Devn 1C 12
Fordcombe. Kent 1G 27
Fordell. Fife 1E 129
Forden. Powy 5E 71
Ford End. Essx 4G 53
Forder Green. Devn 2D 9
Ford Green. Lanc 5D 97
Fordham. Cambs 3F 65
Fordham. Essx 3C 54
Fordham. Norf 1F 65
Fordham Heath. Essx 3C 54
Ford Heath. Shrp 4G 71
Fordhouses. W Mid 5D 72
Fordie. Per 1G 135
Fordingbridge. Hants 1G 15
Fordington. Linc 3D 88
Fordon. E Yor 2E 101
Fordoun. Abers 1G 145
Ford Street. Essx 3C 54
Ford Street. Som 1E 13
Fordton. Devn 3B 12
Fordwells. Oxon 4B 50
Fordwich. Kent 5F 41
Fordyce. Abers 2C 160
Forebridge. Staf 3D 72
Foremark. Derbs 3H 73
Forest. N Yor 4F 105
Forestburn Gate. Nmbd 5E 121
Foresterseat. Mor 3F 159
Forest Green. Glos 2D 34
Forest Green. Surr 1C 26
Forest Hall. Cumb 4G 103
Forest Head. Cumb 4G 113
Forest Hill. Oxon 5D 50
Forest-in-Teesdale. Dur 2B 104
Forest Lodge. Per 1G 143
Forest Mill. Clac 4B 136
Forest Row. E Sus 2F 27
Forestside. W Sus 1F 17
Forest Town. Notts 4C 86
Forfar. Ang 3D 144
Forgandenny. Per 2C 136
Forge. Powy 1G 57
Forge Side. Torf 5F 47
Forge, The. Here 5F 59
Forgewood. N Lan 4A 128
Forgie. Mor 3A 160
Forgue. Abers 4D 160
Forkill. New M 8E 178
Formby. Mers 4A 90
Forncett End. Norf 1D 66
Forncett St Mary. Norf 1D 66
Forncett St Peter. Norf 1D 66
Forneth. Per 4H 143
Fornham All Saints. Suff 4H 65
Fornham St Martin. Suff 4A 66
Forres. Mor 3E 159
Forrestfield. N Lan 3B 128
Forrest Lodge. Dum 1C 110
Forsbrook. Staf 1D 72
Forse. High 5E 169
Forsinard. High 4A 168
Forss. High 2C 168
Forstal, The. Kent 2E 29
Forston. Dors 3B 14
Fort Augustus. High 3F 149
Forteviot. Per 2C 136
Fort George. High 3B 158
Forth. S Lan 4C 128
Forthampton. Glos 2D 48
Forthay. Glos 2C 34
Forth Road Bridge. Fife 2E 129
Fortingall. Per 4E 143
Fort Matilda. Inv 2D 126
Forton. Hants 2C 24
Forton. Lanc 4D 97
Forton. Shrp 4G 71
Forton. Som 2G 13
Forton. Staf 3B 72
Forton Heath. Shrp 4G 71
Fortrie. Abers 4D 160
Fortrose. High 3B 158
Fortuneswell. Dors 5B 14
Fort William. High 1F 141
Forty Green. Buck 1A 38
Forty Hill. G Lon 1E 39
Forward Green. Suff 5C 66
Fosbury. Wilts 1B 24
Foscot. Oxon 3H 49
Fosdyke. Linc 2C 76
Foss. Per 3E 143
Fossebridge. Glos 4F 49
Foster Street. Essx 5E 53
Foston. Derbs 2F 73
Foston. Leics 1D 62
Foston. Linc 1F 75
Foston. N Yor 3A 100
Foston on the Wolds. E Yor 4F 101
Fotherby. Linc 1C 88
Fothergill. Cumb 1B 102
Fotheringhay. Nptn 1H 63
Foubister. Orkn 7E 172
Foula Airport. Shet 8A 173
Foul Anchor. Cambs 4D 76
Foulbridge. Cumb 5F 113
Foulden. Norf 1G 65
Foulden. Bord 4F 131
Foul Mile. E Sus 4H 27
Foulridge. Lanc 5A 98
Foulsham. Norf 3C 78
Fountainhall. Bord 5H 129
Four Alls, The. Shrp 2A 72
Four Ashes. Staf 5D 72 (nr. Cannock)
Four Ashes. Staf 2C 60 (nr. Kinver)
Four Ashes. Suff 3C 66
Four Crosses. Powy 5C 70 (nr. Llanerfyl)
Four Crosses. Powy 4E 71 (nr. Llanymynech)
Four Crosses. Staf 5D 72
Four Elms. Kent 1F 27
Four Forks. Som 3F 21
Four Gotes. Cambs 4D 76
Four Lane End. S Yor 4C 92
Four Lane Ends. Lanc 4E 97
Four Lanes. Corn 5A 6
Fourlanes End. Ches E 5B 84
Four Marks. Hants 3E 25
Four Mile Bridge. IOA 3B 80
Four Oaks. E Sus 3C 28
Four Oaks. Glos 3B 48
Four Oaks. W Mid 2G 61
Four Roads. Carm 5E 45
Four Roads. IOM 5B 108
Fourstones. Nmbd 3B 114
Four Throws. Kent 3B 28
Fovant. Wilts 4F 23
Foveran. Abers 1G 153
Fowey. Corn 3F 7
Fowlershill. Aber 2G 153
Fowley Common. Warr 1A 84
Fowlis. Ang 5C 144
Fowlis Wester. Per 1B 136
Fowlmere. Cambs 1E 53
Fownhope. Here 2A 48
Foxcombe Hill. Oxon 5C 50
Fox Corner. Surr 5A 38
Foxcote. Glos 4F 49
Foxcote. Som 1C 22
Foxdale. IOM 4B 108
Foxearth. Essx 1B 54
Foxfield. Cumb 1B 96
Foxham. Wilts 4E 35
Fox Hatch. Essx 1G 39
Foxhole. Corn 3D 6
Foxholes. N Yor 2E 101
Foxhunt Green. E Sus 4G 27
Fox Lane. Hants 1G 25
Foxley. Norf 3C 78
Foxley. Nptn 5D 62
Foxley. Wilts 3D 35
Foxlydiate. Worc 4E 61
Fox Street. Essx 3D 54
Foxt. Staf 1E 73
Foxton. Cambs 1E 53
Foxton. Dur 2A 106
Foxton. Leics 2D 62
Foxton. N Yor 5B 106
Foxup. N Yor 2A 98
Foxwist Green. Ches W 4A 84
Foxwood. Shrp 3A 60
Foy. Here 3A 48
Foyers. High 1G 149
Foynesfield. High 3C 158
Fraddam. Corn 3C 4
Fraddon. Corn 3D 6
Fradley. Staf 4F 73
Fradley South. Staf 4F 73
Fradswell. Staf 2D 73
Fraisthorpe. E Yor 3F 101
Framfield. E Sus 3F 27
Framingham Earl. Norf 5E 79
Framingham Pigot. Norf 5E 79
Framlingham. Suff 4E 67
Frampton. Dors 3B 14
Frampton. Linc 2C 76
Frampton Cotterell. S Glo 3B 34
Frampton Mansell. Glos 5E 49
Frampton on Severn. Glos 5C 48
Frampton West End. Linc 1B 76
Framsden. Suff 5D 66
Framwellgate Moor. Dur 5F 115
Franche. Worc 3C 60
Frandley. Ches W 3A 84
Frankby. Mers 2E 83
Frankfort. Norf 3F 79
Frankley. Worc 2D 61
Frank's Bridge. Powy 5D 58
Frankton. Warw 3B 62
Frankwell. Shrp 4G 71
Frant. E Sus 2G 27
Fraserburgh. Abers 2G 161
Frating Green. Essx 3D 54
Fratton. Port 2E 17
Freathy. Corn 3A 8
Freckenham. Suff 3F 65
Freckleton. Lanc 2C 90
Freeby. Leics 3F 75
Freefolk Priors. Hants 2C 24
Freehay. Staf 1E 73
Freeland. Oxon 4C 50
Freester. Shet 6F 173
Freethorpe. Norf 5G 79
Freiston. Linc 1C 76
Freiston Shore. Linc 1C 76
Fremington. Devn 3F 19
Fremington. N Yor 5D 104
Frenchbeer. Devn 4G 11
French Street. Kent 5F 39
French. Stir 3D 134
Frensham. Surr 2G 25
Frenze. Norf 2D 66
Fresgoe. High 2B 168
Freshfield. Mers 4A 90
Freshford. Bath 5C 34
Freshwater. IOW 4B 16
Freshwater Bay. IOW 4B 16
Freshwater East. Pemb 5E 43
Fressingfield. Suff 3E 67
Freston. Suff 2E 55
Freswick. High 2F 169
Fretherne. Glos 5C 48
Frettenham. Norf 4E 79
Freuchie. Fife 3E 137
Freystrop. Pemb 3D 42
Friar's Gate. E Sus 2F 27
Friar Waddon. Dors 4B 14
Friday Bridge. Cambs 5D 76
Friday Street. E Sus 5H 27
Friday Street. Surr 1C 26
Fridaythorpe. E Yor 4C 100
Friden. Derbs 4F 85
Friern Barnet. G Lon 1D 39
Friesthorpe. Linc 2H 87
Frieston. Linc 1G 75
Frieth. Buck 2F 37
Friezeland. Notts 5B 86
Frilford. Oxon 2C 36
Frilsham. W Ber 4D 36
Frimley. Surr 1G 25
Frimley Green. Surr 1G 25
Frindsbury. Medw 4B 40
Fring. Norf 2G 77
Fringford. Oxon 3E 50
Frinsted. Kent 5C 40
Frinton-on-Sea. Essx 4F 55
Friockheim. Ang 4E 145
Friog. Gwyn 4F 69
Frisby. Leics 5E 74
Frisby. Linc 4D 88
Frisby on the Wreake. Leics 4D 74
Friskney. Linc 5D 88
Friskney Eaudyke. Linc 5D 88
Friston. E Sus 5G 27
Friston. Suff 4G 67
Fritchley. Derbs 5A 86
Fritham. Hants 1H 15
Frith Bank. Linc 1C 76
Frith Common. Worc 4A 60
Frithelstock. Devn 1E 11
Frithelstock Stone. Devn 1E 11
Frithsden. Herts 5A 52
Frithville. Linc 5C 88
Frittenden. Kent 1C 28
Frittiscombe. Devn 4E 9
Fritton. Norf 5G 79 (nr. Great Yarmouth)
Fritton. Norf 1E 67 (nr. Long Stratton)
Fritwell. Oxon 3D 50
Frizinghall. W Yor 1B 92
Frizington. Cumb 3B 102
Frobost. W Isl 6C 170
Frocester. Glos 5C 48
Frochas. Powy 5D 70
Frodesley. Shrp 5H 71
Frodingham. N Lin 3C 94
Frodsham. Ches W 3H 83
Froggat. Derbs 3G 85
Froghall. Staf 1E 73
Frogham. Hants 1G 15
Frogham. Kent 5G 41
Frogmore. Devn 4D 8
Frogmore. Hants 5G 37
Frogmore. Herts 5B 52
Frognall. Linc 4A 76
Frogshall. Norf 2E 79
Frogwell. Corn 2H 7
Frolesworth. Leics 1C 62
Frome. Som 2C 22
Fromefield. Som 2C 22
Frome St Quintin. Dors 2A 14
Fromes Hill. Here 1B 48
Fron. Carm 2A 46
Fron. Gwyn 2C 68
Fron. Powy 4C 58 (nr. Llandrindod Wells)
Fron. Powy 1D 58 (nr. Newtown)
Fron. Powy 5E 71 (nr. Welshpool)
Froncysyllte. Wrex 1E 71
Frongoch. Gwyn 2B 70
Fron Isaf. Wrex 1E 71
Fronoleu. Gwyn 2G 69
Frosterley. Dur 1D 104
Frotoft. Orkn 5D 172
Froxfield. C Beds 2H 51
Froxfield. Wilts 5A 36
Froxfield Green. Hants 4F 25
Fryern Hill. Hants 4C 24
Fryerning. Essx 5G 53
Fryton. N Yor 2A 100
Fugglestone St Peter. Wilts 3G 23
Fulbeck. Linc 5G 87
Fulbourn. Cambs 5E 65
Fulbrook. Oxon 4A 50
Fulflood. Hants 3C 24
Fulford. Som 4F 21
Fulford. Staf 2D 72
Fulford. York 5A 100
Fulham. G Lon 3D 38
Fulking. W Sus 4D 26
Fuller's Moor. Ches W 5G 83
Fuller Street. Essx 4H 53
Fullerton. Hants 3B 24
Fulletby. Linc 3B 88
Full Sutton. E Yor 4B 100
Fullwood. E Ayr 4F 127
Fulmer. Buck 2A 38
Fulmodestone. Norf 2B 78
Fulnetby. Linc 3H 87
Fulney. Linc 3B 76
Fulstow. Linc 1C 88
Fulthorpe. Stoc T 2B 106
Fulwell. Tyne 4G 115
Fulwood. Lanc 1D 90
Fulwood. Notts 5B 86
Fulwood. Som 1F 13
Fulwood. S Yor 2G 85
Fundenhall. Norf 1D 66
Funtington. W Sus 2G 17
Funtley. Hants 2D 16
Funzie. Shet 2H 173
Furley. Devn 2F 13
Furnace. Arg 3H 133
Furnace. Carm 5F 45
Furnace. Cdgn 1F 57
Furner's Green. E Sus 3F 27
Furness Vale. Derbs 2E 85
Furneux Pelham. Herts 3E 53
Furzebrook. Dors 4E 15
Furzehill. Devn 2H 19
Furzehill. Dors 2F 15
Furzeley Corner. Hants 1E 17
Furzey Lodge. Hants 2B 16
Furzley. Hants 1A 16
Fyfield. Essx 5F 53
Fyfield. Glos 5H 49
Fyfield. Hants 2A 24
Fyfield. Oxon 2C 36
Fyfield. Wilts 5G 35
Fylde, The. Lanc 1B 90
Fylingthorpe. N Yor 4G 107
Fyning. W Sus 4G 25
Fyvie. Abers 5E 161

G

Gabhsann bho Dheas. W Isl 2G 171
Gabhsann bho Thuath. W Isl 2G 171
Gabroc Hill. E Ayr 4F 127
Gadbrook. Surr 1D 26
Gaddesby. Leics 4D 74
Gadfa. IOA 2D 80
Gadgirth. S Ayr 2D 116
Gaer. Powy 3E 47
Gaerwen. IOA 3D 81
Gagingwell. Oxon 3C 50
Gaick Lodge. High 5B 150
Gailey. Staf 4D 72
Gainford. Dur 3E 105
Gainsborough. Linc 1F 87
Gainsborough. Suff 1E 55
Gainsford End. Essx 2H 53
Gairletter. Arg 1C 126
Gairloch. Abers 3E 153
Gairloch. High 1H 155
Gairlochy. High 5D 148
Gairney Bank. Per 4D 136
Gairnshiel Lodge. Abers 3G 151
Gaisgill. Cumb 4H 103
Gaitsgill. Cumb 5E 113
Galashiels. Bord 1G 119
Galgate. Lanc 4D 97
Galgorm. Bmna 6G 175
Galhampton. Som 4B 22
Gallatown. Fife 4E 137
Galley Common. Warw 1H 61
Galleyend. Essx 5H 53
Galleywood. Essx 5H 53
Gallin. Per 4C 142
Gallowfauld. Ang 4D 144
Gallowhill. E Dun 2H 127
Gallowhill. Per 5A 144
Gallowhill. Ren 3F 127
Gallowhills. Abers 3H 161
Gallows Green. Staf 1E 73
Gallows Green. Worc 4D 60
Gallowstree Common. Oxon 3E 37
Galltair. High 1G 147
Gallt Melyd. Den 2C 82
Galmington. Som 4F 21
Galmisdale. High 5C 146
Galmpton. Devn 4C 8
Galmpton. Torb 3E 9
Galmpton Warborough. Torb 3E 9
Galphay. N Yor 2E 99
Galston. E Ayr 1D 117
Galton. Dors 4C 14
Galtrigill. High 3A 154
Gamblesby. Cumb 1H 103
Gamblestown. Cgvn 4F 178
Gamelsby. Cumb 4D 112
Gamesley. Derbs 1E 85
Gamlingay. Cambs 5B 64
Gamlingay Cinques. Cambs 5B 64
Gamlingay Great Heath. C Beds 5B 64
Gammaton. Devn 4E 19
Gammersgill. N Yor 1C 98
Gamston. Notts 2D 74 (nr. Nottingham)
Gamston. Notts 3E 86 (nr. Retford)
Ganarew. Here 4A 48
Ganavan. Arg 5C 140
Ganborough. Glos 3G 49
Gang. Corn 2H 7
Ganllwyd. Gwyn 3G 69
Gannochy. Ang 1E 145
Gannochy. Per 1D 136
Gansclet. High 4F 169
Ganstead. E Yor 1E 95
Ganthorpe. N Yor 2A 100
Ganton. N Yor 2D 101
Gants Hill. G Lon 2F 39
Gappah. Devn 5B 12
Garafad. High 2D 155
Garboldisham. Norf 2C 66
Garden City. Flin 4F 83
Gardeners Green. Wok 5G 37
Gardenstown. Abers 2F 161
Garden Village. S Yor 1G 85
Garden Village. Swan 3E 31
Garderhouse. Shet 7E 173
Gardham. E Yor 5D 100
Gardie. Shet 5C 173 (on Papa Stour)
Gardie. Shet 1H 173 (on Unst)
Gardie Ho. Shet 7F 173
Gare Hill. Som 2C 22
Garelochhead. Arg 4B 134
Garford. Oxon 2C 36
Garforth. W Yor 1E 93
Gargrave. N Yor 4B 98
Gargunnock. Stir 4G 135
Garleffin. S Ayr 1F 109
Garlieston. Dum 5B 110
Garlinge Green. Kent 5F 41
Garlogie. Abers 3E 153
Garmelow. Staf 3B 72
Garmond. Abers 3F 161
Garmondsway. Dur 1A 106
Garmony. Arg 4A 140
Garmouth. Mor 2H 159
Garmston. Shrp 5A 72
Garnant. Carm 4G 45
Garndiffaith. Torf 5F 47
Garndolbenmaen. Gwyn 1D 69
Garnett Bridge. Cumb 5G 103
Garnfadryn. Gwyn 2B 68
Garnkirk. N Lan 3H 127
Garnlydan. Blae 4E 47
Garnsgate. Linc 3D 76
Garnswllt. Swan 5G 45
Garn-yr-erw. Torf 4F 47
Garrabost. W Isl 4H 171
Garrallan. E Ayr 3E 117
Garras. Corn 4E 5
Garreg. Gwyn 1F 69
Garrigill. Cumb 5A 114
Garrison. Ferm 7B 176
Garriston. N Yor 5E 105
Garrogie Lodge. High 2H 149
Garros. High 2D 155
Garrow. Per 4F 143
Garsdale. Cumb 1G 97
Garsdale Head. Cumb 5A 104
Garsdon. Wilts 3E 35
Garshall Green. Staf 2D 72
Garsington. Oxon 5D 50
Garstang. Lanc 5D 97
Garston. Mers 2G 83
Garswood. Mers 1H 83
Gartcosh. N Lan 3H 127
Garth. B'end 2B 32
Garth. Cdgn 2F 57
Garth. Gwyn 2E 69
Garth. IOM 4C 108
Garth. Powy 1C 46 (nr. Builth Wells)
Garth. Powy 3E 59 (nr. Knighton)
Garth. Shet 6D 173 (nr. Sandness)
Garth. Shet 6F 173 (nr. Skellister)
Garth. Wrex 1E 71
Garthamlock. Glas 3H 127
Garthbrengy. Powy 2D 46
Gartheli. Cdgn 5E 57
Garthmyl. Powy 1D 58
Garthorpe. Leics 3F 75
Garthorpe. N Lin 3B 94
Garth Owen. Powy 1D 58
Garth Row. Cumb 5G 103
Gartly. Abers 5C 160
Gartmore. Stir 4E 135
Gartness. N Lan 3A 128
Gartness. Stir 1G 127
Gartocharn. W Dun 1F 127
Garton. E Yor 1F 95
Garton-on-the-Wolds. E Yor 4D 101
Gartsherrie. N Lan 3A 128
Gartymore. High 2H 165
Garvagh. Cole 5E 174
Garvaghy. Omag 3L 177
Garvald. E Lot 2B 130
Garvamore. High 4H 149
Garvard. Arg 4A 132
Garvault. High 5H 167
Garve. High 2F 157
Garvestone. Norf 5C 78
Garvetagh. Strab 4E 176
Garvie. Arg 4H 133
Garvock. Abers 1G 145
Garvock. Inv 2D 126
Garway. Here 3H 47
Garway Common. Here 3H 47
Garway Hill. Here 3H 47
Garwick. Linc 1A 76
Gaskan. High 1C 140
Gasper. Wilts 3C 22
Gastard. Wilts 5D 35
Gasthorpe. Norf 2B 66
Gatcombe. IOW 4C 16
Gateacre. Mers 2G 83
Gatebeck. Cumb 1E 97
Gate Burton. Linc 2F 87
Gateforth. N Yor 2F 93
Gatehead. E Ayr 1C 116
Gate Helmsley. N Yor 4A 100
Gatehouse. Nmbd 1A 114
Gatehouse of Fleet. Dum 4D 110
Gatelawbridge. Dum 5B 118
Gateley. Norf 3B 78
Gatenby. N Yor 1F 99
Gatesgarth. Cumb 3C 102
Gateshead. Tyne 3F 115
Gatesheath. Ches W 4G 83
Gateside. Ang 4D 144 (nr. Forfar)
Gateside. Ang 4C 144 (nr. Kirriemuir)
Gateside. Fife 3D 136
Gateside. N Ayr 4E 127
Gathurst. G Man 4D 90
Gatley. G Man 2C 84
Gatton. Surr 5D 39
Gattonside. Bord 1H 119
Gatwick (London) Airport. W Sus 1D 27 & 205
Gaufron. Powy 4B 58
Gaulby. Leics 5D 74
Gauldry. Fife 1F 137
Gaultree. Norf 5D 77
Gaunt's Common. Dors 2F 15
Gaunt's Earthcott. S Glo 3B 34
Gautby. Linc 3A 88
Gavinton. Bord 4D 130
Gawber. S Yor 4D 92
Gawcott. Buck 2E 51
Gawsworth. Ches E 4C 84
Gawthorpe. W Yor 2C 92
Gawthrop. Cumb 1F 97
Gawthwaite. Cumb 1B 96
Gay Bowers. Essx 5A 54
Gaydon. Warw 5A 62
Gayfield. Orkn 2D 172
Gayhurst. Mil 1G 51
Gayle. N Yor 1A 98
Gayles. N Yor 4E 105
Gay Street. W Sus 3B 26
Gayton. Mers 2E 83
Gayton. Norf 4G 77
Gayton. Nptn 5E 62
Gayton. Staf 3D 73
Gayton le Marsh. Linc 2D 88
Gayton le Wold. Linc 2B 88
Gayton Thorpe. Norf 4G 77
Gaywood. Norf 3F 77
Gazeley. Suff 4G 65
Geanies. High 1C 158
Gearraidh Bhailteas. W Isl 6C 170
Gearraidh Bhaird. W Isl 6F 171
Gearraidh ma Monadh. W Isl 7C 170
Gearraidh na h-Aibhne. W Isl 4E 171
Geary. High 2B 154
Geddes. High 3C 158
Gedding. Suff 5B 66
Geddington. Nptn 2F 63
Gedintailor. High 5E 155
Gedling. Notts 1D 74
Gedney. Linc 3D 76
Gedney Broadgate. Linc 3D 76
Gedney Drove End. Linc 3D 76
Gedney Dyke. Linc 3D 76
Gedney Hill. Linc 4C 76
Gee Cross. G Man 1D 84
Geeston. Rut 5G 75
Geilston. Arg 2E 127
Geirinis. W Isl 4C 170
Geise. High 2D 168
Geisiadar. W Isl 4D 171
Gelder Shiel. Abers 5G 151
Geldeston. Norf 1F 67
Gell. Cnwy 4A 82
Gelli. Pemb 3E 43
Gelli. Rhon 2C 32
Gellifor. Den 4D 82
Gelligaer. Cphy 2E 33
Gellilydan. Gwyn 2F 69
Gellinudd. Neat 5H 45
Gellyburn. Per 5H 143
Gellywen. Carm 2G 43
Gelston. Dum 4E 111
Gelston. Linc 1G 75
Gembling. E Yor 4F 101
Geneva. Cdgn 5D 56
Gentleshaw. Staf 4E 73
Geocrab. W Isl 8D 171
George Best Belfast City Airport. Bel 2H 179
George Green. Buck 2A 38
Georgeham. Devn 3E 19
George Nympton. Devn 4H 19
Georgetown. Blae 5E 47
Georgetown. Ren 3F 127
Georth. Orkn 5C 172
Gerlan. Gwyn 4F 81
Germansweek. Devn 3E 11
Germoe. Corn 4C 4
Gerrans. Corn 5C 6
Gerrard's Bromley. Staf 2B 72
Gerrards Cross. Buck 2A 38
Gerston. High 3D 168
Gestingthorpe. Essx 2B 54
Gethsemane. Pemb 1A 44
Geuffordd. Powy 4E 70
Gibraltar. Buck 4F 51
Gibraltar. Linc 5E 89
Gibraltar. Suff 5D 66
Gibsmere. Notts 1E 74
Giddeahall. Wilts 4D 34
Gidea Park. G Lon 2G 39
Gidleigh. Devn 4G 11
Giffnock. E Ren 4G 127
Gifford. E Lot 3B 130
Giffordtown. Fife 2E 137
Giggetty. Staf 1C 60
Giggleswick. N Yor 3H 97
Gignog. Pemb 2C 42
Gilberdyke. E Yor 2B 94
Gilbert's End. Worc 1D 48
Gilbert's Green. Warw 3F 61
Gilchriston. E Lot 3A 130
Gilcrux. Cumb 1C 102
Gildersome. W Yor 2C 92
Gildingwells. S Yor 2C 86
Gilesgate Moor. Dur 5F 115
Gileston. V Glam 5D 32
Gilfach. Cphy 2E 33
Gilfach Goch. Rhon 2C 32
Gilfachreda. Cdgn 5D 56
Gilford. Ban 5E 178
Gilgarran. Cumb 2B 102
Gillamoor. N Yor 5D 107
Gillan. Corn 4E 5
Gillar's Green. Mers 1G 83
Gillen. High 3B 154
Gilling East. N Yor 2A 100
Gillingham. Dors 4D 22
Gillingham. Medw 4B 40 & Medway 197
Gillingham. Norf 1G 67
Gilling West. N Yor 4E 105
Gillock. High 3E 169
Gillow Heath. Staf 5C 84
Gills. High 1F 169
Gill's Green. Kent 2B 28
Gilmanscleuch. Bord 2F 119
Gilmerton. Edin 3F 129
Gilmerton. Per 1A 136
Gilmonby. Dur 3C 104
Gilmorton. Leics 2C 62
Gilsland. Nmbd 3H 113
Gilsland Spa. Cumb 3H 113
Gilston. Midl 4H 129
Giltbrook. Notts 1B 74
Gilwern. Mon 4F 47
Gimingham. Norf 2E 79
Giosla. W Isl 5D 171
Gipping. Suff 4C 66
Gipsey Bridge. Linc 1B 76
Gipton. W Yor 1D 92
Girdle Toll. N Ayr 5E 127
Girlsta. Shet 6F 173
Girsby. N Yor 4A 106
Girthon. Dum 4D 110
Girton. Cambs 4D 64
Girton. Notts 4F 87
Girvan. S Ayr 5A 116
Gisburn. Lanc 5H 97
Gisleham. Suff 2H 67
Gislingham. Suff 3C 66
Gissing. Norf 2D 66
Gittisham. Devn 3E 13
Gladestry. Powy 5E 59
Gladsmuir. E Lot 2A 130
Glaichbea. High 5H 157
Glais. Swan 5H 45
Glaisdale. N Yor 4E 107
Glame. High 4E 155
Glamis. Ang 4C 144
Glamisdale. High 5C 146
Glanaman. Carm 4G 45
Glan-Conwy. Cnwy 5H 81
Glandford. Norf 1C 78
Glan Duar. Carm 1F 45
Glandwr. Blae 5F 47
Glandwr. Pemb 2F 43
Glan-Dwyfach. Gwyn 1D 69
Glandy Cross. Carm 2F 43
Glandyfi. Cdgn 1F 57
Glangrwyney. Powy 4F 47
Glanmule. Powy 1D 58
Glanrhyd. Gwyn 2B 68
Glanrhyd. Pemb 1B 44 (nr. Cardigan)
Glan-rhyd. Pemb 1F 43 (nr. Crymych)
Glan-rhyd. Powy 5A 46
Glanton. Nmbd 3E 121
Glanton Pyke. Nmbd 3E 121
Glanvilles Wootton. Dors 2B 14
Glan-y-don. Flin 3D 82
Glan-y-nant. Powy 2B 58
Glan-yr-afon. Gwyn 1C 70
Glan-yr-afon. IOA 2F 81
Glan-yr-afon. Powy 5C 70
Glan-y-wern. Gwyn 2F 69
Glapthorn. Nptn 1H 63
Glapwell. Derbs 4B 86
Glarryford. Bmna 5G 175
Glas Aird. Arg 4A 132
Glas-allt Shiel. Abers 5G 151
Glasbury. Powy 2E 47
Glaschoil. Mor 5E 159
Glascoed. Den 3B 82
Glascoed. Mon 5G 47
Glascote. Staf 5G 73
Glascwm. Powy 5D 58
Glasfryn. Cnwy 5B 82
Glasgow. Glas 3G 127 & 195
Glasgow Airport. Ren 3F 127 & 205
Glasgow Prestwick International Airport. S Ayr 2C 116
Glashvin. High 2D 154
Glasinfryn. Gwyn 4E 81
Glas na Cardaich. High 4E 147
Glasnacardoch. High 4E 147
Glasnakille. High 2D 146
Glaspwll. Cdgn 1G 57
Glassburn. High 5F 157
Glassenbury. Kent 2B 28
Glasserton. Dum 5B 110
Glassford. S Lan 5A 128
Glassgreen. Mor 2G 159
Glasshouse. Glos 3C 48
Glasshouses. N Yor 3D 98
Glasson. Cumb 3D 112
Glasson. Lanc 4D 96
Glassonby. Cumb 1G 103
Glasswater. Down 4J 179
Glasterlaw. Ang 3E 145
Glaston. Rut 5F 75
Glastonbury. Som 3H 21
Glatton. Cambs 2A 64
Glazebrook. Warr 1A 84
Glazebury. Warr 1A 84
Glazeley. Shrp 2B 60
Gleadless. S Yor 2A 86
Gleadsmoss. Ches E 4C 84
Gleann Dail bho Dheas. W Isl 7C 170
Gleann Tholastaidh. W Isl 3H 171
Gleann Uige. High 1A 140
Gleaston. Cumb 2B 96
Glebe. Strab 3F 176
Glecknabae. Arg 3B 126
Gledrid. Shrp 2E 71
Gleiniant. Powy 1B 58
Glemsford. Suff 1B 54
Glen. Dum 4C 110
Glenancross. High 4E 147
Glenanne. Arm 6D 178
Glenariff. Moy 4J 175
Glenarm. Lar 5K 175
Glen Audlyn. IOM 2D 108
Glenavy. Lis 2F 179
Glenbarr. Arg 2A 122
Glenbeg. High 2G 139
Glen Bernisdale. High 4D 154
Glenbervie. Abers 5E 153
Glenboig. N Lan 3A 128
Glenborrodale. High 2A 140
Glenbranter. Arg 4A 134
Glenbreck. Bord 2C 118
Glenbrein Lodge. High 2G 149
Glenbrittle. High 1C 146
Glenbuchat Lodge. Abers 2H 151
Glenbuck. E Ayr 2G 117
Glenburn. Ren 3F 127
Glencalvie Lodge. High 5B 164
Glencaple. Dum 3A 112
Glencarron Lodge. High 3C 156
Glencarse. Per 1D 136
Glencassley Castle. High 3B 164
Glencat. Abers 4C 152
Glencoe. High 3F 141
Glen Cottage. High 5E 147
Glencraig. Fife 4D 136
Glendale. High 4A 154
Glendevon. Per 3B 136
Glendoebeg. High 3G 149
Glendoick. Per 1E 136
Glendoune. S Ayr 5A 116
Glenduckie. Fife 2E 137
Gleneagles. Per 3B 136
Glenegedale. Arg 4B 124
Glenegedale Lots. Arg 4B 124
Glenelg. High 2G 147
Glenernie. Mor 4E 159
Glenesslin. Dum 1F 111
Glenfarg. Per 2D 136
Glenfarquhar Lodge. Abers 5E 152
Glenferness Mains. High 4D 158
Glenfeshie Lodge. High 4C 150
Glenfiddich Lodge. Mor 5H 159
Glenfield. Leics 5C 74
Glenfinnan. High 5B 148
Glenfintaig Lodge. High 5E 149
Glenfoot. Per 2D 136
Glenfyne Lodge. Arg 2B 134
Glengap. Dum 4D 110
Glengarnock. N Ayr 4E 126
Glengolly. High 2D 168
Glengorm Castle. Arg 3F 139
Glengormley. Newt 1H 179
Glengrasco. High 4D 154
Glenhead Farm. Ang 2B 144
Glenholm. Bord 1D 118
Glen House. Bord 1E 119
Glenhurich. High 2C 140
Glenkerry. Bord 3E 119
Glenkiln. Dum 2F 111
Glenkindie. Abers 2B 152
Glenkinglass Lodge. Arg 5F 141
Glenkirk. Bord 2C 118
Glenlean. Arg 1B 126
Glenlee. Dum 1D 110
Glenleraig. High 5B 166
Glenlichorn. Per 2G 135
Glenlivet. Mor 1F 151
Glenlochar. Dum 3E 111
Glenlochsie Lodge. Per 1H 143
Glenluce. Dum 4G 109
Glenmarskie. High 3F 157
Glenmassan. Arg 1C 126
Glenmavis. N Lan 3A 128
Glen Maye. IOM 4B 108
Glenmazeran Lodge. High 1B 150
Glenmidge. Dum 1F 111
Glen Mona. IOM 3D 108
Glenmore. High 2G 139 (nr. Glenborrodale)
Glenmore. High 3D 151 (nr. Kingussie)
Glenmore. High 4D 154 (on Isle of Skye)
Glenmoy. Ang 2D 144
Glennoe. Arg 5E 141
Glen of Coachford. Abers 4B 160
Glenogil. Ang 2D 144
Glen Parva. Leics 1C 62
Glenprosen Village. Ang 2C 144
Glenree. N Ayr 3D 122
Glenridding. Cumb 3E 103
Glenrosa. N Ayr 2E 123
Glenrothes. Fife 3E 137
Glensanda. High 4C 140
Glensaugh. Abers 1F 145
Glenshero Lodge. High 4H 149
Glensluain. Arg 4H 133
Glenstockadale. Dum 3F 109
Glenstriven. Arg 2B 126
Glen Tanar House. Abers 4B 152
Glentham. Linc 1H 87
Glenton. Abers 1D 152
Glentress. Bord 1E 119
Glentromie Lodge. High 4B 150
Glentrool Lodge. Dum 1B 110
Glentrool Village. Dum 2A 110
Glentruim House. High 4A 150
Glentworth. Linc 2G 87
Glenuig. High 1A 140
Glen View. New M 6E 178
Glen Village. Falk 2B 128
Glen Vine. IOM 4C 108
Glenwhilly. Dum 2G 109
Glenzierfoot. Dum 2E 113
Glespin. S Lan 2H 117
Gletness. Shet 6F 173
Glewstone. Here 3A 48
Glib Cheois. W Isl 5F 171
Glinton. Pet 5A 76
Glooston. Leics 1E 63
Glossop. Derbs 1E 85
Gloster Hill. Nmbd 4G 121
Gloucester. Glos 4D 48 & 195
Gloucestershire Airport. Glos 3D 49
Gloup. Shet 1G 173
Glusburn. N Yor 5C 98
Glutt Lodge. High 5B 168
Glutton Bridge. Staf 4E 85
Gluvian. Corn 2D 6
Glympton. Oxon 3C 50
Glyn. Cnwy 3A 82
Glynarthen. Cdgn 1D 44
Glynbrochan. Powy 2B 58
Glyn Ceiriog. Wrex 2E 70
Glyncoch. Rhon 2D 32
Glyncorrwg. Neat 2B 32
Glynde. E Sus 5F 27
Glyndebourne. E Sus 4F 27
Glyndyfrdwy. Den 1D 70
Glyn Ebwy. Blae 5E 47
Glynllan. B'end 3C 32
Glynn. Lar 7L 175
Glyn-neath. Neat 5B 46
Glynogwr. B'end 3C 32
Glyntaff. Rhon 3D 32
Glyntawe. Powy 4B 46
Glynteg. Carm 2D 44
Gnosall. Staf 3C 72
Gnosall Heath. Staf 3C 72
Goadby. Leics 1E 63
Goadby Marwood. Leics 3E 75
Goatacre. Wilts 4F 35
Goathill. Dors 1B 14
Goathland. N Yor 4F 107
Goathurst. Som 3F 21
Goathurst Common. Kent 5F 39
Goat Lees. Kent 1E 28
Gobernuisgach Lodge. High 4E 167
Gobernuisgeach. High 5B 168
Gobhaig. W Isl 7C 171
Gobowen. Shrp 2F 71
Godalming. Surr 1A 26
Goddard's Corner. Suff 4E 67
Goddard's Green. Kent 2C 28 (nr. Benenden)
Goddard's Green. Kent 2B 28 (nr. Cranbrook)
Goddards Green. W Sus 3D 27
Godford Cross. Devn 2E 13
Godleybrook. Staf 1D 73
Godmanchester. Cambs 3B 64
Godmanstone. Dors 3B 14
Godmersham. Kent 5E 41
Godolphin Cross. Corn 3D 4
Godre'r-graig. Neat 5A 46
Godshill. Hants 1G 15
Godshill. IOW 4D 16
Godstone. Staf 2E 73
Godstone. Surr 5E 39
Goetre. Mon 5G 47
Goff's Oak. Herts 5D 52
Gogar. Edin 2E 129
Goginan. Cdgn 2F 57
Golan. Gwyn 1E 69
Golant. Corn 3F 7
Golberdon. Corn 5D 10
Golborne. G Man 1A 84
Golcar. W Yor 3A 92

Goldcliff—Harmer Hill

Goldcliff. Newp 3G 33
Golden Cross. E Sus 4G 27
Golden Green. Kent 1H 27
Golden Grove. Carm 4F 45
Golden Grove. N Yor 4F 107
Golden Hill. Pemb 2D 43
Goldenhill. Stoke 5C 84
Golden Pot. Hants 2F 25
Golden Valley. Glos 3E 49
Golders Green. G Lon 2D 38
Goldhanger. Essx 5C 54
Gold Hill. Norf 1E 65
Golding. Shrp 5H 71
Goldington. Bed 5H 63
Goldsborough. N Yor 4F 99 (nr. Harrogate)
Goldsborough. N Yor 3F 107 (nr. Whitby)
Goldsithney. Corn 3C 4
Goldstone. Kent 4G 41
Goldstone. Shrp 3B 72
Goldthorpe. S Yor 4E 93
Goldworthy. Devn 4D 19
Golfa. Powy 3D 70
Gollanfield. High 3C 158
Gollinglith Foot. N Yor 1D 98
Golsoncott. Som 3D 20
Golspie. High 4F 165
Gomeldon. Wilts 3G 23
Gomersal. W Yor 2C 92
Gometra House. Arg 4E 139
Gomshall. Surr 1B 26
Gonalston. Notts 1D 74
Gonerby Hill Foot. Linc 2G 75
Gonfirth. Shet 5E 173
Good Easter. Essx 4G 53
Gooderstone. Norf 5G 77
Goodleigh. Devn 3G 19
Goodmanham. E Yor 5C 100
Goodmayes. G Lon 2F 39
Goodnestone. Kent 5G 41 (nr. Aylesham)
Goodnestone. Kent 4E 41 (nr. Faversham)
Goodrich. Here 4A 48
Goodrington. Torb 3E 9
Goodshaw. Lanc 2G 91
Goodshaw Fold. Lanc 2G 91
Goodstone. Devn 5A 12
Goodwick. Pemb 1D 42
Goodworth Clatford. Hants 2B 24
Goole. E Yor 2H 93
Goom's Hill. Worc 5E 61
Goonabarn. Corn 3D 6
Goonbell. Corn 4B 6
Goonhavern. Corn 3B 6
Goonvrea. Corn 4B 6
Goose Green. Cumb 1E 97
Goose Green. S Glo 3C 34
Gooseham. Corn 1C 10
Goosewell. Plym 3B 8
Goosey. Oxon 2B 36
Goosnargh. Lanc 1D 90
Goostrey. Ches E 3B 84
Gorcott Hill. Warw 4E 61
Gord. Shet 9F 173
Gordon. Bord 5C 130
Gordonbush. High 3F 165
Gordonstown. Abers 3C 160 (nr. Cornhill)
Gordonstown. Abers 5E 160 (nr. Fyvie)
Gorebridge. Midl 3G 129
Gorefield. Cambs 4D 76
Gores. Wilts 1G 23
Gorgie. Edin 2F 129
Goring. Oxon 3E 36
Goring-by-Sea. W Sus 5C 26
Goring Heath. Oxon 4E 37
Gorleston-on-Sea. Norf 5H 79
Gornalwood. W Mid 1D 60
Gorran Churchtown. Corn 4D 6
Gorran Haven. Corn 4E 6
Gorran High Lanes. Corn 4D 6
Gors. Cdgn 3F 57
Gorsedd. Flin 3D 82
Gorseinon. Swan 3E 31
Gorseness. Orkn 6D 172
Gorseybank. Derbs 5G 85
Gorsgoch. Cdgn 5D 57
Gorslas. Carm 4F 45
Gorsley. Glos 3B 48
Gorsley Common. Here 3B 48
Gorstan. High 2F 157
Gorstella. Ches W 4F 83
Gorsty Common. Here 2H 47
Gorsty Hill. Staf 3E 73
Gortantaoid. Arg 2B 124
Gorteneorn. High 2A 140
Gortenfern. High 2A 140
Gortin. Omag 8A 174
Gortnahey. Lim 5C 174
Gorton. G Man 1C 84
Gosbeck. Suff 5D 66
Gosberton. Linc 2B 76
Gosberton Cheal. Linc 3B 76
Gosberton Clough. Linc 3A 76
Goseley Dale. Derbs 3H 73
Gosfield. Essx 3A 54
Gosford. Oxon 4D 50
Gosforth. Cumb 4B 102
Gosforth. Tyne 3F 115
Gosmore. Herts 3B 52
Gospel End Village. Staf 1C 60
Gosport. Hants 2E 16
Gossabrough. Shet 3G 173
Gossington. Glos 5C 48
Gossops Green. W Sus 2D 26
Goswick. Nmbd 5G 131
Gotham. Notts 2C 74
Gotherington. Glos 3E 49
Gott. Arg 4B 138
Gott. Shet 7F 173
Goudhurst. Kent 2B 28
Goulceby. Linc 3B 88
Gourdon. Abers 1H 145
Gourock. Inv 2D 126
Govan. Glas 3G 127
Govanhill. Glas 3G 127
Goverton. Notts 1E 74
Goveton. Devn 4D 8
Govilon. Mon 4F 47
Gowanhill. Abers 2H 161
Gowdall. E Yor 2G 93
Gowdystown. Ban 4F 179
Gowerton. Swan 3E 31
Gowkhall. Fife 1D 128
Gowthorpe. E Yor 4B 100
Goxhill. E Yor 5F 101
Goxhill. N Lin 2E 94
Goxhill Haven. N Lin 2E 94
Goytre. Neat 3A 32
Grabhair. W Isl 6F 171
Graby. Linc 3H 75
Gracehill. Bmna 6G 175
Graffham. W Sus 4A 26
Grafham. Cambs 4A 64
Grafham. Surr 1B 26
Grafton. Here 2H 47
Grafton. N Yor 3G 99
Grafton. Oxon 5A 50
Grafton. Shrp 4G 71
Grafton. Worc 2E 49 (nr. Evesham)
Grafton. Worc 4H 59 (nr. Leominster)
Grafton Flyford. Worc 5D 60
Grafton Regis. Nptn 1F 51
Grafton Underwood. Nptn 2G 63
Grafty Green. Kent 1C 28
Graianrhyd. Den 5E 82
Graig. Carm 5E 45
Graig. Cnwy 3H 81
Graig. Den 3C 82
Graig-fechan. Den 5D 82
Graig Penllyn. V Glam 4C 32
Grain. Medw 3C 40
Grainsby. Linc 1B 88
Grainthorpe. Linc 1C 88
Grainthorpe Fen. Linc 1C 88
Graiselound. N Lin 1E 87
Gramasdail. W Isl 3D 170
Grampound. Corn 4D 6
Grampound Road. Corn 3D 6
Granborough. Buck 3F 51
Granby. Notts 2E 75
Grandborough. Warw 4B 62
Grandpont. Oxon 5D 50
Grandtully. Per 3G 143
Grange. Cumb 3D 102
Grange. E Ayr 1D 116
Grange. Here 3G 59
Grange. Mers 2E 83
Grange. Per 1E 137
Grange Corner. Bmna 7G 175
Grange Crossroads. Mor 3B 160
Grange Hill. G Lon 1F 39
Grangemill. Derbs 5G 85
Grange Moor. W Yor 3C 92
Grangemouth. Falk 1C 128
Grange of Lindores. Fife 2E 137
Grange-over-Sands. Cumb 2D 96
Grangepans. Falk 1D 128
Grange Park. Down 5J 179
Grange, The. N Yor 5C 106
Grangetown. Card 4E 33
Grangetown. Red C 2C 106
Grange Villa. Dur 4F 115
Granish. High 2C 150
Gransmoor. E Yor 4F 101
Granston. Pemb 1C 42
Grantchester. Cambs 5D 64
Grantham. Linc 2G 75
Grantley. N Yor 3E 99
Grantlodge. Abers 2E 152
Granton. Edin 2F 129
Grantown-on-Spey. High 1E 151
Grantshouse. Bord 3E 130
Grappenhall. Warr 2A 84
Grasby. Linc 4D 94
Grasmere. Cumb 4E 103
Grasscroft. G Man 4H 91
Grassendale. Mers 2F 83
Grassgarth. Cumb 5E 113
Grassholme. Dur 2C 104
Grassington. N Yor 3C 98
Grassmoor. Derbs 4B 86
Grassthorpe. Notts 4E 87
Grateley. Hants 2A 24
Gratton. Devn 1D 11
Gratton. Staf 5D 84
Gratwich. Staf 2E 73
Graveley. Cambs 4B 64
Graveley. Herts 3C 52
Gravelhill. Shrp 4G 71
Gravel Hole. G Man 4H 91
Gravelly Hill. W Mid 1F 61
Graven. Shet 4F 173
Graveney. Kent 4E 41
Gravesend. Kent 3H 39
Grayingham. Linc 1G 87
Grayrigg. Cumb 5G 103
Grays. Thur 3H 39
Grayshott. Hants 3G 25
Grayson Green. Cumb 2A 102
Grayswood. Surr 2A 26
Graythorp. Hart 2C 106
Grazeley. Wok 5E 37
Grealin. High 2E 155
Greasbrough. S Yor 1B 86
Greasby. Mers 2E 83
Great Abington. Cambs 1F 53
Great Addington. Nptn 3G 63
Great Alne. Warw 5F 61
Great Altcar. Lanc 4B 90
Great Amwell. Herts 4D 52
Great Asby. Cumb 3H 103
Great Ashfield. Suff 4B 66
Great Ayton. N Yor 3C 106
Great Baddow. Essx 5H 53
Great Bardfield. Essx 2G 53
Great Barford. Bed 5A 64
Great Barr. W Mid 1E 61
Great Barrington. Glos 4H 49
Great Barrow. Ches W 4G 83
Great Barton. Suff 4A 66
Great Barugh. N Yor 2B 100
Great Bavington. Nmbd 1C 114
Great Bealings. Suff 1F 55
Great Bedwyn. Wilts 5A 36
Great Bentley. Essx 3E 54
Great Billing. Nptn 4F 63
Great Bircham. Norf 2G 77
Great Blakenham. Suff 5D 66
Great Blencow. Cumb 1F 103
Great Bolas. Telf 3A 72
Great Bookham. Surr 5C 38
Great Bosullow. Corn 3B 4
Great Bourton. Oxon 1C 50
Great Bowden. Leics 2E 63
Great Bradley. Suff 5F 65
Great Braxted. Essx 4B 54
Great Bricett. Suff 5C 66
Great Brickhill. Buck 2H 51
Great Bridgeford. Staf 3C 72
Great Brington. Nptn 4D 62
Great Bromley. Essx 3D 54
Great Broughton. Cumb 1B 102
Great Broughton. N Yor 4C 106
Great Budworth. Ches W 3A 84
Great Burdon. Darl 3A 106
Great Burstead. Essx 1A 40
Great Busby. N Yor 4C 106
Great Canfield. Essx 4F 53
Great Carlton. Linc 2D 88
Great Casterton. Rut 5H 75
Great Chalfield. Wilts 5D 34
Great Chart. Kent 1D 28
Great Chatwell. Staf 4B 72
Great Chesterford. Essx 1F 53
Great Cheverell. Wilts 1E 23
Great Chilton. Dur 1F 105
Great Chishill. Cambs 2E 53
Great Clacton. Essx 4E 55
Great Cliff. W Yor 3D 92
Great Clifton. Cumb 2B 102
Great Coates. NE Lin 3F 95
Great Comberton. Worc 1E 49
Great Corby. Cumb 4F 113
Great Cornard. Suff 1B 54
Great Cowden. E Yor 5G 101
Great Coxwell. Oxon 2A 36
Great Crakehall. N Yor 1E 99
Great Cransley. Nptn 3F 63
Great Cressingham. Norf 5H 77
Great Crosby. Mers 1F 83
Great Cubley. Derbs 2F 73
Great Dalby. Leics 4E 75
Great Doddington. Nptn 4F 63
Great Doward. Here 4A 48
Great Dunham. Norf 4A 78
Great Dunmow. Essx 3G 53
Great Durnford. Wilts 3G 23
Great Easton. Essx 3G 53
Great Easton. Leics 1F 63
Great Eccleston. Lanc 5D 96
Great Edstone. N Yor 1B 100
Great Ellingham. Norf 1C 66
Great Elm. Som 2C 22
Great Eppleton. Tyne 5G 115
Great Eversden. Cambs 5C 64
Great Fencote. N Yor 5F 105
Great Finborough. Suff 5C 66
Greatford. Linc 4H 75
Great Fransham. Norf 4A 78
Great Gaddesden. Herts 4A 52
Great Gate. Staf 1E 73
Great Gidding. Cambs 2A 64
Great Givendale. E Yor 4C 100
Great Glemham. Suff 4F 67
Great Glen. Leics 1D 62
Great Gonerby. Linc 2G 75
Great Gransden. Cambs 5B 64
Great Green. Norf 2E 67
Great Green. Suff 5B 66 (nr. Lavenham)
Great Green. Suff 3D 66 (nr. Palgrave)
Great Habton. N Yor 2B 100
Great Hale. Linc 1A 76
Great Hallingbury. Essx 4F 53
Greatham. Hants 3F 25
Greatham. Hart 2B 106
Greatham. W Sus 4B 26
Great Hampden. Buck 5G 51
Great Harrowden. Nptn 3F 63
Great Harwood. Lanc 1F 91
Great Haseley. Oxon 5E 51
Great Hatfield. E Yor 5F 101
Great Haywood. Staf 3D 73
Great Heath. W Mid 2H 61
Great Heck. N Yor 2F 93
Great Henny. Essx 2B 54
Great Hinton. Wilts 1E 23
Great Hockham. Norf 1B 66
Great Holland. Essx 4F 55
Great Horkesley. Essx 2C 54
Great Hormead. Herts 2E 53
Great Horton. W Yor 1B 92
Great Horwood. Buck 2F 51
Great Houghton. Nptn 5E 63
Great Houghton. S Yor 4E 93
Great Hucklow. Derbs 3F 85
Great Kelk. E Yor 4F 101
Great Kendale. E Yor 3E 101
Great Kimble. Buck 5G 51
Great Kingshill. Buck 2G 37
Great Langdale. Cumb 4D 102
Great Langton. N Yor 5F 105
Great Leighs. Essx 4H 53
Great Limber. Linc 4E 95
Great Linford. Mil 1G 51
Great Livermere. Suff 3A 66
Great Longstone. Derbs 3G 85
Great Lumley. Dur 5F 115
Great Lyth. Shrp 5G 71
Great Malvern. Worc 1C 48
Great Maplestead. Essx 2B 54
Great Marton. Bkpl 1B 90
Great Massingham. Norf 3G 77
Great Melton. Norf 5D 78
Great Milton. Oxon 5E 51
Great Missenden. Buck 5G 51
Great Mitton. Lanc 1F 91
Great Mongeham. Kent 5H 41
Great Moulton. Norf 1D 66
Great Munden. Herts 3D 52
Great Musgrave. Cumb 3A 104
Great Ness. Shrp 4F 71
Great Notley. Essx 3H 53
Great Oak. Mon 5G 47
Great Oakley. Essx 3E 55
Great Oakley. Nptn 2F 63
Great Offley. Herts 3B 52
Great Ormside. Cumb 3A 104
Great Orton. Cumb 4E 113
Great Ouseburn. N Yor 3G 99
Great Oxendon. Nptn 2E 63
Great Oxney Green. Essx 5G 53
Great Parndon. Essx 5E 53
Great Paxton. Cambs 4B 64
Great Plumpton. Lanc 1B 90
Great Plumstead. Norf 4F 79
Great Ponton. Linc 2G 75
Great Potheridge. Devn 1F 11
Great Preston. W Yor 2E 93
Great Raveley. Cambs 2B 64
Great Rissington. Glos 4G 49
Great Rollright. Oxon 2B 50
Great Ryburgh. Norf 3B 78
Great Ryle. Nmbd 3E 121
Great Ryton. Shrp 5G 71
Great Saling. Essx 3G 53
Great Salkeld. Cumb 1G 103
Great Sampford. Essx 2G 53
Great Sankey. Warr 2H 83
Great Saredon. Staf 5D 72
Great Saxham. Suff 4G 65
Great Shefford. W Ber 4B 36
Great Shelford. Cambs 5D 64
Great Shoddesden. Hants 2A 24
Great Smeaton. N Yor 4A 106
Great Snoring. Norf 2B 78
Great Somerford. Wilts 3E 35
Great Stainton. Darl 2A 106
Great Stambridge. Essx 1C 40
Great Staughton. Cambs 4A 64
Great Steeping. Linc 4D 88
Great Stonar. Kent 5H 41
Greatstone-on-Sea. Kent 3E 29
Great Strickland. Cumb 2G 103
Great Stukeley. Cambs 3B 64
Great Sturton. Linc 3B 88
Great Sutton. Ches W 3F 83
Great Sutton. Shrp 2H 59
Great Swinburne. Nmbd 2C 114
Great Tew. Oxon 3B 50
Great Tey. Essx 3B 54
Great Thirkleby. N Yor 2G 99
Great Thorness. IOW 3C 16
Great Thurlow. Suff 5F 65
Great Torr. Devn 4C 8
Great Torrington. Devn 1E 11
Great Tosson. Nmbd 4E 121
Great Totham North. Essx 4B 54
Great Totham South. Essx 4B 54
Great Tows. Linc 1B 88
Great Urswick. Cumb 2B 96
Great Wakering. Essx 2D 40
Great Waldingfield. Suff 1C 54
Great Walsingham. Norf 2B 78
Great Waltham. Essx 4G 53
Great Warley. Essx 1G 39
Great Washbourne. Glos 2E 49
Great Wenham. Suff 2D 54
Great Whelnetham. Suff 5A 66
Great Whittington. Nmbd 2D 114
Great Wigborough. Essx 4C 54
Great Wilbraham. Cambs 5E 65
Great Wilne. Derbs 2B 74
Great Wishford. Wilts 3F 23
Great Witchingham. Norf 3D 78
Great Witcombe. Glos 4E 49
Great Witley. Worc 4B 60
Great Wolford. Warw 2H 49
Greatworth. Nptn 1D 50
Great Wratting. Suff 1G 53
Great Wymondley. Herts 3C 52
Great Wyrley. Staf 5D 73
Great Wytheford. Shrp 4H 71
Great Yarmouth. Norf 5H 79
Great Yeldham. Essx 2A 54
Grebby. Linc 4D 88
Greeba Castle. IOM 3C 108
Greenbank. Shet 1G 173
Greenbottom. Corn 4B 6
Greenburn. W Lot 3C 128
Greencastle. Omag 1L 177
Greencroft. Dur 4E 115
Greencroft Park. Dur 5E 115
Greendown. Som 1A 22
Greendykes. Nmbd 2E 121
Green End. Bed 1A 52 (nr. Bedford)
Green End. Bed 4A 64 (nr. St Neots)
Green End. Herts 2D 52 (nr. Buntingford)
Green End. Herts 3D 52 (nr. Stevenage)
Green End. N Yor 4F 107
Green End. Warw 2G 61
Greenfield. Arg 4B 134
Greenfield. C Beds 2A 52
Greenfield. Flin 3D 82
Greenfield. G Man 4H 91
Greenfield. Oxon 2F 37
Greenfoot. N Lan 3A 128
Greenford. G Lon 2C 38
Greengairs. N Lan 2A 128
Greengate. Norf 4C 78
Greengill. Cumb 1C 102
Greenhalgh. Lanc 1C 90
Greenham. Dors 2H 13
Greenham. Som 4D 20
Greenham. W Ber 5C 36
Green Hammerton. N Yor 4G 99
Greenhaugh. Nmbd 1A 114
Greenhead. Nmbd 3H 113
Green Heath. Staf 4D 73
Greenhill. Dum 2C 112
Greenhill. Falk 2B 128
Greenhill. Kent 4F 41
Greenhill. S Yor 2H 85
Greenhill. Worc 3C 60
Greenhills. N Ayr 4E 127
Greenhithe. Kent 3G 39
Greenholm. E Ayr 1E 117
Greenhow Hill. N Yor 3D 98
Greenigoe. Orkn 7D 172
Greenisland. Carr 8K 175
Greenland. High 2E 169
Greenland Mains. High 2E 169
Greenlands. Worc 4E 61
Green Lane. Shrp 3A 72
Green Lane. Warw 4E 61
Greenlaw. Bord 5D 130
Greenlea. Dum 2B 112
Greenloaning. Per 3H 135
Greenmount. G Man 3F 91
Greenmow. Shet 9F 173
Greenock. Inv 2D 126
Greenock Mains. E Ayr 2F 117
Greenodd. Cumb 1C 96
Green Ore. Som 1A 22
Greenrow. Cumb 4C 112
Greens. Abers 4F 161
Greensgate. Norf 4D 78
Greenside. Tyne 3E 115
Greensidehill. Nmbd 3D 121
Greens Norton. Nptn 1E 51
Greenstead Green. Essx 3B 54
Greensted Green. Essx 5F 53
Green Street. Herts 1C 38
Green Street. Suff 3D 66
Green Street Green. G Lon 4F 39
Green Street Green. Kent 3G 39
Greenstreet Green. Suff 1D 54
Green, The. Cumb 1A 96
Green, The. Wilts 3D 22
Green Tye. Herts 4E 53
Greenwall. Orkn 7E 172
Greenway. Pemb 2E 43
Greenway. V Glam 4D 32
Greenwell. Cumb 4G 113
Greenwich. G Lon 3E 39
Greet. Glos 2F 49
Greete. Shrp 3H 59
Greetham. Linc 3C 88
Greetham. Rut 4G 75
Greetland. W Yor 2A 92
Gregson Lane. Lanc 2D 90
Grein. W Isl 8B 170
Greinetobht. W Isl 1D 170
Greinton. Som 3H 21
Gremista. Shet 7F 173
Grenaby. IOM 4B 108
Grendon. Nptn 4F 63
Grendon. Warw 1G 61
Grendon Common. Warw 1G 61
Grendon Green. Here 5H 59
Grendon Underwood. Buck 3E 51
Grenofen. Devn 5E 11
Grenoside. S Yor 1H 85
Greosabhagh. W Isl 8D 171
Gresford. Wrex 5F 83
Gresham. Norf 2D 78
Greshornish. High 3C 154
Gressenhall. Norf 4B 78
Gressingham. Lanc 2E 97
Greta Bridge. Dur 3D 105
Gretna. Dum 3E 112
Gretna Green. Dum 3E 112
Gretton. Glos 2F 49
Gretton. Nptn 1G 63
Gretton. Shrp 1H 59
Grewelthorpe. N Yor 2E 99
Greyabbey. Ards 3K 179
Greygarth. N Yor 2D 98
Grey Green. N Lin 4A 94
Greylake. Som 3G 21
Greysouthen. Cumb 2B 102
Greysteel. Lim 4B 174
Greystoke. Cumb 1F 103
Greystoke Gill. Cumb 2F 103
Greystone. Ang 4E 145
Greystones. S Yor 2H 85
Greywell. Hants 1F 25
Griais. W Isl 3G 171
Grianan. W Isl 4G 171
Gribthorpe. E Yor 1A 94
Gribun. Arg 5F 139
Griff. Warw 2A 62
Griffithstown. Torf 2F 33
Griffydam. Leics 4B 74
Griggs Green. Hants 3G 25
Grimbister. Orkn 6C 172
Grimeford Village. Lanc 3E 90
Grimeston. Orkn 6C 172
Grimethorpe. S Yor 4E 93
Griminis. W Isl 3C 170 (on Benbecula)
Griminis. W Isl 1C 170 (on North Uist)
Grimister. Shet 2F 173
Grimley. Worc 4C 60
Grimness. Orkn 8D 172
Grimoldby. Linc 2C 88
Grimpo. Shrp 3F 71
Grimsargh. Lanc 1D 90
Grimsbury. Oxon 1C 50
Grimsby. NE Lin 3F 95
Grimscote. Nptn 5D 62
Grimscott. Corn 2C 10
Grimshaw. Bkbn 2F 91
Grimshaw Green. Lanc 3C 90
Grimsthorpe. Linc 3H 75
Grimston. E Yor 1F 95
Grimston. Leics 3D 74
Grimston. Norf 3G 77
Grimston. York 4A 100
Grimstone. Dors 3B 14
Grimstone End. Suff 4B 66
Grinacombe Moor. Devn 3E 11
Grindale. E Yor 2F 101
Grindhill. Devn 3E 11
Grindiscol. Shet 8F 173
Grindle. Shrp 5B 72
Grindleford. Derbs 3G 85
Grindleton. Lanc 5G 97
Grindley. Staf 3E 73
Grindley Brook. Shrp 1H 71
Grindlow. Derbs 3F 85
Grindon. Nmbd 5F 131
Grindon. Staf 5E 85
Gringley on the Hill. Notts 1E 87
Grinsdale. Cumb 4E 113
Grinshill. Shrp 3H 71
Grinton. N Yor 5D 104
Griomsidar. W Isl 5G 171
Grishipoll. Arg 3C 138
Grisling Common. E Sus 3F 27
Gristhorpe. N Yor 1E 101
Griston. Norf 1B 66
Gritley. Orkn 7E 172
Grittenham. Wilts 3F 35
Grittleton. Wilts 4D 34
Grizebeck. Cumb 1B 96
Grizedale. Cumb 5E 103
Grobister. Orkn 5F 172
Grobsness. Shet 5E 173
Groby. Leics 5C 74
Groes. Cnwy 4C 82
Groes. Neat 3A 32
Groes-faen. Rhon 3D 32
Groesffordd. Gwyn 2B 68
Groesffordd. Powy 3D 46
Groeslon. Gwyn 5D 81
Groes-lwyd. Powy 4E 70
Groes-wen. Cphy 3E 33
Grogport. Arg 5G 125
Groigearraidh. W Isl 4C 170
Gromford. Suff 5F 67
Gronant. Flin 2C 82
Groombridge. E Sus 2G 27
Groomsport. N Dwn 1K 179
Grosmont. Mon 3H 47
Grosmont. N Yor 4F 107
Groton. Suff 1C 54
Grove. Dors 5C 14
Grove. Kent 4G 41
Grove. Notts 3E 87
Grove. Oxon 2B 36
Grovehill. E Yor 1D 94
Grove Park. G Lon 3F 39
Grovesend. Swan 5F 45
Grove, The. Dum 2A 112
Grove, The. Worc 1D 48
Grub Street. Staf 3B 72
Grudie. High 2F 157
Gruids. High 3C 164
Gruinard House. High 4D 162
Gruinart. Arg 3A 124
Grulinbeg. Arg 3A 124
Gruline. Arg 4G 139
Grummore. High 5G 167
Grundisburgh. Suff 5E 66
Gruting. Shet 7D 173
Grutness. Shet 10F 173
Gualachulain. High 4F 141
Gualin House. High 3D 166
Guardbridge. Fife 2G 137
Guarlford. Worc 1D 48
Guay. Per 4H 143
Gubblecote. Herts 4H 51
Guestling Green. E Sus 4C 28
Guestling Thorn. E Sus 4C 28
Guestwick. Norf 3C 78
Guestwick Green. Norf 3C 78
Guide. Bkbn 2F 91
Guide Post. Nmbd 1F 115
Guilden Down. Shrp 2F 59
Guilden Morden. Cambs 1C 52
Guilden Sutton. Ches W 4G 83
Guildford. Surr 1A 26 & 195
Guildtown. Per 5A 144
Guilsborough. Nptn 3D 62
Guilsfield. Powy 4E 70
Guineaford. Devn 3F 19
Guisborough. Red C 3D 106
Guiseley. W Yor 5D 98
Guist. Norf 3B 78
Guiting Power. Glos 3F 49
Gulberwick. Shet 8F 173
Gulladuff. Mag 7F 174
Gullane. E Lot 1A 130
Gulling Green. Suff 5H 65
Gulval. Corn 3B 4
Gumfreston. Pemb 4F 43
Gumley. Leics 1D 62
Gunby. E Yor 1H 93
Gunby. Linc 3G 75
Gundleton. Hants 3E 24
Gun Green. Kent 2B 28
Gun Hill. E Sus 4G 27
Gunn. Devn 3G 19
Gunnerside. N Yor 5C 104
Gunnerton. Nmbd 2C 114
Gunness. N Lin 3B 94
Gunnislake. Corn 5E 11
Gunnista. Shet 7F 173
Gunsgreenhill. Bord 3F 131
Gunstone. Staf 5C 72
Gunthorpe. Norf 2C 78
Gunthorpe. N Lin 1F 87
Gunthorpe. Notts 1D 74
Gunthorpe. Pet 5A 76
Gunville. IOW 4C 16
Gupworthy. Som 3C 20
Gurnard. IOW 3C 16
Gurney Slade. Som 2B 22
Gurnos. Powy 5A 46
Gussage All Saints. Dors 1F 15
Gussage St Andrew. Dors 1E 15
Gussage St Michael. Dors 1E 15
Guston. Kent 1H 29
Gutcher. Shet 2G 173
Guthram Gowt. Linc 3A 76
Guthrie. Ang 3E 145
Guyhirn. Cambs 5D 76
Guyhirn Gull. Cambs 5C 76
Guy's Head. Linc 3D 77
Guy's Marsh. Dors 4D 22
Guyzance. Nmbd 4G 121
Gwaelod-y-garth. Card 3E 32
Gwaenynog Bach. Den 4C 82
Gwaenysgor. Flin 2C 82
Gwalchmai. IOA 3C 80
Gwastad. Pemb 2E 43
Gwaun-Cae-Gurwen. Neat 4H 45
Gwaun-y-bara. Cphy 3E 33
Gwbert. Cdgn 1B 44
Gweek. Corn 4E 5
Gwehelog. Mon 5G 47
Gwenddwr. Powy 1D 46
Gwennap. Corn 4B 6
Gwenter. Corn 5E 5
Gwernaffield. Flin 4E 82
Gwernesney. Mon 5H 47
Gwernogle. Carm 2F 45
Gwern-y-go. Powy 1E 58
Gwernymynydd. Flin 4E 82
Gwersyllt. Wrex 5F 83
Gwespyr. Flin 2D 82
Gwinear. Corn 3C 4
Gwithian. Corn 2C 4
Gwredog. IOA 2D 80
Gwyddelwern. Den 1C 70
Gwyddgrug. Carm 2E 45
Gwynfryn. Wrex 5E 83
Gwystre. Powy 4C 58
Gwytherin. Cnwy 4A 82
Gyfelia. Wrex 1F 71
Gyffin. Cnwy 3G 81

H

Haa of Houlland. Shet 1G 173
Habberley. Shrp 5F 71
Habblesthorpe. Notts 2E 87
Habergham. Lanc 1G 91
Habin. W Sus 4G 25
Habrough. NE Lin 3E 95
Haceby. Linc 2H 75
Hacheston. Suff 5F 67
Hackenthorpe. S Yor 2B 86
Hackford. Norf 5C 78
Hackforth. N Yor 5F 105
Hackland. Orkn 5C 172
Hackleton. Nptn 5F 63
Hackman's Gate. Worc 3C 60
Hackness. N Yor 5G 107
Hackness. Orkn 8C 172
Hackney. G Lon 2E 39
Hackthorn. Linc 2G 87
Hackthorpe. Cumb 2G 103
Haclait. W Isl 4D 170
Haconby. Linc 3A 76
Hadden. Bord 1B 120
Haddenham. Buck 5F 51
Haddenham. Cambs 3D 64
Haddenham End Field. Cambs 3D 64
Haddington. E Lot 2B 130
Haddington. Linc 4G 87
Haddiscoe. Norf 1G 67
Haddo. Abers 5F 161
Haddon. Cambs 1A 64
Hademore. Staf 5F 73
Hadfield. Derbs 1E 85
Hadham Cross. Herts 4E 53
Hadham Ford. Herts 3E 53
Hadleigh. Essx 2C 40
Hadleigh. Suff 1D 54
Hadleigh Heath. Suff 1C 54
Hadley. Telf 4A 72
Hadley. Worc 4C 60
Hadley End. Staf 3F 73
Hadley Wood. G Lon 1D 38
Hadlow. Kent 1H 27
Hadlow Down. E Sus 3G 27
Hadnall. Shrp 3H 71
Hadstock. Essx 1F 53
Hadston. Nmbd 5G 121
Hady. Derbs 3A 86
Hadzor. Worc 4D 60
Haffenden Quarter. Kent 1C 28
Haggate. Lanc 1G 91
Haggbeck. Cumb 2F 113
Haggersta. Shet 7E 173
Haggerston. Nmbd 5G 131
Haggrister. Shet 4E 173
Hagley. Here 1A 48
Hagley. Worc 2D 60
Hagnaby. Linc 4C 88
Hagworthingham. Linc 4C 88
Haigh. G Man 4E 90
Haigh Moor. W Yor 2C 92
Haighton Green. Lanc 1D 90
Haile. Cumb 4B 102
Hailes. Glos 2F 49
Hailey. Herts 4D 52
Hailey. Oxon 4B 50
Hailsham. E Sus 5G 27
Hail Weston. Cambs 4A 64
Hainault. G Lon 1F 39
Hainford. Norf 4E 78
Hainton. Linc 2A 88
Hainworth. W Yor 1A 92
Haisthorpe. E Yor 3F 101
Hakin. Pemb 4C 42
Halam. Notts 5D 86
Halbeath. Fife 1E 129
Halberton. Devn 1D 12
Halcro. High 2E 169
Hale. Cumb 2E 97
Hale. G Man 2B 84
Hale. Hal 2G 83
Hale. Hants 1G 15
Hale. Surr 2G 25
Hale Bank. Hal 2G 83
Halebarns. G Man 2B 84
Hales. Norf 1F 67
Hales. Staf 2B 72
Halesgate. Linc 3C 76
Hales Green. Derbs 1F 73
Halesowen. W Mid 2D 60
Hale Street. Kent 1A 28
Halesworth. Suff 3F 67
Halewood. Mers 2G 83
Halford. Shrp 2G 59
Halford. Warw 1A 50
Halfpenny. Cumb 1E 97
Halfpenny Furze. Carm 3G 43
Halfpenny Green. Shrp 1C 60
Halfway. Carm 2G 45
Halfway. Powy 2B 46
Halfway. S Yor 2B 86
Halfway. W Ber 5C 36
Halfway House. Shrp 4F 71
Halfway Houses. Kent 3D 40
Halgabron. Corn 4A 10
Halifax. W Yor 2A 92
Halistra. High 3B 154
Halket. E Ayr 4F 127
Halkirk. High 3D 168
Halkyn. Flin 3E 82
Hall. E Ren 4F 127
Hallam Fields. Derbs 1B 74
Halland. E Sus 4G 27
Hallands, The. N Lin 2D 94
Hallaton. Leics 1E 63
Hallatrow. Bath 1B 22
Hallbank. Cumb 5H 103
Hallbankgate. Cumb 4G 113
Hall Dunnerdale. Cumb 5D 102
Hallen. S Glo 3A 34
Hall End. Bed 1A 52
Hallgarth. Dur 5G 115
Hall Green. Ches E 5C 84
Hall Green. Norf 2D 66
Hall Green. W Mid 2F 61
Hall Green. W Yor 3D 92
Hall Green. Wrex 1G 71
Halliburton. Bord 5C 130
Hallin. High 3B 154
Halling. Medw 4B 40
Hallington. Linc 2C 88
Hallington. Nmbd 2C 114
Halloughton. Notts 5D 86
Hallow. Worc 5C 60
Hallow Heath. Worc 5C 60
Hallowsgate. Ches W 4H 83
Hallsands. Devn 5E 9
Hall's Green. Herts 3C 52
Hallspill. Devn 4E 19
Hallthwaites. Cumb 1A 96
Hall Waberthwaite. Cumb 5C 102
Hallwood Green. Glos 2B 48
Hallworthy. Corn 4B 10
Hallyne. Bord 5E 129
Halmer End. Staf 1C 72
Halmond's Frome. Here 1B 48
Halmore. Glos 5B 48
Halnaker. W Sus 5A 26
Halsall. Lanc 3B 90
Halse. Nptn 1D 50
Halse. Som 4E 21
Halsetown. Corn 3C 4
Halsham. E Yor 2F 95
Halsinger. Devn 3F 19
Halstead. Essx 2B 54
Halstead. Kent 4F 39
Halstead. Leics 5E 75
Halstock. Dors 2A 14
Halsway. Som 3E 21
Haltcliff Bridge. Cumb 1E 103
Haltham. Linc 4B 88
Haltoft End. Linc 1C 76
Halton. Buck 5G 51
Halton. Hal 2H 83
Halton. Lanc 3E 97
Halton. Nmbd 3C 114
Halton. W Yor 1D 92
Halton. Wrex 2F 71
Halton East. N Yor 4C 98
Halton Fenside. Linc 4D 88
Halton Gill. N Yor 2A 98
Halton Holegate. Linc 4D 88
Halton Lea Gate. Nmbd 4H 113
Halton Moor. W Yor 1D 92
Halton Shields. Nmbd 3D 114
Halton West. N Yor 4H 97
Haltwhistle. Nmbd 3A 114
Halvergate. Norf 5G 79
Halwell. Devn 3D 9
Halwill. Devn 3E 11
Halwill Junction. Devn 3E 11
Ham. Devn 2F 13
Ham. Glos 2B 34
Ham. G Lon 3C 38
Ham. High 1E 169
Ham. Kent 5H 41
Ham. Plym 3A 8
Ham. Shet 8A 173
Ham. Som 1F 13 (nr. Ilminster)
Ham. Som 4F 21 (nr. Taunton)
Ham. Som 4E 21 (nr. Wellington)
Ham. Wilts 5B 36
Hambleden. Buck 3F 37
Hambledon. Hants 1E 17
Hambledon. Surr 2A 26
Hamble-le-Rice. Hants 2C 16
Hambleton. Lanc 5C 96
Hambleton. N Yor 1F 93
Hambridge. Som 4G 21
Hambrook. S Glo 4B 34
Hambrook. W Sus 2F 17
Ham Common. Dors 4D 22
Hameringham. Linc 4C 88
Hamerton. Cambs 3A 64
Ham Green. Here 1C 48
Ham Green. Kent 4C 40
Ham Green. N Som 4A 34
Ham Green. Worc 4E 61
Ham Hill. Kent 4A 40
Hamilton. Leics 5D 74
Hamilton. S Lan 4A 128
Hamiltonsbawn. Arm 5D 178
Hamister. Shet 5G 173
Hammer. W Sus 3G 25
Hammersmith. G Lon 3D 38
Hammerwich. Staf 5E 73
Hammerwood. E Sus 2F 27
Hammill. Kent 5G 41
Hammond Street. Herts 5D 52
Hammoon. Dors 1D 14
Hamnavoe. Shet 3D 173 (nr. Braehoulland)
Hamnavoe. Shet 8E 173 (nr. Burland)
Hamnavoe. Shet 4F 173 (nr. Lunna)
Hamnavoe. Shet 3F 173 (on Yell)
Hamp. Som 3G 21
Hampden Park. E Sus 5H 27
Hampen. Glos 3F 49
Hamperden End. Essx 2F 53
Hamperley. Shrp 2G 59
Hampnett. Glos 4F 49
Hampole. S Yor 3F 93
Hampreston. Dors 3F 15
Hampstead. G Lon 2D 38
Hampstead Norreys. W Ber 4D 36
Hampsthwaite. N Yor 4E 99
Hampton. Devn 3F 13
Hampton. G Lon 3C 38
Hampton. Kent 4F 41
Hampton. Shrp 2B 60
Hampton. Swin 2G 35
Hampton. Worc 1F 49
Hampton Bishop. Here 2A 48
Hampton Fields. Glos 2D 35
Hampton Hargate. Pet 1A 64
Hampton Heath. Ches W 1H 71
Hampton in Arden. W Mid 2G 61
Hampton Loade. Shrp 2B 60
Hampton Lovett. Worc 4C 60
Hampton Lucy. Warw 5G 61
Hampton Magna. Warw 4G 61
Hampton on the Hill. Warw 4G 61
Hampton Poyle. Oxon 4D 50
Hampton Wick. G Lon 4C 38
Hamptworth. Wilts 1H 15
Hamrow. Norf 3B 78
Hamsey. E Sus 4F 27
Hamsey Green. Surr 5E 39
Hamstall Ridware. Staf 4F 73
Hamstead. IOW 3C 16
Hamstead. W Mid 1E 61
Hamstead Marshall. W Ber 5C 36
Hamsterley. Dur 4E 115 (nr. Consett)
Hamsterley. Dur 1E 105 (nr. Wolsingham)
Hamsterley Mill. Dur 4E 115
Hamstreet. Kent 2E 28
Ham Street. Som 3A 22
Hamworthy. Pool 3E 15
Hanbury. Staf 3F 73
Hanbury. Worc 4D 60
Hanbury Woodend. Staf 3F 73
Hanby. Linc 2H 75
Hanchurch. Staf 1C 72
Hand and Pen. Devn 3D 12
Handbridge. Ches W 4G 83
Handcross. W Sus 3D 26
Handforth. Ches E 2C 84
Handley. Ches W 5G 83
Handley. Derbs 4A 86
Handsacre. Staf 4E 73
Handsworth. S Yor 2B 86
Handsworth. W Mid 1E 61
Handy Cross. Buck 2G 37
Hanford. Dors 1D 14
Hanford. Stoke 1C 72
Hangersley. Hants 2G 15
Hanging Houghton. Nptn 3E 63
Hanging Langford. Wilts 3F 23
Hangleton. Brig 5D 26
Hangleton. W Sus 5B 26
Hanham. S Glo 4B 34
Hanham Green. S Glo 4B 34
Hankelow. Ches E 1A 72
Hankerton. Wilts 2E 35
Hankham. E Sus 5H 27
Hanley. Stoke 1C 72 & Stoke 202
Hanley Castle. Worc 1D 48
Hanley Childe. Worc 4A 60
Hanley Swan. Worc 1D 48
Hanley William. Worc 4A 60
Hanlith. N Yor 3B 98
Hanmer. Wrex 2G 71
Hannaborough. Devn 2F 11
Hannaford. Devn 4G 19
Hannah. Linc 3E 89
Hannington. Hants 1D 24
Hannington. Nptn 3F 63
Hannington. Swin 2G 35
Hannington Wick. Swin 2G 35
Hanscombe End. C Beds 2B 52
Hanslope. Mil 1G 51
Hanthorpe. Linc 3H 75
Hanwell. G Lon 2C 38
Hanwell. Oxon 1C 50
Hanwood. Shrp 5G 71
Hanworth. G Lon 3C 38
Hanworth. Norf 2D 78
Happas. Ang 4D 144
Happendon. S Lan 1A 118
Happisburgh. Norf 2F 79
Happisburgh Common. Norf 3F 79
Hapsford. Ches W 3G 83
Hapton. Lanc 1F 91
Hapton. Norf 1D 66
Harberton. Devn 3D 9
Harbertonford. Devn 3D 9
Harbledown. Kent 5F 41
Harborne. W Mid 2E 61
Harborough Magna. Warw 3B 62
Harbottle. Nmbd 4D 120
Harbourneford. Devn 2D 8
Harbours Hill. Worc 4D 60
Harbridge. Hants 1G 15
Harbury. Warw 4A 62
Harby. Leics 2E 75
Harby. Notts 3F 87
Harcombe. Devn 3E 13
Harcombe Bottom. Devn 3G 13
Harcourt. Corn 5C 6
Harden. W Yor 1A 92
Hardenhuish. Wilts 4E 35
Hardgate. Abers 3E 153
Hardgate. Dum 3F 111
Hardham. W Sus 4B 26
Hardingham. Norf 5C 78
Hardingstone. Nptn 5E 63
Hardings Wood. Ches E 5C 84
Hardington. Som 1C 22
Hardington Mandeville. Som 1A 14
Hardington Marsh. Som 2A 14
Hardington Moor. Som 1A 14
Hardley. Hants 2C 16
Hardley Street. Norf 5F 79
Hardmead. Mil 1H 51
Hardraw. N Yor 5B 104
Hardstoft. Derbs 4B 86
Hardway. Hants 2E 16
Hardway. Som 3C 22
Hardwick. Buck 4G 51
Hardwick. Cambs 5C 64
Hardwick. Norf 2E 66
Hardwick. Nptn 4F 63
Hardwick. Oxon 3D 50 (nr. Bicester)
Hardwick. Oxon 5B 50 (nr. Witney)
Hardwick. Shrp 1F 59
Hardwick. S Yor 2B 86
Hardwick. Stoc T 2B 106
Hardwick. W Mid 1E 61
Hardwicke. Glos 3E 49 (nr. Cheltenham)
Hardwicke. Glos 4C 48 (nr. Gloucester)
Hardwicke. Here 1F 47
Hardwick Village. Notts 3D 86
Hardy's Green. Essx 3C 54
Hare. Som 1F 13
Hareby. Linc 4C 88
Hareden. Lanc 4F 97
Harefield. G Lon 1B 38
Hare Green. Essx 3D 54
Hare Hatch. Wok 4G 37
Harehill. Derbs 2F 73
Harehills. W Yor 1D 92
Harehope. Nmbd 2E 121
Harelaw. Dum 2F 113
Harelaw. Dur 4E 115
Hareplain. Kent 2C 28
Haresceugh. Cumb 5H 113
Harescombe. Glos 4D 48
Haresfield. Glos 4D 48
Haresfinch. Mers 1H 83
Hareshaw. N Lan 3B 128
Hare Street. Essx 5E 53
Hare Street. Herts 3D 53
Harewood. W Yor 5F 99
Harewood End. Here 3A 48
Harford. Devn 3C 8
Hargate. Norf 1D 66
Hargatewall. Derbs 3F 85
Hargrave. Ches W 4G 83
Hargrave. Nptn 3H 63
Hargrave. Suff 5G 65
Harker. Cumb 3E 113
Harkland. Shet 3F 173
Harkstead. Suff 2E 55
Harlaston. Staf 4G 73
Harlaxton. Linc 2F 75
Harlech. Gwyn 2E 69
Harlequin. Notts 2D 74
Harlescott. Shrp 4H 71
Harleston. Devn 4D 9
Harleston. Norf 2E 67
Harleston. Suff 4C 66
Harlestone. Nptn 4E 62
Harley. Shrp 5H 71
Harley. S Yor 1A 86
Harling Road. Norf 2B 66
Harlington. C Beds 2A 52
Harlington. G Lon 3B 38
Harlington. S Yor 4E 93
Harlosh. High 4B 154
Harlow. Essx 4E 53
Harlow Hill. Nmbd 3D 115
Harlsey Castle. N Yor 5B 106
Harlthorpe. E Yor 1H 93
Harlton. Cambs 5C 64
Harlyn Bay. Corn 1C 6
Harman's Cross. Dors 4E 15
Harmby. N Yor 1D 98
Harmer Green. Herts 4C 52
Harmer Hill. Shrp 3G 71

Harmondsworth—Holme-on-Spalding-Moor

Harmondsworth. G Lon 3B 38
Harmston. Linc 4G 87
Harnage. Shrp 5H 71
Harnham. Nmbd 1D 115
Harnhill. Glos 5F 49
Harold Hill. G Lon 1G 39
Haroldston West. Pemb 3C 42
Haroldswick. Shet 1H 173
Harold Wood. G Lon 1G 39
Harome. N Yor 1A 100
Harpenden. Herts 4B 52
Harpford. Devn 3D 12
Harpham. E Yor 3E 101
Harpley. Norf 3G 77
Harpley. Worc 4A 60
Harpole. Nptn 4D 62
Harpsdale. High 3D 168
Harpsden. Oxon 3F 37
Harpswell. Linc 2G 87
Harpurhey. G Man 4G 91
Harpur Hill. Derbs 3E 85
Harraby. Cumb 4F 113
Harracott. Devn 4F 19
Harrapool. High 1E 147
Harrapul. High 1E 147
Harrietfield. Per 1B 136
Harrietsham. Kent 5C 40
Harrington. Cumb 2A 102
Harrington. Linc 3C 88
Harrington. Nptn 2E 63
Harringworth. Nptn 1G 63
Harriseahead. Staf 5C 84
Harriston. Cumb 5C 112
Harrogate. N Yor 4F 99 & 196
Harrold. Bed 5G 63
Harrop Dale. G Man 4A 92
Harrow. G Lon 2C 38
Harrowbarrow. Corn 2H 7
Harrowden. Bed 1A 52
Harrowgate Hill. Darl 3F 105
Harrow on the Hill. G Lon 2C 38
Harrow Weald. G Lon 1C 38
Harry Stoke. S Glo 4B 34
Harston. Cambs 5D 64
Harston. Leics 2F 75
Harswell. E Yor 5C 100
Hart. Hart 1B 106
Hartburn. Nmbd 1D 115
Hartburn. Stoc T 3B 106
Hartest. Suff 5H 65
Hartfield. E Sus 2F 27
Hartford. Cambs 3B 64
Hartford. Ches W 3A 84
Hartford. Som 4C 20
Hartfordbridge. Hants 1F 25
Hartford End. Essx 4G 53
Harthill. Ches W 5H 83
Harthill. N Lan 3C 128
Harthill. S Yor 2B 86
Hartington. Derbs 4F 85
Hartland. Devn 4C 18
Hartland Quay. Devn 4C 18
Hartle. Worc 3D 60
Hartlebury. Worc 3C 60
Hartlepool. Hart 1C 106
Hartley. Cumb 4A 104
Hartley. Kent 2B 28
(nr. Cranbrook)
Hartley. Kent 4H 39
(nr. Dartford)
Hartley. Nmbd 2G 115
Hartley Green. Staf 2D 73
Hartley Mauditt. Hants 3F 25
Hartley Wespall. Hants 1E 25
Hartley Wintney. Hants 1F 25
Hartlip. Kent 4C 40
Hartmount. High 1B 158
Hartoft End. N Yor 5E 107
Harton. N Yor 3B 100
Harton. Shrp 2G 59
Harton. Tyne 3G 115
Hartpury. Glos 3C 48
Hartshead. W Yor 2B 92
Hartshill. Warw 1H 61
Hartshorne. Derbs 3H 73
Hartsop. Cumb 3F 103
Hart Station. Hart 1B 106
Hartswell. Som 4D 20
Hartwell. Nptn 5E 63
Hartwood. Lanc 3D 90
Hartwood. N Lan 4B 128
Harvel. Kent 4A 40
Harvington. Worc 1F 49
(nr. Evesham)
Harvington. Worc 3C 60
(nr. Kidderminster)
Harwell. Oxon 3C 36
Harwich. Essx 2F 55 & 204
Harwood. Dur 1B 104
Harwood. G Man 3F 91
Harwood Dale. N Yor 5G 107
Harworth. Notts 1D 86
Hascombe. Surr 2A 26
Haselbech. Nptn 3E 62
Haselbury Plucknett.
Som 1H 13
Haseley. Warw 4G 61
Haselor. Warw 5F 61
Hasfield. Glos 3D 48
Hasguard. Pemb 4C 42
Haskayne. Lanc 4B 90
Hasketon. Suff 5E 67
Hasland. Derbs 4A 86
Haslemere. Surr 2A 26
Haslingden. Lanc 2F 91
Haslingden Grane. Lanc 2F 91
Haslingfield. Cambs 5D 64
Haslington. Ches E 5B 84
Hassall. Ches E 5B 84
Hassall Green. Ches E 5B 84
Hassell Street. Kent 1E 29
Hassendean. Bord 2H 119
Hassingham. Norf 5F 79
Hassness. Cumb 3C 102
Hassocks. W Sus 4E 27
Hassop. Derbs 3G 85
Haster. High 3F 169
Hasthorpe. Linc 4D 89
Hastigrow. High 2E 169
Hastingleigh. Kent 1E 29
Hastings. E Sus 5C 28
Hastingwood. Essx 5E 53
Hastoe. Herts 5H 51
Haston. Shrp 3H 71
Haswell. Dur 5G 115
Haswell Plough. Dur 5G 115
Hatch. C Beds 1B 52
Hatch Beauchamp. Som 4G 21
Hatch End. G Lon 1C 38
Hatch Green. Som 1G 13
Hatching Green. Herts 4B 52
Hatchmere. Ches W 3H 83
Hatch Warren. Hants 2E 24
Hatcliffe. NE Lin 4F 95
Hatfield. Here 5H 59
Hatfield. Herts 5C 52
Hatfield. S Yor 4G 93
Hatfield. Worc 5C 60
Hatfield Broad Oak. Essx 4F 53
Hatfield Garden Village.
Herts 5C 52
Hatfield Heath. Essx 4F 53
Hatfield Hyde. Herts 4C 52
Hatfield Peverel. Essx 4A 54
Hatfield Woodhouse.
S Yor 4G 93
Hatford. Oxon 2B 36
Hatherden. Hants 1B 24
Hatherleigh. Devn 2F 11
Hathern. Leics 3C 74
Hatherop. Glos 5G 49
Hathersage. Derbs 2G 85
Hathersage Booths.
Derbs 2G 85
Hatherton. Ches E 1A 72
Hatherton. Staf 4D 72
Hatley St George. Cambs 5B 64
Hatt. Corn 2H 7
Hattersley. G Man 1D 85
Hattingley. Hants 3E 25
Hatton. Abers 5H 161
Hatton. Derbs 2G 73
Hatton. G Lon 3B 38
Hatton. Linc 3A 88
Hatton. Shrp 1G 59
Hatton. Warr 2H 83
Hatton. Warw 4G 61
Hattoncrook. Abers 1F 153
Hatton Heath. Ches W 4G 83
Hatton of Fintray. Abers 2F 153
Haugh. E Ayr 2D 117
Haugh. Linc 3D 88
Haugham. Linc 2C 88
Haugh Head. Nmbd 2E 121
Haughley. Suff 4C 66
Haughley Green. Suff 4C 66
Haugh of Ballechin. Per 3G 143
Haugh of Glass. Mor 5B 160
Haugh of Urr. Dum 3F 111
Haughton. Ches E 5H 83
Haughton. Notts 3D 86
Haughton. Shrp 1A 60
(nr. Bridgnorth)
Haughton. Shrp 3F 71
(nr. Oswestry)
Haughton. Shrp 5B 72
(nr. Shifnal)
Haughton. Shrp 4H 71
(nr. Shrewsbury)
Haughton. Staf 3C 72
Haughton Green. G Man 1D 84
Haughton le Skerne.
Darl 3A 106
Haultwick. Herts 3D 52
Haunn. Arg 4E 139
Haunn. W Isl 7C 170
Haunton. Staf 4G 73
Hauxton. Cambs 5D 64
Havannah. Ches E 4C 84
Havant. Hants 2F 17
Haven. Here 5G 59
Haven Bank. Linc 5B 88
Havenside. E Yor 2E 95
Havenstreet. IOW 3D 16
Haven, The. W Sus 2B 26
Havercroft. W Yor 3D 93
Haverfordwest. Pemb 3D 42
Haverhill. Suff 1G 53
Haverigg. Cumb 2A 96
Havering-atte-Bower.
G Lon 1G 39
Havering's Grove. Essx 1A 40
Haversham. Mil 1G 51
Haverthwaite. Cumb 1C 96
Haverton Hill. Stoc T 2B 106
Havyatt. Som 3A 22
Hawarden. Flin 4F 83
Hawbridge. Worc 1E 49
Hawcoat. Cumb 2B 96
Hawcross. Glos 2C 48
Hawen. Cdgn 1D 44
Hawes. N Yor 1A 98
Hawes Green. Norf 1E 67
Hawick. Bord 3H 119
Hawkchurch. Devn 2G 13
Hawkedon. Suff 5G 65
Hawkenbury. Kent 1C 28
Hawkeridge. Wilts 1D 22
Hawkerland. Devn 4D 12
Hawkesbury. S Glo 3C 34
Hawkesbury. W Mid 2A 62
Hawkesbury Upton. S Glo 3C 34
Hawkes End. W Mid 2G 61
Hawk Green. G Man 2D 84
Hawkhurst. Kent 2B 28
Hawkhurst Common.
E Sus 4G 27
Hawkinge. Kent 1G 29
Hawkley. Hants 4F 25
Hawkridge. Som 3B 20
Hawksdale. Cumb 5E 113
Hawkshaw. G Man 3F 91
Hawkshead. Cumb 5E 103
Hawkshead Hill. Cumb 5E 103
Hawkswick. N Yor 2B 98
Hawksworth. Notts 1E 75
Hawksworth. W Yor 5D 98
Hawkwell. Essx 1C 40
Hawley. Hants 1G 25
Hawley. Kent 3G 39
Hawling. Glos 3F 49
Hawnby. N Yor 1H 99
Haworth. W Yor 1A 92
Hawstead. Suff 5A 66
Hawthorn. Dur 5H 115
Hawthorn Hill. Brac 4G 37
Hawthorn Hill. Linc 5B 88
Hawthorpe. Linc 3H 75
Hawton. Notts 5E 87
Haxby. York 4A 100
Haxey. N Lin 1E 87
Haybridge. Shrp 3A 60
Haybridge. Som 2A 22
Haydock. Mers 1H 83
Haydon. Bath 1B 22
Haydon. Dors 1B 14
Haydon. Som 4F 21
Haydon Bridge. Nmbd 3B 114
Haydon Wick. Swin 3G 35
Haye. Corn 2H 7
Hayes. G Lon 4F 39
(nr. Bromley)
Hayes. G Lon 2B 38
(nr. Uxbridge)
Hayfield. Derbs 2E 85
Hay Green. Norf 4E 77
Hayhill. E Ayr 3D 116
Haylands. IOW 3D 16
Hayle. Corn 3C 4
Hayley Green. W Mid 2D 60
Hayling Island. Hants 3F 17
Hayne. Devn 2B 12
Haynes. C Beds 1A 52
Haynes West End.
C Beds 1A 52
Hay-on-Wye. Powy 1F 47
Hayscastle. Pemb 2C 42
Hayscastle Cross. Pemb 2D 42
Haysden. Kent 1G 27
Hayshead. Ang 4F 145
Hay Street. Herts 3D 53
Hayton. Aber 3G 153
Hayton. Cumb 5C 112
(nr. Aspatria)
Hayton. Cumb 4G 113
(nr. Brampton)
Hayton. E Yor 5C 100
Hayton. Notts 2E 87
Hayton's Bent. Shrp 2H 59
Haytor Vale. Devn 5A 12
Haytown. Devn 1D 11
Haywards Heath. W Sus 3E 27
Haywood. S Lan 4C 128
Hazelbank. S Lan 5B 128
Hazelbury Bryan. Dors 2C 14
Hazeleigh. Essx 5B 54
Hazeley. Hants 1F 25
Hazel Grove. G Man 2D 84
Hazelhead. S Yor 4B 92
Hazelslade. Staf 4E 73
Hazel Street. Kent 2A 28
Hazelton Walls. Fife 1F 137
Hazelwood. Derbs 1H 73
Hazlemere. Buck 2G 37
Hazler. Shrp 1G 59
Hazlerigg. Tyne 2F 115
Hazles. Staf 1E 73
Hazleton. Glos 4F 49
Hazon. Nmbd 4F 121
Heacham. Norf 2F 77
Headbourne Worthy.
Hants 3C 24
Headcorn. Kent 1C 28
Headingley. W Yor 1C 92
Headington. Oxon 5D 50
Headlam. Dur 3E 105
Headless Cross. Worc 4E 61
Headley. Hants 3G 25
(nr. Haslemere)
Headley. Hants 5D 36
(nr. Kingsclere)
Headley. Surr 5D 38
Headley Down. Hants 3G 25
Headley Heath. Worc 3E 61
Headley Park. Bris 5A 34
Head of Muir. Falk 1B 128
Headon. Notts 3E 87
Heads Nook. Cumb 4F 113
Heage. Derbs 5A 86
Healaugh. N Yor 5D 104
(nr. Grinton)
Healaugh. N Yor 5H 99
(nr. York)
Heald Green. G Man 2C 84
Heale. Devn 2G 19
Healey. G Man 3G 91
Healey. Nmbd 4D 114
Healey. N Yor 1D 98
Healeyfield. Dur 5D 114
Healey Hall. Nmbd 4D 114
Healing. NE Lin 3F 95
Heamoor. Corn 3B 4
Heanish. Arg 4B 138
Heanor. Derbs 1B 74
Heanton Punchardon.
Devn 3F 19
Heapham. Linc 2F 87
Heartsease. Powy 4D 58
Heasley Mill. Devn 3H 19
Heaste. High 2E 147
Heath. Derbs 4B 86
Heath and Reach. C Beds 3H 51
Heath Common. W Sus 4C 26
Heathcote. Derbs 4F 85
Heath Cross. Devn 3H 11
Heathencote. Nptn 1F 51
Heath End. Derbs 3A 74
Heath End. Hants 5D 36
Heath End. W Mid 5E 73
Heather. Leics 4A 74
Heatherfield. High 4D 155
Heatherton. Derb 2H 73
Heathfield. Cambs 1E 53
Heathfield. Cumb 5C 112
Heathfield. Devn 5B 12
Heathfield. E Sus 3G 27
Heathfield. Ren 3E 126
Heathfield. Som 3E 21
(nr. Lydeard St Lawrence)
Heathfield. Som 4E 21
(nr. Norton Fitzwarren)
Heath Green. Worc 3E 61
Heathhall. Dum 2A 112
Heath Hayes. Staf 4E 73
Heath Hill. Shrp 4B 72
Heath House. Som 2H 21
Heathrow (London) Airport.
G Lon 3B 38 & 205
Heathstock. Devn 2F 13
Heath, The. Norf 3E 79
(nr. Buxton)
Heath, The. Norf 3B 78
(nr. Fakenham)
Heath, The. Norf 3D 78
(nr. Hevingham)
Heath, The. Staf 2E 73
Heath, The. Suff 2E 55
Heathton. Shrp 1C 60
Heathtop. Derbs 2F 73
Heath Town. W Mid 1D 60
Heatley. G Man 2B 84
Heatley. Staf 3E 73
Heaton. Lanc 3D 96
Heaton. Staf 4D 84
Heaton. Tyne 3F 115
Heaton. W Yor 1B 92
Heaton Moor. G Man 1C 84
Heaton's Bridge. Lanc 3C 90
Heaverham. Kent 5G 39
Heavitree. Devn 3C 12
Hebburn. Tyne 3G 115
Hebden. N Yor 3C 98
Hebden Bridge. W Yor 2H 91
Hebden Green. Ches W 4A 84
Hebing End. Herts 3D 52
Hebron. Carm 2F 43
Hebron. Nmbd 1E 115
Heck. Dum 1B 112
Heckdyke. Notts 1E 87
Heckfield. Hants 5F 37
Heckfield Green. Suff 3D 66
Heckfordbridge. Essx 3C 54
Heckington. Linc 1A 76
Heckmondwike. W Yor 2C 92
Heddington. Wilts 5E 35
Heddle. Orkn 6C 172
Heddon. Devn 4G 19
Heddon-on-the-Wall.
Nmbd 3E 115
Hedenham. Norf 1F 67
Hedge End. Hants 1C 16
Hedgerley. Buck 2A 38
Hedging. Som 4G 21
Hedley on the Hill.
Nmbd 4D 115
Hednesford. Staf 4E 73
Hedon. E Yor 2E 95
Hegdon Hill. Here 5H 59
Heglibister. Shet 6E 173
Heighington. Darl 2F 105
Heighington. Linc 4H 87
Heightington. Worc 3B 60
Heights of Brae. High 2H 157
Heights of Fodderty.
High 2H 157
Heights of Kinlochewe.
High 2C 156
Heiton. Bord 1B 120
Hele. Devn 2C 12
(nr. Exeter)
Hele. Devn 3D 10
(nr. Holsworthy)
Hele. Devn 2F 19
(nr. Ilfracombe)
Hele. Torb 2F 9
Helen's Bay. N Dwn 1J 179
Helensburgh. Arg 1D 126
Helford. Corn 4E 5
Helhoughton. Norf 3A 78
Helions Bumpstead. Essx 1G 53
Helland. Corn 5A 10
Helland. Som 4G 21
Hellandbridge. Corn 5A 10
Hellesdon. Norf 4E 78
Hellesveor. Corn 2C 4
Hellidon. Nptn 5C 62
Hellifield. N Yor 4A 98
Hellingly. E Sus 4G 27
Hellington. Norf 5F 79
Hellister. Shet 7E 173
Helmdon. Nptn 1D 50
Helmingham. Suff 5D 66
Helmington Row. Dur 1E 105
Helmsdale. High 2H 165
Helmshore. Lanc 2F 91
Helmsley. N Yor 1A 100
Helperby. N Yor 3G 99
Helperthorpe. N Yor 2D 100
Helpringham. Linc 1A 76
Helpston. Pet 5A 76
Helsby. Ches W 3G 83
Helsey. Linc 3E 89
Helston. Corn 4D 4
Helstone. Corn 4A 10
Helton. Cumb 2G 103
Helwith. N Yor 4D 105
Helwith Bridge. N Yor 3H 97
Helygain. Flin 3E 82
Hemblington. Norf 4F 79
Hemel Hempstead. Herts 5A 52
Hemerdon. Devn 3B 8
Hemingbrough. N Yor 1G 93
Hemingby. Linc 3B 88
Hemingfield. S Yor 4D 93
Hemingford Abbots.
Cambs 3B 64
Hemingford Grey. Cambs 3B 64
Hemingstone. Suff 5D 66
Hemington. Leics 3B 74
Hemington. Nptn 2H 63
Hemington. Som 1C 22
Hemley. Suff 1F 55
Hemlington. Midd 3B 106
Hempholme. E Yor 4E 101
Hempnall. Norf 1E 67
Hempnall Green. Norf 1E 67
Hempriggs. High 4F 169
Hemp's Green. Essx 3C 54
Hempstead. Essx 2G 53
Hempstead. Medw 4B 40
Hempstead. Norf 2D 78
(nr. Holt)
Hempstead. Norf 3G 79
(nr. Stalham)
Hempsted. Glos 4D 48
Hempton. Norf 3B 78
Hempton. Oxon 2C 50
Hemsby. Norf 4G 79
Hemswell. Linc 1G 87
Hemswell Cliff. Linc 2G 87
Hemsworth. W Yor 3E 93
Hem, The. Shrp 5B 72
Hemyock. Devn 1E 13
Henallt. Carm 3E 45
Henbury. Bris 4A 34
Henbury. Ches E 3C 84
Hendomen. Powy 1E 58
Hendon. G Lon 2D 38
Hendon. Tyne 4H 115
Hendra. Corn 3D 6
Hendre. B'end 3C 32
Hendreforgan. Rhon 3C 32
Hendy. Carm 5F 45
Heneglwys. IOA 3D 80
Henfeddau Fawr. Pemb 1G 43
Henfield. S Glo 4B 34
Henfield. W Sus 4D 26
Henford. Devn 3D 10
Hengoed. Cphy 2E 33
Hengoed. Shrp 2E 71
Hengrave. Suff 4H 65
Henham. Essx 3F 53
Heniarth. Powy 5D 70
Henlade. Som 4F 21
Henley. Dors 2B 14
Henley. Shrp 2G 59
(nr. Church Stretton)
Henley. Shrp 3H 59
(nr. Ludlow)
Henley. Som 3H 21
Henley. Suff 5D 66
Henley. W Sus 4G 25
Henley-in-Arden. Warw 4F 61
Henley-on-Thames. Oxon 3F 37
Henley's Down. E Sus 4B 28
Henley Street. Kent 4A 40
Henllan. Cdgn 1D 44
Henllan. Den 4C 82
Henllan. Mon 3F 47
Henllan Amgoed. Carm 3F 43
Henllys. Torf 2F 33
Henlow. C Beds 2B 52
Hennock. Devn 4B 12
Henny Street. Essx 2B 54
Henryd. Cnwy 3G 81
Henry's Moat. Pemb 2E 43
Hensall. N Yor 2F 93
Henshaw. Nmbd 3A 114
Hensingham. Cumb 3A 102
Henstead. Suff 2G 67
Hensting. Hants 4C 24
Henstridge. Som 1C 14
Henstridge Ash. Som 4C 22
Henstridge Bowden. Som 4B 22
Henstridge Marsh. Som 4C 22
Henton. Oxon 5F 51
Henton. Som 2H 21
Henwood. Corn 5C 10
Heogan. Shet 7F 173
Heol Senni. Powy 3C 46
Heol-y-Cyw. B'end 3C 32
Hepburn. Nmbd 2E 121
Hepple. Nmbd 4D 121
Hepscott. Nmbd 1F 115
Heptonstall. W Yor 2H 91
Hepworth. Suff 3B 66
Hepworth. W Yor 4B 92
Herbrandston. Pemb 4C 42
Hereford. Here 2A 48
Heribusta. High 1D 154
Heriot. Bord 4H 129
Hermiston. Edin 2E 129
Hermitage. Bord 5H 119
Hermitage. Dors 2B 14
Hermitage. W Ber 4D 36
Hermitage. W Sus 2F 17
Hermon. Carm 3G 45
(nr. Llandeilo)
Hermon. Carm 2D 44
(nr. Newcastle Emlyn)
Hermon. IOA 4C 80
Hermon. Pemb 1G 43
Herne. Kent 4F 41
Herne Bay. Kent 4F 41
Herne Common. Kent 4F 41
Herne Pound. Kent 5A 40
Herner. Devn 4F 19
Hernhill. Kent 4E 41
Herodsfoot. Corn 2G 7
Heronden. Kent 5G 41
Herongate. Essx 1H 39
Heronsford. S Ayr 1G 109
Heronsgate. Herts 1B 38
Heron's Ghyll. E Sus 3F 27
Herra. Shet 2H 173
Herriard. Hants 2E 25
Herringfleet. Suff 1G 67
Herringswell. Suff 4G 65
Herrington. Tyne 4G 115
Hersden. Kent 4G 41
Hersham. Corn 2C 10
Hersham. Surr 4C 38
Herstmonceux. E Sus 4H 27
Herston. Dors 5F 15
Herston. Orkn 8D 172
Hertford. Herts 4D 52
Hertford Heath. Herts 4D 52
Hertingfordbury.
Herts 4D 52
Hesketh. Lanc 2C 90
Hesketh Bank. Lanc 2C 90
Hesketh Lane. Lanc 5F 97
Hesket Newmarket.
Cumb 1E 103
Heskin Green. Lanc 3D 90
Hesleden. Dur 1B 106
Hesleyside. Nmbd 1B 114
Heslington. York 4A 100
Hessay. York 4H 99
Hessenford. Corn 3H 7
Hessett. Suff 4B 66
Hessilhead. N Ayr 4E 127
Hessle. Hull 2D 94
Hestaford. Shet 6D 173
Hest Bank. Lanc 3D 96
Hester's Way. Glos 3E 49
Hestinsetter. Shet 7D 173
Heston. G Lon 3C 38
Hestwall. Orkn 6B 172
Heswall. Mers 2E 83
Hethe. Oxon 3D 50
Hethelpit Cross. Glos 3C 48
Hethersett. Norf 5D 78
Hethersgill. Cumb 3F 113
Hetherside. Cumb 3F 113
Hethpool. Nmbd 2C 120
Hett. Dur 1F 105
Hetton. N Yor 4B 98
Hetton-le-Hole. Tyne 5G 115
Hetton Steads. Nmbd 1E 121
Heugh. Nmbd 2D 115
Heugh-head. Abers 2A 152
Heveningham. Suff 3F 67
Hever. Kent 1F 27
Heversham. Cumb 1D 97
Hevingham. Norf 3D 78
Hewas Water. Corn 4D 6
Hewelsfield. Glos 5A 48
Hewish. N Som 5G 33
Hewish. Som 2H 13
Hewood. Dors 2G 13
Hexham. Nmbd 3C 114
Hextable. Kent 3G 39
Hexton. Herts 2B 52
Hexworthy. Devn 5G 11
Heybridge. Essx 1H 39
(nr. Brentwood)
Heybridge. Essx 5B 54
(nr. Maldon)
Heybridge Basin. Essx 5B 54
Heybrook Bay. Devn 4A 8
Heydon. Cambs 1E 53
Heydon. Norf 3D 78
Heydour. Linc 2H 75
Heylipol. Arg 4A 138
Heyop. Powy 3E 59
Heysham. Lanc 3D 96
Heyshott. W Sus 1G 17
Heytesbury. Wilts 2E 23
Heythrop. Oxon 3B 50
Heywood. G Man 3G 91
Heywood. Wilts 1D 22
Hibaldstow. N Lin 4C 94
Hickleton. S Yor 4E 93
Hickling. Norf 3G 79
Hickling. Notts 3D 74
Hickling Green. Norf 3G 79
Hickling Heath. Norf 3G 79
Hickstead. W Sus 3D 26
Hidcote Bartrim. Glos 1G 49
Hidcote Boyce. Glos 1G 49
Higford. Shrp 5B 72
High Ackworth. W Yor 3E 93
Higham. Derbs 5A 86
Higham. Kent 3B 40
Higham. Lanc 1G 91
Higham. S Yor 4D 92
Higham. Suff 2D 54
(nr. Ipswich)
Higham. Suff 4G 65
(nr. Newmarket)
Higham Dykes. Nmbd 2E 115
Higham Ferrers. Nptn 4G 63
Higham Gobion. C Beds 2B 52
Higham on the Hill. Leics 1A 62
Highampton. Devn 2E 11
Highams Park. G Lon 1E 39
High Angerton. Nmbd 1D 115
High Auldgirth. Dum 1G 111
High Bankhill. Cumb 5G 113
High Banton. N Lan 1A 128
High Barnet. G Lon 1D 38
High Beech. Essx 1F 39
High Bentham. N Yor 3F 97
High Bickington. Devn 4G 19
High Biggins. Cumb 2F 97
High Birkwith. N Yor 2H 97
High Blantyre. S Lan 4H 127
High Bonnybridge. Falk 2B 128
High Borrans. Cumb 4F 103
High Bradfield. S Yor 1G 85
High Bray. Devn 3G 19
Highbridge. Cumb 5E 113
Highbridge. High 5D 148
Highbridge. Som 2G 21
Highbrook. W Sus 2E 27
High Brooms. Kent 1G 27
High Bullen. Devn 4F 19
Highburton. W Yor 3B 92
Highbury. Som 2B 22
High Buston. Nmbd 4G 121
High Callerton. Nmbd 2E 115
High Carlingill. Cumb 4H 103
High Catton. E Yor 4B 100
High Church. Nmbd 1E 115
Highclere. Hants 5C 36
Highcliffe. Dors 3H 15
High Cogges. Oxon 5B 50
High Common. Norf 5B 78
High Coniscliffe. Darl 3F 105
High Crosby. Cumb 4F 113
High Cross. Hants 4F 25
High Cross. Herts 4D 52
High Dougarie. N Ayr 2C 122
High Easter. Essx 4G 53
High Eggborough. N Yor 2F 93
High Ellington. N Yor 1D 98
Higher Alham. Som 2B 22
Higher Ansty. Dors 2C 14
Higher Ashton. Devn 4B 12
Higher Ballam. Lanc 1B 90
Higher Bartle. Lanc 1D 90
Higher Bockhampton.
Dors 3C 14
Higher Bojewyan. Corn 3A 4
High Ercall. Telf 4H 71
Higher Cheriton. Devn 2E 12
Higher Clovelly. Devn 4D 18
Higher Compton. Plym 3A 8
Higher Dinting. Derbs 1E 85
Higher Dunstone. Devn 5H 11
Higher End. G Man 4D 90
Higher Gabwell. Devn 2F 9
Higher Halstock Leigh.
Dors 2A 14
Higher Heysham. Lanc 3D 96
Higher Hurdsfield.
Ches E 3D 84
Higher Kingcombe. Dors 3A 14
Higher Kinnerton. Flin 4F 83
Higher Melcombe. Dors 2C 14
Higher Penwortham.
Lanc 2D 90
Higher Porthpean. Corn 3E 7
Higher Poynton. Ches E 2D 84
Higher Shotton. Flin 4F 83
Higher Shurlach. Ches W 3A 84
Higher Slade. Devn 2F 19
Higher Tale. Devn 2D 12
Highertown. Corn 4C 6
Higher Town. IOS 1B 4
Higher Town. Som 2C 20
Higher Vexford. Som 3E 20
Higher Walton. Lanc 2D 90
Higher Walton. Warr 2H 83
Higher Whatcombe. Dors 2D 14
Higher Wheelton. Lanc 2E 90
Higher Whiteleigh. Corn 3C 10
Higher Whitley. Ches W 2A 84
Higher Wincham. Ches W 3A 84
Higher Wraxall. Dors 2A 14
Higher Wych. Wrex 1G 71
Higher Yalberton. Torb 3E 9
High Etherley. Dur 2E 105
High Ferry. Linc 1C 76
Highfield. E Yor 1H 93
Highfield. N Ayr 4E 126
Highfield. Tyne 4E 115
Highfields Caldecote.
Cambs 5C 64
High Garrett. Essx 3A 54
Highgate. G Lon 2D 39
Highgate. N Ayr 4E 127
Highgate. Powy 1D 58
High Grange. Dur 1E 105
High Green. Cumb 4F 103
High Green. Norf 5D 78
High Green. Shrp 2B 60
High Green. S Yor 1H 85
High Green. W Yor 3B 92
High Green. Worc 1D 49
Highgreen Manor.
Nmbd 5C 120
High Halden. Kent 2C 28
High Halstow. Medw 3B 40
High Ham. Som 3H 21
High Harrington. Cumb 2B 102
High Haswell. Dur 5G 115
High Hatton. Shrp 3A 72
High Hawsker. N Yor 4G 107
High Hesket. Cumb 5F 113
High Hesleden. Dur 1B 106
High Hoyland. S Yor 3C 92
High Hunsley. E Yor 1C 94
High Hurstwood. E Sus 3F 27
High Hutton. N Yor 3B 100
High Ireby. Cumb 1D 102
High Keil. Arg 5A 122
High Kelling. Norf 1D 78
High Kilburn. N Yor 2H 99
High Knipe. Cumb 3G 103
High Lands. Dur 2E 105
Highlands, The. Shrp 2A 60
Highlane. Ches E 4C 84
Highlane. Derbs 2B 86
High Lane. G Man 2D 84
High Lane. Here 4A 60
High Laver. Essx 5F 53
Highlaws. Cumb 5C 112
Highleadon. Glos 3C 48
High Legh. Ches E 2A 84
Highleigh. W Sus 3G 17
High Leven. Stoc T 3B 106
Highley. Shrp 2B 60
High Littleton. Bath 1B 22
High Longthwaite.
Cumb 5D 112
High Lorton. Cumb 2C 102
High Marishes. N Yor 2C 100
High Marnham. Notts 3F 87
High Melton. S Yor 4F 93
High Mickley. Nmbd 3D 115
Highmoor. Cumb 5D 112
High Moor. Lanc 3D 90
Highmoor. Oxon 3F 37
Highmoor Cross. Oxon 3F 37
Highmoor Hill. Mon 3H 33
High Mowthorpe. N Yor 3C 100
Highnam. Glos 4C 48
High Newport. Tyne 4G 115
High Newton. Cumb 1D 96
High Newton-by-the-Sea.
Nmbd 2G 121
High Nibthwaite. Cumb 1B 96
High Offley. Staf 3B 72
High Ongar. Essx 5F 53
High Onn. Staf 4C 72
High Orchard. Glos 4D 48
High Park. Mers 3B 90
High Roding. Essx 4G 53
High Row. Cumb 1E 103
High Salvington. W Sus 5C 26
High Scales. Cumb 5C 112
High Shaw. N Yor 5B 104
High Shincliffe. Dur 5F 115
High Side. Cumb 1D 102
High Spen. Tyne 3E 115
Highsted. Kent 4D 40
High Stoop. Dur 5E 115
High Street. Corn 3D 6
High Street. Suff 5G 67
(nr. Aldeburgh)
High Street. Suff 2F 67
(nr. Bungay)
High Street. Suff 3G 67
(nr. Yoxford)
Highstreet Green. Essx 2A 54
High Street Green. Suff 5C 66
Highstreet Green. Surr 2A 26
Hightae. Dum 2B 112
High Throston. Hart 1B 106
Hightown. Ches E 4C 84
Hightown. Mers 4A 90
High Town. Staf 4D 73
Hightown Green. Suff 5B 66
High Toynton. Linc 4B 88
High Trewhitt. Nmbd 4E 121
High Valleyfield. Fife 1D 128
Highway. Here 1H 47
Highweek. Devn 5B 12
High Westwood. Dur 4E 115
Highwood. Staf 2E 73
Highwood. Worc 4A 60
High Worsall. N Yor 4A 106
Highworth. Swin 2H 35
High Wray. Cumb 5E 103
High Wych. Herts 4E 53
High Wycombe. Buck 2G 37
Hilborough. Norf 5H 77
Hilcott. Wilts 1G 23
Hildenborough. Kent 1G 27
Hildersham. Cambs 1F 53
Hilderstone. Staf 2D 72
Hilderthorpe. E Yor 3F 101
Hilfield. Dors 2B 14
Hilgay. Norf 1F 65
Hill. S Glo 2B 34
Hill. Warw 4B 62
Hill. Worc 1E 49
Hillam. N Yor 2F 93
Hillbeck. Cumb 3A 104
Hillberry. IOM 4C 108
Hillborough. Kent 4G 41
Hillbourne. Pool 3F 15
Hillbrae. Abers 4D 160
(nr. Aberchirder)
Hillbrae. Abers 1E 153
(nr. Inverurie)
Hillbrae. Abers 5F 161
(nr. Methlick)
Hill Brow. Hants 4F 25
Hillbutts. Dors 2E 15
Hillclifflane. Derbs 1G 73
Hillcommon. Som 4E 21
Hill Deverill. Wilts 2D 22
Hilldyke. Linc 1C 76
Hill End. Dur 1D 104
Hillend. Fife 1E 129
(nr. Inverkeithing)
Hill End. Fife 4C 136
(nr. Saline)
Hillend. N Lan 3B 128
Hill End. N Yor 4C 98
Hillend. Shrp 1C 60
Hillend. Swan 3D 30
Hillersland. Glos 4A 48
Hillerton. Devn 3H 11
Hillesden. Buck 3E 51
Hillesley. Glos 3C 34
Hillfarrance. Som 4E 21
Hill Furze. Worc 1E 49
Hill Gate. Here 3H 47
Hill Green. Essx 2E 53
Hillgreen. W Ber 4C 36
Hillhall. Lis 3G 179
Hillhead. Abers 5C 160
Hill Head. Hants 2D 16
Hillhead. S Ayr 3D 116
Hillhead. Torb 3F 9
Hillhead of Auchentumb.
Abers 3G 161
Hilliard's Cross. Staf 4F 73
Hilliclay. High 2D 168
Hillingdon. G Lon 2B 38
Hillington. Norf 3G 77
Hillington. Ren 3G 127
Hillmorton. Warw 3C 62
Hill of Beath. Fife 4D 136
Hill of Fearn. High 1C 158
Hill of Fiddes. Abers 1G 153
Hill of Keillor. Ang 4B 144
Hill of Overbrae. Abers 2F 161
Hill Ridware. Staf 4E 73
Hillsborough. Lis 4G 179
Hillsborough. S Yor 1H 85
Hillside. Abers 4G 153
Hillside. Ang 2G 145
Hillside. Devn 2D 8
Hillside. Mers 3B 90
Hillside. Orkn 5C 172
Hillside. Shet 5F 173
Hillside. Shrp 2A 60
Hill Side. W Yor 3B 92
Hillside. Worc 4B 60
Hillside of Prieston. Ang 5C 144
Hill Somersal. Derbs 2F 73
Hillstown. Derbs 4B 86
Hillstreet. Hants 1B 16
Hillswick. Shet 4D 173
Hill, The. Cumb 1A 96
Hill Top. Dur 2C 104
(nr. Barnard Castle)
Hill Top. Dur 5F 115
(nr. Durham)
Hill Top. Dur 4E 115
(nr. Stanley)
Hill Top. Hants 2C 16
Hill Top. New M 7G 179
Hill View. Dors 3E 15
Hillwell. Shet 10E 173
Hill Wootton. Warw 4H 61
Hillyland. Per 1C 136
Hilmarton. Wilts 4F 35
Hilperton. Wilts 1D 22
Hilperton Marsh. Wilts 1D 22
Hilsea. Port 2E 17
Hilston. E Yor 1F 95
Hiltingbury. Hants 4C 24
Hilton. Cambs 4B 64
Hilton. Cumb 2A 104
Hilton. Derbs 2G 73
Hilton. Dors 2C 14
Hilton. Dur 2E 105
Hilton. High 5E 165
Hilton. Shrp 1B 60
Hilton. Staf 5E 73
Hilton. Stoc T 3B 106
Hilton of Cadboll. High 1C 158
Himbleton. Worc 5D 60
Himley. Staf 1C 60
Hincaster. Cumb 1E 97
Hinchcliffe Mill. W Yor 4B 92
Hinchwick. Glos 2G 49
Hinckley. Leics 1B 62
Hinderclay. Suff 3C 66
Hinderwell. N Yor 3E 107
Hindford. Shrp 2F 71
Hindhead. Surr 3G 25
Hindley. G Man 4E 91
Hindley. Nmbd 4D 114
Hindley Green. G Man 4E 91
Hindlip. Worc 5C 60
Hindolveston. Norf 3C 78
Hindon. Wilts 3E 23
Hindringham. Norf 2B 78
Hingham. Norf 5C 78
Hinksford. Staf 2C 60
Hinstock. Shrp 3A 72
Hintlesham. Suff 1D 54
Hinton. Hants 3H 15
Hinton. Here 2G 47
Hinton. Nptn 5C 62
Hinton. Shrp 5G 71
Hinton. S Glo 4C 34
Hinton Ampner. Hants 4D 24
Hinton Blewett. Bath 1A 22
Hinton Charterhouse.
Bath 1C 22
Hinton-in-the-Hedges.
Nptn 2D 50
Hinton Martell. Dors 2F 15
Hinton on the Green.
Worc 1F 49
Hinton Parva. Swin 3H 35
Hinton St George. Som 1H 13
Hinton St Mary. Dors 1C 14
Hinton Waldrist. Oxon 2B 36
Hints. Shrp 3A 60
Hints. Staf 5F 73
Hinwick. Bed 4G 63
Hinxhill. Kent 1E 29
Hinxton. Cambs 1E 53
Hinxworth. Herts 1C 52
Hipley. Hants 1E 16
Hipperholme. W Yor 2B 92
Hipsburn. Nmbd 3G 121
Hipswell. N Yor 5E 105
Hiraeth. Carm 2F 43
Hirn. Abers 3E 153
Hirnant. Powy 3C 70
Hirst. N Lan 3B 128
Hirst. Nmbd 1F 115
Hirst Courtney. N Yor 2G 93
Hirwaen. Den 4D 82
Hirwaun. Rhon 5C 46
Hiscott. Devn 4F 19
Histon. Cambs 4D 64
Hitcham. Suff 5B 66
Hitchin. Herts 3B 52
Hittisleigh. Devn 3H 11
Hittisleigh Barton. Devn 3H 11
Hive. E Yor 1B 94
Hixon. Staf 3E 73
Hoaden. Kent 5G 41
Hoar Cross. Staf 3F 73
Hoarwithy. Here 3A 48
Hoath. Kent 4G 41
Hobarris. Shrp 3F 59
Hobbister. Orkn 7C 172
Hobbles Green. Suff 5G 65
Hobbs Cross. Essx 1F 39
Hobkirk. Bord 3H 119
Hobson. Dur 4E 115
Hoby. Leics 4D 74
Hockering. Norf 4C 78
Hockering Heath. Norf 4C 78
Hockerton. Notts 5E 86
Hockley. Essx 1C 40
Hockley. Staf 5G 73
Hockley. W Mid 3G 61
Hockley Heath. W Mid 3F 61
Hockliffe. C Beds 3H 51
Hockwold cum Wilton.
Norf 2G 65
Hockworthy. Devn 1D 12
Hoddesdon. Herts 5D 52
Hoddlesden. Bkbn 2F 91
Hoddomcross. Dum 2C 112
Hodgeston. Pemb 5E 43
Hodley. Powy 1D 58
Hodnet. Shrp 3A 72
Hodsoll Street. Kent 4H 39
Hodson. Swin 3G 35
Hodthorpe. Derbs 3C 86
Hoe. Norf 4B 78
Hoe Gate. Hants 1E 17
Hoe, The. Plym 3A 8
Hoff. Cumb 3H 103
Hoffleet Stow. Linc 2B 76
Hogaland. Shet 4E 173
Hogben's Hill. Kent 5E 41
Hoggard's Green. Suff 5A 66
Hoggeston. Buck 3G 51
Hoggrill's End. Warw 1G 61
Hogha Gearraidh. W Isl 1C 170
Hoghton. Lanc 2E 90
Hoghton Bottoms. Lanc 2E 91
Hognaston. Derbs 5G 85
Hogsthorpe. Linc 3E 89
Hogstock. Dors 2E 15
Holbeach. Linc 3C 76
Holbeach Bank. Linc 3C 76
Holbeach Clough. Linc 3C 76
Holbeach Drove. Linc 4C 76
Holbeach Hurn. Linc 3C 76
Holbeach St Johns. Linc 4C 76
Holbeach St Marks. Linc 2C 76
Holbeach St Matthew.
Linc 2D 76
Holbeck. Notts 3C 86
Holbeck. W Yor 1C 92
Holbeck Woodhouse.
Notts 3C 86
Holberrow Green. Worc 5E 61
Holbeton. Devn 3C 8
Holborn. G Lon 2E 39
Holbrook. Derbs 1A 74
Holbrook. S Yor 2B 86
Holbrook. Suff 2E 55
Holburn. Nmbd 1E 121
Holbury. Hants 2C 16
Holcombe. Devn 5C 12
Holcombe. G Man 3F 91
Holcombe. Som 2B 22
Holcombe Brook. G Man 3F 91
Holcombe Rogus. Devn 1D 12
Holcot. Nptn 4E 63
Holden. Lanc 5G 97
Holdenby. Nptn 4D 62
Holder's Green. Essx 3G 53
Holdgate. Shrp 2H 59
Holdingham. Linc 1H 75
Holditch. Dors 2G 13
Holemoor. Devn 2E 11
Hole Street. W Sus 4C 26
Holford. Som 2E 21
Holker. Cumb 2C 96
Holkham. Norf 1A 78
Hollacombe. Devn 2D 11
Holland. Orkn 2D 172
(on Papa Westray)
Holland. Orkn 5F 172
(on Stronsay)
Holland Fen. Linc 1B 76
Holland Lees. Lanc 4D 90
Holland-on-Sea. Essx 4F 55
Holland Park. W Mid 5E 73
Hollandstoun. Orkn 2G 172
Hollesley. Suff 1G 55
Hollinfare. Warr 1A 84
Hollingbourne. Kent 5C 40
Hollingbury. Brig 5E 27
Hollingdon. Buck 3G 51
Hollingrove. E Sus 3A 28
Hollington. Derbs 1G 73
Hollington. E Sus 4B 28
Hollington. Staf 2E 73
Hollington Grove. Derbs 2G 73
Hollingworth. G Man 1E 85
Hollins. Derbs 3H 85
Hollins. G Man 4G 91
(nr. Bury)
Hollins. G Man 4G 91
(nr. Middleton)
Hollinsclough. Staf 4E 85
Hollinswood. Telf 5A 72
Hollinthorpe. W Yor 1D 93
Hollinwood. G Man 4H 91
Hollinwood. Shrp 2H 71
Hollocombe. Devn 1G 11
Holloway. Derbs 5H 85
Hollow Court. Worc 5D 61
Hollowell. Nptn 3D 62
Hollow Meadows. S Yor 2G 85
Hollows. Dum 2E 113
Hollybush. Cphy 5E 47
Hollybush. E Ayr 3C 116
Hollybush. Worc 2C 48
Holly End. Norf 5D 77
Holly Hill. N Yor 4E 105
Hollyhurst. Ches E 1H 71
Hollym. E Yor 2G 95
Hollywood. Worc 3E 61
Holmacott. Devn 4F 19
Holmbridge. W Yor 4B 92
Holmbury St Mary. Surr 1C 26
Holmbush. Corn 3E 7
Holmcroft. Staf 3D 72
Holme. Cambs 2A 64
Holme. Cumb 2E 97
Holme. N Lin 4C 94
Holme. N Yor 1F 99
Holme. Notts 5F 87
Holme. W Yor 4B 92
Holmebridge. Dors 4D 15
Holme Chapel. Lanc 2G 91
Holme Hale. Norf 5A 78
Holme Lacy. Here 2A 48
Holme Marsh. Here 5F 59
Holmend. Dum 4C 118
Holme next the Sea.
Norf 1G 77
Holme-on-Spalding-Moor.
E Yor 1B 94

Holme on the Wolds—Keysoe

Holme on the Wolds.
E Yor 5D 100
Holme Pierrepont. Notts 2D 74
Holmer. Here 1A 48
Holmer Green. Buck 1A 38
Holmes. Lanc 3C 90
Holme St Cuthbert.
Cumb 5C 112
Holmes Chapel. Ches E 4B 84
Holmesfield. Derbs 3H 85
Holmeswood. Lanc 3C 90
Holmewood. Derbs 4B 86
Holmfirth. W Yor 4B 92
Holmhead. E Ayr 2E 117
Holmisdale. High 4A 154
Holm of Drumlanrig.
Dum 5H 117
Holmpton. E Yor 2G 95
Holmrook. Cumb 5B 102
Holmsgarth. Shet 7F 173
Holmside. Dur 5F 115
Holmwrangle. Cumb 5G 113
Holne. Devn 2D 8
Holsworthy. Devn 2D 10
Holsworthy Beacon.
Devn 2D 10
Holt. Dors 2F 15
Holt. Norf 2C 78
Holt. Wilts 5D 34
Holt. Worc 4C 60
Holt. Wrex 5G 83
Holtby. York 4A 100
Holt End. Hants 3E 25
Holt End. Worc 4E 61
Holt Fleet. Worc 4C 60
Holt Green. Lanc 4B 90
Holt Heath. Dors 2F 15
Holt Heath. Worc 4C 60
Holton. Oxon 5E 50
Holton. Som 4B 22
Holton. Suff 3F 67
Holton cum Beckering.
Linc 2A 88
Holton Heath. Dors 3E 15
Holton le Clay. Linc 4F 95
Holton le Moor. Linc 1H 87
Holton St Mary. Suff 2D 54
Holt Pound. Hants 2G 25
Holtsmere End. Herts 4A 52
Holtye. E Sus 2F 27
Holwell. Dors 1C 14
Holwell. Herts 2B 52
Holwell. Leics 3E 75
Holwell. Oxon 5H 49
Holwell. Som 2C 22
Holwick. Dur 2C 104
Holworth. Dors 4C 14
Holybourne. Hants 2F 25
Holy City. Devn 2G 13
Holy Cross. Worc 3D 60
Holyfield. Essx 5D 53
Holyhead. IOA 2B 80
Holy Island. Nmbd 5H 131
Holymoorside. Derbs 4H 85
Holyport. Wind 4G 37
Holystone. Nmbd 4D 120
Holytown. N Lan 3A 128
Holywell. Cambs 3C 64
Holywell. Dors 2A 14
Holywell. Flin 3D 82
Holywell. Glos 2C 34
Holywell. Nmbd 2G 115
Holywell. Warw 4F 61
Holywell Bay. Corn 3B 6
Holywell Green. W Yor 3A 92
Holywell Lake. Som 4E 20
Holywell Row. Suff 3G 65
Holywood. Dum 1G 111
Holywood. N Dwn 2J 179
Homer. Shrp 5A 72
Homer Green. Mers 4B 90
Homersfield. Suff 2E 67
Hom Green. Here 3A 48
Homington. Wilts 4G 23
Honeyborough. Pemb 4D 42
Honeybourne. Worc 1G 49
Honeychurch. Devn 2G 11
Honeydon. Bed 5A 64
Honey Hill. Kent 4F 41
Honey Street. Wilts 5G 35
Honey Tye. Suff 2C 54
Honeywick. C Beds 3H 51
Honiley. Warw 3G 61
Honing. Norf 3F 79
Honingham. Norf 4D 78
Honington. Linc 1G 75
Honington. Suff 3B 66
Honington. Warw 1A 50
Honiton. Devn 2E 13
Honley. W Yor 3B 92
Honnington. Telf 4B 72
Hoo. Suff 5E 67
Hoobrook. Worc 3C 60
Hood Green. S Yor 4D 92
Hooe. E Sus 5A 28
Hooe. Plym 3B 8
Hooe Common. E Sus 4A 28
Hoohill. Bkpl 1B 90
Hook. Cambs 1D 64
Hook. E Yor 2A 94
Hook. G Lon 4C 38
Hook. Hants 1F 25
(nr. Basingstoke)
Hook. Hants 2D 16
(nr. Fareham)
Hook. Pemb 3D 43
Hook. Wilts 3F 35
Hook-a-Gate. Shrp 5G 71
Hook Bank. Worc 1D 48
Hooke. Dors 2A 14
Hooker Gate. Tyne 4E 115
Hookgate. Staf 2B 72
Hook Green. Kent 2A 28
(nr. Lamberhurst)
Hook Green. Kent 3H 39
(nr. Longfield)
Hook Green. Kent 4H 39
(nr. Meopham)
Hook Norton. Oxon 2B 50
Hook's Cross. Herts 3C 52
Hook Street. Glos 2B 34
Hookway. Devn 3B 12
Hookwood. Surr 1D 26
Hoole. Ches W 4G 83
Hooley. Surr 5D 39
Hooley Bridge. G Man 3G 91
Hooley Brow. G Man 3G 91
Hoo St Werburgh. Medw 3B 40
Hooton. Ches W 3F 83
Hooton Levitt. S Yor 1C 86
Hooton Pagnell. S Yor 4E 93
Hooton Roberts. S Yor 1B 86
Hoove. Shet 7E 173
Hope. Derbs 2F 85
Hope. Flin 5F 83
Hope. High 2E 167
Hope. Powy 5E 71
Hope. Shrp 5F 71
Hope. Staf 5F 85
Hope Bagot. Shrp 3H 59
Hope Bowdler. Shrp 1G 59
Hopedale. Staf 5F 85
Hope Green. Ches E 2D 84
Hopeman. Mor 2F 159
Hope Mansell. Here 4B 48
Hopesay. Shrp 2F 59
Hopes Green. Essx 2B 40
Hopetown. W Yor 2D 93
Hope under Dinmore.
Here 5H 59
Hopley's Green. Here 5F 59
Hopperton. N Yor 4G 99
Hop Pole. Linc 4A 76
Hopstone. Shrp 1B 60
Hopton. Derbs 5G 85
Hopton. Powy 1E 59
Hopton. Shrp 3F 71
(nr. Oswestry)
Hopton. Shrp 3H 71
(nr. Wem)
Hopton. Staf 3D 72
Hopton. Suff 3B 66
Hopton Cangeford. Shrp 2H 59
Hopton Castle. Shrp 3F 59
Hoptonheath. Shrp 3F 59
Hopton Heath. Staf 3D 72
Hopton on Sea. Norf 5H 79
Hopton Wafers. Shrp 3A 60
Hopwas. Staf 5F 73
Hopwood. Worc 3E 61
Horam. E Sus 4G 27
Horbling. Linc 2A 76
Horbury. W Yor 3C 92
Horcott. Glos 5G 49
Horden. Dur 5H 115
Horderley. Shrp 2G 59
Hordle. Hants 3A 16
Hordley. Shrp 2F 71
Horeb. Carm 3F 45
(nr. Brechfa)
Horeb. Carm 5E 45
(nr. Llanelli)
Horeb. Cdgn 1D 45
Horfield. Bris 4B 34
Horgabost. W Isl 8C 171
Horham. Suff 3E 66
Horkesley Heath. Essx 3C 54
Horkstow. N Lin 3C 94
Horley. Oxon 1C 50
Horley. Surr 1D 27
Horn Ash. Dors 2G 13
Hornblotton Green. Som 3A 22
Hornby. Lanc 3E 97
Hornby. N Yor 4A 106
(nr. Appleton Wiske)
Hornby. N Yor 5F 105
(nr. Catterick Garrison)
Horncastle. Linc 4B 88
Hornchurch. G Lon 2G 39
Horncliffe. Nmbd 5F 131
Horndean. Hants 1E 17
Horndean. Bord 5E 131
Horndon. Devn 4F 11
Horndon on the Hill. Thur 2A 40
Horne. Surr 1E 27
Horner. Som 2C 20
Horning. Norf 4F 79
Horninghold. Leics 1F 63
Horninglow. Staf 3G 73
Horningsea. Cambs 4D 65
Horningsham. Wilts 2D 22
Horningtoft. Norf 3B 78
Hornsbury. Som 1G 13
Hornsby. Cumb 4G 113
Hornsbygate. Cumb 4G 113
Horns Corner. Kent 3B 28
Horns Cross. Devn 4D 19
Hornsea. E Yor 5G 101
Hornsea Burton. E Yor 5G 101
Hornsey. G Lon 2E 39
Hornton. Oxon 1B 50
Horpit. Swin 3H 35
Horrabridge. Devn 2B 8
Horringer. Suff 4H 65
Horringford. IOW 4D 16
Horrocks Fold. G Man 3F 91
Horrocksford. Lanc 5G 97
Horsbrugh Ford. Bord 1E 119
Horsebridge. Devn 5E 11
Horsebridge. E Sus 4G 27
Horsebridge. Hants 3B 24
Horse Bridge. Staf 5D 84
Horsebrook. Staf 4C 72
Horsecastle. N Som 5H 33
Horsehay. Telf 5A 72
Horseheath. Cambs 1G 53
Horsehouse. N Yor 1C 98
Horsell. Surr 5A 38
Horseman's Green. Wrex 1G 71
Horsenden. Buck 5F 51
Horseway. Cambs 2D 64
Horsey. Norf 3G 79
Horsey. Som 3G 21
Horsford. Norf 4D 78
Horsforth. W Yor 1C 92
Horsham. W Sus 2C 26
Horsham. Worc 5B 60
Horsham St Faith. Norf 4E 78
Horsington. Linc 4A 88
Horsington. Som 4C 22
Horsley. Derbs 1A 74
Horsley. Glos 2D 34
Horsley. Nmbd 3D 115
(nr. Prudhoe)
Horsley. Nmbd 5C 120
(nr. Rochester)
Horsley Cross. Essx 3E 54
Horsleycross Street. Essx 3E 54
Horsleyhill. Bord 3H 119
Horsleyhope. Dur 5D 114
Horsley Woodhouse.
Derbs 1A 74
Horsmonden. Kent 1A 28
Horspath. Oxon 5D 50
Horstead. Norf 4E 79
Horsted Keynes. W Sus 3E 27
Horton. Buck 4H 51
Horton. Dors 2F 15
Horton. Lanc 4A 98
Horton. Nptn 5F 63
Horton. Shrp 2G 71
Horton. S Glo 3C 34
Horton. Som 1G 13
Horton. Staf 5D 84
Horton. Swan 4D 30
Horton. Wilts 5F 35
Horton. Wind 3B 38
Horton Cross. Som 1G 13
Horton-cum-Studley.
Oxon 4D 50
Horton Grange. Nmbd 2F 115
Horton Green. Ches W 1G 71
Horton Heath. Hants 1C 16
Horton in Ribblesdale.
N Yor 2H 97
Horton Kirby. Kent 4G 39
Hortonwood. Telf 4A 72
Horwich. G Man 3E 91
Horwich End. Derbs 2E 85
Horwood. Devn 4F 19
Hoscar. Lanc 3C 90
Hose. Leics 3E 75
Hosh. Per 1A 136
Hosta. W Isl 1C 170
Hoswick. Shet 9F 173
Hotham. E Yor 1B 94
Hothfield. Kent 1D 28
Hoton. Leics 3C 74
Houbie. Shet 2H 173
Hough. Arg 4A 138
Hough. Ches E 5B 84
(nr. Crewe)
Hough. Ches E 3C 84
(nr. Wilmslow)
Hougham. Linc 1F 75
Hough Green. Hal 2G 83
Hough-on-the-Hill. Linc 1G 75
Houghton. Cambs 3B 64
Houghton. Cumb 4F 113
Houghton. Hants 3B 24
Houghton. Nmbd 3E 115
Houghton. Pemb 4D 43
Houghton. W Sus 4B 26
Houghton Bank. Darl 2F 105
Houghton Conquest.
C Beds 1A 52
Houghton Green. E Sus 3D 28
Houghton-le-Side. Darl 2F 105
Houghton-le-Spring.
Tyne 5G 115
Houghton on the Hill.
Leics 5D 74
Houghton Regis. C Beds 3A 52
Houghton St Giles. Norf 2B 78
Houlland. Shet 6E 173
(on Mainland)
Houlland. Shet 4G 173
(on Yell)
Houlsyke. N Yor 4E 107
Hound. Hants 2C 16
Hound Green. Hants 1F 25
Houndslow. Bord 5C 130
Houndsmoor. Som 4E 21
Houndwood. Bord 3E 131
Hounsdown. Hants 1B 16
Hounslow. G Lon 3C 38
Housabister. Shet 6F 173
Housay. Shet 4H 173
Househill. High 3C 158
Housetter. Shet 3E 173
Houss. Shet 8E 173
Houston. Ren 3F 127
Housty. High 5D 168
Houton. Orkn 7C 172
Hove. Brig 5D 27 & 192
Hoveringham. Notts 1E 74
Hoveton. Norf 4F 79
Hovingham. N Yor 2A 100
How. Cumb 4G 113
How Caple. Here 2B 48
Howden. E Yor 2H 93
Howden-le-Wear. Dur 1E 105
Howe. High 2F 169
Howe. Norf 5E 79
Howe. N Yor 1F 99
Howe Green. Essx 5H 53
(nr. Chelmsford)
Howegreen. Essx 5B 54
(nr. Maldon)
Howe Green. Warw 2H 61
Howell. Linc 1A 76
How End. C Beds 1A 52
Howe of Teuchar. Abers 4E 161
Howes. Dum 3C 112
Howe Street. Essx 4G 53
(nr. Chelmsford)
Howe Street. Essx 2G 53
(nr. Finchingfield)
Howe, The. Cumb 1D 96
Howe, The. IOM 5A 108
Howey. Powy 5C 58
Howgate. Midl 4F 129
Howgill. Lanc 5H 97
Howgill. N Yor 4C 98
How Green. Kent 1F 27
How Hill. Norf 4F 79
Howick. Nmbd 3G 121
Howle. Telf 3A 72
Howle Hill. Here 3B 48
Howleigh. Som 1F 13
Howlett End. Essx 2F 53
Howley. Som 2F 13
Howley. Warr 2A 84
Hownam. Bord 3B 120
Howsham. N Lin 4D 94
Howsham. N Yor 3B 100
Howtel. Nmbd 1C 120
Howt Green. Kent 4C 40
Howton. Here 3H 47
Howwood. Ren 3E 127
Hoxne. Suff 3D 66
Hoylake. Mers 2E 82
Hoyland. S Yor 4D 92
Hoylandswaine. S Yor 4C 92
Hoyle. W Sus 4A 26
Hubberholme. N Yor 2B 98
Hubberston. Pemb 4C 42
Hubbert's Bridge. Linc 1B 76
Huby. N Yor 5E 99
(nr. Harrogate)
Huby. N Yor 3H 99
(nr. York)
Hucclecote. Glos 4D 48
Hucking. Kent 5C 40
Hucknall. Notts 1C 74
Huddersfield. W Yor 3B 92
Huddington. Worc 5D 60
Huddlesford. Staf 5F 73
Hudswell. N Yor 4E 105
Huggate. E Yor 4C 100
Hugglescote. Leics 4B 74
Hughenden Valley. Buck 2G 37
Hughley. Shrp 1H 59
Hughton. High 4G 157
Hugh Town. IOS 1B 4
Hugus. Corn 4B 6
Huish. Devn 1F 11
Huish. Wilts 5G 35
Huish Champflower. Som 4D 20
Huish Episcopi. Som 4H 21
Huisinis. W Isl 6B 171
Hulcote. Nptn 5E 62
Hulcott. Buck 4G 51
Hulham. Devn 4D 12
Hull. Hull 2D 94 & 196
Hulland. Derbs 1G 73
Hulland Moss. Derbs 1G 73
Hulland Ward. Derbs 1G 73
Hullavington. Wilts 3D 35
Hullbridge. Essx 1C 40
Hulme. G Man 1C 84
Hulme. Staf 1D 72
Hulme End. Staf 5F 85
Hulme Walfield. Ches E 4C 84
Hulverstone. IOW 4B 16
Hulver Street. Suff 2G 67
Humber. Devn 5C 12
Humber. Here 5H 59
Humber Bridge. N Lin 2D 94
Humberside International Airport.
N Lin 3D 94
Humberston. NE Lin 4G 95
Humberstone. Leic 5D 74
Humbie. E Lot 3A 130
Humbleton. E Yor 1F 95
Humbleton. Nmbd 2D 121
Humby. Linc 2H 75
Hume. Bord 5D 130
Humshaugh. Nmbd 2C 114
Huna. High 1F 169
Huncoat. Lanc 1F 91
Huncote. Leics 1C 62
Hundall. Derbs 3A 86
Hunderthwaite. Dur 2C 104
Hundleby. Linc 4C 88
Hundle Houses. Linc 5B 88
Hundleton. Pemb 4D 42
Hundon. Suff 1H 53
Hundred Acres. Hants 1D 16
Hundred House. Powy 5D 58
Hundred, The. Here 4H 59
Hungarton. Leics 5D 74
Hungerford. Hants 1G 15
Hungerford. Shrp 2H 59
Hungerford. Som 2D 20
Hungerford. W Ber 5B 36
Hungerford Newtown.
W Ber 4B 36
Hunger Hill. G Man 4E 91
Hungerton. Linc 2F 75
Hungladder. High 1C 154
Hungryhatton. Shrp 3A 72
Hunmanby. N Yor 2E 101
Hunmanby Sands. N Yor 2F 101
Hunningham. Warw 4A 62
Hunnington. Worc 2D 60
Hunny Hill. IOW 4C 16
Hunsdon. Herts 4E 53
Hunsdonbury. Herts 4E 53
Hunsingore. N Yor 4G 99
Hunslet. W Yor 1D 92
Hunslet Carr. W Yor 2D 92
Hunsonby. Cumb 1G 103
Hunspow. High 1E 169
Hunstanton. Norf 1F 77
Hunstanworth. Dur 5C 114
Hunston. Suff 4B 66
Hunston. W Sus 2G 17
Hunstrete. Bath 5B 34
Hunt End. Worc 4E 61
Hunterfield. Midl 3G 129
Hunters Forstal. Kent 4F 41
Hunter's Quay. Arg 2C 126
Huntham. Som 4G 21
Hunthill Lodge. Ang 1D 144
Huntingdon. Cambs 3B 64
Huntingfield. Suff 3F 67
Huntingford. Wilts 3D 22
Huntington. Ches W 4G 83
Huntington. E Lot 2A 130
Huntington. Here 5E 59
Huntington. Staf 4D 72
Huntington. Telf 5A 72
Huntington. York 4A 100
Huntingtower. Per 1C 136
Huntley. Glos 4C 48
Huntley. Staf 1E 73
Huntly. Abers 4C 160
Huntlywood. Bord 5C 130
Hunton. Hants 3C 24
Hunton. Kent 1B 28
Hunton. N Yor 5E 105
Hunton Bridge. Herts 5A 52
Hunt's Corner. Norf 2C 66
Huntscott. Som 2C 20
Hunt's Cross. Mers 2G 83
Hunts Green. Warw 1F 61
Huntsham. Devn 4D 20
Huntshaw. Devn 4F 19
Huntspill. Som 2G 21
Huntstile. Som 3F 21
Huntstrete. Bath 5B 34
Huntworth. Som 3G 21
Hunwick. Dur 1E 105
Hunworth. Norf 2C 78
Hurcott. Som 1G 13
(nr. Ilminster)
Hurcott. Som 4A 22
(nr. Somerton)
Hurdcott. Wilts 3G 23
Hurdley. Powy 1E 59
Hurdsfield. Ches E 3D 84
Hurlet. Glas 3G 127
Hurley. Warw 1G 61
Hurley. Wind 3G 37
Hurlford. E Ayr 1D 116
Hurliness. Orkn 9B 172
Hurlston Green. Lanc 3B 90
Hurn. Dors 3G 15
Hursey. Dors 2H 13
Hursley. Hants 4C 24
Hurst. G Man 4H 91
Hurst. N Yor 4D 104
Hurst. Som 1H 13
Hurst. Wok 4F 37
Hurstbourne Priors.
Hants 2C 24
Hurstbourne Tarrant.
Hants 1B 24
Hurst Green. Ches E 1H 71
Hurst Green. E Sus 3B 28
Hurst Green. Essx 4D 54
Hurst Green. Lanc 1E 91
Hurst Green. Surr 5E 39
Hurstley. Here 1G 47
Hurstpierpoint. W Sus 4D 27
Hurstway Common. Here 1F 47
Hurst Wickham. W Sus 4D 27
Hurstwood. Lanc 1G 91
Hurtmore. Surr 1A 26
Hurworth-on-Tees. Darl 3A 106
Hurworth Place. Darl 3F 105
Hury. Dur 3C 104
Husbands Bosworth.
Leics 2D 62
Husborne Crawley.
C Beds 2H 51
Husthwaite. N Yor 2H 99
Hutcherleigh. Devn 3D 9
Hut Green. N Yor 2F 93
Huthwaite. Notts 5B 86
Huttoft. Linc 3E 89
Hutton. Cumb 2F 103
Hutton. E Yor 4E 101
Hutton. Essx 1H 39
Hutton. Lanc 2C 90
Hutton. N Som 1G 21
Hutton. Bord 4F 131
Hutton Bonville. N Yor 4A 106
Hutton Buscel. N Yor 1D 100
Hutton Conyers. N Yor 2F 99
Hutton Cranswick. E Yor 4E 101
Hutton End. Cumb 1F 103
Hutton Gate. Red C 3C 106
Hutton Henry. Dur 1B 106
Hutton-le-Hole. N Yor 5E 107
Hutton Magna. Dur 3E 105
Hutton Mulgrave. N Yor 4F 107
Hutton Roof. Cumb 2E 97
(nr. Kirkby Lonsdale)
Hutton Roof. Cumb 1E 103
(nr. Penrith)
Hutton Rudby. N Yor 4B 106
Huttons Ambo. N Yor 3B 100
Hutton Sessay. N Yor 2G 99
Hutton Village. Red C 3D 106
Hutton Wandesley. N Yor 4H 99
Huxham. Devn 3C 12
Huxham Green. Som 3A 22
Huxley. Ches W 4H 83
Huxter. Shet 6C 173
(on Mainland)
Huxter. Shet 5G 173
(on Whalsay)
Huyton. Mers 1G 83
Hwlffordd. Pemb 3D 42
Hycemoor. Cumb 1A 96
Hyde. Glos 5D 49
(nr. Stroud)
Hyde. Glos 3F 49
(nr. Winchcombe)
Hyde. G Man 1D 84
Hyde Heath. Buck 5H 51
Hyde Lea. Staf 3D 72
Hyde Park. S Yor 4F 93
Hydestile. Surr 1A 26
Hyndford Bridge. S Lan 5C 128
Hynish. Arg 5A 138
Hyssington. Powy 1F 59
Hythe. Hants 2C 16
Hythe. Kent 2F 29
Hythe End. Wind 3B 38
Hythie. Abers 3H 161
Hyton. Cumb 1A 96

I

Ianstown. Mor 2B 160
Iarsiadar. W Isl 4D 171
Ibberton. Dors 2C 14
Ible. Derbs 5G 85
Ibrox. Glas 3G 127
Ibsley. Hants 2G 15
Ibstock. Leics 4B 74
Ibstone. Buck 2F 37
Ibthorpe. Hants 1B 24
Iburndale. N Yor 4F 107
Ibworth. Hants 1D 24
Icelton. N Som 5G 33
Ichrachan. Arg 5E 141
Ickburgh. Norf 1H 65
Ickenham. G Lon 2B 38
Ickenthwaite. Cumb 1C 96
Ickford. Buck 5E 51
Ickham. Kent 5G 41
Ickleford. Herts 2B 52
Icklesham. E Sus 4C 28
Ickleton. Cambs 1E 53
Icklingham. Suff 3G 65
Ickwell. C Beds 1B 52
Icomb. Glos 3H 49
Idbury. Oxon 3H 49
Iddesleigh. Devn 2F 11
Ide. Devn 3B 12
Ideford. Devn 5B 12
Ide Hill. Kent 5F 39
Iden. E Sus 3D 28
Iden Green. Kent 2C 28
(nr. Benenden)
Iden Green. Kent 2B 28
(nr. Goudhurst)
Idle. W Yor 1B 92
Idless. Corn 4C 6
Idlicote. Warw 1A 50
Idmiston. Wilts 3G 23
Idole. Carm 4E 45
Idridgehay. Derbs 1G 73
Idrigill. High 2C 154
Idstone. Oxon 3A 36
Iffley. Oxon 5D 50
Ifield. W Sus 2D 26
Ifieldwood. W Sus 2D 26
Ifold. W Sus 2B 26
Iford. E Sus 5F 27
Ifton Heath. Shrp 2F 71
Ightfield. Shrp 2H 71
Ightham. Kent 5G 39
Iken. Suff 5G 67
Ilam. Staf 5F 85
Ilchester. Som 4A 22
Ilderton. Nmbd 2E 121
Ilford. G Lon 2F 39
Ilford. Som 1G 13
Ilfracombe. Devn 2F 19
Ilkeston. Derbs 1B 74
Ilketshall St Andrew. Suff 2F 67
Ilketshall St Lawrence.
Suff 2F 67
Ilketshall St Margaret.
Suff 2F 67
Ilkley. W Yor 5D 98
Illand. Corn 5C 10
Illey. W Mid 2D 61
Illidge Green. Ches E 4B 84
Illington. Norf 2B 66
Illingworth. W Yor 2A 92
Illogan. Corn 4A 6
Illogan Highway. Corn 4A 6
Illston on the Hill. Leics 1E 62
Ilmer. Buck 5F 51
Ilmington. Warw 1H 49
Ilminster. Som 1G 13
Ilsington. Devn 5A 12
Ilsington. Dors 3C 14
Ilston. Swan 3E 31
Ilton. N Yor 2D 98
Ilton. Som 1G 13
Imachar. N Ayr 5G 125
Imber. Wilts 2E 23
Immingham. NE Lin 3E 95
Immingham Dock. NE Lin 3E 95
Impington. Cambs 4D 64
Ince. Ches W 3G 83
Ince Blundell. Mers 4B 90
Ince-in-Makerfield.
G Man 4D 90
Inchbae Lodge. High 2G 157
Inchbare. Ang 2F 145
Inchberry. Mor 3H 159
Inchbraoch. Ang 3G 145
Inchbrook. Glos 5D 48
Incheril. High 2C 156
Inchinnan. Ren 3F 127
Inchlaggan. High 3D 148
Inchmichael. Per 1E 137
Inchnadamph. High 1G 163
Inchree. High 2E 141
Inchture. Per 1E 137
Inchyra. Per 1D 136
Indian Queens. Corn 3D 6
Ingatestone. Essx 1H 39
Ingbirchworth. S Yor 4C 92
Ingestre. Staf 3D 73
Ingham. Linc 2G 87
Ingham. Norf 3F 79
Ingham. Suff 3A 66
Ingham Corner. Norf 3F 79
Ingleborough. Norf 4D 76
Ingleby. Derbs 3H 73
Ingleby Arncliffe. N Yor 4B 106
Ingleby Barwick. Stoc T 3B 106
Ingleby Greenhow.
N Yor 4C 106
Ingleigh Green. Devn 2G 11
Inglemire. Hull 1D 94
Inglesbatch. Bath 5C 34
Ingleton. Dur 2E 105
Ingleton. N Yor 2F 97
Inglewhite. Lanc 5E 97
Ingoe. Nmbd 2D 114
Ingol. Lanc 1D 90
Ingoldisthorpe. Norf 2F 77
Ingoldmells. Linc 4E 89
Ingoldsby. Linc 2H 75
Ingon. Warw 5G 61
Ingram. Nmbd 3E 121
Ingrave. Essx 1H 39
Ingrow. W Yor 1A 92
Ings. Cumb 5F 103
Ingst. S Glo 3A 34
Ingthorpe. Rut 5G 75
Ingworth. Norf 3D 78
Inishrush. Mag 6F 174
Inkberrow. Worc 5E 61
Inkford. Worc 3E 61
Inkpen. W Ber 5B 36
Inkstack. High 1E 169
Innellan. Arg 3C 126
Inner Hope. Devn 5C 8
Innerleith. Fife 2E 137
Innerleithen. Bord 1F 119
Innerleven. Fife 3F 137
Innermessan. Dum 3F 109
Innerwick. E Lot 2D 130
Innerwick. Per 4C 142
Innsworth. Glos 3D 48
Insch. Abers 1D 152
Insh. High 3C 150
Inshegra. High 3C 166
Inshore. High 1D 166
Inskip. Lanc 1C 90
Instow. Devn 3E 19
Intwood. Norf 5D 78
Inver. Abers 4G 151
Inver. High 5F 165
Inver. Per 4H 143
Inverailort. High 5F 147
Inveralligin. High 3H 155
Inverallochy. Abers 2H 161
Inveramsay. Abers 1E 153
Inveran. High 4C 164
Inveraray. Arg 3H 133
Inverarish. High 5E 155
Inverarity. Ang 4D 144
Inverarnan. Arg 2C 134
Inverarnie. High 5A 158
Inverbeg. Arg 4C 134
Inverbervie. Abers 1H 145
Inverboyndie. Abers 2D 160
Invercassley. High 3B 164
Invercharnan. High 4F 141
Inverchoran. High 3E 157
Invercreran. Arg 4E 141
Inverdruie. High 2D 150
Inverebrie. Abers 5G 161
Invereck. Arg 1C 126
Inveresk. E Lot 2G 129
Inveresragan. Arg 5D 141
Inverey. Abers 5E 151
Inverfarigaig. High 1H 149
Invergarry. High 3F 149
Invergeldie. Per 1G 135
Invergordon. High 2B 158
Invergowrie. Per 5C 144
Inverguseran. High 3F 147
Inverharroch. Mor 5A 160
Inverie. High 3F 147
Inverinan. Arg 2G 133
Inverinate. High 1B 148
Inverkeilor. Ang 4F 145
Inverkeithing. Fife 1E 129
Inverkeithny. Abers 4D 160
Inverkip. Inv 2D 126
Inverkirkaig. High 2E 163
Inverlael. High 5F 163
Inverliever Lodge. Arg 3F 133
Inverliver. Arg 5E 141
Inverloch. High 1F 141
Inverlochlarig. Stir 2D 134
Inverlussa. Arg 1E 125
Inver Mallie. High 5D 148
Invermarkie. Abers 5B 160
Invermoriston. High 2G 149
Invernaver. High 2H 167
Inverneil House. Arg 1G 125
Inverness. High 4A 158 & 196
Inverness Airport. High 3B 158
Invernettie. Abers 4H 161
Inverpolly Lodge. High 2E 163
Inverquhomery. Abers 4H 161
Inverroy. High 5E 149
Inversanda. High 3D 140
Invershiel. High 2B 148
Invershin. High 4C 164
Invershore. High 5E 169
Inversnaid. Stir 3C 134
Inverugie. Abers 4H 161
Inveruglas. Arg 3C 134
Inverurie. Abers 1E 153
Invervar. Per 4D 142
Inverythan. Abers 4E 161
Inwardleigh. Devn 3F 11
Inworth. Essx 4B 54
Iochdar. W Isl 4C 170
Iping. W Sus 4G 25
Ipplepen. Devn 2E 9
Ipsden. Oxon 3E 37
Ipstones. Staf 1E 73
Ipswich. Suff 1E 55 & 196
Irby. Mers 2E 83
Irby in the Marsh. Linc 4D 88
Irby upon Humber.
NE Lin 4E 95
Irchester. Nptn 4G 63
Ireby. Cumb 1D 102
Ireby. Lanc 2F 97
Ireland. Shet 9E 173
Ireleth. Cumb 2B 96
Ireshopeburn. Dur 1B 104
Ireton Wood. Derbs 1G 73
Irlam. G Man 1B 84
Irnham. Linc 3H 75
Iron Acton. S Glo 3B 34
Iron Bridge. Cambs 1D 65
Ironbridge. Telf 5A 72
Iron Cross. Warw 5E 61
Ironville. Derbs 5B 86
Irstead. Norf 3F 79
Irthington. Cumb 3F 113
Irthlingborough. Nptn 3G 63
Irton. N Yor 1E 101
Irvine. N Ayr 1C 116
Irvine Mains. N Ayr 1C 116
Irvinestown. Ferm 7E 176
Isabella Pit. Nmbd 1G 115
Isauld. High 2B 168
Isbister. Orkn 6C 172
Isbister. Shet 2E 173
(on Mainland)
Isbister. Shet 5G 173
(on Whalsay)
Isfield. E Sus 4F 27
Isham. Nptn 3F 63
Island Carr. N Lin 4C 94
Islay Airport. Arg 4B 124
Isle Abbotts. Som 4G 21
Isle Brewers. Som 4G 21
Isleham. Cambs 3F 65
Isle of Man Airport. IOM 5B 108
Isle of Thanet. Kent 4H 41
Isle of Whithorn. Dum 5B 110
Isleornsay. High 2F 147
Islesburgh. Shet 5E 173
Isles of Scilly (St Mary's) Airport.
IOS 1B 4
Islesteps. Dum 2A 112
Isleworth. G Lon 3C 38
Isley Walton. Leics 3B 74
Islibhig. W Isl 5B 171
Islington. G Lon 2E 39
Islington. Telf 3B 72
Islip. Nptn 3G 63
Islip. Oxon 4D 50
Islwyn. Cphy 2F 33
Isombridge. Telf 4A 72
Istead Rise. Kent 4H 39
Itchen. Sotn 1C 16
Itchen Abbas. Hants 3D 24
Itchen Stoke. Hants 3D 24
Itchingfield. W Sus 3C 26
Itchington. S Glo 3B 34
Itlaw. Abers 3D 160
Itteringham. Norf 2D 78
Itteringham Common.
Norf 3D 78
Itton. Devn 3G 11
Itton Common. Mon 2H 33
Ivegill. Cumb 5F 113
Ivelet. N Yor 5C 104
Iverchaolain. Arg 2B 126
Iver Heath. Buck 2B 38
Iveston. Dur 4E 115
Ivetsey Bank. Staf 4C 72
Ivinghoe. Buck 4H 51
Ivinghoe Aston. Buck 4H 51
Ivington. Here 5G 59
Ivington Green. Here 5G 59
Ivybridge. Devn 3C 8
Ivychurch. Kent 3E 29
Ivy Hatch. Kent 5G 39
Ivy Todd. Norf 5A 78
Iwade. Kent 4D 40
Iwerne Courtney. Dors 1D 14
Iwerne Minster. Dors 1D 14
Ixworth. Suff 3B 66
Ixworth Thorpe. Suff 3B 66

J

Jackfield. Shrp 5A 72
Jack Hill. N Yor 4E 98
Jacksdale. Notts 5B 86
Jackton. S Lan 4G 127
Jacobstow. Corn 3B 10
Jacobstowe. Devn 2F 11
Jacobswell. Surr 5A 38
Jameston. Pemb 5E 43
Jamestown. Dum 5F 119
Jamestown. Fife 1E 129
Jamestown. High 3G 157
Jamestown. W Dun 1E 127
Janetstown. High 2C 168
(nr. Thurso)
Janetstown. High 3F 169
(nr. Wick)
Jarrow. Tyne 3G 115
Jarvis Brook. E Sus 3G 27
Jasper's Green. Essx 3H 53
Jaywick. Essx 4E 55
Jedburgh. Bord 2A 120
Jeffreyston. Pemb 4E 43
Jemimaville. High 2B 158
Jenkins Park. High 3F 149
Jersey Marine. Neat 3G 31
Jesmond. Tyne 3F 115
Jevington. E Sus 5G 27
Jingle Street. Mon 4H 47
Jockey End. Herts 4A 52
Jodrell Bank. Ches E 3B 84
Johnby. Cumb 1F 103
John o' Gaunts. W Yor 2D 92
John o' Groats. High 1F 169
John's Cross. E Sus 3B 28
Johnshaven. Abers 2G 145
Johnson Street. Norf 4F 79
Johnston. Pemb 3D 42
Johnstone. Ren 3F 127
Johnstonebridge. Dum 5C 118
Johnstown. Carm 4D 45
Johnstown. Wrex 1F 71
Jonesborough. New M 8E 178
Joppa. Edin 2G 129
Joppa. S Ayr 3D 116
Jordan Green. Norf 3C 78
Jordans. Buck 1A 38
Jordanston. Pemb 1D 42
Jump. S Yor 4D 93
Jumpers Common. Dors 3G 15
Juniper. Nmbd 4C 114
Juniper Green. Edin 3E 129
Jurby East. IOM 2C 108
Jurby West. IOM 2C 108
Jury's Gap. E Sus 4D 28

K

Kaber. Cumb 3A 104
Kaimend. S Lan 5C 128
Kaimes. Edin 3F 129
Kaimrig End. Bord 5D 129
Kames. Arg 2A 126
Kames. E Ayr 2F 117
Katesbridge. Ban 5G 179
Kea. Corn 4C 6
Keadby. N Lin 3B 94
Keady. Arm 6C 178
Keal Cotes. Linc 4C 88
Kearsley. G Man 4F 91
Kearsney. Kent 1G 29
Kearstwick. Cumb 1F 97
Kearton. N Yor 5C 104
Kearvaig. High 1C 166
Keasden. N Yor 3G 97
Keason. Corn 2H 7
Keckwick. Hal 2H 83
Keddington. Linc 2C 88
Keddington Corner. Linc 2C 88
Kedington. Suff 1H 53
Kedleston. Derbs 1H 73
Kedlock Feus. Fife 2F 137
Keelby. Linc 3E 95
Keele. Staf 1C 72
Keeley Green. Bed 1A 52
Keeston. Pemb 3D 42
Keevil. Wilts 1E 23
Kegworth. Leics 3B 74
Kehelland. Corn 2D 4
Keig. Abers 2D 152
Keighley. W Yor 5C 98
Keilarsbrae. Clac 4A 136
Keillmore. Arg 1E 125
Keillor. Per 4B 144
Keillour. Per 1B 136
Keills. Arg 3C 124
Keiloch. Abers 4F 151
Keils. Arg 3D 124
Keinton Mandeville. Som 3A 22
Keir Mill. Dum 5A 118
Keirsleywell Row. Nmbd 4A 114
Keisby. Linc 3H 75
Keisley. Cumb 2A 104
Keiss. High 2F 169
Keith. Mor 3B 160
Keith Inch. Abers 4H 161
Kelbrook. Lanc 5B 98
Kelby. Linc 1H 75
Keld. Cumb 3G 103
Keld. N Yor 4B 104
Keldholme. N Yor 1B 100
Kelfield. N Lin 4B 94
Kelfield. N Yor 1F 93
Kelham. Notts 5E 87
Kellacott. Devn 4E 11
Kellan. Arg 4G 139
Kellas. Ang 5D 144
Kellas. Mor 3F 159
Kellaton. Devn 5E 9
Kelleth. Cumb 4H 103
Kelling. Norf 1C 78
Kellingley. N Yor 2F 93
Kellington. N Yor 2F 93
Kelloe. Dur 1A 106
Kelloholm. Dum 3G 117
Kells. Bmna 7H 175
Kells. Cumb 3A 102
Kelly. Devn 4D 11
Kelly Bray. Corn 5D 10
Kelmarsh. Nptn 3E 63
Kelmscott. Oxon 2A 36
Kelsale. Suff 4F 67
Kelsall. Ches W 4H 83
Kelshall. Herts 2D 52
Kelsick. Cumb 4C 112
Kelso. Bord 1B 120
Kelstedge. Derbs 4H 85
Kelstern. Linc 1B 88
Kelsterton. Flin 3E 83
Kelston. Bath 5C 34
Keltneyburn. Per 4E 143
Kelton. Dum 2A 112
Kelton Hill. Dum 4E 111
Kelty. Fife 4D 136
Kelvedon. Essx 4B 54
Kelvedon Hatch. Essx 1G 39
Kelvinside. Glas 3G 127
Kelynack. Corn 3A 4
Kemback. Fife 2G 137
Kemberton. Shrp 5B 72
Kemble. Glos 2E 35
Kemerton. Worc 2E 49
Kemeys Commander.
Mon 5G 47
Kemnay. Abers 2E 153
Kempe's Corner. Kent 1E 29
Kempley. Glos 3B 48
Kempley Green. Glos 3B 48
Kempsey. Worc 1D 48
Kempsford. Glos 2G 35
Kemps Green. Warw 3F 61
Kempshott. Hants 1E 24
Kempston. Bed 1A 52
Kempston Hardwick. Bed 1A 52
Kempton. Shrp 2F 59
Kemp Town. Brig 5E 27
Kemsing. Kent 5G 39
Kemsley. Kent 4D 40
Kenardington. Kent 2D 28
Kenchester. Here 1H 47
Kencot. Oxon 5A 50
Kendal. Cumb 5G 103
Kendleshire. S Glo 4B 34
Kendray. S Yor 4D 92
Kenfig. B'end 3B 32
Kenfig Hill. B'end 3B 32
Kengharair. Arg 4F 139
Kenilworth. Warw 3G 61
Kenknock. Stir 5B 142
Kenley. G Lon 5E 39
Kenley. Shrp 5H 71
Kenmore. High 3G 155
Kenmore. Per 4E 143
Kenn. Devn 4C 12
Kenn. N Som 5H 33
Kennacraig. Arg 3G 125
Kenneggy Downs. Corn 4C 4
Kennerleigh. Devn 2B 12
Kennet. Clac 4B 136
Kennethmont. Abers 1C 152
Kennett. Cambs 4G 65
Kennford. Devn 4C 12
Kenninghall. Norf 2C 66
Kennington. Kent 1E 29
Kennington. Oxon 5D 50
Kennoway. Fife 3F 137
Kennyhill. Suff 3F 65
Kennythorpe. N Yor 3B 100
Kenovay. Arg 4A 138
Kensaleyre. High 3D 154
Kensington. G Lon 3D 38
Kenstone. Shrp 3H 71
Kensworth. C Beds 4A 52
Kensworth Common.
C Beds 4A 52
Kentallen. High 3E 141
Kentchurch. Here 3H 47
Kentford. Suff 4G 65
Kentisbeare. Devn 2D 12
Kentisbury. Devn 2G 19
Kentisbury Ford. Devn 2G 19
Kentmere. Cumb 4F 103
Kenton. Devn 4C 12
Kenton. G Lon 2C 38
Kenton. Suff 4D 66
Kenton Bankfoot. Tyne 3F 115
Kentra. High 2A 140
Kentrigg. Cumb 5G 103
Kents Bank. Cumb 2C 96
Kent's Green. Glos 3C 48
Kent's Oak. Hants 4B 24
Kent Street. E Sus 4B 28
Kent Street. Kent 5A 40
Kent Street. W Sus 3D 26
Kenwick. Shrp 2G 71
Kenwyn. Corn 4C 6
Kenyon. Warr 1A 84
Keoldale. High 2D 166
Keppoch. High 1B 148
Kepwick. N Yor 5B 106
Keresley. W Mid 2H 61
Keresley Newland. Warw 2H 61
Keristal. IOM 4C 108
Kerne Bridge. Here 4A 48
Kerridge. Ches E 3D 84
Kerris. Corn 4B 4
Kerrow. High 5F 157
Kerry. Powy 2D 58
Kerrycroy. Arg 3C 126
Kerry's Gate. Here 2G 47
Kersall. Notts 4E 86
Kersbrook. Devn 4D 12
Kerse. Ren 4E 127
Kersey. Suff 1D 54
Kershopefoot. Cumb 1F 113
Kersoe. Worc 1E 49
Kerswell. Devn 2D 12
Kerswell Green. Worc 1D 48
Kesgrave. Suff 1F 55
Kesh. Ferm 6D 176
Kessingland. Suff 2H 67
Kessingland Beach. Suff 2H 67
Kestle. Corn 4D 6
Kestle Mill. Corn 3C 6
Keston. G Lon 4F 39
Keswick. Cumb 2D 102
Keswick. Norf 2F 79
(nr. North Walsham)
Keswick. Norf 5E 78
(nr. Norwich)
Ketsby. Linc 3C 88
Kettering. Nptn 3F 63
Ketteringham. Norf 5D 78
Kettins. Per 5B 144
Kettlebaston. Suff 5B 66
Kettlebridge. Fife 3F 137
Kettlebrook. Staf 5G 73
Kettleburgh. Suff 4E 67
Kettleholm. Dum 2C 112
Kettleness. N Yor 3F 107
Kettleshulme. Ches E 3D 85
Kettlesing. N Yor 4E 99
Kettlesing Bottom. N Yor 4E 99
Kettlestone. Norf 2B 78
Kettlethorpe. Linc 3F 87
Kettletoft. Orkn 4F 172
Kettlewell. N Yor 2B 98
Ketton. Rut 5G 75
Kew. G Lon 3C 38
Kewaigue. IOM 4C 108
Kewstoke. N Som 5G 33
Kexbrough. S Yor 4D 92
Kexby. Linc 2F 87
Kexby. York 4B 100
Keyford. Som 2C 22
Key Green. Ches E 4C 84
Key Green. N Yor 4F 107
Keyham. Leics 5D 74
Keyhaven. Hants 3B 16
Keyhead. Abers 3H 161
Keyingham. E Yor 2F 95
Keymer. W Sus 4E 27
Keynsham. Bath 5B 34
Keysoe. Bed 4H 63

Keysoe Row—Ledsham

Keysoe Row. Bed 4H 63
Key's Toft. Linc 5D 89
Keyston. Cambs 3H 63
Key Street. Kent 4C 40
Keyworth. Notts 2D 74
Kibblesworth. Tyne 4F 115
Kibworth Beauchamp. Leics 1D 62
Kibworth Harcourt. Leics 1D 62
Kidbrooke. G Lon 3F 39
Kidburngill. Cumb 2B 102
Kiddemore Green. Staf 5C 72
Kidderminster. Worc 3C 60
Kiddington. Oxon 3C 50
Kidd's Moor. Norf 5D 78
Kidlington. Oxon 4C 50
Kidmore End. Oxon 4E 37
Kidnal. Ches W 1G 71
Kidsgrove. Staf 5C 84
Kidstones. N Yor 1B 98
Kidwelly. Carm 5E 45
Kiel Crofts. Arg 5D 140
Kielder. Nmbd 5A 120
Kilbagie. Fife 4B 136
Kilbarchan. Ren 3F 127
Kilbeg. High 3E 147
Kilberry. Arg 3F 125
Kilbirnie. N Ayr 4E 126
Kilbride. Arg 1F 133
Kilbride. High 1D 147
Kilbucho Place. Bord 1C 118
Kilburn. Derbs 1A 74
Kilburn. G Lon 2D 38
Kilburn. N Yor 2H 99
Kilby. Leics 1D 62
Kilchattan. Arg 4A 132 (on Colonsay)
Kilchattan. Arg 4C 126 (on Isle of Bute)
Kilchattan Bay. Arg 4B 126
Kilchenzie. Arg 3A 122
Kilcheran. Arg 5C 140
Kilchiaran. Arg 3A 124
Kilchoan. High 4F 147 (nr. Inverie)
Kilchoan. High 2F 139 (nr. Tobermory)
Kilchoman. Arg 3A 124
Kilchrenan. Arg 1H 133
Kilclief. Down 5K 179
Kilconquhar. Fife 3G 137
Kilcoo. Down 6G 179
Kilcot. Glos 3B 48
Kilcoy. High 3H 157
Kilcreggan. Arg 1D 126
Kildale. N Yor 4D 106
Kildary. High 1B 158
Kildermorie Lodge. High 1H 157
Kildonan. Dum 4F 109
Kildonan. High 1G 165 (nr. Helmsdale)
Kildonan. High 3C 154 (on Isle of Skye)
Kildonan. N Ayr 3E 123
Kildonnan. High 5C 146
Kildrummy. Abers 2B 152
Kildwick. N Yor 5C 98
Kilfillan. Dum 4H 109
Kilfinan. Arg 2H 125
Kilfinnan. High 4E 149
Kilgetty. Pemb 4F 43
Kilgour. Fife 3E 136
Kilgrammie. S Ayr 4B 116
Kilham. E Yor 3E 101
Kilham. Nmbd 1C 120
Kilkeel. New M 8H 179
Kilkenneth. Arg 4A 138
Kilkhampton. Corn 1C 10
Killadeas. Ferm 7E 176
Killamarsh. Derbs 2B 86
Killandrist. Arg 4C 140
Killay. Swan 3F 31
Killean. Arg 5E 125
Killearn. Stir 1G 127
Killeen. Dngn 3C 178
Killellan. Arg 4A 122
Killen. High 3A 158
Killen. Strab 4E 176
Killerby. Darl 3E 105
Killeter. Strab 4E 176
Killichonan. Per 3C 142
Killiechronan. Arg 4G 139
Killiecrankie. Per 2G 143
Killilan. High 5B 156
Killimster. High 3F 169
Killin. Stir 5C 142
Killinchy. Ards 3K 179
Killinghall. N Yor 4E 99
Killington. Cumb 1F 97
Killingworth. Tyne 2F 115
Killin Lodge. High 3H 149
Killinochonoch. Arg 4F 133
Killochyett. Bord 5A 130
Killough. Down 6K 179
Killowen. New M 8F 179
Killundine. High 4G 139
Killylea. Arm 5B 178
Killyleagh. Down 4K 179
Killyrammer. Bmny 4F 175
Kilmacolm. Inv 3E 127
Kilmahog. Stir 3F 135
Kilmahumaig. Arg 4E 133
Kilmalieu. High 3C 140
Kilmaluag. High 1D 154
Kilmany. Fife 1F 137
Kilmarie. High 2D 146
Kilmarnock. E Ayr 1D 116 & 196
Kilmaron. Fife 2F 137
Kilmartin. Arg 4F 133
Kilmaurs. E Ayr 5F 127
Kilmelford. Arg 2F 133
Kilmeny. Arg 3B 124
Kilmersdon. Som 1B 22
Kilmeston. Hants 4D 24
Kilmichael Glassary. Arg 4F 133
Kilmichael of Inverlussa. Arg 1F 125
Kilmington. Devn 3F 13
Kilmington. Wilts 3C 22
Kilmoluag. Arg 4A 138
Kilmorack. High 4G 157
Kilmore. Arg 1F 133
Kilmore. Arm 4D 178
Kilmore. Down 4J 179
Kilmore. High 3E 147
Kilmory. Arg 2F 125
Kilmory. High 1G 139 (nr. Kilchoan)
Kilmory. High 3B 146 (on Rùm)
Kilmory. N Ayr 3D 122
Kilmory Lodge. Arg 3E 132
Kilmote. High 2G 165
Kilmuir. High 4B 154 (nr. Dunvegan)
Kilmuir. High 1B 158 (nr. Invergordon)
Kilmuir. High 4A 158 (nr. Inverness)
Kilmuir. High 1C 154 (nr. Uig)
Kilmun. Arg 1C 126
Kilnave. Arg 2A 124
Kilncadzow. S Lan 5B 128
Kilndown. Kent 2B 28
Kiln Green. Here 4B 48
Kiln Green. Wind 4G 37
Kilnhill. Cumb 1D 102
Kilnhurst. S Yor 1B 86
Kilninian. Arg 4E 139
Kilninver. Arg 1F 133
Kiln Pit Hill. Nmbd 4D 114
Kilnsea. E Yor 3H 95
Kilnsey. N Yor 3B 98
Kilnwick. E Yor 5D 101
Kiloran. Arg 4A 132
Kilpatrick. N Ayr 3D 122
Kilpeck. Here 2H 47
Kilpin. E Yor 2A 94
Kilpin Pike. E Yor 2A 94
Kilrea. Cole 5F 174
Kilrenny. Fife 3H 137
Kilsby. Nptn 3C 62
Kilspindie. Per 1E 136
Kilsyth. N Lan 2A 128
Kiltarlity. High 4H 157
Kilton. Som 2E 21
Kilton Thorpe. Red C 3D 107
Kilvaxter. High 2C 154
Kilve. Som 2E 21
Kilvington. Notts 1F 75
Kilwinning. N Ayr 5D 126
Kimberley. Norf 5C 78
Kimberley. Notts 1B 74
Kimblesworth. Dur 5F 115
Kimble Wick. Buck 5G 51
Kimbolton. Cambs 4H 63
Kimbolton. Here 4H 59
Kimcote. Leics 2C 62
Kimmeridge. Dors 5E 15
Kimmerston. Nmbd 1D 120
Kimpton. Hants 2A 24
Kimpton. Herts 4B 52
Kinallen. Ban 5G 179
Kinawley. Ferm 6H 177
Kinbeachie. High 2A 158
Kinbrace. High 5A 168
Kinbuck. Stir 3G 135
Kincaple. Fife 2G 137
Kincardine. Fife 1C 128
Kincardine. High 5D 164
Kincardine Bridge. Fife 1C 128
Kincardine O'Neil. Abers 4C 152
Kinchrackine. Arg 1A 134
Kincorth. Aber 3G 153
Kincraig. High 3C 150
Kincraigie. Per 4G 143
Kindallachan. Per 3G 143
Kineton. Glos 3F 49
Kineton. Warw 5H 61
Kinfauns. Per 1D 136
Kingairloch. High 3C 140
Kingarth. Arg 4B 126
Kingcoed. Mon 5H 47
King Edward. Abers 3E 160
Kingerby. Linc 1H 87
Kingham. Oxon 3A 50
Kingholm Quay. Dum 2A 112
Kinghorn. Fife 1F 129
Kingie. High 3D 148
Kinglassie. Fife 4E 137
Kingledores. Bord 2D 118
Kingodie. Per 1F 137
King o' Muirs. Clac 4A 136
King's Acre. Here 1H 47
Kingsand. Corn 3A 8
Kingsash. Buck 5G 51
Kingsbarns. Fife 2H 137
Kingsbridge. Devn 4D 8
Kingsbridge. Som 3C 20
King's Bromley. Staf 4F 73
Kingsburgh. High 3C 154
Kingsbury. G Lon 2C 38
Kingsbury. Warw 1G 61
Kingsbury Episcopi. Som 4H 21
Kings Caple. Here 3A 48
Kingscavil. W Lot 2D 128
Kingsclere. Hants 1D 24
King's Cliffe. Nptn 1H 63
Kings Clipstone. Notts 4D 86
Kingscote. Glos 2D 34
Kingscott. Devn 1F 11
Kings Coughton. Warw 5E 61
Kingscross. N Ayr 3E 123
Kingsdon. Som 4A 22
Kingsdown. Kent 1H 29
Kingsdown. Swin 3G 35
Kingsdown. Wilts 5D 34
Kingseat. Fife 4D 136
Kingsey. Buck 5F 51
Kingsfold. Lanc 2D 90
Kingsfold. W Sus 2C 26
Kingsford. E Ayr 5F 127
Kingsford. Worc 2C 60
Kingsforth. N Lin 3D 94
Kingsgate. Kent 3H 41
King's Green. Glos 2C 48
Kingshall Street. Suff 4B 66
Kingsheanton. Devn 3F 19
King's Heath. W Mid 2E 61
Kings Hill. Kent 5A 40
Kingsholm. Glos 4D 48
Kingshouse. High 3G 141
Kingshouse. Stir 1E 135
Kingshurst. W Mid 2F 61
Kingskerswell. Devn 2E 9
Kingskettle. Fife 3F 137
Kingsland. Here 4G 59
Kingsland. IOA 2B 80
Kings Langley. Herts 5A 52
Kingsley. Ches W 3H 83
Kingsley. Hants 3F 25
Kingsley. Staf 1E 73
Kingsley Green. W Sus 3G 25
Kingsley Holt. Staf 1E 73
King's Lynn. Norf 3F 77
King's Meaburn. Cumb 2H 103
Kings Moss. Mers 4D 90
Kingsmuir. Ang 4D 145
Kingsmuir. Fife 3H 137
Kings Muir. Bord 1E 119
King's Newnham. Warw 3B 62
Kings Newton. Derbs 3A 74
Kingsnorth. Kent 2E 28
Kingsnorth. Medw 3C 40
King's Norton. Leics 5D 74
King's Norton. W Mid 3E 61
King's Nympton. Devn 1G 11
King's Pyon. Here 5G 59
Kings Ripton. Cambs 3B 64
King's Somborne. Hants 3B 24
King's Stag. Dors 1C 14
King's Stanley. Glos 5D 48
King's Sutton. Nptn 2C 50
Kingstanding. W Mid 1E 61
Kingsteignton. Devn 5B 12
Kingsteps. High 3D 158
King's Thorn. Here 2A 48
Kingsthorpe. Nptn 4E 63
Kingston. Cambs 5C 64
Kingston. Devn 4C 8
Kingston. Dors 2C 14 (nr. Sturminster Newton)
Kingston. Dors 5E 15 (nr. Swanage)
Kingston. E Lot 1B 130
Kingston. Hants 2G 15
Kingston. IOW 4C 16
Kingston. Kent 5F 41
Kingston. Mor 2H 159
Kingston. W Sus 5B 26
Kingston Bagpuize. Oxon 2C 36
Kingston Blount. Oxon 2F 37
Kingston by Sea. W Sus 5D 26
Kingston Deverill. Wilts 3D 22
Kingstone. Here 2H 47
Kingstone. Som 1G 13
Kingstone. Staf 3E 73
Kingston Lisle. Oxon 3B 36
Kingston Maurward. Dors 3C 14
Kingston near Lewes. E Sus 5E 27
Kingston on Soar. Notts 3C 74
Kingston Russell. Dors 3A 14
Kingston St Mary. Som 4F 21
Kingston Seymour. N Som 5H 33
Kingston Stert. Oxon 5F 51
Kingston upon Hull. Hull 2D 94 & 196
Kingston upon Thames. G Lon 4C 38
King's Walden. Herts 3B 52
Kingswear. Devn 3E 9
Kingswells. Aber 3F 153
Kingswinford. W Mid 2C 60
Kingswood. Buck 4E 51
Kingswood. Glos 2C 34
Kingswood. Here 5E 59
Kingswood. Kent 5C 40
Kingswood. Per 5H 143
Kingswood. Powy 5E 71
Kingswood. Som 3E 20
Kingswood. S Glo 4B 34
Kingswood. Surr 5D 38
Kingswood. Warw 3F 61
Kingswood Common. Staf 5C 72
Kings Worthy. Hants 3C 24
Kingthorpe. Linc 3A 88
Kington. Here 5E 59
Kington. S Glo 2B 34
Kington. Worc 5D 61
Kington Langley. Wilts 4E 35
Kington Magna. Dors 4C 22
Kington St Michael. Wilts 4E 35
Kingussie. High 3B 150
Kingweston. Som 3A 22
Kinharrachie. Abers 5G 161
Kinhrive. High 1B 158
Kinkell Bridge. Per 2B 136
Kinknockie. Abers 4H 161
Kinkry Hill. Cumb 2G 113
Kinlet. Shrp 2B 60
Kinloch. High 5D 166 (nr. Loch More)
Kinloch. High 3A 140 (nr. Lochaline)
Kinloch. High 4C 146 (on Rùm)
Kinloch. Per 4A 144
Kinlochard. Stir 3D 134
Kinlochbervie. High 3C 166
Kinlocheil. High 1D 141
Kinlochewe. High 2C 156
Kinloch Hourn. High 3B 148
Kinloch Laggan. High 5H 149
Kinlochleven. High 2F 141
Kinloch Lodge. High 3F 167
Kinlochmoidart. High 1B 140
Kinlochmore. High 2F 141
Kinloch Rannoch. Per 3D 142
Kinlochspelve. Arg 1D 132
Kinloid. High 5E 147
Kinloss. Mor 2E 159
Kinmel Bay. Cnwy 2B 82
Kinmuck. Abers 2F 153
Kinnadie. Abers 4G 161
Kinnaird. Per 1E 137
Kinneff. Abers 1H 145
Kinnelhead. Dum 4C 118
Kinnell. Ang 3F 145
Kinnerley. Shrp 3F 71
Kinnernie. Abers 2E 152
Kinnersley. Here 1G 47
Kinnersley. Worc 1D 48
Kinnerton. Powy 4E 59
Kinnerton. Shrp 1F 59
Kinnesswood. Per 3D 136
Kinninvie. Dur 2D 104
Kinnordy. Ang 3C 144
Kinoulton. Notts 2D 74
Kinross. Per 3D 136
Kinrossie. Per 5A 144
Kinsbourne Green. Herts 4B 52
Kinsey Heath. Ches E 1A 72
Kinsham. Here 4F 59
Kinsham. Worc 2E 49
Kinsley. W Yor 3E 93
Kinson. Bour 3F 15
Kintbury. W Ber 5B 36
Kintessack. Mor 2E 159
Kintillo. Per 2D 136
Kinton. Here 3G 59
Kinton. Shrp 4F 71
Kintore. Abers 2E 153
Kintour. Arg 4C 124
Kintra. Arg 2B 132
Kintraw. Arg 3F 133
Kinveachy. High 2D 150
Kinver. Staf 2C 60
Kinwarton. Warw 5F 61
Kiplingcotes. E Yor 5D 100
Kippax. W Yor 1E 93
Kippen. Stir 4F 135
Kippford. Dum 4F 111
Kipping's Cross. Kent 1H 27
Kirbister. Orkn 7C 172 (nr. Hobbister)
Kirbister. Orkn 6B 172 (nr. Quholm)
Kirbuster. Orkn 5F 172
Kirby Bedon. Norf 5E 79
Kirby Bellars. Leics 4E 74
Kirby Cane. Norf 1F 67
Kirby Cross. Essx 3F 55
Kirby Fields. Leics 5C 74
Kirby Green. Norf 1F 67
Kirby Grindalythe. N Yor 3D 100
Kirby Hill. N Yor 4E 105 (nr. Richmond)
Kirby Hill. N Yor 3F 99 (nr. Ripon)
Kirby Knowle. N Yor 1G 99
Kirby-le-Soken. Essx 3F 55
Kirby Misperton. N Yor 2B 100
Kirby Muxloe. Leics 5C 74
Kirby Sigston. N Yor 5B 106
Kirby Underdale. E Yor 4C 100
Kirby Wiske. N Yor 1F 99
Kircubbin. Ards 3L 179
Kirdford. W Sus 3B 26
Kirk. High 3E 169
Kirkabister. Shet 8F 173 (on Bressay)
Kirkabister. Shet 6F 173 (on Mainland)
Kirkandrews. Dum 5D 110
Kirkandrews-on-Eden. Cumb 4E 113
Kirkapol. Arg 4B 138
Kirkbampton. Cumb 4E 112
Kirkbean. Dum 4A 112
Kirk Bramwith. S Yor 3G 93
Kirkbride. Cumb 4D 112
Kirkbridge. N Yor 5F 105
Kirkbuddo. Ang 4E 145
Kirkburn. E Yor 4D 101
Kirkburton. W Yor 3B 92
Kirkby. Linc 1H 87
Kirkby. Mers 1G 83
Kirkby. N Yor 4C 106
Kirkby Fenside. Linc 4C 88
Kirkby Fleetham. N Yor 5F 105
Kirkby Green. Linc 5H 87
Kirkby-in-Ashfield. Notts 5C 86
Kirkby Industrial Estate. Mers 1G 83
Kirkby-in-Furness. Cumb 1B 96
Kirkby la Thorpe. Linc 1A 76
Kirkby Lonsdale. Cumb 2F 97
Kirkby Malham. N Yor 3B 98
Kirkby Mallory. Leics 5B 74
Kirkby Malzeard. N Yor 2E 99
Kirkby Mills. N Yor 1B 100
Kirkbymoorside. N Yor 1A 100
Kirkby on Bain. Linc 4B 88
Kirkby Overblow. N Yor 5F 99
Kirkby Stephen. Cumb 4A 104
Kirkby Thore. Cumb 2H 103
Kirkby Underwood. Linc 3H 75
Kirkby Wharfe. N Yor 5H 99
Kirkcaldy. Fife 4E 137
Kirkcambeck. Cumb 3G 113
Kirkcolm. Dum 3F 109
Kirkconnel. Dum 3G 117
Kirkconnell. Dum 3A 112
Kirkcowan. Dum 3A 110
Kirkcudbright. Dum 4D 111
Kirkdale. Mers 1F 83
Kirk Deighton. N Yor 4F 99
Kirk Ella. E Yor 2D 94
Kirkfieldbank. S Lan 5B 128
Kirkforthar Feus. Fife 3E 137
Kirkgunzeon. Dum 3F 111
Kirk Hallam. Derbs 1B 74
Kirkham. Lanc 1C 90
Kirkham. N Yor 3B 100
Kirkhamgate. W Yor 2C 92
Kirk Hammerton. N Yor 4G 99
Kirkharle. Nmbd 1D 114
Kirkheaton. Nmbd 2D 114
Kirkheaton. W Yor 3B 92
Kirkhill. Ang 2F 145
Kirkhill. High 4H 157
Kirkhope. S Lan 4B 118
Kirkhouse. Bord 1F 119
Kirkibost. High 2D 146
Kirkinch. Ang 4C 144
Kirkinner. Dum 4B 110
Kirkintilloch. E Dun 2H 127
Kirk Ireton. Derbs 5G 85
Kirkland. Cumb 3B 102 (nr. Cleator Moor)
Kirkland. Cumb 1H 103 (nr. Penrith)
Kirkland. Cumb 5D 112 (nr. Wigton)
Kirkland. Dum 3G 117 (nr. Kirkconnel)
Kirkland. Dum 5H 117 (nr. Moniaive)
Kirkland Guards. Cumb 5C 112
Kirk Langley. Derbs 2G 73
Kirklauchline. Dum 4F 109
Kirkleatham. Red C 2C 106
Kirklevington. Stoc T 4B 106
Kirkley. Suff 1H 67
Kirklington. N Yor 1F 99
Kirklington. Notts 5D 86
Kirklinton. Cumb 3F 113
Kirkliston. Edin 2E 129
Kirkmabreck. Dum 4B 110
Kirkmaiden. Dum 5E 109
Kirk Merrington. Dur 1F 105
Kirk Michael. IOM 2C 108
Kirkmichael. Per 2H 143
Kirkmichael. S Ayr 4C 116
Kirkmuirhill. S Lan 5A 128
Kirknewton. Nmbd 1D 120
Kirknewton. W Lot 3E 129
Kirkney. Abers 5C 160
Kirk of Shotts. N Lan 3B 128
Kirkoswald. Cumb 5G 113
Kirkoswald. S Ayr 4B 116
Kirkpatrick. Dum 5B 118
Kirkpatrick Durham. Dum 2E 111
Kirkpatrick-Fleming. Dum 2D 112
Kirk Sandall. S Yor 4G 93
Kirksanton. Cumb 1A 96
Kirk Smeaton. N Yor 3F 93
Kirkstall. W Yor 1C 92
Kirkstile. Dum 5F 119
Kirkstyle. High 1F 169
Kirkthorpe. W Yor 2D 93
Kirkton. Abers 2D 152 (nr. Alford)
Kirkton. Abers 1D 152 (nr. Insch)
Kirkton. Abers 4F 161 (nr. Turriff)
Kirkton. Ang 5D 144 (nr. Dundee)
Kirkton. Ang 4D 144 (nr. Forfar)
Kirkton. Ang 5B 152 (nr. Tarfside)
Kirkton. Dum 1A 112
Kirkton. Fife 1F 137
Kirkton. High 4E 165 (nr. Golspie)
Kirkton. High 1G 147 (nr. Kyle of Lochalsh)
Kirkton. High 4B 156 (nr. Lochcarron)
Kirkton. Bord 3H 119
Kirkton. S Lan 2B 118
Kirktonhill. W Dun 2E 127
Kirkton Manor. Bord 1E 118
Kirkton of Airlie. Ang 3C 144
Kirkton of Auchterhouse. Ang 5C 144
Kirkton of Bourtie. Abers 1F 153
Kirkton of Collace. Per 5A 144
Kirkton of Craig. Ang 3G 145
Kirkton of Culsalmond. Abers 5D 160
Kirkton of Durris. Abers 4E 153
Kirkton of Glenbuchat. Abers 2A 152
Kirkton of Glenisla. Ang 2B 144
Kirkton of Kingoldrum. Ang 3C 144
Kirkton of Largo. Fife 3G 137
Kirkton of Lethendy. Per 4A 144
Kirkton of Logie Buchan. Abers 1G 153
Kirkton of Maryculter. Abers 4F 153
Kirkton of Menmuir. Ang 2E 145
Kirkton of Monikie. Ang 5E 145
Kirkton of Oyne. Abers 1D 152
Kirkton of Rayne. Abers 5D 160
Kirkton of Skene. Abers 3F 153
Kirktown. Abers 2G 161 (nr. Fraserburgh)
Kirktown. Abers 3H 161 (nr. Peterhead)
Kirktown of Alvah. Abers 2D 160
Kirktown of Auchterless. Abers 4E 160
Kirktown of Deskford. Mor 2C 160
Kirktown of Fetteresso. Abers 5F 153
Kirktown of Mortlach. Mor 5H 159
Kirktown of Slains. Abers 1H 153
Kirkurd. Bord 5E 129
Kirkwall. Orkn 6D 172
Kirkwall Airport. Orkn 7D 172
Kirkwhelpington. Nmbd 1C 114
Kirk Yetholm. Bord 2C 120
Kirmington. N Lin 3E 94
Kirmond le Mire. Linc 1A 88
Kirn. Arg 2C 126
Kirriemuir. Ang 3C 144
Kirstead Green. Norf 1E 67
Kirtlebridge. Dum 2D 112
Kirtleton. Dum 2D 112
Kirtling. Cambs 5F 65
Kirtling Green. Cambs 5F 65
Kirtlington. Oxon 4D 50
Kirtomy. High 2H 167
Kirton. Linc 2C 76
Kirton. Notts 4D 86
Kirton. Suff 2F 55
Kirton End. Linc 1B 76
Kirton Holme. Linc 1B 76
Kirton in Lindsey. N Lin 1G 87
Kishorn. High 4H 155
Kislingbury. Nptn 5D 62
Kite Hill. IOW 3D 16
Kites Hardwick. Warw 4B 62
Kittisford. Som 4D 20
Kittle. Swan 4E 31
Kittybrewster. Aber 3G 153
Kitwood. Hants 3E 25
Kivernoll. Here 2H 47
Kiveton Park. S Yor 2B 86
Knaith. Linc 2F 87
Knaith Park. Linc 2F 87
Knaphill. Surr 5A 38
Knapp. Hants 4C 24
Knapp. Per 5B 144
Knapp. Som 4G 21
Knapperfield. High 3E 169
Knapton. Norf 2F 79
Knapton. York 4H 99
Knapton Green. Here 5G 59
Knapwell. Cambs 4C 64
Knaresborough. N Yor 4F 99
Knarsdale. Nmbd 4H 113
Knatts Valley. Kent 4G 39
Knaven. Abers 4F 161
Knayton. N Yor 1G 99
Knebworth. Herts 3C 52
Knedlington. E Yor 2H 93
Kneesall. Notts 4E 86
Kneesworth. Cambs 1D 52
Kneeton. Notts 1E 74
Knelston. Swan 4D 30
Knenhall. Staf 2D 72
Knightacott. Devn 3G 19
Knightcote. Warw 5B 62
Knightcott. N Som 1G 21
Knightley. Staf 3C 72
Knightley Dale. Staf 3C 72
Knightlow Hill. Warw 3B 62
Knighton. Devn 4B 8
Knighton. Dors 1B 14
Knighton. Leic 5D 74
Knighton. Powy 3E 59
Knighton. Som 2E 21
Knighton. Staf 3B 72 (nr. Eccleshall)
Knighton. Staf 1B 72 (nr. Woore)
Knighton. Warw 5H 61
Knighton. Wilts 4A 36
Knighton. Worc 5E 61
Knighton Common. Worc 3A 60
Knight's End. Cambs 1D 64
Knightswood. Glas 3G 127
Knightwick. Worc 5B 60
Knill. Here 4E 59
Knipton. Leics 2F 75
Knitsley. Dur 5E 115
Kniveton. Derbs 5G 85
Knock. Arg 5G 139
Knock. Cumb 2H 103
Knock. Mor 3C 160
Knockally. High 5D 168
Knockan. Arg 1B 132
Knockan. High 2G 163
Knockandhu. Mor 1G 151
Knockando. Mor 4F 159
Knockarthur. High 3E 165
Knockbain. High 3A 158
Knockbreck. High 2B 154
Knockcloghrim. Mag 7E 174
Knockdee. High 2D 168
Knockdolian. S Ayr 1G 109
Knockdon. S Ayr 3C 116
Knockdown. Glos 3D 34
Knockenbaird. Abers 1D 152
Knockenkelly. N Ayr 3E 123
Knockentiber. E Ayr 1C 116
Knockfarrel. High 3H 157
Knockglass. High 2C 168
Knockholt. Kent 5F 39
Knockholt Pound. Kent 5F 39
Knockie Lodge. High 2G 149
Knockin. Shrp 3F 71
Knockinlaw. E Ayr 1D 116
Knockinnon. High 5D 169
Knocknacarry. Moy 3J 175
Knockrome. Arg 2D 124
Knocksharry. IOM 3B 108
Knockshinnoch. E Ayr 3D 116
Knockvennie. Dum 2E 111
Knockvologan. Arg 3B 132
Knodishall. Suff 4G 67
Knole. Som 4H 21
Knollbury. Mon 3H 33
Knolls Green. Ches E 3C 84
Knolton. Wrex 2F 71
Knook. Wilts 2E 23
Knossington. Leics 5F 75
Knott. High 3C 154
Knott End-on-Sea. Lanc 5C 96
Knotting. Bed 4H 63
Knotting Green. Bed 4H 63
Knottingley. W Yor 2E 93
Knotts. Cumb 2F 103
Knotty Ash. Mers 1G 83
Knotty Green. Buck 1A 38
Knowbury. Shrp 3H 59
Knowe. Dum 2A 110
Knowefield. Cumb 4F 113
Knowehead. Dum 5F 117
Knowes. E Lot 2C 130
Knowesgate. Nmbd 1C 114
Knoweside. S Ayr 3B 116
Knowle. Bris 4A 34
Knowle. Devn 3E 19 (nr. Braunton)
Knowle. Devn 4D 12 (nr. Budleigh Salterton)
Knowle. Devn 2A 12 (nr. Crediton)
Knowle. Shrp 3H 59
Knowle. W Mid 3F 61
Knowle Green. Lanc 1E 91
Knowle St Giles. Som 1G 13
Knowlesands. Shrp 1B 60
Knowles of Elrick. Abers 3D 160
Knowle Village. Hants 2D 16
Knowl Hill. Wind 4G 37
Knowlton. Kent 5G 41
Knowsley. Mers 1G 83
Knowstone. Devn 4B 20
Knucklas. Powy 3E 59
Knuston. Nptn 4G 63
Knutsford. Ches E 3B 84
Knypersley. Staf 5C 84
Krumlin. W Yor 3A 92
Kuggar. Corn 5E 5
Kyleakin. High 1F 147
Kyle of Lochalsh. High 1F 147
Kylerhea. High 1F 147
Kylesku. High 5C 166
Kyles Lodge. W Isl 9B 171
Kylesmorar. High 4G 147
Kylestrome. High 5C 166
Kymin. Mon 4A 48
Kynaston. Here 2B 48
Kynaston. Shrp 3F 71
Kynnersley. Telf 4A 72
Kyre Green. Worc 4A 60
Kyre Park. Worc 4A 60
Kyrewood. Worc 4A 60

L

Labost. W Isl 3E 171
Lacasaidh. W Isl 5F 171
Lacasdail. W Isl 4G 171
Laceby. NE Lin 4F 95
Lacey Green. Buck 5G 51
Lach Dennis. Ches W 3B 84
Lache. Ches W 4F 83
Lack. Ferm 6E 176
Lackagh. Lim 5C 174
Lackford. Suff 3G 65
Lacock. Wilts 5E 35
Ladbroke. Warw 5B 62
Laddingford. Kent 1A 28
Lade Bank. Linc 5C 88
Ladock. Corn 3C 6
Lady. Orkn 3F 172
Ladybank. Fife 2F 137
Ladycross. Corn 4D 10
Lady Green. Mers 4B 90
Lady Hall. Cumb 1A 96
Ladykirk. Bord 5E 131
Ladysford. Abers 2G 161
Ladywood. W Mid 2E 61
Ladywood. Worc 4C 60
Laga. High 2A 140
Lagavulin. Arg 5C 124
Lagg. Arg 2D 125
Lagg. N Ayr 3D 122
Laggan. Arg 4A 124
Laggan. High 4E 149 (nr. Fort Augustus)
Laggan. High 4A 150 (nr. Newtonmore)
Laggan. Mor 5H 159
Lagganlia. High 3C 150
Lagganulva. Arg 4F 139
Laglingarten. Arg 3A 134
Lagness. W Sus 2G 17
Laid. High 3E 166
Laide. High 4D 162
Laigh Fenwick. E Ayr 5F 127
Laindon. Essx 2A 40
Lairg. High 3C 164
Lairg Muir. High 3C 164
Laithes. Cumb 1F 103
Laithkirk. Dur 2C 104
Lake. Devn 3F 19
Lake. IOW 4D 16
Lake. Wilts 3G 23
Lake District. Cumb 3E 103
Lakenham. Norf 5E 79
Lakenheath. Suff 2G 65
Lakesend. Norf 1E 65
Lakeside. Cumb 1C 96
Laleham. Surr 4B 38
Laleston. B'end 3B 32
Lamancha. Bord 4F 129
Lamarsh. Essx 2B 54
Lamas. Norf 3E 79
Lamb Corner. Essx 2D 54
Lambden. Bord 5D 130
Lamberhead Green. G Man 4D 90
Lamberhurst. Kent 2A 28
Lamberhurst Quarter. Kent 2A 28
Lamberton. Bord 4F 131
Lambeth. G Lon 3E 39
Lambfell Moar. IOM 3B 108
Lambhill. Glas 3G 127
Lambley. Nmbd 4H 113
Lambley. Notts 1D 74
Lambourn. W Ber 4B 36
Lambourne End. Essx 1F 39
Lambourn Woodlands. W Ber 4B 36
Lambrook. Som 4F 21
Lambs Green. Dors 3E 15
Lambs Green. W Sus 2D 26
Lambston. Pemb 3D 42
Lamellion. Corn 2G 7
Lamerton. Devn 5E 11
Lamesley. Tyne 4F 115
Laminess. Orkn 4F 172
Lamington. High 1B 158
Lamington. S Lan 1B 118
Lamlash. N Ayr 2E 123
Lamonby. Cumb 1F 103
Lamorick. Corn 2E 7
Lamorna. Corn 4B 4
Lamorran. Corn 4C 6
Lampeter. Cdgn 1F 45
Lampeter Velfrey. Pemb 3F 43
Lamphey. Pemb 4E 43
Lamplugh. Cumb 2B 102
Lamport. Nptn 3E 63
Lamyatt. Som 3B 22
Lana. Devn 3D 10 (nr. Ashwater)
Lana. Devn 2D 10 (nr. Holsworthy)
Lanark. S Lan 5B 128
Lanarth. Corn 4E 5
Lancaster. Lanc 3D 97
Lanchester. Dur 5E 115
Lancing. W Sus 5C 26
Landbeach. Cambs 4D 64
Landcross. Devn 4E 19
Landerberry. Abers 3E 153
Landford. Wilts 1A 16
Land Gate. G Man 4D 90
Landhallow. High 5D 169
Landimore. Swan 3D 30
Landkey. Devn 3F 19
Landkey Newland. Devn 3F 19
Landore. Swan 3F 31
Landport. Port 2E 17
Landrake. Corn 2H 7
Landscove. Devn 2D 9
Land's End (St Just) Airport. Corn 4A 4
Landshipping. Pemb 3E 43
Landulph. Corn 2A 8
Landywood. Staf 5D 73
Lane. Corn 2C 6
Laneast. Corn 4C 10
Lane Bottom. Lanc 1G 91
Lane End. Buck 2G 37
Lane End. Hants 4D 24
Lane End. IOW 4E 17
Lane End. Wilts 2D 22
Lane Ends. Derbs 2G 73
Lane Ends. Dur 1E 105
Lane Ends. Lanc 4G 97
Laneham. Notts 3F 87
Lanehead. Dur 5B 114 (nr. Cowshill)
Lane Head. Dur 3E 105 (nr. Hutton Magna)
Lane Head. Dur 2D 105 (nr. Woodland)
Lane Head. G Man 1A 84
Lanehead. Nmbd 1A 114
Lane Head. W Yor 4B 92
Lane Heads. Lanc 1C 90
Lanercost. Cumb 3G 113
Laneshaw Bridge. Lanc 5B 98
Laney Green. Staf 5D 72
Langais. W Isl 2D 170
Langal. High 2B 140
Langar. Notts 2E 74
Langbank. Ren 2E 127
Langbar. N Yor 4C 98
Langburnshiels. Bord 4H 119
Langcliffe. N Yor 3H 97
Langdale End. N Yor 5G 107
Langdon. Corn 3C 10
Langdon Beck. Dur 1B 104
Langdon Cross. Corn 4D 10
Langdon Hills. Essx 2A 40
Langdown. Hants 2C 16
Langdyke. Fife 3F 137
Langenhoe. Essx 4D 54
Langford. C Beds 1B 52
Langford. Devn 2D 12
Langford. Essx 5B 54
Langford. Notts 5F 87
Langford. Oxon 5H 49
Langford. Som 4F 21
Langford Budville. Som 4E 20
Langham. Dors 4C 22
Langham. Essx 2D 54
Langham. Norf 1C 78
Langham. Rut 4F 75
Langham. Suff 4B 66
Langho. Lanc 1F 91
Langholm. Dum 1E 113
Langland. Swan 4F 31
Langleeford. Nmbd 2D 120
Langley. Ches E 3D 84
Langley. Derbs 1B 74
Langley. Essx 2E 53
Langley. Glos 3F 49
Langley. Hants 2C 16
Langley. Herts 3C 52
Langley. Kent 5C 40
Langley. Nmbd 3B 114
Langley. Slo 3B 38
Langley. Som 4D 20
Langley. Warw 4F 61
Langley. W Sus 4G 25
Langley Burrell. Wilts 4E 35
Langleybury. Herts 5A 52
Langley Common. Derbs 2G 73
Langley Green. Derbs 2G 73
Langley Green. Norf 5F 79
Langley Green. Warw 4F 61
Langley Green. W Sus 2D 26
Langley Heath. Kent 5C 40
Langley Marsh. Som 4D 20
Langley Moor. Dur 5F 115
Langley Park. Dur 5F 115
Langley Street. Norf 5F 79
Langney. E Sus 5H 27
Langold. Notts 2C 86
Langore. Corn 4D 10
Langport. Som 4H 21
Langrick. Linc 1B 76
Langridge. Bath 5C 34
Langridgeford. Devn 4F 19
Langrigg. Cumb 5C 112
Langrish. Hants 4F 25
Langsett. S Yor 4C 92
Langshaw. Bord 1H 119
Langstone. Hants 2F 17
Langthorne. N Yor 5F 105
Langthorpe. N Yor 3F 99
Langthwaite. N Yor 4D 104
Langtoft. E Yor 3E 101
Langtoft. Linc 4A 76
Langton. Dur 3E 105
Langton. Linc 4B 88 (nr. Horncastle)
Langton. Linc 3C 88 (nr. Spilsby)
Langton. N Yor 3B 100
Langton by Wragby. Linc 3A 88
Langton Green. Kent 2G 27
Langton Herring. Dors 4B 14
Langton Long Blandford. Dors 2D 15
Langton Matravers. Dors 5E 15
Langtree. Devn 1E 11
Langwathby. Cumb 1G 103
Langwith. Derbs 4C 86
Langworth. Linc 3H 87
Lanivet. Corn 2E 7
Lanjeth. Corn 3D 6
Lank. Corn 5A 10
Lanlivery. Corn 3E 7
Lanner. Corn 5B 6
Lanreath. Corn 3F 7
Lansallos. Corn 3F 7
Lansdown. Bath 5C 34
Lansdown. Glos 3E 49
Lanteglos Highway. Corn 3F 7
Lanton. Nmbd 1D 120
Lanton. Bord 2A 120
Lapford. Devn 2H 11
Lapford Cross. Devn 2H 11
Laphroaig. Arg 5B 124
Lapley. Staf 4C 72
Lapworth. Warw 3F 61
Larachbeg. High 4A 140
Larbert. Falk 1B 128
Larden Green. Ches E 5H 83
Larel. High 3D 169
Largie. Abers 5D 160
Largiemore. Arg 1H 125
Largoward. Fife 3G 137
Largs. N Ayr 4D 126
Largue. Abers 4D 160
Largybeg. N Ayr 3E 123
Largymeanoch. N Ayr 3E 123
Largymore. N Ayr 3E 123
Larkfield. Inv 2D 126
Larkfield. Kent 5B 40
Larkhall. Bath 5C 34
Larkhall. S Lan 4A 128
Larkhill. Wilts 2G 23
Larling. Norf 2B 66
Larne. Lar 6L 175
Larport. Here 2A 48
Lartington. Dur 3D 104
Lary. Abers 3H 151
Lasham. Hants 2E 25
Lashenden. Kent 1C 28
Lassodie. Fife 4D 136
Lasswade. Midl 3G 129
Lastingham. N Yor 5E 107
Latchford. Herts 3D 53
Latchford. Oxon 5E 51
Latchingdon. Essx 5B 54
Latchley. Corn 5E 11
Latchmere Green. Hants 5E 37
Lathbury. Mil 1G 51
Latheron. High 5D 169
Latheronwheel. High 5D 169
Lathom. Lanc 4C 90
Lathones. Fife 3G 137
Latimer. Buck 1B 38
Latteridge. S Glo 3B 34
Lattiford. Som 4B 22
Latton. Wilts 2F 35
Laudale House. High 3B 140
Lauder. Bord 5B 130
Laugharne. Carm 3H 43
Laughterton. Linc 3F 87
Laughton. E Sus 4G 27
Laughton. Leics 2D 62
Laughton. Linc 1F 87 (nr. Gainsborough)
Laughton. Linc 2H 75 (nr. Grantham)
Laughton Common. S Yor 2C 86
Laughton en le Morthen. S Yor 2C 86
Launcells. Corn 2C 10
Launceston. Corn 4D 10
Launcherley. Som 2A 22
Launton. Oxon 3E 50
Laurelvale. Arm 5E 178
Laurencekirk. Abers 1G 145
Laurieston. Dum 3D 111
Laurieston. Falk 2C 128
Lavendon. Mil 5G 63
Lavenham. Suff 1C 54
Laverhay. Dum 5D 118
Laversdale. Cumb 3F 113
Laverstock. Wilts 3G 23
Laverstoke. Hants 2C 24
Laverton. Glos 2F 49
Laverton. N Yor 2E 99
Laverton. Som 1C 22
Lavister. Wrex 5F 83
Law. S Lan 4B 128
Lawers. Per 5D 142
Lawford. Essx 2D 54
Lawhitton. Corn 4D 10
Lawkland. N Yor 3G 97
Lawley. Shrp 5A 72
Lawnhead. Staf 3C 72
Lawrencetown. Ban 5E 178
Lawrenny. Pemb 4E 43
Lawshall. Suff 5A 66
Lawton. Here 5G 59
Laxey. IOM 3D 108
Laxfield. Suff 3E 67
Laxfirth. Shet 6F 173
Laxo. Shet 5F 173
Laxton. E Yor 2A 94
Laxton. Nptn 1G 63
Laxton. Notts 4E 86
Laycock. W Yor 5C 98
Layer Breton. Essx 4C 54
Layer-de-la-Haye. Essx 3C 54
Layer Marney. Essx 4C 54
Layland's Green. W Ber 5B 36
Laymore. Dors 2G 13
Laysters Pole. Here 4H 59
Layter's Green. Buck 1A 38
Laytham. E Yor 1H 93
Lazenby. Red C 3C 106
Lazonby. Cumb 1G 103
Lea. Derbs 5H 85
Lea. Here 3B 48
Lea. Linc 2F 87
Lea. Shrp 2F 59 (nr. Bishop's Castle)
Lea. Shrp 5G 71 (nr. Shrewsbury)
Lea. Wilts 3E 35
Leabrooks. Derbs 5B 86
Leac a Li. W Isl 8D 171
Leachd. Arg 4H 133
Leachkin. High 4A 158
Leachpool. Pemb 3D 42
Leadburn. Midl 4F 129
Leadenham. Linc 5G 87
Leaden Roding. Essx 4F 53
Leaderfoot. Bord 1H 119
Leadgate. Cumb 5A 114
Leadgate. Dur 4E 115
Leadgate. Nmbd 4E 115
Leadhills. S Lan 3A 118
Leadingcross Green. Kent 5C 40
Lea End. Worc 3E 61
Leafield. Oxon 4B 50
Leagrave. Lutn 3A 52
Lea Hall. W Mid 2F 61
Lea Heath. Staf 3E 73
Leake. N Yor 5B 106
Leake Common Side. Linc 5C 88
Leake Fold Hill. Linc 5D 88
Leake Hurn's End. Linc 1D 76
Lealholm. N Yor 4E 107
Lealt. Arg 4D 132
Lealt. High 2E 155
Leam. Derbs 3G 85
Lea Marston. Warw 1G 61
Leamington Hastings. Warw 4B 62
Leamington Spa, Royal. Warw 4H 61
Leamonsley. Staf 5F 73
Leamside. Dur 5G 115
Leargybreck. Arg 2D 124
Lease Rigg. N Yor 4F 107
Leasgill. Cumb 1D 97
Leasingham. Linc 1H 75
Leasingthorne. Dur 1F 105
Leasowe. Mers 1E 83
Leatherhead. Surr 5C 38
Leathley. N Yor 5E 99
Leaths. Dum 3E 111
Leaton. Shrp 4G 71
Leaton. Telf 4A 72
Lea Town. Lanc 1C 90
Leaveland. Kent 5E 40
Leavenheath. Suff 2C 54
Leavening. N Yor 3B 100
Leaves Green. G Lon 4F 39
Lea Yeat. Cumb 1G 97
Leazes. Dur 4E 115
Lebberston. N Yor 1E 101
Lechlade on Thames. Glos 2H 35
Leck. Lanc 2F 97
Leckford. Hants 3B 24
Leckfurin. High 3H 167
Leckgruinart. Arg 3A 124
Leckhampstead. Buck 2F 51
Leckhampstead. W Ber 4C 36
Leckhampstead Street. W Ber 4C 36
Leckhampton. Glos 4E 49
Leckmelm. High 4F 163
Leckwith. V Glam 4E 33
Leconfield. E Yor 5E 101
Ledaig. Arg 5D 140
Ledburn. Buck 3H 51
Ledbury. Here 2C 48
Ledgemoor. Here 5G 59
Ledgowan. High 3D 156
Ledicot. Here 4G 59
Ledmore. High 2G 163
Lednabirichen. High 4E 165
Lednagullin. High 2A 168
Ledsham. Ches W 3F 83

Lochgair—Maydown

Lochgair. Arg 4G 133
Lochgarthside. High 2H 149
Lochgelly. Fife 4D 136
Lochgilphead. Arg 1G 125
Lochgoilhead. Arg 3A 134
Loch Head. Dum 5A 110
Lochhill. Mor 2G 159
Lochindorb Lodge. High 5D 158
Lochinver. High 1E 163
Lochlane. Per 1H 135
Loch Lomond. Arg 3C 134
Loch Loyal Lodge. High 4G 167
Lochluichart. High 2F 157
Lochmaben. Dum 1B 112
Lochmaddy. W Isl 2E 170
Loch nam Madadh.
W Isl 2E 170
Lochore. Fife 4D 136
Lochportain. W Isl 1E 170
Lochranza. N Ayr 4H 125
Loch Sgioport. W Isl 5D 170
Lochside. Abers 2G 145
Lochside. High 5A 168
(nr. Achentoul)
Lochside. High 3C 158
(nr. Nairn)
Lochslin. High 5F 165
Lochstack Lodge. High 4C 166
Lochton. Abers 4E 153
Lochty. Fife 3H 137
Lochuisge. High 3B 140
Lochussie. High 3G 157
Lochwinnoch. Ren 4E 127
Lochyside. High 1F 141
Lockengate. Corn 2E 7
Lockerbie. Dum 1C 112
Lockeridge. Wilts 5G 35
Lockerley. Hants 4A 24
Lockhills. Cumb 5G 113
Locking. N Som 1G 21
Lockington. E Yor 5D 101
Lockington. Leics 3B 74
Lockleywood. Shrp 3A 72
Locksgreen. IOW 3C 16
Locks Heath. Hants 2D 16
Lockton. N Yor 5F 107
Loddington. Leics 5E 75
Loddington. Nptn 3F 63
Loddiswell. Devn 4D 8
Loddon. Norf 1F 67
Lode. Cambs 4E 65
Loders. Dors 3H 13
Lodsworth. W Sus 3A 26
Lofthouse. N Yor 2D 98
Lofthouse. W Yor 2D 92
Lofthouse Gate. W Yor 2D 92
Loftus. Red C 3E 107
Logan. E Ayr 2E 117
Loganlea. W Lot 3C 128
Logaston. Here 5F 59
Loggerheads. Staf 2B 72
Loggie. High 4F 163
Logie. Ang 2F 145
Logie. Fife 1G 137
Logie. Mor 3E 159
Logie Coldstone. Abers 3B 152
Logie Pert. Ang 2F 145
Logierait. Per 3G 143
Login. Carm 2F 43
Lolworth. Cambs 4C 64
Lonbain. High 3F 155
Londesborough. E Yor 5C 100
London.
G Lon 2E 39 & 198-199
London Apprentice. Corn 3E 6
London Ashford (Lydd) Airport.
Kent 3E 29
London City Airport.
G Lon 2F 39
London Colney. Herts 5B 52
Londonderry. Derr 5A 174
Londonderry. N Yor 1F 99
London Gatwick Airport.
W Sus 1D 27 & 205
London Heathrow Airport.
G Lon 3B 38 & 205
London Luton Airport.
Lutn 3B 52 & 205
London Southend Airport.
Essx 2C 40
London Stansted Airport.
Essx 3F 53 & 205
Londonthorpe. Linc 2G 75
Londubh. High 5C 162
Lone. High 4D 166
Lonemore. High 5E 165
(nr. Dornoch)
Lonemore. High 1G 155
(nr. Gairloch)
Long Ashton. N Som 4A 34
Long Bank. Worc 3B 60
Longbar. N Ayr 4E 127
Long Bennington. Linc 1F 75
Longbenton. Tyne 3F 115
Longborough. Glos 3G 49
Long Bredy. Dors 3A 14
Longbridge. Warw 4G 61
Longbridge. W Mid 3E 61
Longbridge Deverill.
Wilts 2D 22
Long Buckby. Nptn 4D 62
Long Buckby Wharf.
Nptn 4D 62
Longburgh. Cumb 4E 112
Longburton. Dors 1B 14
Long Clawson. Leics 3E 74
Longcliffe. Derbs 5G 85
Long Common. Hants 1D 16
Long Compton. Staf 3C 72
Long Compton. Warw 2A 50
Longcot. Oxon 2A 36
Long Crendon. Buck 5E 51
Long Crichel. Dors 1E 15
Longcroft. Cumb 4D 112
Longcroft. Falk 2A 128
Longcross. Surr 4A 38
Longdale. Cumb 4H 103
Longdales. Cumb 5G 113
Longden. Shrp 5G 71
Longden Common. Shrp 5G 71
Long Ditton. Surr 4C 38
Longdon. Staf 4E 73
Longdon. Worc 2D 48
Longdon Green. Staf 4E 73
Longdon on Tern. Telf 4A 72
Longdown. Devn 3B 12
Longdowns. Corn 5B 6
Long Drax. N Yor 2G 93
Long Duckmanton. Derbs 3B 86
Long Eaton. Derbs 2B 74
Longfield. Kent 4H 39
Longfield. Shet 10E 173
Longfield Hill. Kent 4H 39
Longford. Derbs 2G 73
Longford. Glos 3D 48
Longford. G Lon 3B 38
Longford. Shrp 2A 72
Longford. Telf 4B 72
Longford. W Mid 2H 61
Longforgan. Per 1F 137
Longformacus. Bord 4C 130
Longframlington. Nmbd 4F 121
Long Gardens. Essx 2B 54
Long Green. Ches W 3G 83
Long Green. Worc 2D 48
Longham. Dors 3F 15
Longham. Norf 4B 78
Long Hanborough. Oxon 4C 50
Longhedge. Wilts 2D 22
Longhill. Abers 3H 161
Longhirst. Nmbd 1F 115
Longhope. Glos 4B 48
Longhope. Orkn 8C 172
Longhorsley. Nmbd 5F 121
Longhoughton. Nmbd 3G 121
Long Itchington. Warw 4B 62
Longlands. Cumb 1D 102
Longlane. Derbs 2G 73
Long Lane. Telf 4A 72
Longlane. W Ber 4C 36
Long Lawford. Warw 3B 62
Long Lease. N Yor 4G 107
Longley Green. Worc 5B 60
Long Load. Som 4H 21
Longmanhill. Abers 2E 161
Long Marston. Herts 4G 51
Long Marston. N Yor 4H 99
Long Marston. Warw 1G 49
Long Marton. Cumb 2H 103
Long Meadow. Cambs 4E 65
Long Meadowend. Shrp 2G 59
Long Melford. Suff 1B 54
Longmoor Camp. Hants 3F 25
Longmorn. Mor 3G 159
Longmoss. Ches E 3C 84
Long Newnton. Glos 2E 35
Longnewton. Bord 2H 119
Long Newton. Stoc T 3A 106
Longney. Glos 4C 48
Longniddry. E Lot 2H 129
Longnor. Shrp 5G 71
Longnor. Staf 4E 85
(nr. Leek)
Longnor. Staf 4C 72
(nr. Stafford)
Longparish. Hants 2C 24
Longpark. Cumb 3F 113
Long Preston. N Yor 4H 97
Longridge. Lanc 1E 90
Longridge. Staf 4D 72
Longridge. W Lot 3C 128
Longriggend. N Lan 2B 128
Long Riston. E Yor 5F 101
Longrock. Corn 3C 4
Longsdon. Staf 5D 84
Longshaw. G Man 4D 90
Longshaw. Staf 1E 73
Longside. Abers 4H 161
Longslow. Shrp 2A 72
Longstanton. Cambs 4C 64
Longstock. Hants 3B 24
Longstowe. Cambs 5C 64
Long Stratton. Norf 1D 66
Long Street. Mil 1F 51
Longstreet. Wilts 1G 23
Long Sutton. Hants 2F 25
Long Sutton. Linc 3D 76
Long Sutton. Som 4H 21
Longthorpe. Pet 1A 64
Long Thurlow. Suff 4C 66
Longthwaite. Cumb 2F 103
Longton. Lanc 2C 90
Longton. Stoke 1D 72
Longtown. Cumb 3E 113
Longtown. Here 3G 47
Longville in the Dale.
Shrp 1H 59
Long Whatton. Leics 3B 74
Longwick. Buck 5F 51
Long Wittenham. Oxon 2D 36
Longwitton. Nmbd 1D 115
Longworth. Oxon 2B 36
Longyester. E Lot 3B 130
Lonmore. High 4B 154
Looe. Corn 3G 7
Loose. Kent 5B 40
Loosegate. Linc 3C 76
Loosley Row. Buck 5G 51
Lopcombe Corner. Wilts 3A 24
Lopen. Som 1H 13
Loppington. Shrp 3G 71
Lorbottle. Nmbd 4E 121
Lorbottle Hall. Nmbd 4E 121
Lordington. W Sus 2F 17
Loscoe. Derbs 1B 74
Loscombe. Dors 3A 14
Losgaintir. W Isl 8C 171
Lossiemouth. Mor 2G 159
Lossit. Arg 4A 124
Lostock Gralam. Ches W 3A 84
Lostock Green. Ches W 3A 84
Lostock Hall. Lanc 2D 90
Lostock Junction. G Man 4E 91
Lostwithiel. Corn 3F 7
Lothbeg. High 2G 165
Lothersdale. N Yor 5B 98
Lothianbridge. Midl 3G 129
Lothianburn. Edin 3F 129
Lothmore. High 2G 165
Lottisham. Som 3A 22
Loudwater. Buck 1A 38
Loughborough. Leics 4C 74
Loughbrickland. Ban 5F 178
Loughgall. Arm 4D 178
Loughguile. Bmny 4G 175
Loughinisland. Down 5J 179
Loughmacrory. Omag 2L 177
Loughor. Swan 3E 31
Loughton. Essx 1F 39
Loughton. Mil 2G 51
Loughton. Shrp 2A 60
Lound. Linc 4H 75
Lound. Notts 2D 86
Lound. Suff 1H 67
Lount. Leics 4A 74
Loup, The. Cook 1D 178
Louth. Linc 2C 88
Love Clough. Lanc 2G 91
Lovedean. Hants 1E 17
Lover. Wilts 4H 23
Loversall. S Yor 1C 86
Loves Green. Essx 5G 53
Loveston. Pemb 4E 43
Lovington. Som 3A 22
Low Ackworth. W Yor 3E 93
Low Angerton. Nmbd 1D 115
Low Ardwell. Dum 5F 109
Low Ballochdoan. S Ayr 2F 109
Lowbands. Glos 2C 48
Low Barlings. Linc 3H 87
Low Bell End. N Yor 5E 107
Low Bentham. N Yor 3F 97
Low Borrowbridge.
Cumb 4H 103
Low Bradfield. S Yor 1G 85
Low Bradley. N Yor 5C 98
Low Braithwaite. Cumb 5F 113
Low Brunton. Nmbd 2C 114
Low Burnham. N Lin 4A 94
Lowca. Cumb 2A 102
Low Catton. E Yor 4B 100
Low Coniscliffe. Darl 3F 105
Low Coylton. S Ayr 3D 116
Low Crosby. Cumb 4F 113
Low Dalby. N Yor 1C 100
Lowdham. Notts 1D 74
Low Dinsdale. Darl 3A 106
Lowe. Shrp 2H 71
Low Ellington. N Yor 1E 98
Lower Amble. Corn 1D 6
Lower Ansty. Dors 2C 14
Lower Arboll. High 5F 165
Lower Arncott. Oxon 4E 50
Lower Ashton. Devn 4B 12
Lower Assendon. Oxon 3F 37
Lower Auchenreath.
Mor 2A 160
Lower Badcall. High 4B 166
Lower Ballam. Lanc 1B 90
Lower Ballinderry. Lis 3F 178
Lower Basildon. W Ber 4E 36
Lower Beeding. W Sus 3D 26
Lower Benefield. Nptn 2G 63
Lower Bentley. Worc 4D 61
Lower Beobridge. Shrp 1B 60
Lower Bockhampton.
Dors 3C 14
Lower Boddington. Nptn 5B 62
Lower Bordean. Hants 4E 25
Lower Brailes. Warw 2B 50
Lower Breakish. High 1E 147
Lower Broadheath. Worc 5C 60
Lower Brynamman. Neat 4H 45
Lower Bullingham. Here 2A 48
Lower Bullington. Hants 2C 24
Lower Burgate. Hants 1G 15
Lower Cam. Glos 5C 48
Lower Catesby. Nptn 5C 62
Lower Chapel. Powy 2D 46
Lower Cheriton. Devn 2E 12
Lower Chicksgrove. Wilts 3E 23
Lower Chute. Wilts 1B 24
Lower Clopton. Warw 5F 61
Lower Common. Hants 2E 25
Lower Crossings. Derbs 2E 85
Lower Cumberworth.
W Yor 4C 92
Lower Darwen. Bkbn 2E 91
Lower Dean. Bed 4H 63
Lower Dean. Devn 2D 8
Lower Diabaig. High 2G 155
Lower Dicker. E Sus 4G 27
Lower Dounreay. High 2B 168
Lower Down. Shrp 2F 59
Lower Dunsforth. N Yor 3G 99
Lower East Carleton.
Norf 5D 78
Lower Egleton. Here 1B 48
Lower Ellastone. Derbs 1F 73
Lower End. Nptn 4F 63
Lower Everleigh. Wilts 1G 23
Lower Eype. Dors 3H 13
Lower Failand. N Som 4A 34
Lower Faintree. Shrp 2A 60
Lower Farringdon. Hants 3F 25
Lower Foxdale. IOM 4B 108
Lower Frankton. Shrp 2F 71
Lower Froyle. Hants 2F 25
Lower Gabwell. Devn 2F 9
Lower Gledfield. High 4C 164
Lower Godney. Som 2H 21
Lower Gravenhurst.
C Beds 2B 52
Lower Green. Essx 2E 53
Lower Green. Norf 2B 78
Lower Green. Staf 5D 72
Lower Green. W Ber 5B 36
Lower Halstow. Kent 4C 40
Lower Hardres. Kent 5F 41
Lower Hardwick. Here 5G 59
Lower Hartshay. Derbs 5A 86
Lower Hawthwaite. Cumb 1B 96
Lower Hayton. Shrp 2H 59
Lower Hergest. Here 5E 59
Lower Heyford. Oxon 3C 50
Lower Heysham. Lanc 3D 96
Lower Higham. Kent 3B 40
Lower Holbrook. Suff 2E 55
Lower Holditch. Dors 2G 13
Lower Hordley. Shrp 3F 71
Lower Horncroft. W Sus 4B 26
Lower Kilcott. Glos 3C 34
Lower Killeyan. Arg 5A 124
Lower Kingcombe. Dors 3A 14
Lower Kingswood. Surr 5D 38
Lower Kinnerton. Ches W 4F 83
Lower Langford. N Som 5H 33
Lower Largo. Fife 3G 137
Lower Layham. Suff 1D 54
Lower Ledwyche. Shrp 3H 59
Lower Leigh. Staf 2E 73
Lower Lemington. Glos 2H 49
Lower Lenie. High 1H 149
Lower Ley. Glos 4C 48
Lower Llanfadog. Powy 4B 58
Lower Lode. Glos 2D 49
Lower Lovacott. Devn 4F 19
Lower Loxhore. Devn 3G 19
Lower Loxley. Staf 2E 73
Lower Lydbrook. Glos 4A 48
Lower Lye. Here 4G 59
Lower Machen. Newp 3F 33
Lower Maes-coed. Here 2G 47
Lower Meend. Glos 5A 48
Lower Midway. Derbs 3H 73
Lower Milovaig. High 3A 154
Lower Moor. Worc 1E 49
Lower Morton. S Glo 2B 34
Lower Mountain. Flin 5F 83
Lower Nazeing. Essx 5D 53
Lower Netchwood. Shrp 1A 60
Lower Nyland. Dors 4C 22
Lower Oakfield. Fife 4D 136
Lower Oddington. Glos 3H 49
Lower Ollach. High 5E 155
Lower Penarth. V Glam 5E 33
Lower Penn. Staf 1C 60
Lower Pennington. Hants 3B 16
Lower Peover. Ches W 3B 84
Lower Pilsley. Derbs 4B 86
Lower Pitkerrie. High 1C 158
Lower Place. G Man 3H 91
Lower Quinton. Warw 1G 49
Lower Rainham. Medw 4C 40
Lower Raydon. Suff 2D 54
Lower Seagry. Wilts 3E 35
Lower Shelton. C Beds 1H 51
Lower Shiplake. Oxon 4F 37
Lower Shuckburgh.
Warw 4B 62
Lower Sketty. Swan 3F 31
Lower Slade. Devn 2F 19
Lower Slaughter. Glos 3G 49
Lower Soudley. Glos 4B 48
Lower Stanton St Quintin.
Wilts 3E 35
Lower Stoke. Medw 3C 40
Lower Stondon. C Beds 2B 52
Lower Stonnall. Staf 5E 73
Lower Stow Bedon. Norf 1B 66
Lower Street. Norf 2E 79
Lower Strensham. Worc 1E 49
Lower Sundon. C Beds 3A 52
Lower Swanwick. Hants 2C 16
Lower Swell. Glos 3G 49
Lower Tale. Devn 2D 12
Lower Tean. Staf 2E 73
Lower Thurlton. Norf 1G 67
Lower Thurnham. Lanc 4D 96
Lower Thurvaston. Derbs 2G 73
Lowertown. Corn 4D 4
Lower Town. Here 1B 48
Lower Town. IOS 1B 4
Lowertown. Orkn 8D 172
Lower Town. Pemb 1D 42
Lower Tysoe. Warw 1B 50
Lower Upham. Hants 1D 16
Lower Upnor. Medw 3B 40
Lower Vexford. Som 3E 20
Lower Walton. Warr 2A 84
Lower Wear. Devn 4C 12
Lower Weare. Som 1H 21
Lower Welson. Here 5E 59
Lower Whatcombe. Dors 2D 14
Lower Whitley. Ches W 3A 84
Lower Wield. Hants 2E 25
Lower Withington.
Ches E 4C 84
Lower Woodend. Buck 3G 37
Lower Woodford. Wilts 3G 23
Lower Wraxall. Dors 2A 14
Lower Wych. Ches W 1G 71
Lower Wyche. Worc 1C 48
Lowesby. Leics 5E 74
Lowestoft. Suff 1H 67
Loweswater. Cumb 2C 102
Low Etherley. Dur 2E 105
Lowfield Heath. W Sus 1D 26
Lowford. Hants 1C 16
Low Fulney. Linc 3B 76
Low Gate. Nmbd 3C 114
Lowgill. Cumb 5H 103
Lowgill. Lanc 3F 97
Low Grantley. N Yor 2E 99
Low Green. N Yor 4E 98
Low Habberley. Worc 3C 60
Low Ham. Som 4H 21
Low Hameringham. Linc 4C 88
Low Hawkser. N Yor 4G 107
Low Hesket. Cumb 5F 113
Low Hesleyhurst. Nmbd 5E 121
Lowick. Cumb 1B 96
Lowick. Nptn 2G 63
Lowick. Nmbd 1E 121
Lowick Bridge. Cumb 1B 96
Lowick Green. Cumb 1B 96
Low Knipe. Cumb 3G 103
Low Leighton. Derbs 2E 85
Low Lorton. Cumb 2C 102
Low Marishes. N Yor 2C 100
Low Marnham. Notts 4F 87
Low Mill. N Yor 5D 106
Low Moor. Lanc 5G 97
Low Moor. W Yor 2B 92
Low Moorsley. Tyne 5G 115
Low Newton-by-the-Sea.
Nmbd 2G 121
Lownie Moor. Ang 4D 145
Lowood. Bord 1H 119
Low Row. Cumb 3G 113
(nr. Brampton)
Low Row. Cumb 5C 112
(nr. Wigton)
Low Row. N Yor 5C 104
Lowsonford. Warw 4F 61
Low Street. Norf 5C 78
Lowther. Cumb 2G 103
Lowthorpe. E Yor 3E 101
Lowton. Devn 2G 11
Lowton. G Man 1A 84
Lowton. Som 1E 13
Lowton Common. G Man 1A 84
Low Torry. Fife 1D 128
Low Toynton. Linc 3B 88
Low Valleyfield. Fife 1C 128
Low Westwood. Dur 4E 115
Low Whinnow. Cumb 4E 112
Low Wood. Cumb 1C 96
Low Worsall. N Yor 4A 106
Low Wray. Cumb 4E 103
Loxbeare. Devn 1C 12
Loxhill. Surr 2B 26
Loxhore. Devn 3G 19
Loxley. S Yor 2H 85
Loxley. Warw 5G 61
Loxley Green. Staf 2E 73
Loxton. N Som 1G 21
Loxwood. W Sus 2B 26
Lubcroy. High 3A 164
Lubenham. Leics 2E 62
Lubinvullin. High 2F 167
Luccombe. Som 2C 20
Luccombe Village. IOW 4D 16
Lucker. Nmbd 1F 121
Luckett. Corn 5D 11
Luckington. Wilts 3D 34
Lucklawhill. Fife 1G 137
Luckwell Bridge. Som 3C 20
Lucton. Here 4G 59
Ludag. W Isl 7C 170
Ludborough. Linc 1B 88
Ludchurch. Pemb 3F 43
Luddenden. W Yor 2A 92
Luddenden Foot. W Yor 2A 92
Luddenham. Kent 4D 40
Ludderburn. Cumb 5F 103
Luddesdown. Kent 4A 40
Luddington. N Lin 3B 94
Luddington. Warw 5F 61
Luddington in the Brook.
Nptn 2A 64
Ludford. Linc 2A 88
Ludford. Shrp 3H 59
Ludgershall. Buck 4E 51
Ludgershall. Wilts 1A 24
Ludgvan. Corn 3C 4
Ludham. Norf 4F 79
Ludlow. Shrp 3H 59
Ludstone. Shrp 1C 60
Ludwell. Wilts 4E 23
Ludworth. Dur 5G 115
Luffenhall. Herts 3C 52
Luffincott. Devn 3D 10
Lugar. E Ayr 2E 117
Luggate Burn. E Lot 2C 130
Lugg Green. Here 4G 59
Luggiebank. N Lan 2A 128
Lugton. E Ayr 4F 127
Lugwardine. Here 1A 48
Luib. High 1D 146
Luib. Stir 1D 135
Lulham. Here 1H 47
Lullington. Derbs 4G 73
Lullington. E Sus 5G 27
Lullington. Som 1C 22
Lulsgate Bottom. N Som 5A 34
Lulsley. Worc 5B 60
Lulworth Camp. Dors 4D 14
Lumb. Lanc 2G 91
Lumb. W Yor 2A 92
Lumby. N Yor 1E 93
Lumphanan. Abers 3C 152
Lumphinnans. Fife 4D 136
Lumsdaine. Bord 3E 131
Lumsden. Abers 1B 152
Lunan. Ang 3F 145
Lunanhead. Ang 3D 145
Luncarty. Per 1C 136
Lund. E Yor 5D 100
Lund. N Yor 1G 93
Lundie. Ang 5B 144
Lundin Links. Fife 3G 137
Lundy Green. Norf 1E 67
Lunna. Shet 5F 173
Lunning. Shet 5G 173
Lunnon. Swan 4E 31
Lunsford. Kent 5B 40
Lunsford's Cross. E Sus 4B 28
Lunt. Mers 4B 90
Luppitt. Devn 2E 13
Lupridge. Devn 3D 8
Lupset. W Yor 3D 92
Lupton. Cumb 1E 97
Lurgan. Cgvn 4E 178
Lurganare. New M 6E 178
Lurgashall. W Sus 3A 26
Lurley. Devn 1C 12
Lusby. Linc 4C 88
Luscombe. Devn 3D 9
Luson. Devn 4C 8
Luss. Arg 4C 134
Lussagiven. Arg 1E 125
Lusta. High 3B 154
Lustleigh. Devn 4A 12
Luston. Here 4G 59
Luthermuir. Abers 2F 145
Luthrie. Fife 2F 137
Lutley. Staf 2C 60
Luton. Devn 2C 12
(nr. Honiton)
Luton. Devn 5C 12
(nr. Teignmouth)
Luton. Lutn 3A 52
Luton (London) Airport.
Lutn 3B 52 & 205
Lutterworth. Leics 2C 62
Lutton. Devn 3B 8
(nr. Ivybridge)
Lutton. Devn 2C 8
(nr. South Brent)
Lutton. Linc 3D 76
Lutton. Nptn 2A 64
Lutton Gowts. Linc 3D 76
Lutworthy. Devn 1A 12
Luxborough. Som 3C 20
Luxley. Glos 3B 48
Luxulyan. Corn 3E 7
Lybster. High 5E 169
Lydbury North. Shrp 2F 59
Lydcott. Devn 3G 19
Lydd. Kent 3E 29
Lydden. Kent 1G 29
(nr. Dover)
Lydden. Kent 4H 41
(nr. Margate)
Lyddington. Rut 1F 63
Lydd (London Ashford) Airport.
Kent 3E 29
Lydd-on-Sea. Kent 3E 29
Lydeard St Lawrence.
Som 3E 21
Lyde Green. Hants 1F 25
Lydford. Devn 4F 11
Lydford Fair Place. Som 3A 22
Lydgate. G Man 4H 91
Lydgate. W Yor 2H 91
Lydham. Shrp 1F 59
Lydiard Millicent. Wilts 3F 35
Lydiate. Mers 4B 90
Lydiate Ash. Worc 3D 61
Lydlinch. Dors 1C 14
Lydmarsh. Som 2G 13
Lydney. Glos 5B 48
Lydstep. Pemb 5E 43
Lye. W Mid 2D 60
Lye Green. Buck 5H 51
Lye Green. E Sus 2G 27
Lye Head. Worc 3B 60
Lye, The. Shrp 1A 60
Lyford. Oxon 2B 36
Lyham. Nmbd 1E 121
Lylestone. N Ayr 5E 127
Lymbridge Green. Kent 1F 29
Lyme Regis. Dors 3G 13
Lyminge. Kent 1F 29
Lymington. Hants 3B 16
Lyminster. W Sus 5B 26
Lymm. Warr 2A 84
Lymore. Hants 3A 16
Lympne. Kent 2F 29
Lympsham. Som 1G 21
Lympstone. Devn 4C 12
Lynaberack Lodge. High 4B 150
Lynbridge. Devn 2H 19
Lynch. Som 2C 20
Lynchat. High 3B 150
Lynch Green. Norf 5D 78
Lyndhurst. Hants 2B 16
Lyndon. Rut 5G 75
Lyne. Bord 5F 129
Lyne. Surr 4B 38
Lyneal. Shrp 2G 71
Lyne Down. Here 2B 48
Lyneham. Oxon 3A 50
Lyneham. Wilts 4F 35
Lyneholmeford. Cumb 2G 113
Lynemouth. Nmbd 5G 121
Lyne of Gorthleck. High 1H 149
Lyne of Skene. Abers 2E 153
Lynesack. Dur 2D 105
Lyness. Orkn 8C 172
Lyng. Norf 4C 78
Lyngate. Norf 2E 79
(nr. North Walsham)
Lyngate. Norf 3F 79
(nr. Worstead)
Lynmouth. Devn 2H 19
Lynn. Staf 5E 73
Lynn. Telf 4B 72
Lynsted. Kent 4D 40
Lynstone. Corn 2C 10
Lynton. Devn 2H 19
Lynwilg. High 2C 150
Lyon's Gate. Dors 2B 14
Lyonshall. Here 5F 59
Lytchett Matravers. Dors 3E 15
Lytchett Minster. Dors 3E 15
Lyth. High 2E 169
Lytham. Lanc 2B 90
Lytham St Anne's. Lanc 2B 90
Lythe. N Yor 3F 107
Lythes. Orkn 9D 172
Lythmore. High 2C 168

M

Mabe Burnthouse. Corn 5B 6
Mabie. Dum 2A 112
Mablethorpe. Linc 2E 89
Macbiehill. Bord 4E 129
Macclesfield. Ches E 3D 84
Macclesfield Forest.
Ches E 3D 85
Macduff. Abers 2E 160
Machan. S Lan 4A 128
Macharioch. Arg 5B 122
Machen. Cphy 3F 33
Machrie. N Ayr 2C 122
Machrihanish. Arg 3A 122
Machroes. Gwyn 3C 68
Machynlleth. Powy 5G 69
Mackerye End. Herts 4B 52
Mackworth. Derb 2H 73
Macmerry. E Lot 2H 129
Macosquin. Cole 4E 174
Madderty. Per 1B 136
Maddington. Wilts 2F 23
Maddiston. Falk 2C 128
Madehurst. W Sus 4A 26
Madeley. Staf 1B 72
Madeley. Telf 5A 72
Madeley Heath. Staf 1B 72
Madeley Heath. Worc 3D 60
Madford. Devn 1E 13
Madingley. Cambs 4C 64
Madley. Here 2H 47
Madresfield. Worc 1D 48
Madron. Corn 3B 4
Maenaddwyn. IOA 2D 80
Maenclochog. Pemb 2E 43
Maendy. V Glam 4D 32
Maenporth. Corn 4E 5
Maentwrog. Gwyn 1F 69
Maen-y-groes. Cdgn 5C 56
Maer. Staf 2B 72
Maerdy. Carm 3G 45
Maerdy. Cnwy 1C 70
Maerdy. Rhon 2C 32
Maesbrook. Shrp 3F 71
Maesbury. Shrp 3F 71
Maesbury Marsh. Shrp 3F 71
Maes-glas. Flin 3D 82
Maesgwyn-Isaf. Powy 4D 70
Maeshafn. Den 4E 82
Maes Llyn. Cdgn 1D 44
Maesmynis. Powy 1D 46
Maesteg. B'end 2B 32
Maestir. Cdgn 1F 45
Maesybont. Carm 4F 45
Maesycrugiau. Carm 1E 45
Maesycwmmer. Cphy 2E 33
Maesyrhandir. Powy 1C 58
Magdalen Laver. Essx 5F 53
Maggieknockater. Mor 4H 159
Magham Down. E Sus 4H 27
Maghaberry. Lis 3F 179
Maghera. Down 6H 179
Maghera. Mag 6E 174
Magherafelt. Mag 7E 174
Magheralin. Cgvn 4F 178
Magheramason. Strab 1F 176
Magheraveely. Ferm 7K 177
Maghery. Cgvn 3D 178
Maghull. Mers 4B 90
Magor. Mon 3H 33
Magpie Green. Suff 3C 66
Maguiresbridge. Ferm 6J 177
Magwyr. Mon 3H 33
Maidenbower. W Sus 2D 27
Maiden Bradley. Wilts 3D 22
Maidencombe. Torb 2F 9
Maidenhayne. Devn 3F 13
Maidenhead. Wind 3G 37
Maiden Law. Dur 5E 115
Maiden Newton. Dors 3A 14
Maidens. S Ayr 4B 116
Maiden's Green. Brac 4G 37
Maidensgrove. Oxon 3F 37
Maidenwell. Corn 5B 10
Maidenwell. Linc 3C 88
Maiden Wells. Pemb 5D 42
Maidford. Nptn 5D 62
Maids Moreton. Buck 2F 51
Maidstone. Kent 5B 40
Maidwell. Nptn 3E 63
Mail. Shet 9F 173
Maindee. Newp 3G 33
Mainsforth. Dur 1A 106
Mains of Auchindachy.
Mor 4B 160
Mains of Auchnagatt.
Abers 4G 161
Mains of Drum. Abers 4F 153
Mains of Edingight. Mor 3C 160
Mainsriddle. Dum 4G 111
Mainstone. Shrp 2E 59
Maisemore. Glos 3D 48
Major's Green. Worc 3F 61
Makeney. Derbs 1A 74
Makerstoun. Bord 1A 120
Malacleit. W Isl 1C 170
Malaig. High 4E 147
Malaig Bheag. High 4E 147
Malborough. Devn 5D 8
Malcoff. Derbs 2E 85
Malcolmburn. Mor 3A 160
Malden Rushett. G Lon 4C 38
Maldon. Essx 5B 54
Malham. N Yor 3B 98
Maligar. High 2D 155
Malinslee. Telf 5A 72
Mallaig. High 4E 147
Malleny Mills. Edin 3E 129
Mallows Green. Essx 3E 53
Malltraeth. IOA 4D 80
Mallusk. Newt 1G 179
Mallwyd. Gwyn 4A 70
Malmesbury. Wilts 3E 35
Malmsmead. Devn 2A 20
Malpas. Ches W 1G 71
Malpas. Corn 4C 6
Malpas. Newp 2F 33
Malswick. Glos 3C 48
Maltby. S Yor 1C 86
Maltby. Stoc T 3B 106
Maltby le Marsh. Linc 2D 88
Malt Lane. Arg 3H 133
Maltman's Hill. Kent 1D 28
Malton. N Yor 2B 100
Malvern Link. Worc 1C 48
Malvern Wells. Worc 1C 48
Mamble. Worc 3A 60
Mamhilad. Mon 5G 47
Manaccan. Corn 4E 5
Manafon. Powy 5D 70
Manais. W Isl 9D 171
Manaton. Devn 4A 12
Manby. Linc 2C 88
Mancetter. Warw 1H 61
Manchester.
G Man 1C 84 & 197
Manchester International Airport.
G Man 2C 84 & 205
Mancot. Flin 4F 83
Manea. Cambs 2D 65
Maney. W Mid 1F 61
Manfield. N Yor 3F 105
Mangotsfield. S Glo 4B 34
Mangurstadh. W Isl 4C 171
Mankinholes. W Yor 2H 91
Manley. Ches W 3H 83
Manmoel. Cphy 5E 47
Mannal. Arg 4A 138
Mannerston. Falk 2D 128
Manningford Bohune.
Wilts 1G 23
Manningford Bruce. Wilts 1G 23
Manningham. W Yor 1B 92
Mannings Heath. W Sus 3D 26
Mannington. Dors 2F 15
Manningtree. Essx 2E 54
Mannofield. Aber 3G 153
Manorbier. Pemb 5E 43
Manorbier Newton. Pemb 5E 43
Manorowen. Pemb 1D 42
Manor Park. G Lon 2F 39
Mansell Gamage. Here 1G 47
Mansell Lacy. Here 1H 47
Mansergh. Cumb 1F 97
Mansewood. Glas 3G 127
Mansfield. E Ayr 3F 117
Mansfield. Notts 4C 86
Mansfield Woodhouse.
Notts 4C 86
Mansriggs. Cumb 1B 96
Manston. Dors 1D 14
Manston. Kent 4H 41
Manston. W Yor 1D 92
Manswood. Dors 2E 15
Manthorpe. Linc 4H 75
(nr. Bourne)
Manthorpe. Linc 2G 75
(nr. Grantham)
Manton. N Lin 4C 94
Manton. Notts 3C 86
Manton. Rut 5F 75
Manton. Wilts 5G 35
Manuden. Essx 3E 53
Maperton. Som 4B 22
Maplebeck. Notts 4E 86
Maple Cross. Herts 1B 38
Mapledurham. Oxon 4E 37
Mapledurwell. Hants 1E 25
Maplehurst. W Sus 3C 26
Maplescombe. Kent 4G 39
Mapleton. Derbs 1F 73
Mapperley. Derbs 1B 74
Mapperley. Notts 1C 74
Mapperley Park. Notts 1C 74
Mapperton. Dors 3A 14
(nr. Beaminster)
Mapperton. Dors 3E 15
(nr. Poole)
Mappleborough Green.
Warw 4E 61
Mappleton. E Yor 5G 101
Mapplewell. S Yor 4D 92
Mappowder. Dors 2C 14
Maraig. W Isl 7E 171
Marazion. Corn 3C 4
Marbhig. W Isl 6G 171
Marbury. Ches E 1H 71
March. Cambs 1D 64
Marcham. Oxon 2C 36
Marchamley. Shrp 3H 71
Marchington. Staf 2F 73
Marchington Woodlands.
Staf 3F 73
Marchwiel. Wrex 1F 71
Marchwood. Hants 1B 16
Marcross. V Glam 5C 32
Marden. Here 1A 48
Marden. Kent 1B 28
Marden. Wilts 1F 23
Marden Beech. Kent 1B 28
Marden Thorn. Kent 1B 28
Mardu. Shrp 2E 59
Mardy. Mon 4G 47
Marefield. Leics 5E 75
Mareham le Fen. Linc 4B 88
Mareham on the Hill.
Linc 4B 88
Marehay. Derbs 1A 74
Marehill. W Sus 4B 26
Maresfield. E Sus 3F 27
Marfleet. Hull 2E 95
Marford. Wrex 5F 83
Margam. Neat 3A 32
Margaret Marsh. Dors 1D 14
Margaret Roding. Essx 4F 53
Margaretting. Essx 5G 53
Margaretting Tye. Essx 5G 53
Margate. Kent 3H 41
Margery. Surr 5D 38
Margnaheglish. N Ayr 2E 123
Marham. Norf 5G 77
Marhamchurch. Corn 2C 10
Marholm. Pet 5A 76
Marian Cwm. Den 3C 82
Mariandyrys. IOA 2F 81
Marian-glas. IOA 2E 81
Mariansleigh. Devn 4H 19
Marian-y-de. Gwyn 2C 68
Marine Town. Kent 3D 40
Marion-y-mor. Gwyn 2C 68
Marishader. High 2D 155
Marjoriebanks. Dum 1B 112
Mark. Dum 4G 109
Mark. Som 2G 21
Markbeech. Kent 1F 27
Markby. Linc 3D 89
Mark Causeway. Som 2G 21
Mark Cross. E Sus 2G 27
Markeaton. Derb 2H 73
Market Bosworth. Leics 5B 74
Market Deeping. Linc 4A 76
Market Drayton. Shrp 2A 72
Market End. Warw 2H 61
Market Harborough.
Leics 2E 63
Markethill. Arm 6D 178
Markethill. Per 5B 144
Market Lavington. Wilts 1F 23
Market Overton. Rut 4F 75
Market Rasen. Linc 2A 88
Market Stainton. Linc 2B 88
Market Weighton.
E Yor 5C 100
Market Weston. Suff 3B 66
Markfield. Leics 4B 74
Markham. Cphy 5E 47
Markinch. Fife 3E 137
Markington. N Yor 3E 99
Marksbury. Bath 5B 34
Mark's Corner. IOW 3C 16
Marks Tey. Essx 3C 54
Markwell. Corn 3H 7
Markyate. Herts 4A 52
Marlborough. Wilts 5G 35
Marlcliff. Warw 5E 61
Marldon. Devn 2E 9
Marle Green. E Sus 4G 27
Marlesford. Suff 5F 67
Marley Green. Ches E 1H 71
Marley Hill. Tyne 4F 115
Marlingford. Norf 5D 78
Mar Lodge. Abers 5E 151
Marloes. Pemb 4B 42
Marlow. Buck 3G 37
Marlow. Here 3G 59
Marlow Bottom. Buck 3G 37
Marlow Common. Buck 3G 37
Marlpit Hill. Kent 1F 27
Marlpits. E Sus 3F 27
Marlpool. Derbs 1B 74
Marnhull. Dors 1C 14
Marnoch. Abers 3C 160
Marnock. N Lan 3A 128
Marple. G Man 2D 84
Marr. S Yor 4F 93
Marrel. High 2H 165
Marrick. N Yor 5D 105
Marrister. Shet 5G 173
Marros. Carm 4G 43
Marsden. Tyne 3G 115
Marsden. W Yor 3A 92
Marsett. N Yor 1B 98
Marsh. Buck 5G 51
Marsh. Devn 1F 13
Marshall Meadows.
Nmbd 4F 131
Marshalsea. Dors 2G 13
Marshalswick. Herts 5B 52
Marsham. Norf 3D 78
Marshaw. Lanc 4E 97
Marsh Baldon. Oxon 2D 36
Marsh Benham. W Ber 5C 36
Marshborough. Kent 5H 41
Marshbrook. Shrp 2G 59
Marshbury. Essx 4G 53
Marshchapel. Linc 1C 88
Marshfield. Newp 3F 33
Marshfield. S Glo 4C 34
Marshgate. Corn 3B 10
Marsh Gibbon. Buck 3E 51
Marsh Green. Devn 3D 12
Marsh Green. Kent 1F 27
Marsh Green. Staf 5C 84
Marsh Green. Telf 4A 72
Marsh Lane. Derbs 3B 86
Marshside. Kent 4G 41
Marshside. Mers 3B 90
Marsh Side. Norf 1G 77
Marsh Street. Som 2C 20
Marsh, The. Powy 1F 59
Marsh, The. Shrp 3A 72
Marshwood. Dors 3G 13
Marske. N Yor 4E 105
Marske-by-the-Sea.
Red C 2D 106
Marston. Ches W 3A 84
Marston. Here 5F 59
Marston. Linc 1F 75
Marston. Oxon 5D 50
Marston. Staf 3D 72
(nr. Stafford)
Marston. Staf 4C 72
(nr. Wheaton Aston)
Marston. Warw 1G 61
Marston. Wilts 1E 23
Marston Doles. Warw 5B 62
Marston Green. W Mid 2F 61
Marston Hill. Glos 2G 35
Marston Jabbett. Warw 2A 62
Marston Magna. Som 4A 22
Marston Meysey. Wilts 2G 35
Marston Montgomery.
Derbs 2F 73
Marston Moretaine.
C Beds 1H 51
Marston on Dove. Derbs 3G 73
Marston St Lawrence.
Nptn 1D 50
Marston Stannett. Here 5H 59
Marston Trussell. Nptn 2D 62
Marstow. Here 4A 48
Marsworth. Buck 4H 51
Marten. Wilts 5A 36
Marthall. Ches E 3C 84
Martham. Norf 4G 79
Marthwaite. Cumb 5H 103
Martin. Hants 1F 15
Martin. Kent 1H 29
Martin. Linc 4B 88
(nr. Horncastle)
Martin. Linc 5A 88
(nr. Metheringham)
Martindale. Cumb 3F 103
Martin Dales. Linc 4A 88
Martin Drove End. Hants 4F 23
Martinhoe. Devn 2G 19
Martinhoe Cross. Devn 2G 19
Martin Hussingtree. Worc 4C 60
Martin Mill. Kent 1H 29
Martinscroft. Warr 2A 84
Martin's Moss. Ches E 4C 84
Martinstown. Bmna 5H 175
Martinstown. Dors 4B 14
Martlesham. Suff 1F 55
Martlesham Heath. Suff 1F 55
Martletwy. Pemb 3E 43
Martley. Worc 5B 60
Martock. Som 1H 13
Marton. Ches E 4C 84
Marton. Cumb 2B 96
Marton. E Yor 3G 101
(nr. Bridlington)
Marton. E Yor 1E 95
(nr. Hull)
Marton. Linc 2F 87
Marton. Midd 3C 106
Marton. N Yor 3G 99
(nr. Boroughbridge)
Marton. N Yor 1B 100
(nr. Pickering)
Marton. Shrp 3G 71
(nr. Myddle)
Marton. Shrp 5E 71
(nr. Worthen)
Marton. Warw 4B 62
Marton Abbey. N Yor 3H 99
Marton-le-Moor. N Yor 2F 99
Martyr's Green. Surr 5B 38
Martyr Worthy. Hants 3D 24
Marwick. Orkn 5B 172
Marwood. Devn 3F 19
Marybank. High 3G 157
(nr. Dingwall)
Marybank. High 1B 158
(nr. Invergordon)
Maryburgh. High 3H 157
Maryfield. Corn 3A 8
Maryhill. Glas 3G 127
Marykirk. Abers 2F 145
Marylebone. G Lon 2D 39
Marylebone. G Man 4D 90
Marypark. Mor 5F 159
Maryport. Cumb 1B 102
Maryport. Dum 5E 109
Marystow. Devn 4E 11
Mary Tavy. Devn 5F 11
Maryton. Ang 3C 144
(nr. Kirriemuir)
Maryton. Ang 3F 145
(nr. Montrose)
Marywell. Abers 4C 152
Marywell. Ang 4F 145
Masham. N Yor 1E 98
Mashbury. Essx 4G 53
Masongill. N Yor 2F 97
Masons Lodge. Abers 3F 153
Mastin Moor. Derbs 3B 86
Mastrick. Aber 3G 153
Matching. Essx 4F 53
Matching Green. Essx 4F 53
Matching Tye. Essx 4F 53
Matfen. Nmbd 2D 114
Matfield. Kent 1A 28
Mathern. Mon 2A 34
Mathon. Here 1C 48
Mathry. Pemb 1C 42
Matlaske. Norf 2D 78
Matlock. Derbs 4G 85
Matlock Bath. Derbs 5G 85
Matterdale End. Cumb 2E 103
Mattersey. Notts 2D 86
Mattersey Thorpe. Notts 2D 86
Mattingley. Hants 1F 25
Mattishall. Norf 4C 78
Mattishall Burgh. Norf 4C 78
Mauchline. E Ayr 2D 117
Maud. Abers 4G 161
Maudlin. Corn 2E 7
Maugersbury. Glos 3G 49
Maughold. IOM 2D 108
Maulden. C Beds 2A 52
Maulds Meaburn. Cumb 3H 103
Maunby. N Yor 1F 99
Maund Bryan. Here 5H 59
Mautby. Norf 4G 79
Mavesyn Ridware. Staf 4E 73
Mavis Enderby. Linc 4C 88
Mawbray. Cumb 5B 112
Mawdesley. Lanc 3C 90
Mawdlam. B'end 3B 32
Mawgan. Corn 4E 5
Mawgan Porth. Corn 2C 6
Maw Green. Ches E 5B 84
Mawla. Corn 4B 6
Mawnan. Corn 4E 5
Mawnan Smith. Corn 4E 5
Mawsley Village. Nptn 3F 63
Mawthorpe. Linc 3D 88
Maxey. Pet 5A 76
Maxstoke. Warw 2G 61
Maxted Street. Kent 1F 29
Maxton. Kent 1H 29
Maxton. Bord 1A 120
Maxwellheugh. Bord 1B 120
Maxwelltown. Dum 2A 112
Maxworthy. Corn 3C 10
Mayals. Swan 4F 31
Maybole. S Ayr 4C 116
Maybush. Sotn 1B 16
Maydown. Derr 5A 174

Myrelandhorn—Norton Woodseats

Myrelandhorn. High 3E 169
Mytchett. Surr 1G 25
Mythe, The. Glos 2D 49
Mytholmroyd. W Yor 2A 92
Myton-on-Swale. N Yor 3G 99
Mytton. Shrp 4G 71

N

Naast. High 5C 162
Na Buirgh. W Isl 8C 171
Naburn. York 5H 99
Nab Wood. W Yor 1B 92
Nackington. Kent 5F 41
Nacton. Suff 1F 55
Nafferton. E Yor 4E 101
Na Gearrannan. W Isl 3D 171
Nailbridge. Glos 4B 48
Nailsbourne. Som 4F 21
Nailsea. N Som 4H 33
Nailstone. Leics 5B 74
Nailsworth. Glos 2D 34
Nairn. High 3C 158
Nalderswood. Surr 1D 26
Nancegollan. Corn 3D 4
Nancledra. Corn 3B 4
Nangreaves. G Man 3G 91
Nanhyfer. Pemb 1E 43
Nannerch. Flin 4D 82
Nanpantan. Leics 4C 74
Nanpean. Corn 3D 6
Nanstallon. Corn 2E 7
Nant-ddu. Powy 4D 46
Nanternis. Cdgn 5C 56
Nantgaredig. Carm 3E 45
Nantgarw. Rhon 3E 33
Nant Glas. Powy 4B 58
Nantglyn. Den 4C 82
Nantgwyn. Powy 3B 58
Nantile. Gwyn 5E 81
Nantmawr. Shrp 3E 71
Nantmel. Powy 4C 58
Nantmor. Gwyn 1F 69
Nant Peris. Gwyn 5F 81
Nantwich. Ches E 5A 84
Nant-y-bai. Carm 1A 46
Nant-y-bwch. Blae 4E 47
Nant-y-Derry. Mon 5G 47
Nant-y-dugoed. Powy 4B 70
Nant-y-felin. Cnwy 3F 81
Nantyffyllon. B'end 2B 32
Nantyglo. Blae 4E 47
Nant-y-meichiaid. Powy 4D 70
Nant-y-moel. B'end 2C 32
Nant-y-Pandy. Cnwy 3F 81
Naphill. Buck 2G 37
Nappa. Lanc 4A 98
Napton on the Hill. Warw 4B 62
Narberth. Pemb 3F 43
Narberth Bridge. Pemb 3F 43
Narborough. Leics 1C 62
Narborough. Norf 4G 77
Narkurs. Corn 3H 7
Narth, The. Mon 5A 48
Narthwaite. Cumb 5A 104
Nasareth. Gwyn 1D 68
Naseby. Nptn 3D 62
Nash. Buck 2F 51
Nash. Here 4F 59
Nash. Kent 5G 41
Nash. Newp 3G 33
Nash. Shrp 3A 60
Nash Lee. Buck 5G 51
Nassington. Nptn 1H 63
Nasty. Herts 3D 52
Natcott. Devn 4C 18
Nateby. Cumb 4A 104
Nateby. Lanc 5D 96
Nately Scures. Hants 1F 25
Natland. Cumb 1E 97
Naughton. Suff 1D 54
Naunton. Glos 3G 49
Naunton. Worc 2D 49
Naunton Beauchamp. Worc 5D 60
Navenby. Linc 5G 87
Navestock Heath. Essx 1G 39
Navestock Side. Essx 1G 39
Navidale. High 2H 165
Nawton. N Yor 1A 100
Nayland. Suff 2C 54
Nazeing. Essx 5E 53
Neacroft. Hants 3G 15
Nealhouse. Cumb 4E 113
Neal's Green. W Mid 2H 61
Neap House. N Lin 3B 94
Near Sawrey. Cumb 5E 103
Neasden. G Lon 2D 38
Neasham. Darl 3A 106
Neath. Neat 2A 32
Neath Abbey. Neat 3G 31
Neatishead. Norf 3F 79
Neaton. Norf 5B 78
Nebo. Cdgn 4E 57
Nebo. Cnwy 5H 81
Nebo. Gwyn 5D 81
Nebo. IOA 1D 80
Necton. Norf 5A 78
Nedd. High 5B 166
Nedderton. Nmbd 1F 115
Nedging. Suff 1D 54
Nedging Tye. Suff 1D 54
Needham. Norf 2E 67
Needham Market. Suff 5C 66
Needham Street. Suff 4G 65
Needingworth. Cambs 3C 64
Needwood. Staf 3F 73
Neen Savage. Shrp 3A 60
Neen Sollars. Shrp 3A 60
Neenton. Shrp 2A 60
Nefyn. Gwyn 1C 68
Neilston. E Ren 4F 127
Neithrop. Oxon 1C 50
Nelly Andrews Green. Powy 5E 71
Nelson. Cphy 2E 32
Nelson. Lanc 1G 91
Nelson Village. Nmbd 2F 115
Nemphlar. S Lan 5B 128
Nempnett Thrubwell. Bath 5A 34
Nene Terrace. Linc 5B 76
Nenthall. Cumb 5A 114
Nenthead. Cumb 5A 114
Nenthorn. Bord 1A 120
Nercwys. Flin 4E 83
Neribus. Arg 4A 124
Nerston. S Lan 4H 127
Nesbit. Nmbd 1D 121
Nesfield. N Yor 5C 98
Ness. Ches W 3F 83
Nesscliffe. Shrp 4F 71
Ness of Tenston. Orkn 6B 172
Neston. Ches W 3E 83
Neston. Wilts 5D 34
Nethanfoot. S Lan 5B 128
Nether Alderley. Ches E 3C 84
Netheravon. Wilts 2G 23
Nether Blainslie. Bord 5B 130
Netherbrae. Abers 3E 161
Netherbrough. Orkn 6C 172
Nether Broughton. Leics 3D 74
Netherburn. S Lan 5B 128
Nether Burrow. Lanc 2F 97
Netherbury. Dors 3H 13
Netherby. Cumb 2E 113
Nether Careston. Ang 3E 145
Nether Cerne. Dors 3B 14
Nether Compton. Dors 1A 14
Nethercote. Glos 3G 49
Nethercote. Warw 4C 62
Nethercott. Devn 3E 19
Nethercott. Oxon 3C 50
Nether Dallachy. Mor 2A 160
Nether Durdie. Per 1E 136
Nether End. Derbs 3G 85
Netherend. Glos 5A 48
Nether Exe. Devn 2C 12
Netherfield. E Sus 4B 28
Netherfield. Notts 1D 74
Nethergate. Norf 3C 78
Netherhampton. Wilts 4G 23
Nether Handley. Derbs 3B 86
Nether Haugh. S Yor 1B 86
Nether Heage. Derbs 5A 86
Nether Heyford. Nptn 5D 62
Netherhouses. Cumb 1B 96
Nether Howcleugh. Dum 3C 118
Nether Kellet. Lanc 3E 97
Nether Kinmundy. Abers 4H 161
Netherland Green. Staf 2F 73
Nether Langwith. Notts 3C 86
Netherlaw. Dum 5E 111
Netherley. Abers 4F 153
Nethermill. Dum 1B 112
Nethermills. Mor 3C 160
Nether Moor. Derbs 4A 86
Nether Padley. Derbs 3G 85
Netherplace. E Ren 4G 127
Nether Poppleton. York 4H 99
Netherseal. Derbs 4G 73
Nether Silton. N Yor 5B 106
Nether Stowey. Som 3E 21
Nether Street. Essx 4F 53
Netherstreet. Wilts 5E 35
Netherthird. E Ayr 3E 117
Netherthong. W Yor 4B 92
Netherton. Ang 3E 145
Netherton. Cumb 1B 102
Netherton. Devn 5B 12
Netherton. Hants 1B 24
Netherton. Here 3A 48
Netherton. Mers 1F 83
Netherton. N Lan 4A 128
Netherton. Nmbd 4D 121
Netherton. Per 3A 144
Netherton. Shrp 2B 60
Netherton. Stir 2G 127
Netherton. W Mid 2D 60
Netherton. W Yor 3C 92
(nr. Horbury)
Netherton. W Yor 3B 92
(nr. Huddersfield)
Netherton. Worc 1E 49
Nethertown. Cumb 4A 102
Nethertown. High 1F 169
Nethertown. Staf 4F 73
Nether Urquhart. Fife 3D 136
Nether Wallop. Hants 3B 24
Nether Wasdale. Cumb 4C 102
Nether Welton. Cumb 5E 113
Nether Westcote. Glos 3H 49
Nether Whitacre. Warw 1G 61
Netherwhitton. Nmbd 5F 121
Nether Winchendon. Buck 4F 51
Nether Worton. Oxon 2C 50
Nethy Bridge. High 1E 151
Netley. Hants 2C 16
Netley. Shrp 5G 71
Netley Marsh. Hants 1B 16
Nettlebed. Oxon 3F 37
Nettlebridge. Som 2B 22
Nettlecombe. Dors 3A 14
Nettlecombe. IOW 5D 16
Nettleden. Herts 4A 52
Nettleham. Linc 3H 87
Nettlestead. Kent 5A 40
Nettlestead Green. Kent 5A 40
Nettlestone. IOW 3E 16
Nettlesworth. Dur 5F 115
Nettleton. Linc 4E 94
Nettleton. Wilts 4D 34
Netton. Devn 4B 8
Netton. Wilts 3G 23
Neuadd. Carm 3H 45
Neuadd. Powy 5C 70
Neuk, The. Abers 4E 153
Nevendon. Essx 1B 40
Nevern. Pemb 1A 44
New Abbey. Dum 3A 112
New Aberdour. Abers 2F 161
New Addington. G Lon 4E 39
Newall. W Yor 5D 98
New Alresford. Hants 3D 24
New Alyth. Per 4B 144
Newark. Orkn 3G 172
Newark. Pet 5B 76
Newark-on-Trent. Notts 5E 87
New Arley. Warw 2G 61
Newarthill. N Lan 4A 128
New Ash Green. Kent 4H 39
New Balderton. Notts 5F 87
New Barn. Kent 4H 39
New Barnetby. N Lin 3D 94
Newbattle. Midl 3G 129
New Bewick. Nmbd 2E 121
Newbie. Dum 3C 112
Newbiggin. Cumb 2H 103
(nr. Appleby)
Newbiggin. Cumb 3B 96
(nr. Barrow-in-Furness)
Newbiggin. Cumb 5G 113
(nr. Cumrew)
Newbiggin. Cumb 2F 103
(nr. Penrith)
Newbiggin. Cumb 5B 102
(nr. Seascale)
Newbiggin. Dur 5E 115
(nr. Consett)
Newbiggin. Dur 2C 104
(nr. Holwick)
Newbiggin. Nmbd 5C 114
Newbiggin. N Yor 5C 104
(nr. Askrigg)
Newbiggin. N Yor 1F 101
(nr. Filey)
Newbiggin. N Yor 1B 98
(nr. Thoralby)
Newbiggin-by-the-Sea. Nmbd 1G 115
Newbigging. Ang 5D 145
(nr. Monikie)
Newbigging. Ang 4B 144
(nr. Newtyle)
Newbigging. Ang 5D 144
(nr. Tealing)
Newbigging. Edin 2E 129
Newbigging. S Lan 5D 128
Newbiggin-on-Lune. Cumb 4A 104
Newbold. Derbs 3A 86
Newbold. Leics 4B 74
Newbold on Avon. Warw 3B 62
Newbold on Stour. Warw 1H 49
Newbold Pacey. Warw 5G 61
Newbold Verdon. Leics 5B 74
New Bolingbroke. Linc 5C 88
Newborough. IOA 4D 80
Newborough. Pet 5B 76
Newborough. Staf 3F 73
Newbottle. Nptn 2D 50
Newbottle. Tyne 4G 115
New Boultham. Linc 3G 87
Newbourne. Suff 1F 55
New Brancepeth. Dur 5F 115
Newbridge. Cphy 2F 33
Newbridge. Cdgn 5E 57
Newbridge. Corn 3B 4
New Bridge. Dum 2G 111
Newbridge. Edin 2E 129
Newbridge. Hants 1A 16
Newbridge. IOW 4C 16
Newbridge. N Yor 1C 100
Newbridge. Pemb 1D 42
Newbridge. Wrex 1E 71
Newbridge Green. Worc 2D 48
Newbridge-on-Usk. Mon 2G 33
Newbridge on Wye. Powy 5C 58
New Brighton. Flin 4E 83
New Brighton. Hants 2F 17
New Brighton. Mers 1F 83
New Brinsley. Notts 5B 86
Newbrough. Nmbd 3B 114
New Broughton. Wrex 5F 83
New Buckenham. Norf 1C 66
New Buildings. Derr 5A 174
Newbuildings. Devn 2A 12
Newburgh. Abers 1G 153
Newburgh. Fife 2E 137
Newburgh. Lanc 3C 90
Newburn. Tyne 3E 115
Newbury. W Ber 5C 36
Newbury. Wilts 2D 22
Newby. Cumb 2G 103
Newby. N Yor 2G 97
(nr. Ingleton)
Newby. N Yor 1E 101
(nr. Scarborough)
Newby. N Yor 3C 106
(nr. Stokesley)
Newby Bridge. Cumb 1C 96
Newby Cote. N Yor 2G 97
Newby East. Cumb 4F 113
Newby Head. Cumb 2G 103
New Byth. Abers 3F 161
Newby West. Cumb 4E 113
Newby Wiske. N Yor 1F 99
Newcastle. Ards 4L 179
Newcastle. B'end 3B 32
Newcastle. Down 6H 179
Newcastle. Mon 4H 47
Newcastle. Shrp 2E 59
Newcastle Emlyn. Carm 1D 44
Newcastle International Airport. Tyne 2E 115
Newcastleton. Bord 1F 113
Newcastle-under-Lyme. Staf 1C 72
Newcastle Upon Tyne. Tyne 3F 115 & 197
Newchapel. Pemb 1G 43
Newchapel. Powy 2B 58
Newchapel. Staf 5C 84
Newchapel. Surr 1E 27
New Cheriton. Hants 4D 24
Newchurch. Carm 3D 45
Newchurch. Here 5F 59
Newchurch. IOW 4D 16
Newchurch. Kent 2E 29
Newchurch. Lanc 1G 91
(nr. Nelson)
Newchurch. Lanc 2G 91
(nr. Rawtenstall)
Newchurch. Mon 2H 33
Newchurch. Powy 5E 58
Newchurch. Staf 3F 73
New Costessey. Norf 4D 78
Newcott. Devn 2F 13
New Cowper. Cumb 5C 112
Newcraighall. Edin 2G 129
New Crofton. W Yor 3D 93
New Cross. Cdgn 3F 57
New Cross. Som 1H 13
New Cumnock. E Ayr 3F 117
New Deer. Abers 4F 161
New Denham. Buck 2B 38
Newdigate. Surr 1C 26
New Duston. Nptn 4E 62
New Earswick. York 4A 100
New Edlington. S Yor 1C 86
New Elgin. Mor 2G 159
New Ellerby. E Yor 1E 95
Newell Green. Brac 4G 37
New Eltham. G Lon 3F 39
New End. Warw 4F 61
New End. Worc 5E 61
Newenden. Kent 3C 28
New England. Essx 1H 53
New England. Pet 5A 76
Newent. Glos 3C 48
New Ferry. Mers 2F 83
Newfield. Dur 4F 115
(nr. Chester-le-Street)
Newfield. Dur 1F 105
(nr. Willington)
New Forest. Hants 1H 15
Newfound. Hants 1D 24
New Fryston. W Yor 2E 93
New Galloway. Dum 2D 110
Newgate. Norf 1C 78
Newgate. Pemb 2C 42
Newgate Street. Herts 5D 52
New Greens. Herts 5B 52
New Grimsby. IOS 1A 4
New Hainford. Norf 4E 78
Newhall. Ches E 1A 72
Newhall. Staf 3G 73
Newham. Nmbd 2F 121
New Hartley. Nmbd 2G 115
Newhaven. Derbs 4F 85
Newhaven. E Sus 5F 27 & 204
Newhaven. Edin 2F 129
New Haw. Surr 4B 38
New Hedges. Pemb 4F 43
New Herrington. Tyne 4G 115
Newhey. G Man 3H 91
New Holkham. Norf 2A 78
New Holland. N Lin 2D 94
Newholm. N Yor 3F 107
New Houghton. Derbs 4C 86
New Houghton. Norf 3G 77
Newhouse. N Lan 3A 128
New Houses. N Yor 2H 97
New Hutton. Cumb 5G 103
New Hythe. Kent 5B 40
Newick. E Sus 3F 27
Newingreen. Kent 2F 29
Newington. Edin 2F 129
Newington. Kent 2F 29
(nr. Folkestone)
Newington. Kent 4C 40
(nr. Sittingbourne)
Newington. Notts 1D 86
Newington. Oxon 2E 36
Newington Bagpath. Glos 2D 34
New Inn. Carm 2E 45
New Inn. Mon 5H 47
New Inn. N Yor 2H 97
New Inn. Torf 5G 47
New Invention. Shrp 3E 59
New Kelso. High 4B 156
New Lanark. S Lan 5B 128
Newland. Glos 5A 48
Newland. Hull 1D 94
Newland. N Yor 2G 93
Newland. Som 3B 20
Newland. Worc 1C 48
Newlandrig. Midl 3G 129
Newlands. Cumb 1E 103
Newlands. Essx 2C 40
Newlands. High 4B 158
Newlands. Nmbd 4D 115
Newlands. Staf 3E 73
Newlands of Geise. High 2C 168
Newlands of Tynet. Mor 2A 160
Newlands Park. IOA 2B 80
New Lane. Lanc 3C 90
New Lane End. Warr 1A 84
New Langholm. Dum 1E 113
New Leake. Linc 5D 88
New Leeds. Abers 3G 161
New Lenton. Nott 2C 74
New Longton. Lanc 2D 90
Newlot. Orkn 6E 172
New Luce. Dum 3G 109
Newlyn. Corn 4B 4
Newmachar. Abers 2F 153
Newmains. N Lan 4B 128
New Mains of Ury. Abers 5F 153
New Malden. G Lon 4D 38
Newman's Green. Suff 1B 54
Newmarket. Suff 4F 65
Newmarket. W Isl 4G 171
New Marske. Red C 2D 106
New Marton. Shrp 2F 71
New Micklefield. W Yor 1E 93
New Mill. Abers 4E 160
Newmill. Ant 8J 175
New Mill. Corn 3B 4
New Mill. Herts 4H 51
Newmill. Mor 3B 160
Newmill. Bord 3G 119
New Mill. W Yor 4B 92
New Mill. Wilts 5G 35
Newmillerdam. W Yor 3D 92
New Mills. Corn 3C 6
Newmills. Cgvn 4E 178
New Mills. Derbs 2E 85
Newmills. Dngn 3C 178
Newmills. Fife 1D 128
Newmills. High 2A 158
New Mills. Mon 5A 48
New Mills. Powy 5C 70
Newmiln. Per 5A 144
Newmilns. E Ayr 1E 117
New Milton. Hants 3H 15
New Mistley. Essx 2E 54
New Moat. Pemb 2E 43
Newmore. High 3H 157
(nr. Dingwall)
Newmore. High 1A 158
(nr. Invergordon)
Newnham. Cambs 5D 64
Newnham. Glos 4B 48
Newnham. Hants 1F 25
Newnham. Herts 2C 52
Newnham. Kent 5D 40
Newnham. Nptn 5C 62
Newnham. Warw 4F 61
Newnham Bridge. Worc 4A 60
New Ollerton. Notts 4D 86
New Oscott. W Mid 1E 61
Newpark. Fife 2G 137
New Park. N Yor 4E 99
New Pitsligo. Abers 3F 161
New Polzeath. Corn 1D 6
Newport. Corn 4D 10
Newport. Devn 3F 19
Newport. E Yor 1B 94
Newport. Essx 2F 53
Newport. Glos 2B 34
Newport. High 1H 165
Newport. IOW 4D 16
Newport. Newp 3G 33 & 200
Newport. Norf 4H 79
Newport. Pemb 1E 43
Newport. Som 4G 21
Newport. Telf 4B 72
Newport-on-Tay. Fife 1G 137
Newport Pagnell. Mil 1G 51
Newpound Common. W Sus 3B 26
New Prestwick. S Ayr 2C 116
New Quay. Cdgn 5C 56
Newquay. Corn 2C 6
Newquay Cornwall Airport. Corn 2C 6
New Rackheath. Norf 4E 79
New Radnor. Powy 4E 58
New Rent. Cumb 1F 103
New Ridley. Nmbd 4D 114
New Romney. Kent 3E 29
New Rossington. S Yor 1D 86
New Row. Cdgn 3G 57
New Row. Lanc 1E 91
New Row. N Yor 3D 106
Newry. New M 7E 178
New Sauchie. Clac 4A 136
Newsbank. Ches E 4C 84
Newseat. Abers 5E 160
Newsham. Lanc 1D 90
Newsham. Nmbd 2G 115
Newsham. N Yor 3E 105
(nr. Richmond)
Newsham. N Yor 1F 99
(nr. Thirsk)
New Sharlston. W Yor 3D 93
Newsholme. E Yor 2H 93
Newsholme. Lanc 4H 97
New Shoreston. Nmbd 1F 121
New Springs. G Man 4D 90
Newstead. Notts 5C 86
Newstead. Bord 1H 119
New Stevenston. N Lan 4A 128
New Street. Here 5F 59
Newstreet Lane. Shrp 2A 72
New Swanage. Dors 4F 15
New Swannington. Leics 4B 74
Newthorpe. N Yor 1E 93
Newthorpe. Notts 1B 74
Newton. Arg 4H 133
Newton. B'end 4B 32
Newton. Cambs 1E 53
(nr. Cambridge)
Newton. Cambs 4D 76
(nr. Wisbech)
Newton. Ches W 4G 83
(nr. Chester)
Newton. Ches W 5H 83
(nr. Tattenhall)
Newton. Cumb 2B 96
Newton. Derbs 5B 86
Newton. Dors 1C 14
Newton. Dum 2D 112
(nr. Annan)
Newton. Dum 5D 118
(nr. Moffat)
Newton. G Man 1D 84
Newton. Here 2G 47
(nr. Ewyas Harold)
Newton. Here 5H 59
(nr. Leominster)
Newton. High 2B 158
(nr. Cromarty)
Newton. High 4B 158
(nr. Inverness)
Newton. High 5C 166
(nr. Kylestrome)
Newton. High 4F 169
(nr. Wick)
Newton. Lanc 2E 97
(nr. Carnforth)
Newton. Lanc 4F 97
(nr. Clitheroe)
Newton. Lanc 1C 90
(nr. Kirkham)
Newton. Linc 2H 75
Newton. Mers 2E 83
Newton. Mor 2F 159
Newton. Norf 4H 77
Newton. Nptn 2F 63
Newton. Nmbd 3D 114
Newton. Notts 1D 74
Newton. Bord 2A 120
Newton. Shet 8E 173
Newton. Shrp 1B 60
(nr. Bridgnorth)
Newton. Shrp 2G 71
(nr. Wem)
Newton. Som 3E 20
Newton. S Lan 3H 127
(nr. Glasgow)
Newton. S Lan 1B 118
(nr. Lanark)
Newton. Staf 3E 73
Newton. Suff 1C 54
Newton. Swan 4F 31
Newton. Warw 3C 62
Newton. W Lot 2D 129
Newton. Wilts 4H 23
Newton Abbot. Devn 5B 12
Newtonairds. Dum 1F 111
Newton Arlosh. Cumb 4D 112
Newton Aycliffe. Dur 2F 105
Newton Bewley. Hart 2B 106
Newton Blossomville. Mil 5G 63
Newton Bromswold. Bed 4G 63
Newton Burgoland. Leics 5A 74
Newton by Toft. Linc 2H 87
Newton Ferrers. Devn 4B 8
Newton Flotman. Norf 1E 66
Newtongrange. Midl 3G 129
Newton Green. Mon 2A 34
Newton Hall. Dur 5F 115
Newton Hall. Nmbd 3D 114
Newton Harcourt. Leics 1D 62
Newton Heath. G Man 4G 91
Newtonhill. Abers 4G 153
Newtonhill. High 4H 157
Newton Hill. W Yor 2D 92
Newton Ketton. Darl 2A 106
Newton Kyme. N Yor 5G 99
Newton-le-Willows. Mers 1H 83
Newton-le-Willows. N Yor 1E 98
Newton Longville. Buck 2G 51
Newton Mearns. E Ren 4G 127
Newtonmore. High 4B 150
Newton Morrell. N Yor 4F 105
Newton Mulgrave. N Yor 3E 107
Newton of Ardtoe. High 1A 140
Newton of Balcanquhal. Per 2D 136
Newton of Beltrees. Ren 4E 127
Newton of Falkland. Fife 3E 137
Newton of Mountblairy. Abers 3E 160
Newton of Pitcairns. Per 2C 136
Newton-on-Ouse. N Yor 4H 99
Newton-on-Rawcliffe. N Yor 5F 107
Newton on the Hill. Shrp 3G 71
Newton-on-the-Moor. Nmbd 4F 121
Newton on Trent. Linc 3F 87
Newton Poppleford. Devn 4D 12
Newton Purcell. Oxon 2E 51
Newton Regis. Warw 5G 73
Newton Reigny. Cumb 1F 103
Newton Rigg. Cumb 1F 103
Newton St Cyres. Devn 3B 12
Newton St Faith. Norf 4E 78
Newton St Loe. Bath 5C 34
Newton St Petrock. Devn 1E 11
Newton Solney. Derbs 3G 73
Newton Stacey. Hants 2C 24
Newton Stewart. Dum 3B 110
Newton Toney. Wilts 2H 23
Newton Tony. Wilts 2H 23
Newton Tracey. Devn 4F 19
Newton under Roseberry. Red C 3C 106
Newton Unthank. Leics 5B 74
Newton upon Ayr. S Ayr 2C 116
Newton upon Derwent. E Yor 5B 100
Newton Valence. Hants 3F 25
Newton-with-Scales. Lanc 1C 90
Newtown. Abers 2E 160
Newtown. Cambs 4H 63
Newtown. Corn 5C 10
Newtown. Cumb 5B 112
(nr. Aspatria)
Newtown. Cumb 3G 113
(nr. Brampton)
Newtown. Cumb 2G 103
(nr. Penrith)
Newtown. Derbs 2D 85
Newtown. Devn 4A 20
Newtown. Dors 2H 13
(nr. Beaminster)
New Town. Dors 1E 15
(nr. Sixpenny Handley)
New Town. E Lot 2H 129
Newtown. Falk 1C 128
Newtown. Glos 5B 48
(nr. Lydney)
Newtown. Glos 2E 49
(nr. Tewkesbury)
Newtown. Hants 1D 16
(nr. Bishop's Waltham)
Newtown. Hants 3G 25
(nr. Liphook)
Newtown. Hants 1A 16
(nr. Lyndhurst)
Newtown. Hants 5C 36
(nr. Newbury)
Newtown. Hants 4B 24
(nr. Romsey)
Newtown. Hants 2C 16
(nr. Warsash)
Newtown. Hants 1E 16
(nr. Wickham)
Newtown. Here 2A 48
(nr. Little Dewchurch)
Newtown. Here 1B 48
(nr. Stretton Grandison)
Newtown. High 3F 149
Newtown. IOM 4C 108
Newtown. IOW 3C 16
Newtown. Lanc 3D 90
New Town. Lutn 3A 52
Newtown. Nmbd 4E 121
(nr. Rothbury)
Newtown. Nmbd 2E 121
(nr. Wooler)
Newtown. Pool 3F 15
Newtown. Powy 1D 58
Newtown. Rhon 2D 32
Newtown. Shet 3F 173
Newtown. Shrp 2G 71
Newtown. Som 1F 13
Newtown. Staf 4D 84
(nr. Biddulph)
Newtown. Staf 5D 73
(nr. Cannock)
Newtown. Staf 4E 85
(nr. Longnor)
New Town. W Yor 2E 93
Newtown. Wilts 4E 23
Newtownabbey. Newt 1H 179
Newtownards. Ards 2J 179
Newtownbutler. Ferm 7K 177
Newtown-Crommelin. Bmna 5H 175
Newtownhamilton. New M 7D 178
Newtown-in-St Martin. Corn 4E 5
Newtown Linford. Leics 4C 74
Newtown St Boswells. Bord 1H 119
Newtownstewart. Strab 8A 174
New Tredegar. Cphy 5E 47
Newtyle. Ang 4B 144
New Village. E Yor 1D 94
New Village. S Yor 4F 93
New Walsoken. Cambs 5D 76
New Waltham. NE Lin 4F 95
New Winton. E Lot 2H 129
New World. Cambs 1C 64
New Yatt. Oxon 4B 50
Newyears Green. G Lon 2B 38
New York. Linc 5B 88
New York. Tyne 2G 115
Nextend. Here 5F 59
Neyland. Pemb 4D 42
Nib Heath. Shrp 4G 71
Nicholashayne. Devn 1E 12
Nicholaston. Swan 4E 31
Nidd. N Yor 3F 99
Niddrie. Edin 2F 129
Niddry. Edin 2D 129
Nigg. Aber 3G 153
Nigg. High 1C 158
Nigg Ferry. High 2B 158
Nightcott. Som 4B 20
Nimmer. Som 1G 13
Nine Ashes. Essx 5F 53
Ninebanks. Nmbd 4A 114
Nine Elms. Swin 3G 35
Ninemile Bar. Dum 2F 111
Nine Mile Burn. Midl 4E 129
Ninfield. E Sus 4B 28
Ningwood. IOW 4C 16
Nisbet. Bord 2A 120
Nisbet Hill. Bord 4D 130
Niton. IOW 5D 16
Nitshill. E Ren 4G 127
Niwbwrch. IOA 4D 80
Nixon's Corner. Derr 5A 174
Noak Hill. G Lon 1G 39
Nobold. Shrp 4G 71
Nobottle. Nptn 4D 62
Nocton. Linc 4H 87
Nogdam End. Norf 5F 79
Noke. Oxon 4D 50
Nolton. Pemb 3C 42
Nolton Haven. Pemb 3C 42
No Man's Heath. Ches W 1H 71
No Man's Heath. Warw 5G 73
Nomansland. Devn 1B 12
Nomansland. Wilts 1A 16
Noneley. Shrp 3G 71
Noness. Shet 9F 173
Nonikiln. High 1A 158
Nonington. Kent 5G 41
Nook. Cumb 2F 113
(nr. Longtown)
Nook. Cumb 1E 97
(nr. Milnthorpe)
Noranside. Ang 2D 144
Norbreck. Bkpl 5C 96
Norbridge. Here 1C 48
Norbury. Ches E 1H 71
Norbury. Derbs 1F 73
Norbury. Shrp 1F 59
Norbury. Staf 3B 72
Norby. N Yor 1G 99
Norby. Shet 6C 173
Norcross. Lanc 5C 96
Nordelph. Norf 5E 77
Norden. G Man 3G 91
Nordley. Shrp 1A 60
Norfolk Broads. Norf 5G 79
Norham. Nmbd 5F 131
Norland Town. W Yor 2A 92
Norley. Ches W 3H 83
Norleywood. Hants 3B 16
Normanby. N Lin 3B 94
Normanby. N Yor 1B 100
Normanby. Red C 3C 106
Normanby-by-Spital. Linc 2H 87
Normanby le Wold. Linc 1A 88
Norman Cross. Cambs 1A 64
Normandy. Surr 5A 38
Norman's Bay. E Sus 5A 28
Norman's Green. Devn 2D 12
Normanton. Derb 2H 73
Normanton. Leics 1F 75
Normanton. Linc 1G 75
Normanton. Notts 5E 87
Normanton. W Yor 2D 93
Normanton le Heath. Leics 4A 74
Normanton on Soar. Notts 3C 74
Normanton-on-the-Wolds. Notts 2D 74
Normanton on Trent. Notts 4E 87
Normoss. Lanc 1B 90
Norrington Common. Wilts 5D 35
Norris Green. Mers 1F 83
Norris Hill. Leics 4H 73
Norristhorpe. W Yor 2C 92
Northacre. Norf 1B 66
Northall. Buck 3H 51
Northallerton. N Yor 5A 106
Northam. Devn 4E 19
Northam. Sotn 1C 16
Northampton. Nptn 4E 63 & 200
North Anston. S Yor 2C 86
North Ascot. Brac 4A 38
North Aston. Oxon 3C 50
Northaw. Herts 5C 52
Northay. Som 1F 13
North Baddesley. Hants 4B 24
North Balfern. Dum 4B 110
North Ballachulish. High 2E 141
North Barrow. Som 4B 22
North Barsham. Norf 2B 78
Northbeck. Linc 1H 75
North Benfleet. Essx 2B 40
North Bersted. W Sus 5A 26
North Berwick. E Lot 1B 130
North Bitchburn. Dur 1E 105
North Blyth. Nmbd 1G 115
North Boarhunt. Hants 1E 16
North Bockhampton. Dors 3G 15
Northborough. Pet 5A 76
Northbourne. Kent 5H 41
Northbourne. Oxon 3D 36
North Bovey. Devn 4H 11
North Bowood. Dors 3H 13
North Bradley. Wilts 1D 22
North Brentor. Devn 4E 11
North Brewham. Som 3C 22
Northbrook. Oxon 3C 50
North Brook End. Cambs 1C 52
North Broomhill. Nmbd 4G 121
North Buckland. Devn 2E 19
North Burlingham. Norf 4F 79
North Cadbury. Som 4B 22
North Carlton. Linc 3G 87
North Cave. E Yor 1B 94
North Cerney. Glos 5F 49
North Chailey. E Sus 3E 27
Northchapel. W Sus 3A 26
North Charford. Hants 1G 15
North Charlton. Nmbd 2F 121
North Cheriton. Som 4B 22
North Chideock. Dors 3H 13
Northchurch. Herts 5H 51
North Cliffe. E Yor 1B 94
North Clifton. Notts 3F 87
North Close. Dur 1F 105
North Cockerington. Linc 1C 88
North Coker. Som 1A 14
North Collafirth. Shet 3E 173
North Common. E Sus 3E 27
North Commonty. Abers 4F 161
North Coombe. Devn 1B 12
North Cornelly. B'end 3B 32
North Cotes. Linc 4G 95
Northcott. Devn 3D 10
(nr. Boyton)
Northcott. Devn 1D 12
(nr. Culmstock)
Northcourt. Oxon 2D 36
North Cove. Suff 2G 67
North Cowton. N Yor 4F 105
North Craigo. Ang 2F 145
North Crawley. Mil 1H 51
North Cray. G Lon 3F 39
North Creake. Norf 2A 78
North Curry. Som 4G 21
North Dalton. E Yor 4D 100
North Deighton. N Yor 4F 99
North Dronley. Ang 5C 144
North Duffield. N Yor 1G 93
Northdyke. Orkn 5B 172
Northedge. Derbs 4A 86
North Elkington. Linc 1B 88
North Elmham. Norf 3B 78
North Elmsall. W Yor 3E 93
Northend. Buck 2F 37
North End. E Yor 1F 95
North End. Essx 4G 53
(nr. Great Dunmow)
North End. Essx 2A 54
(nr. Great Yeldham)
North End. Hants 5C 36
North End. Leics 4C 74
North End. Linc 1B 76
North End. Norf 1B 66
North End. N Som 5H 33
North End. Port 2E 17
Northend. Warw 5A 62
North End. W Sus 5C 26
North End. Wilts 2F 35
North Erradale. High 5B 162
North Evington. Leic 5D 74
North Fambridge. Essx 1C 40
North Fearns. High 5E 155
North Featherstone. W Yor 2E 93
North Feorline. N Ayr 3D 122
North Ferriby. E Yor 2C 94
Northfield. Aber 3F 153
Northfield. Hull 2D 94
Northfield. Som 3F 21
Northfield. W Mid 3E 61
Northfleet. Kent 3H 39
North Frodingham. E Yor 4F 101
Northgate. Linc 3A 76
North Gluss. Shet 4E 173
North Gorley. Hants 1G 15
North Green. Norf 2E 66
North Green. Suff 4F 67
(nr. Framlingham)
North Green. Suff 3F 67
(nr. Halesworth)
North Green. Suff 4F 67
(nr. Saxmundham)
North Greetwell. Linc 3H 87
North Grimston. N Yor 3C 100
North Halling. Medw 4B 40
North Hayling. Hants 2F 17
North Hazelrigg. Nmbd 1E 121
North Heasley. Devn 3H 19
North Heath. W Sus 3B 26
North Hill. Corn 5C 10
North Hinksey Village. Oxon 5C 50
North Holmwood. Surr 1C 26
North Huish. Devn 3D 8
North Hykeham. Linc 4G 87
Northiam. E Sus 3C 28
Northill. C Beds 1B 52
Northington. Hants 3D 24
North Kelsey. Linc 4D 94
North Kelsey Moor. Linc 4D 94
North Kessock. High 4A 158
North Killingholme. N Lin 3E 95
North Kilvington. N Yor 1G 99
North Kilworth. Leics 2D 62
North Kyme. Linc 5A 88
North Lancing. W Sus 5C 26
Northlands. Linc 5C 88
Northleach. Glos 4G 49
North Lee. Buck 5G 51
North Lees. N Yor 2E 99
Northleigh. Devn 3G 19
(nr. Barnstaple)
Northleigh. Devn 3E 13
(nr. Honiton)
North Leigh. Kent 1F 29
North Leigh. Oxon 4B 50
North Leverton. Notts 2E 87
Northlew. Devn 3F 11
North Littleton. Worc 1F 49
North Lopham. Norf 2C 66
North Luffenham. Rut 5G 75
North Marden. W Sus 1G 17
North Marston. Buck 3F 51
North Middleton. Midl 4G 129
North Middleton. Nmbd 2E 121
North Molton. Devn 4H 19
North Moor. N Yor 1D 100
Northmoor. Oxon 5C 50
Northmoor Green. Som 3G 21
North Moreton. Oxon 3D 36
Northmuir. Ang 3C 144
North Mundham. W Sus 2G 17
North Murie. Per 1E 137
North Muskham. Notts 5E 87
North Ness. Orkn 8C 172
North Newbald. E Yor 1C 94
North Newington. Oxon 2C 50
North Newnton. Wilts 1G 23
North Newton. Som 3F 21
Northney. Hants 2F 17
North Nibley. Glos 2C 34
North Oakley. Hants 1D 24
North Ockendon. G Lon 2G 39
Northolt. G Lon 2C 38
Northop. Flin 4E 83
Northop Hall. Flin 4E 83
North Ormesby. Midd 3C 106
North Ormsby. Linc 1B 88
Northorpe. Linc 4H 75
(nr. Bourne)
Northorpe. Linc 2B 76
(nr. Donington)
Northorpe. Linc 1F 87
(nr. Gainsborough)
North Otterington. N Yor 1F 99
Northover. Som 3H 21
(nr. Glastonbury)
Northover. Som 4A 22
(nr. Yeovil)
North Owersby. Linc 1H 87
Northowram. W Yor 2B 92
North Perrott. Som 2H 13
North Petherton. Som 3F 21
North Petherwin. Corn 4C 10
North Pickenham. Norf 5A 78
North Piddle. Worc 5D 60
North Poorton. Dors 3A 14
North Port. Arg 1H 133
Northport. Dors 4E 15
North Queensferry. Fife 1E 129
North Radworthy. Devn 3A 20
North Rauceby. Linc 1H 75
Northrepps. Norf 2E 79
North Rigton. N Yor 5E 99
North Rode. Ches E 4C 84
North Roe. Shet 3E 173
North Ronaldsay Airport. Orkn 2G 172
North Row. Cumb 1D 102
North Runcton. Norf 4F 77
North Sannox. N Ayr 5B 126
North Scale. Cumb 2A 96
North Scarle. Linc 4F 87
North Seaton. Nmbd 1F 115
North Seaton Colliery. Nmbd 1F 115
North Sheen. G Lon 3C 38
North Shian. Arg 4D 140
North Shields. Tyne 3G 115
North Shoebury. S'end 2D 40
North Shore. Bkpl 1B 90
North Side. Cumb 2B 102
North Skelton. Red C 3D 106
North Somercotes. Linc 1D 88
North Stainley. N Yor 2E 99
North Stainmore. Cumb 3B 104
North Stifford. Thur 2H 39
North Stoke. Bath 5C 34
North Stoke. Oxon 3E 36
North Stoke. W Sus 4B 26
Northstowe. Cambs 4D 64
North Street. Hants 3E 25
North Street. Kent 5E 40
North Street. Medw 3C 40
North Street. W Ber 4E 37
North Sunderland. Nmbd 1G 121
North Tamerton. Corn 3D 10
North Tawton. Devn 2G 11
North Thoresby. Linc 1B 88
North Town. Devn 2F 11
Northtown. Orkn 8D 172
North Town. Shet 10E 173
North Tuddenham. Norf 4C 78
North Walbottle. Tyne 3E 115
Northwall. Orkn 3G 172
North Walney. Cumb 3A 96
North Walsham. Norf 2E 79
North Waltham. Hants 2D 24
North Warnborough. Hants 1F 25
North Water Bridge. Ang 2F 145
North Watten. High 3E 169
Northway. Glos 2E 49
Northway. Swan 4E 31
North Weald Bassett. Essx 5F 53
North Weston. N Som 4H 33
North Weston. Oxon 5E 51
North Wheatley. Notts 2E 87
North Whilborough. Devn 2E 9
Northwich. Ches W 3A 84
North Wick. Bath 5A 34
Northwick. Som 2G 21
Northwick. S Glo 3A 34
North Widcombe. Bath 1A 22
North Willingham. Linc 2A 88
North Wingfield. Derbs 4B 86
North Witham. Linc 3G 75
Northwold. Norf 1G 65
Northwood. Derbs 4G 85
Northwood. G Lon 1B 38
Northwood. IOW 3C 16
Northwood. Kent 4H 41
Northwood. Shrp 2G 71
Northwood. Stoke 1C 72
Northwood Green. Glos 4C 48
North Wootton. Dors 1B 14
North Wootton. Norf 3F 77
North Wootton. Som 2A 22
North Wraxall. Wilts 4D 34
North Wroughton. Swin 3G 35
North Yardhope. Nmbd 4D 120
North York Moors. N Yor 5D 107
Norton. Devn 3E 9
Norton. Glos 3D 48
Norton. Hal 2H 83
Norton. Herts 2C 52
Norton. IOW 4B 16
Norton. Mon 3H 47
Norton. Nptn 4D 62
Norton. Notts 3C 86
Norton. Powy 4F 59
Norton. Shrp 2G 59
(nr. Ludlow)
Norton. Shrp 5B 72
(nr. Madeley)
Norton. Shrp 5H 71
(nr. Shrewsbury)
Norton. S Yor 3F 93
(nr. Askern)
Norton. S Yor 2A 86
(nr. Sheffield)
Norton. Stoc T 2B 106
Norton. Suff 4B 66
Norton. Swan 4F 31
Norton. W Sus 5A 26
(nr. Arundel)
Norton. W Sus 3G 17
(nr. Selsey)
Norton. Wilts 3D 35
Norton. Worc 1F 49
(nr. Evesham)
Norton. Worc 5C 60
(nr. Worcester)
Norton Bavant. Wilts 2E 23
Norton Bridge. Staf 2C 72
Norton Canes. Staf 5E 73
Norton Canon. Here 1G 47
Norton Corner. Norf 3C 78
Norton Disney. Linc 5F 87
Norton East. Staf 5E 73
Norton Ferris. Wilts 3C 22
Norton Fitzwarren. Som 4F 21
Norton Green. IOW 4B 16
Norton Green. Stoke 5D 84
Norton Hawkfield. Bath 5A 34
Norton Heath. Essx 5G 53
Norton in Hales. Shrp 2B 72
Norton in the Moors. Stoke 5C 84
Norton-Juxta-Twycross. Leics 5H 73
Norton-le-Clay. N Yor 2G 99
Norton Lindsey. Warw 4G 61
Norton Little Green. Suff 4B 66
Norton Malreward. Bath 5B 34
Norton Mandeville. Essx 5F 53
Norton-on-Derwent. N Yor 2B 100
Norton St Philip. Som 1C 22
Norton Subcourse. Norf 1G 67
Norton sub Hamdon. Som 1H 13
Norton Woodseats. S Yor 2A 86

Norwell—Peterburn

Norwell. *Notts* 4E **87**
Norwell Woodhouse. *Notts* 4E **87**
Norwich. *Norf* 5E **79** & **200**
Norwich International Airport. *Norf* 4E **79**
Norwick. *Shet* 1H **173**
Norwood. *Derbs* 2B **86**
Norwood Green. *W Yor* 2B **92**
Norwood Hill. *Surr* 1D **26**
Norwood Park. *Som* 3A **22**
Norwoodside. *Cambs* 1D **64**
Noseley. *Leics* 1E **63**
Noss. *Shet* 10E **173**
Noss Mayo. *Devn* 4B **8**
Nosterfield. *N Yor* 1E **99**
Nostie. *High* 1A **148**
Notgrove. *Glos* 3G **49**
Nottage. *B'end* 4B **32**
Nottingham. *Nott* 1C **74** & **200**
Nottington. *Dors* 4B **14**
Notton. *Dors* 3B **14**
Notton. *W Yor* 3D **92**
Notton. *Wilts* 5E **35**
Nounsley. *Essx* 4A **54**
Noutard's Green. *Worc* 4B **60**
Nox. *Shrp* 4G **71**
Noyadd Trefawr. *Cdgn* 1C **44**
Nuffield. *Oxon* 3E **37**
Nunburnholme. *E Yor* 5C **100**
Nuncargate. *Notts* 5B **86**
Nunclose. *Cumb* 5F **113**
Nuneaton. *Warw* 1A **62**
Nuneham Courtenay. *Oxon* 2D **36**
Nun Monkton. *N Yor* 4H **99**
Nunnerie. *S Lan* 3B **118**
Nunney. *Som* 2C **22**
Nunnington. *N Yor* 2A **100**
Nunnykirk. *Nmbd* 5E **121**
Nunsthorpe. *NE Lin* 4F **95**
Nunthorpe. *Red C* 3C **106**
Nunthorpe. *York* 5H **99**
Nunton. *Wilts* 4G **23**
Nunwick. *Nmbd* 2B **114**
Nunwick. *N Yor* 2F **99**
Nupend. *Glos* 5C **48**
Nursling. *Hants* 1B **16**
Nursted. *W Sus* 4F **25**
Nursteed. *Wilts* 5F **35**
Nurston. *V Glam* 5D **32**
Nutbourne. *W Sus* 2F **17** (nr. Chichester)
Nutbourne. *W Sus* 4B **26** (nr. Pulborough)
Nutfield. *Surr* 5E **39**
Nuthall. *Notts* 1C **74**
Nuthampstead. *Herts* 2E **53**
Nuthurst. *Warw* 3F **61**
Nuthurst. *W Sus* 3C **26**
Nutley. *E Sus* 3F **27**
Nuttall. *G Man* 3F **91**
Nutwell. *S Yor* 4G **93**
Nybster. *High* 2F **169**
Nyetimber. *W Sus* 3G **17**
Nyewood. *W Sus* 4G **25**
Nymet Rowland. *Devn* 2H **11**
Nymet Tracey. *Devn* 2H **11**
Nympsfield. *Glos* 5D **48**
Nynehead. *Som* 4E **21**
Nyton. *W Sus* 5A **26**

O

Oadby. *Leics* 5D **74**
Oad Street. *Kent* 4C **40**
Oakamoor. *Staf* 1E **73**
Oakbank. *Arg* 5B **140**
Oakbank. *W Lot* 3D **129**
Oakdale. *Cphy* 2E **33**
Oakdale. *Pool* 3F **15**
Oake. *Som* 4E **21**
Oaken. *Staf* 5C **72**
Oakenclough. *Lanc* 5E **97**
Oakengates. *Telf* 4B **72**
Oakenholt. *Flin* 3E **83**
Oakenshaw. *Dur* 1F **105**
Oakenshaw. *W Yor* 2B **92**
Oakerthorpe. *Derbs* 5A **86**
Oakford. *Cdgn* 5D **56**
Oakford. *Devn* 4C **20**
Oakfordbridge. *Devn* 4C **20**
Oakgrove. *Ches E* 4D **84**
Oakham. *Rut* 5F **75**
Oakhanger. *Ches E* 5B **84**
Oakhanger. *Hants* 3F **25**
Oakhill. *Som* 2B **22**
Oakington. *Cambs* 4D **64**
Oaklands. *Powy* 5C **58**
Oakle Street. *Glos* 4C **48**
Oakley. *Bed* 5H **63**
Oakley. *Buck* 4E **51**
Oakley. *Fife* 1D **128**
Oakley. *Hants* 1D **24**
Oakley. *Suff* 3D **66**
Oakley Green. *Wind* 3A **38**
Oakley Park. *Powy* 2B **58**
Oakmere. *Ches W* 4H **83**
Oakridge. *Glos* 5E **49**
Oaks. *Shrp* 5G **71**
Oaksey. *Wilts* 2E **35**
Oaks Green. *Derbs* 2F **73**
Oakshaw Ford. *Cumb* 2G **113**
Oakshott. *Hants* 4F **25**
Oakthorpe. *Leics* 4H **73**
Oak Tree. *Darl* 3A **106**
Oakwood. *Derb* 2A **74**
Oakwood. *W Yor* 1D **92**
Oakwoodhill. *Surr* 2C **26**
Oakworth. *W Yor* 1A **92**
Oape. *High* 3B **164**
Oare. *Kent* 4E **40**
Oare. *Som* 2B **20**
Oare. *W Ber* 4D **36**
Oare. *Wilts* 5G **35**
Oareford. *Som* 2B **20**
Oasby. *Linc* 2H **75**
Oath. *Som* 4G **21**
Oathlaw. *Ang* 3D **145**
Oatlands. *N Yor* 4F **99**
Oban. *Arg* 1F **133** & **201**
Oban. *W Isl* 7D **171**
Oborne. *Dors* 1B **14**
Obsdale. *High* 2A **158**
Obthorpe. *Linc* 4H **75**
Occlestone Green. *Ches W* 4A **84**
Occold. *Suff* 3D **66**
Ochiltree. *E Ayr* 2E **117**
Ochtermuthill. *Per* 2H **135**
Ochtertyre. *Per* 1H **135**
Ockbrook. *Derbs* 2B **74**
Ockeridge. *Worc* 4B **60**
Ockham. *Surr* 5B **38**
Ockle. *High* 1G **139**
Ockley. *Surr* 1C **26**
Ocle Pychard. *Here* 1A **48**
Octofad. *Arg* 4A **124**
Octomore. *Arg* 4A **124**
Octon. *E Yor* 3E **101**
Odcombe. *Som* 1A **14**
Odd Down. *Bath* 5C **34**
Oddingley. *Worc* 5D **60**
Oddington. *Oxon* 4D **50**
Oddsta. *Shet* 2G **173**
Odell. *Bed* 5G **63**
Odie. *Orkn* 5F **172**
Odiham. *Hants* 1F **25**
Odsey. *Cambs* 2C **52**
Odstock. *Wilts* 4G **23**
Odstone. *Leics* 5A **74**
Offchurch. *Warw* 4A **62**
Offenham. *Worc* 1F **49**
Offenham Cross. *Worc* 1F **49**
Offerton. *G Man* 2D **84**
Offerton. *Tyne* 4G **115**
Offham. *E Sus* 4F **27**
Offham. *Kent* 5A **40**
Offham. *W Sus* 5B **26**
Offleyhay. *Staf* 3C **72**
Offley Hoo. *Herts* 3B **52**
Offleymarsh. *Staf* 3B **72**
Offord Cluny. *Cambs* 4B **64**
Offord D'Arcy. *Cambs* 4B **64**
Offton. *Suff* 1D **54**
Offwell. *Devn* 3E **13**
Ogbourne Maizey. *Wilts* 4G **35**
Ogbourne St Andrew. *Wilts* 4G **35**
Ogbourne St George. *Wilts* 4H **35**
Ogden. *G Man* 3H **91**
Ogle. *Nmbd* 2E **115**
Ogmore. *V Glam* 4B **32**
Ogmore-by-Sea. *V Glam* 4B **32**
Ogmore Vale. *B'end* 2C **32**
Okeford Fitzpaine. *Dors* 1D **14**
Okehampton. *Devn* 3F **11**
Okehampton Camp. *Devn* 3F **11**
Okraquoy. *Shet* 8F **173**
Okus. *Swin* 3G **35**
Old. *Nptn* 3E **63**
Old Aberdeen. *Aber* 3G **153**
Old Alresford. *Hants* 3D **24**
Oldany. *High* 5B **166**
Old Arley. *Warw* 1G **61**
Old Basford. *Nott* 1C **74**
Old Basing. *Hants* 1E **25**
Oldberrow. *Warw* 4F **61**
Old Bewick. *Nmbd* 2E **121**
Old Bexley. *G Lon* 3F **39**
Old Blair. *Per* 2F **143**
Old Bolingbroke. *Linc* 4C **88**
Oldborough. *Devn* 2A **12**
Old Brampton. *Derbs* 3H **85**
Old Bridge of Tilt. *Per* 2F **143**
Old Bridge of Urr. *Dum* 3E **111**
Old Buckenham. *Norf* 1C **66**
Old Burghclere. *Hants* 1C **24**
Oldbury. *Shrp* 1B **60**
Oldbury. *Warw* 1H **61**
Oldbury. *W Mid* 2D **61**
Oldbury-on-Severn. *S Glo* 2B **34**
Oldbury on the Hill. *Glos* 3D **34**
Old Byland. *N Yor* 1H **99**
Old Cassop. *Dur* 1A **106**
Oldcastle. *Mon* 3G **47**
Oldcastle Heath. *Ches W* 1G **71**
Old Catton. *Norf* 4E **79**
Old Clee. *NE Lin* 4F **95**
Old Cleeve. *Som* 2D **20**
Old Colwyn. *Cnwy* 3A **82**
Oldcotes. *Notts* 2C **86**
Old Coulsdon. *G Lon* 5E **39**
Old Dailly. *S Ayr* 5B **116**
Old Dalby. *Leics* 3D **74**
Old Dam. *Derbs* 3F **85**
Old Deer. *Abers* 4G **161**
Old Dilton. *Wilts* 2D **22**
Old Down. *S Glo* 3B **34**
Oldeamere. *Cambs* 1C **64**
Old Edlington. *S Yor* 1C **86**
Old Eldon. *Dur* 2F **105**
Old Ellerby. *E Yor* 1E **95**
Old Fallings. *W Mid* 5D **72**
Oldfallow. *Staf* 4D **72**
Old Felixstowe. *Suff* 2G **55**
Oldfield. *Shrp* 2A **60**
Oldfield. *Worc* 4C **60**
Old Fletton. *Pet* 1A **64**
Oldford. *Som* 1C **22**
Old Forge. *Here* 4A **48**
Old Glossop. *Derbs* 1E **85**
Old Goole. *E Yor* 2H **93**
Old Gore. *Here* 3B **48**
Old Graitney. *Dum* 3E **112**
Old Grimsby. *IOS* 1A **4**
Oldhall. *High* 3E **169**
Old Hall Street. *Norf* 2F **79**
Oldham. *G Man* 4H **91**
Oldhamstocks. *E Lot* 2D **130**
Old Heathfield. *E Sus* 3G **27**
Old Hill. *W Mid* 2D **60**
Old Hunstanton. *Norf* 1F **77**
Old Hurst. *Cambs* 3B **64**
Old Hutton. *Cumb* 1E **97**
Old Kea. *Corn* 4C **6**
Old Kilpatrick. *W Dun* 2F **127**
Old Kinnernie. *Abers* 3E **152**
Old Knebworth. *Herts* 3C **52**
Oldland. *S Glo* 4B **34**
Old Laxey. *IOM* 3D **108**
Old Leake. *Linc* 5D **88**
Old Lenton. *Nott* 2C **74**
Old Llanberis. *Gwyn* 5F **81**
Old Malton. *N Yor* 2B **100**
Oldmeldrum. *Abers* 1F **153**
Old Micklefield. *W Yor* 1E **93**
Old Mill. *Corn* 5D **10**
Oldmixon. *N Som* 1G **21**
Old Monkland. *N Lan* 3A **128**
Old Newton. *Suff* 4C **66**
Old Park. *Telf* 5A **72**
Old Pentland. *Midl* 3F **129**
Old Philpstoun. *W Lot* 2D **128**
Old Quarrington. *Dur* 1A **106**
Old Radnor. *Powy* 5E **59**
Old Rayne. *Abers* 1D **152**
Oldridge. *Devn* 3B **12**
Old Romney. *Kent* 3E **29**
Old Scone. *Per* 1D **136**
Oldshore Beg. *High* 3B **166**
Oldshoremore. *High* 3C **166**
Old Snydale. *W Yor* 2E **93**
Old Sodbury. *S Glo* 3C **34**
Old Somerby. *Linc* 2G **75**
Old Spital. *Dur* 3C **104**
Oldstead. *N Yor* 1H **99**
Old Stratford. *Nptn* 1F **51**
Old Swan. *Mers* 1F **83**
Old Swarland. *Nmbd* 4F **121**
Old Tebay. *Cumb* 4H **103**
Old Town. *Cumb* 5F **113**
Old Town. *E Sus* 5G **27**
Oldtown. *High* 5C **164**
Old Town. *IOS* 1B **4**
Old Town. *Nmbd* 5C **120**
Oldtown of Ord. *Abers* 3D **160**
Old Trafford. *G Man* 1C **84**
Old Tupton. *Derbs* 4A **86**
Oldwall. *Cumb* 3F **113**
Oldwalls. *Swan* 3D **31**
Old Warden. *C Beds* 1B **52**
Oldways End. *Som* 4B **20**
Old Westhall. *Abers* 1D **152**
Old Weston. *Cambs* 3H **63**
Oldwhat. *Abers* 3F **161**
Old Windsor. *Wind* 3A **38**
Old Wives Lees. *Kent* 5E **41**
Old Woking. *Surr* 5B **38**
Oldwood Common. *Worc* 4H **59**
Old Woodstock. *Oxon* 4C **50**
Olgrinmore. *High* 3C **168**
Oliver's Battery. *Hants* 4C **24**
Ollaberry. *Shet* 3E **173**
Ollerton. *Ches E* 3B **84**
Ollerton. *Notts* 4D **86**
Ollerton. *Shrp* 3A **72**
Olmarch. *Cdgn* 5F **57**
Olmstead Green. *Cambs* 1G **53**
Olney. *Mil* 5F **63**
Olrig. *High* 2D **169**
Olton. *W Mid* 2F **61**
Olveston. *S Glo* 3B **34**
Omagh. *Omag* 2K **177**
Ombersley. *Worc* 4C **60**
Ompton. *Notts* 4D **86**
Omunsgarth. *Shet* 7E **173**
Onchan. *IOM* 4D **108**
Onecote. *Staf* 5E **85**
Onehouse. *Suff* 5C **66**
Onen. *Mon* 4H **47**
Ongar Hill. *Norf* 3E **77**
Ongar Street. *Here* 4F **59**
Onibury. *Shrp* 3G **59**
Onich. *High* 2E **141**
Onllwyn. *Neat* 4B **46**
Onneley. *Shrp* 1B **72**
Onslow Green. *Essx* 4G **53**
Onslow Village. *Surr* 1A **26**
Onthank. *E Ayr* 1D **116**
Openwoodgate. *Derbs* 1A **74**
Opinan. *High* 1G **155** (nr. Gairloch)
Opinan. *High* 4C **162** (nr. Laide)
Orasaigh. *W Isl* 6F **171**
Orbost. *High* 4B **154**
Orby. *Linc* 4D **89**
Orchard Hill. *Devn* 4E **19**
Orchard Portman. *Som* 4F **21**
Orcheston. *Wilts* 2F **23**
Orcop. *Here* 3H **47**
Orcop Hill. *Here* 3H **47**
Ord. *High* 2E **147**
Ordale. *Shet* 1H **173**
Ordhead. *Abers* 2D **152**
Ordie. *Abers* 3B **152**
Ordiquish. *Mor* 3H **159**
Ordley. *Nmbd* 4C **114**
Ordsall. *Notts* 3E **86**
Ore. *E Sus* 4C **28**
Oreham Common. *W Sus* 4D **26**
Oreton. *Shrp* 2A **60**
Orford. *Suff* 1H **55**
Orford. *Warr* 1A **84**
Organford. *Dors* 3E **15**
Orgil. *Orkn* 7B **172**
Orgreave. *Staf* 4F **73**
Oridge Street. *Glos* 3C **48**
Orlestone. *Kent* 2D **28**
Orleton. *Here* 4G **59**
Orleton. *Worc* 4A **60**
Orleton Common. *Here* 4G **59**
Orlingbury. *Nptn* 3F **63**
Ormacleit. *W Isl* 5C **170**
Ormathwaite. *Cumb* 2D **102**
Ormesby. *Midd* 3C **106**
Ormesby St Margaret. *Norf* 4G **79**
Ormesby St Michael. *Norf* 4G **79**
Ormiscaig. *High* 4C **162**
Ormiston. *E Lot* 3H **129**
Ormsaigbeg. *High* 2F **139**
Ormsaigmore. *High* 2F **139**
Ormsary. *Arg* 2F **125**
Ormsgill. *Cumb* 2A **96**
Ormskirk. *Lanc* 4C **90**
Orphir. *Orkn* 7C **172**
Orpington. *G Lon* 4F **39**
Orrell. *Lanc* 4D **90**
Orrell. *Mers* 1F **83**
Orrisdale. *IOM* 2C **108**
Orsett. *Thur* 2H **39**
Orslow. *Staf* 4C **72**
Orston. *Notts* 1E **75**
Orthwaite. *Cumb* 1D **102**
Orton. *Cumb* 4H **103**
Orton. *Mor* 3H **159**
Orton. *Nptn* 3F **63**
Orton. *Staf* 1C **60**
Orton Longueville. *Pet* 1A **64**
Orton-on-the-Hill. *Leics* 5H **73**
Orton Waterville. *Pet* 1A **64**
Orton Wistow. *Pet* 1A **64**
Orwell. *Cambs* 5C **64**
Osbaldeston. *Lanc* 1E **91**
Osbaldwick. *York* 4A **100**
Osbaston. *Leics* 5B **74**
Osbaston. *Shrp* 3F **71**
Osbournby. *Linc* 2H **75**
Osclay. *High* 5E **169**
Oscroft. *Ches W* 4H **83**
Ose. *High* 4C **154**
Osgathorpe. *Leics* 4B **74**
Osgodby. *Linc* 1H **87**
Osgodby. *N Yor* 1E **101** (nr. Scarborough)
Osgodby. *N Yor* 1G **93** (nr. Selby)
Oskaig. *High* 5E **155**
Oskamull. *Arg* 4F **139**
Osleston. *Derbs* 2G **73**
Osmaston. *Derb* 2A **74**
Osmaston. *Derbs* 1G **73**
Osmington. *Dors* 4C **14**
Osmington Mills. *Dors* 4C **14**
Osmondthorpe. *W Yor* 1D **92**
Osmondwall. *Orkn* 9C **172**
Osmotherley. *N Yor* 5B **106**
Osnaburgh. *Fife* 2G **137**
Ospisdale. *High* 5E **164**
Ospringe. *Kent* 4E **40**
Ossett. *W Yor* 2C **92**
Ossington. *Notts* 4E **87**
Ostend. *Essx* 1D **40**
Ostend. *Norf* 2F **79**
Osterley. *G Lon* 3C **38**
Oswaldkirk. *N Yor* 2A **100**
Oswaldtwistle. *Lanc* 2F **91**
Oswestry. *Shrp* 3E **71**
Otby. *Linc* 1A **88**
Otford. *Kent* 5G **39**
Otham. *Kent* 5B **40**
Otherton. *Staf* 4D **72**
Othery. *Som* 3G **21**
Otley. *Suff* 5E **66**
Otley. *W Yor* 5E **98**
Otterbourne. *Hants* 4C **24**
Otterburn. *Nmbd* 5C **120**
Otterburn. *N Yor* 4A **98**
Otterburn Camp. *Nmbd* 5C **120**
Otterburn Hall. *Nmbd* 5C **120**
Otter Ferry. *Arg* 1H **125**
Otterford. *Som* 1F **13**
Otterham. *Corn* 3B **10**
Otterhampton. *Som* 2F **21**
Otterham Quay. *Kent* 4C **40**
Ottershaw. *Surr* 4B **38**
Otterspool. *Mers* 2F **83**
Otterswick. *Shet* 3G **173**
Otterton. *Devn* 4D **12**
Otterwood. *Hants* 2C **16**
Ottery St Mary. *Devn* 3E **12**
Ottinge. *Kent* 1F **29**
Ottringham. *E Yor* 2F **95**
Oughterby. *Cumb* 4D **112**
Oughtershaw. *N Yor* 1A **98**
Oughterside. *Cumb* 5C **112**
Oughtibridge. *S Yor* 1H **85**
Oughtrington. *Warr* 2A **84**
Oulston. *N Yor* 2H **99**
Oulton. *Cumb* 4D **112**
Oulton. *Norf* 3D **78**
Oulton. *Staf* 3B **72** (nr. Gnosall Heath)
Oulton. *Staf* 2D **72** (nr. Stone)
Oulton. *Suff* 1H **67**
Oulton. *W Yor* 2D **92**
Oulton Broad. *Suff* 1H **67**
Oulton Street. *Norf* 3D **78**
Oundle. *Nptn* 2H **63**
Ousby. *Cumb* 1H **103**
Ousdale. *High* 1H **165**
Ousden. *Suff* 5G **65**
Ousefleet. *E Yor* 2B **94**
Ouston. *Dur* 4F **115**
Ouston. *Nmbd* 4A **114** (nr. Bearsbridge)
Ouston. *Nmbd* 2D **114** (nr. Stamfordham)
Outer Hope. *Devn* 4C **8**
Outertown. *Orkn* 6B **172**
Outgate. *Cumb* 5E **103**
Outhgill. *Cumb* 4A **104**
Outlands. *Staf* 2B **72**
Outlane. *W Yor* 3A **92**
Out Newton. *E Yor* 2G **95**
Out Rawcliffe. *Lanc* 5D **96**
Outwell. *Norf* 5E **77**
Outwick. *Hants* 1G **15**
Outwood. *Surr* 1E **27**
Outwood. *W Yor* 2D **92**
Outwood. *Worc* 3D **60**
Outwoods. *Leics* 4B **74**
Outwoods. *Staf* 4B **72**
Ouzlewell Green. *W Yor* 2D **92**
Ovenden. *W Yor* 2A **92**
Over. *Cambs* 3C **64**
Over. *Ches W* 4A **84**
Over. *Glos* 4D **48**
Over. *S Glo* 3A **34**
Overbister. *Orkn* 3F **172**
Over Burrows. *Derbs* 2G **73**
Overbury. *Worc* 2E **49**
Overcombe. *Dors* 4B **14**
Over Compton. *Dors* 1A **14**
Over End. *Cambs* 1H **63**
Over Finlarg. *Ang* 4D **144**
Overgreen. *Derbs* 3H **85**
Over Green. *W Mid* 1F **61**
Over Haddon. *Derbs* 4G **85**
Over Hulton. *G Man* 4E **91**
Over Kellet. *Lanc* 2E **97**
Over Kiddington. *Oxon* 3C **50**
Overleigh. *Som* 3H **21**
Overley. *Staf* 4F **73**
Over Monnow. *Mon* 4A **48**
Over Norton. *Oxon* 3B **50**
Over Peover. *Ches E* 3B **84**
Overpool. *Ches W* 3F **83**
Overscaig. *High* 1B **164**
Overseal. *Derbs* 4G **73**
Over Silton. *N Yor* 5B **106**
Oversland. *Kent* 5E **41**
Overstone. *Nptn* 4F **63**
Over Stowey. *Som* 3E **21**
Overstrand. *Norf* 1E **79**
Over Stratton. *Som* 1H **13**
Over Street. *Wilts* 3F **23**
Overthorpe. *Nptn* 1C **50**
Overton. *Aber* 2F **153**
Overton. *Ches W* 3H **83**
Overton. *Hants* 2D **24**
Overton. *High* 5E **169**
Overton. *Lanc* 4D **96**
Overton. *N Yor* 4H **99**
Overton. *Shrp* 2A **60** (nr. Bridgnorth)
Overton. *Shrp* 3H **59** (nr. Ludlow)
Overton. *Swan* 4D **30**
Overton. *W Yor* 3C **92**
Overton. *Wrex* 1F **71**
Overtown. *Lanc* 2F **97**
Overtown. *N Lan* 4B **128**
Overtown. *Swin* 4G **35**
Over Wallop. *Hants* 3A **24**
Over Whitacre. *Warw* 1G **61**
Over Worton. *Oxon* 3C **50**
Oving. *Buck* 3F **51**
Oving. *W Sus* 5A **26**
Ovingdean. *Brig* 5E **27**
Ovingham. *Nmbd* 3D **115**
Ovington. *Dur* 3E **105**
Ovington. *Essx* 1A **54**
Ovington. *Hants* 3D **24**
Ovington. *Norf* 5B **78**
Ovington. *Nmbd* 3D **114**
Owen's Bank. *Staf* 3G **73**
Ower. *Hants* 2C **16** (nr. Holbury)
Ower. *Hants* 1B **16** (nr. Totton)
Owermoigne. *Dors* 4C **14**
Owlbury. *Shrp* 1F **59**
Owler Bar. *Derbs* 3G **85**
Owlerton. *S Yor* 2H **85**
Owlsmoor. *Brac* 5G **37**
Owlswick. *Buck* 5F **51**
Owmby. *Linc* 4D **94**
Owmby-by-Spital. *Linc* 2H **87**
Ownham. *W Ber* 4C **36**
Owrytn. *Wrex* 1F **71**
Owslebury. *Hants* 4D **24**
Owston. *Leics* 5E **75**
Owston. *S Yor* 3F **93**
Owston Ferry. *N Lin* 4B **94**
Owstwick. *E Yor* 1F **95**
Owthorne. *E Yor* 2G **95**
Owthorpe. *Notts* 2D **74**
Owton Manor. *Hart* 2B **106**
Oxborough. *Norf* 5G **77**
Oxbridge. *Dors* 3H **13**
Oxcombe. *Linc* 3C **88**
Oxen End. *Essx* 3G **53**
Oxenhall. *Glos* 3C **48**
Oxenholme. *Cumb* 5G **103**
Oxenhope. *W Yor* 1A **92**
Oxen Park. *Cumb* 1C **96**
Oxenpill. *Som* 2H **21**
Oxenton. *Glos* 2E **49**
Oxenwood. *Wilts* 1B **24**
Oxford. *Oxon* 5D **50** & **200**
Oxgangs. *Edin* 3F **129**
Oxhey. *Herts* 1C **38**
Oxhill. *Warw* 1B **50**
Oxley. *W Mid* 5C **72**
Oxley Green. *Essx* 4C **54**
Oxley's Green. *E Sus* 3A **28**
Oxlode. *Cambs* 2D **65**
Oxnam. *Bord* 3B **120**
Oxshott. *Surr* 4C **38**
Oxspring. *S Yor* 4C **92**
Oxted. *Surr* 5E **39**
Oxton. *Mers* 2E **83**
Oxton. *N Yor* 5H **99**
Oxton. *Notts* 5D **86**
Oxton. *Bord* 4A **130**
Oxwich. *Swan* 4D **31**
Oxwich Green. *Swan* 4D **31**
Oxwick. *Norf* 3B **78**
Oykel Bridge. *High* 3A **164**
Oyne. *Abers* 1D **152**
Oystermouth. *Swan* 4F **31**
Ozleworth. *Glos* 2C **34**

P

Pabail Iarach. *W Isl* 4H **171**
Pabail Uarach. *W Isl* 4H **171**
Pachesham. *Surr* 5C **38**
Packers Hill. *Dors* 1C **14**
Packington. *Leics* 4A **74**
Packmoor. *Stoke* 5C **84**
Packmores. *Warw* 4G **61**
Packwood. *W Mid* 3F **61**
Packwood Gullett. *W Mid* 3F **61**
Padanaram. *Ang* 3D **144**
Padbury. *Buck* 2F **51**
Paddington. *G Lon* 2D **38**
Paddington. *Warr* 2A **84**
Paddlesworth. *Kent* 2F **29**
Paddock. *Kent* 5D **40**
Paddockhole. *Dum* 1D **112**
Paddock Wood. *Kent* 1A **28**
Paddolgreen. *Shrp* 2H **71**
Padeswood. *Flin* 4E **83**
Padiham. *Lanc* 1F **91**
Padside. *N Yor* 4D **98**
Padson. *Devn* 3F **11**
Padstow. *Corn* 1D **6**
Padworth. *W Ber* 5E **36**
Page Bank. *Dur* 1F **105**
Pagham. *W Sus* 3G **17**
Paglesham Churchend. *Essx* 1D **40**
Paglesham Eastend. *Essx* 1D **40**
Paibeil. *W Isl* 2C **170** (on North Uist)
Paibeil. *W Isl* 8C **171** (on Taransay)
Paiblesgearraidh. *W Isl* 2C **170**
Paignton. *Torb* 2E **9**
Pailton. *Warw* 2B **62**
Paine's Corner. *E Sus* 3H **27**
Painleyhill. *Staf* 2E **73**
Painscastle. *Powy* 1E **47**
Painshawfield. *Nmbd* 3D **114**
Painsthorpe. *E Yor* 4C **100**
Painswick. *Glos* 5D **48**
Painter's Forstal. *Kent* 5D **40**
Painthorpe. *W Yor* 3D **92**
Pairc Shiaboist. *W Isl* 3E **171**
Paisley. *Ren* 3F **127**
Pakefield. *Suff* 1H **67**
Pakenham. *Suff* 4B **66**
Pale. *Gwyn* 2B **70**
Palehouse Common. *E Sus* 4F **27**
Palestine. *Hants* 2A **24**
Paley Street. *Wind* 4G **37**
Palgowan. *Dum* 1A **110**
Palgrave. *Suff* 3D **66**
Pallington. *Dors* 3C **14**
Palmarsh. *Kent* 2F **29**
Palmer Moor. *Derbs* 2F **73**
Palmers Cross. *W Mid* 5C **72**
Palmerstown. *V Glam* 5E **33**
Palnackie. *Dum* 4F **111**
Palnure. *Dum* 3B **110**
Palterton. *Derbs* 4B **86**
Pamber End. *Hants* 1E **24**
Pamber Green. *Hants* 1E **24**
Pamber Heath. *Hants* 5E **36**
Pamington. *Glos* 2E **49**
Pamphill. *Dors* 2E **15**
Pampisford. *Cambs* 1E **53**
Panborough. *Som* 2H **21**
Panbride. *Ang* 5E **145**
Pancakehill. *Glos* 4F **49**
Pancrasweek. *Devn* 2C **10**
Pandy. *Gwyn* 3A **70** (nr. Bala)
Pandy. *Gwyn* 5F **69** (nr. Tywyn)
Pandy. *Mon* 3G **47**
Pandy. *Powy* 5B **70**
Pandy. *Wrex* 2D **70**
Pandy Tudur. *Cnwy* 4A **82**
Panfield. *Essx* 3H **53**
Pangbourne. *W Ber* 4E **37**
Pannal. *N Yor* 4F **99**
Pannal Ash. *N Yor* 4E **99**
Pannanich. *Abers* 4A **152**
Pant. *Shrp* 3E **71**
Pant. *Wrex* 1F **71**
Pantasaph. *Flin* 3D **82**
Pant Glas. *Gwyn* 1D **68**
Pant-glas. *Shrp* 2E **71**
Pantgwyn. *Carm* 3F **45**
Pantgwyn. *Cdgn* 1C **44**
Pant-lasau. *Swan* 3F **31**
Panton. *Linc* 3A **88**
Pant-pastynog. *Den* 4C **82**
Pantperthog. *Gwyn* 5G **69**
Pant-teg. *Carm* 3E **45**
Pant-y-Caws. *Carm* 2F **43**
Pant-y-dwr. *Powy* 3B **58**
Pant-y-ffridd. *Powy* 5D **70**
Pantyffynnon. *Carm* 4G **45**
Pantygasseg. *Torf* 5F **47**
Pant-y-llyn. *Carm* 4G **45**
Pant-yr-awel. *B'end* 3C **32**
Pant y Wacco. *Flin* 3D **82**
Panxworth. *Norf* 4F **79**
Papa Stour Airport. *Shet* 6C **173**
Papa Westray Airport. *Orkn* 2D **172**
Papcastle. *Cumb* 1C **102**
Papigoe. *High* 3F **169**
Papil. *Shet* 8E **173**
Papple. *E Lot* 2B **130**
Papplewick. *Notts* 5C **86**
Papworth Everard. *Cambs* 4B **64**
Papworth St Agnes. *Cambs* 4B **64**
Par. *Corn* 3E **7**
Paramour Street. *Kent* 4G **41**
Parbold. *Lanc* 3C **90**
Parbrook. *Som* 3A **22**
Parbrook. *W Sus* 3B **26**
Parc. *Gwyn* 2A **70**
Parcllyn. *Cdgn* 5B **56**
Parc-Seymour. *Newp* 2H **33**
Pardown. *Hants* 2D **24**
Pardshaw. *Cumb* 2B **102**
Parham. *Suff* 4F **67**
Park. *Abers* 4E **153**
Park. *Arg* 4D **140**
Park. *Derr* 6B **174**
Park. *Dum* 5B **118**
Park Bottom. *Corn* 4A **6**
Parkburn. *Abers* 5E **161**
Park Corner. *E Sus* 2G **27**
Park Corner. *Oxon* 3E **37**
Parkend. *Glos* 5B **48**
Park End. *Nmbd* 2B **114**
Parkeston. *Essx* 2F **55**
Parkfield. *Corn* 2H **7**
Parkgate. *Ant* 8J **175**
Parkgate. *Ches W* 3E **83**
Parkgate. *Cumb* 5D **112**
Parkgate. *Dum* 1B **112**
Park Gate. *Hants* 2D **16**
Parkgate. *Surr* 1D **26**
Park Gate. *Worc* 3D **60**
Parkhall. *W Dun* 2F **127**
Parkham. *Devn* 4D **19**
Parkham Ash. *Devn* 4D **18**
Parkhead. *Cumb* 5E **113**
Parkhead. *Glas* 3H **127**
Park Hill. *Mers* 4C **90**
Parkhouse. *Mon* 5H **47**
Parkhurst. *IOW* 3C **16**
Park Lane. *G Man* 4F **91**
Park Lane. *Staf* 5C **72**
Parkmill. *Swan* 4E **31**
Park Mill. *W Yor* 3C **92**
Parkneuk. *Abers* 1G **145**
Parkside. *N Lan* 4B **128**
Parkstone. *Pool* 3F **15**
Park Street. *Herts* 5B **52**
Park Street. *W Sus* 2C **26**
Park Town. *Oxon* 5D **50**
Park Village. *Nmbd* 3H **113**
Parkway. *Here* 2C **48**
Parley Cross. *Dors* 3F **15**
Parmoor. *Buck* 3F **37**
Parr. *Mers* 1H **83**
Parracombe. *Devn* 2G **19**
Parrog. *Pemb* 1E **43**
Parsonage Green. *Essx* 4H **53**
Parsonby. *Cumb* 1C **102**
Parson Cross. *S Yor* 1A **86**
Parson Drove. *Cambs* 5C **76**
Partick. *Glas* 3G **127**
Partington. *G Man* 1B **84**
Partney. *Linc* 4D **88**
Parton. *Cumb* 2A **102** (nr. Whitehaven)
Parton. *Cumb* 4D **112** (nr. Wigton)
Parton. *Dum* 2D **111**
Partridge Green. *W Sus* 4C **26**
Parwich. *Derbs* 5F **85**
Passenham. *Nptn* 2F **51**
Passfield. *Hants* 3G **25**
Passingford Bridge. *Essx* 1G **39**
Paston. *Norf* 2F **79**
Pasturefields. *Staf* 3D **73**
Patchacott. *Devn* 3E **11**
Patcham. *Brig* 5E **27**
Patchetts Green. *Herts* 1C **38**
Patching. *W Sus* 5B **26**
Patchole. *Devn* 2G **19**
Patchway. *S Glo* 3B **34**
Pateley Bridge. *N Yor* 3D **98**
Pathe. *Som* 3G **21**
Pathfinder Village. *Devn* 3B **12**
Pathhead. *Abers* 2G **145**
Pathhead. *E Ayr* 3F **117**
Pathhead. *Fife* 4E **137**
Pathhead. *Midl* 3G **129**
Pathlow. *Warw* 5F **61**
Path of Condie. *Per* 2C **136**
Pathstruie. *Per* 2C **136**
Patmore Heath. *Herts* 3E **53**
Patna. *E Ayr* 3D **116**
Patney. *Wilts* 1F **23**
Patrick. *IOM* 3B **108**
Patrick Brompton. *N Yor* 5F **105**
Patrington. *E Yor* 2G **95**
Patrington Haven. *E Yor* 2G **95**
Patrixbourne. *Kent* 5F **41**
Patterdale. *Cumb* 3E **103**
Pattiesmuir. *Fife* 1D **129**
Pattingham. *Staf* 1C **60**
Pattishall. *Nptn* 5D **62**
Pattiswick. *Essx* 3B **54**
Patton Bridge. *Cumb* 5G **103**
Paul. *Corn* 4B **4**
Paulerspury. *Nptn* 1F **51**
Paull. *E Yor* 2E **95**
Paulton. *Bath* 1B **22**
Pauperhaugh. *Nmbd* 5F **121**
Pave Lane. *Telf* 4B **72**
Pavenham. *Bed* 5G **63**
Pawlett. *Som* 2G **21**
Pawston. *Nmbd* 1C **120**
Paxford. *Glos* 2G **49**
Paxton. *Bord* 4F **131**
Payhembury. *Devn* 2D **12**
Paythorne. *Lanc* 4H **97**
Payton. *Som* 4E **20**
Peacehaven. *E Sus* 5F **27**
Peak Dale. *Derbs* 3E **85**
Peak District. *Derbs* 2F **85**
Peak Forest. *Derbs* 3F **85**
Peak Hill. *Linc* 4B **76**
Peakirk. *Pet* 5A **76**
Pearsie. *Ang* 3C **144**
Peasedown St John. *Bath* 1C **22**
Peaseland Green. *Norf* 4C **78**
Peasemore. *W Ber* 4C **36**
Peasenhall. *Suff* 4F **67**
Pease Pottage. *W Sus* 2D **26**
Peaslake. *Surr* 1B **26**
Peasley Cross. *Mers* 1H **83**
Peasmarsh. *E Sus* 3C **28**
Peasmarsh. *Som* 1G **13**
Peasmarsh. *Surr* 1A **26**
Peaston. *E Lot* 3H **129**
Peastonbank. *E Lot* 3H **129**
Peathill. *Abers* 2G **161**
Peat Inn. *Fife* 3G **137**
Peatling Magna. *Leics* 1C **62**
Peatling Parva. *Leics* 2C **62**
Peaton. *Arg* 1D **126**
Peaton. *Shrp* 2H **59**
Peats Corner. *Suff* 4D **66**
Pebmarsh. *Essx* 2B **54**
Pebworth. *Worc* 1G **49**
Pecket Well. *W Yor* 2H **91**
Peckforton. *Ches E* 5H **83**
Peckham Bush. *Kent* 5A **40**
Peckleton. *Leics* 5B **74**
Pedair-ffordd. *Powy* 3D **70**
Pedham. *Norf* 4F **79**
Pedlinge. *Kent* 2F **29**
Pedmore. *W Mid* 2D **60**
Pedwell. *Som* 3H **21**
Peebles. *Bord* 5F **129**
Peel. *IOM* 3B **108**
Peel. *Bord* 1G **119**
Peel Common. *Hants* 2D **16**
Peening Quarter. *Kent* 3C **28**
Peggs Green. *Leics* 4B **74**
Pegsdon. *C Beds* 2B **52**
Pegswood. *Nmbd* 1F **115**
Peinchorran. *High* 5E **155**
Peinlich. *High* 3D **154**
Pelaw. *Tyne* 3G **115**
Pelcomb Bridge. *Pemb* 3D **42**
Pelcomb Cross. *Pemb* 3D **42**
Peldon. *Essx* 4C **54**
Pelsall. *W Mid* 5E **73**
Pelton. *Dur* 4F **115**
Pelutho. *Cumb* 5C **112**
Pelynt. *Corn* 3G **7**
Pemberton. *Carm* 5F **45**
Pembrey. *Carm* 5E **45**
Pembridge. *Here* 5F **59**
Pembroke. *Pemb* 4D **43**
Pembroke Dock. *Pemb* 4D **42** & **204**
Pembroke Ferry. *Pemb* 4D **43**
Pembury. *Kent* 1H **27**
Penallt. *Mon* 4A **48**
Penally. *Pemb* 5F **43**
Penalt. *Here* 3A **48**
Penalum. *Pemb* 5F **43**
Penare. *Corn* 4D **6**
Penarth. *V Glam* 4E **33**
Penbeagle. *Corn* 3C **4**
Penberth. *Corn* 4B **4**
Pen-bont Rhydybeddau. *Cdgn* 2F **57**
Penbryn. *Cdgn* 5B **56**
Pencader. *Carm* 2E **45**
Pen-cae. *Cdgn* 5D **56**
Pencaenewydd. *Gwyn* 1D **68**
Pencaerau. *Neat* 3G **31**
Pencaitland. *E Lot* 3H **129**
Pencarnisiog. *IOA* 3C **80**
Pencarreg. *Carm* 1F **45**
Pencarrow. *Corn* 4B **10**
Pencelli. *Powy* 3D **46**
Pen-clawdd. *Swan* 3E **31**
Pencoed. *B'end* 3C **32**
Pencombe. *Here* 5H **59**
Pencraig. *Here* 3A **48**
Pencraig. *Powy* 3C **70**
Pendeen. *Corn* 3A **4**
Pendeford. *W Mid* 5D **72**
Penderyn. *Rhon* 5C **46**
Pendine. *Carm* 4G **43**
Pendlebury. *G Man* 4F **91**
Pendleton. *G Man* 1C **84**
Pendleton. *Lanc* 1F **91**
Pendock. *Worc* 2C **48**
Pendoggett. *Corn* 5A **10**
Pendomer. *Som* 1A **14**
Pendoylan. *V Glam* 4D **32**
Pendre. *B'end* 3C **32**
Penegoes. *Powy* 5G **69**
Penelewey. *Corn* 4C **6**
Penffordd. *Pemb* 2E **43**
Penffordd-Lâs. *Powy* 1A **58**
Penfro. *Pemb* 4D **43**
Pengam. *Cphy* 2E **33**
Pengam. *Card* 4F **33**
Penge. *G Lon* 3E **39**
Pengelly. *Corn* 4A **10**
Pengenffordd. *Powy* 2E **47**
Pengorffwysfa. *IOA* 1D **80**
Pengover Green. *Corn* 2G **7**
Pengwern. *Den* 3C **82**
Penhale. *Corn* 5D **5** (nr. Mullion)
Penhale. *Corn* 3D **6** (nr. St Austell)
Penhale Camp. *Corn* 3B **6**
Penhallow. *Corn* 3B **6**
Penhalvean. *Corn* 5B **6**
Penhelig. *Gwyn* 1F **57**
Penhill. *Swin* 3G **35**
Penhow. *Newp* 2H **33**
Penhurst. *E Sus* 4A **28**
Peniarth. *Gwyn* 5F **69**
Penicuik. *Midl* 3F **129**
Peniel. *Carm* 3E **45**
Penifiler. *High* 4D **155**
Peninver. *Arg* 3B **122**
Penisa'r Waun. *Gwyn* 4E **81**
Penistone. *S Yor* 4C **92**
Penketh. *Warr* 2H **83**
Penkill. *S Ayr* 5B **116**
Penkridge. *Staf* 4D **72**
Penley. *Wrex* 2G **71**
Penllech. *Gwyn* 2B **68**
Penllergaer. *Swan* 3F **31**
Pen-llyn. *IOA* 2C **80**
Penmachno. *Cnwy* 5G **81**
Penmaen. *Swan* 4E **31**
Penmaenmawr. *Cnwy* 3G **81**
Penmaenpool. *Gwyn* 4F **69**
Penmaen Rhos. *Cnwy* 3A **82**
Pen-marc. *V Glam* 5D **32**
Penmark. *V Glam* 5D **32**
Penmarth. *Corn* 5B **6**
Penmon. *IOA* 2F **81**
Penmorfa. *Gwyn* 1E **69**
Penmynydd. *IOA* 3E **81**
Penn. *Buck* 1A **38**
Penn. *Dors* 3G **13**
Penn. *W Mid* 1C **60**
Pennal. *Gwyn* 5G **69**
Pennan. *Abers* 2F **161**
Pennant. *Cdgn* 4E **57**
Pennant. *Den* 2C **70**
Pennant. *Gwyn* 3B **70**
Pennant. *Powy* 1A **58**
Pennant Melangell. *Powy* 3C **70**
Pennar. *Pemb* 4D **42**
Pennard. *Swan* 4E **31**
Pennerley. *Shrp* 1F **59**
Pennington. *Cumb* 2B **96**
Pennington. *G Man* 1A **84**
Pennington. *Hants* 3B **16**
Pennorth. *Powy* 3E **46**
Penn Street. *Buck* 1A **38**
Pennsylvania. *Devn* 3C **12**
Pennsylvania. *S Glo* 4C **34**
Penny Bridge. *Cumb* 1C **96**
Pennycross. *Plym* 3A **8**
Pennygate. *Norf* 3F **79**
Pennyghael. *Arg* 1C **132**
Penny Hill. *Linc* 3C **76**
Pennylands. *Lanc* 4C **90**
Pennymoor. *Devn* 1B **12**
Pennyvenie. *E Ayr* 4D **117**
Pennywell. *Tyne* 4G **115**
Penparc. *Cdgn* 1C **44**
Penparcau. *Cdgn* 2E **57**
Penpedairheol. *Cphy* 2E **33**
Penperlleni. *Mon* 5G **47**
Penpillick. *Corn* 3E **7**
Penpol. *Corn* 5C **6**
Penpoll. *Corn* 3F **7**
Penponds. *Corn* 3D **4**
Penpont. *Corn* 5A **10**
Penpont. *Dum* 5H **117**
Penpont. *Powy* 3C **46**
Penprysg. *B'end* 3C **32**
Penquit. *Devn* 3C **8**
Penrherber. *Carm* 1G **43**
Penrhiw. *Pemb* 1C **44**
Penrhiwceiber. *Rhon* 2D **32**
Pen Rhiwfawr. *Neat* 4H **45**
Penrhiw-llan. *Cdgn* 1D **44**
Penrhiw-pal. *Cdgn* 1D **44**
Penrhos. *Gwyn* 2C **68**
Penrhos. *Here* 5F **59**
Penrhos. *IOA* 2B **80**
Penrhos. *Mon* 4H **47**
Penrhos. *Powy* 4A **46**
Penrhos Garnedd. *Gwyn* 3E **81**
Penrhyn. *IOA* 1C **80**
Penrhyn Bay. *Cnwy* 2H **81**
Penrhyn-coch. *Cdgn* 2F **57**
Penrhyndeudraeth. *Gwyn* 2F **69**
Penrhyn Side. *Cnwy* 2H **81**
Penrice. *Swan* 4D **31**
Penrith. *Cumb* 2G **103**
Penrose. *Corn* 1C **6**
Penruddock. *Cumb* 2F **103**
Penryn. *Corn* 5B **6**
Pensarn. *Carm* 4E **45**
Pen-sarn. *Gwyn* 3E **69**
Pensax. *Worc* 4B **60**
Pensby. *Mers* 2E **83**
Penselwood. *Som* 3C **22**
Pensford. *Bath* 5B **34**
Pensham. *Worc* 1E **49**
Penshaw. *Tyne* 4G **115**
Penshurst. *Kent* 1G **27**
Pensilva. *Corn* 2G **7**
Pensnett. *W Mid* 2D **60**
Penston. *E Lot* 2H **129**
Penstone. *Devn* 2A **12**
Pente-tafarn-y-fedw. *Cnwy* 4H **81**
Pentewan. *Corn* 4E **6**
Pentir. *Gwyn* 4E **81**
Pentire. *Corn* 2B **6**
Pentlepoir. *Pemb* 4F **43**
Pentlow. *Essx* 1B **54**
Pentney. *Norf* 4G **77**
Penton Mewsey. *Hants* 2B **24**
Pentraeth. *IOA* 3E **81**
Pentre. *Powy* 1E **59** (nr. Church Stoke)
Pentre. *Powy* 2D **58** (nr. Kerry)
Pentre. *Powy* 2C **58** (nr. Mochdre)
Pentre. *Rhon* 2C **32**
Pentre. *Shrp* 4F **71**
Pentre. *Wrex* 2D **70** (nr. Llanfyllin)
Pentre. *Wrex* 1E **71** (nr. Rhosllanerchrugog)
Pentrebach. *Carm* 2B **46**
Pentre-bach. *Cdgn* 1F **45**
Pentrebach. *Mer T* 5D **46**
Pentre-bach. *Powy* 2C **46**
Pentrebach. *Swan* 5G **45**
Pentre Berw. *IOA* 3D **80**
Pentre-bont. *Cnwy* 5G **81**
Pentrecagal. *Carm* 1D **44**
Pentre-celyn. *Den* 5D **82**
Pentre-clawdd. *Shrp* 2E **71**
Pentreclwydau. *Neat* 5B **46**
Pentre-cwrt. *Carm* 2D **45**
Pentre Dolau Honddu. *Powy* 1C **46**
Pentre-dwr. *Swan* 3F **31**
Pentrefelin. *Carm* 3F **45**
Pentrefelin. *Cdgn* 1G **45**
Pentrefelin. *Cnwy* 3H **81**
Pentrefelin. *Gwyn* 2E **69**
Pentrefoelas. *Cnwy* 5A **82**
Pentre Galar. *Pemb* 1F **43**
Pentregat. *Cdgn* 5C **56**
Pentre Gwenlais. *Carm* 4G **45**
Pentre Gwynfryn. *Gwyn* 3E **69**
Pentre Halkyn. *Flin* 3E **82**
Pentre Hodre. *Shrp* 3F **59**
Pentre-Llanrhaeadr. *Den* 4C **82**
Pentre Llifior. *Powy* 1D **58**
Pentrellwyn. *IOA* 2E **81**
Pentre-llwyn-llwyd. *Powy* 5B **58**
Pentre-llyn-cymmer. *Cnwy* 5B **82**
Pentre Meyrick. *V Glam* 4C **32**
Pentre-piod. *Gwyn* 2A **70**
Pentre-poeth. *Newp* 3F **33**
Pentre'r Beirdd. *Powy* 4D **70**
Pentre'r-felin. *Powy* 2C **46**
Pentre-ty-gwyn. *Carm* 2B **46**
Pentre-uchaf. *Gwyn* 2C **68**
Pentrich. *Derbs* 5A **86**
Pentridge. *Dors* 1F **15**
Pen-twyn. *Cphy* 5F **47** (nr. Oakdale)
Pentwyn. *Cphy* 5E **46** (nr. Rhymney)
Pentwyn. *Card* 3F **33**
Pentyrch. *Card* 3E **32**
Pentywyn. *Carm* 4G **43**
Penuwch. *Cdgn* 4E **57**
Penwithick. *Corn* 3E **7**
Penwyllt. *Powy* 4B **46**
Penybanc. *Carm* 4G **45** (nr. Ammanford)
Pen-y-banc. *Carm* 3G **45** (nr. Llandeilo)
Pen-y-bont. *Carm* 2H **43**
Penybont. *Powy* 4D **58** (nr. Llandrindod Wells)
Pen-y-bont. *Powy* 3E **70** (nr. Llanfyllin)
Pen-y-Bont Ar Ogwr. *B'end* 3C **32**
Penybontfawr. *Powy* 3C **70**
Penybryn. *Cphy* 2E **33**
Pen-y-bryn. *Pemb* 1B **44**
Pen-y-bryn. *Wrex* 1E **71**
Pen-y-cae. *Powy* 4B **46**
Penycae. *Wrex* 1E **71**
Pen-y-cae-mawr. *Mon* 2H **33**
Penycaerau. *Gwyn* 3A **68**
Pen-y-cefn. *Flin* 3D **82**
Pen-y-clawdd. *Mon* 5H **47**
Pen-y-coedcae. *Rhon* 3D **32**
Penycwm. *Pemb* 2C **42**
Pen-y-Darren. *Mer T* 5D **46**
Pen-y-fai. *B'end* 3B **32**
Penyffordd. *Flin* 4F **83** (nr. Mold)
Pen-y-ffordd. *Flin* 2D **82** (nr. Prestatyn)
Penyffridd. *Gwyn* 5E **81**
Pen-y-garn. *Cdgn* 2F **57**
Pen-y-garnedd. *IOA* 3E **81**
Penygarnedd. *Powy* 3D **70**
Pen-y-graig. *Gwyn* 2B **68**
Penygraig. *Rhon* 2C **32**
Penygraigwen. *IOA* 2D **80**
Pen-y-groes. *Carm* 4F **45**
Penygroes. *Gwyn* 5D **80**
Penygroes. *Pemb* 1F **43**
Pen-y-Mynydd. *Carm* 5E **45**
Penymynydd. *Flin* 4F **83**
Penyrheol. *Cphy* 3E **33**
Pen-yr-heol. *Mon* 4H **47**
Penyrheol. *Swan* 3E **31**
Pen-yr-Heolgerrig. *Mer T* 5D **46**
Penysarn. *IOA* 1D **80**
Pen-y-stryt. *Den* 5E **82**
Penywaun. *Rhon* 5C **46**
Penzance. *Corn* 3B **4**
Peopleton. *Worc* 5D **60**
Peover Heath. *Ches E* 3B **84**
Peper Harow. *Surr* 1A **26**
Peplow. *Shrp* 3A **72**
Pepper Arden. *N Yor* 4F **105**
Perceton. *N Ayr* 5E **127**
Percyhorner. *Abers* 2G **161**
Perham Down. *Wilts* 2A **24**
Periton. *Som* 2C **20**
Perkinsville. *Dur* 4F **115**
Perlethorpe. *Notts* 3D **86**
Perranarworthal. *Corn* 5B **6**
Perranporth. *Corn* 3B **6**
Perranuthnoe. *Corn* 4C **4**
Perranwell. *Corn* 5B **6**
Perranzabuloe. *Corn* 3B **6**
Perrott's Brook. *Glos* 5F **49**
Perry. *W Mid* 1E **61**
Perry Barr. *W Mid* 1E **61**
Perry Crofts. *Staf* 5G **73**
Perry Green. *Essx* 3B **54**
Perry Green. *Herts* 4E **53**
Perry Green. *Wilts* 3E **35**
Perry Street. *Kent* 3H **39**
Perry Street. *Som* 2G **13**
Perrywood. *Kent* 5E **41**
Pershall. *Staf* 3C **72**
Pershore. *Worc* 1E **49**
Pertenhall. *Bed* 4H **63**
Perth. *Per* 1D **136** & **201**
Perthy. *Shrp* 2F **71**
Perton. *Staf* 1C **60**
Pertwood. *Wilts* 3D **23**
Peterborough. *Pet* 1A **64** & **201**
Peterburn. *High* 5B **162**

Peterchurch—Reymerston

Peterchurch. Here 2G 47
Peterculter. Aber 3F 153
Peterhead. Abers 4H 161
Peterlee. Dur 5H 115
Petersfield. Hants 4F 25
Petersfinger. Wilts 4G 23
Peter's Green. Herts 4B 52
Peters Marland. Devn 1E 11
Peterstone Wentlooge. Newp 3F 33
Peterston-super-Ely. V Glam 4D 32
Peterstow. Here 3A 48
Peter Tavy. Devn 5F 11
Petertown. Orkn 7C 172
Petham. Kent 5F 41
Petherwin Gate. Corn 4C 10
Petrockstowe. Devn 2F 11
Petsoe End. Mil 1G 51
Pett. E Sus 4C 28
Pettaugh. Suff 5D 66
Pett Bottom. Kent 5F 41
Petteridge. Kent 1A 28
Pettinain. S Lan 5C 128
Pettistree. Suff 5E 67
Petton. Devn 4D 20
Petton. Shrp 3G 71
Petts Wood. G Lon 4F 39
Pettycur. Fife 1F 129
Pettywell. Norf 3C 78
Petworth. W Sus 3A 26
Pevensey. E Sus 5A 28
Pevensey Bay. E Sus 5A 28
Pewsey. Wilts 5G 35
Pheasants Hill. Buck 3F 37
Philadelphia. Tyne 4G 115
Philham. Devn 4C 18
Philiphaugh. Bord 2G 119
Phillack. Corn 3C 4
Philleigh. Corn 5C 6
Philpstoun. W Lot 2D 128
Phocle Green. Here 3B 48
Phoenix Green. Hants 1F 25
Pibsbury. Som 4H 21
Pibwrlwyd. Carm 4E 45
Pica. Cumb 2B 102
Piccadilly. Warw 1G 61
Piccadilly Corner. Norf 2E 67
Piccotts End. Herts 5A 52
Pickering. N Yor 1B 100
Picket Piece. Hants 2B 24
Picket Post. Hants 2G 15
Pickford. W Mid 2G 61
Pickhill. N Yor 1F 99
Picklenash. Glos 3C 48
Picklescott. Shrp 1G 59
Pickletillem. Fife 1G 137
Pickmere. Ches E 3A 84
Pickstock. Telf 3B 72
Pickwell. Devn 2E 19
Pickwell. Leics 4E 75
Pickworth. Linc 2H 75
Pickworth. Rut 4G 75
Picton. Ches W 3G 83
Picton. Flin 2D 82
Picton. N Yor 4B 106
Pict's Hill. Som 4H 21
Piddinghoe. E Sus 5F 27
Piddington. Buck 2G 37
Piddington. Nptn 5F 63
Piddington. Oxon 4E 51
Piddlehinton. Dors 3C 14
Piddletrenthide. Dors 2C 14
Pidley. Cambs 3C 64
Pidney. Dors 2C 14
Pie Corner. Here 4A 60
Piercebridge. Darl 3F 105
Pierowall. Orkn 3D 172
Pigdon. Nmbd 1E 115
Pightley. Som 3F 21
Pikehall. Derbs 5F 85
Pikeshill. Hants 2A 16
Pilford. Dors 2F 15
Pilgrims Hatch. Essx 1G 39
Pilham. Linc 1F 87
Pill. N Som 4A 34
Pillaton. Corn 2H 7
Pillaton. Staf 4D 72
Pillerton Hersey. Warw 1A 50
Pillerton Priors. Warw 1A 50
Pilleth. Powy 4E 59
Pilley. Hants 3B 16
Pilley. S Yor 4D 92
Pillgwenlly. Newp 3G 33
Pilling. Lanc 5D 96
Pilling Lane. Lanc 5C 96
Pillowell. Glos 5B 48
Pill, The. Mon 3H 33
Pillwell. Dors 1C 14
Pilning. S Glo 3A 34
Pilsbury. Derbs 4F 85
Pilsdon. Dors 3H 13
Pilsgate. Pet 5H 75
Pilsley. Derbs 3G 85
(nr. Bakewell)
Pilsley. Derbs 4B 86
(nr. Clay Cross)
Pilson Green. Norf 4F 79
Piltdown. E Sus 3F 27
Pilton. Edin 2F 129
Pilton. Nptn 2H 63
Pilton. Rut 5G 75
Pilton. Som 2A 22
Pilton Green. Swan 4D 30
Pimperne. Dors 2E 15
Pinchbeck. Linc 3B 76
Pinchbeck Bars. Linc 3A 76
Pinchbeck West. Linc 3B 76
Pinfold. Lanc 3B 90
Pinford End. Suff 5H 65
Pinged. Carm 5E 45
Pinhoe. Devn 3C 12
Pinkerton. E Lot 2D 130
Pinkneys Green. Wind 3G 37
Pinley. W Mid 3A 62
Pinley Green. Warw 4G 61
Pinmill. Suff 2F 55
Pinmore. S Ayr 5B 116
Pinner. G Lon 2C 38
Pins Green. Worc 1C 48
Pinsley Green. Ches E 1H 71
Pinvin. Worc 1E 49
Pinwherry. S Ayr 1G 109
Pinxton. Derbs 5B 86
Pipe and Lyde. Here 1A 48
Pipe Aston. Here 3G 59
Pipe Gate. Shrp 1B 72
Pipehill. Staf 5E 73
Piperhill. High 3C 158
Pipe Ridware. Staf 4E 73
Pipers Pool. Corn 4C 10
Pipewell. Nptn 2F 63
Pippacott. Devn 3F 19
Pipton. Powy 2E 47
Pirbright. Surr 5A 38
Pirnmill. N Ayr 5G 125
Pirton. Herts 2B 52
Pirton. Worc 1D 49
Pisgah. Stir 3G 135
Pishill. Oxon 3F 37
Pistyll. Gwyn 1C 68
Pitagowan. Per 2F 143
Pitcairn. Per 3F 143
Pitcairngreen. Per 1C 136
Pitcalnie. High 1C 158
Pitcaple. Abers 1E 152
Pitchcombe. Glos 5D 48
Pitchcott. Buck 3F 51
Pitchford. Shrp 5H 71
Pitch Green. Buck 5F 51
Pitch Place. Surr 5A 38
Pitcombe. Som 3B 22
Pitcox. E Lot 2C 130
Pitcur. Per 5B 144
Pitfichie. Abers 2D 152
Pitgrudy. High 4E 165
Pitkennedy. Ang 3E 145
Pitlessie. Fife 3F 137
Pitlochry. Per 3G 143
Pitmachie. Abers 1D 152
Pitmaduthy. High 1B 158
Pitmedden. Abers 1F 153
Pitminster. Som 1F 13
Pitnacree. Per 3G 143
Pitney. Som 4H 21
Pitroddie. Per 1E 136
Pitscottie. Fife 2G 137
Pitsea. Essx 2B 40
Pitsford. Nptn 4E 63
Pitsford Hill. Som 3E 20
Pitsmoor. S Yor 2A 86
Pitstone. Buck 4H 51
Pitt. Hants 4C 24
Pitt Court. Glos 2C 34
Pittentrail. High 3E 164
Pittenweem. Fife 3H 137
Pittington. Dur 5G 115
Pitton. Swan 4D 30
Pitton. Wilts 3H 23
Pittswood. Kent 1H 27
Pittulie. Abers 2G 161
Pittville. Glos 3E 49
Pitversie. Per 2D 136
Pityme. Corn 1D 6
Pity Me. Dur 5F 115
Pixey Green. Suff 3E 67
Pixley. Here 2B 48
Place Newton. N Yor 2C 100
Plaidy. Abers 3E 161
Plaidy. Corn 3G 7
Plain Dealings. Pemb 3E 43
Plains. N Lan 3A 128
Plainsfield. Som 3E 21
Plaish. Shrp 1H 59
Plaistow. Here 2B 48
Plaistow. W Sus 2B 26
Plaitford. Wilts 1A 16
Plas Llwyd. Cnwy 3B 82
Plastow Green. Hants 5D 36
Plas yn Cefn. Den 3C 82
Platt. Kent 5H 39
Platt Bridge. G Man 4E 90
Platt Lane. Shrp 2H 71
Platts Common. S Yor 4D 92
Platt's Heath. Kent 5C 40
Platt, The. E Sus 2G 27
Plawsworth. Dur 5F 115
Plaxtol. Kent 5H 39
Playden. E Sus 3D 28
Playford. Suff 1F 55
Play Hatch. Oxon 4F 37
Playing Place. Corn 4C 6
Playley Green. Glos 2C 48
Plealey. Shrp 5G 71
Plean. Stir 1B 128
Pleasington. Bkbn 2E 91
Pleasley. Derbs 4C 86
Pledgdon Green. Essx 3F 53
Plenmeller. Nmbd 3A 114
Pleshey. Essx 4G 53
Plockton. High 5H 155
Plocrapol. W Isl 8D 171
Ploughfield. Here 1G 47
Plowden. Shrp 2F 59
Ploxgreen. Shrp 5F 71
Pluckley. Kent 1D 28
Plucks Gutter. Kent 4G 41
Plumbland. Cumb 1C 102
Plumbridge. Strab 7A 174
Plumgarths. Cumb 5F 103
Plumley. Ches E 3B 84
Plummers Plain. W Sus 3D 26
Plumpton. Cumb 1F 103
Plumpton. E Sus 4E 27
Plumpton. Nptn 1D 50
Plumpton Foot. Cumb 1F 103
Plumpton Green. E Sus 4E 27
Plumpton Head. Cumb 1G 103
Plumstead. G Lon 3F 39
Plumstead. Norf 2D 78
Plumtree. Notts 2D 74
Plumtree Park. Notts 2D 74
Plungar. Leics 2E 75
Plush. Dors 2C 14
Plushabridge. Corn 5D 10
Plwmp. Cdgn 5C 56
Plymouth. Plym 3A 8 & 201
Plympton. Plym 3B 8
Plymstock. Plym 3B 8
Plymtree. Devn 2D 12
Pockley. N Yor 1A 100
Pocklington. E Yor 5C 100
Pode Hole. Linc 3B 76
Podimore. Som 4A 22
Podington. Bed 4G 63
Podmore. Staf 2B 72
Poffley End. Oxon 4B 50
Point Clear. Essx 4D 54
Pointon. Linc 2A 76
Pokesdown. Bour 3G 15
Polbae. Dum 2H 109
Polbain. High 3E 163
Polbathic. Corn 3H 7
Polbeth. W Lot 3D 128
Polbrock. Corn 2E 6
Polchar. High 3C 150
Polebrook. Nptn 2H 63
Pole Elm. Worc 1D 48
Polegate. E Sus 5G 27
Pole Moor. W Yor 3A 92
Poles. High 4E 165
Polesworth. Warw 5G 73
Polglass. High 3E 163
Polgooth. Corn 3D 6
Poling. W Sus 5B 26
Poling Corner. W Sus 5B 26
Polio. High 1B 158
Polkerris. Corn 3E 7
Polla. High 3D 166
Pollard Street. Norf 2F 79
Pollicott. Buck 4F 51
Pollington. E Yor 3G 93
Polloch. High 2B 140
Pollok. Glas 3G 127
Pollokshaws. Glas 3G 127
Pollokshields. Glas 3G 127
Polmaily. High 5G 157
Polmassick. Corn 4D 6
Polmont. Falk 2C 128
Polnessan. E Ayr 3D 116
Polnish. High 5F 147
Polperro. Corn 3G 7
Polruan. Corn 3F 7
Polscoe. Corn 2F 7
Polsham. Som 2A 22
Polskeoch. Dum 4F 117
Polstead. Suff 2C 54
Polstead Heath. Suff 1C 54
Poltesco. Corn 5E 5
Poltimore. Devn 3C 12
Polton. Midl 3G 129
Polwarth. Bord 4D 130
Polyphant. Corn 4C 10
Polzeath. Corn 1D 6
Pomeroy. Cook 2A 178
Ponde. Powy 2E 46
Pondersbridge. Cambs 1B 64
Ponders End. G Lon 1E 39
Pond Street. Essx 2E 53
Pondtail. Hants 1G 25
Ponsanooth. Corn 5B 6
Ponsongath. Corn 5E 5
Ponsworthy. Devn 5H 11
Pontamman. Carm 4G 45
Pontantwn. Carm 4E 45
Pontardawe. Neat 5H 45
Pontarddulais. Swan 5F 45
Pontarfynach. Cdgn 3G 57
Pont-ar-gothi. Carm 3F 45
Pont ar Hydfer. Powy 3B 46
Pontarllechau. Carm 3H 45
Pontarsais. Carm 3E 45
Pontblyddyn. Flin 4E 83
Pontbren Llwyd. Rhon 5C 46
Pont Cyfyng. Cnwy 5G 81
Pontdolgoch. Powy 1C 58
Pontefract. W Yor 2E 93
Ponteland. Nmbd 2E 115
Ponterwyd. Cdgn 2G 57
Pontesbury. Shrp 5G 71
Pontesford. Shrp 5G 71
Pontfadog. Wrex 2E 71
Pontfaen. Pemb 1E 43
Pont-faen. Powy 2C 46
Pont-Faen. Shrp 2E 71
Pontgarreg. Cdgn 5C 56
Pont-Henri. Carm 5E 45
Ponthir. Torf 2G 33
Ponthirwaun. Cdgn 1C 44
Pont-iets. Carm 5E 45
Pontllanfraith. Cphy 2E 33
Pontlliw. Swan 5G 45
Pont Llogel. Powy 4C 70
Pontllyfni. Gwyn 5D 80
Pontlottyn. Cphy 5E 46
Pontneddfechan. Neat 5C 46
Pont-newydd. Carm 5E 45
Pont-newydd. Flin 4D 82
Pontnewydd. Torf 2F 33
Ponton. Shet 6E 173
Pont Pen-y-benglog. Gwyn 4F 81
Pontrhydfendigaid. Cdgn 4G 57
Pont Rhyd-y-cyff. B'end 3B 32
Pontrhydyfen. Neat 2A 32
Pont-rhyd-y-groes. Cdgn 3G 57
Pontrhydyrun. Torf 2F 33
Pont Rhythallt. Gwyn 4E 81
Pontrilas. Here 3G 47
Pontrilas Road. Here 3G 47
Pontrobert. Powy 4D 70
Pont-rug. Gwyn 4E 81
Ponts Green. E Sus 4A 28
Pontshill. Here 3B 48
Pont-Sian. Cdgn 1E 45
Pontsticill. Mer T 4D 46
Pont-Walby. Neat 5B 46
Pontwelly. Carm 2E 45
Pontwgan. Cnwy 3G 81
Pontyates. Carm 5E 45
Pontyberem. Carm 4F 45
Pontybodkin. Flin 5E 83
Pontyclun. Rhon 3D 32
Pontycymer. B'end 2C 32
Pontyglazier. Pemb 1F 43
Pontygwaith. Rhon 2D 32
Pont-y-pant. Cnwy 5G 81
Pontypool. Torf 2G 33
Pontypridd. Rhon 2D 32
Pontypwl. Torf 2G 33
Pontywaun. Cphy 2F 33
Pooksgreen. Hants 1B 16
Pool. Corn 4A 6
Pool. W Yor 5E 99
Poole. Pool 3F 15 & 204
Poole. Som 4E 21
Poole Keynes. Glos 2E 35
Poolend. Staf 5D 84
Poolewe. High 5C 162
Pooley Bridge. Cumb 2F 103
Poolfold. Staf 5C 84
Pool Head. Here 5H 59
Pool Hey. Lanc 3B 90
Poolhill. Glos 3C 48
Poolmill. Here 3A 48
Pool o' Muckhart. Clac 3C 136
Pool Quay. Powy 4E 71
Poolsbrook. Derbs 3B 86
Pool Street. Essx 2A 54
Pootings. Kent 1F 27
Pope Hill. Pemb 3D 42
Pope's Hill. Glos 4B 48
Popeswood. Brac 5G 37
Popham. Hants 2D 24
Poplar. G Lon 2E 39
Popley. Hants 1E 25
Porchfield. IOW 3C 16
Porin. High 3F 157
Poringland. Norf 5E 79
Porkellis. Corn 5A 6
Porlock. Som 2B 20
Porlock Weir. Som 2B 20
Portachoillan. Arg 4F 125
Port Adhair Bheinn na Faoghla. W Isl 3C 170
Port Adhair Thirlodh. Arg 4B 138
Portadown. Cgvn 4E 178
Portaferry. Ards 4K 179
Port Ann. Arg 1H 125
Port Appin. Arg 4D 140
Port Asgaig. Arg 3C 124
Port Askaig. Arg 3C 124
Portavadie. Arg 3H 125
Portavogie. Ards 3L 179
Portballintrae. Cole 2F 174
Port Bannatyne. Arg 3B 126
Portbury. N Som 4A 34
Port Carlisle. Cumb 3D 112
Port Charlotte. Arg 4A 124
Portchester. Hants 2E 16
Port Clarence. Stoc T 2B 106
Port Dinorwig. Gwyn 4E 81
Port Driseach. Arg 2A 126
Port Dundas. Glas 3H 127
Port Ellen. Arg 5B 124
Port Elphinstone. Abers 1E 153
Portencalzie. Dum 2F 109
Portencross. N Ayr 5C 126
Port Erin. IOM 5A 108
Port Erroll. Abers 5H 161
Porter's Fen Corner. Norf 5E 77
Portesham. Dors 4B 14
Portessie. Mor 2B 160
Port e Vullen. IOM 2D 108
Port-Eynon. Swan 4D 30
Portfield. Som 4H 21
Portfield Gate. Pemb 3D 42
Portgate. Devn 4E 11
Port Gaverne. Corn 4A 10
Port Glasgow. Inv 2E 127
Portglenone. Bmna 6F 175
Portgordon. Mor 2A 160
Portgower. High 2H 165
Porth. Corn 2C 6
Porth. Rhon 2D 32
Porthaethwy. IOA 3E 81
Porthallow. Corn 3G 7
(nr. Looe)
Porthallow. Corn 4E 5
(nr. St Keverne)
Porthalong. High 5C 154
Porthcawl. B'end 4B 32
Porthceri. V Glam 5D 32
Porthcothan. Corn 1C 6
Porthcurno. Corn 4A 4
Port Henderson. High 1G 155
Porthgain. Pemb 1C 42
Porthgwarra. Corn 4A 4
Porthill. Shrp 4G 71
Porthkerry. V Glam 5D 32
Porthleven. Corn 4D 4
Porthllechog. IOA 1D 80
Porthmadog. Gwyn 2E 69
Porthmeirion. Gwyn 2E 69
Porthmeor. Corn 3B 4
Porth Navas. Corn 4E 5
Portholland. Corn 4D 6
Porthoustock. Corn 4F 5
Porthtowan. Corn 4A 6
Porth Tywyn. Carm 5E 45
Porth-y-felin. IOA 2B 80
Porthyrhyd. Carm 4F 45
(nr. Carmarthen)
Porthyrhyd. Carm 2H 45
(nr. Llandovery)
Porth-y-waen. Shrp 3E 71
Portincaple. Arg 4B 134
Portington. E Yor 1A 94
Portinnisherrich. Arg 2G 133
Portinscale. Cumb 2D 102
Port Isaac. Corn 1D 6
Portishead. N Som 4H 33
Portknockie. Mor 2B 160
Port Lamont. Arg 2B 126
Portlethen. Abers 4G 153
Portlethen Village. Abers 4G 153
Portling. Dum 4F 111
Port Lion. Pemb 4D 43
Portloe. Corn 5D 6
Port Logan. Dum 5F 109
Portmahomack. High 5G 165
Port Mead. Swan 3F 31
Portmellon. Corn 4E 6
Port Mholair. W Isl 4H 171
Port Mor. High 1F 139
Portmore. Hants 3B 16
Port Mulgrave. N Yor 3E 107
Portnacroish. Arg 4D 140
Portnahaven. Arg 4A 124
Portnalong. High 5C 154
Portnaluchaig. High 5E 147
Portnancon. High 2E 167
Port Nan Giuran. W Isl 4H 171
Port nan Long. W Isl 1D 170
Port Nis. W Isl 1H 171
Portobello. Edin 2G 129
Portobello. W Yor 3D 92
Port of Menteith. Stir 3E 135
Porton. Wilts 3G 23
Portormin. High 5D 168
Portpatrick. Dum 4F 109
Port Quin. Corn 1D 6
Port Ramsay. Arg 4C 140
Portreath. Corn 4A 6
Portree. High 4D 155
Port Righ. High 4D 155
Portrush. Cole 3E 174
Port St Mary. IOM 5B 108
Portscatho. Corn 5C 6
Portsea. Port 2E 17
Port Seton. E Lot 2H 129
Portskerra. High 2A 168
Portskewett. Mon 3A 34
Portslade-by-Sea. Brig 5D 26
Portsmouth. Port 3E 17 & 201
Portsmouth. W Yor 2H 91
Port Soderick. IOM 4C 108
Port Solent. Port 2E 17
Portsonachan. Arg 1H 133
Portsoy. Abers 2C 160
Portstewart. Cole 3E 174
Port Sunlight. Mers 2F 83
Portswood. Sotn 1C 16
Port Talbot. Neat 4G 31
Porttannachy. Mor 2A 160
Port Tennant. Swan 3F 31
Portuairk. High 2F 139
Portway. Here 1H 47
Portway. Worc 3E 61
Port Wemyss. Arg 4A 124
Port William. Dum 5A 110
Portwrinkle. Corn 3H 7
Poslingford. Suff 1A 54
Postbridge. Devn 5G 11
Postcombe. Oxon 2F 37
Post Green. Dors 3E 15
Postling. Kent 2F 29
Postlip. Glos 3F 49
Post-Mawr. Cdgn 5D 56
Postwick. Norf 5E 79
Potarch. Abers 4D 152
Potsgrove. C Beds 3H 51
Potten End. Herts 5A 52
Potter Brompton. N Yor 2D 101
Pottergate Street. Norf 1D 66
Potterhanworth. Linc 4H 87
Potterhanworth Booths. Linc 4H 87
Potter Heigham. Norf 4G 79
Potter Hill. Leics 3E 75
Potteries, The. Stoke 1C 72
Potterne. Wilts 1E 23
Potterne Wick. Wilts 1E 23
Potternewton. W Yor 1D 92
Potters Bar. Herts 5C 52
Potters Brook. Lanc 4D 97
Potter's Cross. Staf 2C 60
Potters Crouch. Herts 5B 52
Potter Somersal. Derbs 2F 73
Potterspury. Nptn 1F 51
Potter Street. Essx 5E 53
Potterton. Abers 2G 153
Potthorpe. Norf 3B 78
Pottle Street. Wilts 2D 22
Potto. N Yor 4B 106
Potton. C Beds 1C 52
Pott Row. Norf 3G 77
Pott Shrigley. Ches E 3D 84
Poughill. Corn 2C 10
Poughill. Devn 2B 12
Poulner. Hants 2G 15
Poulshot. Wilts 1E 23
Poulton. Glos 5G 49
Poulton-le-Fylde. Lanc 1B 90
Pound Bank. Worc 3B 60
Poundbury. Dors 3B 14
Poundfield. E Sus 2G 27
Poundgate. E Sus 3F 27
Pound Green. E Sus 3G 27
Pound Green. Suff 5G 65
Pound Hill. W Sus 2D 27
Poundland. S Ayr 1G 109
Poundon. Buck 3E 51
Poundsgate. Devn 5H 11
Poundstock. Corn 3C 10
Pound Street. Hants 5C 36
Pounsley. E Sus 3G 27
Powburn. Nmbd 3E 121
Powderham. Devn 4C 12
Powerstock. Dors 3A 14
Powfoot. Dum 3C 112
Powick. Worc 5C 60
Powmill. Per 4C 136
Poxwell. Dors 4C 14
Poyle. Slo 3B 38
Poynings. W Sus 4D 26
Poyntington. Dors 4B 22
Poynton. Ches E 2D 84
Poynton. Telf 4H 71
Poynton Green. Telf 4H 71
Poyntz Pass. Arm 6E 178
Poystreet Green. Suff 5B 66
Praa Sands. Corn 4C 4
Pratt's Bottom. G Lon 4F 39
Praze-an-Beeble. Corn 3D 4
Prees. Shrp 2H 71
Preesall. Lanc 5C 96
Preesall Park. Lanc 5C 96
Prees Green. Shrp 2H 71
Prees Higher Heath. Shrp 2H 71
Prendergast. Pemb 3D 42
Prendwick. Nmbd 3E 121
Pren-gwyn. Cdgn 1E 45
Prenteg. Gwyn 1E 69
Prenton. Mers 2F 83
Prescot. Mers 1G 83
Prescott. Devn 1D 12
Prescott. Shrp 3G 71
Preshute. Wilts 5G 35
Pressen. Nmbd 1C 120
Prestatyn. Den 2C 82
Prestbury. Ches E 3D 84
Prestbury. Glos 3E 49
Presteigne. Powy 4F 59
Presthope. Shrp 1H 59
Prestleigh. Som 2B 22
Preston. Brig 5E 27
Preston. Devn 5B 12
Preston. Dors 4C 14
Preston. E Lot 2B 130
(nr. East Linton)
Preston. E Lot 2G 129
(nr. Prestonpans)
Preston. E Yor 1E 95
Preston. Glos 5F 49
Preston. Herts 3B 52
Preston. Kent 4G 41
(nr. Canterbury)
Preston. Kent 4E 40
(nr. Faversham)
Preston. Lanc 2D 90 & 201
Preston. Nmbd 2F 121
Preston. Rut 5F 75
Preston. Bord 4D 130
Preston. Shrp 4H 71
Preston. Suff 5B 66
Preston. Wilts 4A 36
(nr. Aldbourne)
Preston. Wilts 4F 35
(nr. Lyneham)
Preston Bagot. Warw 4F 61
Preston Bissett. Buck 3E 51
Preston Bowyer. Som 4E 21
Preston Brockhurst. Shrp 3H 71
Preston Brook. Hal 2H 83
Preston Candover. Hants 2E 24
Preston Capes. Nptn 5C 62
Preston Cross. Glos 2B 48
Preston Gubbals. Shrp 4G 71
Preston-le-Skerne. Dur 2A 106
Preston Marsh. Here 1A 48
Prestonmill. Dum 4A 112
Preston on Stour. Warw 5G 61
Preston on the Hill. Hal 2H 83
Preston on Wye. Here 1G 47
Prestonpans. E Lot 2G 129
Preston Plucknett. Som 1A 14
Preston-under-Scar. N Yor 5D 104
Preston upon the Weald Moors. Telf 4A 72
Preston Wynne. Here 1A 48
Prestwich. G Man 4G 91
Prestwick. Nmbd 2E 115
Prestwick. S Ayr 2C 116
Prestwold. Leics 3C 74
Prestwood. Buck 5G 51
Prestwood. Staf 1E 73
Price Town. B'end 2C 32
Prickwillow. Cambs 2E 65
Priddy. Som 1A 22
Priestcliffe. Derbs 3F 85
Priesthill. Glas 3G 127
Priest Hutton. Lanc 2E 97
Priestland. E Ayr 1E 117
Priest Weston. Shrp 1E 59
Priestwood. Brac 4G 37
Priestwood. Kent 4A 40
Primethorpe. Leics 1C 62
Primrose Green. Norf 4C 78
Primrose Hill. Derbs 5B 86
Primrose Hill. Glos 5B 48
Primrose Hill. Lanc 4B 90
Primrose Valley. N Yor 2F 101
Primsidemill. Bord 2C 120
Princes Gate. Pemb 3F 43
Princes Risborough. Buck 5G 51
Princethorpe. Warw 3B 62
Princetown. Devn 5F 11
Prinsted. W Sus 2F 17
Prion. Den 4C 82
Prior Muir. Fife 2H 137
Prior's Frome. Here 2A 48
Priors Halton. Shrp 3G 59
Priors Hardwick. Warw 5B 62
Priorslee. Telf 4B 72
Priors Marston. Warw 5B 62
Prior's Norton. Glos 3D 48
Priory, The. W Ber 5B 36
Priory Wood. Here 1F 47
Priston. Bath 5B 34
Pristow Green. Norf 2D 66
Prittlewell. S'end 2C 40
Privett. Hants 4E 25
Prixford. Devn 3F 19
Probus. Corn 4D 6
Prospect. Cumb 5C 112
Prospect Village. Staf 4E 73
Provanmill. Glas 3H 127
Prudhoe. Nmbd 3D 115
Publow. Bath 5B 34
Puckeridge. Herts 3D 53
Puckington. Som 1G 13
Pucklechurch. S Glo 4B 34
Puckrup. Glos 2D 49
Puddinglake. Ches W 4B 84
Puddington. Ches W 3F 83
Puddington. Devn 1B 12
Puddlebrook. Glos 4B 48
Puddledock. Norf 1C 66
Puddletown. Dors 3C 14
Pudleston. Here 5H 59
Pudsey. W Yor 1C 92
Pulborough. W Sus 4B 26
Puleston. Telf 3B 72
Pulford. Ches W 5F 83
Pulham. Dors 2C 14
Pulham Market. Norf 2D 66
Pulham St Mary. Norf 2E 66
Pulley. Shrp 5G 71
Pulloxhill. C Beds 2A 52
Pulpit Hill. Arg 1F 133
Pulverbatch. Shrp 5G 71
Pumpherston. W Lot 3D 128
Pumsaint. Carm 1G 45
Puncheston. Pemb 2E 43
Puncknowle. Dors 4A 14
Punnett's Town. E Sus 3H 27
Purbrook. Hants 2E 17
Purfleet. Thur 3G 39
Puriton. Som 2G 21
Purleigh. Essx 5B 54
Purley. G Lon 4E 39
Purley on Thames. W Ber 4E 37
Purlogue. Shrp 3E 59
Purl's Bridge. Cambs 2D 65
Purse Caundle. Dors 1B 14
Purslow. Shrp 2F 59
Purston Jaglin. W Yor 3E 93
Purtington. Som 2G 13
Purton. Glos 5B 48
(nr. Lydney)
Purton. Glos 5B 48
(nr. Sharpness)
Purton. Wilts 3F 35
Purton Stoke. Wilts 2F 35
Pury End. Nptn 1F 51
Pusey. Oxon 2B 36
Putley. Here 2B 48
Putney. G Lon 3D 38
Putsborough. Devn 2E 19
Puttenham. Herts 4G 51
Puttenham. Surr 1A 26
Puttock End. Essx 1B 54
Puttock's End. Essx 4F 53
Puxey. Dors 1C 14
Puxton. N Som 5H 33
Pwll. Carm 5E 45
Pwll. Powy 5D 70
Pwllcrochan. Pemb 4D 42
Pwll-glas. Den 5D 82
Pwllgloyw. Powy 2D 46
Pwllheli. Gwyn 2C 68
Pwllmeyric. Mon 2A 34
Pwlltrap. Carm 3G 43
Pwll-y-glaw. Neat 2A 32
Pyecombe. W Sus 4D 27
Pye Corner. Herts 4E 53
Pye Corner. Newp 3G 33
Pye Green. Staf 4D 73
Pyewipe. NE Lin 3F 95
Pyle. B'end 3B 32
Pyle. IOW 5C 16
Pylle. Som 3B 22
Pymoor. Cambs 2D 65
Pymoor. Dors 3H 13
Pyrford. Surr 5B 38
Pyrford Village. Surr 5B 38
Pyrton. Oxon 2E 37
Pytchley. Nptn 3F 63
Pyworthy. Devn 2D 10

Q

Quabbs. Shrp 2E 58
Quadring. Linc 2B 76
Quadring Eaudike. Linc 2B 76
Quainton. Buck 3F 51
Quaking Houses. Dur 4E 115
Quarley. Hants 2A 24
Quarndon. Derbs 1H 73
Quarrendon. Buck 4G 51
Quarrier's Village. Inv 3E 127
Quarrington. Linc 1H 75
Quarrington Hill. Dur 1A 106
Quarry Bank. W Mid 2D 60
Quarry, The. Glos 2C 34
Quarrywood. Mor 2F 159
Quartalehouse. Abers 4G 161
Quarter. N Ayr 3C 126
Quarter. S Lan 4A 128
Quatford. Shrp 1B 60
Quatt. Shrp 2B 60
Quebec. Dur 5E 115
Quedgeley. Glos 4D 48
Queen Adelaide. Cambs 2E 65
Queenborough. Kent 3D 40
Queen Camel. Som 4A 22
Queen Charlton. Bath 5B 34
Queen Dart. Devn 1B 12
Queenhill. Worc 2D 48
Queen Oak. Dors 3C 22
Queensbury. W Yor 2B 92
Queensferry. Flin 4F 83
Queenstown. Bkpl 1B 90
Queen Street. Kent 1A 28
Queenzieburn. N Lan 2H 127
Quemerford. Wilts 5F 35
Quendale. Shet 10E 173
Quendon. Essx 2F 53
Queniborough. Leics 4D 74
Quenington. Glos 5G 49
Quernmore. Lanc 3E 97
Quethiock. Corn 2H 7
Quholm. Orkn 6B 172
Quick's Green. W Ber 4D 36
Quidenham. Norf 2C 66
Quidhampton. Hants 1D 24
Quidhampton. Wilts 3G 23
Quilquox. Abers 5G 161
Quina Brook. Shrp 2H 71
Quindry. Orkn 8D 172
Quine's Hill. IOM 4C 108
Quinton. Nptn 5E 63
Quinton. W Mid 2D 61
Quintrell Downs. Corn 2C 6
Quixhill. Staf 1F 73
Quoditch. Devn 3E 11
Quorn. Leics 4C 74
Quorndon. Leics 4C 74
Quothquan. S Lan 1B 118
Quoyloo. Orkn 5B 172
Quoyness. Orkn 7B 172
Quoys. Shet 5F 173
(on Mainland)
Quoys. Shet 1H 173
(on Unst)

R

Rableyheath. Herts 4C 52
Raby. Cumb 4C 112
Raby. Mers 3F 83
Rachan Mill. Bord 1D 118
Rachub. Gwyn 4F 81
Rack End. Oxon 5C 50
Rackenford. Devn 1B 12
Rackham. W Sus 4B 26
Rackheath. Norf 4E 79
Racks. Dum 2B 112
Rackwick. Orkn 8A 172
(on Hoy)
Rackwick. Orkn 3D 172
(on Westray)
Radbourne. Derbs 2G 73
Radcliffe. G Man 4F 91
Radcliffe. Nmbd 4G 121
Radcliffe on Trent. Notts 2D 74
Radclive. Buck 2E 51
Radernie. Fife 2G 137
Radfall. Kent 4F 41
Radford. Bath 1B 22
Radford. Nott 1C 74
Radford. Oxon 3C 50
Radford. W Mid 2H 61
Radford. Worc 5E 61
Radford Semele. Warw 4H 61
Radipole. Dors 4B 14
Radlett. Herts 1C 38
Radley. Oxon 2D 36
Radnage. Buck 2F 37
Radstock. Bath 1B 22
Radstone. Nptn 1D 50
Radway. Warw 1B 50
Radway Green. Ches E 5B 84
Radwell. Bed 5H 63
Radwell. Herts 2C 52
Radwinter. Essx 2G 53
Radyr. Card 3E 33
RAF Coltishall. Norf 3E 79
Rafford. Mor 3E 159
Raffrey. Down 4J 179
Ragdale. Leics 4D 74
Ragdon. Shrp 1G 59
Ragged Appleshaw. Hants 2B 24
Raggra. High 4F 169
Raglan. Mon 5H 47
Ragnall. Notts 3F 87
Rahoy. Down 5K 179
Raigbeg. High 1C 150
Rainford. Mers 4C 90
Rainford Junction. Mers 4C 90
Rainham. G Lon 2G 39
Rainham. Medw 4C 40
Rainhill. Mers 1G 83
Rainow. Ches E 3D 84
Rainton. N Yor 2F 99
Rainworth. Notts 5C 86
Raisbeck. Cumb 4H 103
Raise. Cumb 5A 114
Rait. Per 1E 137
Raithby. Linc 2C 88
Raithby by Spilsby. Linc 4C 88
Raithwaite. N Yor 3F 107
Rake. W Sus 4G 25
Rake End. Staf 4E 73
Rakeway. Staf 1E 73
Rakewood. G Man 3H 91
Ralia. High 4B 150
Ram Alley. Wilts 5H 35
Ramasaig. High 4A 154
Rame. Corn 4A 8
(nr. Millbrook)
Rame. Corn 5B 6
(nr. Penryn)
Ram Lane. Kent 1D 28
Ramnageo. Shet 1H 173
Rampisham. Dors 2A 14
Rampside. Cumb 3B 96
Rampton. Cambs 4D 64
Rampton. Notts 3E 87
Ramsbottom. G Man 3F 91
Ramsburn. Mor 3C 160
Ramsbury. Wilts 4A 36
Ramscraigs. High 1H 165
Ramsdean. Hants 4F 25
Ramsdell. Hants 1D 24
Ramsden. Oxon 4B 50
Ramsden. Worc 1E 49
Ramsden Bellhouse. Essx 1B 40
Ramsden Heath. Essx 1B 40
Ramsey. Cambs 2B 64
Ramsey. Essx 2F 55
Ramsey. IOM 2D 108
Ramsey Forty Foot. Cambs 2C 64
Ramsey Heights. Cambs 2B 64
Ramsey Island. Essx 5C 54
Ramsey Mereside. Cambs 2B 64
Ramsey St Mary's. Cambs 2B 64
Ramsgate. Kent 4H 41
Ramsgill. N Yor 2D 98
Ramshaw. Dur 5C 114
Ramshorn. Staf 1E 73
Ramsley. Devn 3G 11
Ramsnest Common. Surr 2A 26
Ramstone. Abers 2D 152
Ranais. W Isl 5G 171
Ranby. Linc 3B 88
Ranby. Notts 2D 86
Rand. Linc 3A 88
Randalstown. Ant 7G 175
Randwick. Glos 5D 48
Ranfurly. Ren 3E 127
Rangag. High 4D 168
Rangemore. Staf 3F 73
Rangeworthy. S Glo 3B 34
Rankinston. E Ayr 3D 116
Rank's Green. Essx 4H 53
Ranmore Common. Surr 5C 38
Rannoch Station. Per 3B 142
Ranochan. High 5G 147
Ranskill. Notts 2D 86
Ranton. Staf 3C 72
Ranton Green. Staf 3C 72
Ranworth. Norf 4F 79
Raploch. Stir 4G 135
Rapness. Orkn 3E 172
Rapps. Som 1G 13
Rascal Moor. E Yor 1B 94
Rascarrel. Dum 5E 111
Rasharkin. Bmny 5F 175
Rashfield. Arg 1C 126
Rashwood. Worc 4D 60
Raskelf. N Yor 2G 99
Rassau. Blae 4E 47
Rastrick. W Yor 2B 92
Ratagan. High 2B 148
Ratby. Leics 5C 74
Ratcliffe Culey. Leics 1H 61
Ratcliffe on Soar. Notts 3B 74
Ratcliffe on the Wreake. Leics 4D 74
Rathen. Abers 2H 161
Rathfriland. Ban 6F 179
Rathillet. Fife 1F 137
Rathmell. N Yor 4H 97
Ratho. Edin 2E 129
Ratho Station. Edin 2E 129
Rathven. Mor 2B 160
Ratley. Hants 4B 24
Ratley. Warw 1B 50
Ratlinghope. Shrp 1G 59
Rattar. High 1E 169
Ratten Row. Cumb 5E 113
Ratten Row. Lanc 5D 96
Rattery. Devn 2D 8
Rattlesden. Suff 5B 66
Ratton Village. E Sus 5G 27
Rattray. Abers 3H 161
Rattray. Per 4A 144
Raughton. Cumb 5E 113
Raughton Head. Cumb 5E 113
Raunds. Nptn 3G 63
Ravenfield. S Yor 1B 86
Ravenfield Common. S Yor 1B 86
Ravenglass. Cumb 5B 102
Ravenhills Green. Worc 5B 60
Raveningham. Norf 1F 67
Ravenscar. N Yor 4G 107
Ravensdale. IOM 2C 108
Ravensden. Bed 5H 63
Ravenseat. N Yor 4B 104
Ravenshead. Notts 5C 86
Ravensmoor. Ches E 5A 84
Ravensthorpe. Nptn 3D 62
Ravensthorpe. W Yor 2C 92
Ravenstone. Leics 4B 74
Ravenstone. Mil 5F 63
Ravenstonedale. Cumb 4A 104
Ravenstown. Cumb 2C 96
Ravenstruther. S Lan 5C 128
Ravensworth. N Yor 4E 105
Ravernet. Lis 3G 179
Raw. N Yor 4G 107
Rawcliffe. E Yor 2G 93
Rawcliffe. York 4H 99
Rawcliffe Bridge. E Yor 2G 93
Rawdon. W Yor 1C 92
Rawgreen. Nmbd 4C 114
Rawmarsh. S Yor 1B 86
Rawnsley. Staf 4E 73
Rawreth. Essx 1B 40
Rawridge. Devn 2F 13
Rawson Green. Derbs 1A 74
Rawtenstall. Lanc 2F 91
Raydon. Suff 2D 54
Raylees. Nmbd 5D 120
Rayleigh. Essx 1C 40
Raymond's Hill. Devn 3G 13
Rayne. Essx 3H 53
Rayners Lane. G Lon 2C 38
Reach. Cambs 4E 65
Read. Lanc 1F 91
Reading. Read 4F 37 & 201
Reading Green. Suff 3D 66
Reading Street. Kent 2D 28
Readymoney. Corn 3F 7
Reagill. Cumb 3H 103
Rea Hill. Torb 3F 9
Rearquhar. High 4E 165
Rearsby. Leics 4D 74
Reasby. Linc 3H 87
Reaseheath. Ches E 5A 84
Reaster. High 2E 169
Reawick. Shet 7E 173
Reay. High 2B 168
Rechullin. High 3A 156
Reculver. Kent 4G 41
Redberth. Pemb 4E 43
Redbourn. Herts 4B 52
Redbourne. N Lin 4C 94
Redbrook. Glos 4A 48
Redbrook. Wrex 1H 71
Redburn. High 4D 158
Redburn. Nmbd 3A 114
Redcar. Red C 2D 106
Redcastle. High 4H 157
Redcliff Bay. N Som 4H 33
Red Dial. Cumb 5D 112
Redding. Falk 2C 128
Reddingmuirhead. Falk 2C 128
Reddings, The. Glos 3E 49
Reddish. G Man 1C 84
Redditch. Worc 4E 61
Rede. Suff 5H 65
Redenhall. Norf 2E 67
Redesdale Camp. Nmbd 5C 120
Redesmouth. Nmbd 1B 114
Redford. Ang 4E 145
Redford. Dur 1D 105
Redford. W Sus 4G 25
Redfordgreen. Bord 3F 119
Redgate. Corn 2G 7
Redgrave. Suff 3C 66
Redhill. Abers 3E 153
Redhill. Herts 2C 52
Redhill. N Som 5H 33
Redhill. Shrp 4B 72
Redhill. Surr 5D 39
Red Hill. Warw 5F 61
Red Hill. W Yor 2E 93
Redhouses. Arg 3B 124
Redisham. Suff 2G 67
Redland. Bris 4A 34
Redland. Orkn 5C 172
Redlingfield. Suff 3D 66
Red Lodge. Suff 3F 65
Redlynch. Som 3C 22
Redlynch. Wilts 4H 23
Redmain. Cumb 1C 102
Redmarley. Worc 4B 60
Redmarley D'Abitot. Glos 2C 48
Redmarshall. Stoc T 2A 106
Redmile. Leics 2E 75
Redmire. N Yor 5D 104
Rednal. Shrp 3F 71
Redpath. Bord 1H 119
Redpoint. High 2G 155
Red Post. Corn 2C 10
Red Rock. G Man 4D 90
Red Roses. Carm 3G 43
Red Row. Nmbd 5G 121
Redruth. Corn 4B 6
Red Street. Staf 5C 84
Redvales. G Man 4F 91
Red Wharf Bay. IOA 2E 81
Redwick. Newp 3H 33
Redwick. S Glo 3A 34
Redworth. Darl 2F 105
Reed. Herts 2D 52
Reed End. Herts 2D 52
Reedham. Linc 5B 88
Reedham. Norf 5G 79
Reedness. E Yor 2B 94
Reeds Beck. Linc 4B 88
Reemshill. Abers 4E 161
Reepham. Linc 3H 87
Reepham. Norf 3C 78
Reeth. N Yor 5D 104
Regaby. IOM 2D 108
Regil. N Som 5A 34
Regoul. High 3C 158
Reiff. High 2D 162
Reigate. Surr 5D 38
Reighton. N Yor 2F 101
Reilth. Shrp 2E 59
Reinigeadal. W Isl 7E 171
Reisque. Abers 1F 153
Reiss. High 3F 169
Rejerrah. Corn 3B 6
Releath. Corn 5A 6
Relubbus. Corn 3C 4
Relugas. Mor 4D 159
Remenham. Wok 3F 37
Remenham Hill. Wok 3F 37
Rempstone. Notts 3C 74
Rendcomb. Glos 5F 49
Rendham. Suff 4F 67
Rendlesham. Suff 5F 67
Renfrew. Ren 3G 127
Renhold. Bed 5H 63
Renishaw. Derbs 3B 86
Rennington. Nmbd 3G 121
Renton. W Dun 2E 127
Renwick. Cumb 5G 113
Repps. Norf 4G 79
Repton. Derbs 3H 73
Resaurie. High 4B 158
Rescassa. Corn 4D 6
Rescobie. Ang 3E 145
Rescorla. Corn 3E 7
(nr. Rosevean)
Rescorla. Corn 4D 6
(nr. St Ewe)
Resipole. High 2B 140
Resolfen. Neat 5B 46
Resolis. High 2A 158
Resolven. Neat 5B 46
Rest and be thankful. Arg 3B 134
Reston. Bord 3E 131
Restrop. Wilts 3F 35
Retford. Notts 2E 86
Retire. Corn 2E 6
Rettendon. Essx 1B 40
Revesby. Linc 4C 88
Rew. Devn 5D 8
Rewe. Devn 3C 12
Rew Street. IOW 3C 16
Rexon. Devn 4E 11
Reybridge. Wilts 5E 35
Reydon. Suff 3H 67
Reymerston. Norf 5C 78

Reynalton—Sarratt

Reynalton. Pemb 4E 43
Reynoldston. Swan 4D 31
Rezare. Corn 5D 10
Rhadyr. Mon 5G 47
Rhaeadr Gwy. Powy 4B 58
Rhandirmwyn. Carm 1A 46
Rhayader. Powy 4B 58
Rheindown. High 4H 157
Rhemore. High 3G 139
Rhenetra. High 3D 154
Rhewl. Den 1D 70
(nr. Llangollen)
Rhewl. Den 4D 82
(nr. Ruthin)
Rhewl. Shrp 2F 71
Rhewl-Mostyn. Flin 3D 82
Rhian. High 2C 164
Rhian Breck. High 3C 164
Rhicarn. High 1E 163
Rhiconich. High 3C 166
Rhicullen. High 1A 158
Rhidorroch. High 4F 163
Rhifail. High 4H 167
Rhigos. Rhon 5C 46
Rhilochan. High 3E 165
Rhiroy. High 5F 163
Rhitongue. High 3G 167
Rhiw. Gwyn 3B 68
Rhiwabon. Wrex 1F 71
Rhiwbina. Card 3E 33
Rhiwbryfdir. Gwyn 1F 69
Rhiwderin. Newp 3F 33
Rhiwlas. Gwyn 2B 70
(nr. Bala)
Rhiwlas. Gwyn 4E 81
(nr. Bangor)
Rhiwlas. Powy 2D 70
Rhodes. G Man 4G 91
Rhodesia. Notts 2C 86
Rhodes Minnis. Kent 1F 29
Rhodiad-y-Brenin. Pemb 2B 42
Rhondda. Rhon 2C 32
Rhonehouse. Dum 4E 111
Rhoose. V Glam 5D 32
Rhos. Carm 2D 45
Rhos. Neat 5H 45
Rhosaman. Carm 4H 45
Rhoscefnhir. IOA 3E 81
Rhoscolyn. IOA 3B 80
Rhos Common. Powy 4E 71
Rhoscrowther. Pemb 4D 42
Rhos-ddu. Gwyn 2B 68
Rhosdylluan. Gwyn 3A 70
Rhosesmor. Flin 4E 82
Rhos-fawr. Gwyn 2C 68
Rhosgadfan. Gwyn 5E 81
Rhosgoch. IOA 2D 80
Rhosgoch. Powy 1E 47
Rhos Haminiog. Cdgn 4E 57
Rhos-hill. Pemb 1B 44
Rhoshirwaun. Gwyn 3A 68
Rhoslan. Gwyn 1D 69
Rhoslefain. Gwyn 5E 69
Rhosllanerchrugog.
Wrex 1E 71
Rhos Lligwy. IOA 2D 81
Rhosmaen. Carm 3G 45
Rhosmeirch. IOA 3D 80
Rhosneigr. IOA 3C 80
Rhos-on-Sea. Cnwy 2H 81
Rhossili. Swan 4D 30
Rhosson. Pemb 2B 42
Rhos, The. Pemb 3E 43
Rhostrenwfa. IOA 3D 80
Rhostryfan. Gwyn 5D 81
Rhostyllen. Wrex 1F 71
Rhoswiel. Shrp 2E 71
Rhosybol. IOA 2D 80
Rhos-y-brithdir. Powy 3D 70
Rhos-y-garth. Cdgn 3F 57
Rhos-y-gwaliau. Gwyn 2B 70
Rhos-y-llan. Gwyn 2B 68
Rhos-y-meirch. Powy 4E 59
Rhu. Arg 1D 126
Rhualt. Den 3C 82
Rhubadach. Arg 2B 126
Rhubha Stoer. High 1E 163
Rhuddall Heath. Ches W 4H 83
Rhuddlan. Cdgn 1E 45
Rhuddlan. Den 3C 82
Rhue. High 4E 163
Rhulen. Powy 1E 47
Rhunahaorine. Arg 5F 125
Rhuthun. Den 5D 82
Rhuvoult. High 3C 166
Rhyd. Gwyn 1F 69
Rhydaman. Carm 4G 45
Rhydargaeau. Carm 3E 45
Rhydcymerau. Carm 2F 45
Rhydd. Worc 1D 48
Rhyd-Ddu. Gwyn 5E 81
Rhydding. Neat 3G 31
Rhydfudr. Cdgn 4E 57
Rhydlanfair. Cnwy 5H 81
Rhydlewis. Cdgn 1D 44
Rhydlios. Gwyn 2A 68
Rhydlydan. Cnwy 5A 82
Rhyd-meirionydd. Cdgn 2F 57
Rhydowen. Cdgn 1E 45
Rhyd-Rosser. Cdgn 4E 57
Rhydspence. Powy 1F 47
Rhydtalog. Flin 5E 83
Rhyd-uchaf. Gwyn 2B 70
Rhydwyn. IOA 2C 80
Rhyd-y-clafdy. Gwyn 2C 68
Rhydycroesau. Shrp 2E 71
Rhydyfelin. Cdgn 3E 57
Rhydyfelin. Rhon 3E 32
Rhyd-y-foel. Cnwy 3B 82
Rhyd-y-fro. Neat 5H 45
Rhydymain. Gwyn 3H 69
Rhyd-y-meirch. Mon 5G 47
Rhyd-y-meudwy. Den 5D 82
Rhydymwyn. Flin 4E 82
Rhyd-yr-onen. Gwyn 5F 69
Rhyd-y-sarn. Gwyn 1F 69
Rhyl. Den 2C 82
Rhymney. Cphy 5E 46
Rhymni. Cphy 5E 46
Rhynd. Per 1D 136
Rhynie. Abers 1B 152
Ribbesford. Worc 3B 60
Ribbleton. Lanc 1D 90
Ribby. Lanc 1C 90
Ribchester. Lanc 1E 91
Riber. Derbs 5H 85
Ribigill. High 3F 167
Riby. Linc 4E 95
Riccall. N Yor 1G 93
Riccarton. E Ayr 1D 116
Richards Castle. Here 4G 59
Richborough Port. Kent 4H 41
Richhill. Arm 5D 178
Richings Park. Buck 3B 38
Richmond. G Lon 3C 38
Richmond. N Yor 4E 105
Rickarton. Abers 5F 153
Rickerby. Cumb 4F 113
Rickerscote. Staf 3D 72
Rickford. N Som 1H 21
Rickham. Devn 5D 8
Rickinghall. Suff 3C 66
Rickleton. Tyne 4F 115
Rickling. Essx 2E 53
Rickling Green. Essx 3F 53
Rickmansworth. Herts 1B 38
Riddings. Derbs 5B 86
Riddlecombe. Devn 1G 11
Riddlesden. W Yor 5C 98
Ridge. Dors 4E 15
Ridge. Herts 5C 52
Ridge. Wilts 3E 23
Ridgebourne. Powy 4C 58
Ridge Lane. Warw 1G 61
Ridgeway. Derbs 5A 86
(nr. Alfreton)
Ridgeway. Derbs 2B 86
(nr. Sheffield)
Ridgeway. Staf 5C 84
Ridgeway Cross. Here 1C 48
Ridgeway Moor. Derbs 2B 86
Ridgewell. Essx 1H 53
Ridgewood. E Sus 3F 27
Ridgmont. C Beds 2H 51
Ridgwardine. Shrp 2A 72
Riding Mill. Nmbd 3D 114
Ridley. Kent 4H 39
Ridley. Nmbd 3A 114
Ridlington. Norf 2F 79
Ridlington. Rut 5F 75
Ridsdale. Nmbd 1C 114
Riemore Lodge. Per 4H 143
Rievaulx. N Yor 1H 99
Rift House. Hart 1B 106
Rigg. Dum 3D 112
Riggend. N Lan 2A 128
Rigsby. Linc 3D 88
Rigside. S Lan 1A 118
Riley Green. Lanc 2E 90
Rileyhill. Staf 4F 73
Rilla Mill. Corn 5C 10
Rillington. N Yor 2C 100
Rimington. Lanc 5H 97
Rimpton. Som 4B 22
Rimsdale. High 4H 167
Rimswell. E Yor 2G 95
Ringasta. Shet 10E 173
Ringford. Dum 4D 111
Ringing Hill. Leics 4B 74
Ringinglow. S Yor 2G 85
Ringland. Norf 4D 78
Ringlestone. Kent 5C 40
Ringmer. E Sus 4F 27
Ringmore. Devn 4C 8
(nr. Kingsbridge)
Ringmore. Devn 5C 12
(nr. Teignmouth)
Ring o' Bells. Lanc 3C 90
Ring's End. Cambs 5C 76
Ringsfield. Suff 2G 67
Ringsfield Corner. Suff 2G 67
Ringshall. Buck 4H 51
Ringshall. Suff 5C 66
Ringshall Stocks. Suff 5C 66
Ringstead. Norf 1G 77
Ringstead. Nptn 3G 63
Ringwood. Hants 2G 15
Ringwould. Kent 1H 29
Rinmore. Abers 2B 152
Rinnigill. Orkn 8C 172
Rinsey. Corn 4C 4
Riof. W Isl 4D 171
Ripe. E Sus 4G 27
Ripley. Derbs 1B 74
Ripley. Hants 3G 15
Ripley. N Yor 3E 99
Ripley. Surr 5B 38
Riplingham. E Yor 1C 94
Riplington. Hants 4E 25
Ripon. N Yor 2F 99
Rippingale. Linc 3H 75
Ripple. Kent 1H 29
Ripple. Worc 2D 48
Ripponden. W Yor 3A 92
Rireavach. High 4E 163
Risabus. Arg 5B 124
Risbury. Here 5H 59
Risby. E Yor 1D 94
Risby. N Lin 3C 94
Risby. Suff 4G 65
Risca. Cphy 2F 33
Rise. E Yor 5F 101
Riseden. E Sus 2H 27
Riseden. Kent 2B 28
Rise End. Derbs 5G 85
Risegate. Linc 2B 76
Riseholme. Linc 3G 87
Riseley. Bed 4H 63
Riseley. Wok 5F 37
Rishangles. Suff 4D 66
Rishton. Lanc 1F 91
Rishworth. W Yor 3A 92
Risley. Derbs 2B 74
Risley. Warr 1A 84
Risplith. N Yor 3E 99
Rispond. High 2E 167
Rivar. Wilts 5B 36
Rivenhall. Essx 4B 54
Rivenhall End. Essx 4B 54
River. Kent 1G 29
River. W Sus 3A 26
River Bank. Cambs 4E 65
Riverhead. Kent 5G 39
Rivington. Lanc 3E 91
Roach Bridge. Lanc 2D 90
Roachill. Devn 4B 20
Roade. Nptn 5E 63
Road Green. Norf 1E 67
Roadhead. Cumb 2G 113
Roadmeetings. S Lan 5B 128
Roadside. High 2D 168
Roadside of Catterline.
Abers 1H 145
Roadside of Kinneff.
Abers 1H 145
Roadwater. Som 3D 20
Road Weedon. Nptn 5D 62
Roag. High 4B 154
Roa Island. Cumb 3B 96
Roath. Card 4E 33
Roberton. Bord 3G 119
Roberton. S Lan 2B 118
Robertsbridge. E Sus 3B 28
Robertstown. Mor 4G 159
Robertstown. Rhon 5C 46
Roberttown. W Yor 2B 92
Robeston Back. Pemb 3E 43
Robeston Wathen. Pemb 3E 43
Robeston West. Pemb 4C 42
Robin Hood. Lanc 3D 90
Robin Hood. W Yor 2D 92
Robin Hood Airport
Doncaster Sheffield.
S Yor 1D 86
Robinhood End. Essx 2H 53
Robin Hood's Bay.
N Yor 4G 107
Roborough. Devn 1F 11
(nr. Great Torrington)
Roborough. Devn 2B 8
(nr. Plymouth)
Rob Roy's House. Arg 2A 134
Roby Mill. Lanc 4D 90
Rocester. Staf 2F 73
Roch. Pemb 2C 42
Rochdale. G Man 3G 91
Roche. Corn 2D 6
Rochester. Medw 4B 40 & **Medway** 197
Rochester. Nmbd 5C 120
Rochford. Essx 1C 40
Rock. Corn 1D 6
Rock. Nmbd 2G 121
Rock. W Sus 4C 26
Rock. Worc 3B 60
Rockbeare. Devn 3D 12
Rockbourne. Hants 1G 15
Rockcliffe. Cumb 3E 113
Rockcliffe. Dum 4F 111
Rockcliffe Cross. Cumb 3E 113
Rock Ferry. Mers 2F 83
Rockfield. High 5G 165
Rockfield. Mon 4H 47
Rockford. Hants 2G 15
Rockgreen. Shrp 3H 59
Rockhampton. S Glo 2B 34
Rockhead. Corn 4A 10
Rockingham. Nptn 1F 63
Rockland All Saints. Norf 1B 66
Rockland St Mary. Norf 5F 79
Rockland St Peter. Norf 1B 66
Rockley. Wilts 4G 35
Rock, The. Cook 2B 178
Rockwell End. Buck 3F 37
Rockwell Green. Som 1E 13
Rodborough. Glos 5D 48
Rodbourne. Wilts 3E 35
Rodd. Here 4F 59
Roddam. Nmbd 2E 121
Rodden. Dors 4B 14
Roddenloft. E Ayr 2D 117
Roddymoor. Dur 1E 105
Rode. Som 1D 22
Rodeheath. Ches E 4C 84
(nr. Congleton)
Rode Heath. Ches E 5C 84
(nr. Kidsgrove)
Roden. Telf 4H 71
Rodhuish. Som 3D 20
Rodington. Telf 4H 71
Rodington Heath. Telf 4H 71
Rodley. Glos 4C 48
Rodmarton. Glos 2E 35
Rodmell. E Sus 5F 27
Rodmersham. Kent 4D 40
Rodmersham Green.
Kent 4D 40
Rodney Stoke. Som 2H 21
Rodsley. Derbs 1G 73
Rodway. Som 2F 21
Rodway. Telf 4A 72
Rodwell. Dors 5B 14
Roecliffe. N Yor 3F 99
Roe Green. Herts 2D 52
Roehampton. G Lon 3D 38
Roesound. Shet 5E 173
Roffey. W Sus 2C 26
Rogart. High 3E 165
Rogate. W Sus 4G 25
Roger Ground. Cumb 5E 103
Rogerstone. Newp 3F 33
Rogiet. Mon 3H 33
Rohallion Lodge. Per 4H 143
Rogue's Alley. Cambs 5C 76
Roke. Oxon 2E 37
Rokemarsh. Oxon 2E 36
Roker. Tyne 4H 115
Rollesby. Norf 4G 79
Rolleston. Leics 5E 75
Rolleston. Notts 5E 87
Rolleston on Dove. Staf 3G 73
Rolston. E Yor 5G 101
Rolvenden. Kent 2C 28
Rolvenden Layne. Kent 2C 28
Romaldkirk. Dur 2C 104
Roman Bank. Shrp 1H 59
Romanby. N Yor 5A 106
Roman Camp. W Lot 2D 129
Romannobridge. Bord 5E 129
Romansleigh. Devn 4H 19
Romers Common. Worc 4H 59
Romesdal. High 3D 154
Romford. Dors 2F 15
Romford. G Lon 2G 39
Romiley. G Man 1D 84
Romsey. Hants 4B 24
Romsley. Shrp 2B 60
Romsley. Worc 3D 60
Ronague. IOM 4B 108
Ronaldsvoe. Orkn 8D 172
Rookby. Cumb 3B 104
Rookhope. Dur 5C 114
Rooking. Cumb 3F 103
Rookley. IOW 4D 16
Rooks Bridge. Som 1G 21
Rooksey Green. Suff 5B 66
Rook's Nest. Som 3D 20
Rookwood. W Sus 3F 17
Roos. E Yor 1F 95
Roosebeck. Cumb 3B 96
Roosecote. Cumb 3B 96
Rootfield. High 3H 157
Rootham's Green. Bed 5A 64
Rootpark. S Lan 4C 128
Ropley. Hants 3E 25
Ropley Dean. Hants 3E 25
Ropsley. Linc 2G 75
Rora. Abers 3H 161
Rorandle. Abers 2D 152
Rorrington. Shrp 5F 71
Rose. Corn 3B 6
Roseacre. Lanc 1C 90
Rose Ash. Devn 4A 20
Rosebank. S Lan 5B 128
Rosebush. Pemb 2E 43
Rosedale Abbey. N Yor 5E 107
Roseden. Nmbd 2E 121
Rose Green. Essx 3C 54
Rose Green. Suff 1C 54
Rosehall. High 3B 164
Rosehearty. Abers 2G 161
Rose Hill. E Sus 4F 27
Rose Hill. Lanc 1G 91
Rosehill. Shrp 2A 72
(nr. Market Drayton)
Rosehill. Shrp 4G 71
(nr. Shrewsbury)
Roseisle. Mor 2F 159
Rosemarket. Pemb 4D 42
Rosemarkie. High 3B 158
Rosemary Lane. Devn 1E 13
Rosemount. Per 4A 144
Rosenannon. Corn 2D 6
Roser's Cross. E Sus 3G 27
Rosevean. Corn 3E 6
Rosewell. Midl 3F 129
Roseworth. Stoc T 2B 106
Roseworthy. Corn 3D 4
Rosgill. Cumb 3G 103
Roshven. High 1B 140
Roskhill. High 4B 154
Roskorwell. Corn 4E 5
Rosley. Cumb 5E 113
Roslin. Midl 3F 129
Rosliston. Derbs 4G 73
Rosneath. Arg 1D 126
Ross. Dum 5D 110
Ross. Nmbd 1F 121
Ross. Per 1G 135
Ross. Bord 3F 131
Rossendale. Lanc 2F 91
Rossett. Wrex 5F 83
Rossington. S Yor 1D 86
Rosskeen. High 2A 158
Rossland. Ren 2F 127
Rosslea. Ferm 6L 177
Ross-on-Wye. Here 3B 48
Roster. High 4E 169
Rostherne. Ches E 2B 84
Rostholme. S Yor 4F 93
Rosthwaite. Cumb 3D 102
Roston. Derbs 1F 73
Rostrevor. New M 8F 179
Rosudgeon. Corn 4C 4
Rosyth. Fife 1E 129
Rothbury. Nmbd 4E 121
Rotherby. Leics 4D 74
Rotherfield. E Sus 3G 27
Rotherfield Greys. Oxon 3F 37
Rotherfield Peppard.
Oxon 3F 37
Rotherham. S Yor 1B 86
Rothersthorpe. Nptn 5E 62
Rotherwick. Hants 1F 25
Rothes. Mor 4G 159
Rothesay. Arg 3B 126
Rothienorman. Abers 5E 160
Rothiesholm. Orkn 5F 172
Rothley. Leics 4C 74
Rothley. Nmbd 1D 114
Rothwell. Linc 1A 88
Rothwell. Nptn 2F 63
Rothwell. W Yor 2D 92
Rothwell Haigh. W Yor 2D 92
Rotsea. E Yor 4E 101
Rottal. Ang 2C 144
Rotten End. Suff 4F 67
Rotten Row. Norf 4C 78
Rotten Row. W Ber 4D 36
Rotten Row. W Mid 3F 61
Rottingdean. Brig 5E 27
Rottington. Cumb 3A 102
Roud. IOW 4D 16
Rougham. Norf 3H 77
Rougham. Suff 4B 66
Rough Close. Staf 2D 72
Rough Common. Kent 5F 41
Roughcote. Staf 1D 72
Roughfort. Newt 1G 179
Rough Haugh. High 4H 167
Rough Hay. Staf 3G 73
Roughlee. Lanc 5H 97
Roughley. W Mid 1F 61
Roughsike. Cumb 2G 113
Roughton. Linc 4B 88
Roughton. Norf 2E 78
Roughton. Shrp 1B 60
Roundbush Green. Essx 4F 53
Roundham. Som 2H 13
Roundhay. W Yor 1D 92
Round Hill. Torb 2F 9
Roundhurst. W Sus 2A 26
Round Maple. Suff 1C 54
Round Oak. Shrp 2F 59
Roundstreet Common.
W Sus 3B 26
Roundthwaite. Cumb 4H 103
Roundway. Wilts 5F 35
Roundyhill. Ang 3C 144
Rousdon. Devn 3F 13
Rousham. Oxon 3C 50
Rousky. Omag 8B 174
Rous Lench. Worc 5E 61
Routh. E Yor 5E 101
Rout's Green. Buck 2F 37
Row. Corn 5A 10
Row. Cumb 1D 96
(nr. Kendal)
Row. Cumb 1H 103
(nr. Penrith)
Rowanburn. Dum 2F 113
Rowanhill. Abers 3H 161
Rowardennan. Stir 4C 134
Rowarth. Derbs 2E 85
Row Ash. Hants 1D 16
Rowberrow. Som 1H 21
Rowde. Wilts 5E 35
Rowden. Devn 3G 11
Rowen. Cnwy 3G 81
Rowfoot. Nmbd 3H 113
Row Green. Essx 3H 53
Row Heath. Essx 4E 55
Rowhedge. Essx 3D 54
Rowhook. W Sus 2C 26
Rowington. Warw 4G 61
Rowland. Derbs 3G 85
Rowland's Castle. Hants 1F 17
Rowlands Gill. Tyne 4E 115
Rowledge. Surr 2G 25
Rowley. Dur 5D 115
Rowley. E Yor 1C 94
Rowley. Shrp 5F 71
Rowley Hill. W Yor 3B 92
Rowley Regis. W Mid 2D 60
Rowlstone. Here 3G 47
Rowly. Surr 1B 26
Rowner. Hants 2D 16
Rowney Green. Worc 3E 61
Rownhams. Hants 1B 16
Rowrah. Cumb 3B 102
Rowsham. Buck 4G 51
Rowsley. Derbs 4G 85
Rowstock. Oxon 3C 36
Rowston. Linc 5H 87
Row, The. Lanc 2D 96
Rowthorne. Derbs 4B 86
Rowton. Ches W 4G 83
Rowton. Shrp 2A 60
(nr. Ludlow)
Rowton. Shrp 4F 71
(nr. Shrewsbury)
Rowton. Telf 4A 72
Row Town. Surr 4B 38
Roxburgh. Bord 1B 120
Roxby. N Lin 3C 94
Roxby. N Yor 3E 107
Roxhill. Ant 7G 175
Roxton. Bed 5A 64
Roxwell. Essx 5G 53
Royal Leamington Spa.
Warw 4H 61
Royal Oak. Darl 2F 105
Royal Oak. Lanc 4C 90
Royal Oak. N Yor 2F 101
Royal's Green. Ches E 1A 72
Royal Tunbridge Wells.
Kent 2G 27
Royal Wootton Bassett.
Wilts 3F 35
Roybridge. High 5E 149
Roydon. Essx 4E 53
Roydon. Norf 2C 66
(nr. Diss)
Roydon. Norf 3G 77
(nr. King's Lynn)
Roydon Hamlet. Essx 5E 53
Royston. Herts 1D 52
Royston. S Yor 3D 92
Royston Water. Som 1F 13
Royton. G Man 4H 91
Ruabon. Wrex 1F 71
Ruaig. Arg 4B 138
Ruan High Lanes. Corn 5D 6
Ruan Lanihorne. Corn 4C 6
Ruan Major. Corn 5E 5
Ruan Minor. Corn 5E 5
Ruarach. High 1B 148
Ruardean. Glos 4B 48
Ruardean Hill. Glos 4B 48
Ruardean Woodside.
Glos 4B 48
Rubery. W Mid 3D 61
Ruchazie. Glas 3H 127
Ruckcroft. Cumb 5G 113
Ruckinge. Kent 2E 29
Ruckland. Linc 3C 88
Rucklers Lane. Herts 5A 52
Ruckley. Shrp 5H 71
Rudbaxton. Pemb 2D 42
Rudby. N Yor 4B 106
Ruddington. Notts 2C 74
Rudford. Glos 3C 48
Rudge. Shrp 1C 60
Rudge. Wilts 1D 22
Rudge Heath. Shrp 1B 60
Rudgeway. S Glo 3B 34
Rudgwick. W Sus 2B 26
Rudhall. Here 3B 48
Rudheath. Ches W 3A 84
Rudley Green. Essx 5B 54
Rudloe. Wilts 4D 34
Rudry. Cphy 3E 33
Rudston. E Yor 3E 101
Rudyard. Staf 5D 84
Rufford. Lanc 3C 90
Rufforth. York 4H 99
Rugby. Warw 3C 62
Rugeley. Staf 4E 73
Ruglen. S Ayr 4B 116
Ruilick. High 4H 157
Ruisaurie. High 4G 157
Ruishton. Som 4F 21
Ruisigearraidh. W Isl 1E 170
Ruislip. G Lon 2B 38
Ruislip Common.
G Lon 2B 38
Rumbling Bridge. Per 4C 136
Rumburgh. Suff 2F 67
Rumford. Corn 1C 6
Rumford. Falk 2C 128
Rumney. Card 4F 33
Rumwell. Som 4E 21
Runcorn. Hal 2H 83
Runcton. W Sus 2G 17
Runcton Holme. Norf 5F 77
Rundlestone. Devn 5F 11
Runfold. Surr 2G 25
Runhall. Norf 5C 78
Runham. Norf 4G 79
Runnington. Som 4E 20
Runshaw Moor. Lanc 3D 90
Runswick. N Yor 3F 107
Runtaleave. Ang 2B 144
Runwell. Essx 1B 40
Ruscombe. Wok 4F 37
Rushall. Here 2B 48
Rushall. Norf 2D 66
Rushall. W Mid 5E 73
Rushall. Wilts 1G 23
Rushbrooke. Suff 4A 66
Rushbury. Shrp 1H 59
Rushden. Herts 2D 52
Rushden. Nptn 4G 63
Rushenden. Kent 3D 40
Rushford. Devn 5E 11
Rushford. Suff 2B 66
Rush Green. Herts 3C 52
Rushlake Green. E Sus 4H 27
Rushmere. Suff 2G 67
Rushmere St Andrew.
Suff 1E 55
Rushmoor. Surr 2G 25
Rushock. Worc 3C 60
Rusholme. G Man 1C 84
Rushton. Ches W 4H 83
Rushton. Nptn 2F 63
Rushton. Shrp 5A 72
Rushton Spencer. Staf 4D 84
Rushwick. Worc 5C 60
Rushyford. Dur 2F 105
Ruskie. Stir 3F 135
Ruskington. Linc 5H 87
Rusland. Cumb 1C 96
Rusper. W Sus 2D 26
Ruspidge. Glos 4B 48
Russell's Water. Oxon 3F 37
Russel's Green. Suff 3E 67
Russ Hill. Surr 1D 26
Russland. Orkn 6C 172
Rusthall. Kent 2G 27
Rustington. W Sus 5B 26
Ruston. N Yor 1D 100
Ruston Parva. E Yor 3E 101
Ruswarp. N Yor 4F 107
Rutherglen. S Lan 3H 127
Ruthernbridge. Corn 2E 6
Ruthin. Den 5D 82
Ruthin. V Glam 4C 32
Ruthrieston. Aber 3G 153
Ruthven. Abers 4C 160
Ruthven. Ang 4B 144
Ruthven. High 5C 158
(nr. Inverness)
Ruthven. High 4B 150
(nr. Kingussie)
Ruthvoes. Corn 2D 6
Ruthwaite. Cumb 1D 102
Ruthwell. Dum 3C 112
Ruxton Green. Here 4A 48
Ruyton-XI-Towns. Shrp 3F 71
Ryal. Nmbd 2D 114
Ryall. Dors 3H 13
Ryall. Worc 1D 48
Ryarsh. Kent 5A 40
Rychraggan. High 5G 157
Rydal. Cumb 4E 103
Ryde. IOW 3D 16
Rye. E Sus 3D 28
Ryecroft Gate. Staf 4D 84
Ryeford. Here 3B 48
Rye Foreign. E Sus 3D 28
Rye Harbour. E Sus 4D 28
Ryehill. E Yor 2F 95
Rye Street. Worc 2C 48
Ryhall. Rut 4H 75
Ryhill. W Yor 3D 93
Ryhope. Tyne 4H 115
Ryhope Colliery. Tyne 4H 115
Rylands. Notts 2C 74
Rylstone. N Yor 4B 98
Ryme Intrinseca. Dors 1A 14
Ryther. N Yor 1F 93
Ryton. Glos 2C 48
Ryton. N Yor 2B 100
Ryton. Shrp 5B 72
Ryton. Tyne 3E 115
Ryton. Warw 2A 62
Ryton-on-Dunsmore.
Warw 3A 62
Ryton Woodside. Tyne 3E 115

S

Saasaig. High 3E 147
Sabden. Lanc 1F 91
Sacombe. Herts 4D 52
Sacriston. Dur 5F 115
Sadberge. Darl 3A 106
Saddell. Arg 2B 122
Saddington. Leics 1D 62
Saddle Bow. Norf 4F 77
Saddlescombe. W Sus 4D 26
Saddleworth. G Man 4H 91
Sadgill. Cumb 4F 103
Saffron Walden. Essx 2F 53
Sageston. Pemb 4E 43
Saham Hills. Norf 5B 78
Saham Toney. Norf 5A 78
Saighdinis. W Isl 2D 170
Saighton. Ches W 4G 83
Sain Dunwyd. V Glam 5C 32
Sain Hilari. V Glam 4D 32
St Abbs. Bord 3F 131
St Agnes. Corn 3B 6
St Albans. Herts 5B 52
St Allen. Corn 3C 6
St Andrews. Fife 2H 137
St Andrews Major.
V Glam 4E 33
St Anne's. Lanc 2B 90
St Ann's. Dum 5C 118
St Ann's Chapel.
Corn 5E 11
St Ann's Chapel. Devn 4C 8
St Anthony. Corn 5C 6
St Anthony-in-Meneage.
Corn 4E 5
St Arvans. Mon 2A 34
St Asaph. Den 3C 82
Sain Tathan. V Glam 5D 32
St Athan. V Glam 5D 32
St Austell. Corn 3E 6
St Bartholomew's Hill.
Wilts 4E 23
St Bees. Cumb 3A 102
St Blazey. Corn 3E 7
St Blazey Gate. Corn 3E 7
St Boswells. Bord 1A 120
St Breock. Corn 1D 6
St Breward. Corn 5A 10
St Briavels. Glos 5A 48
St Brides. Pemb 3B 42
St Bride's Major.
V Glam 4B 32
St Bride's Netherwent.
Mon 3H 33
St Bride's-super-Ely.
V Glam 4D 32
St Brides Wentlooge.
Newp 3F 33
St Budeaux. Plym 3A 8
Saintbury. Glos 2G 49
St Buryan. Corn 4B 4
St Catherine. Bath 4C 34
St Catherines. Arg 3A 134
St Clears. Carm 3G 43
St Cleer. Corn 2G 7
St Clement. Corn 4C 6
St Clether. Corn 4C 10
St Colmac. Arg 3B 126
St Columb Major. Corn 2D 6
St Columb Minor. Corn 2C 6
St Columb Road. Corn 3D 6
St Combs. Abers 2H 161
St Cross. Hants 4C 24
St Cross South Elmham.
Suff 2E 67
St Cyrus. Abers 2G 145
St David's. Per 1B 136
St David's. Pemb 2B 42
St Day. Corn 4B 6
St Dennis. Corn 3D 6
St Dogmaels. Pemb 1B 44
St Dominick. Corn 2H 7
St Donat's. V Glam 5C 32
St Edith's Marsh. Wilts 5E 35
St Endellion. Corn 1D 6
St Enoder. Corn 3C 6
St Erme. Corn 4C 6
St Erney. Corn 3H 7
St Erth. Corn 3C 4
St Erth Praze. Corn 3C 4
St Ervan. Corn 1C 6
St Eval. Corn 2C 6
St Ewe. Corn 4D 6
St Fagans. Card 4E 32
St Fergus. Abers 3H 161
Saintfield. Down 4J 179
St Fillans. Per 1F 135
St Florence. Pemb 4E 43
St Gennys. Corn 3B 10
St George. Cnwy 3B 82
St Georges. N Som 5G 33
St Georges. V Glam 4D 32
St George's Hill. Surr 4B 38
St Germans. Corn 3H 7
St Giles in the Wood.
Devn 1F 11
St Giles on the Heath.
Devn 3D 10
St Giles's Hill. Hants 4C 24
St Gluvias. Corn 5B 6
St Harmon. Powy 3B 58
St Helena. Warw 5G 73
St Helen Auckland. Dur 2E 105
St Helens. Cumb 1B 102
St Helens. E Sus 4C 28
St Helens. IOW 4E 17
St Helens. Mers 1G 83
St Hilary. Corn 3C 4
St Hilary. V Glam 4D 32
Saint Hill. Devn 2D 12
Saint Hill. W Sus 2E 27
St Illtyd. Blae 5F 47
St Ippolyts. Herts 3B 52
St Ishmael. Carm 5D 44
St Ishmael's. Pemb 4C 42
St Issey. Corn 1D 6
St Ive. Corn 2H 7
St Ives. Cambs 3C 64
St Ives. Corn 2C 4
St Ives. Dors 2G 15
St James' End. Nptn 4E 63
St James South Elmham.
Suff 2F 67
St Jidgey. Corn 2D 6
St John. Corn 3A 8
St John's. IOM 3B 108
St Johns. Worc 5C 60
St John's Chapel. Devn 4F 19
St John's Chapel. Dur 1B 104
St John's Fen End. Norf 4E 77
St John's Hall. Dur 1D 104
St John's Town of Dalry.
Dum 1D 110
St Judes. IOM 2C 108
St Just. Corn 5C 6
(nr. Falmouth)
St Just. Corn 3A 4
(nr. Penzance)
St Just in Roseland. Corn 5C 6
St Katherines. Abers 5E 161
St Keverne. Corn 4E 5
St Kew. Corn 5A 10
St Kew Highway. Corn 5A 10
St Keyne. Corn 2G 7
St Lawrence. Corn 2E 6
St Lawrence. Essx 5C 54
St Lawrence. IOW 5D 16
St Leonards. Buck 5H 51
St Leonards. Dors 2G 15
St Leonards. E Sus 5B 28
St Levan. Corn 4A 4
St Lythans. V Glam 4E 32
St Mabyn. Corn 5A 10
St Madoes. Per 1D 136
St Margarets. Here 2G 47
St Margarets. Herts 4A 52
(nr. Hemel Hempstead)
St Margarets. Herts 4D 53
(nr. Hoddesdon)
St Margaret's. Wilts 5G 35
St Margaret's at Cliffe.
Kent 1H 29
St Margaret's Hope.
Orkn 8D 172
St Margaret South Elmham.
Suff 2F 67
St Mark's. IOM 4B 108
St Martin. Corn 4E 5
(nr. Helston)
St Martin. Corn 3G 7
(nr. Looe)
St Martins. Per 5A 144
St Martin's. Shrp 2F 71
St Mary Bourne. Hants 1C 24
St Marychurch. Torb 2F 9
St Mary Church. V Glam 4D 32
St Mary Cray. G Lon 4F 39
St Mary Hill. V Glam 4C 32
St Mary Hoo. Medw 3C 40
St Mary in the Marsh.
Kent 3E 29
St Mary's. Orkn 7D 172
St Mary's Bay. Kent 3E 29
St Maughan's Green.
Mon 4H 47
St Mawes. Corn 5C 6
St Mawgan. Corn 2C 6
St Mellion. Corn 2H 7
St Mellons. Card 3F 33
St Merryn. Corn 1C 6
St Mewan. Corn 3D 6
St Michael Caerhays. Corn 4D 6
St Michael Penkevil. Corn 4C 6
St Michaels. Kent 2C 28
St Michaels. Torb 3E 9
St Michaels. Worc 4H 59
St Michael's on Wyre.
Lanc 5D 96
St Michael South Elmham.
Suff 2F 67
St Minver. Corn 1D 6
St Monans. Fife 3H 137
St Neot. Corn 2F 7
St Neots. Cambs 4A 64
St Newlyn East. Corn 3C 6
St Nicholas. Pemb 1D 42
St Nicholas. V Glam 4D 32
St Nicholas at Wade.
Kent 4G 41
St Nicholas South Elmham.
Suff 2F 67
St Ninians. Stir 4H 135
St Olaves. Norf 1G 67
St Osyth. Essx 4E 54
St Osyth Heath. Essx 4E 55
St Owen's Cross. Here 3A 48
St Paul's Cray. G Lon 4F 39
St Paul's Walden. Herts 3B 52
St Peter's. Kent 4H 41
St Peter The Great. Worc 5C 60
St Petrox. Pemb 5D 42
St Pinnock. Corn 2G 7
St Quivox. S Ayr 2C 116
St Ruan. Corn 5E 5
St Stephen. Corn 3D 6
St Stephens. Corn 4D 10
(nr. Launceston)
St Stephens. Corn 3A 8
(nr. Saltash)
St Teath. Corn 4A 10
St Thomas. Devn 3C 12
St Thomas. Swan 3F 31
St Tudy. Corn 5A 10
St Twynnells. Pemb 5D 42
St Veep. Corn 3F 7
St Vigeans. Ang 4F 145
St Wenn. Corn 2D 6
St Weonards. Here 3H 47
St Winnolls. Corn 3H 7
St Winnow. Corn 3F 7
Salcombe. Devn 5D 8
Salcombe Regis. Devn 4E 13
Salcott. Essx 4C 54
Sale. G Man 1B 84
Saleby. Linc 3D 88
Sale Green. Worc 5D 60
Salehurst. E Sus 3B 28
Salem. Carm 3G 45
Salem. Cdgn 2F 57
Salen. Arg 4G 139
Salen. High 2A 140
Salesbury. Lanc 1E 91
Saleway. Worc 5D 60
Salford. C Beds 2H 51
Salford. G Man
1C 84 & **Manchester** 197
Salford. Oxon 3A 50
Salford Priors. Warw 5E 61
Salfords. Surr 1D 27
Salhouse. Norf 4F 79
Saligo. Arg 3A 124
Saline. Fife 4C 136
Salisbury. Wilts 3G 23 & 201
Salkeld Dykes. Cumb 1G 103
Sallachan. High 2D 141
Sallachy. High 3C 164
(nr. Lairg)
Sallachy. High 5B 156
(nr. Stromeferry)
Salle. Norf 3D 78
Salmonby. Linc 3C 88
Salmond's Muir. Ang 5E 145
Salperton. Glos 3F 49
Salph End. Bed 5H 63
Salsburgh. N Lan 3B 128
Salt. Staf 3D 72
Salta. Cumb 5B 112
Saltaire. W Yor 1B 92
Saltash. Corn 3A 8
Saltburn. High 2B 158
Saltburn-by-the-Sea.
Red C 2D 106
Saltby. Leics 3F 75
Saltcoats. N Ayr 5D 126
Saltdean. Brig 5E 27
Salt End. E Yor 2E 95
Salter. Lanc 3F 97
Salterforth. Lanc 5A 98
Salters Lode. Norf 5E 77
Salterswall. Ches W 4A 84
Salterton. Wilts 3G 23
Saltfleet. Linc 1D 88
Saltfleetby All Saints.
Linc 1D 88
Saltfleetby St Clements.
Linc 1D 88
Saltfleetby St Peter. Linc 2D 88
Saltford. Bath 5B 34
Salthouse. Norf 1C 78
Saltmarshe. E Yor 2A 94
Saltmead. Card 4E 33
Saltness. Orkn 9B 172
Saltness. Shet 7D 173
Saltney. Flin 4F 83
Salton. N Yor 2B 100
Saltrens. Devn 4E 19
Saltwick. Nmbd 2E 115
Saltwood. Kent 2F 29
Salum. Arg 4B 138
Salwarpe. Worc 4C 60
Salwayash. Dors 3H 13
Samalaman. High 1A 140
Sambourne. Warw 4E 61
Sambourne. Wilts 2D 22
Sambrook. Telf 3B 72
Samhia. W Isl 2C 170
Samlesbury. Lanc 1D 90
Samlesbury Bottoms.
Lanc 2E 90
Sampford Arundel. Som 1E 12
Sampford Brett. Som 2D 20
Sampford Courtenay.
Devn 2G 11
Sampford Peverell. Devn 1D 12
Sampford Spiney. Devn 5F 11
Samsonlane. Orkn 5F 172
Samuelston. E Lot 2A 130
Sanaigmore. Arg 2A 124
Sancreed. Corn 4B 4
Sancton. E Yor 1C 94
Sand. High 4D 162
Sand. Shet 7E 173
Sand. Som 2H 21
Sandaig. Arg 4A 138
Sandaig. High 3F 147
Sandale. Cumb 5D 112
Sandal Magna. W Yor 3D 92
Sandavore. High 5C 146
Sanday Airport. Orkn 3F 172
Sandbach. Ches E 4B 84
Sandbank. Arg 1C 126
Sandbanks. Pool 4F 15
Sandend. Abers 2C 160
Sanderstead. G Lon 4E 39
Sandfields. Neat 3G 31
Sandford. Cumb 3A 104
Sandford. Devn 2B 12
Sandford. Dors 4E 15
Sandford. Hants 2G 15
Sandford. IOW 4D 16
Sandford. N Som 1H 21
Sandford. Shrp 3F 71
(nr. Oswestry)
Sandford. Shrp 2H 71
(nr. Whitchurch)
Sandford. S Lan 5A 128
Sandfordhill. Abers 4H 161
Sandford-on-Thames.
Oxon 5D 50
Sandford Orcas. Dors 4B 22
Sandford St Martin. Oxon 3C 50
Sandgate. Kent 2F 29
Sandgreen. Dum 4C 110
Sandhaven. Abers 2G 161
Sandhead. Dum 4F 109
Sandhill. Cambs 2E 65
Sandhills. Dors 1B 14
Sandhills. Oxon 5D 50
Sandhills. Surr 2A 26
Sandhoe. Nmbd 3C 114
Sand Hole. E Yor 1B 94
Sandholes. Cook 2B 178
Sandholme. E Yor 1B 94
Sandholme. Linc 2C 76
Sandhurst. Brac 5G 37
Sandhurst. Glos 3D 48
Sandhurst. Kent 3B 28
Sandhurst Cross. Kent 3B 28
Sandhutton. N Yor 1F 99
(nr. Thirsk)
Sand Hutton. N Yor 4A 100
(nr. York)
Sandiacre. Derbs 2B 74
Sandilands. Linc 2E 89
Sandiway. Ches W 3A 84
Sandleheath. Hants 1G 15
Sandling. Kent 5B 40
Sandlow Green. Ches E 4B 84
Sandness. Shet 6C 173
Sandon. Essx 5H 53
Sandon. Herts 2D 52
Sandon. Staf 3D 72
Sandonbank. Staf 3D 72
Sandown. IOW 4D 16
Sandplace. Corn 3G 7
Sandridge. Herts 4B 52
Sandridge. Wilts 5E 35
Sandringham. Norf 3F 77
Sandsend. N Yor 3F 107
Sandside. Cumb 2C 96
Sandsound. Shet 7E 173
Sands, The. Surr 2G 25
Sandtoft. N Lin 4H 93
Sandvoe. Shet 2E 173
Sandway. Kent 5C 40
Sandwell Green. Suff 3D 66
Sandwich. Kent 5H 41
Sandwick. Cumb 3F 103
Sandwick. Orkn 6B 172
(on Mainland)
Sandwick. Orkn 9D 172
(on South Ronaldsay)
Sandwick. Shet 9F 173
(on Mainland)
Sandwick. Shet 5G 173
(on Whalsay)
Sandwith. Cumb 3A 102
Sandy. Carm 5E 45
Sandy. C Beds 1B 52
Sandy Bank. Linc 5B 88
Sandycroft. Flin 4F 83
Sandy Cross. Here 5A 60
Sandygate. Devn 5B 12
Sandygate. IOM 2C 108
Sandy Haven. Pemb 4C 42
Sandyhills. Dum 4F 111
Sandylands. Lanc 3D 96
Sandylane. Swan 4E 31
Sandy Lane. Wilts 5E 35
Sandystones. Bord 2H 119
Sandyway. Here 3H 47
Sangobeg. High 2E 167
Sangomore. High 2E 166
Sankyn's Green. Worc 4B 60
Sanna. High 2F 139
Sanndabhaig. W Isl 4G 171
(on Isle of Lewis)
Sanndabhaig. W Isl 4D 170
(on South Uist)
Sannox. N Ayr 5B 126
Sanquhar. Dum 3G 117
Santon. Cumb 4B 102
Santon Bridge. Cumb 4C 102
Santon Downham. Suff 2H 65
Sapcote. Leics 1B 62
Sapey Common. Here 4B 60
Sapiston. Suff 3B 66
Sapley. Cambs 3B 64
Sapperton. Derbs 2F 73
Sapperton. Glos 5E 49
Sapperton. Linc 2H 75
Saracen's Head. Linc 3C 76
Sarclet. High 4F 169
Sardis. Carm 5F 45
Sardis. Pemb 4D 42
(nr. Milford Haven)
Sardis. Pemb 4F 43
(nr. Tenby)
Sarisbury. Hants 2D 16
Sarn. B'end 3C 32
Sarn. Powy 1E 58
Sarnau. Carm 3E 45
Sarnau. Cdgn 5C 56
Sarnau. Gwyn 2B 70
Sarnau. Powy 2D 46
(nr. Brecon)
Sarnau. Powy 4E 71
(nr. Welshpool)
Sarn Bach. Gwyn 3C 68
Sarnesfield. Here 5F 59
Sarn Meyllteyrn. Gwyn 2B 68
Saron. Carm 4G 45
(nr. Ammanford)
Saron. Carm 2D 45
(nr. Newcastle Emlyn)
Saron. Gwyn 4E 81
(nr. Bethel)
Saron. Gwyn 5D 80
(nr. Bontnewydd)
Sarratt. Herts 1B 38

Sarre—South Elkington

Sarre. Kent 4G 41
Sarsden. Oxon 3A 50
Satley. Dur 5E 115
Satron. N Yor 5C 104
Satterleigh. Devn 4G 19
Satterthwaite. Cumb 5E 103
Satwell. Oxon 3F 37
Sauchen. Abers 2D 152
Saucher. Per 5A 144
Saughall. Ches W 4F 83
Saughtree. Bord 5H 119
Saul. Down 5K 179
Saul. Glos 5C 48
Saundby. Notts 2E 87
Saundersfoot. Pemb 4F 43
Saunderton. Buck 5F 51
Saunderton Lee. Buck 2G 37
Saunton. Devn 3E 19
Sausthorpe. Linc 4C 88
Saval. High 3C 164
Saverley Green. Staf 2D 72
Sawbridge. Warw 4C 62
Sawbridgeworth. Herts 4E 53
Sawdon. N Yor 1D 100
Sawley. Derbs 2B 74
Sawley. Lanc 5G 97
Sawley. N Yor 3E 99
Sawston. Cambs 1E 53
Sawtry. Cambs 2A 64
Saxby. Leics 3F 75
Saxby. Linc 2H 87
Saxby All Saints. N Lin 3C 94
Saxelby. Leics 3D 74
Saxelbye. Leics 3D 74
Saxham Street. Suff 4C 66
Saxilby. Linc 3F 87
Saxlingham. Norf 2C 78
Saxlingham Green. Norf 1E 67
Saxlingham Nethergate.
Norf 1E 67
Saxlingham Thorpe. Norf 1E 66
Saxmundham. Suff 4F 67
Saxondale. Notts 1D 74
Saxon Street. Cambs 5F 65
Saxtead. Suff 4E 67
Saxtead Green. Suff 4E 67
Saxthorpe. Norf 2D 78
Saxton. N Yor 1E 93
Sayers Common. W Sus 4D 26
Scackleton. N Yor 2A 100
Scadabhagh. W Isl 8D 171
Scaddy. Down 5J 179
Scaftworth. Notts 1D 86
Scagglethorpe. N Yor 2C 100
Scaitcliffe. Lanc 2F 91
Scaladal. W Isl 6D 171
Scalasaig. Arg 4A 132
Scalby. E Yor 2B 94
Scalby. N Yor 5H 107
Scalby Mills. N Yor 5H 107
Scaldwell. Nptn 3E 63
Scaleby. Cumb 3F 113
Scaleby Hill. Cumb 3F 113
Scale Houses. Cumb 5G 113
Scales. Cumb 2B 96
(nr. Barrow-in-Furness)
Scales. Cumb 2E 103
(nr. Keswick)
Scalford. Leics 3E 75
Scaling. Red C 3E 107
Scaling Dam. Red C 3E 107
Scalloway. Shet 8E 173
Scalpaigh. W Isl 8E 171
Scalpay House. High 1E 147
Scamblesby. Linc 3B 88
Scamodale. High 1C 140
Scampston. N Yor 2C 100
Scampton. Linc 3G 87
Scaniport. High 5A 158
Scapa. Orkn 7D 172
Scapegoat Hill. W Yor 3A 92
Scar. Orkn 3F 172
Scarasta. W Isl 8C 171
Scarborough. N Yor 1E 101
Scarcliffe. Derbs 4B 86
Scarcroft. W Yor 5F 99
Scardroy. High 3E 156
Scarfskerry. High 1E 169
Scargill. Dur 3D 104
Scarinish. Arg 4B 138
Scarisbrick. Lanc 3B 90
Scarning. Norf 4B 78
Scarrington. Notts 1E 75
Scarth Hill. Lanc 4C 90
Scartho. NE Lin 4F 95
Scarva. Ban 5E 178
Scarvister. Shet 7E 173
Scatness. Shet 10E 173
Scatwell. High 3F 157
Scaur. Dum 4F 111
Scawby. N Lin 4C 94
Scawby Brook. N Lin 4C 94
Scawsby. S Yor 4F 93
Scawton. N Yor 1H 99
Scayne's Hill. W Sus 3E 27
Scethrog. Powy 3E 46
Scholar Green. Ches E 5C 84
Scholes. G Man 4D 90
Scholes. W Yor 2B 92
(nr. Bradford)
Scholes. W Yor 4B 92
(nr. Holmfirth)
Scholes. W Yor 1D 93
(nr. Leeds)
Scholey Hill. W Yor 2D 93
School Aycliffe. Dur 2F 105
School Green. Ches W 4A 84
School Green. Essx 2H 53
Scissett. W Yor 3C 92
Scleddau. Pemb 1D 42
Scofton. Notts 2D 86
Scole. Norf 3D 66
Scollogstown. Down 6J 179
Scolpaig. W Isl 1C 170
Scolton. Pemb 2D 43
Scone. Per 1D 136
Sconser. High 5E 155
Scoonie. Fife 3F 137
Scopwick. Linc 5H 87
Scoraig. High 4E 163
Scorborough. E Yor 5E 101
Scorrier. Corn 4B 6
Scorriton. Devn 2D 8
Scorton. Lanc 5E 97
Scorton. N Yor 4F 105
Sco Ruston. Norf 3E 79
Scotbheinn. W Isl 3D 170
Scotby. Cumb 4F 113
Scotch Corner. N Yor 4F 105
Scotch Street. Cgvn 4D 178
Scotforth. Lanc 3D 97
Scot Hay. Staf 1C 72
Scothern. Linc 3H 87
Scotland End. Oxon 2B 50
Scotlandwell. Per 3D 136
Scot Lane End. G Man 4E 91
Scotsburn. High 1B 158
Scotsburn. Mor 2G 159
Scotsdike. Cumb 2E 113
Scots Gap. Nmbd 1D 114
Scotstoun. Glas 3G 127
Scotstown. High 2C 140
Scotswood. Tyne 3F 115
Scottas. High 3F 147
Scotter. Linc 4B 94
Scotterthorpe. Linc 4B 94
Scottlethorpe. Linc 3H 75
Scotton. Linc 1F 87
Scotton. N Yor 5E 105
(nr. Catterick Garrison)
Scotton. N Yor 4F 99
(nr. Harrogate)
Scottow. Norf 3E 79
Scoulton. Norf 5B 78
Scounslow Green. Staf 3E 73
Scourie. High 4B 166
Scourie More. High 4B 166
Scousburgh. Shet 10E 173
Scout Green. Cumb 4G 103
Scouthead. G Man 4H 91
Scrabster. High 1C 168
Scrafield. Linc 4C 88
Scrainwood. Nmbd 4D 121
Scrane End. Linc 1C 76
Scraptoft. Leic 5D 74
Scratby. Norf 4H 79
Scrayingham. N Yor 3B 100
Scredington. Linc 1H 75
Scremby. Linc 4D 88
Scremerston. Nmbd 5G 131
Screveton. Notts 1E 75
Scrivelsby. Linc 4B 88
Scriven. N Yor 4F 99
Scronkey. Lanc 5D 96
Scrooby. Notts 1D 86
Scropton. Derbs 2F 73
Scrub Hill. Linc 5B 88
Scruton. N Yor 5F 105
Scuggate. Cumb 2F 113
Sculamus. High 1E 147
Sculcoates. Hull 1D 94
Sculthorpe. Norf 2A 78
Scunthorpe. N Lin 3B 94
Scurlage. Swan 4D 30
Sea. Som 1G 13
Seaborough. Dors 2H 13
Seabridge. Staf 1C 72
Seabrook. Kent 2F 29
Seaburn. Tyne 3H 115
Seacombe. Mers 1F 83
Seacroft. Linc 4E 89
Seacroft. W Yor 1D 92
Seadyke. Linc 2C 76
Seafield. High 5G 165
Seafield. Midl 3F 129
Seafield. S Ayr 2C 116
Seafield. W Lot 3D 128
Seaford. E Sus 5F 27
Seaforde. Down 5J 179
Seaforth. Mers 1F 83
Seagrave. Leics 4D 74
Seaham. Dur 5H 115
Seahouses. Nmbd 1G 121
Seal. Kent 5G 39
Sealand. Flin 4F 83
Seale. Surr 2G 25
Seamer. N Yor 1E 101
(nr. Scarborough)
Seamer. N Yor 3B 106
(nr. Stokesley)
Seamill. N Ayr 5C 126
Sea Mills. Bris 4A 34
Sea Palling. Norf 3G 79
Seapatrick. Ban 5F 178
Searby. Linc 4D 94
Seasalter. Kent 4E 41
Seascale. Cumb 4B 102
Seaside. Per 1E 137
Seater. High 1F 169
Seathorne. Linc 4E 89
Seathwaite. Cumb 3D 102
(nr. Buttermere)
Seathwaite. Cumb 5D 102
(nr. Ulpha)
Seatle. Cumb 1C 96
Seatoller. Cumb 3D 102
Seaton. Corn 3H 7
Seaton. Cumb 1B 102
Seaton. Devn 3F 13
Seaton. Dur 4G 115
Seaton. E Yor 5G 101
Seaton. Nmbd 2G 115
Seaton. Rut 1G 63
Seaton Burn. Tyne 2F 115
Seaton Carew. Hart 2C 106
Seaton Delaval. Nmbd 2G 115
Seaton Junction. Devn 3F 13
Seaton Ross. E Yor 5B 100
Seaton Sluice. Nmbd 2G 115
Seatown. Abers 2C 160
Seatown. Dors 3H 13
Seatown. Mor 2C 160
(nr. Cullen)
Seatown. Mor 1G 159
(nr. Lossiemouth)
Seave Green. N Yor 4C 106
Seaview. IOW 3E 17
Seaville. Cumb 4C 112
Seavington St Mary. Som 1H 13
Seavington St Michael.
Som 1H 13
Seawick. Essx 4E 55
Sebastopol. Torf 2F 33
Sebergham. Cumb 5E 113
Seckington. Warw 5G 73
Second Coast. High 4D 162
Sedbergh. Cumb 5H 103
Sedbury. Glos 2A 34
Sedbusk. N Yor 5B 104
Sedgeberrow. Worc 2F 49
Sedgebrook. Linc 2F 75
Sedgefield. Dur 2A 106
Sedgeford. Norf 2G 77
Sedgehill. Wilts 4D 22
Sedgley. W Mid 1D 60
Sedgwick. Cumb 1E 97
Sedlescombe. E Sus 4B 28
Seend. Wilts 5E 35
Seend Cleeve. Wilts 5E 35
Seer Green. Buck 1A 38
Seething. Norf 1F 67
Sefster. Shet 6E 173
Sefton. Mers 4B 90
Sefton Park. Mers 2F 83
Segensworth. Hants 2D 16
Seggat. Abers 4E 161
Seghill. Nmbd 2F 115
Seifton. Shrp 2G 59
Seighford. Staf 3C 72
Seilebost. W Isl 8C 171
Seisdon. Staf 1C 60
Seisiadar. W Isl 4H 171
Selattyn. Shrp 2E 71
Selborne. Hants 3F 25
Selby. N Yor 1G 93
Selham. W Sus 3A 26
Selkirk. Bord 2G 119
Sellack. Here 3A 48
Sellafirth. Shet 2G 173
Sellick's Green. Som 1F 13
Sellindge. Kent 2F 29
Selling. Kent 5E 41
Sells Green. Wilts 5E 35
Selly Oak. W Mid 2E 61
Selmeston. E Sus 5G 27
Selsdon. G Lon 4E 39
Selsey. W Sus 3G 17
Selsfield Common.
W Sus 2E 27
Selside. Cumb 5G 103
Selside. N Yor 2G 97
Selsley. Glos 5D 48
Selsted. Kent 1G 29
Selston. Notts 5B 86
Selworthy. Som 2C 20
Semblister. Shet 6E 173
Semer. Suff 1D 54
Semington. Wilts 5D 35
Semley. Wilts 4D 23
Sempringham. Linc 2A 76
Send. Surr 5B 38
Send Marsh. Surr 5B 38
Senghenydd. Cphy 2E 32
Sennen. Corn 4A 4
Sennen Cove. Corn 4A 4
Sennicotts. W Sus 2G 17
Sennybridge. Powy 3C 46
Serlby. Notts 2D 86
Seskinore. Omag 3K 177
Sessay. N Yor 2G 99
Setchey. Norf 4F 77
Setley. Hants 2B 16
Setter. Shet 3F 173
Settiscarth. Orkn 6C 172
Settle. N Yor 3H 97
Settrington. N Yor 2C 100
Seven Ash. Som 3E 21
Sevenhampton. Glos 3F 49
Sevenhampton. Swin 2H 35
Sevenoaks. Kent 5G 39
Sevenoaks Weald. Kent 5G 39
Seven Sisters. Neat 5B 46
Seven Springs. Glos 4E 49
Severn Beach. S Glo 3A 34
Severn Stoke. Worc 1D 48
Sevington. Kent 1E 29
Sewards End. Essx 2F 53
Sewardstone. Essx 1E 39
Sewell. C Beds 3H 51
Sewerby. E Yor 3G 101
Seworgan. Corn 5B 6
Sewstern. Leics 3F 75
Sgallairidh. W Isl 9B 170
Sgarasta Mhor. W Isl 8C 171
Sgiogarstaigh. W Isl 1H 171
Sgreadan. Arg 4A 132
Shabbington. Buck 5E 51
Shackerley. Shrp 5C 72
Shackerstone. Leics 5A 74
Shackleford. Surr 1A 26
Shadforth. Dur 5G 115
Shadingfield. Suff 2G 67
Shadoxhurst. Kent 2D 28
Shadsworth. Bkbn 2E 91
Shadwell. Norf 2B 66
Shadwell. W Yor 1D 92
Shaftesbury. Dors 4D 22
Shafton. S Yor 3D 93
Shafton Two Gates. S Yor 3D 93
Shaggs. Dors 4D 14
Shakesfield. Glos 2B 48
Shalbourne. Wilts 5B 36
Shalcombe. IOW 4B 16
Shalden. Hants 2E 25
Shaldon. Devn 5C 12
Shalfleet. IOW 4C 16
Shalford. Essx 3H 53
Shalford. Surr 1B 26
Shalford Green. Essx 3H 53
Shallowford. Devn 2H 19
Shallowford. Staf 3C 72
Shalmsford Street. Kent 5E 41
Shalstone. Buck 2E 51
Shamley Green. Surr 1B 26
Shandon. Arg 1D 126
Shandwick. High 1C 158
Shangton. Leics 1E 62
Shankhouse. Nmbd 2F 115
Shanklin. IOW 4D 16
Shannochie. N Ayr 3D 122
Shap. Cumb 3G 103
Shapwick. Dors 2E 15
Shapwick. Som 3H 21
Sharcott. Wilts 1G 23
Shardlow. Derbs 2B 74
Shareshill. Staf 5D 72
Sharlston. W Yor 3D 93
Sharlston Common.
W Yor 3D 93
Sharnal Street. Medw 3B 40
Sharnbrook. Bed 5G 63
Sharneyford. Lanc 2G 91
Sharnford. Leics 1B 62
Sharnhill Green. Dors 2C 14
Sharoe Green. Lanc 1D 90
Sharow. N Yor 2F 99
Sharpe Green. Lanc 1D 90
Sharpenhoe. C Beds 2A 52
Sharperton. Nmbd 4D 120
Sharpness. Glos 5B 48
Sharp Street. Norf 3F 79
Sharpthorne. W Sus 2E 27
Sharrington. Norf 2C 78
Shatterford. Worc 2B 60
Shatton. Derbs 2F 85
Shaugh Prior. Devn 2B 8
Shavington. Ches E 5B 84
Shaw. G Man 4H 91
Shaw. W Ber 5C 36
Shaw. Wilts 5D 35
Shawbirch. Telf 4A 72
Shawbury. Shrp 3H 71
Shawdon Hall. Nmbd 3E 121
Shawell. Leics 2C 62
Shawford. Hants 4C 24
Shawforth. Lanc 2G 91
Shaw Green. Lanc 3D 90
Shawhead. Dum 2F 111
Shaw Mills. N Yor 3E 99
Shawwood. E Ayr 2E 117
Shearington. Dum 3B 112
Shearsby. Leics 1D 62
Shearston. Som 3F 21
Shebbear. Devn 2E 11
Shebdon. Staf 3B 72
Shebster. High 2C 168
Sheddocksley. Aber 3F 153
Shedfield. Hants 1D 16
Shedog. N Ayr 2D 122
Sheen. Staf 4F 85
Sheepbridge. Derbs 3A 86
Sheep Hill. Tyne 4E 115
Sheepscar. W Yor 1D 92
Sheepscombe. Glos 4D 49
Sheepstor. Devn 2B 8
Sheepwash. Devn 2E 11
Sheepwash. Nmbd 1F 115
Sheepway. N Som 4H 33
Sheepy Magna. Leics 5H 73
Sheepy Parva. Leics 5H 73
Sheering. Essx 4F 53
Sheerness. Kent 3D 40
Sheerwater. Surr 4B 38
Sheet. Hants 4F 25
Sheffield. S Yor 2H 85 & 202
Sheffield Bottom. W Ber 5E 37
Sheffield Green. E Sus 3F 27
Shefford. C Beds 2B 52
Shefford Woodlands.
W Ber 4B 36
Sheigra. High 2B 166
Sheinton. Shrp 5A 72
Shelderton. Shrp 3G 59
Sheldon. Derbs 4F 85
Sheldon. Devn 2E 12
Sheldon. W Mid 2F 61
Sheldwich. Kent 5E 40
Sheldwich Lees. Kent 5E 40
Shelf. W Yor 2B 92
Shelfanger. Norf 2D 66
Shelfield. Warw 4F 61
Shelfield. W Mid 5E 73
Shelford. Notts 1D 74
Shelford. Warw 2B 62
Shell. Worc 5D 60
Shelley. Suff 2D 54
Shelley. W Yor 3C 92
Shell Green. Hal 2H 83
Shellingford. Oxon 2B 36
Shellow Bowells. Essx 5G 53
Shelsley Beauchamp.
Worc 4B 60
Shelsley Walsh. Worc 4B 60
Shelthorpe. Leics 4C 74
Shelton. Bed 4H 63
Shelton. Norf 1E 67
Shelton. Notts 1E 75
Shelton. Shrp 4G 71
Shelton Green. Norf 1E 67
Shelton Lock. Derb 2A 74
Shelve. Shrp 1F 59
Shelwick. Here 1A 48
Shelwick Green. Here 1A 48
Shenfield. Essx 1H 39
Shenington. Oxon 1B 50
Shenley. Herts 5B 52
Shenley Brook End. Mil 2G 51
Shenleybury. Herts 5B 52
Shenley Church End. Mil 2G 51
Shenmore. Here 2G 47
Shennanton. Dum 3A 110
Shenstone. Staf 5F 73
Shenstone. Worc 3C 60
Shenstone Woodend. Staf 5F 73
Shenton. Leics 5A 74
Shenval. Mor 1G 151
Shepeau Stow. Linc 4C 76
Shephall. Herts 3C 52
Shepherd's Bush. G Lon 2D 38
Shepherd's Gate. Norf 4E 77
Shepherd's Green. Oxon 3F 37
Shepherd's Port. Norf 2F 77
Shepherdswell. Kent 1G 29
Shepley. W Yor 4B 92
Sheppardstown. High 4D 169
Shepperdine. S Glo 2B 34
Shepperton. Surr 4B 38
Shepreth. Cambs 1D 53
Shepshed. Leics 4B 74
Shepton Beauchamp.
Som 1H 13
Shepton Mallet. Som 2B 22
Shepton Montague. Som 3B 22
Shepway. Kent 5B 40
Sheraton. Dur 1B 106
Sherborne. Bath 1A 22
Sherborne. Dors 1B 14
Sherborne. Glos 4G 49
Sherborne Causeway.
Dors 4D 22
Sherborne St John. Hants 1E 24
Sherbourne. Warw 4G 61
Sherburn. Dur 5G 115
Sherburn. N Yor 2D 100
Sherburn Hill. Dur 5G 115
Sherburn in Elmet. N Yor 1E 93
Shere. Surr 1B 26
Shereford. Norf 3A 78
Sherfield English. Hants 4A 24
Sherfield on Loddon.
Hants 1E 25
Sherford. Devn 4D 9
Sherford. Dors 3E 15
Sheriffhales. Shrp 4B 72
Sheriff Hutton. N Yor 3A 100
Sheriffston. Mor 2G 159
Sheringham. Norf 1D 78
Sherington. Mil 1G 51
Shermanbury. W Sus 4D 26
Shernal Green. Worc 4D 60
Shernborne. Norf 2G 77
Sherrington. Wilts 3E 23
Sherston. Wilts 3D 34
Sherwood. Nott 1C 74
Sherwood Green. Devn 4F 19
Shettleston. Glas 3H 127
Shevington. G Man 4D 90
Shevington Moor. G Man 3D 90
Shevington Vale. G Man 4D 90
Sheviock. Corn 3H 7
Shide. IOW 4C 16
Shiel Bridge. High 2B 148
Shieldaig. High 1H 155
(nr. Charlestown)
Shieldaig. High 3H 155
(nr. Torridon)
Shieldhill. Dum 1B 112
Shieldhill. Falk 2B 128
Shieldhill. S Lan 5D 128
Shieldmuir. N Lan 4A 128
Shielfoot. High 2A 140
Shielhill. Abers 3H 161
Shielhill. Ang 3D 144
Shifnal. Shrp 5B 72
Shilbottle. Nmbd 4F 121
Shilbottle Grange.
Nmbd 4G 121
Shildon. Dur 2F 105
Shillford. E Ren 4F 127
Shillingford. Devn 4C 20
Shillingford. Oxon 2D 36
Shillingford St George.
Devn 4C 12
Shillingstone. Dors 1D 14
Shillington. C Beds 2B 52
Shillmoor. Nmbd 4C 120
Shilton. Oxon 5A 50
Shilton. Warw 2B 62
Shilvinghampton. Dors 4B 14
Shilvington. Nmbd 1E 115
Shimpling. Norf 2D 66
Shimpling. Suff 5A 66
Shimpling Street. Suff 5A 66
Shincliffe. Dur 5F 115
Shiney Row. Tyne 4G 115
Shinfield. Wok 5F 37
Shingay. Cambs 1D 52
Shingham. Norf 5G 77
Shingle Street. Suff 1G 55
Shinner's Bridge. Devn 2D 9
Shinness. High 2C 164
Shipbourne. Kent 5G 39
Shipdham. Norf 5B 78
Shipham. Som 1H 21
Shiphay. Torb 2E 9
Shiplake. Oxon 4F 37
Shipley. Derbs 1B 74
Shipley. Nmbd 3F 121
Shipley. Shrp 1C 60
Shipley. W Sus 3C 26
Shipley. W Yor 1B 92
Shipley Bridge. Surr 1E 27
Shipmeadow. Suff 1F 67
Shippon. Oxon 2C 36
Shipston-on-Stour. Warw 1A 50
Shipton. Buck 3F 51
Shipton. Glos 4F 49
Shipton. N Yor 4H 99
Shipton. Shrp 1H 59
Shipton Bellinger. Hants 2H 23
Shipton Gorge. Dors 3H 13
Shipton Green. W Sus 3G 17
Shipton Moyne. Glos 3D 35
Shipton-on-Cherwell.
Oxon 4C 50
Shiptonthorpe. E Yor 5C 100
Shipton-under-Wychwood.
Oxon 4A 50
Shirburn. Oxon 2E 37
Shirdley Hill. Lanc 3B 90
Shire. Cumb 1H 103
Shirebrook. Derbs 4C 86
Shiregreen. S Yor 1A 86
Shirehampton. Bris 4A 34
Shiremoor. Tyne 2G 115
Shirenewton. Mon 2H 33
Shireoaks. Notts 2C 86
Shires Mill. Fife 1D 128
Shirkoak. Kent 2D 28
Shirland. Derbs 5A 86
Shirley. Derbs 1G 73
Shirley. Sotn 1C 16
Shirley. W Mid 3F 61
Shirleywich. Staf 3D 73
Shirl Heath. Here 5G 59
Shirrell Heath. Hants 1D 16
Shirwell. Devn 3F 19
Shiskine. N Ayr 3D 122
Shobdon. Here 4F 59
Shobnall. Staf 3G 73
Shobrooke. Devn 2B 12
Shoby. Leics 3D 74
Shocklach. Ches W 1G 71
Shoeburyness. S'end 2D 40
Sholden. Kent 5H 41
Sholing. Sotn 1C 16
Sholver. G Man 4H 91
Shoot Hill. Shrp 4G 71
Shop. Corn 1C 10
(nr. Bude)
Shop. Corn 1C 6
(nr. Padstow)
Shop. Devn 1D 11
Shopford. Cumb 2G 113
Shoreditch. G Lon 2E 39
Shoreditch. Som 4F 21
Shoregill. Cumb 4A 104
Shoreham. Kent 4G 39
Shoreham-by-Sea.
W Sus 5D 26
Shoresdean. Nmbd 5F 131
Shoreswood. Nmbd 5F 131
Shore, The. Fife 2E 137
Shorncote. Glos 2F 35
Shorne. Kent 3A 40
Shorne Ridgeway. Kent 3A 40
Shortacombe. Devn 4F 11
Shortbridge. E Sus 3F 27
Shortgate. E Sus 4F 27
Short Green. Norf 2C 66
Shorthampton. Oxon 3B 50
Short Heath. Leics 4H 73
Short Heath. W Mid 1E 61
(nr. Erdington)
Short Heath. W Mid 5D 73
(nr. Wednesfield)
Shortlanesend. Corn 4C 6
Shorton. Torb 2E 9
Shortstown. Bed 1A 52
Shortwood. S Glo 4B 34
Shorwell. IOW 4C 16
Shoscombe. Bath 1C 22
Shotesham. Norf 1E 67
Shotgate. Essx 1B 40
Shotley. Suff 2F 55
Shotley Bridge. Dur 4D 115
Shotleyfield. Nmbd 4D 114
Shotley Gate. Suff 2F 55
Shottenden. Kent 5E 41
Shottermill. Surr 3G 25
Shottery. Warw 5F 61
Shotteswell. Warw 1C 50
Shottisham. Suff 1G 55
Shottle. Derbs 1H 73
Shotton. Dur 1B 106
(nr. Peterlee)
Shotton. Dur 2A 106
(nr. Sedgefield)
Shotton. Flin 4E 83
Shotton. Nmbd 2F 115
(nr. Morpeth)
Shotton. Nmbd 1C 120
(nr. Town Yetholm)
Shotton Colliery. Dur 5G 115
Shotts. N Lan 3B 128
Shotwick. Ches W 3F 83
Shouldham. Norf 5F 77
Shouldham Thorpe. Norf 5F 77
Shoulton. Worc 5C 60
Shrawardine. Shrp 4G 71
Shrawley. Worc 4C 60
Shreding Green. Buck 2B 38
Shrewley. Warw 4G 61
Shrewsbury. Shrp 4G 71 & 202
Shrewton. Wilts 2F 23
Shrigley. Down 4K 179
Shripney. W Sus 5A 26
Shrivenham. Oxon 3H 35
Shropham. Norf 1B 66
Shroton. Dors 1D 14
Shrub End. Essx 3C 54
Shucknall. Here 1A 48
Shudy Camps. Cambs 1G 53
Shulishadermor. High 4D 155
Shulista. High 1D 154
Shurdington. Glos 4E 49
Shurlock Row. Wind 4G 37
Shurrery. High 3C 168
Shurton. Som 2F 21
Shustoke. Warw 1G 61
Shute. Devn 3F 13
(nr. Axminster)
Shute. Devn 2B 12
(nr. Crediton)
Shutford. Oxon 1B 50
Shut Heath. Staf 3C 72
Shuthonger. Glos 2D 49
Shutlanehead. Staf 1C 72
Shutlanger. Nptn 1F 51
Shutt Green. Staf 5C 72
Shuttington. Warw 5G 73
Shuttlewood. Derbs 3B 86
Shuttleworth. G Man 3G 91
Siabost. W Isl 3E 171
Siabost bho Dheas.
W Isl 3E 171
Siabost bho Thuath.
W Isl 3E 171
Siadar. W Isl 2F 171
Siadar Uarach. W Isl 2F 171
Sibbaldbie. Dum 1C 112
Sibbertoft. Nptn 2D 62
Sibdon Carwood. Shrp 2G 59
Sibertswold. Kent 1G 29
Sibford Ferris. Oxon 2B 50
Sibford Gower. Oxon 2B 50
Sible Hedingham. Essx 2A 54
Sibsey. Linc 5C 88
Sibsey Fen Side. Linc 5C 88
Sibson. Cambs 1H 63
Sibson. Leics 5A 74
Sibster. High 3F 169
Sibthorpe. Notts 1E 75
Sibton. Suff 4F 67
Sicklesmere. Suff 4A 66
Sicklinghall. N Yor 5F 99
Sid. Devn 4E 13
Sidbury. Devn 3E 13
Sidbury. Shrp 2A 60
Sidcot. N Som 1H 21
Sidcup. G Lon 3F 39
Siddick. Cumb 1B 102
Siddington. Ches E 3C 84
Siddington. Glos 2F 35
Side of the Moor. G Man 3F 91
Sidestrand. Norf 2E 79
Sidford. Devn 3E 13
Sidlesham. W Sus 3G 17
Sidley. E Sus 5B 28
Sidlow. Surr 1D 26
Sidmouth. Devn 4E 13
Sigford. Devn 5A 12
Sigglesthorne. E Yor 5F 101
Sighthill. Edin 2E 129
Sigingstone. V Glam 4C 32
Signet. Oxon 4H 49
Silchester. Hants 5E 37
Sildinis. W Isl 6E 171
Sileby. Leics 4D 74
Silecroft. Cumb 1A 96
Silfield. Norf 1D 66
Silian. Cdgn 5E 57
Silkstone. S Yor 4C 92
Silkstone Common. S Yor 4C 92
Silksworth. Tyne 4G 115
Silk Willoughby. Linc 1H 75
Silloth. Cumb 4C 112
Sills. Nmbd 4C 120
Sillyearn. Mor 3C 160
Silpho. N Yor 5G 107
Silsden. W Yor 5C 98
Silsoe. C Beds 2A 52
Silverbank. Abers 4E 152
Silverbridge. New M 8D 178
Silverburn. Midl 3F 129
Silverdale. Lanc 2D 96
Silverdale. Staf 1C 72
Silverdale Green. Lanc 2D 96
Silver End. Essx 4B 54
Silver End. W Mid 2D 60
Silvergate. Norf 3D 78
Silver Green. Norf 1E 67
Silverhillocks. Abers 2E 161
Silverley's Green. Suff 3E 67
Silverstone. Nptn 1E 51
Silverton. Devn 2C 12
Silverton. W Dun 2F 127
Silvington. Shrp 3A 60
Simm's Cross. Hal 2H 83
Simm's Lane End. Mers 1H 83
Simonburn. Nmbd 2B 114
Simonsbath. Som 3A 20
Simonstone. Lanc 1F 91
Simprim. Bord 5E 131
Simpson. Pemb 3C 42
Simpson Cross. Pemb 3C 42
Sinclairston. E Ayr 3D 116
Sinclairtown. Fife 4E 137
Sinderby. N Yor 1F 99
Sinderhope. Nmbd 4B 114
Sindlesham. Wok 5F 37
Sinfin. Derb 2A 74
Singleborough. Buck 2F 51
Singleton. Kent 1D 28
Singleton. Lanc 1B 90
Singleton. W Sus 1G 17
Singlewell. Kent 3A 40
Sinkhurst Green. Kent 1C 28
Sinnahard. Abers 2B 152
Sinnington. N Yor 1B 100
Sinton Green. Worc 4C 60
Sion Mills. Strab 3F 176
Sipson. G Lon 3B 38
Sirhowy. Blae 4E 47
Sisland. Norf 1F 67
Sissinghurst. Kent 2B 28
Siston. S Glo 4B 34
Sithney. Corn 4D 4
Sittingbourne. Kent 4D 40
Six Ashes. Staf 2B 60
Six Bells. Blae 5F 47
Six Hills. Leics 3D 74
Sixhills. Linc 2A 88
Six Mile Bottom. Cambs 5E 65
Sixpenny Handley. Dors 1E 15
Sizewell. Suff 4G 67
Skail. High 4H 167
Skaill. Orkn 6B 172
Skaills. Orkn 7E 172
Skares. E Ayr 3E 117
Skateraw. E Lot 2D 130
Skaw. Shet 5G 173
Skeabost. High 4D 154
Skeabrae. Orkn 5B 172
Skeeby. N Yor 4E 105
Skeffington. Leics 5E 75
Skeffling. E Yor 3G 95
Skegby. Notts 4B 86
(nr. Mansfield)
Skegby. Notts 3E 87
(nr. Tuxford)
Skegness. Linc 4E 89
Skelberry. Shet 10E 173
(nr. Boddam)
Skelberry. Shet 3E 173
(nr. Housetter)
Skelbo. High 4E 165
Skelbo Street. High 4E 165
Skelbrooke. S Yor 3F 93
Skeldyke. Linc 2C 76
Skellingthorpe. Linc 3G 87
Skellister. Shet 6F 173
Skellorn Green. Ches E 2D 84
Skellow. S Yor 3F 93
Skelmanthorpe. W Yor 3C 92
Skelmersdale. Lanc 4C 90
Skelmorlie. N Ayr 3C 126
Skelpick. High 3H 167
Skelton. Cumb 1F 103
Skelton. E Yor 2A 94
Skelton. N Yor 4D 105
(nr. Richmond)
Skelton. N Yor 3F 99
(nr. Ripon)
Skelton. Red C 3D 106
Skelton. York 4H 99
Skelton Green. Red C 3D 106
Skelwick. Orkn 3D 172
Skelwith Bridge. Cumb 4E 103
Skendleby. Linc 4D 88
Skendleby Psalter. Linc 3D 88
Skenfrith. Mon 3H 47
Skerne. E Yor 4E 101
Skeroblingarry. Arg 3B 122
Skerray. High 2G 167
Skerricha. High 3C 166
Skerries Airport. Shet 4H 173
Skerton. Lanc 3D 97
Sketchley. Leics 1B 62
Sketty. Swan 3F 31
Skewen. Neat 3G 31
Skewsby. N Yor 2A 100
Skeyton. Norf 3E 79
Skeyton Corner. Norf 3E 79
Skiall. High 2C 168
Skidbrooke. Linc 1D 88
Skidbrooke North End.
Linc 1D 88
Skidby. E Yor 1D 94
Skilgate. Som 4C 20
Skillington. Linc 3F 75
Skinburness. Cumb 4C 112
Skinflats. Falk 1C 128
Skinidin. High 4B 154
Skinnet. High 2F 167
Skinningrove. Red C 2E 107
Skipness. Arg 4G 125
Skippool. Lanc 5C 96
Skiprigg. Cumb 5E 113
Skipsea. E Yor 4F 101
Skipsea Brough. E Yor 4F 101
Skipton. N Yor 4B 98
Skipton-on-Swale. N Yor 2F 99
Skipwith. N Yor 1G 93
Skirbeck. Linc 1C 76
Skirbeck Quarter. Linc 1C 76
Skirlaugh. E Yor 1E 95
Skirling. Bord 1C 118
Skirmett. Buck 2F 37
Skirpenbeck. E Yor 4B 100
Skirwith. Cumb 1H 103
Skirwith. N Yor 2G 97
Skirza. High 2F 169
Skitby. Cumb 3F 113
Skitham. Lanc 5D 96
Skroo. Shet 1B 172
Skulamus. High 1E 147
Skullomie. High 2G 167
Skyborry Green. Shrp 3E 59
Skye Green. Essx 3B 54
Skye of Curr. High 1D 151
Slack. W Yor 2H 91
Slackhall. Derbs 2E 85
Slack Head. Cumb 2D 97
Slackhead. Mor 2B 160
Slackholme End. Linc 3E 89
Slacks of Cairnbanno.
Abers 4F 161
Slack, The. Dur 2E 105
Slad. Glos 5D 48
Slade. Swan 4D 31
Slade End. Oxon 2D 36
Slade Field. Cambs 2C 64
Slade Green. G Lon 3G 39
Slade Heath. Staf 5D 72
Slade Hooton. S Yor 2C 86
Sladesbridge. Corn 5A 10
Slade, The. W Ber 5D 36
Slaggyford. Nmbd 4H 113
Slaidburn. Lanc 4G 97
Slaid Hill. W Yor 5F 99
Slaithwaite. W Yor 3A 92
Slaley. Derbs 5G 85
Slaley. Nmbd 4C 114
Slamannan. Falk 2B 128
Slapton. Buck 3H 51
Slapton. Devn 4E 9
Slapton. Nptn 1E 51
Slattock. G Man 4G 91
Slaugham. W Sus 3D 26
Slaughterbridge. Corn 4B 10
Slaughterford. Wilts 4D 34
Slawston. Leics 1E 63
Sleaford. Hants 3G 25
Sleaford. Linc 1H 75
Sleagill. Cumb 3G 103
Sleap. Shrp 3G 71
Sledmere. E Yor 3D 100
Sleightholme. Dur 3C 104
Sleights. N Yor 4F 107
Slepe. Dors 3E 15
Slickly. High 2E 169
Sliddery. N Ayr 3D 122
Sligachan. High 1C 146
Slimbridge. Glos 5C 48
Slindon. Staf 2C 72
Slindon. W Sus 5A 26
Slinfold. W Sus 2C 26
Slingsby. N Yor 2A 100
Slip End. C Beds 4A 52
Slipton. Nptn 3G 63
Slitting Mill. Staf 4E 73
Slochd. High 1C 150
Slockavullin. Arg 4F 133
Sloley. Norf 3E 79
Sloncombe. Devn 4H 11
Sloothby. Linc 3D 89
Slough. Slo 3A 38
Slough Green. Som 4F 21
Slough Green. W Sus 3D 27
Sluggan. High 1C 150
Slyne. Lanc 3D 97
Smailholm. Bord 1A 120
Smallbridge. G Man 3H 91
Smallbrook. Devn 3B 12
Smallburgh. Norf 3F 79
Smallburn. E Ayr 2F 117
Smalldale. Derbs 3E 85
Small Dole. W Sus 4D 26
Smalley. Derbs 1B 74
Smallfield. Surr 1E 27
Small Heath. W Mid 2E 61
Small Hythe. Kent 2C 28
Smallrice. Staf 2D 72
Smallridge. Devn 2G 13
Smallwood Hey. Lanc 5C 96
Smallworth. Norf 2C 66
Smannell. Hants 2B 24
Smardale. Cumb 4A 104
Smarden. Kent 1C 28
Smarden Bell. Kent 1C 28
Smart's Hill. Kent 1G 27
Smeatharpe. Devn 1F 13
Smeeth. Kent 2E 29
Smeeth, The. Norf 4E 77
Smeeton Westerby. Leics 1D 62
Smeircleit. W Isl 7C 170
Smerral. High 5D 168
Smestow. Staf 1C 60
Smethwick. W Mid 2E 61
Smirisary. High 1A 140
Smisby. Derbs 4H 73
Smitham Hill. Bath 1A 22
Smith End Green. Worc 5B 60
Smithfield. Cumb 3F 113
Smith Green. Lanc 4D 97
Smithies, The. Shrp 1A 60
Smithincott. Devn 1D 12
Smith's Green. Essx 3F 53
Smithstown. High 1G 155
Smithton. High 4B 158
Smithwood Green. Suff 5B 66
Smithy Bridge. G Man 3H 91
Smithy Green. Ches E 3B 84
Smithy Lane Ends. Lanc 3C 90
Smockington. Warw 2B 62
Smoogro. Orkn 7C 172
Smyth's Green. Essx 4C 54
Snaigow House. Per 4H 143
Snailbeach. Shrp 5F 71
Snailwell. Cambs 4F 65
Snainton. N Yor 1D 100
Snaith. E Yor 2G 93
Snape. N Yor 1E 99
Snape. Suff 5F 67
Snape Green. Lanc 3B 90
Snapper. Devn 3F 19
Snarestone. Leics 5H 73
Snarford. Linc 2H 87
Snargate. Kent 3D 28
Snave. Kent 3E 28
Sneachill. Worc 5D 60
Snead. Powy 1F 59
Snead Common. Worc 4B 60
Sneaton. N Yor 4F 107
Sneatonthorpe. N Yor 4G 107
Snelland. Linc 2H 87
Snelston. Derbs 1F 73
Snetterton. Norf 1B 66
Snettisham. Norf 2F 77
Snibston. Leics 4B 74
Sniseabhal. W Isl 5C 170
Snitter. Nmbd 4E 121
Snitterby. Linc 1G 87
Snitterfield. Warw 5G 61
Snitton. Shrp 3H 59
Snodhill. Here 1G 47
Snodland. Kent 4A 40
Snods Edge. Nmbd 4D 114
Snowdonia. Gwyn 2G 69
Snowshill. Glos 2F 49
Snow Street. Norf 2C 66
Snydale. W Yor 3E 93
Soake. Hants 1E 17
Soar. Carm 3G 45
Soar. Gwyn 2F 69
Soar. IOA 3C 80
Soar. Powy 2C 46
Soberton. Hants 1E 16
Soberton Heath. Hants 1E 16
Sockbridge. Cumb 2F 103
Sockburn. Darl 4A 106
Sodom. Den 3C 82
Sodom. Shet 5G 173
Soham. Cambs 3E 65
Soham Cotes. Cambs 3E 65
Solas. W Isl 1D 170
Soldon Cross. Devn 1D 10
Soldridge. Hants 3E 25
Solent Breezes. Hants 2D 16
Sole Street. Kent 4A 40
(nr. Meopham)
Sole Street. Kent 1E 29
(nr. Waltham)
Solihull. W Mid 3F 61
Sollers Dilwyn. Here 5G 59
Sollers Hope. Here 2B 48
Sollom. Lanc 3C 90
Solva. Pemb 2B 42
Somerby. Leics 4E 75
Somerby. Linc 4D 94
Somercotes. Derbs 5B 86
Somerford. Dors 3G 15
Somerford. Staf 5C 72
Somerford Keynes. Glos 2F 35
Somerley. W Sus 3G 17
Somerleyton. Suff 1G 67
Somersal Herbert. Derbs 2F 73
Somersby. Linc 3C 88
Somersham. Cambs 3C 64
Somersham. Suff 1D 54
Somerton. Oxon 3C 50
Somerton. Som 4H 21
Somerton. Suff 5H 65
Sompting. W Sus 5C 26
Sonning. Wok 4F 37
Sonning Common. Oxon 3F 37
Sonning Eye. Oxon 4F 37
Sookholme. Notts 4C 86
Sopley. Hants 3G 15
Sopworth. Wilts 3D 34
Sorbie. Dum 5B 110
Sordale. High 2D 168
Sorisdale. Arg 2D 138
Sorn. E Ayr 2E 117
Sornhill. E Ayr 1E 117
Sortat. High 2E 169
Sotby. Linc 3B 88
Sots Hole. Linc 4A 88
Sotterley. Suff 2G 67
Soudley. Shrp 1G 59
(nr. Church Stretton)
Soudley. Shrp 3B 72
(nr. Market Drayton)
Soughton. Flin 4E 83
Soulbury. Buck 3G 51
Soulby. Cumb 3A 104
(nr. Appleby)
Soulby. Cumb 2F 103
(nr. Penrith)
Souldern. Oxon 2D 50
Souldrop. Bed 4G 63
Sound. Ches E 1A 72
Sound. Shet 7F 173
(nr. Lerwick)
Sound. Shet 6E 173
(nr. Tresta)
Soundwell. Bris 4B 34
Sourhope. Bord 2C 120
Sourin. Orkn 4D 172
Sour Nook. Cumb 5E 113
Sourton. Devn 3F 11
Soutergate. Cumb 1B 96
South Acre. Norf 4H 77
Southall. G Lon 3C 38
South Allington. Devn 5D 9
South Alloa. Falk 4A 136
Southam. Glos 3E 49
Southam. Warw 4B 62
South Ambersham.
W Sus 3A 26
Southampton.
Sotn 1C 16 & 202
Southampton International Airport.
Hants 1C 16
Southannan. N Ayr 4D 126
South Anston. S Yor 2C 86
South Ascot. Wind 4A 38
South Baddesley. Hants 3B 16
South Balfern. Dum 4B 110
South Ballachulish. High 3E 141
South Bank. Red C 2C 106
South Barrow. Som 4B 22
South Benfleet. Essx 2B 40
South Bents. Tyne 3H 115
South Bersted. W Sus 5A 26
Southborough. Kent 1G 27
Southbourne. Bour 3G 15
Southbourne. W Sus 2F 17
South Bowood. Dors 3H 13
South Brent. Devn 2D 8
South Brewham. Som 3C 22
South Broomage. Falk 1B 128
South Broomhill. Nmbd 4G 121
Southburgh. Norf 5B 78
South Burlingham. Norf 5F 79
Southburn. E Yor 4D 101
South Cadbury. Som 4B 22
South Carlton. Linc 3G 87
South Cave. E Yor 1C 94
South Cerney. Glos 2F 35
South Chard. Som 2G 13
South Charlton. Nmbd 2F 121
South Cheriton. Som 4B 22
South Church. Dur 2F 105
Southchurch. S'end 2D 40
South Cleatlam. Dur 3E 105
South Cliffe. E Yor 1B 94
South Clifton. Notts 3F 87
South Clunes. High 4H 157
South Cockerington. Linc 2C 88
South Common. Devn 2G 13
South Common. E Sus 4E 27
South Cornelly. B'end 3B 32
Southcott. Devn 1E 11
(nr. Great Torrington)
Southcott. Devn 3F 11
(nr. Okehampton)
Southcott. Wilts 1G 23
Southcourt. Buck 4G 51
South Cove. Suff 2G 67
South Creagan. Arg 4D 141
South Creake. Norf 2A 78
South Crosland. W Yor 3B 92
South Croxton. Leics 4D 74
South Dalton. E Yor 5D 100
South Darenth. Kent 4G 39
Southdean. Bord 4A 120
Southdown. Bath 5C 34
South Downs. W Sus 5D 26
South Duffield. N Yor 1G 93
Southease. E Sus 5F 27
South Elkington. Linc 2B 88

South Elmsall—Sutton

South Elmsall. W Yor 3E 93
Southend. Arg 5A 122
South End. Cumb 3B 96
Southend. Glos 2C 34
South End. N Lin 2E 94
South End. W Ber 4D 36
Southend (London) Airport. Essx 2C 40
Southend-on-Sea. S'end 2C 40
Southerfield. Cumb 5C 112
Southerhouse. Shet 8E 173
Southerly. Devn 4F 11
Southernden. Kent 1C 28
Southerndown. V Glam 4B 32
Southerness. Dum 4A 112
South Erradale. High 1G 155
Southerton. Devn 3D 12
Southery. Norf 1F 65
Southey Green. Essx 2A 54
South Fambridge. Essx 1C 40
South Fawley. W Ber 3B 36
South Feorline. N Ayr 3D 122
South Ferriby. N Lin 2C 94
South Field. E Yor 2D 94
Southfleet. Kent 3H 39
South Garvan. High 1D 141
Southgate. Cdgn 2E 57
Southgate. G Lon 1E 39
Southgate. Norf .....3D 78 (nr. Aylsham)
Southgate. Norf .....2A 78 (nr. Fakenham)
Southgate. Swan 4E 31
South Gluss. Shet 4E 173
South Godstone. Surr 1E 27
South Gorley. Hants 1G 15
South Green. Essx .....1A 40 (nr. Billericay)
South Green. Essx .....4D 54 (nr. Colchester)
South Green. Kent 4C 40
South Hanningfield. Essx 1B 40
South Harting. W Sus 1F 17
South Hayling. Hants 3F 17
South Hazelrigg. Nmbd 1E 121
South Heath. Buck 5H 51
South Heath. Essx 4E 54
South Heighton. E Sus 5F 27
South Hetton. Dur 5G 115
South Hiendley. W Yor 3D 93
South Hill. Corn 5D 10
South Hill. Som 4H 21
South Hinksey. Oxon 5D 50
South Hole. Devn 4C 18
South Holme. N Yor 2B 100
South Holmwood. Surr 1C 26
South Hornchurch. G Lon 2G 39
South Huish. Devn 4C 8
South Hykeham. Linc 4G 87
South Hylton. Tyne 4G 115
Southill. C Beds 1B 52
Southington. Hants 2D 24
South Kelsey. Linc 1H 87
South Kessock. High 4A 158
South Killingholme. N Lin 3E 95
South Kilvington. N Yor 1G 99
South Kilworth. Leics 2D 62
South Kirkby. W Yor 3E 93
South Kirton. Abers 3E 153
South Knighton. Devn 5B 12
South Kyme. Linc 1A 76
South Lancing. W Sus 5C 26
South Ledaig. Arg 5D 140
Southleigh. Devn 3F 13
South Leigh. Oxon 5B 50
South Leverton. Notts 2E 87
South Littleton. Worc 1F 49
South Lopham. Norf 2C 66
South Luffenham. Rut 5G 75
South Malling. E Sus 4F 27
South Marston. Swin 3G 35
South Middleton. Nmbd 2E 121
South Milford. N Yor 1E 93
South Milton. Devn 4D 8
South Mimms. Herts 5C 52
Southminster. Essx 1D 40
South Molton. Devn 4H 19
South Moor. Dur 4E 115
Southmoor. Oxon 2B 36
South Moreton. Oxon 3D 36
South Mundham. W Sus 2G 17
South Muskham. Notts 5E 87
South Newbald. E Yor 1C 94
South Newington. Oxon 2C 50
South Newsham. Nmbd 2G 115
South Newton. N Ayr 4H 125
South Newton. Wilts 3F 23
South Normanton. Derbs 5B 86
South Norwood. G Lon 4E 39
South Nutfield. Surr 1E 27
South Ockendon. Thur 2G 39
Southoe. Cambs 4A 64
Southolt. Suff 4D 66
South Ormsby. Linc 3C 88
Southorpe. Pet 5H 75
South Otterington. N Yor 1F 99
South Owersby. Linc 1H 87
Southowram. W Yor 2B 92
South Oxhey. Herts 1C 38
South Perrott. Dors 2H 13
South Petherton. Som 1H 13
South Petherwin. Corn 4D 10
South Pickenham. Norf 5A 78
South Pool. Devn 4D 9
South Poorton. Dors 3A 14
South Port. Arg 1H 133
Southport. Mers 3B 90
Southpunds. Shet 10F 173
South Queensferry. Edin 2E 129
South Radworthy. Devn 3A 20
South Rauceby. Linc 1H 75
South Raynham. Norf 3A 78
Southrepps. Norf 2E 79
South Reston. Linc 2D 88
Southrey. Linc 4A 88
Southrop. Glos 5G 49
Southrope. Hants 2E 25
South Runcton. Norf 5F 77
South Scarle. Notts 4F 87
Southsea. Port 3E 17
South Shields. Tyne 3G 115
South Shore. Bkpl 1B 90
Southside. Orkn 5E 172
South Somercotes. Linc 1D 88
South Stainley. N Yor 3F 99
South Stainmore. Cumb 3B 104
South Stifford. Thur 3G 39
Southstoke. Bath 5C 34
South Stoke. Oxon 3D 36
South Stoke. W Sus 4B 26
South Street. E Sus 4E 27
South Street. Kent .....5E 41 (nr. Faversham)
South Street. Kent .....4F 41 (nr. Whitstable)
South Tawton. Devn 3G 11
South Thoresby. Linc 3D 88
South Tidworth. Wilts 2H 23
South Town. Devn 4C 12
South Town. Hants 3E 25
Southtown. Norf 5H 79
Southtown. Orkn 8D 172
South View. Shet 7E 173
Southwaite. Cumb 5F 113
South Walsham. Norf 4F 79
South Warnborough. Hants 2F 25
Southwater. W Sus 3C 26
Southwater Street. W Sus 3C 26
Southway. Som 2A 22
South Weald. Essx 1G 39
South Weirs. Hants 2A 16
Southwell. Dors 5B 14
Southwell. Notts 5D 86
South Weston. Oxon 2F 37
South Wheatley. Corn 3C 10
South Wheatley. Notts 2E 87
Southwick. Hants 2E 17
Southwick. Nptn 1H 63
Southwick. Tyne 4G 115
Southwick. W Sus 5D 26
Southwick. Wilts 1D 22
South Widcombe. Bath 1A 22
South Wigston. Leics 1C 62
South Willingham. Linc 2A 88
South Wingfield. Derbs 5A 86
South Witham. Linc 4G 75
Southwold. Suff 3H 67
South Wonston. Hants 3C 24
Southwood. Norf 5F 79
Southwood. Som 3A 22
South Woodham Ferrers. Essx 1C 40
South Wootton. Norf 3F 77
South Wraxall. Wilts 5D 34
South Zeal. Devn 3G 11
Soval Lodge. W Isl 5F 171
Sowerby. N Yor 1G 99
Sowerby. W Yor 2A 92
Sowerby Bridge. W Yor 2A 92
Sowerby Row. Cumb 5E 113
Sower Carr. Lanc 5C 96
Sowley Green. Suff 5G 65
Sowood. W Yor 3A 92
Sowton. Devn 3C 12
Soyal. High 4C 164
Soyland Town. W Yor 2A 92
Spacey Houses. N Yor 4F 99
Spa Common. Norf 2E 79
Spalding. Linc 3B 76
Spaldington. E Yor 1A 94
Spaldwick. Cambs 3A 64
Spalford. Notts 4F 87
Spamount. Strab 4E 176
Spanby. Linc 2H 75
Sparham. Norf 4C 78
Sparhamhill. Norf 4C 78
Spark Bridge. Cumb 1C 96
Sparket. Cumb 2F 103
Sparkford. Som 4B 22
Sparkwell. Devn 3B 8
Sparrow Green. Norf 4B 78
Sparrowpit. Derbs 2E 85
Sparrow's Green. E Sus 2H 27
Sparsholt. Hants 3C 24
Sparsholt. Oxon 3B 36
Spartylea. Nmbd 5B 114
Spath. Staf 2E 73
Spa, The. Down 5H 179
Spaunton. N Yor 1B 100
Spaxton. Som 3F 21
Spean Bridge. High 5E 149
Spear Hill. W Sus 4C 26
Speen. Buck 2G 37
Speen. W Ber 5C 36
Speeton. N Yor 2F 101
Speke. Mers 2G 83
Speldhurst. Kent 1G 27
Spellbrook. Herts 4E 53
Spelsbury. Oxon 3B 50
Spencers Wood. Wok 5F 37
Spennithorne. N Yor 1D 98
Spennymoor. Dur 1F 105
Spernall. Warw 4E 61
Sperrin. Strab 7C 174
Spetchley. Worc 5C 60
Spetisbury. Dors 2E 15
Spexhall. Suff 2F 67
Speybank. High 3C 150
Spey Bay. Mor 2A 160
Speybridge. High 1E 151
Speyview. Mor 4G 159
Spilsby. Linc 4C 88
Spindlestone. Nmbd 1F 121
Spinkhill. Derbs 3B 86
Spinney Hills. Leic 5D 74
Spinningdale. High 5D 164
Spital. Mers 2F 83
Spitalhill. Derbs 1F 73
Spital in the Street. Linc 1G 87
Spithurst. E Sus 4F 27
Spittal. Dum 4A 110
Spittal. E Lot 2A 130
Spittal. High 3D 168
Spittal. Nmbd 4G 131
Spittal. Pemb 2D 43
Spittalfield. Per 4A 144
Spittal of Glenmuick. Abers 5H 151
Spittal of Glenshee. Per 1A 144
Spittal-on-Rule. Bord 3H 119
Spixworth. Norf 4E 79
Splatt. Corn 4C 10
Spofforth. N Yor 4F 99
Spondon. Derb 2B 74
Spon End. W Mid 3H 61
Spooner Row. Norf 1C 66
Sporle. Norf 4H 77
Spott. E Lot 2C 130
Spratton. Nptn 3E 62
Spreakley. Surr 2G 25
Spreyton. Devn 3H 11
Spridlington. Linc 2H 87
Springburn. Glas 3H 127
Springfield. Dum 3E 113
Springfield. Fife 2F 137
Springfield. High 2A 158
Springfield. W Mid 2E 61
Springhill. Staf 5D 73
Springholm. Dum 2F 111
Springside. N Ayr 1C 116
Springthorpe. Linc 2F 87
Spring Vale. IOW 3E 16
Spring Valley. IOM 4C 108
Springwell. Tyne 4F 115
Sproatley. E Yor 1E 95
Sproston Green. Ches W 4B 84
Sprotbrough. S Yor 4F 93
Sproughton. Suff 1E 55
Sprouston. Bord 1B 120
Sprowston. Norf 4E 79
Sproxton. Leics 3F 75
Sproxton. N Yor 1A 100
Sprunston. Cumb 5E 113
Spurstow. Ches E 5H 83
Squires Gate. Bkpl 1B 90
Sraid Ruadh. Arg 4A 138
Srannda. W Isl 9C 171
Sron an t-Sithein. High 2C 140
Sronphadruig Lodge. Per 1E 142
Sruth Mor. W Isl 2E 170
Stableford. Shrp 1B 60
Stackhouse. N Yor 3H 97
Stackpole. Pemb 5D 43
Stackpole Elidor. Pemb 5D 43
Stacksford. Norf 1C 66
Stacksteads. Lanc 2G 91
Staddiscombe. Plym 3B 8
Staddlethorpe. E Yor 2B 94
Staddon. Devn 2D 10
Staden. Derbs 3E 85
Stadhampton. Oxon 2E 36
Stadhlaigearraidh. W Isl 5C 170
Stafainn. High 2D 155
Staffield. Cumb 5G 113
Staffin. High 2D 155
Stafford. Staf 3D 72
Stafford Park. Telf 5B 72
Stagden Cross. Essx 4G 53
Stagsden. Bed 1H 51
Stag's Head. Devn 4G 19
Stainburn. Cumb 2B 102
Stainburn. N Yor 5E 99
Stainby. Linc 3G 75
Staincliffe. W Yor 2C 92
Staincross. S Yor 3D 92
Staindrop. Dur 2E 105
Staines-Upon-Thames. Surr 3B 38
Stainfield. Linc .....3H 75 (nr. Bourne)
Stainfield. Linc .....3A 88 (nr. Lincoln)
Stainforth. N Yor 3H 97
Stainforth. S Yor 3G 93
Staining. Lanc 1B 90
Stainland. W Yor 3A 92
Stainsacre. N Yor 4G 107
Stainton. Cumb .....4E 113 (nr. Carlisle)
Stainton. Cumb .....1E 97 (nr. Kendal)
Stainton. Cumb .....2F 103 (nr. Penrith)
Stainton. Dur 3D 104
Stainton. Midd 3B 106
Stainton. N Yor 5E 105
Stainton. S Yor 1C 86
Stainton by Langworth. Linc 3H 87
Staintondale. N Yor 5G 107
Stainton le Vale. Linc 1A 88
Stainton with Adgarley. Cumb 2B 96
Stair. Cumb 2D 102
Stair. E Ayr 2D 116
Stairhaven. Dum 4H 109
Staithes. N Yor 3E 107
Stakeford. Nmbd 1F 115
Stake Pool. Lanc 5D 96
Stakes. Hants 2E 17
Stalbridge. Dors 1C 14
Stalbridge Weston. Dors 1C 14
Stalham. Norf 3F 79
Stalham Green. Norf 3F 79
Stalisfield Green. Kent 5D 40
Stallen. Dors 1B 14
Stallingborough. NE Lin 3F 95
Stalling Busk. N Yor 1B 98
Stallington. Staf 2D 72
Stalmine. Lanc 5C 96
Stalybridge. G Man 1D 84
Stambourne. Essx 2H 53
Stamford. Linc 5H 75
Stamford. Nmbd 3G 121
Stamford Bridge. Ches W 4G 83
Stamford Bridge. E Yor 4B 100
Stamfordham. Nmbd 2D 115
Stamperland. E Ren 4G 127
Stanah. Lanc 5C 96
Stanborough. Herts 4C 52
Stanbridge. C Beds 3H 51
Stanbridge. Dors 2F 15
Stanbury. W Yor 1A 92
Stand. N Lan 3A 128
Standburn. Falk 2C 128
Standeford. Staf 5D 72
Standen. Kent 1C 28
Standen Street. Kent 2C 28
Standerwick. Som 1D 22
Standford. Hants 3G 25
Standford Bridge. Telf 3B 72
Standingstone. Cumb 5D 112
Standish. Glos 5D 48
Standish. G Man 3D 90
Standish Lower Ground. G Man 4D 90
Standlake. Oxon 5B 50
Standon. Hants 4C 24
Standon. Herts 3D 53
Standon. Staf 2C 72
Standon Green End. Herts 4D 52
Stane. N Lan 4B 128
Stanecastle. N Ayr 1C 116
Stanfield. Norf 3B 78
Stanford. C Beds 1B 52
Stanford. Kent 2F 29
Stanford Bishop. Here 5A 60
Stanford Bridge. Worc 4B 60
Stanford Dingley. W Ber 4D 36
Stanford in the Vale. Oxon 2B 36
Stanford-le-Hope. Thur 2A 40
Stanford on Avon. Nptn 3C 62
Stanford on Soar. Notts 3C 74
Stanford on Teme. Worc 4B 60
Stanford Rivers. Essx 5F 53
Stanfree. Derbs 3B 86
Stanghow. Red C 3D 107
Stanground. Pet 1B 64
Stanhoe. Norf 2H 77
Stanhope. Dur 1C 104
Stanhope. Bord 1D 118
Stanion. Nptn 2G 63
Stanley. Derbs 1B 74
Stanley. Dur 4E 115
Stanley. Per 5A 144
Stanley. Shrp 2B 60
Stanley. Staf 5D 84
Stanley. W Yor 2D 92
Stanley Common. Derbs 1B 74
Stanley Crook. Dur 1E 105
Stanley Hill. Here 1B 48
Stanlow. Ches W 3G 83
Stanmer. Brig 5E 27
Stanmore. G Lon 1C 38
Stanmore. Hants 4C 24
Stanmore. W Ber 4C 36
Stannersburn. Nmbd 1A 114
Stanningfield. Suff 5A 66
Stannington. Nmbd 2F 115
Stannington. S Yor 2H 85
Stansbatch. Here 4F 59
Stansfield. Suff 5G 65
Stanshope. Staf 5F 85
Stanstead. Suff 1B 54
Stanstead Abbotts. Herts 4D 53
Stansted. Kent 4H 39
Stansted (London) Airport. Essx .....3F 53 & 205
Stansted Mountfitchet. Essx 3F 53
Stanthorne. Ches W 4A 84
Stanton. Derbs 4G 73
Stanton. Glos 2F 49
Stanton. Nmbd 5F 121
Stanton. Staf 1F 73
Stanton. Suff 3B 66
Stanton by Bridge. Derbs 3A 74
Stanton-by-Dale. Derbs 2B 74
Stanton Chare. Suff 3B 66
Stanton Drew. Bath 5A 34
Stanton Fitzwarren. Swin 2G 35
Stanton Harcourt. Oxon 5C 50
Stanton Hill. Notts 4B 86
Stanton in Peak. Derbs 4G 85
Stanton Lacy. Shrp 3G 59
Stanton Long. Shrp 1H 59
Stanton-on-the-Wolds. Notts 2D 74
Stanton Prior. Bath 5B 34
Stanton St Bernard. Wilts 5F 35
Stanton St John. Oxon 5D 50
Stanton St Quintin. Wilts 4E 35
Stanton Street. Suff 4B 66
Stanton under Bardon. Leics 4B 74
Stanton upon Hine Heath. Shrp 3H 71
Stanton Wick. Bath 5B 34
Stanwardine in the Fields. Shrp 3G 71
Stanwardine in the Wood. Shrp 3G 71
Stanway. Essx 3C 54
Stanway. Glos 2F 49
Stanwell. Surr 3B 38
Stanwell Moor. Surr 3B 38
Stanwick. Nptn 3G 63
Stanydale. Shet 6D 173
Staoinebrig. W Isl 5C 170
Stape. N Yor 5E 107
Stapehill. Dors 2F 15
Stapeley. Ches E 1A 72
Stapenhill. Staf 3G 73
Staple. Kent 5G 41
Staple Cross. Devn 4D 20
Staplecross. E Sus 3B 28
Staplefield. W Sus 3D 27
Staple Fitzpaine. Som 1F 13
Stapleford. Cambs 5D 64
Stapleford. Herts 4D 52
Stapleford. Leics 4F 75
Stapleford. Linc 5F 87
Stapleford. Notts 2B 74
Stapleford. Wilts 3F 23
Stapleford Abbotts. Essx 1G 39
Stapleford Tawney. Essx 1G 39
Staplegrove. Som 4F 21
Staplehay. Som 4F 21
Staple Hill. S Glo 4B 34
Staplehurst. Kent 1B 28
Staplers. IOW 4D 16
Stapleton. Bris 4B 34
Stapleton. Cumb 2G 113
Stapleton. Here 4F 59
Stapleton. Leics 1B 62
Stapleton. N Yor 3F 105
Stapleton. Shrp 5G 71
Stapleton. Som 4H 21
Stapley. Som 1E 13
Staploe. Bed 4A 64
Staplow. Here 1B 48
Star. Fife 3F 137
Star. Pemb 1G 43
Starbeck. N Yor 4F 99
Starbotton. N Yor 2B 98
Starcross. Devn 4C 12
Stareton. Warw 3H 61
Starkholmes. Derbs 5H 85
Starling. G Man 3F 91
Starling's Green. Essx 2E 53
Starston. Norf 2E 67
Start. Devn 4E 9
Startforth. Dur 3D 104
Start Hill. Essx 3F 53
Startley. Wilts 3E 35
Stathe. Som 4G 21
Stathern. Leics 2E 75
Station Town. Dur 1B 106
Staughton Green. Cambs 4A 64
Staughton Highway. Cambs 4A 64
Staunton. Glos .....3C 48 (nr. Cheltenham)
Staunton. Glos .....4A 48 (nr. Monmouth)
Staunton in the Vale. Notts 1F 75
Staunton on Arrow. Here 4F 59
Staunton on Wye. Here 1G 47
Staveley. Cumb 5F 103
Staveley. Derbs 3B 86
Staveley. N Yor 3F 99
Staveley-in-Cartmel. Cumb 1C 96
Staverton. Devn 2D 9
Staverton. Glos 3D 49
Staverton. Nptn 4C 62
Staverton. Wilts 5D 35
Stawell. Som 3G 21
Stawley. Som 4D 20
Staxigoe. High 3F 169
Staxton. N Yor 2E 101
Staylittle. Powy 1A 58
Staynall. Lanc 5C 96
Staythorpe. Notts 5E 87
Stean. N Yor 2C 98
Stearsby. N Yor 2A 100
Steart. Som 2F 21
Stebbing. Essx 3G 53
Stebbing Green. Essx 3G 53
Stedham. W Sus 4G 25
Steel. Nmbd 4C 114
Steel Cross. E Sus 2G 27
Steelend. Fife 4C 136
Steele Road. Bord 5H 119
Steel Heath. Shrp 2H 71
Steen's Bridge. Here 5H 59
Steep. Hants 4F 25
Steep Lane. W Yor 2A 92
Steeple. Dors 4E 15
Steeple. Essx 5C 54
Steeple Ashton. Wilts 1E 23
Steeple Aston. Oxon 3C 50
Steeple Barton. Oxon 3C 50
Steeple Bumpstead. Essx 1G 53
Steeple Claydon. Buck 3E 51
Steeple Gidding. Cambs 2A 64
Steeple Langford. Wilts 3F 23
Steeple Morden. Cambs 1C 52
Steeton. W Yor 5C 98
Stein. High 3B 154
Steinmanhill. Abers 4E 161
Stelling Minnis. Kent 1F 29
Stembridge. Som 4H 21
Stemster. High .....2D 169 (nr. Halkirk)
Stemster. High .....2C 168 (nr. Westfield)
Stenalees. Corn 3E 6
Stenhill. Devn 1D 12
Stenhouse. Edin 2F 129
Stenhousemuir. Falk 1B 128
Stenigot. Linc 2B 88
Stenscholl. High 2D 155
Stenso. Orkn 5C 172
Stenson. Derbs 3H 73
Stenson Fields. Derbs 2H 73
Stenton. E Lot 2C 130
Stenwith. Linc 2F 75
Steòrnabhagh. W Isl 4G 171
Stepaside. Pemb 4F 43
Stepford. Dum 1F 111
Stepney. G Lon 2E 39
Steppingley. C Beds 2A 52
Stepps. N Lan 3H 127
Sterndale Moor. Derbs 4F 85
Sternfield. Suff 4F 67
Stert. Wilts 1F 23
Stetchworth. Cambs 5F 65
Stevenage. Herts 3C 52
Stevenston. N Ayr 5D 126
Stevenstone. Devn 1F 11
Steventon. Hants 2D 24
Steventon. Oxon 2C 36
Steventon End. Cambs 1G 53
Stevington. Bed 5G 63
Stewartby. Bed 1A 52
Stewarton. Arg 4A 122
Stewarton. E Ayr 5F 127
Stewartstown. Cook 2C 178
Stewkley. Buck 3G 51
Stewkley Dean. Buck 3G 51
Stewley. Som 1G 13
Stewton. Linc 2C 88
Steyning. W Sus 4C 26
Steynton. Pemb 4D 42
Stibb. Corn 1C 10
Stibbard. Norf 3B 78
Stibb Cross. Devn 1E 11
Stibb Green. Wilts 5H 35
Stibbington. Cambs 1H 63
Stichill. Bord 1B 120
Sticker. Corn 3D 6
Stickford. Linc 5C 88
Sticklepath. Devn 3G 11
Sticklinch. Som 3A 22
Stickling Green. Essx 2E 53
Stickney. Linc 5C 88
Stiffkey. Norf 1B 78
Stifford's Bridge. Here 1C 48
Stileway. Som 2H 21
Stillingfleet. N Yor 5H 99
Stillington. N Yor 3H 99
Stillington. Stoc T 2A 106
Stilton. Cambs 2A 64
Stinchcombe. Glos 2C 34
Stinsford. Dors 3C 14
Stiperstones. Shrp 5F 71
Stirchley. Telf 5B 72
Stirchley. W Mid 2E 61
Stirling. Abers 4H 161
Stirling. Stir .....4G 135 & 202
Stirton. N Yor 4B 98
Stisted. Essx 3A 54
Stitchcombe. Wilts 5H 35
Stithians. Corn 5B 6
Stittenham. High 1A 158
Stivichall. W Mid 3H 61
Stixwould. Linc 4A 88
Stoak. Ches W 3G 83
Stobo. Bord 1D 118
Stobo Castle. Bord 1D 118
Stoborough. Dors 4E 15
Stoborough Green. Dors 4E 15
Stobs Castle. Bord 4H 119
Stobswood. Nmbd 5G 121
Stock. Essx 1A 40
Stockbridge. Hants 3B 24
Stockbridge. W Yor 5C 98
Stockbury. Kent 4C 40
Stockcross. W Ber 5C 36
Stockdalewath. Cumb 5E 113
Stocker's Head. Kent 5D 40
Stockerston. Leics 1F 63
Stock Green. Worc 5D 61
Stocking. Here 2B 48
Stockingford. Warw 1H 61
Stocking Green. Essx 2F 53
Stocking Pelham. Herts 3E 53
Stockland. Devn 2F 13
Stockland Bristol. Som 2F 21
Stockleigh English. Devn 2B 12
Stockleigh Pomeroy. Devn 2B 12
Stockley. Wilts 5F 35
Stocklinch. Som 1G 13
Stockport. G Man 2D 84
Stocksbridge. S Yor 1G 85
Stocksfield. Nmbd 3D 114
Stocks, The. Kent 3D 28
Stockstreet. Essx 3B 54
Stockton. Here 4H 59
Stockton. Norf 1F 67
Stockton. Shrp .....1B 60 (nr. Bridgnorth)
Stockton. Shrp .....5E 71 (nr. Chirbury)
Stockton. Telf 4B 72
Stockton. Warw 4B 62
Stockton. Wilts 3E 23
Stockton Brook. Staf 5D 84
Stockton Cross. Here 4H 59
Stockton Heath. Warr 2A 84
Stockton-on-Tees. Stoc T 3B 106
Stockton on Teme. Worc 4B 60
Stockton-on-the-Forest. York 4A 100
Stockwell Heath. Staf 3E 73
Stockwood. Bris 5B 34
Stock Wood. Worc 5E 61
Stodmarsh. Kent 4G 41
Stody. Norf 2C 78
Stoer. High 1E 163
Stoford. Som 1A 14
Stoford. Wilts 3F 23
Stogumber. Som 3D 20
Stogursey. Som 2F 21
Stoke. Devn 4C 18
Stoke. Hants .....1C 16 (nr. Andover)
Stoke. Hants .....2F 17 (nr. South Hayling)
Stoke. Medw 3C 40
Stoke. W Mid 3A 62
Stoke Abbott. Dors 2H 13
Stoke Albany. Nptn 2F 63
Stoke Ash. Suff 3D 66
Stoke Bardolph. Notts 1D 74
Stoke Bliss. Worc 4A 60
Stoke Bruerne. Nptn 1F 51
Stoke by Clare. Suff 1H 53
Stoke-by-Nayland. Suff 2C 54
Stoke Canon. Devn 3C 12
Stoke Charity. Hants 3C 24
Stoke Climsland. Corn 5D 10
Stoke Cross. Here 5A 60
Stoke D'Abernon. Surr 5C 38
Stoke Doyle. Nptn 2H 63
Stoke Dry. Rut 1F 63
Stoke Edith. Here 1B 48
Stoke Farthing. Wilts 4F 23
Stoke Ferry. Norf 1G 65
Stoke Fleming. Devn 4E 9
Stokeford. Dors 4D 14
Stoke Gabriel. Devn 3E 9
Stoke Gifford. S Glo 4B 34
Stoke Golding. Leics 1A 62
Stoke Goldington. Mil 1G 51
Stokeham. Notts 3E 87
Stoke Hammond. Buck 3G 51
Stoke Heath. Shrp 3A 72
Stoke Holy Cross. Norf 5E 79
Stokeinteignhead. Devn 5C 12
Stoke Lacy. Here 1B 48
Stoke Lyne. Oxon 3D 50
Stoke Mandeville. Buck 4G 51
Stokenchurch. Buck 2F 37
Stoke Newington. G Lon 2E 39
Stokenham. Devn 4E 9
Stoke on Tern. Shrp 3A 72
Stoke-on-Trent. Stoke .....1C 72 & 202
Stoke Orchard. Glos 3E 49
Stoke Pero. Som 2B 20
Stoke Poges. Buck 2A 38
Stoke Prior. Here 5H 59
Stoke Prior. Worc 4D 60
Stoke Rivers. Devn 3G 19
Stoke Rochford. Linc 3G 75
Stoke Row. Oxon 3E 37
Stoke St Gregory. Som 4G 21
Stoke St Mary. Som 4F 21
Stoke St Michael. Som 2B 22
Stoke St Milborough. Shrp 2H 59
Stokesay. Shrp 2G 59
Stokesby. Norf 4G 79
Stokesley. N Yor 4C 106
Stoke sub Hamdon. Som 1H 13
Stoke Talmage. Oxon 2E 37
Stoke Town. Stoke .....1C 72 & 202
Stoke Trister. Som 4C 22
Stoke Wake. Dors 2C 14
Stolford. Som 2F 21
Stondon Massey. Essx 5F 53
Stone. Buck 4F 51
Stone. Glos 2B 34
Stone. Kent 3G 39
Stone. Som 3A 22
Stone. Staf 2D 72
Stone. Worc 3C 60
Stoneacton. Shrp 1H 59
Stone Allerton. Som 1H 21
Ston Easton. Som 1B 22
Stonebridge. N Som 1G 21
Stonebridge. Som 2C 22
Stonebridge. W Mid 2G 61
Stone Bridge Corner. Pet 5B 76
Stonebroom. Derbs 5B 86
Stonebyres. S Lan 5B 128
Stone Chair. W Yor 2B 92
Stone Cross. E Sus 5H 27
Stone Cross. Kent 2G 27
Stone-edge-Batch. N Som 4H 33
Stoneferry. Hull 1D 94
Stonefield. Arg 5D 140
Stonefield. S Lan 4H 127
Stonegate. E Sus 3A 28
Stonegate. N Yor 4E 107
Stonegrave. N Yor 2A 100
Stonehall. Worc 1D 49
Stonehaugh. Nmbd 2A 114
Stonehaven. Abers 5F 153
Stone Heath. Staf 2D 72
Stone Hill. Kent 2E 29
Stone House. Cumb 1G 97
Stonehouse. Glos 5D 48
Stonehouse. Nmbd 4H 113
Stonehouse. S Lan 5A 128
Stone in Oxney. Kent 3D 28
Stoneleigh. Warw 3H 61
Stoneley Green. Ches E 5A 84
Stonely. Cambs 4A 64
Stonepits. Worc 5E 61
Stoner Hill. Hants 4F 25
Stonesby. Leics 3F 75
Stonesfield. Oxon 4B 50
Stones Green. Essx 3E 55
Stone Street. Kent 5G 39
Stone Street. Suff .....2C 54 (nr. Boxford)
Stone Street. Suff .....2F 67 (nr. Halesworth)
Stonethwaite. Cumb 3D 102
Stoneyburn. W Lot 3C 128
Stoney Cross. Hants 1A 16
Stoneyford. Devn 2D 12
Stoneygate. Leic 5D 74
Stoneyhills. Essx 1D 40
Stoneykirk. Dum 4F 109
Stoney Middleton. Derbs 3G 85
Stoney Stanton. Leics 1B 62
Stoney Stoke. Som 3C 22
Stoney Stratton. Som 3B 22
Stoney Stretton. Shrp 5F 71
Stoneywood. Aber 2F 153
Stonham Aspal. Suff 5D 66
Stonnall. Staf 5E 73
Stonor. Oxon 3F 37
Stonton Wyville. Leics 1E 63
Stonybreck. Shet 1B 172
Stony Cross. Devn 4F 19
Stony Cross. Here .....1C 48 (nr. Great Malvern)
Stony Cross. Here .....4H 59 (nr. Leominster)
Stonyford. Lis 2G 179
Stony Houghton. Derbs 4B 86
Stony Stratford. Mil 1F 51
Stoodleigh. Devn .....3G 19 (nr. Barnstaple)
Stoodleigh. Devn .....1C 12 (nr. Tiverton)
Stopham. W Sus 4B 26
Stopsley. Lutn 3B 52
Stoptide. Corn 1D 6
Storeton. Mers 2F 83
Stormontfield. Per 1D 136
Stornoway. W Isl 4G 171
Stornoway Airport. W Isl 4G 171
Storridge. Here 1C 48
Storrington. W Sus 4B 26
Storrs. Cumb 5E 103
Storth. Cumb 1D 97
Storwood. E Yor 5B 100
Stotfield. Mor 1G 159
Stotfold. C Beds 2C 52
Stottesdon. Shrp 2A 60
Stoughton. Leics 5D 74
Stoughton. Surr 5A 38
Stoughton. W Sus 1G 17
Stoul. High 4F 147
Stoulton. Worc 1E 49
Stourbridge. W Mid 2C 60
Stourpaine. Dors 2D 14
Stourport-on-Severn. Worc 3C 60
Stour Provost. Dors 4C 22
Stour Row. Dors 4D 22
Stourton. Staf 2C 60
Stourton. Warw 2A 50
Stourton. W Yor 1D 92
Stourton. Wilts 3C 22
Stourton Caundle. Dors 1C 14
Stove. Orkn 4F 172
Stove. Shet 9F 173
Stoven. Suff 2G 67
Stow. Linc .....2H 75 (nr. Billingborough)
Stow. Linc .....2F 87 (nr. Gainsborough)
Stow. Bord 5A 130
Stow Bardolph. Norf 5F 77
Stow Bedon. Norf 1B 66
Stowbridge. Norf 5F 77
Stow cum Quy. Cambs 4E 65
Stowe. Glos 5A 48
Stowe. Shrp 3F 59
Stowe. Staf 4F 73
Stowe-by-Chartley. Staf 3E 73
Stowell. Som 4B 22
Stowey. Bath 1A 22
Stowford. Devn .....2G 19 (nr. Combe Martin)
Stowford. Devn .....4D 12 (nr. Exmouth)
Stowford. Devn .....4E 11 (nr. Tavistock)
Stowlangtoft. Suff 4B 66
Stow Longa. Cambs 3A 64
Stow Maries. Essx 1C 40
Stowmarket. Suff 5C 66
Stow-on-the-Wold. Glos 3G 49
Stowting. Kent 1F 29
Stowupland. Suff 5C 66
Straad. Arg 3B 126
Strabane. Strab 3F 176
Strachan. Abers 4D 152
Stradbroke. Suff 3E 67
Stradbrook. Wilts 1E 23
Stradishall. Suff 5G 65
Stradsett. Norf 5F 77
Stragglethorpe. Linc 5G 87
Stragglethorpe. Notts 2D 74
Straid. Bmna 7G 175
Straid. Newt 7K 175
Straid. S Ayr 5A 116
Straight Soley. Wilts 4B 36
Straiton. Edin 3F 129
Straiton. S Ayr 4C 116
Straloch. Per 2H 143
Stramshall. Staf 2E 73
Strang. IOM 4C 108
Strangford. Down 5K 179
Strangford. Here 3A 48
Stranocum. Bmny 3G 175
Stranraer. Dum 3F 109
Strata Florida. Cdgn 4G 57
Stratfield Mortimer. W Ber 5E 37
Stratfield Saye. Hants 5E 37
Stratfield Turgis. Hants 1E 25
Stratford. Glos 2D 49
Stratford. G Lon 2E 39
Stratford St Andrew. Suff 4F 67
Stratford St Mary. Suff 2D 54
Stratford sub Castle. Wilts 3G 23
Stratford Tony. Wilts 4F 23
Stratford-upon-Avon. Warw .....5G 61 & 202
Strath. High .....1G 155 (nr. Gairloch)
Strath. High .....3E 169 (nr. Wick)
Strathan. High .....4B 148 (nr. Fort William)
Strathan. High .....1E 163 (nr. Lochinver)
Strathan. High .....2F 167 (nr. Tongue)
Strathan Skerray. High 2G 167
Strathaven. S Lan 5A 128
Strathblane. Stir 2G 127
Strathcanaird. High 3F 163
Strathcarron. High 4B 156
Strathcoil. Arg 5A 140
Strathdon. Abers 2A 152
Strathkinness. Fife 2G 137
Strathmashie House. High 4H 149
Strathmiglo. Fife 2E 136
Strathmore Lodge. High 4D 168
Strathpeffer. High 3G 157
Strathrannoch. High 1F 157
Strathtay. Per 3G 143
Strathvaich Lodge. High 1F 157
Strathwhillan. N Ayr 2E 123
Strathy. High .....1A 158 (nr. Invergordon)
Strathy. High .....2A 168 (nr. Melvich)
Strathyre. Stir 2E 135
Stratton. Corn 2C 10
Stratton. Dors 3B 14
Stratton. Glos 5F 49
Stratton Audley. Oxon 3E 50
Stratton-on-the-Fosse. Som 1B 22
Stratton St Margaret. Swin 3G 35
Stratton St Michael. Norf 1E 66
Stratton Strawless. Norf 3E 78
Stravithie. Fife 2H 137
Straw. Mag 7D 174
Stream. Som 3D 20
Streat. E Sus 4E 27
Streatham. G Lon 3D 39
Streatley. C Beds 3A 52
Streatley. W Ber 3D 36
Street. Corn 3C 10
Street. Lanc 4E 97
Street. N Yor 4E 107
Street. Som .....2G 13 (nr. Chard)
Street. Som .....3H 21 (nr. Glastonbury)
Street Ash. Som 1F 13
Street Dinas. Shrp 2F 71
Street End. Kent 5F 41
Street End. W Sus 3G 17
Street Gate. Tyne 4F 115
Streethay. Staf 4F 73
Streethouse. W Yor 3D 93
Streetlam. N Yor 5A 106
Street Lane. Derbs 1A 74
Streetly. W Mid 1E 61
Streetly End. Cambs 1G 53
Street on the Fosse. Som 3B 22
Strefford. Shrp 2G 59
Strelley. Notts 1C 74
Strensall. York 3A 100
Strensall Camp. York 4A 100
Stretcholt. Som 2F 21
Strete. Devn 4E 9
Stretford. G Man 1C 84
Stretford. Here 5H 59
Strethall. Essx 2E 53
Stretham. Cambs 3E 65
Stretton. Ches W 5G 83
Stretton. Derbs 4A 86
Stretton. Rut 4G 75
Stretton. Staf .....4C 72 (nr. Brewood)
Stretton. Staf .....3G 73 (nr. Burton upon Trent)
Stretton. Warr 2A 84
Stretton en le Field. Leics 4H 73
Stretton Grandison. Here 1B 48
Stretton Heath. Shrp 4F 71
Stretton-on-Dunsmore. Warw 3B 62
Stretton-on-Fosse. Warw 2H 49
Stretton Sugwas. Here 1H 47
Stretton under Fosse. Warw 2B 62
Stretton Westwood. Shrp 1H 59
Strichen. Abers 3G 161
Strines. G Man 2D 84
Stringston. Som 2E 21
Strixton. Nptn 4G 63
Stroanfreggan. Dum 5F 117
Stroat. Glos 2A 34
Stromeferry. High 5A 156
Stromemore. High 5A 156
Stromness. Orkn 7B 172
Stronachie. Per 3C 136
Stronachlachar. Stir 2D 134
Stronchreggan. High 1E 141
Strone. Arg 1C 126
Strone. High .....1H 149 (nr. Drumnadrochit)
Strone. High .....3B 150 (nr. Kingussie)
Stronenaba. High 5E 148
Stronganess. Shet 1G 173
Stronmilchan. Arg 1A 134
Stronsay Airport. Orkn 5F 172
Strontian. High 2C 140
Strood. Kent 2C 28
Strood. Medw 4B 40
Strood Green. Surr 1D 26
Strood Green. W Sus .....3B 26 (nr. Billingshurst)
Strood Green. W Sus .....2C 26 (nr. Horsham)
Strothers Dale. Nmbd 4C 114
Stroud. Glos 5D 48
Stroud. Hants 4F 25
Stroud Green. Essx 1C 40
Stroxton. Linc 2G 75
Struan. High 5C 154
Struan. Per 2F 143
Struanmore. High 5C 154
Strubby. Linc 2D 88
Strugg's Hill. Linc 2B 76
Strumpshaw. Norf 5F 79
Strutherhill. S Lan 4A 128
Struy. High 5F 157
Stryd. IOA 2B 80
Stryt-issa. Wrex 1E 71
Stuartfield. Abers 4G 161
Stubbington. Hants 2D 16
Stubbins. Lanc 3F 91
Stubble Green. Cumb 5B 102
Stubb's Cross. Kent 2D 28
Stubbs Green. Norf 1F 67
Stubhampton. Dors 1E 15
Stubton. Linc 1F 75
Stubwood. Staf 2E 73
Stuckton. Hants 1G 15
Studham. C Beds 4A 52
Studland. Dors 4F 15
Studley. Warw 4E 61
Studley. Wilts 4E 35
Studley Roger. N Yor 2E 99
Stuntney. Cambs 3E 65
Stunts Green. E Sus 4H 27
Sturbridge. Staf 2C 72
Sturgate. Linc 2F 87
Sturmer. Essx 1G 53
Sturminster Marshall. Dors 2E 15
Sturminster Newton. Dors 1C 14
Sturry. Kent 4F 41
Sturton. N Lin 4C 94
Sturton by Stow. Linc 2F 87
Sturton le Steeple. Notts 2E 87
Stuston. Suff 3D 66
Stutton. N Yor 5G 99
Stutton. Suff 2E 55
Styal. Ches E 2C 84
Stydd. Lanc 1E 91
Styrrup. Notts 1D 86
Suainebost. W Isl 1H 171
Suardail. W Isl 4G 171
Succoth. Abers 5B 160
Succoth. Arg 3B 134
Suckley. Worc 5B 60
Suckley Knowl. Worc 5B 60
Sudborough. Nptn 2G 63
Sudbourne. Suff 5G 67
Sudbrook. Linc 1G 75
Sudbrook. Mon 3A 34
Sudbrooke. Linc 3H 87
Sudbury. Derbs 2F 73
Sudbury. Suff 1B 54
Sudgrove. Glos 5E 49
Suffield. Norf 2E 79
Suffield. N Yor 5G 107
Sugnall. Staf 2B 72
Sugwas Pool. Here 1H 47
Suisnish. High 5E 155
Sulaisiadar. W Isl 4H 171
Sùlaisiadar Mòr. High 4D 155
Sulby. IOM 2C 108
Sulgrave. Nptn 1D 50
Sulham. W Ber 4E 37
Sulhamstead. W Ber 5E 37
Sullington. W Sus 4B 26
Sullom. Shet 4E 173
Sully. V Glam 5E 33
Sumburgh. Shet 10F 173
Sumburgh Airport. Shet 10E 173
Summer Bridge. N Yor 3E 98
Summercourt. Corn 3C 6
Summergangs. Hull 1E 95
Summerhill. Aber 3G 153
Summerhill. Pemb 4F 43
Summer Hill. W Mid 1D 60
Summerhouse. Darl 3F 105
Summersdale. W Sus 2G 17
Summerseat. G Man 3F 91
Summit. G Man 3H 91
Sunbury. Surr 4C 38
Sunderland. Cumb 1C 102
Sunderland. Lanc 4D 96
Sunderland. Tyne .....4G 115 & 202
Sunderland Bridge. Dur 1F 105
Sundon Park. Lutn 3A 52
Sundridge. Kent 5F 39
Sunk Island. E Yor 3F 95
Sunningdale. Wind 4A 38
Sunninghill. Wind 4A 38
Sunningwell. Oxon 5C 50
Sunniside. Dur 1E 105
Sunniside. Tyne 4F 115
Sunny Bank. Cumb 5D 102
Sunny Hill. Derb 2H 73
Sunnyhurst. Bkbn 2E 91
Sunnylaw. Stir 4G 135
Sunnymead. Oxon 5D 50
Sunnyside. S Yor 1B 86
Sunnyside. W Sus 2E 27
Sunton. Wilts 1H 23
Surbiton. G Lon 4C 38
Surby. IOM 4B 108
Surfleet. Linc 3B 76
Surfleet Seas End. Linc 3B 76
Surlingham. Norf 5F 79
Surrex. Essx 3B 54
Sustead. Norf 2D 78
Susworth. Linc 4B 94
Sutcombe. Devn 1D 10
Suton. Norf 1C 66
Sutors of Cromarty. High 2C 158
Sutterby. Linc 3C 88
Sutterton. Linc 2B 76
Sutterton Dowdyke. Linc 2B 76
Sutton. Buck 3B 38
Sutton. Cambs 3D 64
Sutton. C Beds 1C 52
Sutton. E Sus 5F 27
Sutton. G Lon 4D 38
Sutton. Kent 1H 29
Sutton. Norf 3F 79
Sutton. Notts 2E 75
Sutton. Oxon 5C 50
Sutton. Pemb 3D 42
Sutton. Pet 1H 63
Sutton. Shrp .....2B 60 (nr. Bridgnorth)
Sutton. Shrp .....2A 72 (nr. Market Drayton)
Sutton. Shrp .....3F 71 (nr. Oswestry)
Sutton. Shrp .....4H 71 (nr. Shrewsbury)

Sutton—Trealaw

Sutton. Som 3B 22
Sutton. S Yor 3F 93
Sutton. Staf 3B 72
Sutton. Suff 1G 55
Sutton. W Sus 4A 26
Sutton. Worc 4A 60
Sutton Abinger. Surr 1C 26
Sutton at Hone. Kent 4G 39
Sutton Bassett. Nptn 1E 63
Sutton Benger. Wilts 4E 35
Sutton Bingham. Som 1A 14
Sutton Bonington. Notts 3C 74
Sutton Bridge. Linc 3D 76
Sutton Cheney. Leics 5B 74
Sutton Coldfield. W Mid 1F 61
Sutton Corner. Linc 3D 76
Sutton Courtenay. Oxon 2D 36
Sutton Crosses. Linc 3D 76
Sutton cum Lound. Notts 2D 86
Sutton Gault. Cambs 3D 64
Sutton Grange. N Yor 2E 99
Sutton Green. Surr 5B 38
Sutton Howgrave. N Yor 2F 99
Sutton in Ashfield. Notts 5B 86
Sutton-in-Craven. N Yor 5C 98
Sutton Ings. Hull 1E 94
Sutton in the Elms. Leics 1C 62
Sutton Lane Ends. Ches E 3D 84
Sutton Leach. Mers 1H 83
Sutton Maddock. Shrp 5B 72
Sutton Mallet. Som 3G 21
Sutton Mandeville. Wilts 4E 23
Sutton Montis. Som 4B 22
Sutton-on-Hull. Hull 1E 94
Sutton on Sea. Linc 2E 89
Sutton-on-the-Forest. N Yor 3H 99
Sutton on the Hill. Derbs 2G 73
Sutton on Trent. Notts 4E 87
Sutton Poyntz. Dors 4C 14
Sutton St Edmund. Linc 4C 76
Sutton St Edmund's Common. Linc 5C 76
Sutton St James. Linc 4C 76
Sutton St Michael. Here 1A 48
Sutton St Nicholas. Here 1A 48
Sutton Scarsdale. Derbs 4B 86
Sutton Scotney. Hants 3C 24
Sutton-under-Brailes. Warw 2B 50
Sutton-under-Whitestonecliffe. N Yor 1G 99
Sutton upon Derwent. E Yor 5B 100
Sutton Valence. Kent 1C 28
Sutton Veny. Wilts 2E 23
Sutton Waldron. Dors 1D 14
Sutton Weaver. Ches W 3H 83
Swaby. Linc 3C 88
Swadlincote. Derbs 4G 73
Swaffham. Norf 5H 77
Swaffham Bulbeck. Cambs 4E 65
Swaffham Prior. Cambs 4E 65
Swafield. Norf 2E 79
Swainby. N Yor 4B 106
Swainshill. Here 1H 47
Swainsthorpe. Norf 5E 78
Swainswick. Bath 5C 34
Swalcliffe. Oxon 2B 50
Swalecliffe. Kent 4F 41
Swallow. Linc 4E 95
Swallow Beck. Linc 4G 87
Swallowcliffe. Wilts 4E 23
Swallowfield. Wok 5F 37
Swallownest. S Yor 2B 86
Swampton. Hants 1C 24
Swanage. Dors 5F 15
Swanbister. Orkn 7C 172
Swanbourne. Buck 3G 51
Swanbridge. V Glam 5E 33
Swan Green. Ches W 3B 84
Swanland. E Yor 2C 94
Swanley. Kent 4G 39
Swanmore. Hants 1D 16
Swannington. Leics 4B 74
Swannington. Norf 4D 78
Swanpool. Linc 3G 87
Swanscombe. Kent 3G 39
Swansea. Swan 3F 31 & 203
Swansmoor. Staf 3E 73
Swan Street. Essx 3B 54
Swanton Abbott. Norf 3E 79
Swanton Morley. Norf 4C 78
Swanton Novers. Norf 2C 78
Swanton Street. Kent 5C 40
Swanwick. Derbs 5B 86
Swanwick. Hants 2D 16
Swanwick Green. Ches E 1H 71
Swarby. Linc 1H 75
Swardeston. Norf 5E 78
Swarister. Shet 3G 173
Swarkestone. Derbs 3A 74
Swarland. Nmbd 4F 121
Swarraton. Hants 3D 24
Swartha. W Yor 5C 98
Swarthmoor. Cumb 2B 96
Swaton. Linc 2A 76
Swatragh. Mag 6E 174
Swavesey. Cambs 4C 64
Sway. Hants 3A 16
Swayfield. Linc 3G 75
Swaythling. Sotn 1C 16
Sweet Green. Worc 4A 60
Sweetham. Devn 3B 12
Sweetholme. Cumb 3G 103
Sweets. Corn 3B 10
Sweetshouse. Corn 2E 7
Swefling. Suff 4F 67
Swell. Som 4G 21
Swepstone. Leics 4A 74
Swerford. Oxon 2B 50
Swettenham. Ches E 4C 84
Swetton. N Yor 2D 98
Swffyrd. Cphy 2F 33
Swiftsden. E Sus 3B 28
Swilland. Suff 5D 66
Swillington. W Yor 1D 93
Swimbridge. Devn 4G 19
Swimbridge Newland. Devn 3G 19
Swinbrook. Oxon 4A 50
Swincliffe. N Yor 4E 99
Swincliffe. W Yor 2C 92
Swinderby. Linc 4F 87
Swindon. Glos 3E 49
Swindon. Nmbd 5D 121
Swindon. Staf 1C 60
Swindon. Swin 3G 35 & 203
Swine. E Yor 1E 95
Swinefleet. E Yor 2A 94
Swineford. S Glo 5B 34
Swineshead. Bed 4H 63
Swineshead. Linc 1B 76
Swineshead Bridge. Linc 1B 76
Swiney. High 5E 169
Swinford. Leics 3C 62
Swinford. Oxon 5C 50
Swingate. Notts 1C 74
Swingbrow. Cambs 2C 64
Swingfield Minnis. Kent 1G 29
Swingfield Street. Kent 1G 29
Swingleton Green. Suff 1C 54
Swinhill. S Lan 5A 128
Swinhoe. Nmbd 2G 121
Swinhope. Linc 1B 88
Swinister. Shet 3E 173
Swinithwaite. N Yor 1C 98
Swinmore Common. Here 1B 48
Swinscoe. Staf 1F 73
Swinside Hall. Bord 3B 120
Swinstead. Linc 3H 75
Swinton. G Man 4F 91
Swinton. N Yor 2B 100 (nr. Malton)
Swinton. N Yor 2E 98 (nr. Masham)
Swinton. Bord 5E 131
Swinton. S Yor 1B 86
Swithland. Leics 4C 74
Swordale. High 2H 157
Swordly. High 2H 167
Sworton Heath. Ches E 2A 84
Swyddffynnon. Cdgn 4F 57
Swyffrd. Cphy 2F 33
Swynnerton. Staf 2C 72
Swyre. Dors 4A 14
Sycharth. Powy 3E 70
Sychdyn. Flin 4E 83
Sychnant. Powy 3B 58
Sychtyn. Powy 5B 70
Syde. Glos 4E 49
Sydenham. G Lon 3E 39
Sydenham. Oxon 5F 51
Sydenham. Som 3G 21
Sydenham Damerel. Devn 5E 11
Syderstone. Norf 2H 77
Sydling St Nicholas. Dors 3B 14
Sydmonton. Hants 1C 24
Sydney. Ches E 5B 84
Syerston. Notts 1E 75
Syke. G Man 3G 91
Sykehouse. S Yor 3G 93
Sykes. Lanc 4F 97
Syleham. Suff 3E 66
Sylen. Carm 5F 45
Sylfaen. Powy 5D 70
Symbister. Shet 5G 173
Symington. S Ayr 1C 116
Symington. S Lan 1B 118
Symondsbury. Dors 3H 13
Symonds Yat. Here 4A 48
Synod Inn. Cdgn 5D 56
Syre. High 4G 167
Syreford. Glos 3F 49
Syresham. Nptn 1E 51
Syston. Leics 4D 74
Syston. Linc 1G 75
Sytchampton. Worc 4C 60
Sywell. Nptn 4F 63

T

Tabost. W Isl 6F 171 (nr. Cearsiadar)
Tabost. W Isl 1H 171 (nr. Suainebost)
Tachbrook Mallory. Warw 4H 61
Tackley. Oxon 3C 50
Tacleit. W Isl 4D 171
Tacolneston. Norf 1D 66
Tadcaster. N Yor 5G 99
Taddington. Derbs 3F 85
Taddington. Glos 2F 49
Taddiport. Devn 1E 11
Tadley. Hants 5E 36
Tadlow. Cambs 1C 52
Tadmarton. Oxon 2B 50
Tadwick. Bath 4C 34
Tadworth. Surr 5D 38
Tafarnaubach. Blae 4E 46
Tafarn-y-bwlch. Pemb 1E 43
Tafarn-y-Gelyn. Den 4D 82
Taff's Well. Rhon 3E 33
Tafolwern. Powy 5A 70
Taibach. Neat 3A 32
Tai-bach. Powy 3D 70
Taigh a Ghearraidh. W Isl 1C 170
Taigh Bhuirgh. W Isl 8C 171
Tain. High 5E 165 (nr. Invergordon)
Tain. High 2E 169 (nr. Thurso)
Tai-Nant. Wrex 1E 71
Tai'n Lon. Gwyn 5D 80
Tairbeart. W Isl 8D 171
Tairgwaith. Neat 4H 45
Takeley. Essx 3F 53
Takeley Street. Essx 3F 53
Talachddu. Powy 2D 46
Talacre. Flin 2D 82
Talardd. Gwyn 3A 70
Talaton. Devn 3D 12
Talbenny. Pemb 3C 42
Talbot Green. Rhon 3D 32
Taleford. Devn 3D 12
Talerddig. Powy 5B 70
Talgarreg. Cdgn 5D 56
Talgarth. Powy 2E 47
Talisker. High 5C 154
Talke. Staf 5C 84
Talkin. Cumb 4G 113
Talladale. High 1B 156
Talla Linnfoots. Bord 2D 118
Tallaminnock. S Ayr 5D 116
Tallarn Green. Wrex 1G 71
Tallentire. Cumb 1C 102
Talley. Carm 2G 45
Tallington. Linc 5H 75
Talmine. High 2F 167
Talog. Carm 2H 43
Talsarn. Carm 3A 46
Talsarn. Cdgn 5E 57
Talsarnau. Gwyn 2F 69
Talskiddy. Corn 2D 6
Talwrn. IOA 3D 81
Talwrn. Wrex 1E 71
Tal-y-bont. Cdgn 2F 57
Tal-y-Bont. Cnwy 4G 81
Tal-y-bont. Gwyn 3F 81 (nr. Bangor)
Tal-y-bont. Gwyn 3E 69 (nr. Barmouth)
Talybont-on-Usk. Powy 3E 46
Tal-y-cafn. Cnwy 3G 81
Tal-y-coed. Mon 4H 47
Tal-y-llyn. Gwyn 5G 69
Talyllyn. Powy 3E 46
Talysarn. Gwyn 5D 81
Tal-y-waenydd. Gwyn 1F 69
Talywain. Torf 5F 47
Talywern. Powy 5H 69
Tamerton Foliot. Plym 2A 8
Tamlaght. Ferm 8E 176
Tamlaght O'Crilly. Mag 6F 174
Tamnamore. Dngn 3C 178
Tamworth. Staf 5G 73
Tamworth Green. Linc 1C 76
Tandlehill. Ren 3F 127
Tandragee. Arm 5E 178
Tandridge. Surr 5E 39
Tanerdy. Carm 3E 45
Tanfield. Dur 4E 115
Tanfield Lea. Dur 4E 115
Tangasdale. W Isl 8B 170
Tang Hall. York 4A 100
Tangiers. Pemb 3D 42
Tangley. Hants 1B 24
Tangmere. W Sus 5A 26
Tangwick. Shet 4D 173
Tankerness. Orkn 7E 172
Tankersley. S Yor 1H 85
Tankerton. Kent 4F 41
Tan-lan. Cnwy 4G 81
Tan-lan. Gwyn 1F 69
Tannach. High 4F 169
Tannadice. Ang 3D 145
Tanner's Green. Worc 3E 61
Tannington. Suff 4E 67
Tannochside. N Lan 3A 128
Tan Office Green. Suff 5G 65
Tansley. Derbs 5H 85
Tansley Knoll. Derbs 4H 85
Tansor. Nptn 1H 63
Tantobie. Dur 4E 115
Tanton. N Yor 3C 106
Tanvats. Linc 4A 88
Tanworth-in-Arden. Warw 3F 61
Tan-y-bwlch. Gwyn 1F 69
Tan-y-fron. Cnwy 4B 82
Tanyfron. Wrex 5E 83
Tan-y-goes. Cdgn 1C 44
Tanygrisiau. Gwyn 1F 69
Tan-y-pistyll. Powy 3C 70
Tan-yr-allt. Den 2C 82
Taobh a Chaolais. W Isl 7C 170
Taobh a Deas Loch Aineort. W Isl 6C 170
Taobh a Ghlinne. W Isl 6F 171
Taobh a Tuath Loch Aineort. W Isl 6C 170
Taplow. Buck 2A 38
Tapton. Derbs 3A 86
Tarbert. Arg 1E 125 (on Jura)
Tarbert. Arg 3G 125 (on Kintyre)
Tarbert. W Isl 8D 171
Tarbet. Arg 3C 134
Tarbet. High 4F 147 (nr. Mallaig)
Tarbet. High 4B 166 (nr. Scourie)
Tarbock Green. Mers 2G 83
Tarbolton. S Ayr 2D 116
Tarbrax. S Lan 4D 128
Tardebigge. Worc 4E 61
Tarfside. Ang 1D 145
Tarland. Abers 3B 152
Tarleton. Lanc 2C 90
Tarlogie. High 5E 165
Tarlscough. Lanc 3C 90
Tarlton. Glos 2E 35
Tarnbrook. Lanc 4E 97
Tarnock. Som 1G 21
Tarns. Cumb 5C 112
Tarporley. Ches W 4H 83
Tarpots. Essx 2B 40
Tarr. Som 3E 20
Tarrant Crawford. Dors 2E 15
Tarrant Gunville. Dors 1E 15
Tarrant Hinton. Dors 1E 15
Tarrant Keyneston. Dors 2E 15
Tarrant Launceston. Dors 2E 15
Tarrant Monkton. Dors 2E 15
Tarrant Rawston. Dors 2E 15
Tarrant Rushton. Dors 2E 15
Tarrel. High 5F 165
Tarring Neville. E Sus 5F 27
Tarrington. Here 1B 48
Tarsappie. Per 1D 136
Tarscabhaig. High 3D 147
Tarskavaig. High 3D 147
Tarves. Abers 5F 161
Tarvie. High 3G 157
Tarvin. Ches W 4G 83
Tasburgh. Norf 1E 66
Tasley. Shrp 1A 60
Tassagh. Arm 6C 178
Taston. Oxon 3B 50
Tatenhill. Staf 3G 73
Tathall End. Mil 1G 51
Tatham. Lanc 3F 97
Tathwell. Linc 2C 88
Tatling End. Buck 2B 38
Tatsfield. Surr 5F 39
Tattenhall. Ches W 5G 83
Tatterford. Norf 3A 78
Tattersett. Norf 2H 77
Tattershall. Linc 5B 88
Tattershall Bridge. Linc 5A 88
Tattershall Thorpe. Linc 5B 88
Tattingstone. Suff 2E 55
Tattingstone White Horse. Suff 2E 55
Tattle Bank. Warw 4F 61
Tatworth. Som 2G 13
Taunton. Som 4F 21 & 203
Taverham. Norf 4D 78
Taverners Green. Essx 4F 53
Tavernspite. Pemb 3F 43
Tavistock. Devn 5E 11
Tavool House. Arg 1B 132
Taw Green. Devn 3G 11
Tawstock. Devn 4F 19
Taxal. Derbs 2E 85
Tayinloan. Arg 5E 125
Taynish. Arg 1F 125
Taynton. Glos 3C 48
Taynton. Oxon 4H 49
Taynuilt. Arg 5E 141
Tayport. Fife 1G 137
Tay Road Bridge. Fife 1G 137
Tayvallich. Arg 1F 125
Tealby. Linc 1A 88
Tealing. Ang 5D 144
Teams. Tyne 3F 115
Teangue. High 3E 147
Teanna Machair. W Isl 2C 170
Tebay. Cumb 4H 103
Tebworth. C Beds 3H 51
Tedburn St Mary. Devn 3B 12
Teddington. Glos 2E 49
Teddington. G Lon 3C 38
Tedsmore. Shrp 3F 71
Tedstone Delamere. Here 5A 60
Tedstone Wafer. Here 5A 60
Teemore. Ferm 7J 177
Teesport. Red C 2C 106
Teesside. Stoc T 2C 106
Teeton. Nptn 3D 62
Teffont Evias. Wilts 3E 23
Teffont Magna. Wilts 3E 23
Tegryn. Pemb 1G 43
Teigh. Rut 4F 75
Teigncombe. Devn 4G 11
Teigngrace. Devn 5B 12
Teignmouth. Devn 5C 12
Telford. Telf 4A 72
Telham. E Sus 4B 28
Tellisford. Som 1D 22
Telscombe. E Sus 5F 27
Telscombe Cliffs. E Sus 5E 27
Tempar. Per 3D 142
Templand. Dum 1B 112
Temple. Corn 5B 10
Temple. Glas 3G 127
Temple. Midl 4G 129
Temple Balsall. W Mid 3G 61
Temple Bar. Carm 4F 45
Temple Bar. Cdgn 5E 57
Temple Cloud. Bath 1B 22
Templecombe. Som 4C 22
Temple Ewell. Kent 1G 29
Temple Grafton. Warw 5F 61
Temple Guiting. Glos 3F 49
Templehall. Fife 4E 137
Temple Hirst. N Yor 2G 93
Temple Normanton. Derbs 4B 86
Templepatrick. Ant 8J 175
Temple Sowerby. Cumb 2H 103
Templeton. Devn 1B 12
Templeton. Pemb 3F 43
Templeton. W Ber 5B 36
Templetown. Dur 5E 115
Tempo. Ferm 8F 176
Tempsford. C Beds 5A 64
Tenandry. Per 2G 143
Tenbury Wells. Worc 4H 59
Tenby. Pemb 4F 43
Tendring. Essx 3E 55
Tendring Green. Essx 3E 55
Tenga. Arg 4G 139
Ten Mile Bank. Norf 1F 65
Tenterden. Kent 2C 28
Terfyn. Cnwy 3B 82
Terhill. Som 3E 21
Terling. Essx 4A 54
Termon Rock. Omag 2A 178
Ternhill. Shrp 2A 72
Terregles. Dum 2G 111
Terrick. Buck 5G 51
Terrington. N Yor 2A 100
Terrington St Clement. Norf 3E 77
Terrington St John. Norf 4E 77
Terry's Green. Warw 3F 61
Teston. Kent 5B 40
Testwood. Hants 1B 16
Tetbury. Glos 2D 35
Tetbury Upton. Glos 2D 35
Tetchill. Shrp 2F 71
Tetcott. Devn 3D 10
Tetford. Linc 3C 88
Tetney. Linc 4G 95
Tetney Lock. Linc 4G 95
Tetsworth. Oxon 5E 51
Tettenhall. W Mid 1C 60
Teversal. Notts 4B 86
Teversham. Cambs 5D 65
Teviothead. Bord 4G 119
Tewel. Abers 5F 153
Tewin. Herts 4C 52
Tewkesbury. Glos 2D 49
Teynham. Kent 4D 40
Teynham Street. Kent 4D 40
Thackthwaite. Cumb 2F 103
Thakeham. W Sus 4C 26
Thame. Oxon 5F 51
Thames Ditton. Surr 4C 38
Thames Haven. Thur 2B 40
Thamesmead. G Lon 2F 39
Thamesport. Medw 3C 40
Thanington Without. Kent 5F 41
Thankerton. S Lan 1B 118
Tharston. Norf 1D 66
Thatcham. W Ber 5D 36
Thatto Heath. Mers 1H 83
Thaxted. Essx 2G 53
Theakston. N Yor 1F 99
Thealby. N Lin 3B 94
Theale. Som 2H 21
Theale. W Ber 4E 37
Thearne. E Yor 1D 94
Theberton. Suff 4G 67
Theddingworth. Leics 2D 62
Theddlethorpe All Saints. Linc 2D 88
Theddlethorpe St Helen. Linc 2D 89
Thelbridge Barton. Devn 1A 12
Thelnetham. Suff 3C 66
Thelveton. Norf 2D 66
Thelwall. Warr 2A 84
Themelthorpe. Norf 3C 78
Thenford. Nptn 1D 50
Therfield. Herts 2D 52
Thetford. Linc 4A 76
Thetford. Norf 2A 66
Thethwaite. Cumb 5E 113
Theydon Bois. Essx 1F 39
Thick Hollins. W Yor 3B 92
Thickwood. Wilts 4D 34
Thimbleby. Linc 3B 88
Thimbleby. N Yor 5B 106
Thingwall. Mers 2E 83
Thirlby. N Yor 1G 99
Thirlestane. Bord 5B 130
Thirn. N Yor 1E 98
Thirsk. N Yor 1G 99
Thirtleby. E Yor 1E 95
Thistleton. Lanc 1C 90
Thistleton. Rut 4G 75
Thistley Green. Suff 3F 65
Thixendale. N Yor 3C 100
Thockrington. Nmbd 2C 114
Tholomas Drove. Cambs 5D 76
Tholthorpe. N Yor 3G 99
Thomas Chapel. Pemb 4F 43
Thomas Close. Cumb 5F 113
Thomastown. Abers 4E 160
Thomastown. Rhon 3D 32
Thompson. Norf 1B 66
Thomshill. Mor 3G 159
Thong. Kent 3A 40
Thongsbridge. W Yor 4B 92
Thoralby. N Yor 1C 98
Thoresby. Notts 3D 86
Thoresway. Linc 1A 88
Thorganby. Linc 1B 88
Thorganby. N Yor 5A 100
Thorgill. N Yor 5E 107
Thorington. Suff 3G 67
Thorington Street. Suff 2D 54
Thorlby. N Yor 4B 98
Thorley. Herts 4E 53
Thorley Street. Herts 4E 53
Thorley Street. IOW 4B 16
Thormanby. N Yor 2G 99
Thorn. Powy 4E 59
Thornaby-on-Tees. Stoc T 3B 106
Thornage. Norf 2C 78
Thornborough. Buck 2F 51
Thornborough. N Yor 2E 99
Thornbury. Devn 2E 11
Thornbury. Here 5A 60
Thornbury. S Glo 3B 34
Thornby. Cumb 4D 112
Thornby. Nptn 3D 62
Thorncliffe. Staf 5E 85
Thorncombe. Dors 2G 13
Thorncombe Street. Surr 1A 26
Thorncote Green. C Beds 1B 52
Thorndon. Suff 4D 66
Thorndon Cross. Devn 3F 11
Thorne. S Yor 3G 93
Thornehillhead. Devn 1E 11
Thorner. W Yor 5F 99
Thorne St Margaret. Som 4D 20
Thorney. Notts 3F 87
Thorney. Pet 5B 76
Thorney. Som 4H 21
Thorney Hill. Hants 3G 15
Thorney Toll. Cambs 5C 76
Thornfalcon. Som 4F 21
Thornford. Dors 1B 14
Thorngrafton. Nmbd 3A 114
Thorngrove. Som 3G 21
Thorngumbald. E Yor 2F 95
Thornham. Norf 1G 77
Thornham Magna. Suff 3D 66
Thornham Parva. Suff 3D 66
Thornhaugh. Pet 5H 75
Thornhill. Cphy 3E 33
Thornhill. Cumb 4B 102
Thornhill. Derbs 2G 85
Thornhill. Dum 5A 118
Thornhill. Sotn 1C 16
Thornhill. Stir 4F 135
Thornhill. W Yor 3C 92
Thornhill Lees. W Yor 3C 92
Thornhills. W Yor 2B 92
Thornholme. E Yor 3F 101
Thornicombe. Dors 2D 14
Thornington. Nmbd 1C 120
Thornley. Dur 1A 106 (nr. Durham)
Thornley. Dur 1E 105 (nr. Tow Law)
Thornley Gate. Nmbd 4B 114
Thornliebank. E Ren 4G 127
Thornroan. Abers 5F 161
Thorns. Suff 5G 65
Thornsett. Derbs 2E 85
Thornthwaite. Cumb 2D 102
Thornthwaite. N Yor 4D 98
Thornton. Ang 4C 144
Thornton. Buck 2F 51
Thornton. E Yor 5B 100
Thornton. Fife 4E 137
Thornton. Lanc 5C 96
Thornton. Leics 5B 74
Thornton. Linc 4B 88
Thornton. Mers 4B 90
Thornton. Midd 3B 106
Thornton. Nmbd 5F 131
Thornton. Pemb 4D 42
Thornton. W Yor 1A 92
Thornton Curtis. N Lin 3D 94
Thorntonhall. S Lan 4G 127
Thornton Heath. G Lon 4E 39
Thornton Hough. Mers 2F 83
Thornton in Craven. N Yor 5B 98
Thornton in Lonsdale. N Yor 2F 97
Thornton-le-Beans. N Yor 5A 106
Thornton-le-Clay. N Yor 3A 100
Thornton-le-Dale. N Yor 1C 100
Thornton le Moor. Linc 1H 87
Thornton-le-Moor. N Yor 1F 99
Thornton-le-Moors. Ches W 3G 83
Thornton-le-Street. N Yor 1G 99
Thorntonloch. E Lot 2D 130
Thornton Rust. N Yor 1B 98
Thornton Steward. N Yor 1D 98
Thornton Watlass. N Yor 1E 99
Thornwood Common. Essx 5E 53
Thornythwaite. Cumb 2E 103
Thoroton. Notts 1E 75
Thorp Arch. W Yor 5G 99
Thorpe. Derbs 5F 85
Thorpe. E Yor 5D 101
Thorpe. Linc 2D 89
Thorpe. Norf 1G 67
Thorpe. N Yor 3C 98
Thorpe. Notts 1E 75
Thorpe. Surr 4B 38
Thorpe Abbotts. Norf 3D 66
Thorpe Acre. Leics 3C 74
Thorpe Arnold. Leics 3E 75
Thorpe Audlin. W Yor 3E 93
Thorpe Bassett. N Yor 2C 100
Thorpe Bay. S'end 2D 40
Thorpe by Water. Rut 1F 63
Thorpe Common. S Yor 1A 86
Thorpe Common. Suff 2F 55
Thorpe Constantine. Staf 5G 73
Thorpe End. Norf 4E 79
Thorpe Fendike. Linc 4D 88
Thorpe Green. Essx 3E 55
Thorpe Green. Suff 5B 66
Thorpe Hall. N Yor 2H 99
Thorpe Hamlet. Norf 5E 79
Thorpe Hesley. S Yor 1A 86
Thorpe in Balne. S Yor 3F 93
Thorpe in the Fallows. Linc 2G 87
Thorpe Langton. Leics 1E 63
Thorpe Larches. Dur 2A 106
Thorpe Latimer. Linc 1A 76
Thorpe-le-Soken. Essx 3E 55
Thorpe le Street. E Yor 5C 100
Thorpe Malsor. Nptn 3F 63
Thorpe Mandeville. Nptn 1D 50
Thorpe Market. Norf 2E 79
Thorpe Marriott. Norf 4D 78
Thorpe Morieux. Suff 5B 66
Thorpeness. Suff 4G 67
Thorpe on the Hill. Linc 4G 87
Thorpe on the Hill. W Yor 2D 92
Thorpe St Andrew. Norf 5E 79
Thorpe St Peter. Linc 4D 89
Thorpe Salvin. S Yor 2C 86
Thorpe Satchville. Leics 4E 75
Thorpe Thewles. Stoc T 2B 106
Thorpe Tilney. Linc 5A 88
Thorpe Underwood. N Yor 4G 99
Thorpe Waterville. Nptn 2H 63
Thorpe Willoughby. N Yor 1F 93
Thorpland. Norf 5F 77
Thorrington. Essx 3D 54
Thorverton. Devn 2C 12
Thrandeston. Suff 3D 66
Thrapston. Nptn 3G 63
Thrashbush. N Lan 3A 128
Threapland. Cumb 1C 102
Threapland. N Yor 3B 98
Threapwood. Ches W 1G 71
Threapwood. Staf 1E 73
Three Ashes. Here 3A 48
Three Bridges. Linc 2D 88
Three Bridges. W Sus 2D 27
Three Burrows. Corn 4B 6
Three Chimneys. Kent 2C 28
Three Cocks. Powy 2E 47
Three Crosses. Swan 3E 31
Three Cups Corner. E Sus 3H 27
Threehammer Common. Norf 3F 79
Three Holes. Norf 5E 77
Threekingham. Linc 2H 75
Three Leg Cross. E Sus 2A 28
Three Legged Cross. Dors 2F 15
Three Mile Cross. Wok 5F 37
Threemilestone. Corn 4B 6
Three Oaks. E Sus 4C 28
Threlkeld. Cumb 2E 102
Threshfield. N Yor 3B 98
Thrigby. Norf 4G 79
Thringarth. Dur 2C 104
Thringstone. Leics 4B 74
Thrintoft. N Yor 5A 106
Thriplow. Cambs 1E 53
Throckenholt. Linc 5C 76
Throcking. Herts 2D 52
Throckley. Tyne 3E 115
Throckmorton. Worc 1E 49
Throop. Bour 3G 15
Throphill. Nmbd 1E 115
Thropton. Nmbd 4E 121
Throsk. Stir 4A 136
Througham. Glos 5E 49
Throughgate. Dum 1F 111
Throwleigh. Devn 3G 11
Throwley. Kent 5D 40
Throwley Forstal. Kent 5D 40
Throxenby. N Yor 1E 101
Thrumpton. Notts 2C 74
Thrumster. High 4F 169
Thrunton. Nmbd 3E 121
Thrupp. Glos 5D 48
Thrupp. Oxon 4C 50
Thrushelton. Devn 4E 11
Thrushgill. Lanc 3F 97
Thrussington. Leics 4D 74
Thruxton. Hants 2A 24
Thruxton. Here 2H 47
Thrybergh. S Yor 1B 86
Thulston. Derbs 2B 74
Thundergay. N Ayr 5G 125
Thundersley. Essx 2B 40
Thundridge. Herts 4D 52
Thurcaston. Leics 4C 74
Thurcroft. S Yor 2B 86
Thurdon. Corn 1C 10
Thurgarton. Norf 2D 78
Thurgarton. Notts 1D 74
Thurgoland. S Yor 4C 92
Thurlaston. Leics 1C 62
Thurlaston. Warw 3B 62
Thurlbear. Som 4F 21
Thurlby. Linc 3D 89 (nr. Alford)
Thurlby. Linc 4A 76 (nr. Baston)
Thurlby. Linc 4G 87 (nr. Lincoln)
Thurleigh. Bed 5H 63
Thurlestone. Devn 4C 8
Thurloxton. Som 3F 21
Thurlstone. S Yor 4C 92
Thurlton. Norf 1G 67
Thurmaston. Leics 5D 74
Thurnby. Leics 5D 74
Thurne. Norf 4G 79
Thurnham. Kent 5C 40
Thurning. Norf 3C 78
Thurning. Nptn 2H 63
Thurnscoe. S Yor 4E 93
Thursby. Cumb 4E 113
Thursford. Norf 2B 78
Thursford Green. Norf 2B 78
Thursley. Surr 2A 26
Thurso. High 2D 168
Thurso East. High 2D 168
Thurstaston. Mers 2E 83
Thurston. Suff 4B 66
Thurston End. Suff 5G 65
Thurstonfield. Cumb 4E 112
Thurstonland. W Yor 3B 92
Thurton. Norf 5F 79
Thurvaston. Derbs 2F 73 (nr. Ashbourne)
Thurvaston. Derbs 2G 73 (nr. Derby)
Thuxton. Norf 5C 78
Thwaite. Dur 3D 104
Thwaite. N Yor 5B 104
Thwaite. Suff 4D 66
Thwaite Head. Cumb 5E 103
Thwaites. W Yor 5C 98
Thwaite St Mary. Norf 1F 67
Thwing. E Yor 2E 101
Tibbermore. Per 1C 136
Tibberton. Glos 3C 48
Tibberton. Telf 3A 72
Tibberton. Worc 5D 60
Tibenham. Norf 2D 66
Tibshelf. Derbs 4B 86
Tibthorpe. E Yor 4D 100
Ticehurst. E Sus 2A 28
Tichborne. Hants 3D 24
Tickencote. Rut 5G 75
Tickenham. N Som 4H 33
Tickhill. S Yor 1C 86
Ticklerton. Shrp 1G 59
Ticknall. Derbs 3H 73
Tickton. E Yor 5E 101
Tidbury Green. W Mid 3F 61
Tidcombe. Wilts 1A 24
Tiddington. Oxon 5E 51
Tiddington. Warw 5G 61
Tiddleywink. Wilts 4D 34
Tidebrook. E Sus 3H 27
Tideford. Corn 3H 7
Tideford Cross. Corn 2H 7
Tidenham. Glos 2A 34
Tideswell. Derbs 3F 85
Tidmarsh. W Ber 4E 37
Tidmington. Warw 2A 50
Tidpit. Hants 1F 15
Tidworth. Wilts 2H 23
Tidworth Camp. Wilts 2H 23
Tiers Cross. Pemb 3D 42
Tiffield. Nptn 5D 62
Tifty. Abers 4E 161
Tigerton. Ang 2E 145
Tighnabruaich. Arg 2A 126
Tigley. Devn 2D 8
Tilbrook. Cambs 4H 63
Tilbury. Thur 3H 39
Tilbury Green. Essx 1H 53
Tilbury Juxta Clare. Essx 1A 54
Tile Hill. W Mid 3G 61
Tilehurst. Read 4E 37
Tilford. Surr 2G 25
Tilgate Forest Row. W Sus 2D 26
Tillathrowie. Abers 5B 160
Tillers Green. Glos 2B 48
Tillery. Abers 1G 153
Tilley. Shrp 3H 71
Tillicoultry. Clac 4B 136
Tillingham. Essx 5C 54
Tillington. Here 1H 47
Tillington. W Sus 3A 26
Tillington Common. Here 1H 47
Tillybirloch. Abers 3D 152
Tillyfourie. Abers 2D 152
Tilmanstone. Kent 5H 41
Tilney All Saints. Norf 4E 77
Tilney Fen End. Norf 4E 77
Tilney High End. Norf 4E 77
Tilney St Lawrence. Norf 4E 77
Tilshead. Wilts 2F 23
Tilstock. Shrp 2H 71
Tilston. Ches W 5G 83
Tilstone Fearnall. Ches W 4H 83
Tilsworth. C Beds 3H 51
Tilton on the Hill. Leics 5E 75
Tiltups End. Glos 2D 34
Timberland. Linc 5A 88
Timbersbrook. Ches E 4C 84
Timberscombe. Som 2C 20
Timble. N Yor 4D 98
Timperley. G Man 2B 84
Timsbury. Bath 1B 22
Timsbury. Hants 4B 24
Timsgearraidh. W Isl 4C 171
Timworth Green. Suff 4A 66
Tincleton. Dors 3C 14
Tindale. Cumb 4H 113
Tindale Crescent. Dur 2F 105
Tingewick. Buck 2E 51
Tingrith. C Beds 2A 52
Tingwall. Orkn 5D 172
Tinhay. Devn 4D 11
Tinshill. W Yor 1C 92
Tinsley. S Yor 1B 86
Tinsley Green. W Sus 2D 27
Tintagel. Corn 4A 10
Tintern. Mon 5A 48
Tintinhull. Som 1A 14
Tintwistle. Derbs 1E 85
Tinwald. Dum 1B 112
Tinwell. Rut 5H 75
Tippacott. Devn 2A 20
Tipperty. Abers 1G 153
Tipps End. Cambs 1E 65
Tiptoe. Hants 3A 16
Tipton. W Mid 1D 60
Tipton St John. Devn 3D 12
Tiptree. Essx 4B 54
Tiptree Heath. Essx 4B 54
Tirabad. Powy 1B 46
Tircoed. Swan 5G 45
Tiree Airport. Arg 4B 138
Tirinie. Per 2F 143
Tirley. Glos 3D 48
Tirnewydd. Flin 3D 82
Tiroran. Arg 1B 132
Tirphil. Cphy 5E 47
Tirril. Cumb 2G 103
Tirryside. High 2C 164
Tir-y-dail. Carm 4G 45
Tisbury. Wilts 4E 23
Tisman's Common. W Sus 2B 26
Tissington. Derbs 5F 85
Titchberry. Devn 4C 18
Titchfield. Hants 2D 16
Titchmarsh. Nptn 3H 63
Titchwell. Norf 1G 77
Tithby. Notts 2D 74
Titley. Here 5F 59
Titlington. Nmbd 3F 121
Titsey. Surr 5F 39
Titson. Corn 2C 10
Tittensor. Staf 2C 72
Tittleshall. Norf 3A 78
Titton. Worc 4C 60
Tiverton. Ches W 4H 83
Tiverton. Devn 1C 12
Tivetshall St Margaret. Norf 2D 66
Tivetshall St Mary. Norf 2D 66
Tivington. Som 2C 20
Tixall. Staf 3D 73
Tixover. Rut 5G 75
Toab. Orkn 7E 172
Toab. Shet 10E 173
Toadmoor. Derbs 5H 85
Tobermore. Mag 7E 174
Tobermory. Arg 3G 139
Toberonochy. Arg 3E 133
Tobha-Beag. W Isl 1E 170 (on North Uist)
Tobha Beag. W Isl 5C 170 (on South Uist)
Tobha Mor. W Isl 5C 170
Tobhtarol. W Isl 4D 171
Tobson. W Isl 4D 171
Tocabhaig. High 2E 147
Tocher. Abers 5D 160
Tockenham. Wilts 4F 35
Tockenham Wick. Wilts 3F 35
Tockholes. Bkbn 2E 91
Tockington. S Glo 3B 34
Tockwith. N Yor 4G 99
Todber. Dors 4D 22
Todding. Here 3G 59
Toddington. C Beds 3A 52
Toddington. Glos 2F 49
Todenham. Glos 2H 49
Todhills. Cumb 3E 113
Todmorden. W Yor 2H 91
Todwick. S Yor 2B 86
Toft. Cambs 5C 64
Toft. Linc 4H 75
Toft Hill. Dur 2E 105
Toft Monks. Norf 1G 67
Toft next Newton. Linc 2H 87
Toftrees. Norf 3A 78
Tofts. High 2F 169
Toftwood. Norf 4B 78
Togston. Nmbd 4G 121
Tokavaig. High 2E 147
Tokers Green. Oxon 4F 37
Tolastadh a Chaolais. W Isl 4D 171
Tolladine. Worc 5C 60
Tolland. Som 3E 20
Tollard Farnham. Dors 1E 15
Tollard Royal. Wilts 1E 15
Toll Bar. S Yor 4F 93
Toller Fratrum. Dors 3A 14
Toller Porcorum. Dors 3A 14
Tollerton. N Yor 3H 99
Tollerton. Notts 2D 74
Toller Whelme. Dors 2A 14
Tollesbury. Essx 4C 54
Tolleshunt D'Arcy. Essx 4C 54
Tolleshunt Knights. Essx 4C 54
Tolleshunt Major. Essx 4C 54
Tollie. High 3H 157
Tollie Farm. High 1A 156
Tolm. W Isl 4G 171
Tolpuddle. Dors 3C 14
Tolstadh bho Thuath. W Isl 3H 171
Tolworth. G Lon 4C 38
Tomachlaggan. Mor 1F 151
Tomaknock. Per 1A 136
Tomatin. High 1C 150
Tombuidhe. Arg 3H 133
Tomdoun. High 3D 148
Tomich. High 1F 149 (nr. Cannich)
Tomich. High 1B 158 (nr. Invergordon)
Tomich. High 3D 164 (nr. Lairg)
Tomintoul. Mor 2F 151
Tomnavoulin. Mor 1G 151
Tomsleibhe. Arg 5A 140
Ton. Mon 2G 33
Tonbridge. Kent 1G 27
Tondu. B'end 3B 32
Tonedale. Som 4E 21
Tonfanau. Gwyn 5E 69
Tong. Shrp 5B 72
Tonge. Leics 3B 74
Tong Forge. Shrp 5B 72
Tongham. Surr 2G 25
Tongland. Dum 4D 111
Tong Norton. Shrp 5B 72
Tongue. High 3F 167
Tongue End. Linc 4A 76
Tongwynlais. Card 3E 33
Tonmawr. Neat 2B 32
Tonna. Neat 2A 32
Tonnau. Neat 2A 32
Ton-Pentre. Rhon 2C 32
Ton-Teg. Rhon 3D 32
Tonwell. Herts 4D 52
Tonypandy. Rhon 2C 32
Tonyrefail. Rhon 3D 32
Toome. Ant 7F 175
Toot Baldon. Oxon 5D 50
Toot Hill. Essx 5F 53
Toot Hill. Hants 1B 16
Topcliffe. N Yor 2G 99
Topcliffe. W Yor 2C 92
Topcroft. Norf 1E 67
Topcroft Street. Norf 1E 67
Toppesfield. Essx 2H 53
Toppings. G Man 3F 91
Toprow. Norf 1D 66
Topsham. Devn 4C 12
Torbay. Torb 2F 9
Torbeg. N Ayr 3C 122
Torbothie. N Lan 3B 128
Torbryan. Devn 2E 9
Torcross. Devn 4E 9
Tore. High 3A 158
Torgyle. High 2F 149
Torinturk. Arg 3G 125
Torksey. Linc 3F 87
Torlum. W Isl 3C 170
Torlundy. High 1F 141
Tormarton. S Glo 4C 34
Tormitchell. S Ayr 5B 116
Tormore. High 3E 147
Tormore. N Ayr 2C 122
Tornagrain. High 4B 158
Tornaveen. Abers 3D 152
Torness. High 1H 149
Toronto. Dur 1E 105
Torpenhow. Cumb 1D 102
Torphichen. W Lot 2C 128
Torphins. Abers 3D 152
Torpoint. Corn 3A 8
Torquay. Torb 2F 9
Torr. Devn 3B 8
Torra. Arg 4B 124
Torran. High 4E 155
Torrance. E Dun 2H 127
Torrans. Arg 1B 132
Torranyard. E Ayr 5E 127
Torre. Som 3D 20
Torre. Torb 2E 9
Torridon. High 3B 156
Torrin. High 1D 147
Torrisdale. Arg 2B 122
Torrisdale. High 2G 167
Torrish. High 2G 165
Torrisholme. Lanc 3D 96
Torroble. High 3C 164
Torroy. High 4C 164
Torry. Aber 3G 153
Torryburn. Fife 1D 128
Torthorwald. Dum 2B 112
Tortington. W Sus 5B 26
Tortworth. S Glo 2C 34
Torvaig. High 4D 155
Torver. Cumb 5D 102
Torwood. Falk 1B 128
Torworth. Notts 2D 86
Toscaig. High 5G 155
Toseland. Cambs 4B 64
Tosside. Lanc 4G 97
Tostock. Suff 4B 66
Totaig. High 3B 154
Totardor. High 5C 154
Tote. High 4D 154
Totegan. High 2A 168
Tothill. Linc 2D 88
Totland. IOW 4B 16
Totley. S Yor 3H 85
Totnell. Dors 2B 14
Totnes. Devn 2E 9
Toton. Derbs 2B 74
Totronald. Arg 3C 138
Totscore. High 2C 154
Tottenham. G Lon 1E 39
Tottenhill. Norf 4F 77
Tottenhill Row. Norf 4F 77
Totteridge. G Lon 1D 38
Totternhoe. C Beds 3H 51
Tottington. G Man 3F 91
Totton. Hants 1B 16
Touchen-end. Wind 4G 37
Toulvaddie. High 5F 165
Towans, The. Corn 3C 4
Toward. Arg 3C 126
Towcester. Nptn 1E 51
Towednack. Corn 3B 4
Tower End. Norf 4F 77
Tower Hill. Mers 4C 90
Tower Hill. W Sus 3C 26
Towersey. Oxon 5F 51
Towie. Abers 2B 152
Towiemore. Mor 4A 160
Tow Law. Dur 1E 105
Town End. Cambs 1D 64
Town End. Cumb 4F 103 (nr. Ambleside)
Town End. Cumb 2H 103 (nr. Kirkby Thore)
Town End. Cumb 1D 96 (nr. Lindale)
Town End. Cumb 1C 96 (nr. Newby Bridge)
Town End. Mers 2G 83
Townend. W Dun 2F 127
Townfield. Dur 5C 114
Towngate. Cumb 5G 113
Towngate. Linc 4A 76
Town Green. Lanc 4B 90
Town Head. Cumb 4E 103 (nr. Grasmere)
Town Head. Cumb 3H 103 (nr. Great Asby)
Townhead. Cumb 1G 103 (nr. Lazonby)
Townhead. Cumb 1B 102 (nr. Maryport)
Townhead. Cumb 1H 103 (nr. Ousby)
Townhead. Dum 5D 111
Townhead of Greenlaw. Dum 3E 111
Townhill. Fife 1E 129
Townhill. Swan 3F 31
Townjoy. Dngn 3D 178
Town Kelloe. Dur 1A 106
Town Littleworth. E Sus 4F 27
Town Row. E Sus 2G 27
Towns End. Hants 1D 24
Townsend. Herts 5B 52
Townshend. Corn 3C 4
Town Street. Suff 2G 65
Town, The. IOS 1A 4
Town Yetholm. Bord 2C 120
Towthorpe. E Yor 3C 100
Towthorpe. York 4A 100
Towton. N Yor 1E 93
Towyn. Cnwy 3B 82
Toxteth. Mers 2F 83
Toynton All Saints. Linc 4C 88
Toynton Fen Side. Linc 4C 88
Toynton St Peter. Linc 4D 88
Toy's Hill. Kent 5F 39
Trabboch. E Ayr 2D 116
Traboe. Corn 4E 5
Tradespark. High 3C 158
Tradespark. Orkn 7D 172
Trafford Park. G Man 1B 84
Trallong. Powy 3C 46
Tranent. E Lot 2H 129
Tranmere. Mers 2F 83
Trantlebeg. High 3A 168
Trantlemore. High 3A 168
Tranwell. Nmbd 1E 115
Trapp. Carm 4G 45
Traquair. Bord 1F 119
Trash Green. W Ber 5E 37
Trawden. Lanc 1H 91
Trawscoed. Powy 2D 46
Trawsfynydd. Gwyn 2G 69
Trawsgoed. Cdgn 3F 57
Treaddow. Here 3A 48
Trealaw. Rhon 2D 32

Treales—Wareside

Treales. Lanc 1C 90
Trearddur. IOA 3B 80
Treaslane. High 3C 154
Treator. Corn 1D 6
Trebanog. Rhon 2D 32
Trebanos. Neat 5H 45
Trebarber. Corn 2C 6
Trebartha. Corn 5C 10
Trebarwith. Corn 4A 10
Trebetherick. Corn 1D 6
Treborough. Som 3D 20
Trebudannon. Corn 2C 6
Trebullett. Corn 5D 10
Treburley. Corn 5D 10
Treburrick. Corn 1C 6
Trebyan. Corn 2E 7
Trecastle. Powy 3B 46
Trecenydd. Cphy 3E 33
Trecott. Devn 2G 11
Trecwn. Pemb 1D 42
Trecynon. Rhon 5C 46
Tredaule. Corn 4C 10
Tredavoe. Corn 4B 4
Tredegar. Blae 5E 47
Trederwen. Powy 4E 71
Tredington. Glos 3E 49
Tredington. Warw 1A 50
Tredinnick. Corn 2F 7 (nr. Bodmin)
Tredinnick. Corn 3G 7 (nr. Looe)
Tredinnick. Corn 1D 6 (nr. Padstow)
Tredogan. V Glam 5D 32
Tredomen. Powy 2E 46
Tredunnock. Mon 2G 33
Tredustan. Powy 2E 47
Treen. Corn 4A 4 (nr. Land's End)
Treen. Corn 3B 4 (nr. St Ives)
Treeton. S Yor 2B 86
Trefaldwyn. Powy 1E 58
Trefasser. Pemb 1C 42
Trefdraeth. IOA 3D 80
Trefdraeth. Pemb 1E 43
Trefecca. Powy 2E 47
Trefechan. Mer T 5D 46
Trefeglwys. Powy 1B 58
Trefeitha. Powy 2E 46
Trefenter. Cdgn 4F 57
Treffgarne. Pemb 2D 42
Treffynnon. Flin 3D 82
Treffynnon. Pemb 2C 42
Trefil. Blae 4E 46
Trefilan. Cdgn 5E 57
Trefin. Pemb 1C 42
Treflach. Shrp 3E 71
Trefnant. Den 3C 82
Trefonen. Shrp 3E 71
Trefor. Gwyn 1C 68
Trefor. IOA 2C 80
Treforest. Rhon 3D 32
Trefrew. Corn 4B 10
Trefriw. Cnwy 4G 81
Tref-y-Clawdd. Powy 3E 59
Trefynwy. Mon 4A 48
Tregada. Corn 4D 10
Tregadillett. Corn 4D 10
Tregare. Mon 4H 47
Tregarne. Corn 4E 5
Tregaron. Cdgn 5F 57
Tregarth. Gwyn 4F 81
Tregear. Corn 3C 6
Tregeare. Corn 4C 10
Tregeiriog. Wrex 2D 70
Tregele. IOA 1C 80
Tregeseal. Corn 3A 4
Tregiskey. Corn 4E 6
Tregole. Corn 3B 10
Tregolwyn. V Glam 4C 32
Tregonetha. Corn 2D 6
Tregonhawke. Corn 3A 8
Tregony. Corn 4D 6
Tregoodwell. Corn 4B 10
Tregorrick. Corn 3E 6
Tregoss. Corn 2D 6
Tregowris. Corn 4E 5
Tregoyd. Powy 2E 47
Tregrehan Mills. Corn 3E 7
Tre-groes. Cdgn 1E 45
Tregullon. Corn 2E 7
Tregurrian. Corn 2C 6
Tregynon. Powy 1C 58
Trehafod. Rhon 2D 32
Trehan. Corn 3A 8
Treharris. Mer T 2E 32
Treherbert. Rhon 2C 32
Trehunist. Corn 2H 7
Trekenner. Corn 5D 10
Trekenning. Corn 2D 6
Treknow. Corn 4A 10
Trelales. B'end 3B 32
Trelan. Corn 5E 5
Trelash. Corn 3B 10
Trelassick. Corn 3C 6
Trelawnyd. Flin 3C 82
Trelech. Carm 1G 43
Treleddyd-fawr. Pemb 2B 42
Trelewis. Mer T 2E 32
Treligga. Corn 4A 10
Trelights. Corn 1D 6
Trelill. Corn 5A 10
Trelissick. Corn 5C 6
Trellech. Mon 5A 48
Trelleck Grange. Mon 5H 47
Trelogan. Flin 2D 82
Trelystan. Powy 5E 71
Tremadog. Gwyn 1E 69
Tremail. Corn 4B 10
Tremain. Cdgn 1C 44
Tremaine. Corn 4C 10
Tremar. Corn 2G 7
Trematon. Corn 3H 7
Tremeirchion. Den 3C 82
Tremore. Corn 2E 6
Tremorfa. Card 4F 33
Trenance. Corn 2C 6 (nr. Newquay)
Trenance. Corn 1D 6 (nr. Padstow)
Trenarren. Corn 4E 7
Trench. Telf 4A 72
Trencreek. Corn 2C 6
Trendeal. Corn 3C 6
Trenear. Corn 5A 6
Treneglos. Corn 4C 10
Trenewan. Corn 3F 7
Trengune. Corn 3B 10
Trent. Dors 1A 14
Trentham. Stoke 1C 72
Trentishoe. Devn 2G 19
Trentlock. Derbs 2B 74
Treoes. V Glam 4C 32
Treorchy. Rhon 2C 32
Treorci. Rhon 2C 32
Tre'r-ddol. Cdgn 1F 57
Tre'r llai. Powy 5E 71
Trerulefoot. Corn 3H 7
Tresaith. Cdgn 5B 56
Trescott. Staf 1C 60
Trescowe. Corn 3C 4
Tresham. Glos 2C 34
Tresigin. V Glam 4C 32
Tresillian. Corn 4C 6
Tresimwn. V Glam 4D 32
Tresinney. Corn 4B 10
Treskillard. Corn 5A 6
Treskinnick Cross. Corn 3C 10
Tresmeer. Corn 4C 10
Tresparrett. Corn 3B 10
Tresparrett Posts. Corn 3B 10
Tressady. High 3D 164
Tressait. Per 2F 143
Tresta. Shet 2H 173 (on Fetlar)
Tresta. Shet 6E 173 (on Mainland)
Treswell. Notts 3E 87
Treswithian. Corn 3D 4
Tre Taliesin. Cdgn 1F 57
Trethomas. Cphy 3E 33
Trethosa. Corn 3D 6
Trethurgy. Corn 3E 7
Tretio. Pemb 2B 42
Tretire. Here 3A 48
Tretower. Powy 3E 47
Treuddyn. Flin 5E 83
Trevadlock. Corn 5C 10
Trevalga. Corn 3A 10
Trevalyn. Wrex 5F 83
Trevance. Corn 1D 6
Trevanger. Corn 1D 6
Trevanson. Corn 1D 6
Trevarrack. Corn 3B 4
Trevarren. Corn 2D 6
Trevarrian. Corn 2C 6
Trevarrick. Corn 4D 6
Tre-vaughan. Carm 3E 45 (nr. Carmarthen)
Trevaughan. Carm 3F 43 (nr. Whitland)
Treveighan. Corn 5A 10
Trevellas. Corn 3B 6
Trevelmond. Corn 2G 7
Treverva. Corn 5B 6
Trevescan. Corn 4A 4
Trevethin. Torf 5F 47
Trevia. Corn 4A 10
Trevigro. Corn 2H 7
Trevilley. Corn 4A 4
Treviscoe. Corn 3D 6
Trevivian. Corn 4B 10
Trevone. Corn 1C 6
Trevor. Wrex 1E 71
Trevor Uchaf. Den 1E 71
Trew. Corn 4D 4
Trewalder. Corn 4A 10
Trewarlett. Corn 4D 10
Trewarmett. Corn 4A 10
Trewassa. Corn 4B 10
Treween. Corn 4C 10
Trewellard. Corn 3A 4
Trewen. Corn 4C 10
Trewennack. Corn 4D 5
Trewern. Powy 4E 71
Trewetha. Corn 5A 10
Trewidland. Corn 2G 7
Trewint. Corn 3B 10
Trewithian. Corn 5C 6
Trewoofe. Corn 4B 4
Trewoon. Corn 3D 6
Treworthal. Corn 5C 6
Trewyddel. Pemb 1B 44
Treyarnon. Corn 1C 6
Treyford. W Sus 1G 17
Triangle. Staf 5E 73
Triangle. W Yor 2A 92
Trickett's Cross. Dors 2F 15
Trillick. Omag 7F 176
Trimdon. Dur 1A 106
Trimdon Colliery. Dur 1A 106
Trimdon Grange. Dur 1A 106
Trimingham. Norf 2E 79
Trimley Lower Street. Suff 2F 55
Trimley St Martin. Suff 2F 55
Trimley St Mary. Suff 2F 55
Trimpley. Worc 3B 60
Trimsaran. Carm 5E 45
Trimstone. Devn 2F 19
Trinafour. Per 2E 142
Trinant. Cphy 2F 33
Tring. Herts 4H 51
Trinity. Ang 2F 145
Trinity. Edin 2F 129
Trisant. Cdgn 3G 57
Triscombe. Som 3E 21
Trislaig. High 1E 141
Trispen. Corn 3C 6
Tritlington. Nmbd 5G 121
Trochry. Per 4G 143
Troedrhiwdalar. Powy 5B 58
Troedrhiwfuwch. Cphy 5E 47
Troedrhiwgwair. Blae 5E 47
Troedyraur. Cdgn 1D 44
Troedyrhiw. Mer T 5D 46
Trondavoe. Shet 4E 173
Troon. Corn 5A 6
Troon. S Ayr 1C 116
Troqueer. Dum 2A 112
Troston. Suff 3A 66
Trottiscliffe. Kent 4H 39
Trotton. W Sus 4G 25
Troutbeck. Cumb 4F 103 (nr. Ambleside)
Troutbeck. Cumb 2E 103 (nr. Penrith)
Troutbeck Bridge. Cumb 4F 103
Troway. Derbs 3A 86
Trowbridge. Wilts 1D 22
Trowell. Notts 2B 74
Trowle Common. Wilts 1D 22
Trowley Bottom. Herts 4A 52
Trowse Newton. Norf 5E 79
Trudoxhill. Som 2C 22
Trull. Som 4F 21
Trumaisgearraidh. W Isl 1D 170
Trumpan. High 2B 154
Trumpet. Here 2B 48
Trumpington. Cambs 5D 64
Trumps Green. Surr 4A 38
Trunch. Norf 2E 79
Trunnah. Lanc 5C 96
Truro. Corn 4C 6
Trusham. Devn 4B 12
Trusley. Derbs 2G 73
Trusthorpe. Linc 2E 89
Tryfil. IOA 2D 80
Trysull. Staf 1C 60
Tubney. Oxon 2C 36
Tuckenhay. Devn 3E 9
Tuckhill. Staf 2B 60
Tuckingmill. Corn 4A 6
Tuckton. Bour 3G 15
Tuddenham. Suff 3G 65
Tuddenham St Martin. Suff 1E 55
Tudeley. Kent 1H 27
Tudhoe. Dur 1F 105
Tudhoe Grange. Dur 1F 105
Tudorville. Here 3A 48
Tudweiliog. Gwyn 2B 68
Tuesley. Surr 1A 26
Tufton. Hants 2C 24
Tufton. Pemb 2E 43
Tugby. Leics 5E 75
Tugford. Shrp 2H 59
Tughall. Nmbd 2G 121
Tulchan. Per 1B 136
Tullibardine. Per 2B 136
Tullibody. Clac 4A 136
Tullich. Arg 2H 133
Tullich. High 4B 156 (nr. Lochcarron)
Tullich. High 1C 158 (nr. Tain)
Tullich. Mor 4H 159
Tullich Muir. High 1B 158
Tulliemet. Per 3G 143
Tulloch. Abers 5F 161
Tulloch. High 4D 164 (nr. Bonar Bridge)
Tulloch. High 5F 149 (nr. Fort William)
Tulloch. High 2D 151 (nr. Grantown-on-Spey)
Tulloch. Per 1C 136
Tullochgorm. Arg 4G 133
Tullybeagles Lodge. Per 5H 143
Tullyhogue. Cook 2C 178
Tullymurdoch. Per 3A 144
Tullynessle. Abers 2C 152
Tumble. Carm 4F 45
Tumbler's Green. Essx 3B 54
Tumby. Linc 4B 88
Tumby Woodside. Linc 5B 88
Tummel Bridge. Per 3E 143
Tunbridge Wells, Royal. Kent 2G 27
Tunga. W Isl 4G 171
Tungate. Norf 3E 79
Tunley. Bath 1B 22
Tunstall. E Yor 1G 95
Tunstall. Kent 4C 40
Tunstall. Lanc 2F 97
Tunstall. Norf 5G 79
Tunstall. N Yor 5F 105
Tunstall. Staf 3B 72
Tunstall. Stoke 5C 84
Tunstall. Suff 5F 67
Tunstall. Tyne 4G 115
Tunstead. Derbs 3F 85
Tunstead. Norf 3E 79
Tunstead Milton. Derbs 2E 85
Tunworth. Hants 2E 25
Tupsley. Here 1A 48
Tupton. Derbs 4A 86
Turfholm. S Lan 1H 117
Turfmoor. Devn 2F 13
Turgis Green. Hants 1E 25
Turkdean. Glos 4G 49
Turkey Island. Hants 1D 16
Tur Langton. Leics 1E 62
Turleigh. Wilts 5D 34
Turlin Moor. Pool 3E 15
Turnant. Here 3G 47
Turnastone. Here 2G 47
Turnberry. S Ayr 4B 116
Turnchapel. Plym 3A 8
Turnditch. Derbs 1G 73
Turners Hill. W Sus 2E 27
Turners Puddle. Dors 3D 14
Turnford. Herts 5D 52
Turnhouse. Edin 2E 129
Turnworth. Dors 2D 14
Turriff. Abers 4E 161
Tursdale. Dur 1A 106
Turton Bottoms. Bkbn 3F 91
Turtory. Mor 4C 160
Turves Green. W Mid 3E 61
Turvey. Bed 5G 63
Turville. Buck 2F 37
Turville Heath. Buck 2F 37
Turweston. Buck 2E 50
Tushielaw. Bord 3F 119
Tutbury. Staf 3G 73
Tutnall. Worc 3D 61
Tutshill. Glos 2A 34
Tuttington. Norf 3E 79
Tutts Clump. W Ber 4D 36
Tutwell. Corn 5D 11
Tuxford. Notts 3E 87
Twatt. Orkn 5B 172
Twatt. Shet 6E 173
Twechar. E Dun 2A 128
Tweedale. Telf 5B 72
Tweedmouth. Nmbd 4F 131
Tweedsmuir. Bord 2C 118
Twelveheads. Corn 4B 6
Twemlow Green. Ches E 4B 84
Twenty. Linc 3A 76
Twerton. Bath 5C 34
Twickenham. G Lon 3C 38
Twigworth. Glos 3D 48
Twineham. W Sus 3D 26
Twinhoe. Bath 1C 22
Twinstead. Essx 2B 54
Twinstead Green. Essx 2B 54
Twiss Green. Warr 1A 84
Twiston. Lanc 5H 97
Twitchen. Devn 3A 20
Twitchen. Shrp 3F 59
Two Bridges. Devn 5G 11
Two Bridges. Glos 5B 48
Two Dales. Derbs 4G 85
Two Gates. Staf 5G 73
Two Mile Oak. Devn 2E 9
Twycross. Leics 5H 73
Twyford. Buck 3E 51
Twyford. Derbs 3H 73
Twyford. Dors 1D 14
Twyford. Hants 4C 24
Twyford. Leics 4E 75
Twyford. Norf 3C 78
Twyford. Wok 4F 37
Twyford Common. Here 2A 48
Twyncarno. Cphy 5E 46
Twynholm. Dum 4D 110
Twyning. Glos 2D 49
Twyning Green. Glos 2E 49
Twynllanan. Carm 3A 46
Twyn-y-Sheriff. Mon 5H 47
Twywell. Nptn 3G 63
Tyberton. Here 2G 47
Tyburn. W Mid 1F 61
Tyby. Norf 3C 78
Tycroes. Carm 4G 45
Tycrwyn. Powy 4D 70
Tyddewi. Pemb 2B 42
Tydd Gote. Linc 4D 76
Tydd St Giles. Cambs 4D 76
Tydd St Mary. Linc 4D 76
Tye. Hants 2F 17
Tye Green. Essx 3F 53 (nr. Bishop's Stortford)
Tye Green. Essx 3A 54 (nr. Braintree)
Tye Green. Essx 2F 53 (nr. Saffron Walden)
Tyersal. W Yor 1B 92
Ty Issa. Powy 3D 70
Tyldesley. G Man 4E 91
Tyle. Carm 3G 45
Tyler Hill. Kent 4F 41
Tylers Green. Buck 2G 37
Tyler's Green. Essx 5F 53
Tylorstown. Rhon 2D 32
Tylwch. Powy 2B 58
Tynan. Arm 5B 178
Ty-nant. Cnwy 1B 70
Tyndrum. Stir 5H 141
Tyneham. Dors 4D 15
Tynehead. Midl 4G 129
Tynemouth. Tyne 3G 115
Tyneside. Tyne 3F 115
Tyne Tunnel. Tyne 3G 115
Tynewydd. Rhon 2C 32
Tyninghame. E Lot 2C 130
Tynron. Dum 5H 117
Ty'n-y-bryn. Rhon 3D 32
Tyn-y-celyn. Wrex 2D 70
Tyn-y-cwm. Swan 5G 45
Tyn-y-ffridd. Powy 2D 70
Tynygongl. IOA 2E 81
Tynygraig. Cdgn 4F 57
Tyn-y-groes. Cnwy 3G 81
Ty'n-yr-eithin. Cdgn 4F 57
Tyn-y-rhyd. Powy 4C 70
Tyn-y-wern. Powy 3C 70
Tyrie. Abers 2G 161
Tyringham. Mil 1G 51
Tythecott. Devn 1E 11
Tythegston. B'end 4B 32
Tytherington. Ches E 3D 84
Tytherington. Som 2C 22
Tytherington. S Glo 3B 34
Tytherington. Wilts 2E 23
Tytherleigh. Devn 2G 13
Tywardreath. Corn 3E 7
Tywardreath Highway. Corn 3E 7
Tywyn. Cnwy 3G 81
Tywyn. Gwyn 5E 69

U

Uachdar. W Isl 3D 170
Uags. High 5G 155
Ubbeston Green. Suff 3F 67
Ubley. Bath 1A 22
Uckerby. N Yor 4F 105
Uckfield. E Sus 3F 27
Uckinghall. Worc 2D 48
Uckington. Glos 3E 49
Uckington. Shrp 5H 71
Uddingston. S Lan 3H 127
Uddington. S Lan 1A 118
Udimore. E Sus 4C 28
Udny Green. Abers 1F 153
Udny Station. Abers 1G 153
Udston. S Lan 4A 128
Udstonhead. S Lan 5A 128
Uffcott. Wilts 4G 35
Uffculme. Devn 1D 12
Uffington. Linc 5H 75
Uffington. Oxon 3B 36
Uffington. Shrp 4H 71
Ufford. Pet 5H 75
Ufford. Suff 5E 67
Ufton. Warw 4A 62
Ufton Nervet. W Ber 5E 37
Ugadale. Arg 3B 122
Ugborough. Devn 3C 8
Ugford. Wilts 3F 23
Uggeshall. Suff 2G 67
Ugglebarnby. N Yor 4F 107
Ugley. Essx 3F 53
Ugley Green. Essx 3F 53
Ugthorpe. N Yor 3E 107
Uidh. W Isl 9B 170
Uig. Arg 3C 138
Uig. High 2C 154 (nr. Balgown)
Uig. High 3A 154 (nr. Dunvegan)
Uigshader. High 4D 154
Uisken. Arg 2A 132
Ulbster. High 4F 169
Ulcat Row. Cumb 2F 103
Ulceby. Linc 3D 88
Ulceby. N Lin 3E 94
Ulceby Skitter. N Lin 3E 94
Ulcombe. Kent 1C 28
Uldale. Cumb 1D 102
Uley. Glos 2C 34
Ulgham. Nmbd 5G 121
Ullapool. High 4F 163
Ullenhall. Warw 4F 61
Ulleskelf. N Yor 1F 93
Ullesthorpe. Leics 2C 62
Ulley. S Yor 2B 86
Ullingswick. Here 1A 48
Ullinish. High 5C 154
Ullock. Cumb 2B 102
Ulpha. Cumb 5C 102
Ulrome. E Yor 4F 101
Ulsta. Shet 3F 173
Ulting. Essx 5B 54
Ulva House. Arg 5F 139
Ulverston. Cumb 2B 96
Ulwell. Dors 4F 15
Umberleigh. Devn 4G 19
Unapool. High 5C 166
Underbarrow. Cumb 5F 103
Undercliffe. W Yor 1B 92
Underdale. Shrp 4H 71
Underhoull. Shet 1G 173
Underriver. Kent 5G 39
Under Tofts. S Yor 2H 85
Underton. Shrp 1A 60
Underwood. Newp 3G 33
Underwood. Notts 5B 86
Underwood. Plym 3B 8
Undley. Suff 2F 65
Undy. Mon 3H 33
Union Mills. IOM 4C 108
Union Street. E Sus 2B 28
Unstone. Derbs 3A 86
Unstone Green. Derbs 3A 86
Unthank. Cumb 5E 113 (nr. Carlisle)
Unthank. Cumb 5H 113 (nr. Gamblesby)
Unthank. Cumb 1F 103 (nr. Penrith)
Unthank End. Cumb 1F 103
Upavon. Wilts 1G 23
Up Cerne. Dors 2B 14
Upchurch. Kent 4C 40
Upcott. Devn 2F 11
Upcott. Here 5F 59
Upend. Cambs 5G 65
Up Exe. Devn 2C 12
Upgate. Norf 4D 78
Upgate Street. Norf 1C 66
Uphall. Dors 2A 14
Uphall. W Lot 2D 128
Uphall Station. W Lot 2D 128
Upham. Devn 2B 12
Upham. Hants 4D 24
Uphampton. Here 4F 59
Uphampton. Worc 4C 60
Up Hatherley. Glos 3E 49
Uphill. N Som 1G 21
Up Holland. Lanc 4D 90
Uplawmoor. E Ren 4F 127
Upleadon. Glos 3C 48
Upleatham. Red C 3D 106
Uplees. Kent 4D 40
Uploders. Dors 3A 14
Uplowman. Devn 1D 12
Uplyme. Devn 3G 13
Up Marden. W Sus 1F 17
Upminster. G Lon 2G 39
Up Nately. Hants 1E 25
Upottery. Devn 2F 13
Uppat. High 3F 165
Upper Affcot. Shrp 2G 59
Upper Arley. Worc 2B 60
Upper Armley. W Yor 1C 92
Upper Arncott. Oxon 4E 50
Upper Astrop. Nptn 2D 50
Upper Badcall. High 4B 166
Upper Ballinderry. Lis 3F 179
Upper Bangor. Gwyn 3E 81
Upper Basildon. W Ber 4D 36
Upper Batley. W Yor 2C 92
Upper Beeding. W Sus 4C 26
Upper Benefield. Nptn 2G 63
Upper Bentley. Worc 4D 61
Upper Bighouse. High 3A 168
Upper Boddam. Abers 5D 160
Upper Boddington. Nptn 5B 62
Upper Bogside. Mor 3G 159
Upper Booth. Derbs 2F 85
Upper Borth. Cdgn 2F 57
Upper Boyndlie. Abers 2G 161
Upper Brailes. Warw 2B 50
Upper Breinton. Here 1H 47
Upper Broadheath. Worc 5C 60
Upper Broughton. Notts 3D 74
Upper Brynamman. Carm 4H 45
Upper Bucklebury. W Ber 5D 36
Upper Bullington. Hants 2C 24
Upper Burgate. Hants 1G 15
Upper Caldecote. C Beds 1B 52
Upper Canterton. Hants 1A 16
Upper Catesby. Nptn 5C 62
Upper Chapel. Powy 1D 46
Upper Cheddon. Som 4F 21
Upper Chicksgrove. Wilts 4E 23
Upper Church Village. Rhon 3D 32
Upper Chute. Wilts 1A 24
Upper Clatford. Hants 2B 24
Upper Coberley. Glos 4E 49
Upper Coedcae. Torf 5F 47
Upper Cokeham. W Sus 5C 26
Upper Common. Hants 2E 25
Upper Cound. Shrp 5H 71
Upper Cudworth. S Yor 4D 93
Upper Cumberworth. W Yor 4C 92
Upper Cuttlehill. Abers 4B 160
Upper Cwmbran. Torf 2F 33
Upper Dallachy. Mor 2A 160
Upper Dean. Bed 4H 63
Upper Dean. Devn 2D 8
Upper Denby. W Yor 4C 92
Upper Derraid. High 5E 159
Upper Diabaig. High 2H 155
Upper Dicker. E Sus 5G 27
Upper Dinchope. Shrp 2G 59
Upper Dochcarty. High 2H 157
Upper Dounreay. High 2B 168
Upper Dovercourt. Essx 2F 55
Upper Dunsforth. N Yor 3G 99
Upper Dunsley. Herts 4H 51
Upper Eastern Green. W Mid 2G 61
Upper Elkstone. Staf 5E 85
Upper Ellastone. Staf 1F 73
Upper End. Derbs 3E 85
Upper Enham. Hants 2B 24
Upper Farmcote. Shrp 1B 60
Upper Farringdon. Hants 3F 25
Upper Framilode. Glos 4C 48
Upper Froyle. Hants 2F 25
Upper Gills. High 1F 169
Upper Glenfintaig. High 5E 149
Upper Godney. Som 2H 21
Upper Gravenhurst. C Beds 2B 52
Upper Green. Essx 2E 53
Upper Green. W Ber 5B 36
Upper Green. W Yor 2C 92
Upper Grove Common. Here 3A 48
Upper Hackney. Derbs 4G 85
Upper Hale. Surr 2G 25
Upper Halliford. Surr 4B 38
Upper Halling. Medw 4A 40
Upper Hambleton. Rut 5G 75
Upper Hardres Court. Kent 5F 41
Upper Hardwick. Here 5G 59
Upper Hartfield. E Sus 2F 27
Upper Haugh. S Yor 1B 86
Upper Hayton. Shrp 2H 59
Upper Heath. Shrp 2H 59
Upper Hellesdon. Norf 4E 79
Upper Helmsley. N Yor 4A 100
Upper Hengoed. Shrp 2E 71
Upper Hergest. Here 5E 59
Upper Heyford. Nptn 5D 62
Upper Heyford. Oxon 3C 50
Upper Hill. Here 5G 59
Upper Hindhope. Bord 4B 120
Upper Hopton. W Yor 3B 92
Upper Howsell. Worc 1C 48
Upper Hulme. Staf 4E 85
Upper Inglesham. Swin 2H 35
Upper Kilcott. Glos 3C 34
Upper Killay. Swan 3E 31
Upper Kirkton. Abers 5E 161
Upper Kirkton. N Ayr 4C 126
Upper Knockando. Mor 4F 159
Upper Knockchoilum. High 2G 149
Upper Lambourn. W Ber 3B 36
Upperlands. Mag 6E 174
Upper Langford. N Som 1H 21
Upper Langwith. Derbs 4C 86
Upper Largo. Fife 3G 137
Upper Latheron. High 5D 169
Upper Layham. Suff 1D 54
Upper Leigh. Staf 2E 73
Upper Lenie. High 1H 149
Upper Lochton. Abers 4E 152
Upper Longdon. Staf 4E 73
Upper Longwood. Shrp 5A 72
Upper Lybster. High 5E 169
Upper Lydbrook. Glos 4B 48
Upper Lye. Here 4F 59
Upper Maes-coed. Here 2G 47
Upper Midway. Derbs 3G 73
Uppermill. G Man 4H 91
Upper Millichope. Shrp 2H 59
Upper Milovaig. High 4A 154
Upper Minety. Wilts 2F 35
Upper Mitton. Worc 3C 60
Upper Nash. Pemb 4E 43
Upper Neepaback. Shet 3G 173
Upper Netchwood. Shrp 1A 60
Upper Nobut. Staf 2E 73
Upper North Dean. Buck 2G 37
Upper Norwood. W Sus 4A 26
Upper Nyland. Dors 4C 22
Upper Oddington. Glos 3H 49
Upper Ollach. High 5E 155
Upper Outwoods. Staf 3G 73
Upper Padley. Derbs 3G 85
Upper Pennington. Hants 3B 16
Upper Poppleton. York 4H 99
Upper Quinton. Warw 1G 49
Upper Rochford. Worc 4A 60
Upper Rusko. Dum 3C 110
Upper Sandaig. High 2F 147
Upper Sanday. Orkn 7E 172
Upper Sapey. Here 4A 60
Upper Seagry. Wilts 3E 35
Upper Shelton. C Beds 1H 51
Upper Sheringham. Norf 1D 78
Upper Skelmorlie. N Ayr 3C 126
Upper Slaughter. Glos 3G 49
Upper Sonachan. Arg 1H 133
Upper Soudley. Glos 4B 48
Upper Staploe. Bed 5A 64
Upper Stoke. Norf 5E 79
Upper Stondon. C Beds 2B 52
Upper Stowe. Nptn 5D 62
Upper Street. Hants 1G 15
Upper Street. Norf 4F 79 (nr. Horning)
Upper Street. Norf 4F 79 (nr. Hoveton)
Upper Street. Suff 2E 55
Upper Strensham. Worc 2E 49
Upper Studley. Wilts 1D 22
Upper Sundon. C Beds 3A 52
Upper Swell. Glos 3G 49
Upper Tankersley. S Yor 1H 85
Upper Tean. Staf 2E 73
Upperthong. W Yor 4B 92
Upperthorpe. N Lin 4A 94
Upper Thurnham. Lanc 4D 96
Upper Tillyrie. Per 3D 136
Upperton. W Sus 3A 26
Upper Tooting. G Lon 3D 38
Uppertown. Derbs 4H 85 (nr. Ashover)
Upper Town. Derbs 5G 85 (nr. Bonsall)
Upper Town. Derbs 5G 85 (nr. Hognaston)
Upper Town. Here 1A 48
Uppertown. High 1F 169
Upper Town. N Som 5A 34
Uppertown. Nmbd 2B 114
Uppertown. Orkn 8D 172
Upper Tysoe. Warw 1B 50
Upper Upham. Wilts 4H 35
Upper Upnor. Medw 3B 40
Upper Urquhart. Fife 3D 136
Upper Wardington. Oxon 1C 50
Upper Weald. Mil 2G 51
Upper Weedon. Nptn 5D 62
Upper Wellingham. E Sus 4F 27
Upper Whiston. S Yor 2B 86
Upper Wield. Hants 3E 25
Upper Winchendon. Buck 4F 51
Upperwood. Derbs 5G 85
Upper Woodford. Wilts 3G 23
Upper Wootton. Hants 1D 24
Upper Wraxall. Wilts 4D 34
Upper Wyche. Here 1C 48
Uppincott. Devn 2B 12
Uppingham. Rut 1F 63
Uppington. Shrp 5H 71
Upsall. N Yor 1G 99
Upsettlington. Bord 5E 131
Upshire. Essx 5E 53
Up Somborne. Hants 3B 24
Upstreet. Kent 4G 41
Up Sydling. Dors 2B 14
Upthorpe. Suff 3B 66
Upton. Buck 4F 51
Upton. Cambs 3A 64
Upton. Ches W 4G 83
Upton. Corn 2C 10 (nr. Bude)
Upton. Corn 5C 10 (nr. Liskeard)
Upton. Cumb 1E 102
Upton. Devn 2D 12 (nr. Honiton)
Upton. Devn 4D 8 (nr. Kingsbridge)
Upton. Dors 3E 15 (nr. Poole)
Upton. Dors 4C 14 (nr. Weymouth)
Upton. E Yor 4F 101
Upton. Hants 1B 24 (nr. Andover)
Upton. Hants 1B 16 (nr. Southampton)
Upton. IOW 3D 16
Upton. Leics 1A 62
Upton. Linc 2F 87
Upton. Mers 2E 83
Upton. Norf 4F 79
Upton. Nptn 4E 62
Upton. Notts 3E 87 (nr. Retford)
Upton. Notts 5E 87 (nr. Southwell)
Upton. Oxon 3D 36
Upton. Pemb 4E 43
Upton. Pet 5A 76
Upton. Slo 3A 38
Upton. Som 4H 21 (nr. Somerton)
Upton. Som 4C 20 (nr. Wiveliscombe)
Upton. Warw 5F 61
Upton. W Yor 3E 93
Upton. Wilts 3D 22
Upton Bishop. Here 3B 48
Upton Cheyney. S Glo 5B 34
Upton Cressett. Shrp 1A 60
Upton Crews. Here 3B 48
Upton Cross. Corn 5C 10
Upton End. C Beds 2B 52
Upton Grey. Hants 2E 25
Upton Heath. Ches W 4G 83
Upton Hellions. Devn 2B 12
Upton Lovell. Wilts 2E 23
Upton Magna. Shrp 4H 71
Upton Noble. Som 3C 22
Upton Pyne. Devn 3C 12
Upton St Leonards. Glos 4D 48
Upton Scudamore. Wilts 2D 22
Upton Snodsbury. Worc 5D 60
Upton upon Severn. Worc 1D 48
Upton Warren. Worc 4D 60
Upwaltham. W Sus 4A 26
Upware. Cambs 3E 65
Upwell. Cambs 5D 77
Upwey. Dors 4B 14
Upwick Green. Herts 3E 53
Upwood. Cambs 2B 64
Urafirth. Shet 4E 173
Uragaig. Arg 4A 132
Urchany. High 4C 158
Urchfont. Wilts 1F 23
Urdimarsh. Here 1A 48
Ure. Shet 4D 173
Ure Bank. N Yor 2F 99
Urgha. W Isl 8D 171
Urlay Nook. Stoc T 3B 106
Urmston. G Man 1B 84
Urquhart. Mor 2G 159
Urra. N Yor 4C 106
Urray. High 3H 157
Usan. Ang 3G 145
Ushaw Moor. Dur 5F 115
Usk. Mon 5G 47
Usselby. Linc 1H 87
Usworth. Tyne 4G 115
Utkinton. Ches W 4H 83
Uton. Devn 3B 12
Utterby. Linc 1C 88
Uttoxeter. Staf 2E 73
Uwchmynydd. Gwyn 3A 68
Uxbridge. G Lon 2B 38
Uyeasound. Shet 1G 173
Uzmaston. Pemb 3D 42

V

Valley. IOA 3B 80
Valley End. Surr 4A 38
Valley Truckle. Corn 4B 10
Valsgarth. Shet 1H 173
Valtos. High 2E 155
Van. Powy 2B 58
Vange. Essx 2B 40
Varteg. Torf 5F 47
Vatsetter. Shet 3G 173
Vatten. High 4B 154
Vaul. Arg 4B 138
Vauld,The. Here 1A 48
Vaynol. Gwyn 3E 81
Vaynor. Mer T 4D 46
Veensgarth. Shet 7F 173
Velindre. Powy 2E 47
Vellow. Som 3D 20
Velly. Devn 4C 18
Veness. Orkn 5E 172
Venhay. Devn 1A 12
Venn. Devn 4D 8
Venngreen. Devn 1D 11
Vennington. Shrp 5F 71
Venn Ottery. Devn 3D 12
Venn's Green. Here 1A 48
Venny Tedburn. Devn 3B 12
Venterdon. Corn 5D 10
Ventnor. IOW 5D 16
Vernham Dean. Hants 1B 24
Vernham Street. Hants 1B 24
Vernolds Common. Shrp 2G 59
Verwood. Dors 2F 15
Veryan. Corn 5D 6
Veryan Green. Corn 4D 6
Vicarage. Devn 4F 13
Vickerstown. Cumb 3A 96
Victoria. Corn 2D 6
Victoria Bridge. Strab 3F 176
Vidlin. Shet 5F 173
Viewpark. N Lan 3A 128
Vigo. W Mid 5E 73
Vigo Village. Kent 4H 39
Village Bay. High 3B 154
Vinehall Street. E Sus 3B 28
Vine's Cross. E Sus 4G 27
Viney Hill. Glos 5B 48
Virginia Water. Surr 4A 38
Virginstow. Devn 3D 11
Vobster. Som 2C 22
Voe. Shet 5F 173 (nr. Hillside)
Voe. Shet 3E 173 (nr. Swinister)
Vole. Som 2G 21
Vowchurch. Here 2G 47
Voxter. Shet 4E 173
Voy. Orkn 6B 172
Vulcan Village. Warr 1H 83

W

Waberthwaite. Cumb 5C 102
Wackerfield. Dur 2E 105
Wacton. Norf 1D 66
Wadbister. Shet 7F 173
Wadborough. Worc 1E 49
Wadbrook. Devn 2G 13
Waddesdon. Buck 4F 51
Waddeton. Devn 3E 9
Waddicar. Mers 1F 83
Waddingham. Linc 1G 87
Waddington. Lanc 5G 97
Waddington. Linc 4G 87
Waddon. Devn 5B 12
Wadebridge. Corn 1D 6
Wadeford. Som 1G 13
Wadenhoe. Nptn 2H 63
Wadesmill. Herts 4D 52
Wadhurst. E Sus 2H 27
Wadshelf. Derbs 3H 85
Wadsley. S Yor 1H 85
Wadsley Bridge. S Yor 1H 85
Wadswick. Wilts 5D 34
Wadwick. Hants 1C 24
Wadworth. S Yor 1C 86
Waen. Den 4C 82 (nr. Bodfari)
Waen. Den 4B 82 (nr. Llandyrnog)
Waen. Den 4B 82 (nr. Nantglyn)
Waen. Powy 1B 58
Waen Fach. Powy 4E 70
Waen Goleugoed. Den 3C 82
Wag. High 1H 165
Wainfleet All Saints. Linc 5D 89
Wainfleet Bank. Linc 5D 88
Wainfleet St Mary. Linc 5D 89
Wainhouse Corner. Corn 3B 10
Wainscott. Medw 3B 40
Wainstalls. W Yor 2A 92
Waitby. Cumb 4A 104
Waithe. Linc 4F 95
Wakefield. W Yor 2D 92
Wakerley. Nptn 1G 63
Wakes Colne. Essx 3B 54
Walberswick. Suff 3G 67
Walberton. W Sus 5A 26
Walbottle. Tyne 3E 115
Walby. Cumb 3F 113
Walcombe. Som 2A 22
Walcot. Linc 2H 75
Walcot. N Lin 2B 94
Walcot. Swin 3G 35
Walcot. Telf 4H 71
Walcot. Warw 5F 61
Walcote. Leics 2C 62
Walcot Green. Norf 2D 66
Walcott. Linc 5A 88
Walcott. Norf 2F 79
Walden. N Yor 1C 98
Walden Head. N Yor 1B 98
Walden Stubbs. N Yor 3F 93
Walderslade. Medw 4B 40
Walderton. W Sus 1F 17
Walditch. Dors 3H 13
Waldley. Derbs 2F 73
Waldridge. Dur 4F 115
Waldringfield. Suff 1F 55
Waldron. E Sus 4G 27
Wales. S Yor 2B 86
Walesby. Linc 1A 88
Walesby. Notts 3D 86
Walford. Here 3F 59 (nr. Leintwardine)
Walford. Here 3A 48 (nr. Ross-on-Wye)
Walford. Shrp 3G 71
Walford. Staf 2C 72
Walford Heath. Shrp 4G 71
Walgherton. Ches E 1A 72
Walgrave. Nptn 3F 63
Walhampton. Hants 3B 16
Walkden. G Man 4F 91
Walker. Tyne 3F 115
Walkerburn. Bord 1F 119
Walker Fold. Lanc 5F 97
Walkeringham. Notts 1E 87
Walkerith. Linc 1E 87
Walkern. Herts 3C 52
Walker's Green. Here 1A 48
Walkerton. Fife 3E 137
Walkerville. N Yor 5F 105
Walkford. Dors 3H 15
Walkhampton. Devn 2B 8
Walkington. E Yor 1C 94
Walkley. S Yor 2H 85
Walk Mill. Lanc 1G 91
Wall. Corn 3D 4
Wall. Nmbd 3C 114
Wall. Staf 5F 73
Wallaceton. Dum 1F 111
Wallacetown. Shet 6E 173
Wallacetown. S Ayr 2C 116 (nr. Ayr)
Wallacetown. S Ayr 4B 116 (nr. Dailly)
Wallands Park. E Sus 4F 27
Wallasey. Mers 1F 83
Wallaston Green. Pemb 4D 42
Wallbrook. W Mid 1D 60
Wallcrouch. E Sus 2A 28
Wall End. Cumb 1B 96
Wallend. Medw 3C 40
Wall Heath. W Mid 2C 60
Wallingford. Oxon 3E 36
Wallington. G Lon 4D 39
Wallington. Hants 2D 16
Wallington. Herts 2C 52
Wallis. Pemb 2E 43
Wallisdown. Pool 3F 15
Walliswood. Surr 2C 26
Wall Nook. Dur 5F 115
Walls. Shet 7D 173
Wallsend. Tyne 3G 115
Wallsworth. Glos 3D 48
Wall under Heywood. Shrp 1H 59
Wallyford. E Lot 2G 129
Walmer. Kent 5H 41
Walmer Bridge. Lanc 2C 90
Walmersley. G Man 3G 91
Walmley. W Mid 1F 61
Walnut Grove. Per 1D 136
Walpole. Suff 3F 67
Walpole Cross Keys. Norf 4E 77
Walpole Gate. Norf 4E 77
Walpole Highway. Norf 4E 77
Walpole Marsh. Norf 4D 77
Walpole St Andrew. Norf 4E 77
Walpole St Peter. Norf 4E 77
Walsall. W Mid 1E 61
Walsall Wood. W Mid 5E 73
Walsden. W Yor 2H 91
Walsgrave on Sowe. W Mid 2A 62
Walsham le Willows. Suff 3C 66
Walshaw. G Man 3F 91
Walshford. N Yor 4G 99
Walsoken. Cambs 4D 76
Walston. S Lan 5D 128
Walsworth. Herts 2B 52
Walter's Ash. Buck 2G 37
Walterston. V Glam 4D 32
Walterstone. Here 3G 47
Waltham. Kent 1F 29
Waltham. NE Lin 4F 95
Waltham Abbey. Essx 5D 53
Waltham Chase. Hants 1D 16
Waltham Cross. Herts 5D 52
Waltham on the Wolds. Leics 3F 75
Waltham St Lawrence. Wind 4G 37
Waltham's Cross. Essx 2G 53
Walthamstow. G Lon 2E 39
Walton. Cumb 3G 113
Walton. Derbs 4A 86
Walton. Leics 2C 62
Walton. Mers 1F 83
Walton. Mil 2G 51
Walton. Pet 5A 76
Walton. Powy 5E 59
Walton. Som 3H 21
Walton. Staf 3C 72 (nr. Eccleshall)
Walton. Staf 2C 72 (nr. Stone)
Walton. Suff 2F 55
Walton. Telf 4H 71
Walton. Warw 5G 61
Walton. W Yor 3D 92 (nr. Wakefield)
Walton. W Yor 5G 99 (nr. Wetherby)
Walton Cardiff. Glos 2E 49
Walton East. Pemb 2E 43
Walton Elm. Dors 1C 14
Walton Highway. Norf 4D 77
Walton-in-Gordano. N Som 4H 33
Walton-le-Dale. Lanc 2D 90
Walton-on-Thames. Surr 4C 38
Walton-on-the-Hill. Staf 3D 72
Walton on the Hill. Surr 5D 38
Walton-on-the-Naze. Essx 3F 55
Walton on the Wolds. Leics 4C 74
Walton-on-Trent. Derbs 4G 73
Walton West. Pemb 3C 42
Walwick. Nmbd 2C 114
Walworth. Darl 3F 105
Walworth Gate. Darl 2F 105
Walwyn's Castle. Pemb 3C 42
Wambrook. Som 2F 13
Wampool. Cumb 4D 112
Wanborough. Surr 1A 26
Wanborough. Swin 3H 35
Wandel. S Lan 2B 118
Wandsworth. G Lon 3D 38
Wangford. Suff 2G 65 (nr. Lakenheath)
Wangford. Suff 3G 67 (nr. Southwold)
Wanlip. Leics 4D 74
Wanlockhead. Dum 3A 118
Wannock. E Sus 5G 27
Wansford. E Yor 4E 101
Wansford. Pet 1H 63
Wanshurst Green. Kent 1B 28
Wanstead. G Lon 2F 39
Wanstrow. Som 2C 22
Wanswell. Glos 5B 48
Wantage. Oxon 3C 36
Wapley. S Glo 4C 34
Wappenbury. Warw 4A 62
Wappenham. Nptn 1E 51
Warbleton. E Sus 4H 27
Warblington. Hants 2F 17
Warborough. Oxon 2D 36
Warboys. Cambs 2C 64
Warbreck. Bkpl 1B 90
Warbstow. Corn 3C 10
Warburton. G Man 2A 84
Warcop. Cumb 3A 104
Warden. Kent 3E 40
Warden. Nmbd 3C 114
Ward End. W Mid 2F 61
Ward Green. Suff 4C 66
Ward Green Cross. Lanc 1E 91
Wardhedges. C Beds 2A 52
Wardhouse. Abers 5C 160
Wardington. Oxon 1C 50
Wardle. Ches E 5A 84
Wardle. G Man 3H 91
Wardley. Rut 5F 75
Wardley. W Sus 4G 25
Wardlow. Derbs 3F 85
Wardsend. Ches E 2D 84
Wardy Hill. Cambs 2D 64
Ware. Herts 4D 52
Ware. Kent 4G 41
Wareham. Dors 4E 15
Warehorne. Kent 2D 28
Warenford. Nmbd 2F 121
Waren Mill. Nmbd 1F 121
Warenton. Nmbd 1F 121
Wareside. Herts 4D 53

Waresley—Wicken

Waresley. *Cambs* 5B 64
Waresley. *Worc* 4C 60
Warfield. *Brac* 4G 37
Warfleet. *Devn* 3E 9
Wargate. *Linc* 2B 76
Wargrave. *Wok* 4F 37
Warham. *Norf* 1B 78
Waringsford. *Ban* 5G 179
Waringstown. *Cgvn* 4F 178
Wark. *Nmbd* 1C 120 (nr. Coldstream)
Wark. *Nmbd* 2B 114 (nr. Hexham)
Warkleigh. *Devn* 4G 19
Warkton. *Nptn* 3F 63
Warkworth. *Nptn* 1C 50
Warkworth. *Nmbd* 4G 121
Warlaby. *N Yor* 5A 106
Warland. *W Yor* 2H 91
Warleggan. *Corn* 2F 7
Warlingham. *Surr* 5E 39
Warmanbie. *Dum* 3C 112
Warmfield. *W Yor* 2D 93
Warmingham. *Ches E* 4B 84
Warminghurst. *W Sus* 4C 26
Warmington. *Nptn* 1H 63
Warmington. *Warw* 1C 50
Warminster. *Wilts* 2D 23
Warmley. *S Glo* 4B 34
Warmsworth. *S Yor* 4F 93
Warmwell. *Dors* 4C 14
Warndon. *Worc* 5C 60
Warners End. *Herts* 5A 52
Warnford. *Hants* 4E 24
Warnham. *W Sus* 2C 26
Warningcamp. *W Sus* 5B 26
Warninglid. *W Sus* 3D 26
Warren. *Ches E* 3C 84
Warren. *Pemb* 5D 42
Warrenby. *Red C* 2C 106
Warren Corner. *Hants* 2G 25 (nr. Aldershot)
Warren Corner. *Hants* 4F 25 (nr. Petersfield)
Warrenpoint. *New M* 8F 178
Warren Row. *Wind* 3G 37
Warren Street. *Kent* 5D 40
Warrington. *Mil* 5F 63
Warrington. *Warr* 2A 84
Warsash. *Hants* 2C 16
Warse. *High* 1F 169
Warslow. *Staf* 5E 85
Warsop. *Notts* 4C 86
Warsop Vale. *Notts* 4C 86
Warter. *E Yor* 4C 100
Warthermarske. *N Yor* 2E 98
Warthill. *N Yor* 4A 100
Wartling. *E Sus* 5A 28
Wartnaby. *Leics* 3E 74
Warton. *Lanc* 2D 97 (nr. Carnforth)
Warton. *Lanc* 2C 90 (nr. Freckleton)
Warton. *Nmbd* 4E 121
Warton. *Warw* 5G 73
Warwick. *Warw* 4G 61
Warwick Bridge. *Cumb* 4F 113
Warwick-on-Eden. *Cumb* 4F 113
Warwick Wold. *Surr* 5E 39
Wasbister. *Orkn* 4C 172
Wasdale Head. *Cumb* 4C 102
Wash. *Derbs* 2E 85
Washaway. *Corn* 2E 7
Washbourne. *Devn* 3E 9
Washbrook. *Suff* 1E 54
Wash Common. *W Ber* 5C 36
Washerwall. *Staf* 1D 72
Washfield. *Devn* 1C 12
Washfold. *N Yor* 4D 104
Washford. *Som* 2D 20
Washford Pyne. *Devn* 1B 12
Washingborough. *Linc* 3H 87
Washington. *Tyne* 4G 115
Washington. *W Sus* 4C 26
Washington Village. *Tyne* 4G 115
Waskerley. *Dur* 5D 114
Wasperton. *Warw* 5G 61
Wasp Green. *Surr* 1E 27
Wasps Nest. *Linc* 4H 87
Wass. *N Yor* 2H 99
Watchet. *Som* 2D 20
Watchfield. *Oxon* 2H 35
Watchgate. *Cumb* 5G 103
Watchhill. *Cumb* 5C 112
Watcombe. *Torb* 2F 9
Watendlath. *Cumb* 3D 102
Water. *Devn* 4A 12
Water. *Lanc* 2G 91
Waterbeach. *Cambs* 4D 65
Waterbeach. *W Sus* 2G 17
Waterbeck. *Dum* 2D 112
Waterditch. *Hants* 3G 15
Water End. *C Beds* 2A 52
Water End. *E Yor* 1A 94
Water End. *Essx* 1F 53
Water End. *Herts* 5C 52 (nr. Hatfield)
Water End. *Herts* 4A 52 (nr. Hemel Hempstead)
Waterfall. *Staf* 5E 85
Waterfoot. *E Ren* 4G 127
Waterfoot. *Lanc* 2G 91
Waterfoot. *Moy* 4J 175
Waterford. *Herts* 4D 52
Water Fryston. *W Yor* 2E 93
Waterhead. *Cumb* 4E 103
Waterhead. *E Ayr* 3E 117
Waterhead. *S Ayr* 5C 116
Waterheads. *Bord* 4F 129
Waterhouses. *Dur* 5E 115
Waterhouses. *Staf* 5E 85
Wateringbury. *Kent* 5A 40
Waterlane. *Glos* 5E 49
Waterlip. *Som* 2B 22
Waterloo. *Cphy* 3E 33
Waterloo. *Corn* 5B 10
Waterloo. *Here* 1G 47
Waterloo. *High* 1E 147
Waterloo. *Mers* 1F 83
Waterloo. *Norf* 4E 78
Waterloo. *N Lan* 4B 128
Waterloo. *Pemb* 4D 42
Waterloo. *Per* 5H 143
Waterloo. *Pool* 3F 15
Waterloo. *Shrp* 2G 71
Waterlooville. *Hants* 2E 17
Watermead. *Buck* 4G 51
Watermillock. *Cumb* 2F 103
Water Newton. *Cambs* 1A 64
Water Orton. *Warw* 1F 61
Waterperry. *Oxon* 5E 51
Waterrow. *Som* 4D 20
Watersfield. *W Sus* 4B 26
Waterside. *Buck* 5H 51
Waterside. *Cambs* 3F 65
Waterside. *Cumb* 5D 112
Waterside. *E Ayr* 4D 116 (nr. Ayr)
Waterside. *E Ayr* 5F 127 (nr. Kilmarnock)
Waterside. *E Dun* 2H 127
Waterstein. *High* 4A 154
Waterstock. *Oxon* 5E 51
Waterston. *Pemb* 4D 42
Water Stratford. *Buck* 2E 51
Waters Upton. *Telf* 4A 72
Water Yeat. *Cumb* 1B 96
Watford. *Herts* 1B 38
Watford. *Nptn* 4D 62
Wath. *Cumb* 4H 103
Wath. *N Yor* 3D 98 (nr. Pateley Bridge)
Wath. *N Yor* 2F 99 (nr. Ripon)
Wath Brow. *Cumb* 3B 102
Wath upon Dearne. *S Yor* 1B 86
Watlington. *Norf* 4F 77
Watlington. *Oxon* 2E 37
Watten. *High* 3E 169
Wattisfield. *Suff* 3C 66
Wattisham. *Suff* 5C 66
Wattlesborough Heath. *Shrp* 4F 71
Watton. *Dors* 3H 13
Watton. *E Yor* 4E 101
Watton. *Norf* 5B 78
Watton at Stone. *Herts* 4C 52
Wattston. *N Lan* 2A 128
Wattstown. *Rhon* 2D 32
Wattsville. *Cphy* 2F 33
Wauldby. *E Yor* 2C 94
Waulkmill. *Abers* 4D 152
Waun. *Powy* 4E 71
Waunarlwydd. *Swan* 3F 31
Waun Fawr. *Cdgn* 2F 57
Waunfawr. *Gwyn* 5E 81
Waungilwen. *Carm* 1H 43
Waunlwyd. *Blae* 5E 47
Waun-y-Clyn. *Carm* 5E 45
Wavendon. *Mil* 2H 51
Waverbridge. *Cumb* 5D 112
Waverley. *Surr* 2G 25
Waverton. *Ches W* 4G 83
Waverton. *Cumb* 5D 112
Wavertree. *Mers* 2F 83
Wawne. *E Yor* 1D 94
Waxham. *Norf* 3G 79
Waxholme. *E Yor* 2G 95
Wayford. *Som* 2H 13
Way Head. *Cambs* 2D 65
Waytown. *Dors* 3H 13
Way Village. *Devn* 1B 12
Wdig. *Pemb* 1D 42
Wealdstone. *G Lon* 2C 38
Weardley. *W Yor* 5E 99
Weare. *Som* 1H 21
Weare Giffard. *Devn* 4E 19
Wearhead. *Dur* 1B 104
Wearne. *Som* 4H 21
Weasdale. *Cumb* 4H 103
Weasenham All Saints. *Norf* 3H 77
Weasenham St Peter. *Norf* 3A 78
Weaverham. *Ches W* 3A 84
Weaverthorpe. *N Yor* 2D 100
Webheath. *Worc* 4E 61
Webton. *Here* 2H 47
Wedderlairs. *Abers* 5F 161
Weddington. *Warw* 1A 62
Wedhampton. *Wilts* 1F 23
Wedmore. *Som* 2H 21
Wednesbury. *W Mid* 1D 61
Wednesfield. *W Mid* 5D 72
Weecar. *Notts* 4F 87
Weedon. *Buck* 4G 51
Weedon Bec. *Nptn* 5D 62
Weedon Lois. *Nptn* 1E 50
Weeford. *Staf* 5F 73
Week. *Devn* 4F 19 (nr. Barnstaple)
Week. *Devn* 2G 11 (nr. Okehampton)
Week. *Devn* 1H 11 (nr. South Molton)
Week. *Devn* 2D 9 (nr. Totnes)
Week. *Som* 3C 20
Weeke. *Devn* 2A 12
Weeke. *Hants* 3C 24
Week Green. *Corn* 3C 10
Weekley. *Nptn* 2F 63
Week St Mary. *Corn* 3C 10
Weel. *E Yor* 1D 94
Weeley. *Essx* 3E 55
Weeley Heath. *Essx* 3E 55
Weem. *Per* 4F 143
Weeping Cross. *Staf* 3D 72
Weethly. *Warw* 5E 61
Weeting. *Norf* 2G 65
Weeton. *E Yor* 2G 95
Weeton. *Lanc* 1B 90
Weeton. *N Yor* 5E 99
Weetwood Hall. *Nmbd* 2E 121
Weir. *Lanc* 2G 91
Welborne. *Norf* 4C 78
Welbourn. *Linc* 5G 87
Welburn. *N Yor* 1A 100 (nr. Kirkbymoorside)
Welburn. *N Yor* 3B 100 (nr. Malton)
Welbury. *N Yor* 4A 106
Welby. *Linc* 2G 75
Welches Dam. *Cambs* 2D 64
Welcombe. *Devn* 1C 10
Weld Bank. *Lanc* 3D 90
Weldon. *Nptn* 2G 63
Weldon. *Nmbd* 5F 121
Welford. *Nptn* 2D 62
Welford. *W Ber* 4C 36
Welford-on-Avon. *Warw* 5F 61
Welham. *Leics* 1E 63
Welham. *Notts* 2E 87
Welham Green. *Herts* 5C 52
Well. *Hants* 2F 25
Well. *Linc* 3D 88
Well. *N Yor* 1E 99
Welland. *Worc* 1C 48
Wellbank. *Ang* 5D 144
Well Bottom. *Dors* 1E 15
Welldale. *Dum* 3C 112
Wellesbourne. *Warw* 5G 61
Well Hill. *Kent* 4F 39
Wellhouse. *W Ber* 4D 36
Welling. *G Lon* 3F 39
Wellingborough. *Nptn* 4F 63
Wellingham. *Norf* 3A 78
Wellingore. *Linc* 5G 87
Wellington. *Cumb* 4B 102
Wellington. *Here* 1H 47
Wellington. *Som* 4E 21
Wellington. *Telf* 4A 72
Wellington Heath. *Here* 1C 48
Wellow. *Bath* 1C 22
Wellow. *IOW* 4B 16
Wellow. *Notts* 4D 86
Wellpond Green. *Herts* 3E 53
Wells. *Som* 2A 22
Wellsborough. *Leics* 5A 74
Wells Green. *Ches E* 5A 84
Wells-next-the-Sea. *Norf* 1B 78
Wells of Ythan. *Abers* 5D 160
Wellswood. *Torb* 2F 9
Wellwood. *Fife* 1D 129
Welney. *Norf* 1E 65
Welsford. *Devn* 4C 18
Welshampton. *Shrp* 2G 71
Welsh End. *Shrp* 2H 71
Welsh Frankton. *Shrp* 2F 71
Welsh Hook. *Pemb* 2D 42
Welsh Newton. *Here* 4H 47
Welsh Newton Common. *Here* 4A 48
Welshpool. *Powy* 5E 70
Welsh St Donats. *V Glam* 4D 32
Welton. *Bath* 1B 22
Welton. *Cumb* 5E 113
Welton. *E Yor* 2C 94
Welton. *Linc* 2H 87
Welton. *Nptn* 4C 62
Welton Hill. *Linc* 2H 87
Welton le Marsh. *Linc* 4D 88
Welton le Wold. *Linc* 2B 88
Welwick. *E Yor* 2G 95
Welwyn. *Herts* 4C 52
Welwyn Garden City. *Herts* 4C 52
Wem. *Shrp* 3H 71
Wembdon. *Som* 3F 21
Wembley. *G Lon* 2C 38
Wembury. *Devn* 4B 8
Wembworthy. *Devn* 2G 11
Wemyss Bay. *Inv* 2C 126
Wenallt. *Cdgn* 3F 57
Wenallt. *Gwyn* 1B 70
Wendens Ambo. *Essx* 2F 53
Wendlebury. *Oxon* 4D 50
Wendling. *Norf* 4B 78
Wendover. *Buck* 5G 51
Wendron. *Corn* 5A 6
Wendy. *Cambs* 1D 52
Wenfordbridge. *Corn* 5A 10
Wenhaston. *Suff* 3G 67
Wennington. *Cambs* 3B 64
Wennington. *G Lon* 2G 39
Wennington. *Lanc* 2F 97
Wensley. *Derbs* 4G 85
Wensley. *N Yor* 1C 98
Wentbridge. *W Yor* 3E 93
Wentnor. *Shrp* 1F 59
Wentworth. *Cambs* 3D 65
Wentworth. *S Yor* 1A 86
Wenvoe. *V Glam* 4E 32
Weobley. *Here* 5G 59
Weobley Marsh. *Here* 5G 59
Wepham. *W Sus* 5B 26
Wereham. *Norf* 5F 77
Wergs. *W Mid* 5C 72
Wern. *Gwyn* 1E 69
Wern. *Powy* 4E 46 (nr. Brecon)
Wern. *Powy* 4E 71 (nr. Guilsfield)
Wern. *Powy* 4B 70 (nr. Llangadfan)
Wern. *Powy* 3E 71 (nr. Llanymynech)
Wernffrwd. *Swan* 3E 31
Wernyrheolydd. *Mon* 4G 47
Werrington. *Corn* 4D 10
Werrington. *Pet* 5A 76
Werrington. *Staf* 1D 72
Wervin. *Ches W* 3G 83
Wesham. *Lanc* 1C 90
Wessington. *Derbs* 5A 86
West Aberthaw. *V Glam* 5D 32
West Acre. *Norf* 4G 77
West Allerdean. *Nmbd* 5F 131
West Alvington. *Devn* 4D 8
West Amesbury. *Wilts* 2G 23
West Anstey. *Devn* 4B 20
West Appleton. *N Yor* 5F 105
West Ardsley. *W Yor* 2C 92
West Arthurlie. *E Ren* 4F 127
West Ashby. *Linc* 3B 88
West Ashling. *W Sus* 2G 17
West Ashton. *Wilts* 1D 23
West Auckland. *Dur* 2E 105
West Ayton. *N Yor* 1D 101
West Bagborough. *Som* 3E 21
West Bank. *Hal* 2H 83
West Barkwith. *Linc* 2A 88
West Barnby. *N Yor* 3F 107
West Barns. *E Lot* 2C 130
West Barsham. *Norf* 2B 78
West Bay. *Dors* 3H 13
West Beckham. *Norf* 2D 78
West Bennan. *N Ayr* 3D 123
Westbere. *Kent* 4F 41
West Bergholt. *Essx* 3C 54
West Bexington. *Dors* 4A 14
West Bilney. *Norf* 4G 77
West Blackdene. *Dur* 1B 104
West Blatchington. *Brig* 5D 27
Westborough. *Linc* 1F 75
Westbourne. *Bour* 3F 15
Westbourne. *W Sus* 2F 17
West Bowling. *W Yor* 1B 92
West Brabourne. *Kent* 1E 29
West Bradford. *Lanc* 5G 97
West Bradley. *Som* 3A 22
West Bretton. *W Yor* 3C 92
West Bridgford. *Notts* 2C 74
West Briggs. *Norf* 4F 77
West Bromwich. *W Mid* 1D 61
Westbrook. *Here* 1F 47
Westbrook. *Kent* 3H 41
Westbrook. *Wilts* 5E 35
West Buckland. *Devn* 3G 19 (nr. Barnstaple)
West Buckland. *Devn* 4C 8 (nr. Thurlestone)
West Buckland. *Som* 4E 21
West Burnside. *Abers* 1G 145
West Burrafirth. *Shet* 6D 173
West Burton. *N Yor* 1C 98
West Burton. *W Sus* 4B 26
Westbury. *Buck* 2E 50
Westbury. *Shrp* 5F 71
Westbury. *Wilts* 1D 22
Westbury Leigh. *Wilts* 2D 22
Westbury-on-Severn. *Glos* 4C 48
Westbury on Trym. *Bris* 4A 34
Westbury-sub-Mendip. *Som* 2A 22
West Butsfield. *Dur* 5E 115
West Butterwick. *N Lin* 4B 94
Westby. *Linc* 3G 75
West Byfleet. *Surr* 4B 38
West Caister. *Norf* 4H 79
West Calder. *W Lot* 3D 128
West Camel. *Som* 4A 22
West Carr. *N Lin* 4H 93
West Chaldon. *Dors* 4C 14
West Challow. *Oxon* 3B 36
West Charleton. *Devn* 4D 8
West Chelborough. *Dors* 2A 14
West Chevington. *Nmbd* 5G 121
West Chiltington. *W Sus* 4B 26
West Chiltington Common. *W Sus* 4B 26
West Chinnock. *Som* 1H 13
West Chisenbury. *Wilts* 1G 23
West Clandon. *Surr* 5B 38
West Cliffe. *Kent* 1H 29
Westcliff-on-Sea. *S'end* 2C 40
West Clyne. *High* 3F 165
West Coker. *Som* 1A 14
Westcombe. *Som* 3B 22 (nr. Evercreech)
Westcombe. *Som* 4H 21 (nr. Somerton)
West Compton. *Dors* 3A 14
West Compton. *Som* 2A 22
West Cornforth. *Dur* 1A 106
Westcot. *Oxon* 3B 36
Westcott. *Buck* 4F 51
Westcott. *Devn* 2D 12
Westcott. *Surr* 1C 26
Westcott Barton. *Oxon* 3C 50
West Cowick. *E Yor* 2G 93
West Cranmore. *Som* 2B 22
West Croftmore. *High* 2D 150
West Cross. *Swan* 4F 31
West Cullerlie. *Abers* 3E 153
West Culvennan. *Dum* 3H 109
West Curry. *Corn* 3C 10
West Curthwaite. *Cumb* 5E 113
Westdean. *E Sus* 5G 27
West Dean. *W Sus* 1G 17
West Dean. *Wilts* 4A 24
West Deeping. *Linc* 5A 76
West Derby. *Mers* 1F 83
West Dereham. *Norf* 5F 77
West Down. *Devn* 2F 19
Westdowns. *Corn* 4A 10
West Drayton. *G Lon* 3B 38
West Drayton. *Notts* 3E 86
West Dunnet. *High* 1E 169
West Ella. *E Yor* 2D 94
West End. *Bed* 5G 63
West End. *Cambs* 1D 64
West End. *Dors* 2E 15
West End. *E Yor* 3E 101 (nr. Kilham)
West End. *E Yor* 1E 95 (nr. Preston)
West End. *E Yor* 1C 94 (nr. South Cove)
West End. *E Yor* 4F 101 (nr. Ulrome)
West End. *G Lon* 2D 39
West End. *Hants* 1C 16
West End. *Herts* 5C 52
West End. *Kent* 4F 41
West End. *Lanc* 3D 96
West End. *Linc* 1C 76
West End. *Norf* 4G 79
West End. *N Som* 5H 33
West End. *N Yor* 4D 98
West End. *S Glo* 3C 34
West End. *S Lan* 5C 128
West End. *Surr* 4A 38
West End. *Wilts* 4E 23
West End. *Wind* 4G 37
West End. *Worc* 2F 49
West End Green. *Hants* 5E 37
Westenhanger. *Kent* 2F 29
Wester Aberchalder. *High* 2H 149
Wester Balgedie. *Per* 3D 136
Wester Brae. *High* 2A 158
Wester Culbeuchly. *Abers* 2D 160
Westerdale. *High* 3D 168
Westerdale. *N Yor* 4D 106
Wester Dechmont. *W Lot* 2D 128
Wester Fearn. *High* 5D 164
Westerfield. *Suff* 1E 55
Wester Galcantray. *High* 4C 158
Westergate. *W Sus* 5A 26
Wester Gruinards. *High* 4C 164
Westerham. *Kent* 5F 39
Westerleigh. *S Glo* 4B 34
Westerloch. *High* 3F 169
Wester Mandally. *High* 3E 149
Wester Quarff. *Shet* 8F 173
Wester Rarichie. *High* 1C 158
Wester Shian. *Per* 5F 143
Wester Skeld. *Shet* 7D 173
Westerton. *Ang* 3F 145
Westerton. *Dur* 1F 105
Westerton. *W Sus* 2G 17
Westerwick. *Shet* 7D 173
West Farleigh. *Kent* 5B 40
West Farndon. *Nptn* 5C 62
West Felton. *Shrp* 3F 71
Westfield. *Cumb* 2A 102
Westfield. *E Sus* 4C 28
Westfield. *High* 2C 168
Westfield. *Norf* 5B 78
Westfield. *N Lan* 2A 128
Westfield. *W Lot* 2C 128
Westfields. *Dors* 2C 14
Westfields of Rattray. *Per* 4A 144
West Fleetham. *Nmbd* 2F 121
Westford. *Som* 1E 13
West Garforth. *W Yor* 1D 93
Westgate. *Dur* 1C 104
Westgate. *Norf* 1B 78
Westgate. *N Lin* 4A 94
Westgate on Sea. *Kent* 3H 41
West Ginge. *Oxon* 3C 36
West Grafton. *Wilts* 5H 35
West Green. *Hants* 1F 25
West Grimstead. *Wilts* 4H 23
West Grinstead. *W Sus* 3C 26
West Haddlesey. *N Yor* 2F 93
West Haddon. *Nptn* 3D 62
West Hagbourne. *Oxon* 3D 36
West Hagley. *Worc* 2C 60
West Hall. *Cumb* 3G 113
Westhall. *Suff* 2G 67
West Hallam. *Derbs* 1B 74
Westhall Terrace. *Ang* 5D 144
West Halton. *N Lin* 2C 94
Westham. *Dors* 5B 14
Westham. *E Sus* 5H 27
West Ham. *G Lon* 2E 39
Westham. *Som* 2H 21
Westhampnett. *W Sus* 2G 17
West Handley. *Derbs* 3A 86
West Hanney. *Oxon* 2C 36
West Hanningfield. *Essx* 1B 40
West Hardwick. *W Yor* 3E 93
West Harnham. *Wilts* 4G 23
West Harptree. *Bath* 1A 22
West Harting. *W Sus* 4F 25
West Harton. *Tyne* 3G 115
West Hatch. *Som* 4F 21
Westhay. *Som* 2H 21
Westhead. *Lanc* 4C 90
West Head. *Norf* 5E 77
West Heath. *Hants* 1D 24 (nr. Basingstoke)
West Heath. *Hants* 1G 25 (nr. Farnborough)
West Helmsdale. *High* 2H 165
West Hendred. *Oxon* 3C 36
West Heogaland. *Shet* 4D 173
West Heslerton. *N Yor* 2D 100
West Hewish. *N Som* 5G 33
Westhide. *Here* 1A 48
Westhill. *Abers* 3F 153
West Hill. *Devn* 3D 12
West Hill. *E Yor* 3F 101
Westhill. *High* 4B 158
West Hill. *N Som* 4H 33
West Hill. *W Sus* 2E 27
West Hoathly. *W Sus* 2E 27
West Holme. *Dors* 4D 15
Westhope. *Here* 5G 59
Westhope. *Shrp* 2G 59
West Horndon. *Essx* 2H 39
Westhorp. *Nptn* 5C 62
Westhorpe. *Linc* 2B 76
Westhorpe. *Suff* 4C 66
West Horrington. *Som* 2A 22
West Horsley. *Surr* 5B 38
West Horton. *Nmbd* 1E 121
West Hougham. *Kent* 1G 29
Westhoughton. *G Man* 4E 91
West Houlland. *Shet* 6D 173
Westhouse. *N Yor* 2F 97
Westhouses. *Derbs* 5B 86
West Howe. *Bour* 3F 15
Westhumble. *Surr* 5C 38
West Huntspill. *Som* 2G 21
West Hyde. *Herts* 1B 38
West Hynish. *Arg* 5A 138
West Hythe. *Kent* 2F 29
West Ilsley. *W Ber* 3C 36
Westing. *Shet* 1G 173
West Itchenor. *W Sus* 2G 17
West Keal. *Linc* 4C 88
West Kennett. *Wilts* 5G 35
West Kilbride. *N Ayr* 5D 126
West Kingsdown. *Kent* 4G 39
West Kington. *Wilts* 4D 34
West Kirby. *Mers* 2E 82
West Knapton. *N Yor* 2C 100
West Knighton. *Dors* 4C 14
West Knoyle. *Wilts* 3D 22
West Kyloe. *Nmbd* 5G 131
Westlake. *Devn* 3C 8
West Lambrook. *Som* 1H 13
West Langdon. *Kent* 1H 29
West Langwell. *High* 3D 164
West Lavington. *W Sus* 4G 25
West Lavington. *Wilts* 1F 23
West Layton. *N Yor* 4E 105
West Leake. *Notts* 3C 74
West Learmouth. *Nmbd* 1C 120
Westleigh. *Devn* 4E 19 (nr. Bideford)
Westleigh. *Devn* 1D 12 (nr. Tiverton)
West Leigh. *Devn* 2G 11 (nr. Winkleigh)
Westleigh. *G Man* 4E 91
West Leith. *Buck* 4H 51
Westleton. *Suff* 4G 67
West Lexham. *Norf* 4H 77
Westley. *Shrp* 5F 71
Westley. *Suff* 4H 65
Westley Waterless. *Cambs* 5F 65
West Lilling. *N Yor* 3A 100
West Lingo. *Fife* 3G 137
Westlington. *Buck* 4F 51
Westlinton. *Cumb* 3E 113
West Linton. *Bord* 4E 129
West Littleton. *S Glo* 4C 34
West Looe. *Corn* 3G 7
West Lulworth. *Dors* 4D 14
West Lutton. *N Yor* 3D 100
West Lydford. *Som* 3A 22
West Lyng. *Som* 4G 21
West Lynn. *Norf* 4F 77
West Mains. *Per* 2B 136
West Malling. *Kent* 5A 40
West Malvern. *Worc* 1C 48
Westmancote. *Worc* 2E 49
West Marden. *W Sus* 1F 17
West Markham. *Notts* 3E 86
Westmarsh. *Kent* 4G 41
West Marsh. *NE Lin* 4F 95
West Marton. *N Yor* 4A 98
West Meon. *Hants* 4E 25
West Mersea. *Essx* 4D 54
Westmeston. *E Sus* 4E 27
Westmill. *Herts* 3D 52 (nr. Buntingford)
Westmill. *Herts* 2B 52 (nr. Hitchin)
West Milton. *Dors* 3A 14
Westminster. *G Lon* 3D 39
West Molesey. *Surr* 4C 38
West Monkton. *Som* 4F 21
Westmoor End. *Cumb* 1B 102
West Moors. *Dors* 2F 15
West Morden. *Dors* 3E 15
West Muir. *Ang* 2E 145 (nr. Brechin)
Westmuir. *Ang* 3C 144 (nr. Forfar)
West Murkle. *High* 2D 168
West Ness. *N Yor* 2A 100
Westness. *Orkn* 5C 172
Westnewton. *Cumb* 5C 112
West Newton. *E Yor* 1E 95
West Newton. *Norf* 3F 77
Westnewton. *Nmbd* 1D 120
West Newton. *Som* 4F 21
West Norwood. *G Lon* 3E 39
Westoe. *Tyne* 3G 115
West Ogwell. *Devn* 2E 9
Weston. *Bath* 5C 34
Weston. *Ches E* 5B 84 (nr. Crewe)
Weston. *Ches E* 3D 84 (nr. Macclesfield)
Weston. *Devn* 2E 13 (nr. Honiton)
Weston. *Devn* 4E 13 (nr. Sidmouth)
Weston. *Dors* 5B 14 (nr. Weymouth)
Weston. *Dors* 2A 14 (nr. Yeovil)
Weston. *Hal* 2H 83
Weston. *Hants* 4F 25
Weston. *Here* 5F 59
Weston. *Herts* 2C 52
Weston. *Linc* 3B 76
Weston. *Nptn* 1D 50
Weston. *Notts* 4E 87
Weston. *Shrp* 1H 59 (nr. Bridgnorth)
Weston. *Shrp* 3F 59 (nr. Knighton)
Weston. *Shrp* 3H 71 (nr. Wem)
Weston. *S Lan* 5D 128
Weston. *Staf* 3D 73
Weston. *Suff* 2G 67
Weston. *W Ber* 4B 36
Weston Bampfylde. *Som* 4B 22
Weston Beggard. *Here* 1A 48
Westonbirt. *Glos* 3D 34
Weston by Welland. *Nptn* 1E 63
Weston Colville. *Cambs* 5F 65
Westoncommon. *Shrp* 3G 71
Weston Coyney. *Stoke* 1D 72
Weston Ditch. *Suff* 3F 65
Weston Favell. *Nptn* 4E 63
Weston Green. *Cambs* 5F 65
Weston Green. *Norf* 4D 78
Weston Heath. *Shrp* 4B 72
Weston Hills. *Linc* 4B 76
Weston in Arden. *Warw* 2A 62
Westoning. *C Beds* 2A 52
Weston-in-Gordano. *N Som* 4H 33
Weston Jones. *Staf* 3B 72
Weston Longville. *Norf* 4D 78
Weston Lullingfields. *Shrp* 3G 71
Weston-on-Avon. *Warw* 5F 61
Weston-on-the-Green. *Oxon* 4D 50
Weston-on-Trent. *Derbs* 3B 74
Weston Patrick. *Hants* 2E 25
Weston Rhyn. *Shrp* 2E 71
Weston-sub-Edge. *Glos* 1G 49
Weston-super-Mare. *N Som* 5G 33
Weston Town. *Som* 2C 22
Weston Turville. *Buck* 4G 51
Weston under Lizard. *Staf* 4C 72
Weston under Penyard. *Here* 3B 48
Weston under Wetherley. *Warw* 4A 62
Weston Underwood. *Derbs* 1G 73
Weston Underwood. *Mil* 5F 63
Westonzoyland. *Som* 3G 21
West Orchard. *Dors* 1D 14
West Overton. *Wilts* 5G 35
Westow. *N Yor* 3B 100
Westown. *Per* 1E 137
West Panson. *Devn* 3D 10
West Park. *Hart* 1B 106
West Parley. *Dors* 3F 15
West Peckham. *Kent* 5H 39
West Pelton. *Dur* 4F 115
West Pennard. *Som* 3A 22
West Pentire. *Corn* 2B 6
West Perry. *Cambs* 4A 64
West Pitcorthie. *Fife* 3H 137
West Plean. *Stir* 1B 128
West Poringland. *Norf* 5E 79
West Porlock. *Som* 2B 20
Westport. *Som* 1G 13
West Putford. *Devn* 1D 10
West Quantoxhead. *Som* 2E 20
Westra. *V Glam* 4E 33
West Rainton. *Dur* 5G 115
West Rasen. *Linc* 2H 87
West Ravendale. *NE Lin* 1B 88
Westray Airport. *Orkn* 2D 172
West Raynham. *Norf* 3A 78
Westrigg. *W Lot* 3C 128
West Rounton. *N Yor* 4B 106
West Row. *Suff* 3F 65
West Rudham. *Norf* 3H 77
West Runton. *Norf* 1D 78
Westruther. *Bord* 4C 130
Westry. *Cambs* 1C 64
West Saltoun. *E Lot* 3A 130
West Sandford. *Devn* 2B 12
West Sandwick. *Shet* 3F 173
West Scrafton. *N Yor* 1C 98
Westside. *Orkn* 5C 172
West Sleekburn. *Nmbd* 1F 115
West Somerton. *Norf* 4G 79
West Stafford. *Dors* 4C 14
West Stockwith. *Notts* 1E 87
West Stoke. *W Sus* 2G 17
West Stonesdale. *N Yor* 4B 104
West Stoughton. *Som* 2H 21
West Stour. *Dors* 4C 22
West Stourmouth. *Kent* 4G 41
West Stow. *Suff* 3H 65
West Stowell. *Wilts* 5G 35
West Strathan. *High* 2F 167
West Stratton. *Hants* 2D 24
West Street. *Kent* 5D 40
West Tanfield. *N Yor* 2E 99
West Taphouse. *Corn* 2F 7
West Tarbert. *Arg* 3G 125
West Thirston. *Nmbd* 4F 121
West Thorney. *W Sus* 2F 17
West Thurrock. *Thur* 3G 39
West Tilbury. *Thur* 3A 40
West Tisted. *Hants* 4E 25
West Tofts. *Norf* 1H 65
West Torrington. *Linc* 2A 88
West Town. *Bath* 5A 34
West Town. *Hants* 3F 17
West Town. *N Som* 5H 33
West Tytherley. *Hants* 4A 24
West Tytherton. *Wilts* 4E 35
West View. *Hart* 1C 106
Westville. *Notts* 1C 74
West Walton. *Norf* 4D 76
Westward. *Cumb* 5D 112
Westward Ho!. *Devn* 4E 19
Westwell. *Kent* 1D 28
Westwell. *Oxon* 5H 49
Westwell Leacon. *Kent* 1D 28
West Wellow. *Hants* 1A 16
West Wemyss. *Fife* 4F 137
Westwick. *Cambs* 4D 64
Westwick. *Dur* 3D 104
Westwick. *Norf* 3E 79
West Wick. *N Som* 5G 33
West Wickham. *Cambs* 1G 53
West Wickham. *G Lon* 4E 39
West Williamston. *Pemb* 4E 43
West Willoughby. *Linc* 1G 75
West Winch. *Norf* 4F 77
West Winterslow. *Wilts* 3H 23
West Wittering. *W Sus* 3F 17
West Witton. *N Yor* 1C 98
Westwood. *Devn* 3D 12
Westwood. *Kent* 4H 41
Westwood. *Pet* 1A 64
Westwood. *S Lan* 4H 127
Westwood. *Wilts* 1D 22
West Woodburn. *Nmbd* 1B 114
West Woodhay. *W Ber* 5B 36
West Woodlands. *Som* 2C 22
West Woodside. *Cumb* 5E 112
Westwoodside. *N Lin* 4H 93
West Worldham. *Hants* 3F 25
West Worlington. *Devn* 1A 12
West Worthing. *W Sus* 5C 26
West Wratting. *Cambs* 5F 65
West Wycombe. *Buck* 2G 37
West Wylam. *Nmbd* 3E 115
West Yatton. *Wilts* 4D 34
West Yell. *Shet* 3F 173
West Youlstone. *Corn* 1C 10
Wetheral. *Cumb* 4F 113
Wetherby. *W Yor* 5G 99
Wetherden. *Suff* 4C 66
Wetheringsett. *Suff* 4D 66
Wethersfield. *Essx* 2H 53
Wethersta. *Shet* 5E 173
Wetherup Street. *Suff* 4D 66
Wetley Rocks. *Staf* 1D 72
Wettenhall. *Ches E* 4A 84
Wetton. *Staf* 5F 85
Wetwang. *E Yor* 4D 100
Wetwood. *Staf* 2B 72
Wexcombe. *Wilts* 1A 24
Wexham Street. *Buck* 2A 38
Weybourne. *Norf* 1D 78
Weybourne. *Surr* 2G 25
Weybread. *Suff* 2E 67
Weybridge. *Surr* 4B 38
Weycroft. *Devn* 3G 13
Weydale. *High* 2D 168
Weyhill. *Hants* 2B 24
Weymouth. *Dors* 5B 14 & 204
Weythel. *Powy* 5E 59
Whaddon. *Buck* 2G 51
Whaddon. *Cambs* 1D 52
Whaddon. *Glos* 4D 48
Whaddon. *Wilts* 4G 23
Whale. *Cumb* 2G 103
Whaley. *Derbs* 3C 86
Whaley Bridge. *Derbs* 2E 85
Whaley Thorns. *Derbs* 3C 86
Whalley. *Lanc* 1F 91
Whalton. *Nmbd* 1E 115
Wham. *N Yor* 3G 97
Whaplode. *Linc* 3C 76
Whaplode Drove. *Linc* 4C 76
Whaplode St Catherine. *Linc* 3C 76
Wharfe. *N Yor* 3G 97
Wharles. *Lanc* 1C 90
Wharley End. *C Beds* 1H 51
Wharncliffe Side. *S Yor* 1G 85
Wharram-le-Street. *N Yor* 3C 100
Wharton. *Ches W* 4A 84
Wharton. *Here* 5H 59
Whashton. *N Yor* 4E 105
Whasset. *Cumb* 1E 97
Whatcote. *Warw* 1A 50
Whateley. *Warw* 1G 61
Whatfield. *Suff* 1D 54
Whatley. *Som* 2G 13 (nr. Chard)
Whatley. *Som* 2C 22 (nr. Frome)
Whatlington. *E Sus* 4B 28
Whatmore. *Shrp* 3A 60
Whatstandwell. *Derbs* 5H 85
Whatton. *Notts* 2E 75
Whauphill. *Dum* 5B 110
Whaw. *N Yor* 4C 104
Wheatacre. *Norf* 1G 67
Wheatcroft. *Derbs* 5A 86
Wheathampstead. *Herts* 4B 52
Wheathill. *Shrp* 2A 60
Wheatley. *Devn* 3B 12
Wheatley. *Hants* 2F 25
Wheatley. *Oxon* 5D 50
Wheatley. *S Yor* 4F 93
Wheatley. *W Yor* 2A 92
Wheatley Hill. *Dur* 1A 106
Wheatley Lane. *Lanc* 1G 91
Wheatley Park. *S Yor* 4F 93
Wheaton Aston. *Staf* 4C 72
Wheatstone Park. *Staf* 5C 72
Wheddon Cross. *Som* 3C 20
Wheelerstreet. *Surr* 1A 26
Wheelock. *Ches E* 5B 84
Wheelock Heath. *Ches E* 5B 84
Wheelton. *Lanc* 2E 90
Wheldrake. *York* 5A 100
Whelford. *Glos* 2G 35
Whelpley Hill. *Buck* 5H 51
Whelpo. *Cumb* 1E 102
Whelston. *Flin* 3E 82
Whenby. *N Yor* 3A 100
Whepstead. *Suff* 5H 65
Wherstead. *Suff* 1E 55
Wherwell. *Hants* 2B 24
Wheston. *Derbs* 3F 85
Whetsted. *Kent* 1A 28
Whetstone. *G Lon* 1D 38
Whetstone. *Leics* 1C 62
Whicham. *Cumb* 1A 96
Whichford. *Warw* 2B 50
Whickham. *Tyne* 3F 115
Whiddon. *Devn* 2E 11
Whiddon Down. *Devn* 3G 11
Whigstreet. *Ang* 4D 145
Whilton. *Nptn* 4D 62
Whimble. *Devn* 2D 10
Whimple. *Devn* 3D 12
Whimpwell Green. *Norf* 3F 79
Whinburgh. *Norf* 5C 78
Whin Lane End. *Lanc* 5C 96
Whinnyfold. *Abers* 5H 161
Whinny Hill. *Stoc T* 3A 106
Whippingham. *IOW* 3D 16
Whipsnade. *C Beds* 4A 52
Whipton. *Devn* 3C 12
Whirlow. *S Yor* 2H 85
Whisby. *Linc* 4G 87
Whissendine. *Rut* 4F 75
Whissonsett. *Norf* 3B 78
Whisterfield. *Ches E* 3C 84
Whistley Green. *Wok* 4F 37
Whiston. *Mers* 1G 83
Whiston. *Nptn* 4F 63
Whiston. *S Yor* 1B 86
Whiston. *Staf* 1E 73 (nr. Cheadle)
Whiston. *Staf* 4C 72 (nr. Penkridge)
Whiston Cross. *Shrp* 5B 72
Whiston Eaves. *Staf* 1E 73
Whitacre Heath. *Warw* 1G 61
Whitbeck. *Cumb* 1A 96
Whitbourne. *Here* 5B 60
Whitburn. *Tyne* 3H 115
Whitburn. *W Lot* 3C 128
Whitburn Colliery. *Tyne* 3H 115
Whitby. *Ches W* 3F 83
Whitby. *N Yor* 3F 107
Whitbyheath. *Ches W* 3F 83
Whitchester. *Bord* 4D 130
Whitchurch. *Bath* 5B 34
Whitchurch. *Buck* 3G 51
Whitchurch. *Card* 4E 33
Whitchurch. *Devn* 5E 11
Whitchurch. *Hants* 2C 24
Whitchurch. *Here* 4A 48
Whitchurch. *Pemb* 2C 42
Whitchurch. *Shrp* 1H 71
Whitchurch Canonicorum. *Dors* 3G 13
Whitchurch Hill. *Oxon* 4E 37
Whitchurch-on-Thames. *Oxon* 4E 37
Whitcombe. *Dors* 4C 14
Whitcot. *Shrp* 1F 59
Whitcott Keysett. *Shrp* 2E 59
Whiteabbey. *Newt* 1H 179
Whiteash Green. *Essx* 2A 54
Whitebog. *High* 2B 158
Whitebridge. *High* 2G 149
Whitebrook. *Mon* 5A 48
Whitecairns. *Abers* 2G 153
White Chapel. *Lanc* 5E 97
Whitechurch. *Pemb* 1F 43
White Colne. *Essx* 3B 54
White Coppice. *Lanc* 3E 90
White Corries. *High* 3G 141
Whitecraig. *E Lot* 2G 129
Whitecroft. *Glos* 5B 48
White Cross. *Corn* 4D 5 (nr. Mullion)
Whitecross. *Corn* 1D 6 (nr. Wadebridge)
Whitecross. *Falk* 2C 128
Whitecross. *New M* 6D 178
White End. *Worc* 2C 48
Whiteface. *High* 5E 164
Whitefarland. *N Ayr* 5G 125
Whitefaulds. *S Ayr* 4B 116
Whitefield. *Dors* 3E 15
Whitefield. *G Man* 4G 91
Whitefield. *Som* 4D 20
Whiteford. *Abers* 1E 152
Whitegate. *Ches W* 4A 84
Whitehall. *Devn* 1E 13
Whitehall. *Hants* 1F 25
Whitehall. *Orkn* 5F 172
Whitehall. *W Sus* 3C 26
Whitehaven. *Cumb* 3A 102
Whitehaven. *Shrp* 3E 71
Whitehead. *Carr* 7L 175
Whitehill. *Hants* 3F 25
Whitehill. *N Ayr* 4D 126
Whitehills. *Abers* 2D 160
Whitehills. *Ang* 3D 144
White Horse Common. *Norf* 3F 79
Whitehough. *Derbs* 2E 85
Whitehouse. *Abers* 2D 152
Whitehouse. *Arg* 3G 125
Whiteinch. *Glas* 3G 127
Whitekirk. *E Lot* 1B 130
White Kirkley. *Dur* 1D 104
White Lackington. *Dors* 3C 14
Whitelackington. *Som* 1G 13
White Ladies Aston. *Worc* 5D 60
White Lee. *W Yor* 2C 92
Whiteley. *Hants* 1D 16
Whiteley Bank. *IOW* 4D 16
Whiteley Village. *Surr* 4B 38
Whitemans Green. *W Sus* 3E 27
White Mill. *Carm* 3E 45
Whitemire. *Mor* 3D 159
Whitemoor. *Corn* 3D 6
Whitenap. *Hants* 4B 24
Whiteness. *Shet* 7F 173
White Notley. *Essx* 4A 54
Whiteoak Green. *Oxon* 4B 50
Whiteparish. *Wilts* 4H 23
White Pit. *Linc* 3C 88
Whiterashes. *Abers* 1F 153
Whiterock. *Ards* 3K 179
White Rocks. *Here* 3H 47
White Roding. *Essx* 4F 53
Whiterow. *High* 4F 169
Whiterow. *Mor* 3E 159
Whiteshill. *Glos* 5D 48
Whiteside. *Nmbd* 3A 114
Whiteside. *W Lot* 3C 128
Whitesmith. *E Sus* 4G 27
Whitestaunton. *Som* 1F 13
Whitestone. *Abers* 4D 152
Whitestone. *Devn* 3B 12
White Stone. *Here* 1A 48
Whitestones. *Abers* 3F 161
Whitestreet Green. *Suff* 2C 54
Whitewall Corner. *N Yor* 2B 100
White Waltham. *Wind* 4G 37
Whiteway. *Glos* 4E 49
Whitewell. *Lanc* 5F 97
Whitewell Bottom. *Lanc* 2G 91
Whiteworks. *Devn* 5G 11
Whitewreath. *Mor* 3G 159
Whitfield. *D'dee* 5D 144
Whitfield. *Kent* 1H 29
Whitfield. *Nptn* 2E 50
Whitfield. *Nmbd* 4A 114
Whitfield. *S Glo* 2B 34
Whitford. *Devn* 3F 13
Whitford. *Flin* 3D 82
Whitgift. *E Yor* 2B 94
Whitgreave. *Staf* 3C 72
Whithorn. *Dum* 5B 110
Whiting Bay. *N Ayr* 3E 123
Whitington. *Norf* 1G 65
Whitkirk. *W Yor* 1D 92
Whitland. *Carm* 3G 43
Whitleigh. *Plym* 3A 8
Whitletts. *S Ayr* 2C 116
Whitley. *N Yor* 2F 93
Whitley. *Wilts* 5D 35
Whitley Bay. *Tyne* 2G 115
Whitley Chapel. *Nmbd* 4C 114
Whitley Heath. *Staf* 3C 72
Whitley Lower. *W Yor* 3C 92
Whitley Thorpe. *N Yor* 2F 93
Whitlock's End. *W Mid* 3F 61
Whitminster. *Glos* 5C 48
Whitmore. *Dors* 2F 15
Whitmore. *Staf* 1C 72
Whitnage. *Devn* 1D 12
Whitnash. *Warw* 4H 61
Whitney. *Here* 1F 47
Whitrigg. *Cumb* 4D 112 (nr. Kirkbride)
Whitrigg. *Cumb* 1D 102 (nr. Torpenhow)
Whitsbury. *Hants* 1G 15
Whitsome. *Bord* 4E 131
Whitson. *Newp* 3G 33
Whitstable. *Kent* 4F 41
Whitstone. *Corn* 3C 10
Whittingham. *Nmbd* 3E 121
Whittingslow. *Shrp* 2G 59
Whittington. *Derbs* 3B 86
Whittington. *Glos* 3F 49
Whittington. *Lanc* 2F 97
Whittington. *Shrp* 2F 71
Whittington. *Staf* 2C 60 (nr. Kinver)
Whittington. *Staf* 5F 73 (nr. Lichfield)
Whittington. *Warw* 1G 61
Whittington. *Worc* 5C 60
Whittington Barracks. *Staf* 5F 73
Whittlebury. *Nptn* 1E 51
Whittleford. *Warw* 1H 61
Whittle-le-Woods. *Lanc* 2D 90
Whittlesey. *Cambs* 1B 64
Whittlesford. *Cambs* 1E 53
Whittlestone Head. *Bkbn* 3F 91
Whitton. *N Lin* 2C 94
Whitton. *Nmbd* 4E 121
Whitton. *Powy* 4E 59
Whitton. *Bord* 2B 120
Whitton. *Shrp* 3H 59
Whitton. *Stoc T* 2A 106
Whittonditch. *Wilts* 4A 36
Whittonstall. *Nmbd* 4D 114
Whitway. *Hants* 1C 24
Whitwell. *Derbs* 3C 86
Whitwell. *Herts* 3B 52
Whitwell. *IOW* 5D 16
Whitwell. *N Yor* 5F 105
Whitwell. *Rut* 5G 75
Whitwell-on-the-Hill. *N Yor* 3B 100
Whitwick. *Leics* 4B 74
Whitwood. *W Yor* 2E 93
Whitworth. *Lanc* 3G 91
Whixall. *Shrp* 2H 71
Whixley. *N Yor* 4G 99
Whoberley. *W Mid* 3G 61
Whorlton. *Dur* 3E 105
Whorlton. *N Yor* 4B 106
Whygate. *Nmbd* 2A 114
Whyle. *Here* 4H 59
Whyteleafe. *Surr* 5E 39
Wibdon. *Glos* 2A 34
Wibtoft. *Warw* 2B 62
Wichenford. *Worc* 4B 60
Wichling. *Kent* 5D 40
Wick. *Bour* 3G 15
Wick. *Devn* 2E 13
Wick. *High* 3F 169
Wick. *Shet* 8F 173 (on Mainland)
Wick. *Shet* 1G 173 (on Unst)
Wick. *Som* 2F 21 (nr. Bridgwater)
Wick. *Som* 1G 21 (nr. Burnham-on-Sea)
Wick. *Som* 4H 21 (nr. Somerton)
Wick. *S Glo* 4C 34
Wick. *V Glam* 4C 32
Wick. *W Sus* 5B 26
Wick. *Wilts* 4G 23
Wick. *Worc* 1E 49
Wick Airport. *High* 3F 169
Wicken. *Cambs* 3E 65

INDEX TO SELECTED PLACES OF INTEREST

(1) A strict alphabetical order is used e.g. Benmore Botanic Gdn. follows Ben Macdui but precedes Ben Nevis.

(2) Entries shown without a main map index reference have the name of the appropriate Town Plan and its page number;
e.g. Ashmolean Mus. (OX1 2PH) .... **Oxford 200**
The Town Plan title is not given when this is included in the name of the Place of Interest.

(3) Entries in italics are not named on the map but are shown with a symbol only.
Entries in italics and enclosed in brackets are not shown on the map.
Where this occurs the nearest town or village may also be given, unless that name is already included in the name of the Place of Interest.

SAT NAV POSTCODES

Postcodes (in brackets) are included as a navigation aid to assist Sat Nav users and are supplied on this basis.
It should be noted that postcodes have been selected by their proximity to the Place of Interest and that they may not form part of the actual postal address. Drivers should follow the Tourist Brown Signs where available.

ABBREVIATIONS USED IN THIS INDEX

Garden : Gdn.	Museum : Mus.	Park : Pk.
Gardens : Gdns.	National : Nat	

INDEX

Flamingo Land—Prior Pk. Landscape Gdn.

Flamingo Land (YO17 6UX) 2B 100
Fleet Air Arm Mus. (BA22 8HT) 4A 22
Flint Castle (CH6 5PE) 3E 83
Floors Castle & Gdns. (TD5 7SF) 1B 120
Florence Court (BT92 1DB) 6G 177
Fonmon Castle (CF62 3ZN) 5D 32
Forde Abbey & Gdns. (TA20 4LU) 2G 13
Ford Green Hall (ST6 1NG) 5C 84
Forest of Dean (GL15 4SL) 5B 48
Fort George (IV2 7TD) 3B 158
Forth Bridge (EH30 9TB) 2E 129
Fort Nelson (Royal Armouries) (PO17 6AN) 2E 16
Fountains Abbey & Studley Royal (HG4 3DY) 3E 99
Foxfield Steam Railway (ST11 9BG) 1D 72
Foxton Locks (LE16 7RA) 2D 62
Framlingham Castle (IP13 9BP) 4E 67
Froghall Wharf (ST10 2HH) 1E 73
Furness Abbey (LA13 0PG) 2B 96
Furzey Gdns. (SO43 7GL) 1A 16
Fyne Court (TA5 2EQ) 3F 21
Fyvie Castle (AB53 8JS) 5E 161

G

Gainsborough Old Hall (DN21 2NB) 1F 87
Gainsborough's House (CO10 2EU) 1B 54
Gallery of Modern Art (G1 3AH) **Glasgow 195**
Galloway Forest Pk. (DG8 6TA) 1B 110
Galloway House Gdns. (DG8 8HF) 5B 110
Galloway Wildlife Conservation Pk. (DG6 4XX) 4E 111
Garden House, The (PL20 7LQ) 2A 8
Gdns. of the Rose (AL2 3NR) 5B 52
Gawsworth Hall (SK11 9RN) 4C 84
Gawthorpe Hall (BB12 8UA) 1G 91
Geevor Tin Mine Mus. (TR19 7EW) 3A 4
George Stephenson's Birthplace (NE41 8BP) 3E 115
Georgian House (EH2 4DR) **Edinburgh 195**
Giant's Causeway (BT57 8SU) 2F 174
Gibside (NE16 6BG) 4E 115
Gilbert White's House & Gdn. (GU34 3JH) 3F 25
Gisborough Priory (TS14 6BU) 3D 106
Gladstone Pottery Mus. (ST3 1PQ) 1D 72
Gladstone's Land (EH1 2NT) **Edinburgh 195**
Glamis Castle (DD8 1QJ) 4C 144
Glastonbury Abbey (BA6 9EL) 3A 22
Glastonbury Tor (BA6 8BG) 3A 22
Glenarn (G84 8LL) 1D 126
Glenbuchat Castle (AB36 8TN) 2A 152
Glencoe Gorge (PH50 4SG) 3F 141
Glendurgan Gdn. (TR11 5JZ) 4E 5
Glenfinnan Monument (PH37 4LT) 5B 148
Glenluce Abbey (DG8 0LW) 4G 109
Glenmore Forest Pk. Visitor Centre (PH22 1QY) 3D 150
Glenwhan Gdns. (DG9 8PH) 4G 109
Gloucester Cathedral (GL1 2LR) 195
Gloucestershire Warwickshire Railway (GL54 5DT) 2F 49
Gloucester Waterways Mus. (GL1 2EH) 195
Glynde Place (BN8 6SX) 5F 27
Godinton House & Gdns. (TN23 3BP) 1D 28
Godolphin (TR13 9RE) 3D 4
Goodnestone Pk. Gdns. (CT3 1PL) 5G 41
Goodrich Castle (HR9 6HY) 3A 48
Goodwood House (PO18 0PX) 2G 17
Goodwood Racecourse (PO18 0PS) 1G 17
Gordale Scar (BD23 4DL) 3B 98
Grampian Transport Mus. (AB33 8AE) 2C 152
Grange at Northington, The (SO24 9TG) 4D 24
Graves Gallery (S1 1XZ) **Sheffield 202**
Gray's Printing Press (BT82 8AU) 3F 176
Graythwaite Hall Gdns. (LA12 8BA) 5E 103
Great Central Railway (LE11 1RW) 4C 74
Great Central Railway (Nottingham) (NG11 6NX) 2C 74
Great Chalfield Manor & Gdn. (SN12 8NH) 5D 34
Great Comp Gdn. (TN15 8QS) 5H 39
Great Dixter (TN31 6PH) 3C 28
Great North Mus. : Hancock (NE2 4PT) **Newcastle 197**
Greenbank House & Gdn. (G76 8RB) 4G 127
Greenknowe Tower (TD3 6JL) 5C 130
Greenway (TQ5 0ES) 3E 9
Gretna Green Old Blacksmith's Shop (DG16 5EA) 3E 112
Grey Mare's Tail Waterfall (DG10 9LH) 3E 119
Greys Court (RG9 4PG) 3F 37
Grimes Graves (IP26 5DE) 1H 65
Grimsby Fishing Heritage Centre (DN31 1UZ) 4F 95
Grimspound (PL20 6TB) 4H 11
Grimsthorpe Castle (PE10 0LZ) 3H 75
Grizedale Forest (LA22 0QJ) 5E 103
Groombridge Place Gdns. (TN3 9QG) 2G 27
Grove Mus. (IM8 3UA) 2D 108
Gulliver's Dinosaur & Farm Pk. (MK15 0DT) 2G 51
Gulliver's Matlock Bath (DE4 3PG) 5G 85
Gulliver's Milton Keynes (MK15 0DT) 200
Gulliver's Warrington (WA5 9YZ) 1H 83
Gunby Hall (PE23 5SS) 4D 88
Gwydir Castle (LL26 0PN) 4G 81

H

Haddo House (AB41 7EQ) 5F 161
Haddon Hall (DE45 1LA) 4G 85
Hadleigh Castle (SS7 2AR) 2C 40
Hadrian's Wall (NE47 6NN) 3A 114
Hailes Abbey (GL54 5PB) 2F 49
Hailes Castle (EH41 3SB) 2B 130
Hall i' th' Wood Mus. (BL1 8UA) 3F 91
Hall Place & Gdns. (DA5 1PQ) 3G 39
Hamerton Zoo Pk. (PE28 5RE) 2A 64
Ham House & Gdn. (TW10 7RS) 3C 38
Hammerwood Pk. (RH19 3QE) 2F 27
Hampden Pk. (G42 9AY) 3G 127
Hampton Court Castle & Gdns. (HR6 0PN) 5H 59
Hampton Court Palace (KT8 9AU) 4C 38
Hanbury Hall (WR9 7EA) 4D 60
Handel House Mus. (W1K 4HB) **London 199**
Hardknott Roman Fort (LA20 6EQ) 4D 102
Hardwick Hall (S44 5QJ) 4B 86
Hardy Monument (DT2 9HY) 4B 14
Hardy's Cottage (DT2 8QJ) 3C 14
Hare Hill (SK10 4QA) 3C 84
Harewood House (LS17 9LG) 5F 99
Harlech Castle (LL46 2YH) 2E 69
Harley Gallery (S80 3LW) 3C 86
Hartland Abbey & Gdns. (EX39 6DT) 4C 18
Harvington Hall (DY10 4LR) 3C 60
Harwich Redoubt (CO12 3NL) 2F 55
Hatchlands Pk. (GU4 7RT) 5B 38
Hatfield House (AL9 5NQ) 5C 52
Haughmond Abbey (SY4 4RW) 4H 71
Haverfordwest Castle (SA61 2BW) 3D 42
Haverfordwest Priory (SA61 1RN) 3D 42
Hawk Conservancy Trust (SP11 8DY) 2B 24
Haydock Pk. Racecourse (WA12 0HQ) 1H 83
Head of Steam - Darlington Railway Mus. (DL3 6ST) 3F 105
Heale Gdns. (SP4 6NT) 3G 23
Heaton Hall (M25 2SW) 4G 91
Hedingham Castle (CO9 3DJ) 2A 54
Heights of Abraham (DE4 3PB) 5G 85
Hellens (HR8 2LY) 2B 48
Helmingham Hall Gdns. (IP14 6EF) 5D 66
Helmshore Mills Textile Mus. (BB4 4NP) 2F 91
Helmsley Castle (YO62 5AB) 1A 100
Helvellyn (CA12 4TP) 3E 103
[Henry Moore Institute, Leeds (LS1 3AH)] **Leeds 196**
Heptonstall Mus. (HX7 7PL) 2H 91
Hereford Cathedral (HR1 2NG) 2A 48
Hereford Cider Mus. (HR4 0LW) 2A 48
Hergest Croft Gdns. (HR5 3EG) 5E 59
Heritage Motor Centre (CV35 0BJ) 5A 62
Hermitage Castle (TD9 0LU) 5H 119
Herstmonceux Castle & Gdn. (BN27 1RN) 4H 27
Hestercombe Gdns. (TA2 8LG) 4F 21
Hever Castle & Gdns. (TN8 7NG) 1F 27
Hexham Abbey (NE46 3NB) 3C 114
Hidcote (GL55 6LR) 1G 49
High Beeches Gdns. (RH17 6HQ) 2D 27
Highclere Castle (RG20 9RN) 1C 24
Highland Folk Mus. (PH20 1AY) 4B 150
Highland Wildlife Pk. (PH21 1NL) 3C 150
Hill House (G84 9AJ) 1D 126
Hill of Tarvit Mansionhouse & Gdns. (KY15 5PB) 2F 137
Hill Top (LA22 0LF) 5E 103
Hinton Ampner (SO24 0LA) 4D 24
Hirsel (TD12 4LP) 5E 131
Historic Dockyard Chatham (ME4 4TZ) **Medway 197**
HMS Victory (PO1 3LJ) **Portsmouth 201**
HMS Warrior 1860 (PO1 3QX) **Portsmouth 201**
Hodnet Hall Gdns. (TF9 3NN) 3A 72
Hoghton Tower (PR5 0SH) 2E 90
Hog's Back (GU3 1AQ) 1A 26
Holburne Mus. of Art (BA2 4DB) **Bath 192**
Holdenby House Gdns. & Falconry Centre (NN6 8DJ) 4D 62
Holehird Gdns. (LA23 1NP) 4F 103
Holker Hall & Gdns. (LA11 7PL) 2C 96
Holkham (NR23 1AB) 1A 78
Hollycombe (GU30 7LP) 4G 25
Holst Birthplace Mus. (GL52 2AY) **Cheltenham 193**
Holy Jesus Hospital (NE1 2AS) **Newcastle 197**
Holyrood Abbey (EH8 8DX) **Edinburgh 195**
Hopetoun (EH30 9SL) 2D 129
Hop Farm Family Pk. (TN12 6PY) 1A 28
Houghton Hall (PE31 6TZ) 3G 77
Houghton House (MK45 2EZ) 2A 52
Houghton Lodge Gdns. (SO20 6LQ) 3B 24
House of Dun (DD10 9LQ) 3F 145
House of Manannan Mus., Peel (IM5 1TA) 3B 108
House of the Binns (EH49 7NA) 2D 128
Houses of Parliament (SW1A 0RS) **London 199**
Housesteads Roman Fort & Mus. (NE47 6NN) 3A 114
Hoveton Hall Gdns. (NR12 8RJ) 3F 79
Hovingham Hall (YO62 4LU) 2A 100
Howick Hall Gdns. (NE66 3LB) 3G 121
Howletts Wild Animal Pk. (CT4 5EL) 5F 41
Hughenden Manor (HP14 4LA) 2G 37
Hugh Miller Mus. & Birthplace Cottage (IV11 8XA) 2B 158
Hunstanton Sea Life Sanctuary (PE36 5BH) 1F 77
Hunterian Mus. (G12 8QQ) 3G 127
Huntingtower Castle (PH1 3JL) 1C 136
Huntly Castle (AB54 4SH) 4C 160
Hurst Castle (SO41 0TP) 4B 16
Hutton-in-the-Forest (CA11 9TH) 1F 103
Hylands House & Gdns. (CM2 8WQ) 5G 53

I

Iceni Village & Mus. (PE37 8AG) 5G 77
Ickworth (IP29 5QE) 4H 65
Iford Manor (Peto Gdn.) (BA15 2BA) 1D 22
Ightham Mote (TN15 0NT) 5G 39
Ilam Pk. (DE6 2AZ) 5F 85
Ilfracombe Aquarium (EX34 9EQ) 2F 19
Imperial War Mus. Duxford (CB22 4QR) 1E 53
Imperial War Mus. London (SE1 6HZ) 199
Imperial War Mus. North, Trafford Park (M17 1TZ) 1C 84
Inchcolm Abbey (KY3 0XR) 1E 129
Inchmahome Priory (FK8 3RD) 3E 135
Ingatestone Hall (CM4 9NS) 1A 40
International Centre for Birds of Prey (GL18 1JJ) 3C 48
Inveraray Castle (PA32 8XE) 3H 133
Inveresk Lodge Gdn. (EH21 7TE) 2G 129
Inverewe Gdn. (IV22 2LG) 5C 162
Inverlochy Castle (PH33 6TQ) 1F 141
Inverness Mus. & Art Gallery (IV2 3EB) 196
Iona (PA76 6SP) 2A 132
Iron Bridge (TF8 7JP) 5A 72
Isel Hall (CA13 0QG) 1C 102
Isle of Man Steam Railway (IM1 4LL) 4C 108
Isle of Wight Steam Railway (PO33 4DS) 4D 16
Ivinghoe Beacon (LU6 2EG) 4H 51
Izaak Walton's Cottage (ST15 0PA) 3C 72

J

Jackfield Tile Mus. (TF8 7ND) 5A 72
Jane Austen Centre (BA1 2NT) **Bath 192**
Jane Austen's House Mus. (GU34 1SD) 3F 25
Jarlshof Prehistoric & Norse Settlement (ZE3 9JN) 10E 173
Jedburgh Abbey (TD8 6JQ) 3A 120
Jervaulx Abbey (HG4 4PH) 1D 98
JM Barrie's Birthplace (DD8 4BX) 3C 144
Jodrell Bank Discovery Centre (SK11 9DL) 3B 84
Jorvik Viking Centre (YO1 9WT) **York 203**

K

Kedleston Hall (DE22 5JH) 1H 73
Keighley & Worth Valley Railway (BD22 8NJ) 1A 92
Kelburn Castle & Country Centre (KA29 0BE) 4D 126
Keld Chapel (CA10 3QF) 3G 103
Kelham Island Mus. (S3 8RY) **Sheffield 202**
Kellie Castle & Gdn. (KY10 2RF) 3H 137
Kelmarsh Hall & Gdns. (NN6 9LY) 3E 63
Kelmscott Manor (GL7 3HJ) 2A 36
Kelso Abbey (TD5 7BB) 1B 120
Kelvingrove Art Gallery & Mus., Glasgow (G3 8AG) 3G 127
Kempton Pk. Racecourse (TW16 5AE) 3C 38
Kenilworth Castle (CV8 1NE) 3G 61
Kent & East Sussex Railway (TN30 6HE) 3C 28
Kentwell (CO10 9BA) 1B 54
Kenwood House (NW3 7JR) 2D 38
Keswick Mus. & Gallery (CA12 4NF) 2D 102
Kettle's Yard (CB3 0AQ) **Cambridge 193**
Kew Gdns. (TW9 3AB) 3C 38
Kidwelly Castle (SA17 5BQ) 5E 45
Kielder Water & Forest Pk. (NE48 1QZ) 1H 113
Kiftsgate Court Gdns. (GL55 6LN) 1G 49
Kilchurn Castle (PA33 1AF) 1A 134
Kildrummy Castle (AB33 8RA) 2B 152
Killerton (EX5 3LE) 2C 12
Kilmartin Glen Prehistoric Sites (PA31 8RQ) 4F 133
Kilmartin House Mus. (PA31 8RQ) 4F 133
Kinder Scout (S33 7ZJ) 2E 85
King's College Chapel (CB2 1TN) **Cambridge 193**
Kingston Bagpuize House & Gdn. (OX13 5AX) 2C 36
Kingston Lacy (BH21 4EA) 2E 15
Kingston Maurward Animal Pk. & Gdns. (DT2 8PY) 3C 14
Kinnersley Castle (HR3 6QF) 1G 47
Kinver Edge (DY7 5NP) 2C 60
Kiplin Hall (DL10 6AT) 5F 105
Kirby Hall (NN17 3EN) 1G 63
Kirby Muxloe Castle (LE9 2DH) 5C 74
Kirkham Priory (YO60 7JS) 3B 100
Kirklees Light Railway (HD8 9XJ) 3C 92
Kirkstall Abbey (LS5 3EH) 1C 92
Kirkwall Cathedral (KW15 1JF) 6D 172
Knaresborough Castle (HG5 8BB) 4F 99
Knebworth House (SG3 6PY) 3C 52
Knightshayes Court (EX16 7RQ) 1C 12
Knockhill Motor Circuit (KY12 9TF) 4C 136
Knole (TN15 0RP) 5G 39
Knoll Gdns. (BH21 7ND) 2F 15
Knowsley Safari Pk. (L34 4AN) 1G 83

L

Lacock Abbey (SN15 2LG) 5E 35
Lady Lever Art Gallery (CH62 5EQ) 2F 83
Laing Art Gallery (NE1 8AG) **Newcastle 197**
Lake District Nat. Pk. (LA9 7RL) 3E 103
Lakeside & Haverthwaite Railway (LA12 8AL) 1C 96
Lamb House (TN31 7ES) 3D 28
Lamphey Bishop's Palace (SA71 5NT) 4E 43
Lamport Hall & Gdns. (NN6 9HD) 3E 63
Lancaster Castle (LA1 1YJ) 3D 96
Landmark Forest Adventure Pk. (PH23 3AJ) 1D 150
Land's End (TR19 7AA) 4A 4
Lanercost Priory (CA8 2HQ) 3G 113
Langdale Pikes (LA22 9JY) 4D 102
Langley Chapel (SY5 7HU) 1H 59
Lanhydrock (PL30 5AD) 2E 7
Lappa Valley Steam Railway (TR8 5LX) 3C 6
Larmer Tree Gdns. (SP5 5PZ) 1E 15
Laugharne Castle (SA33 4SA) 3H 43
Launceston Castle (PL15 7DR) 4D 10
Launceston Steam Railway (PL15 8DA) 4D 10
Lauriston Castle (EH4 5QD) 2F 129
Lavenham Guildhall (CO10 9QZ) 1C 54
Laxey Wheel (IM4 7NL) 3D 108
Layer Marney Tower (CO5 9US) 4C 54
Leeds Castle (Kent) (ME17 1PL) 5C 40
Leeds City Mus. (LS1 3AA) 196
Legoland (SL4 4AY) 3A 38
Leighton Buzzard Railway (LU7 4TN) 3H 51
Leighton Hall (LA5 9ST) 2E 97
Leiston Abbey (IP16 4TD) 4G 67
Leith Hall (AB54 4NQ) 1C 152
Leith Hill (RH5 6LX) 1C 26
Lennoxlove House (EH41 4NZ) 2B 130
Levant Mine & Beam Engine (TR19 7SX) 3A 4
Levens Hall & Gdns. (LA8 0PD) 1D 97
Lewes Castle (BN7 1YE) 4F 27
Lichfield Cathedral (WS13 7LD) 4F 73
Life (NE1 4EP) **Newcastle 197**
Lightwater Valley (HG4 3HT) 2E 99
Lilleshall Abbey (TF10 9HW) 4B 72
Lincoln Castle (LN1 3AA) 197
Lincoln Cathedral (LN2 1PZ) 197
Lincoln Medieval Bishops' Palace (LN2 1PU) 197
Lincolnshire Road Transport Mus. (LN6 3QT) 4G 87
Lindisfarne (TD15 2SF) 5H 131
Lindisfarne Castle (TD15 2SH) 5H 131
Lindisfarne Priory (TD15 2RX) 5H 131
Linlithgow Palace (EH49 7AL) 2D 128
Linton Zoo (CB21 4XN) 1F 53
Little Clarendon (SP3 5DZ) 3F 23
Little Malvern Court (WR14 4JN) 1C 48
Little Moreton Hall (CW12 4SD) 5C 84
Liverpool Cathedral (L1 7AZ) 2F 83
Liverpool Metropolitan RC Cathedral (L3 5TQ) 197
Lizard Point (TR12 7NU) 5E 5
Llanberis Lake Railway (LL55 3HB) 4E 81
Llanerchaeron (SA48 8DG) 5D 57
Llangollen Railway (LL20 7AJ) 1D 70
Llansteffan Castle (SA33 5JX) 4D 44
Llawhaden Castle (SA67 8HL) 3E 43
Llechwedd Slate Caverns (LL41 3NB) 1G 69
Llywernog Silver-Lead Mine (SY23 3AB) 2G 57
Lochalsh Woodland Gdn. (IV40 8DN) 1F 147
Loch Doon Castle (KA6 7QE) 5D 117
Lochleven Castle (KY13 8ET) 3D 136
Loch Lomond (G83 8PA) 4C 134
Loch Lomond & The Trossachs Nat. Pk. (FK8 3UA) 2D 134
Lochmaben Castle (DG11 1JE) 1B 112
Loch Ness Exhibition Centre (IV63 6TU) 5H 157
"Locomotion" Nat. Railway Mus. Shildon (DL4 1PQ) 2F 105
Lodge Pk. (GL54 3PP) 4G 49
Lodge RSPB Nature Reserve, The (SG19 2DL) 1B 52
Logan Botanic Gdn. (DG9 9ND) 5F 109
Logan Fish Pond & Marine Life Centre (DG9 9NF) 5F 109
London 2012 Olympic Pk. (E20 2ST) 2E 39
London Dungeon (SE1 2SZ) 199
London Eye (SE1 7PB) 199
London Film Mus. (Se1 3PB) 199
London Zoo (NW1 4RY) 198
Long Cross Victorian Gdns. (PL29 3TF) 1D 6
Longleat Safari & Adventure Pk. (BA12 7NW) 2D 22
Long Mynd (SY7 8BH) 1G 59
Longthorpe Tower (PE3 6SU) 1A 64
Longtown Castle (HR2 0LE) 3G 47
Lord Leycester Hospital & The Master's Gdn., Warwick (CV34 4BH) 4G 61
Loseley Pk. (GU3 1HS) 1A 26
Lost Gdns. of Heligan (PL26 6EN) 4D 6
Lotherton Hall (LS25 3EB) 1E 93
Lough Neagh Discovery Centre (BT66 6NJ) 3E 178
Loughwood Meeting House (EX13 7DU) 3F 13
[Lowry, The, Salford (M50 3AZ)] 1C 84
Ludgershall Castle (SP11 9QS) 1A 24
Ludlow Castle (SY8 1AY) 3H 59
Lullingstone Castle & World Gdn. (DA4 0JA) 4G 39
Lullingstone Roman Villa (DA4 0JA) 4G 39
Lulworth Castle (BH20 5QS) 4D 14
Lundy Island (EX39 2LY) 2B 18
Lyddington Bede House (LE15 9LZ) 1F 63
Lydford Castle & Saxon Town (EX20 4BH) 4F 11
Lydford Gorge (EX20 4BH) 4F 11
Lydiard House & Pk. (SN5 3PA) 3G 35
Lydney Pk. Gdns. (GL15 6BU) 5B 48
Lyme Pk. (SK12 2NX) 2D 84
Lytes Cary Manor (TA11 7HU) 4A 22
Lyveden New Bield (PE8 5AT) 2G 63

M

Macclesfield Silk Museums (SK11 6PD) 3D 84
Macduff Marine Aquarium (AB44 1SL) 2E 160
MacLellan's Castle (DG6 4JD) 4D 111
Madame Tussaud's (NW1 5LR) **London 198**
Maeshowe Chambered Cairn (KW16 3HQ) 6C 172
MAGNA Science Adventure Centre (S60 1DX) 1B 86
Maiden Castle (DT2 9PP) 4B 14
Major Oak (NG21 9HN) 4D 86
Malham Cove (BD23 4DJ) 3A 98
Malham Tarn (BD24 9PU) 3A 98
Malleny Gdn. (EH14 7AF) 3E 129
Malton Mus. (YO17 7LP) 2B 100
Malvern Hills (HR8 1EN) 2C 48
Manchester Art Gallery (M2 3JL) 197
M & D's (Scotland's Theme Pk.), Motherwell (ML1 3RT) 4A 128
Manderston (TD11 3PP) 4E 131
Mannington Gdns. (NR11 7BB) 2D 78
Manorbier Castle (SA70 7SY) 5E 43
Manx Electric Railway (IM2 4NR) 3D 108
Manx Mus. (IM1 3LY) 4C 108
Mapledurham House (RG4 7TR) 4E 37
Marble Arch Caves Global Geopark (BT92 1EW) 6G 177
Marble Hill House (TW1 2NL) 3C 38
Markenfield Hall (HG4 3AD) 3E 99
Mar Lodge Estate (AB35 5YJ) 5E 151
Martin Mere Wetland Centre (L40 0TA) 3C 90
Marwell Wildlife (SO21 1JH) 4D 24
Marwood Hill Gdns. (EX31 4EB) 3F 19
Mary Arden's Farm (CV37 9UN) 5F 61
Mary, Queen of Scots' House (TD8 6EN) 2A 120
Mary Rose Ship & Mus. (PO1 3LX) **Portsmouth 201**
Max Gate (DT1 2AB) 3C 14
Megginch Castle Gdns. (PH2 7SW) 1E 137
Melbourne Hall (DE73 8EN) 3A 74
Melford Hall (CO10 9AA) 1B 54
Mellerstain House (TD3 6LG) 1A 120
Melrose Abbey (TD6 9LG) 1H 119
Menai Suspension Bridge (LL59 5HH) 3E 81
Mendip Hills (BS40 7XS) 1H 21
Merriments Gdns. (TN19 7RA) 3B 28
Merseyside Maritime Mus. (L3 4AQ) **Liverpool 197**
Mertoun Gdns. (TD6 0EA) 1A 120
Michelham Priory (BN27 3QS) 5G 27
Middleham Castle (DL8 4QR) 1D 98
Midland Railway Centre (DE5 3QZ) 5B 86
Mid-Norfolk Railway (NR19 1DF) 5C 78
Millennium Coastal Pk. (SA15 2LG) 3D 44
Millennium Stadium (CF10 1NS) **Cardiff 193**
Milton Manor House (OX14 4EN) 2C 36
Milton's Cottage (HP8 4JH) 1A 38
Minack Theatre (TR19 6JU) 4A 4
Minsmere (IP17 3BY) 4G 67
Minterne Gdns. (DT2 7AU) 2B 14
Mirehouse (CA12 4QE) 2D 102
Misarden Pk. Gdns. (GL6 7JA) 5E 49
Mistley Towers (CO11 1ET) 2E 54
Mompesson House (SP1 2EL) **Salisbury 201**
Monk Bretton Priory (S71 5QE) 4D 93
Monkey Forest at Trentham (ST4 8AY) 2C 72
Monkey Sanctuary (PL13 1NZ) 3G 7
Monkey World (BH20 6HH) 4D 14
Monk's House (BN7 3HF) 5F 27
Montacute House (TA15 6XP) 1H 13
Monteviot House (TD8 6UH) 2A 120
Montgomery Castle (SY15 6HN) 1E 58
Moreton Corbet Castle, Shawbury (SY4 4DW) 3H 71
Morwellham Quay (PL19 8JL) 2A 8
Moseley Old Hall, Wolverhampton (WV10 7HY) 5D 72
Mother Shipton's Cave & the Petrifying Well (HG5 8DD) 4F 99
Mottisfont (SO51 0LP) 4B 24
Mount Edgcumbe House (PL10 1HZ) 3A 8
Mount Ephraim Gdns. (ME13 9TX) 4E 41
Mountfitchet Castle (CM24 8SY) 3F 53
Mount Grace Priory (DL6 3JG) 5B 106
Mount Stewart House and Gdns. (BT22 2AD) 2K 179
Mount Stuart (PA20 9LR) 4C 126
Mr Straw's House (S81 0JG) 2C 86
Muchelney Abbey (TA10 0DQ) 4H 21
Muchelney Priest's House (TA10 0DQ) 4H 21
Mull of Kintyre (PA28 6RU) 5A 122
Muncaster Castle & Gdns. (CA18 1RQ) 5C 102
Murlough Nat. Nature Reserve (BT33 0NQ) 6J 179
Mus. of Army Flying (SO20 8DY) 3B 24
Mus. of East Anglian Life (IP14 1DL) 5C 66
Mus. of Lakeland Life & Industry, Kendal (LA9 5AL) 5G 103
Mus. of Lincolnshire Life (LN1 3LY) **Lincoln 197**
Mus. of London (EC2Y 5HN) 199
Mus. of Science & Industry (M3 4FP) **Manchester 197**
Mus. of Scottish Lighthouses (AB43 9DU) 2G 161
Mus. of the Gorge (TF8 7NH) 5A 72
Mus. of the Isles (IV45 8RS) 3E 147
Mus. of the Jewellery Quarter (B18 6HA) **Birmingham 192**

N

Nat. Botanic Gdn. of Wales (SA32 8HG) 4F 45
Nat. Coal Mining Mus. for England (WF4 4RH) 3C 92
Nat. Coracle Centre (SA38 9JL) 1C 44
Nat. Exhibition Centre (NEC) (B40 1NT) 2F 61
Nat. Football Mus. (M4 3BG) **Manchester 197**
Nat. Forest, The (DE12 6HZ) 4H 73
Nat. Gallery (WC2N 5DN) **London 199**
Nat. Gallery of Scotland (EH2 2EL) **Edinburgh 195**
Nat. Glass Centre (SR6 0GL) 4H 115
Nat. Horseracing Mus. (CB8 8JL) 4F 65
Nat. Marine Aquarium (PL4 0LF) **Plymouth 201**
Nat. Maritime Mus., Greenwich (SE10 9NF) 3E 39
Nat. Maritime Mus. Cornwall, Falmouth (TR11 3QY) 5C 6
Nat. Media Mus. (BD1 1NQ) **Bradford 192**
Nat. Memorial Arboretum (DE13 7AR) 4F 73
National Mining Mus. Scotland (EH22 4QN) 3G 129
Nat. Motorcycle Mus. (B92 0EJ) 2G 61
Nat. Motor Mus., (Beaulieu) (SO42 7ZN) 2B 16
Nat. Mus. Cardiff (CF10 3NP) 193
Nat. Mus. of Costume (DG2 8HQ) 3A 112
Nat. Mus. of Flight (EH39 5LF) 2B 130
Nat. Mus. of Rural Life Scotland (G76 9HR) 4H 127
Nat. Mus. of Scotland (EH1 1JF) **Edinburgh 195**
Nat. Portrait Gallery (WC2H 0HE) **London 199**
Nat. Railway Mus. (YO26 4XJ) **York 203**
Nat. Roman Legion Mus., Caerleon, Caerleon (NP18 1AE) 2G 33
Nat. Sea Life Centre (B1 2HL) **Birmingham 192**
Nat. Seal Sanctuary (TR12 6UG) 4E 5
Nat. Showcaves Centre for Wales (SA9 1GJ) 4B 46
Nat. Slate Mus. (LL55 4TY) 4E 81
Nat. Space Centre (LE4 5NS) 5C 74
Nat. Waterfront Mus. (SA1 3RD) **Swansea 203**
Nat. Waterways Mus. (CH65 4FW) 3G 83
Nat. Wool Mus. (SA44 5UP) 2D 44
Natural History Mus. (SW7 5BD) **London 198**
Natural History Mus. at Tring (HP23 6AP) 4H 51
Neath Abbey (SA10 7DW) 3G 31
Needles, The (PO39 0JH) 4A 16
Nene Valley Railway (PE8 6LR) 1A 64
Ness Botanic Gdns. (CH64 4AY) 3F 83
Nessieland Castle Monster Centre (IV63 6TU) 5H 157
Nether Winchendon House (HP18 0DY) 4F 51
Netley Abbey (SO31 5HB) 2C 16
New Abbey Corn Mill (DG2 8DX) 3A 112
Newark Air Mus. (NG24 2NY) 5F 87
Newark Castle (Newark-on-Trent) (NG24 1BN) 5E 87
Newark Castle (Port Glasgow) (PA14 5NG) 2E 127
Newark Pk. (GL12 7PZ) 2C 34
New Art Gallery Walsall (WS2 8LG) 1E 61
Newburgh Priory (YO61 4AS) 2H 99
Newbury Racecourse (RG14 7NZ) 5C 36
Newby Hall & Gdns. (HG4 5AE) 3F 99
Newcastle Castle (Bridgend) (CF31 4JW) 3B 32
Newcastle Upon Tyne Castle Keep (NE1 1RQ) 197
New Forest Nat. Pk. (SO43 7BD) 2H 15
New Lanark World Heritage Site Visitor Centre (ML11 9DB) 5B 128
Newmarket Racecourse (CB8 0TG) 4F 65
Newquay Zoo (TR7 2LZ) 2C 6
Newstead Abbey (NG15 8NA) 5C 86
Nine Ladies Stone Circle (DE4 2LF) 4G 85
Norfolk Lavender (PE31 7JE) 2F 77
Norham Castle (TD15 2LL) 5F 131
Normanby Hall Mus. (DN15 9HU) 3B 94
North Downs (GU10 5QE) 5C 38
North Norfolk Railway (NR26 8RA) 1D 78
Northumberland Nat. Pk. (NE46 1BS) 1A 114
North York Moors Nat. Pk. (YO18 8RN) 5E 107
North Yorkshire Moors Railway (YO18 7AJ) 1C 100
Norton Conyers (HG4 5EQ) 2F 99
Norton Priory Mus. & Gdns. (WA7 1SX) 2H 83
Norwich Castle Mus. & Art Gallery (NR1 3JU) 200
Norwich Cathedral (NR1 4DH) 200
Nostell Priory (WF4 1QE) 3E 93
Nunney Castle (BA11 4LN) 2C 22
Nunnington Hall (YO62 5UY) 2A 100
Nymans (RH17 6EB) 3D 26

O

Oakham Castle (LE15 6DR) 5F 75
Oakwell Hall, Birstall (WF17 9LG) 2C 92
Oakwood Theme Pk. (SA67 8DE) 3E 43
Observatory Science Centre (BN27 1RN) 4A 28
Oceanarium (BH2 5AA) **Bournemouth 192**
Offa's Dyke (NP16 7NQ) 5A 48
Okehampton Castle (EX20 1JA) 3F 11
Old Beaupre Castle (CF71 7LT) 4D 32
Old Gorhambury House (AL3 6AH) 5B 52
Old Oswestry Hill Fort (SY10 7AA) 2E 71
Old Sarum (SP1 3SD) 3G 23
Old Wardour Castle (SP3 6RR) 4E 23
Old Winchester Hill Hill Fort (GU32 1HN) 4E 25
Olympic Pk. (London 2012) (E20 2ST) 2E 39
Orford Castle (IP12 2NF) 1H 55
Orford Ness (IP12 2NU) 1H 55
Ormesby Hall (TS7 9AS) 3C 106
Osborne House (PO32 6JX) 3D 16
Osterley Pk. & House (TW7 4RB) 3C 38
Oulton Pk. Motor Circuit (CW6 9BW) 4H 83
Our Dynamic Earth (EH8 8AS) **Edinburgh 195**
Overbeck's (TQ8 8LW) 5D 8
Owletts (DA12 3AP) 4A 40
Oxburgh Hall (PE33 9PS) 5G 77
Oxford Christ Church Cathedral (OX1 4JF) 200
Oxford Island Nat. Nature Reserve (BT66 6NJ) 3E 178
Oxwich Castle (SA3 1LU) 4D 31
Oystermouth Castle (SA3 5TA) 4F 31

P

Packwood House (B94 6AT) 3F 61
Paignton Zoo (TQ4 7EU) 3E 9
Painshill Pk. (KT11 1JE) 5B 38
Painswick Rococo Gdn. (GL6 6TH) 4D 48
Palace of Holyroodhouse (EH8 8DX) **Edinburgh 195**
Papplewick Pumping Station (NG15 9AJ) 5C 86
Paradise Pk. (Hayle) (TR27 4HB) 3C 4
Paradise Wildlife Pk. (EN10 7QZ) 5D 52
Parcevall Hall Gdns. (BD23 6DE) 3C 98
Parham (RH20 4HS) 4B 26
Pashley Manor Gdns. (TN5 7HE) 3A 28
Patterson's Spade Mill (BT39 0AP) 8J 175
Paul Corin's Magnificent Music Machines (PL14 4SH) 2G 7
Paultons Pk. (SO51 6AL) 1B 16
Paxton House (TD15 1SZ) 4F 131
Paycocke's (CO6 1NS) 3B 54
Peak Cavern (S33 8WS) 2F 85
Peak District Nat. Pk. (DE45 1AE) 3F 85
Peak Rail (DE4 3NA) 4G 85
Peckover House & Gdn. (PE13 1JR) 5D 76
Peel Castle (IM5 1AB) 3B 108
Pembroke Castle (SA71 4LA) 4D 43
Pembrokeshire Coast Nat. Pk. (SA41 3XD) 3C 42
Pencarrow (PL30 3AG) 5A 10
Pendennis Castle (TR11 4LP) 5C 6
Penhow Castle (NP26 3AD) 2H 33
Penrhyn Castle (LL57 4HN) 3F 81
Penrith Castle (CA11 7JB) 2G 103
Penshurst Place & Gdns. (TN11 8DG) 1G 27
Peover Hall (WA16 9HW) 3B 84
Perth Mus. & Art Gallery (PH1 5LB) 201
Peterborough Cathedral (PE1 1XZ) 201
Petworth House & Pk. (GU28 0AE) 3A 26
Pevensey Castle (BN24 5LE) 5H 27
Peveril Castle (S33 8WQ) 2F 85
Philipps House (SP3 5HH) 3F 23
Pickering Castle (YO18 7AX) 1C 100
Picton Castle (SA62 4AS) 3E 43
Piel Castle (LA13 0QN) 3B 96
Pistyll Rhaeadr (SY10 0BZ) 3D 70
Pitmedden Gdn. (AB41 7PD) 1F 153
Pitt Rivers Mus. (OX1 3PP) **Oxford 200**
Plantasia (SA1 2AL) **Swansea 203**
Plas Brondanw Gdn. (LL48 6SW) 1F 69
Plas Newydd (Llanfairpwllgwyngyll) (LL61 6DQ) 4E 81
Plas Newydd (Llangollen) (LL20 8AW) 1E 70
Plas yn Rhiw (LL53 8AB) 3B 68
Pleasurewood Hills (NR32 5DZ) 1H 67
Poldark Mine (TR13 0ES) 5A 6
Polesden Lacey (RH5 6BD) 5C 38
Pollok House, Glasgow (G43 1AT) 3G 127
Pontcysyllte Aqueduct (LL20 7YS) 1E 71
Portchester Castle (PO16 9QW) 2E 17
Portland Castle (DT5 1AZ) 5B 14
Port Lympne Wild Animal Pk. (CT21 4PD) 2F 29
Portsmouth Historic Dockyard (PO1 3LJ) 201
Potteries Mus. & Art Gallery (ST1 3DW) **Stoke 202**
Powderham Castle (EX6 8JQ) 4C 12
Powis Castle & Gdn. (SY21 8RF) 5E 71
Prebendal Manor House (PE8 6QG) 1H 63
Prestongrange Mus. (EH32 9RX) 2G 129
Preston Manor (BN1 6SD) 5E 27
Preston Mill & Phantassie Doocot (EH40 3DS) 2B 130
Preston Tower (Northumberland) (NE67 5DH) 2F 121
Preston Tower, Prestonpans (EH32 9NN) 2G 129
Prideaux Place (PL28 8RP) 1D 6
Prior Pk. Landscape Gdn. (BA2 5AH) 5C 34

Limited Interchange Motorway Junctions are shown on the mapping pages by red junction indicators **2**

M1

Junction		
2	Northbound	No exit, access from A1 only
	Southbound	No exit, access to A1 only
4	Northbound	No exit, access from A41 only
	Southbound	No access, exit to A41 only
6a	Northbound	No exit, access from M25 only
	Southbound	No access, exit to M25 only
17	Northbound	No access, exit to M45 only
	Southbound	No exit, access from M45 only
19	Northbound	Exit to M6 only, access from A14 only
	Southbound	Access from M6 only, exit to A14 only
21a	Northbound	No access, exit to A46 only
	Southbound	No exit, access from A46 only
24a	Northbound	No access from A50 only
	Southbound	Exit to A50 only
35a	Northbound	No access, exit to A616 only
	Southbound	No exit, access from A616 only
43	Northbound	Exit to M621 only
	Southbound	Access from M621 only
48	Northbound	Exit to A1(M) northbound only
	Westbound	Access from A1(M) southbound only

M2

Junction		
1	Eastbound	Access from A2 eastbound only
	Westbound	Exit to A2 westbound only

M3

Junction		
8	Eastbound	No exit, access from A303 only
	Westbound	No access, exit to A303 only
10	Northbound	No access from A31
	Southbound	No exit to A31
13	Southbound	No access from A335 to M3 leading to M27 Eastbound

M4

Junction		
1	Eastbound	Exit to A4 eastbound only
	Westbound	Access from A4 westbound only
21	Eastbound	No exit to M48
	Westbound	No access from M48
23	Eastbound	No access from M48
	Westbound	No exit to M48
25	Eastbound	No exit
	Westbound	No access
25a	Eastbound	No exit
	Westbound	No access
29	Eastbound	No exit, access from A48(M) only
	Westbound	No access, exit to A48(M) only
38	Westbound	No access, exit to A48 only
39	Eastbound	No access or exit
	Westbound	No exit, access from A48 only
42	Eastbound	No access from A48
	Westbound	No exit to A48

M5

Junction		
10	Northbound	No exit, access from A4019 only
	Southbound	No access, exit to A4019 only
11a	Southbound	No exit to A417 westbound
18a	Northbound	No access from M49
	Southbound	No exit to M49

M6

Junction		
3a	Eastbound	No exit to M6 Toll
	Westbound	No access from M6 Toll
4	Northbound	No exit to M42 northbound
		No access from M42 southbound
	Southbound	No exit to M42
		No access from M42 southbound
4a	Northbound	No exit, access from M42 southbound only
	Southbound	No access, exit to M42 only
5	Northbound	No access, exit to A452 only
	Southbound	No exit, access from A452 only
10a	Northbound	No access, exit to M54 only
	Southbound	No exit, access from M54 only
11a	Northbound	No exit to M6 Toll
	Southbound	No access from M6 Toll
20	Northbound	No exit to M56 eastbound
	Southbound	No access from M56 westbound
24	Northbound	No exit, access from A58 only
	Southbound	No access, exit to A58 only
25	Northbound	No access, exit to A49 only
	Southbound	No exit, access from A49 only
30	Northbound	No exit, access from M61 northbound only
	Southbound	No access, exit to M61 northbound only
31a	Northbound	No access, exit to B6242 only
	Southbound	No exit, access from B6242 only
45	Northbound	No access onto A74(M)
	Southbound	No exit from A74(M)

M6 Toll

Junction		
T1	Northbound	No exit
	Southbound	No access or exit
T2	Northbound	No access or exit
	Southbound	No access
T5	Northbound	No exit
	Southbound	No access
T7	Northbound	No access from A5
	Southbound	No exit
T8	Northbound	No exit to A460 northbound
	Southbound	No exit

M8

Junction		
8	Eastbound	No exit to M73 northbound
	Westbound	No access from M73 southbound
9	Eastbound	No access, exit only
	Westbound	No exit, access only
13	Eastbound	No access from M80 southbound
	Westbound	No exit to M80 northbound
14	Eastbound	No access, exit only
	Westbound	No exit, access only
16	Eastbound	No access, exit only
	Westbound	No exit, access only
17	Eastbound	No exit, access from A82 only
	Westbound	No access, exit to A82 only
18	Westbound	No exit, access only
19	Eastbound	No exit to A814 eastbound
	Westbound	No access from A814 westbound
20	Eastbound	No exit, access only
	Westbound	No access, exit only
21	Eastbound	No access, exit only
	Westbound	No exit, access only
22	Eastbound	No exit, access from M77 only
	Westbound	No access, exit to M77 only
23	Eastbound	No exit, access from B768 only
	Westbound	No access, exit to B768 only
25	Eastbound & Westbound	Access from A739 southbound only Exit to A739 northbound only
25a	Eastbound	Access only
	Westbound	Exit only
28	Eastbound	No access from airport only
	Westbound	No access, exit to airport only

M9

Junction		
1a	Northbound	No exit, access to M9 spur only
	Southbound	No access from M9 spur only
2	Northbound	No exit, access from B8046 only
	Southbound	No access, exit to B8046 only
3	Northbound	No access, exit to A803 only
	Southbound	No exit, access from A803 only
6	Northbound	No exit, access only
	Southbound	No access, exit to A905 only
8	Northbound	No access, exit to M876 only
	Southbound	No exit, access from M876 only
Junction with A90	Northbound	Exit onto A90 northbound only
	Southbound	Access from A90 eastbound only

M11

Junction		
4	Northbound	No exit, access from A406 eastbound only
	Southbound	No access, exit to A406 westbound only
5	Northbound	No access, exit to A1168 only
	Southbound	No exit, access from A1168 only
8a	Northbound	No access, exit only
	Southbound	No exit, access only
9	Northbound	No access, exit only
	Southbound	No exit, access only
13	Northbound	No access, exit only
	Southbound	No exit, access only
14	Northbound	No access from A428 eastbound
		No exit to A428 westbound
	Southbound	No exit, access from A428 eastbound only

M20

Junction		
2	Eastbound	No access, exit to A20 only (access via M26 Junction 2a)
	Westbound	No exit, access only (exit via M26 Jun.2a)
3	Eastbound	No exit, access from M26 eastbound
	Westbound	No access, exit to M26 westbound only
11a	Eastbound	No access from Channel Tunnel
	Westbound	No exit to Channel Tunnel

M23

Junction		
7	Northbound	No exit to A23 southbound
	Southbound	No access from A23 northbound

M25

Junction		
5	Clockwise	No exit to M26 eastbound
	Anti-clockwise	No access from M26 westbound
Spur to A21	Northbound	No exit to M26 eastbound
	Southbound	No access from M26 westbound
19	Clockwise	No access, exit only
	Anti-clockwise	No exit, access only
21	Clockwise & Anti-clockwise	No exit to M1 southbound No access from M1 northbound
31	Northbound	No access, exit only (access via Jun.30)
	Southbound	No exit, access only (exit via Jun.30)

M26

Junction with M25 (M25 Jun.5)		
	Eastbound	No access from M25 clockwise or spur from A21 northbound
	Westbound	No exit to M25 anti-clockwise or spur to A21 southbound

Junction with M20 (M20 Jun.3)		
	Eastbound	No exit to M20 westbound
	Westbound	No access from M20 eastbound

M27

Junction		
4	Eastbound & Westbound	No exit to A33 southbound (Southampton) No access from A33 northbound
10	Eastbound	No exit, access from A32 only
	Westbound	No access, exit to A32 only

M40

Junction		
3	N.W bound	No access, exit to A40 only
	S.E bound	No exit, access from A40 only

M40 continued

7	N.W bound	No access, exit only
	S.E bound	No exit, access only
13	N.W bound	No access, exit only
	S.E bound	No exit, access only
14	N.W bound	No exit, access only
	S.E bound	No access, exit only
16	N.W bound	No access, exit only
	S.E bound	No exit, access only

M42

Junction		
1	Eastbound	No exit
	Westbound	No access
7	Northbound	No access, exit to M6 only
	Southbound	No exit, access from M6 northbound only
8	Northbound	No exit, access from M6 southbound only
		Exit to M6 northbound only
	Southbound	Access from M6 southbound only

M45

Junction with M1 (M1 Jun.17)		
	Eastbound	No exit to M1 northbound
	Westbound	No access from M1 southbound

Junction with A45 east of Dunchurch		
	Eastbound	No access, exit to A45 only
	Westbound	No exit, access from A45 northbound only

M48

Junction with M4 (M4 Jun.21)		
	Eastbound	No exit, access from M4 westbound
	Westbound	No access from M4 eastbound

Junction with M4 (M4 Jun.23)		
	Eastbound	No access from M4 westbound
	Westbound	No exit to M4 eastbound

M53

Junction		
11	Northbound & Southbound	No access from M56 eastbound, no exit to M56 westbound

M56

Junction		
1	Eastbound	No exit to M60 N.W bound
		No exit to A34 southbound
	S.E bound	No access from A34 northbound
	Westbound	No access from M60
2	Eastbound	No access, exit to A560 only
	Westbound	No access, exit to A560 only
3	Eastbound	No access, exit only
	Westbound	No exit, access only
4	Eastbound	No exit, access only
	Westbound	No access, exit only
7	Westbound	No access, exit only
8	Eastbound	No access or exit
	Westbound	No exit, access from A556 only
9	Eastbound	No access from M6 northbound
	Westbound	No exit to M60 southbound
10a	Northbound	No access, exit only
	Southbound	No exit, access only
15	Eastbound	No exit to M53
	Westbound	No access from M53

M57

Junction		
3	Northbound	No exit, access only
	Southbound	No access, exit only
5	Northbound	No exit, access from A580 westbound only
	Southbound	No access, exit to A580 eastbound only

M58

Junction		
1	Eastbound	No exit, access from A506 only
	Westbound	No access, exit to A506 only

M60

Junction		
2	N.E bound	No access, exit to A560 only
	S.W bound	No exit, access from A560 only
3	Eastbound	No access from A34 southbound
	Westbound	No exit to A34 northbound
4	Eastbound	No exit to M56 S.W bound
		No access to A34 northbound
	Westbound	No access from A34 southbound No access from M56 eastbound
5	N.W bound	No access from or exit to A5103 southbound
	S.E bound	No access from or exit to A5103 northbound
14	Eastbound	No exit to A580
		No access from A580 westbound
	Westbound	No exit to A580 eastbound No access from A580
16	Eastbound	No access from A666 only
	Westbound	No access, exit to A666 only
20	Eastbound	No access from A664
	Westbound	No exit to A664
22	Westbound	No access from A62
25	S.W bound	No access from A560 / A6017
26	N.E bound	No access or exit
27	N.E bound	No access, exit only
	S.W bound	No exit, access only

M61

Junction		
2&3	N.W bound	No access from A580 eastbound
	S.E bound	No exit to A580 westbound

Junction with M6 (M6 Jun.30)		
	N.W bound	No exit to M6 southbound
	S.E bound	No access from M6 northbound

M62

Junction		
23	Eastbound	No access, exit to A640 only
	Westbound	No exit, access from A640 only

M65

Junction		
9	N.E bound	No access, exit to A679 only
	S.W bound	No exit, access from A679 only
11	N.E bound	No exit, access only
	S.W bound	No access, exit only

M66

Junction		
1	Northbound	No access, exit to A56 only
	Southbound	No exit, access from A56 only

M67

Junction		
1	Eastbound	Access from A57 eastbound only
	Westbound	Exit to A57 westbound only
1a	Eastbound	No access, exit to A6017 only
	Westbound	No exit, access from A6017 only
2	Eastbound	No access from A57 only
	Westbound	No exit, access to A57 only

M69

Junction		
2	N.E bound	No access from B4669 only
	S.W bound	No exit, access to B4669 only

M73

Junction		
1	Southbound	No exit to A721 eastbound
2	Northbound	No access from M8 eastbound
		No exit to A89 eastbound
	Southbound	No exit to M8 westbound No access from A89 westbound
3	Northbound	No exit to A80 S.W bound
	Southbound	No access from A80 N.E bound

M74

Junction		
1	Eastbound	No access from M8 Westbound
	Westbound	No exit to M8 Westbound
3	Eastbound	No exit
	Westbound	No access
3a	Eastbound	No access
	Westbound	No exit
7	Northbound	No exit, access from A72 only
	Southbound	No access, exit to A72 only
9	Northbound	No access or exit
	Southbound	No access, exit to B7078 only
10	Southbound	No exit, access from B7078 only
11	Northbound	No exit, access from B7078 only
	Southbound	No access, exit to B7078 only
12	Northbound	No access, exit to A70 only
	Southbound	No exit, access from A70 only

M77

Junction with M8 (M8 Jun.22)		
	Northbound	No exit to M8 westbound
	Southbound	No access from M8 eastbound
4	Northbound	No exit
	Southbound	No access
6	Northbound	No exit to A77
	Southbound	No access from A77
7	Northbound	No access from A77 No exit to A77

M80

Junction		
1	Northbound	No access from M8 westbound
	Southbound	No exit to M8 eastbound
4a	Northbound	No access
	Southbound	No exit
6a	Northbound	No exit
	Southbound	No access
8	Northbound	No access from M876
	Southbound	No exit to M876

M90

Junction		
2a	Northbound	No access, exit to A92 only
	Southbound	No exit, access from A92 only
7	Northbound	No exit, access from A91 only
	Southbound	No access, exit to A91 only
8	Northbound	No access, exit to A91 only
	Southbound	No exit, access from A91 only
10	Northbound	No access from A912
		Exit to A912 northbound only
	Southbound	No exit to A912 Access from A912 southbound only

M180

Junction		
1	Eastbound	No access, exit only
	Westbound	No exit, access from A18 only

M606

Junction		
2	Northbound	No access, exit only

M621

Junction		
2a	Eastbound	No access, exit only
	Westbound	No exit, access only
4	Southbound	No exit
5	Northbound	No access, exit to A61 only
	Southbound	No exit, access from A61 only
6	Northbound	No exit, access only
	Southbound	No access, exit only
7	Eastbound	No access, exit only
	Westbound	No exit, access only
8	Northbound	No access, exit only
	Southbound	No exit, access only

M876

Junction with M80 (M80 Jun.5)		
	N.E bound	No access from M80 southbound
	S.W bound	No exit to M80 northbound

Junction with M9 (M9 Jun.8)		
	N.E bound	No exit to M9 northbound
	S.W bound	No access from M9 southbound

A1(M)

Junction		
Hertfordshire Section		
2	Northbound	No access, exit only
	Southbound	No exit, access from A1001 only
3	Southbound	No access, exit only
5	Northbound	No exit, access only
	Southbound	No access or exit
Cambridgeshire Section		
13a	Northbound	No exit to B1043
	Southbound	No access from B1043
14	Northbound	No exit, access only
	Southbound	No access, exit only
Leeds Section		
40	Southbound	Exit to A1 southbound only
Durham Section		
57	Northbound	No access, exit to A66(M) only
	Southbound	No exit, access from A66(M)
65	Northbound	Exit to A1 N.W bound and to A194(M) only
	Southbound	Access from A1 S.E bound and from A194(M) only

A3(M)

Junction		
4	Northbound	No access, exit only
	Southbound	No exit, access only

A38(M)

Aston Expressway

Junction with Victoria Road, Aston		
	Northbound	No access, exit only
	Southbound	No exit, access only

A48(M)

Junction with M4 (M4 Jun.29)		
	N.E bound	Exit to M4 eastbound only
	S.W bound	Access from M4 westbound only
29a	N.E bound	Access from A48 eastbound only
	S.W bound	Exit to A48 westbound only

A57(M)

Mancunian Way

Junction with A34 Brook Street, Manchester		
	Eastbound	No access, exit to A34 Brook Street, southbound only
	Westbound	No exit, access only

A58(M)

Leeds Inner Ring Road

Junction with Park Lane / Westgate		
	Southbound	No access, exit only

A64(M)

Leeds Inner Ring Road (continuation of A58(M))

Junction with A58 Clay Pit Lane		
	Eastbound	No access
	Westbound	No exit

A66(M)

Junction with A1(M) (A1(M) Jun.57)		
	N.E bound	Access from A1(M) northbound only
	S.W bound	Exit to A1(M) southbound only

A74(M)

Junction		
18	Northbound	No access
	Southbound	No exit

A167(M)

Newcastle Central Motorway

Junction with Camden Street		
	Northbound	No exit, access only
	Southbound	No access or exit

A194(M)

Junction with A1(M) (A1(M) Jun.65) and A1 Gateshead Western By-Pass		
	Northbound	Access from A1(M) only
	Southbound	Exit to A1(M) only

Northern Ireland

M1

Junction		
3	Northbound	No access, exit only
	Southbound	No access, exit only
7	Westbound	No access, exit only

M2

Junction		
2	Eastbound	No access to M5 northbound
	Westbound	No exit to M5 southbound

M5

Junction		
2	Northbound	No access from M2 eastbound
	Southbound	No exit to M2 westbound